LONELY PLANET PUBLICATIONS

W9-CDX-799

STEVE FALLON
NICOLA WILLIAMS

PARIS
CITY GUIDE

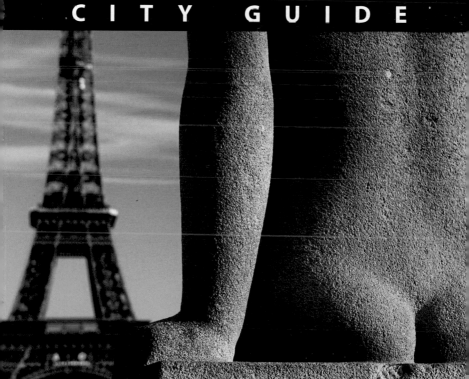

INTRODUCING PARIS

Snap an iconic shot of the Eiffel Tower (p131)

Well informed, eloquent and oh-so-romantic, the 'City of Light' is a philosopher, a poet, a crooner. As it always has been, Paris is a million different things to a million different people.

Paris has all but exhausted the superlatives that can reasonably be applied to any city. Notre Dame and the Eiffel Tower – at sunrise, at sunset, at night – have been described countless times, as have the Seine and the subtle (and not-so-subtle) differences between the Left and Right Banks. But what writers have been unable to capture is the grandness and even the magic.

Paris probably has more familiar landmarks than any other city in the world. As a result, first-time visitors often arrive in the French capital with all sorts of expectations: of grand vistas, of intellectuals discussing weighty matters in cafés, of romance along the Seine, of naughty nightclub revues, of rude people who won't speak English. If you look hard enough, you can probably find all of those. But another approach is to set aside the preconceptions of Paris and to explore the city's avenues and backstreets as if the tip of the Eiffel Tower or the spire of Notre Dame wasn't about to pop into view at any moment.

You'll soon discover (as so many others before you have) that Paris is enchanting almost everywhere, at any time, even 'in the summer, when it sizzles' and 'in the winter, when it drizzles', as Cole Porter put it. And you'll be back. Trust us.

PARIS LIFE

In the build-up to the 40th anniversary of May 1968, the month and year that rocked Paris and the world, it was fitting that the French capital was once again visited by strikes, riots and protests and the slogan, *'Sous les pavés, la plage'* (Under the cobblestones, the beach). But while your average Parisian enjoys nothing (well almost nothing) better than a good *râle* (a moan or a whinge) the city is a different –

> **'the infinitely successful Paris Plage just keeps on a-growin' and is now called Paris Plages'**

almost unrecognisable – place four decades on. The transport strike? Sorted. Everyone just jumped on the closest Vélib' cycle, having learned how sweet was a seat on a bicycle built for 2.2 million. And a return to 2005-style riots in the *banlieue* (suburbs) after two youths on a motorbike died in a crash with a police patrol car? Neighbourhoods did burn, baby, but for days, not weeks. The mass demonstrations expected after President Nicolas Sarkozy announced his overhaul of the crumbling university system in 2007 never happened. And what about that 'beach'? Well, the infinitely successful Paris Plage just keeps on a-growin' and is now called Paris Plages.

Most of the reforms (but not the popular ban on smoking in public places) were the work of Mayor Bernard Delanoë – according to the polls France's most popular politician – who beat his Sarkozy-backed opponent in the March 2008 municipal election. Delanoë is hard-working, capable, modest and earnest. He gets on with business while President Bling-Bling (p33) entertains (in spite of himself). From hobnobbing with the rich and famous to – *sacré bleu!* – holidaying in the USA, the mercurial right-wing son of an immigrant from Budapest kept left-wing Parisians shocked, stunned and maybe even a little amused. Then along came Carla Bruni – supermodel, folk singer, public undresser and now Madame Sarkozy. With his popularity in the polls at the lowest ever recorded by a *président de la république,* Sarko crossed the Channel to fly the flag and his trophy wife. *Les rosbifs* fell in love with La Carla at first sight. 'Je Thames' gushed the *Sun* in a headline that has begged to be written since Waterloo. *Touché!*

Typical Parisian café life (p226)

3

HIGHLIGHTS

FOOD

The French think mainly about two things, it is said: their two main meals. An inordinate amount of time is spent thinking about, talking about and consuming lunch and dinner. Breakfast barely gets a passing thought (or comment).

Pommes de terre, lardons, reblochon, crème fraîche, oignons.

❶ Busy Outdoor Tables at a Café
The *terrasse* (pavement terrace) is the best vantage point from which to see and be seen (p226).

❷ Tajine
A Moroccan favourite, *tajine* (a slow-cooked meat stew) is now a staple of the Parisian diet, appearing in many restaurants, such as 404 (p240).

❸ Food Stalls at the Marché Bastille
Neighbourhood markets are very much a part of life in Paris (p231).

❹ Boucherie
Buy everything at a French *boucherie* (butcher shop) – from nose to tail of the cow, calf, lamb or pig (p230).

❺ Cheese
The choice on offer at a *fromagerie* (cheese shop) in France can be overwhelming (p223).

❻ Crêpes Stand
The sweet *crêpe* and its savoury cousin, the *galette*, are the street snack of choice (p226).

❼ Poissonnerie
A *poissonnerie* (fishmonger's shop) dispenses fresh fish and seafood (p230).

❽ A Chalkboard Menu
A restaurant *carte* (menu) outside on a *l'ardoise* (chalkboard) will help you to decide before going in whether it is to your taste and budget (p233).

❾ A Plate of Steak-Frites
A standard feature of tourist menus in Paris, *steak-frites* is a deceptively simple dish (p225).

ART & MUSEUMS

With more than a hundred museums in central Paris, there's something here for every interest, however obscure. And art is not just 'bullion' stashed away in safe houses but also found out on the streets and down in the metro.

❶ Musée de l'Orangerie
Monet's *Decorations des Nymphéas* (Water Lilies) are housed in two purpose-built rooms (p87).

❷ Musée du Quai Branly
The 'vertical garden' puts new meaning to the phrase 'growing up' in Paris (p134).

❸ Artists in Montmartre
Art takes to the streets – literally – throughout Paris, but especially up in Montmartre (p168).

❹ Louvre Pyramid
Lambasted when it opened in 1989, IM Pei's Grande Pyramide (Great Pyramid) opens up the Louvre to everyone (p81).

❺ Louvre–Rivoli Metro Station
Art is everywhere in Paris, including the Louvre–Rivoli metro station (p156)

❻ Musée d'Orsay
This erstwhile train station contains some of the most important works by impressionists and postimpressionists (p130).

❶ Couple on the Banks of the Seine

Paris Je T'aime (Paris, I love you)– it's a phrase, a film and a lifetime commitment (p44).

❷ The Seine

A boat from Bateaux-Parisiens glides quietly past the quays on the Seine (p407).

❸ Paris Plages

The Seine is at its most amusing when 5km of its banks are transformed into the 'beaches' of Paris Plages (p14).

THE SEINE

Paris' playground, backdrop and dustless highway, the Seine is beautiful at any time of day and in any season. The best way to view it is from one of the three dozen bridges spanning the river.

CONTENTS

Continued from previous page.

THE AUTHORS

Steve Fallon

Steve, who has worked on every edition of *Paris* and *France* except the first, visited the 'City of Light' for the first time at age 16 with his half-French best friend, where they spent a week drinking *vin ordinaire* from plastic bottles, keeping several paces ahead of irate café waiters demanding to be paid, and learning French swear words that shocked even them. Despite this inexcusable behaviour, the PAF (border police) let him back in five years later to complete a degree in French at the Sorbonne. Now based in East London, Steve will be just one Underground stop away from Paris when Eurostar trains begin departing from Stratford in 2010. *C'est si bon…* Steve was the coordinating author and wrote the Introducing Paris, Getting Started, Background, Sleeping, Gay & Lesbian Paris and Directory chapters. He also cowrote the Neighbourhoods, Shopping, Eating, Drinking and Nightlife & the Arts chapters.

Nicola Williams

For Nicola, a British journalist living and working in France for the past 12 years (home is a hillside house with Lake Geneva view in Haute Savoie), it is an easy flit to Paris where she has spent endless amounts of time eating her way around and revelling in the city's extraordinary art and architecture. When she's not working for Lonely Planet, she can be found in the Alps skiing or hiking, strolling around Florence or having fun with family in Britain and Germany. Nicola has worked on numerous other Lonely Planet titles including *France, Provence & the Côte d'Azur* and *The Loire*. Nicola wrote the Sports & Activities, Excursions and Transport chapters. She also cowrote the Neighbourhoods, Shopping, Eating, Drinking and Nightlife & the Arts chapters.

PHOTOGRAPHER
Will Salter

In the last 12 years, Will has worked on assignment in over 50 countries in Africa, Asia, Europe, and the Pacific region as well as Antarctica. He has produced a body of award-winning work that includes evocative images of travel, portraits and sport. He sees photography as a privilege, a rare opportunity to become intimately involved in people's lives. Will is based in Melbourne, Australia, with his wife and two children. His website is www .willsalter.com.

Paris is a dream destination for countless reasons, but among the most obvious is that it requires so very little advance planning. Tourist literature abounds, maps are excellent and readily available, and the staff at tourist offices are usually helpful and efficient. Paris is so well developed and organised that you don't have to plan much of anything before your trip.

But this is fine only if your budget is unlimited, you don't have an interest in any particular period of architecture or type of music, and you'll eat or drink anything put down in front of you. This is Paris, one of the most visited cities of the world, and everyone wants a piece of the action. First and foremost, book your accommodation well ahead. And if you have specific interests – live big-name jazz, blockbuster art exhibitions, top-end restaurants – you'll certainly want to make sure that the things you expect to see and do will be available or open to you when you arrive. The key here is advance planning (see p17).

WHEN TO GO

As the old song says, Paris is lovely in springtime – though winterlike relapses and heavy rains are not uncommon in the otherwise beautiful month of April. The best months are probably May and June – but early, before the hordes of tourists descend. Autumn is also pleasant – some people say the best months of the year to visit are September and October – but of course the days are getting shorter and in October hotels are booked solid by businesspeople attending conferences and trade shows. In winter Paris has all sorts of cultural events going on, while in summer the weather is warm – sometimes sizzling. In any case, in August Parisians flee for the beaches to the west and south, and many restaurateurs and café owners lock up and leave town too. It's true that you will find more places open in August than even a decade ago, but it still can feel like a ghost town in certain districts. For more information on Paris' climate, see p397.

To ensure that your trip does (or perhaps does *not*) coincide with a public holiday, see p401. For a list of festivals and other events to plan around, see below.

FESTIVALS & EVENTS

Innumerable festivals, cultural and sporting events and trade shows take place in Paris throughout the year; weekly details appear in *Pariscope* and *L'Officiel des Spectacles* (p302). You can also find them listed under 'What's On' on the website of the Paris Convention & Visitors Bureau (www.parisinfo.com). The following abbreviated list gives you a taste of what to expect throughout the year.

January & February

FESTIVAL DES MUSIQUES DU NOVEL AN
www.parisparade.com
The New Year Music Festival, relatively subdued after the previous night's shenanigans (p15) with marching and carnival bands, dance acts and so on, takes place on the afternoon of New Year's Day at the Palais de Chaillot (p131) at Trocadéro.

LOUIS XVI COMMEMORATIVE MASS
www.monuments-nationaux.fr
On the Sunday closest to 21 January, royalists and right-wingers attend a mass at the Chapelle Expiatoire (p142 marking the execution by guillotine of King Louis XVI in 1793.

DON'T LEAVE HOME WITHOUT...

- an adaptor plug for electrical appliances
- binoculars for viewing detail on churches and other buildings
- an immersion water heater or small kettle for an impromptu cup of tea or coffee
- tea bags if you need that cuppa since the French drink buckets of the herbal variety but not much of the black stuff
- premoistened towelettes or a large cotton handkerchief to soak in fountains and use to cool off in the hot weather
- sunglasses and sun block, even in the cooler months
- swimsuit and thongs (flip-flops) for Paris Plages or swimming pool
- a Swiss Army knife, with such essentials as a bottle opener and strong corkscrew

FASHION WEEK
www.pretparis.com
Prêt-à-Porter, the ready-to-wear fashion salon that is held twice a year in late January and again in September, is a must for fashion buffs and is held at the Parc des Expositions at Porte de Versailles in the 15e arrondissement (metro Porte de Versailles), southwest of the city centre.

CHINESE NEW YEAR
www.paris.fr
Dragon parades and other festivities are held in late January or early February in two Chinatowns: the smaller, more authentic one in the 3e, taking in rue du Temple, rue au Maire and rue de Turbigo (metro Temple or Arts et Métiers); and the larger, flashier one in the 13e in between porte de Choisy, porte d'Ivry and blvd Masséna (metro Porte de Choisy, Port d'Ivry or Tolbiac).

SALON INTERNATIONAL DE L'AGRICULTURE
www.salon-agriculture.com
A 10-day international agricultural fair with produce and animals turned into dishes from all over France, held at the Parc des Expositions at Porte de Versailles in the 15e (metro Porte de Versailles) from late February to early March.

March–May

BANLIEUES BLEUES
www.banlieuesbleues.org, in French
The 'Suburban Blues' jazz and blues festival is held over five weeks in March and April in the northern suburbs of Paris, including St-Denis (p182), and attracts some big-name talent.

PRINTEMPS DU CINÉMA
www.printempsducinema.com, in French
Cinemas across Paris offer filmgoers a unique entry fee of €3.50 over three days (usually Sunday, Monday and Tuesday) sometime around 21 March.

FOIRE DU TRÔNE
www.foiredutrone.com, in French
This huge funfair, with 350 attractions spread over 10 hectares, is held on the pelouse de Reuilly of the Bois de Vincennes

(metro Porte Dorée) for eight weeks from late March to mid-May.

MARATHON INTERNATIONAL DE PARIS
www.parismarathon.com
The Paris International Marathon, usually held on the first Sunday of early April, starts on the av des Champs-Élysées, 8e, and finishes on av Foch, in the 16e. The Semi-Marathon de Paris is a half-marathon held in early March; see the website for map and registration details.

FOIRE DE PARIS
www.foiredeparis.fr
This huge modern-living fair, including crafts, gadgets and widgets, and food and wine, is held from late April to early May at the Parc des Expositions at Porte de Versailles in the 15e (metro Porte de Versailles).

ATELIERS D'ARTISTES DE BELLEVILLE: LES PORTES OUVERTES
www.ateliers-artistes-belleville.org, in French
More than 200 painters, sculptors and other artists in Belleville (metro Belleville) in the 10e open their studio doors to visitors over four days (Friday to Monday) in mid-May in an event that has now been going for two decades.

LA NUIT DES MUSÉES
www.nuitdesmusees.culture.fr, in French
Key museums across Paris throw open their doors at 6pm for one Saturday night in mid-May on 'Museums Night' and don't close till late. Some also organise special events.

FRENCH TENNIS OPEN
www.rolandgarros.com
The glitzy Internationaux de France de Tennis – the Grand Slam – takes place from late May to mid-June at Stade Roland Garros (metro Porte d'Auteuil) at the southern edge of the Bois de Boulogne in the 16e.

June–August

FOIRE ST-GERMAIN
www.foiresaintgermain.org, in French
This month-long festival of concerts and theatre from early June to early July takes place on the place St-Sulpice, 6e (metro

St-Sulpice) and various other venues (see website) in the quartier St-Germain.

FÊTE DE LA MUSIQUE
www.fetedelamusique.fr, in French
This national music festival welcomes in summer on Midsummer's Night (21 June) and caters to a great diversity of tastes (including jazz, reggae and classical) and features staged and impromptu live performances all over the city.

GAY PRIDE MARCH
www.gaypride.fr, in French
This colourful Saturday-afternoon parade in very late June through the Marais to Bastille celebrates Gay Pride Day, with various bars and clubs sponsoring floats, and participants in some pretty outrageous costumes.

PARIS JAZZ FESTIVAL
www.parcfloraldeparis.com; www.paris.fr
There are free jazz concerts every Saturday and Sunday afternoon in June and July in the Parc Floral de Paris (metro Château de Vincennes).

LA GOUTTE D'OR EN FÊTE
www.gouttedorenfete.org, in French
This week-long world-music festival (featuring rai, reggae and rap) is held at square Léon, 18e (metro Barbès Rochechouart or Château Rouge) from late June to early July.

PARIS CINÉMA
www.pariscinema.org
This two-week festival in the first half of July sees rare and restored films screened in selected cinemas across Paris.

BASTILLE DAY (14 JULY)
www.paris.fr
Paris is *the* place to be on France's national day. Late on the night of the 13th, *bals des sapeurs-pompiers* (dances sponsored by Paris' firefighters, who are considered sex symbols in France) are held at fire stations around the city. At 10am on the 14th, there's a military and fire-brigade parade along av des Champs-Élysées, accompanied by a fly-past of fighter aircraft and helicopters. In the evening, a huge display of *feux d'artifice* (fireworks) is held at around 11pm on the Champ de Mars, 7e.

PARIS PLAGES
www.paris.fr
Initiated in 2002, 'Paris Beaches' is one of the most inspired and successful city recreational events in the world. Across four weeks, from mid-July to mid-August, three waterfront areas are transformed into sand and pebble 'beaches', complete with sun beds, beach umbrellas, atomisers, lounge chairs and palm trees. They make up the 3km-long stretch along the Right Bank embankment from the quai Henri IV at the Pont de Sully (metro Sully Morland) in the 4e to the quai des Tuileries (metro Tuileries) below the Louvre in the 1er; a 1km-long 'beach' below the Bibliothèque Nationale de France and across from the Parc de Bercy in the 13e on the Left Bank; and the area around the Bassin de la Villette in the 19e (metro Jaurès). The beaches are open from 8am to midnight daily.

TOUR DE FRANCE
www.letour.fr
The last of 21 stages of this prestigious, 3500km-long cycling event finishes with a race up av des Champs-Élysées on the third or fourth Sunday of July, as it has done since 1975.

September & October

JAZZ À LA VILLETTE
www.villette.com, in French
This super 10-day jazz festival in early September has sessions in Parc de la Villette, at the Cité de la Musique and in surrounding bars.

FESTIVAL D'AUTOMNE
www.festival-automne.com
The Autumn Festival of arts has painting, music, dance and theatre at venues throughout the city from mid-September to mid-December.

EUROPEAN HERITAGE DAYS
www.journeesdupatrimoine.culture.fr, in French
As elsewhere in Europe on the third weekend in September, Paris opens the doors to buildings (eg embassies, government ministries, corporate offices – even the Palais de l'Élysée) normally off-limits to outsiders.

TECHNOPARADE

www.technopol.net, in French

Part of the annual festival called Rendez-vous Électroniques (Electronic Meeting), this parade involving some 20 floats and carrying 150 musicians and DJs wends its way on the periphery of the Marais on the third Saturday of September, starting and ending at place de la Bastille, 12e.

NUIT BLANCHE

www.paris.fr

'White Night' (or more accurately 'All Nighter') is when Paris 'does' New York and becomes 'the city that doesn't sleep at all'. It's a cultural festival that lasts from sundown until sunrise on the first Saturday and Sunday of October, with museums and recreational facilities in town joining bars and clubs and staying open till the very wee hours.

FÊTE DES VENDANGES DE MONTMARTRE

www.fetedesvendangesdemontmartre.com, in French

This festival is held over the second weekend in October following the harvesting of grapes from the Close du Montmartre (p185), with costumes, speeches and a parade.

FOIRE INTERNATIONALE D'ART CONTEMPORAIN

www.fiacparis.com

Better known as FIAC, this huge contemporary art fair is held over five days in late October, with some 160 galleries represented at the Louvre and the Grand Palais.

November & December

AFRICOLOR

www.africolor.com, in French

This African music festival is held for the most part in venues in the suburbs surrounding Paris from late November to late December.

JUMPING INTERNATIONAL DE PARIS

www.salon-cheval.com, in French

This annual showjumping tournament features the world's most celebrated jumpers at the Palais Omnisports de Paris-Bercy in the 12e arrondissement (metro Bercy) in the first half of December. The annual Inter-

top picks

UNUSUAL EVENTS

- Paris Plages (opposite) – the next best thing to the seaside along France's smallest urban beaches
- Gay Pride March (opposite) – feathers and beads and participants in and out of same
- Fête des Vendanges de Montmartre (left) – lots of noise for a bunch of old (and some say sour) grapes
- Louis XVI Commemorative Mass (p12) – right-wing sob-fest for aristocrats, pretenders and hangers-on
- Salon Internationale de l'Agriculture (p13) – lots to smell (cowpats) and hear (braying donkeys) and coo (lambs gambolling) and eat and drink at Europe's largest agricultural fair

national Showjumping Competition forms part of the Salon du Cheval at the Parc des Expositions at Porte de Versailles in the 15e (metro Porte de Versailles).

CHRISTMAS EVE MASS

Mass is celebrated at midnight on Christmas Eve at many Paris churches, including Notre Dame, but get there by 11pm to find a place.

NEW YEAR'S EVE

Blvd St-Michel (5e), place de la Bastille (11e), the Eiffel Tower (7e) and especially av des Champs-Élysées (8e) are the places to be to welcome in the New Year.

COSTS & MONEY

If you stay in a hostel or in a showerless, toiletless room in a bottom-end hotel and have picnics rather than dining out, it is possible to stay in Paris for €50 a day per person. A couple staying in a two-star hotel and eating one cheap restaurant meal each day should count on spending at least €75 a day per person. Eating out frequently, ordering wine and treating yourself to any of the many luxuries on offer in Paris will increase these figures considerably.

If greater Paris were a country, its economy would rank as one of the world's largest (in fact, placing at No 17). The 617,000 companies employing just over five million people in

Île de France contribute to the region's €415 billion GDP, which accounts for upwards of a third of the total for all of France. The service industries employ the most people – almost 82% of the workforce, of which 4% are in tourism. Not surprisingly, only 0.5% of Parisians are involved in the primary industries of agriculture, forestry or fishing.

Manufacturers – software developers, electronic industries, pharmaceuticals, publishers – employ about 18% of the workforce. As most industry is located outside the Périphérique (p51), about the only factories you're likely to see during your visit are those lining the highway from Charles de Gaulle airport. As a result, 50% of Parisians commute out of – rather than into – the city every day to work.

That is, those who have a job to commute to do. Unemployment is currently at a low of around 7.5% nationally, and the jobless rate for Paris is about half that figure. However, for youths living in the dire housing estates surrounding the city, the figure reaches more than 20%, one of the reasons that the *banlieues* (suburbs) erupted into violence at the end of 2005 (p30). Bids by the previous government to reduce the number of jobless youth through its controversial CPE plan (p30) were stymied early the following year when a million workers and students took to the streets in protest. They argued that the law, which would allow companies with more than 20 employees to fire workers under 26 within the first two years of employment with no severance pay, encouraged a regular turnover of cut-rate

staff and did not allow young people to build careers. The French government decided to withdraw the CPE altogether later in 2006.

To a certain extent the government's ability to boost employment through training and aid is crimped: it simply doesn't have the money. First and foremost is the need to reduce debt, which stood at almost 67% of GDP in 2007. The country was also in danger of breaching EU rules regulating national debt – again – if it didn't cut its spending. The national public deficit was expected to rise to over 3% of GDP in 2008, which is above the EU limit.

To fill the national coffers, France has raised billions of euros by selling stakes in state-owned companies. In late 2007 and early 2008 it sold a stake of 2.5% in the power company Électricité de France and one of 3.3% in Aéroports de Paris, the company that manages Charles de Gaulle and Orly airports. It's not the first time that the government has flogged the family silver.

INTERNET RESOURCES

Wi-fi is widely available at midrange and top-end hotels in Paris (sometimes for free but more usually for something like €5 per one-off connection) and occasionally in public spaces such as train stations and tourist offices. For a list of almost 100 free-access wi-fi cafés in Paris, visit www.cafes-wifi.com (in French).

If you don't have a laptop or wi-fi access, don't fret: Paris is awash with internet cafés with their own computers, and you'll probably find at least one in your immediate neighbourhood.

In terms of websites to consult before you go, Lonely Planet (www.lonelyplanet.com) is a good start for many of the city's more useful links. The following English-language websites are useful when wanting learn more about Paris (and France).

Expatica (www.expatica.com) Lifestyle website for internationals living in countries worldwide, including France, with regularly updated news, features and blogs.

French Government Tourism Office (www.francetourism .com) Official tourism site with all manner of information on and about travel in France, with lots and lots on Paris too.

Go Go Paris! Culture! (www.gogoparis.com) Clubs, hangouts, art gigs, dance around town, eat and drink – everything a culture vulture living in Paris needs.

Mairie de Paris (www.paris.fr) Your primary source of information about Paris, with everything from opening

HOW MUCH?

An hour's car parking: from €1 (street), €2.40 (garage)

Average fair/good seat at the opera: €40/60

Cinema ticket: €5.90 to €9.90 (adult)

Copy of Le Monde newspaper: €1.30

Coffee at a café bar: from €1.20

Grand crème at Champs-Élysées café terrace: €4.50

Metro/bus ticket: €1.50 (€10 for 10)

Entry to the Louvre: €9 (adult)

Litre of bottled mineral water: from €0.70 (supermarket), €1 (corner shop)

Pint of local beer: from €6.50 (€5 at happy hour)

Pop music CD: €13 to €18

Street snack: from €2.50 (basic crêpe or galette)

ADVANCE PLANNING

A couple of months before you go Try to book your accommodation months ahead, especially if it's high season and you want to stay in a boutique hotel like the Hôtel Caron de Beaumarchais (p339), a 'find' such as the Hôtel Jeanne d'Arc (p340) or some place offering exceptional value for money like the Hôtel du Champ-du-Mars (p351). Take a look at some of the 'what's on' websites listed on opposite or the entertainment magazines *Pariscope* and *L'Officiel des Spectacles* (p302).

A month before you go If you're interested in serious fine dining at places like Le Grand Véfour (p232) or the Casa Olympe (p264) and there's more than one of you, book a table now. Now is also the time to visit the Fnac and/or Virgin Megastore websites (p302) to get seats for a big-ticket concert, musical or play.

Two weeks before you go Blockbuster exhibitions at venues such as the Grand Palais (p139) or Centre Pompidou (p88) – or even a visit to the Louvre (p80) – can be booked in advance via Fnac or Virgin Megastore for a modest fee. Sign up for an email newsletter via Expatica (opposite) and read some up-to-date blogs.

A day or two before you go Make sure your bookings are in order and you've followed all the instructions outlined in this chapter.

times and what's on to the latest statistics direct from the Hôtel de Ville.

Paris Convention & Visitors Bureau (www.parisinfo.com) The official site of the Office de Tourisme et de Congrès – the city's tourist office – is super, with more links than you'll ever need.

Paris Digest (www.parisdigest.com) Useful site for making pretravel arrangements and for its forum.

Paris Pages (www.paris.org) Has good links to museums and cultural events.

Paris Woman (www.pariswoman.com) Deals with news and issues and events affecting expatriate women in Paris.

RATP (www.ratp.com) This invaluable (and easy to use) website from the city's transport network will help you negotiate your way around town.

BLOGS

If there's one country in Europe where blogging is a national pastime (so *that's* what they do outside their 35-hour work week) it's France. The underbelly of what French people think right now, the French blogosphere is gargantuan, with everyone and everything from streets and metro stops to bands, bars and the president having their own blog. For an informative overview (did someone say three million bloggers in France and counting?) see LeMondeduBlog.com (www.lemondedublog.com in English & French). Parisian *star du blog* Loïc Le Meur (www.loiclemeur.com in English & French) – one of

France's most widely read and watched (this serial entrepreneur vid-blogs like mad at www.loic.tv) – considerably blogs a best-of-blog list at www.eu.socialtext.net/loicwiki/index.cgi?french_blogosphere.

For clubbing, music and nightlife links see p302. Blogroll to tune into politics, fashion/kitchen gossip, happenings and bags more in the capital (in English):

Chocolate & Zucchini (http://chocolateandzucchini.com) Food-driven blog by a 28-year-old foodie called Clotilde from Montmartre.

Le Blageur à Paris (www.parisblagueur.blogspot.com) On-the-ball, engaging and inspirational snapshots of Parisian life from one of the city's most enigmatic bloggers, a 32-year-old French *fille* called Meg Zimbeck.

Paris Daily Photo (www.parisdailyphoto.com) An image a day with detailed comment, enjoyed by 2000-odd a day, from friendly Eric in the 9e arrondissement.

Petite Brigitte (http://petitebrigitte.com) 'Inside Paris: Gossip, News, Fashion' with a savvy Parisian gal in St-Germain des Prés.

Secrets of Paris (www.secretsofparis.com) OK, OK, she writes for lots of our competitors but this site is a great resource, full of venue recommendations, lots of great bar/nightlife info.

The Paris Blog (www.theparisblog.com) Insightful portrait of Parisian life by a blogger collective.

Voice of a City (www.voiceofacity.com) Eurostar-vetted voices blog about their Paris.

HISTORY

With upwards of 12 million inhabitants, the greater metropolitan area of Paris is home to almost 19% of France's total population (central Paris counts just under 2.2 million souls). Since before the Revolution, Paris has been what urban planners like to call a 'hypertrophic city' – the enlarged 'head' of a nation-state's 'body'. The urban area of the next biggest city – Marseilles – is just over a third the size of central Paris.

As the capital city, Paris is the administrative, business and cultural centre; virtually everything of importance in the republic starts, finishes or is currently taking place here. The French have always said *'Quand Paris éternue, la France s'en rhume'* (When Paris sneezes, France catches cold) but there have been conscious efforts – going back at least four decades – by governments to decentralise Paris' role, and during that time the population, and thus to a certain extent the city's authority, has actually shrunk. The pivotal year was 1968, a watershed not just in France but throughout Western Europe.

Paris has a timeless quality, a condition that can often be deceiving. And while the cobbled backstreets of Montmartre, the terraced cafés of Montparnasse, the iconic structure of the Eiffel Tower and the placid waters of the Seine may all have some visitors believing that the city has been here since time immemorial, that's hardly the case.

EARLY SETTLEMENT

The early history of the Celts is murky, but it is thought that they originated somewhere in the eastern part of central Europe around the 2nd millennium BC and began to migrate across the continent, arriving in France sometime in the 7th century BC. In the 3rd century a group of Celtic Gauls called the Parisii settled here.

Centuries of conflict between the Gauls and Romans ended in 52 BC, with the latter taking control of the territory. The settlement on the Seine prospered as the Roman town of Lutetia (from the Latin for 'midwater dwelling', in French, Lutèce), counting some 10,000 inhabitants by the 3rd century AD.

The Great Migrations, beginning around the middle of the 3rd century AD with raids by the Franks and then by the Alemanii from the east, left the settlement on the south bank scorched and pillaged, and its inhabitants fled to the Île de la Cité, which was subsequently fortified with stone walls. Christianity (as well as Mithraism; see opposite) had been introduced early in the previous century, and the first church, probably made of wood, was built on the western part of the island.

INVASIONS & DYNASTIES

The Romans occupied what would become known as Paris (after its first settlers) from AD 212 to the late 5th century. It was at this time that a second wave of Franks and other Germanic groups under Merovius from the north and northeast overran the territory. Merovius' grandson,

TIMELINE

3rd century BC	52 BC	AD 845–86
Celtic Gauls called Parisii – believed to mean 'boat men' – arrive in the Paris area and set up a few wattle-and-daub huts on what is now the Île de la Cité. Here they engage in fishing and trading.	Roman legions under Julius Caesar crush a Celtic revolt led by Vercingétorix on the Mons Lutetius (now the site of the Panthéon) and establish the town of Lutetia.	Paris is repeatedly raided by Vikings for more than four decades including the siege of 885–86 by Siegfried the Saxon, which lasts 10 months but ends in victory for the French.

MITHRA & THE GREAT SACRIFICE

Mithraism, the worship of the god Mithra, originated in Persia. As Roman rule extended into the west, the religion became extremely popular with traders, imperial slaves and mercenaries of the Roman army and spread rapidly throughout the empire in the 2nd and 3rd centuries AD. In fact, Mithraism was the principal rival of Christianity until Constantine came to the throne in the 4th century.

Mithraism was a mysterious religion with its devotees (mostly males) sworn to secrecy. What little is known of Mithra, the god of justice and social contract, has been deduced from reliefs and icons found in sanctuaries and temples, particularly in Eastern and Central European countries. Most of these portray Mithra clad in a Persian-style cap and tunic, sacrificing a white bull in front of Sol, the sun god. From the bull's blood sprout grain and grapes and from its semen animals. Sol's wife Luna, the moon, begins her cycle and time is born.

Mithraism and Christianity were close competitors partly because of the striking similarity of many of their rituals. Both involve the birth of a deity on winter solstice (25 December), shepherds, death and resurrection, and a form of baptism. Devotees knelt when they worshipped and a common meal – a 'communion' of bread and water – was a regular feature of both liturgies.

Clovis I, converted to Christianity, making Paris his seat in 508. Childeric II, Clovis' son and successor, founded the Abbey of St-Germain des Prés a half-century later, and the dynasty's most productive ruler, Dagobert, established an abbey at St-Denis. This abbey soon became the richest, most important monastery in France and became the final resting place of its kings.

The militaristic rulers of the Carolingian dynasty, beginning with Charles 'the Hammer' Martel (688–741) were almost permanently away fighting wars in the east, and Paris languished, controlled mostly by the counts of Paris. When Charles Martel's grandson, Charlemagne (768–814), moved his capital to Aix-la-Chapelle (today's Aachen in Germany), Paris' fate was sealed. Basically a group of separate villages with its centre on the island, Paris was badly defended throughout the second half of the 9th century and suffered a succession of raids by the 'Norsemen' (Vikings).

CONSOLIDATION OF POWER

The counts of Paris, whose powers had increased as the Carolingians feuded among themselves, elected one of their own, Hugh Capet, as king at Senlis in 987. He made Paris the royal seat and resided in the renovated palace of the Roman governor on the Île de la Cité (the site of the present Palais de Justice). Under Capetian rule, which would last for the next 800 years, Paris prospered as a centre of politics, commerce, trade, religion and culture. By the time Hugh Capet had assumed the throne, the Norsemen (or Normans, descendants of the Vikings) were in control of northern and western French territory. In 1066 they mounted a successful invasion of England from their base in Normandy.

Paris' strategic riverside position ensured its importance throughout the Middle Ages, although settlement remained centred on the Île de la Cité, with the *rive gauche* (left bank) to the south given over to fields and vineyards; the Marais area on the *rive droite* (right bank) to the north was a waterlogged marsh. The first guilds were established in the 11th century, and rapidly grew in importance; in the mid-12th century the ship merchants' guild bought the principal river port, by today's Hôtel de Ville (city hall), from the crown.

1066	1163	1253
The so-called Norman Conquest (and subsequent occupation) of England ignites almost 300 years of conflict between the Normans in western and northern France and the Capetians in Paris.	Two centuries of nonstop building reaches its zenith with the start of Notre Dame Cathedral under Maurice de Sully, the bishop of Paris; construction will continue for more than a century and a half.	La Sorbonne is founded by Robert de Sorbon, confessor to Louis IX, as a theological college for impoverished students in the area of the Left Bank known as the Latin Quarter, where students and their teachers communicated in that language exclusively.

GOING UP & UP

The 12th and 13th centuries were a time of frenetic building activity in Paris. Abbot Suger, both confessor and minister to several Capetian kings, was one of the powerhouses of this period; in 1136 he commissioned the basilica at St-Denis (p182). Less than three decades later, work started on the cathedral of Notre Dame, the greatest creation of medieval Paris. At the same time Philippe-Auguste (r 1180–1223) expanded the city wall, adding 25 gates and hundreds of protective towers.

The Marais, whose name means 'swamp', was drained for agricultural use and settlement moved to the north (or right) bank of the Seine. this would soon become the mercantile centre, especially around place de Grève (today's place de l'Hôtel de Ville). The food markets at Les Halles first came into existence in 1183 and the Louvre began its existence as a riverside fortress in the 13th century. In a bid to do something about the city's horrible traffic congestion and stinking excrement (the population numbered about 200,000 by the year 1200), Philippe-Auguste paved four of Paris' main streets for the first time since the Roman occupation, using metre-square sandstone blocks. By 1292 Paris counted 352 streets, 10 squares and 11 crossroads.

The area south of the Seine – today's Left Bank – was by contrast developing not as a trade centre but as the centre of European learning and erudition, particularly in the so-called Latin Quarter. The ill-fated lovers Pierre Abélard and Héloïse (see the boxed text, p33) wrote the finest poetry of the age and their treatises on philosophy, and Thomas Aquinas taught at the new University of Paris. About 30 other colleges were established, including the Sorbonne.

In 1337 some three centuries of hostility between the Capetians and the Anglo-Normans degenerated into the Hundred Years' War, which would be fought on and off until the middle of the 15th century. The Black Death (1348–49) killed more than a third (an estimated 80,000 souls) of Paris' population but only briefly interrupted the fighting. Paris would not see its population reach 200,000 again until the beginning of the 16th century.

The Hundred Years' War and the plague, along with the development of free, independent cities elsewhere in Europe, brought political tension and open insurrection to Paris. In 1358 the provost of the merchants, a wealthy draper named Étienne Marcel, allied himself with peasants revolting against the dauphin (the future Charles V) and seized Paris in a bid to limit the power of the throne and secure a city charter. But the dauphin's supporters recaptured it within two years, and Marcel and his followers were executed at place de Grève. Charles then completed the right-bank city wall begun by Marcel and turned the Louvre into a sumptuous palace for himself.

After the French forces were defeated by the English at Agincourt in 1415, Paris was once again embroiled in revolt. The dukes of Burgundy, allied with the English, occupied the capital in 1420. Two years later John Plantagenet, duke of Bedford, was installed as regent of France for the English king, Henry VI, who was then an infant. Henry was crowned king of France at Notre Dame less than 10 years later, but Paris was almost continuously under siege from the French for much of that time.

Around that time a 17-year-old peasant girl known to history as Jeanne d'Arc (Joan of Arc) persuaded the French pretender Charles VII that she'd received a divine mission from God to expel the English from France and bring about Charles' coronation. She rallied French troops and defeated the English at Patay, north of Orléans, and Charles was crowned at Reims. But Joan of Arc failed to take Paris. In 1430 she was captured, convicted of witchcraft and heresy by a tribunal of French ecclesiastics and burned at the stake.

1358	1429	1532–64
The Hundred Years' War (1337–1453) between France and England and the devastation and poverty caused by the plague lead to the ill-fated peasants' revolt led by Étienne Marcel.	French forces under Joan of Arc defeat the English near Orléans but three years later Joan is captured by the Burgundians, allies of the English, and burned at the stake in Rouen.	The 16th century is a period of heightened literary activity which sees the publication of Rabelais' five-part satirical work *Gargantua and Panagruel* over more than three decades.

Charles VII returned to Paris in 1436, ending more than 16 years of occupation, but the English were not entirely driven from French territory (with the exception of Calais) for another 17 years. The occupation had left Paris a disaster zone. Conditions improved while the restored monarchy moved to consolidate its power under Louis XI (r 1461–83), the first Renaissance king under whose reign the city's first printing press was installed at the Sorbonne. Churches were rehabilitated or built in the Flamboyant Gothic style (see p46) and a number of *hôtels particuliers* (private mansions) such as the Hôtel de Cluny (now the Musée National du Moyen Age, p114) and the Hôtel de Sens (now the Bibliothèque Forney, p191) were erected.

A CULTURAL 'REBIRTH'

The culture of the Italian Renaissance (French for 'rebirth') arrived in full swing in France during the reign of François I in the early 16th century partly because of a series of indecisive French military operations in Italy. For the first time, the French aristocracy was exposed to Renaissance ideas of scientific and geographical scholarship and discovery as well as the value of secular over religious life. The population of Paris at the start of François' reign in 1515 was 170,000 – still almost 20% less than it had been some three centuries before, when the Black Death had decimated the population.

Writers such as François Rabelais, Clément Marot and Pierre de Ronsard of La Pléiade were influential at this time, as were the architectural disciples of Michelangelo and Raphael. Evidence of this architectural influence can be seen in François I's chateau at Fontainebleau (p368) and the Petit Château at Chantilly (p373). In the city itself, a prime example of the period is the Pont Neuf, the 'New Bridge' that is, in fact, the oldest span in Paris. This new architecture was meant to reflect the splendour of the monarchy, which was fast moving towards absolutism, and of Paris as the capital of a powerful centralised state. But all this grandeur and show of strength was not enough to stem the tide of Protestantism that was flowing into France.

REFORM & REACTION

The position of the Protestant Reformation sweeping across Europe in the 1530s had been strengthened in France by the ideas of John Calvin, a Frenchman exiled to Geneva. The edict of January 1562, which afforded the Protestants certain rights, was met by violent opposition from ultra-Catholic nobles whose fidelity to their faith was mixed with a desire to strengthen their power bases in the provinces. Paris remained very much a Catholic stronghold, and executions continued apace up to the outbreak of religious civil war.

The Wars of Religion (1562–98) involved three groups: the Huguenots (French Protestants supported by the English), the Catholic League and the Catholic king. The fighting severely weakened the position of the monarchy and brought the kingdom of France close to disintegration. On 7 May 1588, on the 'Day of the Barricades', Henri III, who had granted many concessions to the Huguenots, was forced to flee from the Louvre when the Catholic League rose up against him. He was assassinated the following year.

Henri III was succeeded by Henri IV, who inaugurated the Bourbon dynasty and was a Huguenot when he ascended the throne. Catholic Paris refused to allow its new Protestant king entry into the city, and a siege of the capital continued for almost five years. Only when Henri embraced Catholicism at St-Denis did the capital welcome him. In 1598 he promulgated the

1547–50	1572	1589
Some 39 Huguenots (French Protestants) are burned at the stake in place de Grève (today's place de l'Hôtel de Ville), which spurs a nationwide religious civil war.	Some 3000 Huguenots in Paris to celebrate the wedding of the Protestant Henri of Navarre (the future Henri IV) are slaughtered on 23–24 August, in what is now called the St Bartholomew's Day Massacre.	Henry IV, the first Bourbon king, ascends the throne after renouncing Protestantism; *'Paris vaut bien une messe'* (Paris is well worth a Mass), he is reputed to have said upon taking communion at the basilica in St-Denis.

Edict of Nantes, which guaranteed the Huguenots religious freedom as well as many civil and political rights, but this was not universally accepted.

Henri consolidated the monarchy's power and began to rebuild Paris (the city's population was now about 450,000) after more than 30 years of fighting. The magnificent place Royale (today's place des Vosges in the Marais) and place Dauphine at the western end of the Île de la Cité are prime examples of the new era of town planning. But Henri's rule ended as abruptly and violently as that of his predecessor. In 1610 he was assassinated by a Catholic fanatic named François Ravaillac when his coach became stuck in traffic along rue de la Ferronnerie in the Marais. Ravaillac was executed by an irate mob of Parisians (who were mightily sick of religious turmoil by this time) by being quartered – after a thorough scalding.

Henri IV's son, the future Louis XIII, was too young to assume the throne, so his mother, Marie de Médici, was named regent. She set about building the magnificent Palais du Luxembourg and its enormous gardens for herself just outside the city wall. Louis XIII ascended the throne at age 16 but throughout most of his undistinguished reign he remained under the control of Cardinal Richelieu, his ruthless chief minister. Richelieu is best known for his untiring efforts to establish an all-powerful monarchy in France, opening the door to the absolutism of Louis XIV, and French supremacy in Europe. Under Louis XIII's reign two uninhabited islets in the Seine – Île Notre Dame and Île aux Vaches – were joined to form the Île de St-Louis, and Richelieu commissioned a number of palaces and churches, including the Palais Royal and the Église Notre Dame du Val-de-Grâce.

ANCIEN RÉGIME & ENLIGHTENMENT

Le Roi Soleil (the Sun King) – Louis XIV – ascended the throne in 1643 at the age of five. His mother, Anne of Austria, was appointed regent, and Cardinal Mazarin, a protégé of Richelieu, was named chief minister. One of the decisive events of Louis XIV's early reign was the War of the Fronde (1648–53), a rebellion by the bourgeoisie and some of the nobility opposed to taxation and the increasing power of the monarchy. The revolt forced the royal court to flee Paris for a time.

When Mazarin died in 1661, Louis XIV assumed absolute power until his own death in 1715. Throughout his long reign, characterised by 'glitter and gloom' as one historian has put it, Louis sought to project the power of the French monarchy – bolstered by claims of divine right – both at home and abroad. He involved France in a long series of costly, almost continuous wars with Holland, Austria and England, which gained France territory but terrified its neighbours and nearly bankrupted the treasury. State taxation to fill the coffers caused widespread poverty and vagrancy in Paris, which was by then a city of almost 600,000 people.

But Louis was able to quash the ambitious, feuding aristocracy and create the first truly centralised French state, elements of which can still be seen in France today. While he did pour huge sums of money into building his extravagant palace at Versailles, by doing so he was able to turn his nobles into courtiers, forcing them to compete with one another for royal favour and reducing them to ineffectual sycophants.

Louis mercilessly persecuted his Protestant subjects, whom he considered a threat to the unity of the state and thus his power. In 1685 he revoked the Edict of Nantes, which had guaranteed the Huguenots freedom of conscience.

It was Louis XIV who said 'Après moi, le déluge' (After me, the flood); in hindsight his words were more than prophetic. His grandson and successor, Louis XV, was an oafish, incompetent

1635	1682	14 July 1789
Cardinal Richelieu, de facto ruler during the undistinguished reign of Louis XIII (1617–43), founds the Académie Française, the first and best known of France's five institutes of arts and sciences.	Louis XIV, the 'Sun King', moves his court from the Palais des Tuileries in Paris to Versailles in a bid to sidestep the endless intrigues of the capital; the cunning plan works.	The French Revolution begins when a mob arms itself with weapons taken from the Hôtel des Invalides and storms the prison at Bastille, freeing a total of just seven prisoners.

buffoon, and grew to be universally despised. However, Louis XV's regent, Philippe of Orléans, did move the court from Versailles back to Paris; in the Age of Enlightenment, the French capital had become, in effect, the centre of Europe.

As the 18th century progressed, new economic and social circumstances rendered the *ancien régime* (old order) dangerously out of step with the needs of the country and its capital. The regime was further weakened by the antiestablishment and anticlerical ideas of the Enlightenment, whose leading lights included Voltaire (François-Marie Arouet), Jean-Jacques Rousseau and Denis Diderot. But entrenched vested interests, a cumbersome power structure and royal lassitude prevented change from starting until the 1770s, by which time the monarchy's moment had passed.

The Seven Years' War (1756–63) was one of a series of ruinous military engagements pursued by Louis XV. It led to the loss of France's flourishing colonies in Canada, the West Indies and India. It was in part to avenge these losses that Louis XVI sided with the colonists in the American War of Independence (1775–83). But the Seven Years' War cost France a fortune and, more disastrously for the monarchy, it helped to disseminate at home the radical democratic ideas that were thrust upon the world stage by the American Revolution.

COME THE REVOLUTION

By the late 1780s, the indecisive Louis XVI and his dominating Vienna-born queen, Marie-Antoinette, known to her subjects disparagingly as *l'Autrichienne* (the Austrian), had managed to alienate virtually every segment of society – from the enlightened bourgeoisie to the conservatives – and the king became increasingly isolated as unrest and dissatisfaction reached boiling point. When he tried to neutralise the power of the more reform-minded delegates at a meeting of the États-Généraux (States-General) at the Jeu de Paume in Versailles from May to June 1789 (see p360), the masses – spurred on by the oratory and inflammatory tracts circulating at places like the Café de Foy (p188) at Palais Royal – took to the streets of Paris. On 14 July, a mob raided the armoury at the Hôtel des Invalides for rifles, seizing 32,000 muskets, and then stormed the prison at Bastille – the ultimate symbol of the despotic *ancien régime*. The French Revolution had begun.

At first, the Revolution was in the hands of moderate republicans called the Girondins. France was declared a constitutional monarchy and various reforms were introduced, including the adoption of the *Déclaration des Droits de l'Homme and du Citoyen* (Declaration of the Rights of Man and of the Citizen). This document set forth the principles of the Revolution in a preamble and 17 articles, and was modelled on the American Declaration of Independence. A forward-thinking document called *Les Droits des Femmes* (The Rights of Women) was also published. But as the masses armed themselves against the external threat to the new government – posed by Austria, Prussia and the exiled French nobles – patriotism and nationalism mixed with extreme fervour and then popularised and radicalised the Revolution. It was not long before the Girondins lost out to the extremist Jacobins, led by Maximilien Robespierre, Georges-Jacques Danton and Jean-Paul Marat. The Jacobins abolished the monarchy and declared the First Republic in September 1792 after Louis XVI proved unreliable as a constitutional monarch. The Assemblée Nationale (National Assembly) was replaced by an elected Revolutionary Convention.

In January 1793 Louis XVI, who had tried to flee the country with his family but only got as far as Varennes, was convicted of 'conspiring against the liberty of the nation' and guillotined

1793	1799	1815
Louis XVI is tried and convicted as citizen 'Louis Capet' (as all kings since Hugh Capet were declared to have ruled illegally) and executed; Marie-Antoinette's turn comes nine months later.	Napoleon Bonaparte overthrows the Directory and seizes control of the government in a coup d'état, opening the doors to 16 years of despotic rule, victory and then defeat on the battlefield.	British and Prussian forces under the Duke of Wellington defeat Napoleon at Waterloo; he is sent into exile for the second time, this time to a remote island in the South Atlantic where he dies six years later.

A DATE WITH THE REVOLUTION

Along with standardising France's – and, later, most of the world's – system of weights and measures with the almost universal metric system, the Revolutionary government adopted a new, 'more rational' calendar from which all 'superstitious' associations (ie saints' days and mythology) were removed. Year 1 began on 22 September 1792, the day the First Republic was proclaimed. The names of the 12 months – Vendémaire, Brumaire, Frimaire, Nivôse, Pluviôse, Ventôse, Germinal, Floréal, Prairial, Messidor, Thermidor and Fructidor – were chosen according to the seasons. The autumn months, for instance, were Vendémaire, derived from *vendange* (grape harvest); Brumaire, derived from *brume* (mist or fog); and Frimaire, derived from *frimas* (wintry weather). In turn, each month was divided into three 10-day 'weeks' called *décades*, the last day of which was a rest day. The five remaining days of the year were used to celebrate Virtue, Genius, Labour, Opinion and Rewards. While the republican calendar worked well in theory, it caused no end of confusion for France in its communications and trade abroad because the months and days kept changing in relation to those of the Gregorian calendar. The Revolutionary calendar was abandoned and the old system was restored in France in 1806 by Napoleon Bonaparte.

at place de la Révolution, today's place de la Concorde. His consort, Marie-Antoinette, was executed in October of the same year.

In March 1793 the Jacobins set up the notorious Committee of Public Safety to deal with national defence and to apprehend and try 'traitors'. This body had dictatorial control over the city and the country during the so-called Reign of Terror (September 1793 to July 1794), which saw most religious freedoms revoked and churches closed to worship and desecrated. Paris during the Reign of Terror was not unlike Moscow under Joseph Stalin.

Jacobin propagandist Marat was assassinated in his bathtub by the Girondin Charlotte Corday in July 1793 and by autumn the Reign of Terror was in full swing; by mid-1794 some 2500 people had been beheaded in Paris and more than 14,500 executed elsewhere in France. In the end, the Revolution turned on itself, 'devouring its own children' in the words of an intimate of Robespierre, Jacobin Louis Antoine Léon de Saint-Just. Robespierre sent Danton to the guillotine; Saint-Just and Robespierre eventually met the same fate. Paris celebrated for days afterwards.

After the Reign of Terror faded, a five-man delegation of moderate republicans led by Paul Barras, who had ordered the arrests of Robespierre and Saint-Just, set itself up to rule the republic as the Directoire (Directory). On 5 October 1795 (or 13 Vendémaire in year 6 – see the boxed text, above), a group of royalist *jeunesse dorée* (gilded youth) bent on overthrowing the Directory was intercepted in front of the Église St-Roch on rue St-Honoré. They were met by loyalist forces led by a young Corsican general named Napoleon Bonaparte, who fired into the crowd. For this 'whiff of grapeshot' Napoleon was put in command of the French forces in Italy, where he was particularly successful in the campaign against Austria. His victories would soon turn him into an independent political force.

LITTLE BIG MAN & EMPIRE

The post-Revolutionary government led by the five-man Directory was far from stable, and when Napoleon returned to Paris in 1799 he found a chaotic republic in which few citizens had any faith. In November, when it appeared that the Jacobins were again on the ascend-

1848	1852–70	1870–1
After more than three decades of monarchy, King Louis-Philippe is ousted and the short-lived Second Republic is established with Napoleon's incompetent nephew at the helm.	Paris enjoys significant economic growth during the Second Empire of Napoleon III and much of the city is redesigned or rebuilt by Baron Haussmann as the Paris we know today.	Harsh terms inflicted on France by victor Prussia in the Franco-Prussian War leads to open revolt and the establishment of the insurrectionary Paris Commune.

ancy in the legislature, Napoleon tricked the delegates into leaving Paris for St-Cloud to the southwest ('for their own protection'), overthrew the discredited Directory and assumed power himself.

At first, Napoleon took the post of First Consul, chosen by popular vote. In a referendum three years later he was named 'Consul for Life' and his birthday became a national holiday. By December 1804, when he crowned himself 'Emperor of the French' in the presence of Pope Pius VII at Notre Dame, the scope and nature of Napoleon's ambitions were obvious to all. But to consolidate and legitimise his authority Napoleon needed more victories on the battlefield. So began a seemingly endless series of wars and victories by which France would come to control most of Europe.

In 1812 Napoleon invaded Russia in an attempt to do away with his last major rival on the Continent, Tsar Alexander I. Although his Grande Armée managed to capture Moscow, it was wiped out by the brutal Russian winter; of the 600,000 soldiers mobilised, only 90,000 – a mere 15% – returned. Prussia and Napoleon's other adversaries quickly recovered from their earlier defeats, and less than two years after the fiasco in Russia the Prussians, backed by Russia, Austria and Britain, entered Paris. Napoleon abdicated and was exiled to the island of Elba off the coast of Italy. The Senate then formally deposed him as emperor.

At the Congress of Vienna (1814–15), the victorious allies restored the House of Bourbon to the French throne, installing Louis XVI's brother as Louis XVIII (Louis XVI's second son, Charles, had been declared Louis XVII by monarchists in exile but he died while under arrest by the Revolutionary government). But in February 1815 Napoleon escaped from Elba, landed in southern France and gathered a large army as he marched towards Paris. On 1 June he reclaimed the throne at celebrations held at the Champs de Mars. But his reign came to an end just three weeks later when his forces were defeated at Waterloo in Belgium. Napoleon was exiled again, this time to St Helena in the South Atlantic, where he died in 1821.

Although reactionary in some ways – he re-established slavery in France's colonies, for example – Napoleon instituted a number of important reforms, including a reorganisation of the judicial system; the promulgation of a new legal code, the Code Napoléon (or civil code), which forms the basis of the French legal system to this day; and the establishment of a new educational system. More importantly, he preserved the essence of the changes brought about by the Revolution. Napoleon is therefore remembered by many French people as the nation's greatest hero.

Few of Napoleon's grand architectural plans for Paris were completed, but the Arc de Triomphe, Arc de Triomphe du Carrousel, La Madeleine, Pont des Arts, rue de Rivoli and some buildings within the Louvre complex as well as the Canal St-Martin all date from this period.

THE RETURN OF THE MONARCHY

The reign of 'the gouty old gentleman' Louis XVIII (1814–24) was dominated by the struggle between extreme monarchists who wanted a return to the *ancien régime*, liberals who saw the changes wrought by the Revolution as irreversible, and the radicals of the working-class neighbourhoods of Paris (by 1817 the population of Paris stood at 715,000). Louis' successor, the reactionary Charles X (r 1824–30), handled this struggle with great incompetence and was overthrown in the so-called July Revolution of 1830 when a motley group of revolutionaries seized the Hôtel de Ville. The Colonne de Juillet in the centre of the place de la Bastille honours

1889	1894	1905
The Eiffel Tower is completed in time for the opening of the 1889 Exposition Universelle (World Exhibition) but is vilified in the press and on the street as the 'metal asparagus' – or worse.	Army Captain Alfred Dreyfus is convicted and sentenced to life imprisonment on trumped-up charges of spying for Germany but is later exonerated despite widespread conservative opposition.	The emotions aroused by the Dreyfus affair and the interference of the Catholic Church leads to the promulgation of *laïcité* (secularism), the legal separation of church and state.

those killed in the street battles that accompanied this revolution; they are buried in vaults under the column.

Louis-Philippe (r 1830–48), an ostensibly constitutional monarch of bourgeois sympathies and tastes, was then chosen by parliament to head what became known as the July Monarchy. His tenure was marked by inflation, corruption and rising unemployment and was overthrown in the February Revolution of 1848, in whose wake the Second Republic was established. The population of Paris had reached one million by 1844.

FROM PRESIDENT TO EMPEROR

In presidential elections held in 1848, Napoleon's inept nephew, the German-accented Louis Napoleon Bonaparte, was overwhelmingly elected. Legislative deadlock caused Louis Napoleon to lead a coup d'état in 1851, after which he was proclaimed Emperor Napoleon III (Bonaparte had conferred the title Napoleon II on his son upon his abdication in 1814, but the latter never ruled). A plebiscite overwhelmingly approved the motion (7.8 million in favour and 250,000 against), and Napoleon III moved into the Palais des Tuileries.

The Second Empire lasted from 1852 until 1870. During this period France enjoyed significant economic growth, and Paris was transformed by town planner Haussmann (see the boxed text, opposite) into the modern city it now is today. The city's first department stores were also built at this time – the now defunct La Ville de Paris in 1834 followed by Le Bon Marché in 1852 – as were the *passages couverts,* Paris' delightful covered shopping arcades (p188).

Like his uncle before him, Napoleon III embroiled France in a number of costly conflicts, including the disastrous Crimean War (1854–56). In 1870 Otto von Bismarck goaded Napoleon III into declaring war on Prussia. Within months the thoroughly unprepared French army was defeated and the emperor taken prisoner. When news of the debacle reached Paris the masses took to the streets and demanded that a republic be declared.

THE COMMUNE & THE 'BEAUTIFUL AGE'

The Third Republic began as a provisional government of national defence in September 1870. The Prussians were, at the time, advancing on Paris and would subsequently lay siege to the capital, forcing starving Parisians to bake bread partially with sawdust and consume most of the animals on display in the Ménagerie at the Jardin des Plantes. In January 1871 the government negotiated an armistice with the Prussians, who demanded that National Assembly elections be held immediately. The republicans, who had called on the nation to continue to resist the Prussians and were overwhelmingly supported by Parisians, lost to the monarchists, who had campaigned on a peace platform.

As expected, the monarchist-controlled assembly ratified the Treaty of Frankfurt. However, when ordinary Parisians heard of its harsh terms – a huge war indemnity, cession of the provinces of Alsace and Lorraine, and the occupation of Paris by 30,000 Prussian troops – they revolted against the government.

Following the withdrawal of Prussian troops on 18 March 1871, an insurrectionary government, known to history as the Paris Commune, was established and its supporters, the Communards, seized control of the capital (the legitimate government had fled to Versailles). In late May, after the Communards had tried to burn the centre of the city, the Versailles government launched an offensive on the Commune known as La Semaine Sanglante (Bloody Week), in which several

1918	1922	1940
Armistice ending WWI signed at Fôret de Compiègne near Paris sees the return of lost territories (Alsace and Lorraine); the war, however, had seen the loss of over a million French soldiers.	The doyenne at the centre of expatriate literary activity in Paris, Sylvia Beach of the Shakespeare & Company bookshop in rue de l'Odéon, publishes James Joyce's *Ulysses*.	After more than 10 months of *le drôle de guerre* (phoney war) Germany launches the battle for France, and the four-year occupation of Paris under direct German rule begins.

HAUSSMANN'S HOUSING

Few town planners anywhere in the world have had as great an impact on the city of their birth as did Baron Georges-Eugène Haussmann (1809–91) on Paris. As Prefect of the Seine *département* under Napoleon III between 1853 and 1870, Haussmann and his staff of engineers and architects completely rebuilt huge swaths of Paris. He is best known (and most bitterly attacked) for having demolished much of medieval Paris, replacing the chaotic narrow streets – easy to barricade in an uprising – with the handsome, arrow-straight thoroughfares for which the city is now celebrated. He also revolutionised Paris' water-supply and sewerage systems and laid out many of the city's loveliest parks, including large areas of the Bois de Boulogne (p177) and Bois de Vincennes (p176) as well as the Parc des Buttes-Chaumont (p173) and Parc Montsouris (Map pp162–3). The 12 avenues leading out from the Arc de Triomphe were also his work.

thousand rebels were killed. After a mop-up of the Parc des Buttes-Chaumont, the last of the Communard insurgents – cornered by government forces in the Cimetière du Père Lachaise – fought a hopeless, all-night battle among the tombstones. In the morning, the 147 survivors were lined up against what is now known as the Mur des Fédérés (Wall of the Federalists). They were then shot, and buried in a mass grave. A further 20,000 or so Communards, mostly working class, were rounded up throughout the city and executed. As many as 13,000 were jailed or transported to Devil's Island penal colony off French Guiana in South America.

Karl Marx, in his *The Civil War in France,* interpreted the Communard insurrection as the first great proletarian uprising against the bourgeoisie, and socialists came to see its victims as martyrs of the class struggle. Among the buildings destroyed in the fighting were the original Hôtel de Ville, the Palais des Tuileries and the Cours des Comptes (site of the present-day Musée d'Orsay). Both Ste-Chapelle and Notre Dame were slated to be torched but those in charge apparently had a change of heart at the last minute.

Despite this disastrous start, the Third Republic ushered in the glittering *belle époque* (beautiful age), with Art Nouveau architecture, a whole field of artistic 'isms' from impressionism onwards and advances in science and engineering, including the construction of the first metro line, which opened in 1900. *Expositions universelles* (world exhibitions) were held in Paris in 1889 – showcasing the then maligned Eiffel Tower – and again in 1900 in the purpose-built Petit Palais. The Paris of nightclubs and artistic cafés made its first appearance around this time, and Montmartre became a magnet for artists, writers, pimps and prostitutes (see p184).

But France was consumed with a desire for revenge after its defeat by Germany, and jingoistic nationalism, scandals and accusations were the order of the day. The most serious crisis – morally and politically – of the Third Republic, however, was the infamous Dreyfus Affair. This began in 1894 when a Jewish army captain named Alfred Dreyfus was accused of betraying military secrets to Germany – he was then court-martialled and sentenced to life imprisonment on Devil's Island. Liberal politicians, artists and writers, including the novelist Émile Zola, who penned his celebrated 'J'accuse!' (I Accuse!) open letter in support of the captain, succeeded in having the case reopened – despite bitter opposition from the army command, right-wing politicians and many Catholic groups – and Dreyfus was vindicated in 1900. When he died in 1935 Dreyfus was laid to rest in the Cimetière de Montparnasse. The Dreyfus affair discredited the army and the Catholic Church in France. This resulted in more-rigorous civilian control of the military and, in 1905, the legal separation of the Catholic Church and the French state.

25 August 1944	1949	1954
Spearheaded by Free French units, Allied forces liberate Paris and the city escapes destruction, despite Hitler's orders that it be torched; the war in Europe ends nine months later.	Simone de Beauvoir publishes her ground-breaking and very influential study *Le Deuxième Sexe* (The Second Sex) just four years after French women win the right to vote.	As a portent of what is to happen to the rest of its overseas empire, France loses its bid to reassert colonial control over Indochina when its forces are soundly defeated at Dien Bien Phu in Vietnam.

THE GREAT WAR & ITS AFTERMATH

Central to France's entry into WWI was the desire to regain the provinces of Alsace and Lorraine, lost to Germany in the Franco-Prussian War. Indeed, Raymond Poincaré, president of the Third Republic from 1913 to 1920 and later prime minister, was a native of Lorraine and a firm supporter of war with Germany. But when the heir to the Austrian throne, Archduke Franz Ferdinand, was assassinated by a Bosnian Serb in Sarajevo on 28 June 1914, Germany and Austria-Hungary – precipitating what would erupt into the first-ever global war – jumped the gun. Within a month, they had declared war on Russia *and* France.

By early September German troops had reached the River Marne, just 15km east of Paris, and the central government moved to Bordeaux. But Marshal Joffre's troops, transported to the front by Parisian taxicabs, brought about the 'Miracle of the Marne', and Paris was safe within a month. In November 1918 the armistice was finally signed in a railway carriage in a clearing of the Forêt de Compiègne, 82km northeast of Paris.

The defeat of Austria-Hungary and Germany in WWI, which regained Alsace and Lorraine for France, was achieved at an unimaginable human cost. Of the eight million French men who were called to arms, 1.3 million were killed and almost one million crippled. In other words, two of every 10 Frenchmen aged between 20 and 45 years of age were killed in WWI. At the Battle of Verdun (1916) alone, the French, led by General Philippe Pétain, and the Germans each lost about 400,000 men.

The 1920s and '30s saw Paris as a centre of the avant-garde, with artists pushing into new fields of cubism and surrealism, Le Corbusier rewriting the textbook for architecture, foreign writers such as Ernest Hemingway and James Joyce drawn by the city's liberal atmosphere (p193) and nightlife establishing a cutting-edge reputation for everything from jazz clubs to striptease.

France's efforts to promote a separatist movement in the Rhineland, and its occupation of the Ruhr in 1923 to enforce German reparations payments, proved disastrous. But it did lead to almost a decade of accommodation and compromise with Germany over border guarantees, and to Germany's admission to the League of Nations. The naming of Adolf Hitler as German chancellor in 1933, however, would put an end to all that.

WWII & OCCUPATION

During most of the 1930s, the French, like the British, had done their best to appease Hitler. However, two days after the German invasion of Poland on 1 September 1939, Britain and France declared war on Germany. For the first nine months Parisians joked about *le drôle de guerre* – what Britons called 'the phoney war' – in which nothing happened. But the battle for France began in earnest in May 1940 and by 14 June France had capitulated. Paris was occupied, and almost half the population of just under five million fled the city by car, by bicycle or on foot. The British expeditionary force sent to help the French barely managed to avoid capture by retreating to Dunkirk, described so vividly in Ian McEwan's *Atonement* (2001) and in a dreamlike sequence in Joe Wright's 2007 film of the book, and crossing the English Channel in small boats. The Maginot Line, a supposedly impregnable wall of fortifications along the Franco-German border, had proved useless – the German armoured divisions simply outflanked it by going through Belgium.

The Germans divided France into a zone under direct German rule (along the western coast and the north, including Paris), and into a puppet-state based in the spa town of Vichy and led by General Philippe Pétain, the ageing WWI hero of the Battle of Verdun. Pétain's collabora-

1958	1962	1968
De Gaulle returns to power after more than a dozen years in the opposition to form the Fifth Republic, in which power is weighted in the presidency at the expense of the National Assembly.	War in Algeria is brought to an end after claiming the lives of more than 12,000 people; three-quarters of a million Algeria-born French citizens arrive in France and many taken up residency in Paris.	Paris is rocked by student-led riots that bring the nation and the city to the brink of civil war; as a result de Gaulle is forced to resign the following year.

tionist government, whose leaders and supporters assumed that the Nazis were Europe's new masters and had to be accommodated, as well as French police forces in German-occupied areas (including Paris) helped the Nazis round up 160,000 French Jews and others for deportation to concentration and extermination camps in Germany and Poland. (In 2006 the state railway SNCF was found guilty of colluding in the deportation of Jews during WWII and was ordered to pay compensation to the families of two victims.)

After the fall of Paris, General Charles de Gaulle, France's undersecretary of war, fled to London. In a radio broadcast on 18 June 1940, he appealed to French patriots to continue resisting the Germans. He set up a French government-in-exile and established the Forces Françaises Libres (Free French Forces), a military force dedicated to fighting the Germans.

The underground movement known as the Résistance (Resistance), whose active members never amounted to more than about 5% of the French population, engaged in such activities as sabotaging railways, collecting intelligence for the Allies, helping Allied airmen who had been shot down, and publishing anti-German leaflets. The vast majority of the rest of the population did little or nothing to resist the occupiers or assist their victims or were collaborators, such as the film stars Maurice Chevalier and Arletty, and the designer Coco Chanel.

The liberation of France began with the Allied landings in Normandy on D-day (Jour-J in French): 6 June 1944. On 15 August Allied forces also landed in southern France. After a brief insurrection by the Résistance, Paris was liberated on 25 August by an Allied force spearheaded by Free French units – these units were sent in ahead of the Americans so that the French would have the honour of liberating the capital the following day. Hitler, who visited Paris in June 1940 and loved it, ordered that the city be burned toward the end of the war. It was an order that, gratefully, had not been obeyed.

POSTWAR INSTABILITY

De Gaulle returned to Paris and set up a provisional government, but in January 1946 he resigned as president, wrongly believing that the move would provoke a popular outcry for his return. A few months later, a new constitution was approved by referendum. De Gaulle formed his own party (Rassemblement du Peuple Française) and would spend the next 13 years in opposition.

The Fourth Republic was a period that saw unstable coalition cabinets follow one another with bewildering speed (on average, one every six months), and economic recovery that was helped immeasurably by massive American aid. France's disastrous defeat at Dien Bien Phu in Vietnam in 1954 ended its colonial supremacy in Indochina. France also tried to suppress an uprising by Arab nationalists in Algeria, where over one million French settlers lived.

The Fourth Republic came to an end in 1958, when extreme right-wingers, furious at what they saw as defeatism rather than tough action in dealing with the uprising in Algeria, began conspiring to overthrow the government. De Gaulle was brought back to power to prevent a military coup and even possible civil war. He soon drafted a new constitution that gave considerable powers to the president at the expense of the National Assembly.

CHARLES DE GAULLE & THE FIFTH REPUBLIC

The Fifth Republic was rocked in 1961 by an attempted coup staged in Algiers by a group of right-wing military officers. When it failed, the Organisation de l'Armée Secrète (OAS) – a group of French colons (colonists) and sympathisers opposed to Algerian independence – turned to

1977	1986	1989
The Centre Pompidou, the first of a string of grands projets, huge public edifices through which French leaders seek to immortalise themselves, opens to great controversy near Les Halles.	Victory for the opposition in the National Assembly elections forces President Mitterrand to work with a prime minister and cabinet from the right wing.	President Mitterrand's grand projet, Opéra Bastille, opens to mark the bicentennial of the French Revolution; IM Pei's Grande Pyramide is unveiled at the Louvre.

terrorism, trying several times to assassinate de Gaulle and nearly succeeding in August 1962 in the Parisian suburb of Petit Clamart. The book and film *The Day of the Jackal* portrayed a fictional OAS attempt on de Gaulle's life.

In 1962, after more than 12,000 had died as a result of this 'civil war', de Gaulle negotiated an end to the war in Algeria. Some 750,000 *pied-noir* (black feet), as Algerian-born French people are known in France, flooded into France and the capital. Meanwhile, almost all of the other French colonies and protectorates in Africa had demanded and achieved independence. Shrewdly, the French government began a programme of economic and military aid to its former colonies to bolster France's waning importance internationally and to create a bloc of French-speaking nations – *la francophonie* – in the developing world.

Paris retained its position as a creative and intellectual centre, particularly in philosophy and film-making, and the 1960s saw large parts of the Marais beautifully restored. But the loss of the colonies, the surge in immigration, economic difficulties and an increase in unemployment weakened de Gaulle's government.

In March 1968 a large demonstration in Paris against the war in Vietnam was led by student Daniel 'Danny the Red' Cohn-Bendit, who is today copresident of the Green/Free European Alliance Group in the European Parliament. This gave impetus to the student movement, and protests were staged throughout the spring. A seemingly insignificant incident in May 1968, in which police broke up yet another in a long series of demonstrations by students of the University of Paris, sparked a violent reaction on the streets of the capital; students occupied the Sorbonne and barricades were erected in the Latin Quarter. Workers joined in the protests and six million people across France participated in a general strike that virtually paralysed the country and the city. It was a period of much creativity and new ideas with slogans appearing everywhere, such as *'L'Imagination au Pouvoir'* (Put Imagination in Power) and *'Sous les Pavés, la Plage'* (Under the Cobblestones, the Beach), a reference to Parisians' favoured material for building barricades and what they could expect to find beneath them.

The alliance between workers and students couldn't last long. While the former wanted to reap greater benefits from the consumer market, the latter wanted (or at least said they wanted) to destroy it – and were called 'fascist *provocateurs*' and 'mindless anarchists' by the French Communist leadership. De Gaulle took advantage of this division and appealed to people's fear of anarchy. Just as Paris and the rest of France seemed on the brink of revolution, 100,000 Gaullists demonstrated on the av des Champs-Élysées in support of the government and stability was restored.

POMPIDOU TO CHIRAC

There is no underestimating the effect the student riots of 1968 had on France and the French people, and on the way they govern themselves today. After stability was restored the government made a number of immediate changes, including the decentralisation of the higher education system, and reforms (eg lowering the voting age to 18, an abortion law and workers' self-management) continued through the 1970s, creating, in effect, the modern society that is France today.

President Charles de Gaulle resigned in 1969 and was succeeded by the Gaullist leader Georges Pompidou, who was in turn replaced by Valéry Giscard d'Estaing in 1974. François Mitterrand, long-time head of the Partie Socialiste (PS), was elected president in 1981 and, as the business

1994	1998	2001
Eurostar trains link Waterloo station in London with the Gare du Nord in Paris in just over three hours.	France beats Brazil to win the World Cup at the spanking-new Stade de France (Stadium of France) in St-Denis north of central Paris.	Socialist Bertrand Delanoë becomes the first openly gay mayor of Paris (and of any European capital) but is wounded in a knife attack by a homophobic assailant the following year.

community had feared, immediately set out to nationalise privately owned banks, large industrial groups and various other parts of the economy. However, during the mid-1980s Mitterrand followed a generally moderate economic policy and in 1988, aged 69, he was re-elected for a second seven-year term.

In the 1986 parliamentary elections the right-wing opposition led by Jacques Chirac, mayor of Paris since 1977, received a majority in the National Assembly; for the next two years Mitterrand was forced to work with a prime minister and cabinet from the opposition, an unprecedented arrangement in French governance known as *cohabitation*.

In the May 1995 presidential elections Chirac enjoyed a comfortable victory (Mitterrand, who would die in January 1996, decided not to run again because of failing health). In his first few months in office Chirac received high marks for his direct words and actions in matters relating to the EU and the war in Bosnia. His cabinet choices, including the selection of 'whiz kid' foreign minister Alain Juppé as prime minister, were well received. But Chirac's decision to resume nuclear testing on the French Polynesian island of Mururoa and a nearby atoll was met with outrage in France and abroad. On the home front, Chirac's moves to restrict welfare payments (designed to bring France closer to meeting the criteria for the European Monetary Union; EMU) led to the largest protests since 1968. For three weeks in late 1995 Paris was crippled by public-sector strikes, battering the economy.

In 1997 Chirac took a big gamble and called an early parliamentary election for June. The move backfired. Chirac remained president but his party, the Rassemblement Pour la République (RPR; Rally for the Republic), lost support, and a coalition of Socialists, Communists and Greens came to power. Lionel Jospin, a former minister of education in the Mitterrand government (who, most notably,

top picks

HISTORICAL READS

- Paris: The Secret History, Andrew Hussey (2006) – a book not unlike Peter Ackroyd's *London: The Biography*, this colourful historical tour of Paris opens the door to (but does not solve) many of the city's mysteries.
- Paris Changing, Christopher Rauschenberg (2007) – modern-day photographer follows in the footsteps of early-20th-century snapper Eugène Atget in this 'spot the difference' album of before-and-after photos.
- The Flâneur: A Stroll Through the Paradoxes of Paris, Edmund White (2001) – doyen of American literature and long-term resident (and *flâneur* – 'stroller') of Paris, White notices things rarely noticed by others – veritable footnotes of footnotes – in this loving portrait of his adopted city.
- The Seven Ages of Paris: Portrait of a City, Alistair Horne (2002) – this superb, very idiosyncratic 'biography' of Paris divides the city's history into seven ages – from the 13th-century reign of Philippe-Auguste to President Charles de Gaulle's retirement in 1969.
- Is Paris Burning? Larry Collins & Dominique Lapierre (1965) – this is a tense and very intelligent reportage of the last days of the Nazi occupation of Paris.
- Paris: The Biography of a City, Colin Jones (2005) – although written by a University of Warwick professor, this one-volume history is not at all academic. Instead, it's rather chatty, and goes into much detail on the physical remains of history as the author walks the reader through the centuries and the city.
- Cross Channel, Julien Barnes (1997) – This is a witty collection of key moments in shared Anglo-French history – from Joan of Arc to a trip via Eurostar from London to Paris – by one of Britain's most talented novelists.

BACKGROUND HISTORY

2002	2003	2004
President Jacques Chirac overwhelmingly defeats Front National leader Jean-Marie Le Pen to win second term.	Hundreds of mostly elderly and housebound Parisians die from complications arising from an unusually hot summer; a review of the health and emergency-response systems gets under way.	France bans the wearing of Muslim headscarves and other religious symbols in schools.

promised the French people a shorter working week for the same pay), became prime minister. France had once again entered into a period of *cohabitation* – with Chirac on the other side of the table this time around.

For the most part Jospin and his government continued to enjoy the electorate's approval, thanks largely to a recovery in economic growth and the introduction of a 35-hour working week, which created thousands of (primarily part-time) jobs. But this period of *cohabitation,* the longest-lasting government in the history of the Fifth Republic, ended in May 2002 when Chirac was returned to the presidency for a second five-year term with 82% of the vote. This reflected less Chirac's popularity than the fear of Jean-Marie Le Pen, leader of the right-wing Front National, who had garnered nearly 17% of the first round of voting against Chirac's 20%.

Chirac appointed Jean-Pierre Raffarin, a popular regional politician, as prime minister and pledged to lower taxes with declining revenues from a sluggish economy. But in May 2005 the electorate handed Chirac an embarrassing defeat when it overwhelmingly rejected, by referendum, the international treaty that was to create a constitution for the EU.

In the autumn of the same year riots broke out in Paris' *cités*, the enormous housing estates or projects encircling the capital, home to a dispossessed population of mostly blacks and Muslims. In some of the worst violence seen since WWII, there thankfully was no deaths but 3000 arrests and millions of euros in property damage. Parisians began to talk about and debate ethnic origin and affirmative action but this remained essentially a problem 'out there' in the *banlieues* (suburbs).

The trouble became more central – both literally and figuratively – in March 2006 after parliament passed the controversial Contrat de Première Embauche (CPE; First Employment Contract). Supporters argued that the plan would reduce unemployment by 20% while detractors said it would encourage a regular turnover of cut-rate staff and not allow young people to build careers. The majority of the nation's universities went on strike, workers and students mobilised and 1.5 million protesters took to the streets nationwide. In Paris, demonstrators torched cars and clashed with police, who responded with tear gas and water cannons. The government decided to withdraw the CPE altogether later in 2006.

PARIS TODAY

With this backdrop it came as no surprise that Prime Minister Dominique de Villepin, President Chirac's loyal henchman and heir apparent who had never even been elected to public office, did not even make it to the first post in the national elections of spring 2007. Instead, the get-tough Interior Minister Nicolas 'Sarko' Sarkozy, who famously fanned the flames during the 2005 race riots by calling the rioters *racaille* (rabble or riffraff) and whose loyalty to Chirac seemed to blow with the prevailing wind, stood as the UMP (Union for a Popular Movement) candidate against Socialist Ségolène 'Ségo' Royal, who appeared to be the left's only hope of ending a dozen years of right-wing incumbency. Neither candidate received an absolute majority in the first round of voting but in the second Sarkozy took 53% of the popular vote.

In his first year as president, Sarkozy succeeded where his predecessors failed in getting unions and employee groups to compromise on benefits and saw the national unemployment rate fall to 7.5%, the lowest level in more than two decades. But many of even his staunchest supporters were less than impressed with his performance and his popularity in the polls one year on stood at less than 40% (against 67% just after the May 2007 election). That's partly due to what the

2005	2007	2008
The French electorate overwhelmingly rejects EU Constitution; the suburbs surrounding Paris are wracked by rioting by Arab and African youths.	Pro-American pragmatist, Nicolas Sarkozy, Interior Minister under Chirac, beats Socialist candidate Ségolène Royal to become France's new president.	Mayor Bertrand Delanoë wins re-election to a second term of office.

STAR-CROSSED LOVERS

He was a brilliant 39-year-old philosopher and logician who had gained a reputation for his controversial ideas. She was the beautiful niece of a canon at Notre Dame. And like Bogart and Bergman in Casablanca and Romeo and Juliet in Verona, they had to fall in love in medieval Paris of all damned times and places.

In 1118, the wandering scholar Pierre Abélard (1079–1142) found his way to Paris, having clashed with yet another theologian in the provinces. There he was employed by Canon Fulbert of Notre Dame to tutor his niece Héloïse (1101–64). One thing led to another and a son, Astrolabe, was born. Abélard did the gentlemanly thing and married his sweetheart. But they wed in secret and when Fulbert learned of it he was outraged. The canon had Abélard castrated and sent Héloïse packing to a nunnery. Abélard took monastic vows at the abbey in St-Denis and continued his studies and controversial writings. Héloïse, meanwhile, was made abbess of a convent.

All the while, however, the star-crossed lovers continued to correspond: he sending tender advice on how to run the convent and she writing passionate, poetic letters to her lost lover. The two were reunited only in death; in 1817 their remains were disinterred and brought to Père Lachaise cemetery (p154) in the 20e, where they lie together beneath a neo-Gothic tombstone in Division 7.

French now calling *peopolisation,* another Anglo-French neologism, this one meaning excessive media interest in and coverage of politicians' private lives. Mind you, Sarkozy's divorcing his wife of 18 years just three months after taking office and his subsequent marriage to Italian-French model/pop singer Carla Bruni would have tongues wagging in even the most taciturn of societies. Indeed, his well-publicised holidays with the rich and famous and what some French people see as his extravagance have earned him the sobriquet 'President Bling-Bling', a reference to an American hip-hop term meaning showy, often crass jewellery. Waiting in the wings are the Socialists, encouraged by their successes in the March 2008 local elections, which included holding on to the power base of Paris. But will it be a replay of the 'Sarko-Ségo' show next time around in 2012, or will the president be eclipsed by Mayor Bertrand Delanoë's rising star?

ARTS

Paris is a bottomless well when it comes to the arts. There are philharmonic orchestras, ballet and opera troupes, theatre companies and copious cinemas from which to choose your art form. And its museums are among the richest in the world, with artwork representing the best of every historical period and school from the Romans to postmodernism. Generous government funding allows local venues to attract top international performers, and the number of international arts festivals hosted here seems to grow each year.

LITERATURE

Literature is something that matters deeply to French people, and it is an important focus in their sense of identity. Problem is, nowadays there are no schools or clear literary trends emerging, some authors are impossible to read and, relatively speaking, little contemporary literature finds its way into English translation. Much French writing today tends to focus in a rather nihilistic way on what the nation has lost in recent decades (such as identity, international prestige etc), particularly in the work of Michel Houellebecq, who rose to national prominence in 1998 with his *Les Particules Élémentaires* (Atomised). And accessibility? In 2002 the winner of the Prix Goncourt (Goncourt Prize; see the boxed text, p37) – *Les Ombres Errantes* by Pascal Quignard – was denounced even by some of the prestigious prize's judges as 'over-erudite' and 'inaccessible' to the average reader.

Such novels do not help the traveller get into the head of Paris, to see and feel how the city thinks and works. For now perhaps it is better to stick with the classics of French literature or even those writers who are more descriptive and thus accessible. The *roman policier* (detective novel), for example, has always been a great favourite with the French, and among its greatest exponents has been Belgian-born Georges Simenon, author of the Inspector Maigret novels. *La Nuit du Carrefour* (Maigret at the Crossroads) portrays Montmartre at its 1930s sleaziest and seediest best. And then there are the works of all those foreigners, such as Gertrude Stein and George Orwell (p36) and, more recently, Cara Black (p35).

Going back in time, in the history of early medieval French literature Paris does not figure largely, though the misadventures of Pierre Abélard and Héloïse (see the boxed text, p33) took place in the capital as did their mutual correspondence, which ended only with their deaths. And here they lie.

François Villon, considered the finest poet – in any language – of the late Middle Ages, received the equivalent of a Master of Arts degree from the Sorbonne before he turned 20 years of age. Involved in a series of brawls, robberies and generally illicit escapades, 'Master Villon' (as he became known) was sentenced to be hanged in 1462 supposedly for stabbing a lawyer. However, the sentence was commuted to banishment from Paris for 10 years, and he disappeared forever. As well as a long police record, Villon left behind a body of poems charged with a highly personal lyricism, among them the *Ballade des Pendus* (Ballad of the Hanged Men), in which he writes his own epitaph, and the *Ballade des Femmes du Temps Jadis*, which was translated by the English poet and painter Dante Gabriel Rossetti as the 'Ballad of Dead Ladies'.

The great landmarks of French Renaissance literature are the works of François Rabelais, Pierre de Ronsard and other poets of the group referred to as of La Pléiade and Michel de Montaigne. The exuberant narratives of the erstwhile monk Rabelais blend coarse humour with erudition in a vast *œuvre* that seems to include every kind of person, occupation and jargon to be found in the France of the mid-16th century. Rabelais had friends in high places in Paris, including Archbishop Jean du Bellay, whom he accompanied to Rome on two occasions. But some of Rabelais' friends and associates fell afoul of the clergy, including his publisher Étienne Dolet. After being convicted of heresy and blasphemy in 1546, Dolet was hanged and then burned at place Maubert in the 5e arrondissement.

During the 17th century, François de Malherbe, court poet under Henri IV, brought a new rigour to the treatment of rhythm in literature. One of his better-known works is his sycophantic *Ode* (1600) to Marie de Médici. Transported by the perfection of Malherbe's verses, Jean de La Fontaine went on to write his charming *Fables* in the manner of Aesop – though he fell afoul of the Académie Française (French Academy) in the process. The mood of classical tragedy permeates *La Princesse de Clèves* by Marie de La Fayette, which is widely regarded as the precursor of the modern character novel.

The literature of the 18th century is dominated by philosophers (see p38), among them Voltaire (François-Marie Arouet) and Jean-Jacques Rousseau. Voltaire's political writings, arguing that society is fundamentally opposed to nature, had a profound and lasting influence on the

top picks

BOOKS ABOUT PARISIANS & THE FRENCH

- *An Englishman in Paris: L'Éducation Continentale*, Michael Sadler (2003) – rollicking, *very* funny (mis)adventures of a self-proclaimed Francophile teacher in the City of Light with a preface from Peter Mayle.
- *Culture Shock France*, Sally Adamson Taylor (2005) – subtitled 'A Survival Guide to Customs and Etiquette', this was the first (and remains the best) introductory handbook to France and its foibles, Parisians and their peculiarities.
- *The Last Time I Saw Paris*, Elliot Paul (2001) – a superb classic work by an American expat that looks back on the working-class Paris of the interwar years in a series of interwoven episodes.
- *The French*, Theodore Zeldin (1983) – dated but highly acclaimed survey of French passions, peculiarities and perspectives by British scholar now advising the Sarkozy government.
- *Un Peu de Paris*, Jean-Jacques Sempé (2001) – wordless, very gentle portrait of Paris and Parisians in cartoons from a national institution whose work appears frequently in *The New Yorker*.
- *Savoir Flair*, Polly Platt (2000) – subtitled '211 Tips for Enjoying France and the French', this book by a 30-year Paris expat resident will help you understand what makes the French tick.
- *Paris in Mind*, Jennifer Lee (2003) – an anthology of essays and excerpts by 29 American writers – from Edith Wharton and James Baldwin to David Sedaris and Dave Barry (who discusses how to pronounce the French 'r').
- *Sixty Million Frenchmen Can't Be Wrong*, Jean-Benoit Nadeau and Julie Barlow (2003) – a Paris-based Canadian journalist couple explains the essence of what it means to be French and how they got to be the way they are.
- *The House in Paris*, Elizabeth Bowen (1949) – Paris through the eyes and ears of an 11-year-old English girl sequestered for 24 hours in a Parisian townhouse. Dark, evocative, classic.

century, and he is buried in the Panthéon. Rousseau's sensitivity to landscape and its moods anticipate romanticism, and the insistence on his own singularity in *Les Confessions* made it the first modern autobiography. He, too, is buried in the Panthéon.

The 19th century brought Victor Hugo, as much acclaimed for his poetry as for his novels, who lived on the place des Vosges before fleeing to the Channel Islands during the Second Empire. *Les Misérables* (1862) describes life among the poor and marginalised of Paris during the first half of the 19th century; the 20-page flight of the central character, Jean Valjean, through the sewers of the capital is memorable. *Notre Dame de Paris* (The Hunchback of Notre Dame; 1831), a medieval romance and tragedy revolving around the life of the celebrated cathedral, made Hugo the key figure of French romanticism.

Other influential 19th-century novelists include Stendhal (Marie-Henri Beyle), Honoré de Balzac, Amandine Aurore Lucile Dupin (better known as George Sand) and, of course, Alexandre Dumas, who wrote the swashbuckling adventures *Le Compte de Monte Cristo* (The Count of Monte Cristo) and *Les Trois Mousquetaires* (The Three Musketeers). The latter tells the story of d'Artagnan (based on the historical personage Charles de Baatz d'Artagnan, 1623–73), who arrives in Paris as a young Gascon determined to become one of the guardsmen of Louis XIII.

In 1857 two landmarks of French literature were published in book form: *Madame Bovary* by Gustave Flaubert and *Les Fleurs du Mal* by Charles Baudelaire. Both writers were tried for the supposed immorality of their works. Flaubert won his case, and his novel was distributed without censorship. Baudelaire, who moonlighted as a translator in Paris (he introduced the works of the American writer Edgar Allan Poe to Europe in editions that have since become classics of English-to-French translation), was obliged to cut a half-dozen poems from his work and was fined 300 francs, and he died an early and painful death, practically unknown. Flaubert's second-most popular novel, *L'Éducation Sentimentale* (Sentimental Education), presents a vivid picture of life among Parisian dilettantes, intellectuals and revolutionaries during the decline and fall of Louis-Philippe's monarchy and the February Revolution of 1848.

CARA BLACK

Cara Black (www.carablack.com), who divides her time between Paris and San Francisco, is the author of a best-selling murder-by-arrondissement series set in Paris and featuring the intrepid, half-French-half-American sleuth Aimée Leduc. The latest is *Murder in the Rue de Paradis*.

A Francophile from California... How does that work? Francophilia goes way back. I had French nuns in school, my uncle studied under Georges Braque on the GI Bill after the war and in 1971, while travelling through Paris, I went to Rue du Bac and knocked on the door of my favourite writer, [two-times Prix Goncourt winner] Romain Gary. He invited me to his café for an espresso and a cigar. We both had both.

Ah, smoke – but fire? All this murder and darkness in the City of Light? That all came about much later, in 1993. I was walking around the place des Vosges and remembered a visit to Paris almost a decade before when I stayed with my friend Sarah. She had taken me on a tour of the pregentrified Marais and shown me the ancient abandoned building where her Jewish mother had hidden during the war and from where the rest of the family had been deported to Auschwitz. The idea for my first book *Murder in the Marais* came to me on the plane going home.

Does your research get down and dirty? I crawl under buildings, explore restrooms in old cafés, visit ghost metro stations, go down into the city sewers and even the tunnels under the Palais Royal. I interview police – I'm one of only two American women writers to have spent time in the Préfecture – and private detectives. Some of them have become friends and I take them to dinner.

Now we're cooking! What's on the menu? Murder most fowl? Steak saignant ('bleeding', or rare)? Anything but the *écrevisse* [freshwater crayfish] that come from the Seine. They feed on corpses. I discovered that while researching *Murder on the Île Saint-Louis*. One restaurant was still selling them.

Why are you always Right and not Left? How about murder in the sexy 6e or the louche Latin Quarter? I don't write about the Paris of tourists, where people wear berets and carry baguettes. I'm not really comfortable on the Left Bank. I feel better where my friends live – the Marais, Belleville, Montmartre. I understand these places better.

I wish I could... Tie a scarf the way French women do.

I wish I hadn't... Buried Baudelaire in Père Lachaise cemetery. He's actually in Montparnasse.

I'll always come back to Paris for... Hot chocolate at Ladurée, bicycle rides along the Canal St-Martin, the old stones of the Place des Vosges and the ghosts. Paris is full of ghosts and they communicate. You only need listen.

Interviewed by Steve Fallon

STRANGERS IN PARIS

Foreigners (*étrangers,* or strangers, to the French) have found inspiration in Paris since Charles Dickens used the city alongside London as the backdrop to his novel on the French Revolution, *A Tale of Two Cities,* in 1859. The glory days of Paris as a literary setting, however, were without a doubt the interwar years (p193).

Both Ernest Hemingway's *The Sun Also Rises* and *A Moveable Feast* portray bohemian life in Paris between the wars; many of the vignettes in the latter – dissing Ford Maddox Ford in a café, 'sizing up' F Scott Fitzgerald in a toilet in the Latin Quarter and overhearing Gertrude Stein and her lover, Alice B Toklas, bitchin' at one another from the sitting room of their salon near the Jardin du Luxembourg – are classic and *très parisien.*

Language guru Stein, who could be so tiresome with her wordplays and endless repetitions ('A rose is a rose is a rose', 'Pigeons on the grass, alas') in books like *The Making of Americans,* was able to let her hair down by assuming her lover's identity in *The Autobiography of Alice B Toklas.* It's a fascinating account of the author's many years in Paris, her salon on the rue de Fleurus in the 6e and her friendships with Matisse, Picasso, Braque, Hemingway and others. It's also where you'll find that classic recipe for hashish brownies. Stein's *Wars I Have Seen* is a personal account of life in German-occupied Paris.

Down and Out in Paris and London is George Orwell's account of the time he spent working as a *plongeur* (dishwasher) in Paris and living with tramps in Paris and London in the early 1930s. Both *Tropic of Cancer* and *Quiet Days in Clichy* by Henry Miller are steamy novels set partly in the French capital. Mention should also be made of Anaïs Nin's voluminous diaries and fiction, especially her published correspondence with Miller, which is highly evocative of 1930s Paris.

For a taste of Paris in the 1950s try *Giovanni's Room,* James Baldwin's poignant account of a young American in Paris who falls in love with an Italian bartender, and his struggle with his sexuality. *Satori in Paris* by Jack Kerouac is the sometimes entertaining (eg the scene in the Montparnasse gangster bar) but often irritating account of the American Beat writer's last trip to France.

The aim of Émile Zola, who came to Paris with his close friend Paul Cézanne in 1858, was to transform novel-writing from an art to a science by the application of experimentation. His theory may now seem naive, but his work influenced most significant French writers of the late 19th century and is reflected in much 20th-century fiction as well. His novel *Nana* tells the decadent tale of a young woman who resorts to prostitution to survive the Paris of the Second Empire.

Paul Verlaine and Stéphane Mallarmé created the symbolist movement, which strove to express states of mind rather than simply detail daily reality. Arthur Rimbaud, apart from crowding an extraordinary amount of exotic travel into his 37 years and having a tempestuous sexual relationship with Verlaine, produced two enduring pieces of work: *Illuminations* and *Une Saison en Enfer* (A Season in Hell). Rimbaud stopped writing and deserted Europe for Africa in 1874, never to return. Verlaine died at 39 rue Descartes (5e) in 1896.

Marcel Proust dominated the early 20th century with his giant seven-volume novel *À la Recherche du Temps Perdu* (Remembrance of Things Past), which is largely autobiographical and explores in evocative detail the true meaning of past experience recovered from the unconscious by 'involuntary memory'. In 1907 Proust moved from the family home near av des Champs-Élysées to the apartment on blvd Haussmann that was famous for its cork-lined bedroom (now on display at the Musée Carnavalet in the Marais, p96) from which he almost never stirred. André Gide found his voice in the celebration of gay sensuality and, later, left-wing politics. *Les Faux-Monnayeurs* (The Counterfeiters) exposes the hypocrisy and self-deception to which people resort in order to fit in or deceive themselves.

André Breton led the group of French surrealists and wrote its three manifestos, although the first use of the word 'surrealist' is attributed to the poet Guillaume Apollinaire, a fellow traveller of surrealism who was killed in action in WWI. As a poet, Breton was overshadowed by Paul Éluard and Louis Aragon, whose most famous surrealist novel was *Le Paysan de Paris* (Nightwalker). Colette (Sidonie-Gabrielle Colette) enjoyed tweaking the nose of conventionally moral readers with titillating novels that detailed the amorous exploits of such heroines as the schoolgirl Claudine. Her best-known work is *Gigi* but far more interesting is *Paris de Ma Fenêtre* (Paris from My Window), dealing with the German occupation of Paris. Her view, by the way, was from 9 rue de Beaujolais in the 1er, overlooking the Jardin du Palais Royal.

After WWII, existentialism developed as a significant literary movement around Jean-Paul Sartre (see p38), Simone de Beauvoir and Albert Camus, who worked and conversed in the cafés of blvd St-Germain in the 6e. All three stressed the importance of the writer's political engagement. *L'Âge de Raison* (The Age of Reason), the first volume of Sartre's trilogy *Les Chemins de la Liberté* (The Roads to Freedom), is a superb Parisian novel; the subsequent volumes recall Paris immediately before and during WWII. De Beauvoir, author of *Le Deuxième Sexe* (The Second Sex), had a profound influence on feminist thinking. Camus' novel *L'Étranger* (The Stranger) reveals that the absurd is the condition of modern man, who feels himself a stranger – more accurately translated as 'outsider' in English – in his world.

In the late 1950s certain novelists began to look for new ways of organising narrative. The so-called *nouveau roman* (new novel) refers to the works of Nathalie Sarraute, Alain Robbe-Grillet, Boris Vian, Julien Gracq, Michel Butor and others. However, these writers never formed a close-knit group, and their experiments took them in divergent directions. Today the *nouveau roman* is very much out of favour in France though the authors' names often appear in print and conversation.

Mention must also be made of *Histoire d'O* (Story of O), the highly erotic sadomasochistic novel written by Dominique Aury under a pseudonym in 1954. It sold more copies than any other contemporary French novel outside France.

In 1980 Marguerite Yourcenar, best known for her memorable historical novels such as *Mémoires d'Hadrien* (Hadrian's Memoirs), became the first woman to be elected to the Académie Française. Several years later Marguerite Duras came to the notice of a larger public when she won the Prix Goncourt (see the boxed text, below) for her novel *L'Amant* (The Lover) in 1984.

Philippe Sollers was one of the editors of *Tel Quel*, a highbrow, then left-wing, Paris-based review that was very influential in the 1960s and early 1970s. His 1960s novels were highly experimental, but with *Femmes* (Women) he returned to a conventional narrative style.

Another editor of *Tel Quel* was Julia Kristeva, best known for her theoretical writings on literature and psychoanalysis. In recent years she has turned her hand to fiction, and *Les Samuraï* (The Samurai; 1990), a fictionalised account of the heady days of *Tel Quel*, is an interesting document on the life of the Paris intelligentsia. Roland Barthes and Michel Foucault are other authors and philosophers associated with the 1960s and '70s.

So-called accessible contemporary authors who enjoy a wide following include Patrick Modiano, Yann Queffélec, Pascal Quignard, Denis Tillinac and Nicole de Buron, a very popular mainstream humour writer whose books sell in the hundreds of thousands. Fred Vargas is a popular writer of crime fiction.

More-serious authors whose careers and works are closely scrutinised by the literary establishment and the well-read include Jean Echenoz, Nina Bouraoui, Jean-Philippe Toussaint, Annie Ernaux and Erik Orsenna. Others are Christine Angot, '*la reine de l'autofiction*' famous for her autobiographical novels, the best-selling novelist Marc Levy, and Yasmina Khadra, a former colonel in the Algerian army who adopted his wife's name as a nom de plume.

Two recent winners of the Prix Goncourt have been controversial for rather less than literary reasons. Jonathan Littell, who took the prize in 2006 for *Les Bienveillantes*, is actually a New

AND THE WINNER IS...

Like the UK's Booker or the Pulitzer in the USA, the Prix Goncourt (Goncourt Prize) is the most highly respected and coveted literary prize in France, awarded annually since 1903 to the best volume of imaginative work in prose published during that year. In the event of a tie, novels are to be given preference over collections of short stories or sketches. The winner is announced by the 10-strong Académie Goncourt each year at the Drouant (p233), a swanky restaurant in the 2e arrondissement. Though the prize comes with a purse of less than €10, it guarantees much media attention and soaring sales.

Among writers who have won the Prix Goncourt in the past and are still read are Marcel Proust (1919), André Malraux (1933), Julien Gracq (1951), Simone de Beauvoir (1954) and Marguerite Duras (1984). Winners in recent years:

2002 Pascal Quignard, *Les Ombres Errantes* (Wandering Shadows)
2003 Jacques-Pierre Amette, *La Maîtresse de Brecht* (Brecht's Mistress)
2004 Laurent Gaudé, *Le Soleil des Scorta* (The House of Scorta)
2005 François Weyergans, *Trois Jours chez Ma Mère* (Three Days at My Mother's)
2006 Jonathan Littell, *Les Bienveillantes* (The Kindly Ones)
2007 Gilles Leroy, *Alabama Song*

York–born American, though he was largely educated in France and writes in French. And it wasn't enough that the original title of Gilles Leroy's award-winning *Alabama Song* was in English, the theme – the story of the descent into madness of Zelda Fitzgerald, wife of novelist F Scott Fitzgerald and written in the first person – is centred squarely on the other side of the puddle.

PHILOSOPHY

France may be one of the few countries in the world to require its secondary-school students to demonstrate a solid mastery of philosophical concepts before pursuing an academic career. Forced to expostulate upon such brain ticklers as 'Can demands for justice be separated from demands for liberty?' (discuss) or 'Do passions prevent us from doing our duty?' (elaborate) in order to receive a *baccalauréat* (school-leaving certificate), many people here develop a lifelong passion for philosophical discourse. Most French towns of any size have at least one bar or café that will sponsor a regular *'philocafé'* in which anyone may contribute their ideas on a particular philosophical question; in Paris one of the most popular *philocafés* is at Café des Phares (p288), which goes into debate from 11am to 1pm on Sunday.

Left Bank philosophers Bernard-Henri Levy, Jean-François Revel, André Glucksmann and the late Marc Sautet, who founded the Café des Phares and died in 1998 at the age of 51, have achieved a level of celebrity normally reserved for film stars. Even politicians are expected to show a philosophical bent. In 2003 then Foreign (and later Prime) Minister Dominique de Villepin quietly published *Éloge des Voleurs de Feu* (translated as 'On Poetry'), an 824-page critique and homage to such 'Promethean rebels' as Villon and Rimbaud (p33) in French poetry.

René Descartes, who lived in the first half of the 17th century, was the founder of modern philosophy and one of the greatest thinkers since Aristotle. After making important contributions to analytical geometry and algebra, Descartes sought to establish certainty from a position of absolute doubt. Descartes' famed aphorism 'Cogito, ergo sum' (I think, therefore I am) is the basis of modern philosophical thought. His method and systems of thought came to be known as Cartesianism. In positing that there is an external reality that can be grasped through reason, Descartes rendered possible the development of modern science.

Blaise Pascal, a contemporary of Descartes, was also a mathematician, but addressed the absurdity of the human predicament in a manner that foreshadowed the existentialists of the 20th century. Pascal's central concern was in reconciling his religious devotion – he was a convert to Jansenism, an almost Calvinist branch of Roman Catholicism – with his scientific background. Thus, in *Pensées* (Thoughts) he put forth 'Pascal's Razor', which stated that the most logical approach is to believe in God. If God does not exist, one has lost nothing; if God does exist one has assured oneself of a favourable afterlife. The difficulty in this argument is that it makes it possible to argue that one should believe in all religions.

As one of the major thinkers of the 18th century, the so-called Age of Enlightenment, Jean-Jacques Rousseau addressed the relationship of the individual to society. His 1762 work *Le Contrat Social* (The Social Contract) laid the foundations for modern democracy by arguing that sovereignty resides with the people who express their will through majority vote. Liberty is an inalienable 'natural' right that cannot be exchanged for civil peace.

In the late 19th century the philosopher Henri Bergson abandoned reason as a tool towards discovering the truth, arguing that direct intuition is deeper than intellect. He developed the concept of *élan vital* (creative impulse), a spirit of energy and life that moves all living things, as the heart of evolution – not Darwin's theory of natural selection. His thoughts about the subjective experience of time greatly influenced his brother-in-law, Marcel Proust, and the writer's *À la Recherche du Temps Perdu* (Remembrance of Things Past; p33).

The 20th century's most famous French thinker was Jean-Paul Sartre, the quintessential Parisian intellectual who was born in the capital in 1905 and died there in 1980. For most people he embodied an obscure idea known as existentialism. It's one of the great 'isms' of popular culture, but even philosophers have trouble explaining what existentialism really means. The word derives from Sartre's statement, 'Existence precedes (or, more accurately in English, takes priority over) essence', meaning that man must create himself because there is no eternal 'natural self' or 'meaning of life'. Realising that there is no meaning of life provokes 'existential dread' and 'alienation'.

Simone de Beauvoir, Sartre's lifelong companion, applied existentialist concepts to the predicament of women in French society. There is no essential 'female' or 'male' nature, she opined in her seminal work *Le Deuxième Sexe* (The Second Sex), published in 1949. According to Beauvoir, women's status as the perpetual 'other' relegates them to remaining 'objects' of the subjective male gaze.

Sartre and de Beauvoir were strong advocates of communism until 1956 and the Soviet invasion of Hungary. Disillusionment with communism and with the political engagement implied by existentialism led a new generation towards the social science called structuralism. Coined by the anthropologist Claude Levi-Strauss, structuralists believe that sociological, psychological and linguistic structures shape individuals. Individuals do not shape themselves as the existentialists believe. Beginning as a scientific method for studying differences between cultures, structuralism soon came to represent a rejection of all the universal ideas – reason, progress, democracy – that had held sway since the Age of Enlightenment.

As a poststructuralist, Michel Foucault rejected the idea that it was possible to step outside the 'discursive practices' that claim to reveal knowledge and arrive at an ultimate truth. The search for knowledge cannot be separated from the power relationships that lie at the heart of every social and political relationship.

Jacques Derrida, first published in the influential *Tel Quel* (p33) in the 1960s, introduced the concept of deconstructionism. This concept suggests that outside language there is nothing to which we can refer directly, since all language is indicative only of itself (*il n'y a pas de hors-texte* – there is no subtext). So knowledge outside of language is literally unthinkable; it is not a natural reflection of the world. Each text allows for multiple interpretations, making it impossible to find certainty in textual analysis. But deconstructionism posed an obvious paradox: how can one use language to claim that language is meaningless?

In recent decades French philosophers have returned to political commitment and moral philosophy. Bernard-Henri Levy was an outspoken critic of the war in Bosnia and made several films on the subject in the 1990s. Known as France's No 1 'anti-anti-Americanist', Levy's recent (and most popular work in English) is *American Vertigo: Travelling America in the Footsteps of Tocqueville* (2006), in which he follows in the footsteps of his compatriot and forerunner, Alexis de Tocqueville, crisscrossing America and commenting on the state of the union. André Glucksmann's *Ouest contre Ouest* (West against West; 2003) looked at the Iraq war and the paradox that those groups for and against the war both claimed to be inspired by the same principles. In fact he was one of the few French intellectuals to back the invasion of Iraq. He supported Sarkozy in the 2007 national elections.

PAINTING

The philosopher Voltaire wrote that French painting began with Nicolas Poussin, the greatest representative of 17th-century classicism who frequently set scenes from ancient Rome, classical mythology and the Bible in ordered landscapes bathed in golden light. It's not a bad starting point.

In the 18th century Jean-Baptiste Chardin brought the humbler domesticity of the Dutch masters to French art. In 1785 the public reacted with enthusiasm to two large paintings with clear republican messages: *The Oath of the Horatii* and *Brutus Condemning His Son* by Jacques-Louis David. David became one of the leaders of the French Revolution, and a virtual dictator in matters of art, where he advocated a precise, severe classicism. He was made official state painter by Napoleon Bonaparte, glorifying him as general, first consul and then emperor, and is best remembered for his *Death of Marat*, depicting the Jacobin propagandist lying dead in his bath.

Jean-Auguste-Dominique Ingres, David's most gifted pupil in Paris, continued in the neoclassical tradition. The historical pictures to which he devoted most of his life (eg *Oedipus and the Sphinx*) are now generally regarded as inferior to his portraits. The name of Ingres, who played the violin for enjoyment, lives on in the phrase *violon d'Ingres*, which means 'hobby' in French.

The gripping *Raft of the Medusa* by Théodore Géricault is on the threshold of romanticism; if Géricault had not died early aged 33 he would probably have become a leader of the movement, along with his friend Eugène Delacroix. Delacroix's most famous – if not best – work is *Liberty Leading the People*, which commemorates the July Revolution of 1830 (p25).

The members of the Barbizon School brought about a parallel transformation of landscape painting. The school derived its name from a village near the Forêt de Fontainebleau (Forest of Fontainebleau; p371), where Camille Corot and Jean-François Millet, among others, gathered to paint *en plein air* (in the open air). Corot is best known for his landscapes *(The Bridge at Nantes, Chartres Cathedral);* Millet took many of his subjects from peasant life *(The Gleaners)* and had a great influence on Van Gogh.

Millet anticipated the realist programme of Gustave Courbet, a prominent member of the Paris Commune (he was accused of – and imprisoned for – destroying the Vendôme Column), whose paintings show the drudgery of manual labour and dignity of ordinary life *(Funeral at Ornans, The Angelus)*.

Édouard Manet used realism to depict the life of the Parisian middle classes, yet he included in his pictures numerous references to the Old Masters. His *Déjeuner sur l'Herbe* and *Olympia* both were considered scandalous, largely because they broke with the traditional treatment of their subject matter.

Impressionism, initially a term of derision, was taken from the title of an 1874 experimental painting by Claude Monet, *Impression: Soleil Levant* (Impression: Sunrise). Monet was the leading figure of the school, which counted among its members Alfred Sisley, Camille Pissarro, Pierre-Auguste Renoir and Berthe Morisot. The impressionists' main aim was to capture the effects of fleeting light, painting almost universally in the open air – and light came to dominate the content of their painting.

Edgar Degas was a fellow traveller of the impressionists, but he preferred painting at the racecourse *(At the Races)* and in ballet studios *(The Dance Class)* than the great outdoors. Henri de Toulouse-Lautrec was a great admirer of Degas, but chose subjects one or two notches below: people in the bistros, brothels and music halls of Montmartre (eg *Au Moulin Rouge*). He is best known for his posters and lithographs, in which the distortion of the figures is both satirical and decorative.

Paul Cézanne is celebrated for his still lifes and landscapes depicting the south of France, though he spent many years in Paris after breaking with the impressionists. The name of Paul Gauguin immediately conjures up studies of Tahitian and Breton women. Both painters are usually referred to as postimpressionists, something of a catch-all term for the diverse styles that flowed from impressionism.

In the late 19th century Gauguin worked for a time in Arles in Provence with the Dutch-born Vincent Van Gogh, who spent most of his painting life in France and died in the town of Auvers-sur-Oise (p382) north of Paris in 1890. A brilliant, innovative artist, Van Gogh produced haunting self-portraits and landscapes in which bold colour assumes an expressive and emotive quality.

Van Gogh's later technique paralleled pointillism, developed by Georges Seurat, who applied paint in small dots or uniform brush strokes of unmixed colour, producing fine mosaics of warm and cool tones in such tableaux as *Une Baignade, Asnières* (Bathers at Asnières). Henri Rousseau was a contemporary of the postimpressionists but his 'naïve' art was totally unaffected by them. His dreamlike pictures of the Paris suburbs and of jungle and desert scenes (eg *The Snake Charmer*) have had a lasting influence on art right up to this century.

Gustave Moreau was a member of the symbolist school. His eerie treatment of mythological subjects can be seen in his old studio, which is now the Musée National Gustave Moreau (p150) in the 9e. Fauvism took its name from the slight of a critic who compared the exhibitors at the 1905 Salon d'Automne (Autumn Salon) with *fauves* (beasts) because of their radical use of intensely bright colours. Among these 'beastly' painters were Henri Matisse, André Derain and Maurice de Vlaminck.

Cubism was effectively launched in 1907 with *Les Demoiselles d'Avignon* by the Spanish prodigy Pablo Picasso. Cubism, as developed by Picasso, Georges Braque and Juan Gris, deconstructed the subject into a system of intersecting planes and presented various aspects simultaneously. A good example is Braque's *Houses at l'Estaque*.

In the 1920s and '30s the so-called École de Paris (School of Paris) was formed by a group of expressionists, mostly foreign born, including Amedeo Modigliani from Italy, Foujita from Japan and Marc Chagall from Russia, whose works combined fantasy and folklore.

Dada, both a literary and artistic movement of revolt, started in Zürich in 1915. In Paris, one of the key Dadaists was Marcel Duchamp, whose *Mona Lisa* adorned with moustache and goatee epitomises the spirit of the movement. Surrealism, an offshoot of Dada, flourished between the wars. Drawing on the theories of Sigmund Freud, it attempted to reunite the conscious and unconscious realms, to permeate everyday life with fantasies and dreams. Among the most important proponents of this style in Paris were Chagall, as well as René Magritte, André Masson, Max Ernst, André Breton and Piet Mondrian. The most influential, however, was the Spanish-born artist Salvador Dalí, who arrived in the French capital in 1929 and painted some of his most seminal works (eg *Sleep, Paranoia*) while residing here (see Dalí Espace Montmartre, p170).

top picks

ART & SCULPTURE MUSEUMS

- Musée du Louvre (p80)
- Musée Rodin (p130)
- Musée d'Orsay (p130)
- Musée Atelier Zadkine (p121)
- Musée d'Art Moderne de la Ville de Paris (p135)

WWII ended Paris' role as the world's artistic capital. Many artists left France, and though some returned after the war, the city never regained its old magnetism, with New York and then London picking up the baton. A few postwar Parisian artists worth noting have been Jean Fautrier, Nicolas de Staël, Bernard Buffet and Robert Combas. Popular installation artists include Christian Boltanski, Xavier Veilhan and Ben Vautier.

SCULPTURE

By the 14th century, sculpture was increasingly commissioned for the tombs of the nobility. In Renaissance Paris, Pierre Bontemps decorated the beautiful tomb of François I at the Basilique de St-Denis (p182), and Jean Goujon created the Fontaine des Innocents (p89). The baroque style is exemplified by Guillaume Coustou's *Horses of Marly* at the entrance to the av des Champs-Élysées.

In the mid-19th century, memorial statues in public places came to replace sculpted tombs (see the boxed text, p120). One of the best artists in the new mode was François Rude, who sculpted the Maréchal Ney statue (Map pp116–17), *Maréchal under Napoleon*, outside La Closerie des Lilas, and the relief on the Arc de Triomphe. Another sculptor was Jean-Baptiste Carpeaux, who began as a romantic, but whose work – such as *The Dance* on the Palais Garnier and his fountain in the Jardin du Luxembourg – look back to the warmth and gaiety of the baroque era. At the end of the 19th century Auguste Rodin's work overcame the conflict between neoclassicism and romanticism; his sumptuous bronze and marble figures of men and women did much to revitalise sculpture as an expressive medium. One of Rodin's most gifted pupils was Camille Claudel, whose work can be seen along with that of Rodin in the Musée Rodin (p130).

Both Braque and Picasso experimented with sculpture, and in the spirit of Dada, Marcel Duchamp exhibited 'found objects', one of which was a urinal, which he mounted, signed and dubbed *Fountain* in 1917.

One of the most influential sculptors to emerge before WWII was the Romanian-born and Paris-based Constantin Brancusi, whose work can be seen in the Atelier Brancusi outside the Centre Pompidou (p88). After the war César Baldaccini – known simply as César to the world – used iron and scrap metal to create his imaginary insects and animals, later graduating to pliable plastics. Among his best-known works are the *Centaur* statue (Map pp116–17) in the 6e and the statuette handed to actors at the Césars (French cinema's equivalent to the Oscars). Two sculptors who lived and worked most of their adult lives in Paris and each have a museum devoted to their life and work are Ossip Zadkine (p121) and Antoine Bourdelle (p165), though the museum of the latter was under renovation at the time of research.

In 1936 France put forward a bill providing for 'the creation of monumental decorations in public buildings' by allotting 1% of all building costs to public art, but this did not really get off the ground for another half-century when Daniel Buren's *Les Deux Plateaux* sculpture (p88) was commissioned at Palais Royal. The whole concept mushroomed, and artwork appeared everywhere: in the Jardin des Tuileries (*The Welcoming Hands;* p85), throughout La Défense (p179), Parc de la Villette (eg *Bicyclette Ensevelie,* 1990; p172) and even in the metro (see boxed text, p156). In addition, Paris counts some 120 commissioned murals, including a fine set of wall paintings by a group of four artists at 52 rue de Belleville, 20e (Map p155); and one by Robert Combas at 3 rue des Haudriettes, 3e (Map pp98–9).

MUSIC

In the 17th and 18th centuries French baroque music influenced much of Europe's musical output. Composers François Couperin and Jean Philippe Rameau were two luminaries of this period.

France produced and cultivated a number of brilliant composers in the 19th century, including Hector Berlioz, Charles Gounod, César Franck, Camille Saint-Saëns and Georges Bizet. Berlioz was the founder of modern orchestration, while Franck's organ compositions sparked a musical renaissance in France that would go on to produce such greats as Gabriel Fauré, and the musical impressionists Maurice Ravel and Claude Debussy. The latter's adaptations of poems are among the greatest contributions to the world of music.

More-recent classical composers include Olivier Messiaen, for decades the chief organist at the Église de la Trinité in the 9e, who (until his death in 1992 at the age of 84) combined modern, almost mystical music with natural sounds such as birdsong. His student, the radical Pierre Boulez, includes computer-generated sound in his compositions.

Jazz hit Paris with a bang in the 1920s and has remained popular ever since. France's contribution to the world of jazz has been great, including the violinist Stéphane Grapelli and the legendary three-fingered Roma guitarist Django Reinhardt.

The most popular form of indigenous music is the *chanson française*, with a tradition going back to the troubadours of the Middle Ages. 'French songs' have always emphasised lyrics over music and rhythm, which may explain the enormous success of rap in France in the 1990s, especially of groups like MC Solaar, NTM and I Am. The *chanson* tradition, celebrated by street singers such as Lucienne Delisle and Dahlia, was revived from the 1930s onwards by the likes of Édith Piaf and Charles Trénet. In the 1950s singers such as Georges Brassens, Léo Ferré, Claude Nougaro, Jacques Brel and Barbara became national stars; the music of balladeer/folk singer Serge Gainsbourg – very charming, very sexy and very French – remains enormously popular a decade and a half after his death.

The turn of the new millennium saw a revival of this genre called *la nouvelle chanson française*. Among the most exciting performers of this old-fashioned, slightly wordy genre are Vincent Delerm, Bénabar, Jeanne Cherhal, Camille, Soha and a group called Les Têtes Raides.

France was among the first countries to 'discover' *sono mondiale* (world music). You'll hear everything from Algerian rai and other North African popular music (Khaled, Cheb Mami, Rachid Taha) and Senegalese *mbalax* (Youssou N'Dour) to West Indian *zouk* (Kassav, Zouk Machine) and Cuban salsa. In the late 1980s, Mano Negra and Les Négresses

top picks

CDS

- Édith Piaf: Live at the Paris Olympia – a collation of live recordings made in the 1950s and '60s, this album contains 20 of the belle of Belleville's classics, including 'Milord', 'Hymne à l'Amour' and, of course, 'Non, Je Ne Regrette Rien'.
- M: Le Tour de M – everybody's favourite sing-along gives a little Prince and a titch of Zappa, and even gives Brel a nod with 'Au Suivant' in this double CD with two-dozen tracks.
- Georges Brassens: Le Disque d'Or – everything you need to know about one of France's greatest performers (and the inspiration for Jacques Brel) is in this 21-track double helping.
- Anthologie Serge Gainsbourg – three-CD anthology includes the metro man's most famous tracks, including 'Le Poinçonneur des Lilas' and 'Je t'aime…Moi Non Plus' in duet with Brigitte Bardot.
- Carla Bruni: No Promises – OK, the breathy voice might not do much for you but Italian-French model-cum-singer Carla Bruni's only album thus far in English in which she sets to (her own) music a dozen poems by the likes of WB Yeats, Emily Dickinson, WH Auden and Dorothy Parker is more than just a *curiosité* now that said model-cum-singer is Mme Sarkozy.
- Luaka Bop Présente Cuisine Non-Stop – there's something for everyone in David Byrne's homage to *la nouvelle chanson française*, with Arthur H coming over all Serge Gainsbourg on 'Naïve Derviche', and Têtes Raides light and breezy on 'Un P'tit Air'.
- La Nouvelle Chanson Française – like it or not, this five-pack by various artists gives directions to the way vocals are heading in French music, with everything from traditional and cabaret to folk-electronic and Paris club sound.

Vertes were two bands that combined many of these elements – often with brilliant results. Magic System from Côte d'Ivoire has helped popularise *zouglou* (a kind of West African rap and dance music) with its album *Premier Gaou,* and Congolese Koffi Olomide still packs the halls.

In recent years a distinctly urban and highly exportable Parisian sound has developed, often mixing computer-enhanced Chicago blues and Detroit techno with 1960s lounge music and vintage tracks from the likes of Gainsbourg and Brassens. Among those playing now are Parisian duo Daft Punk, who adapt first-wave acid House and techno to their younger roots in pop, indie rock and hip-hop; Air; and erstwhile Mano Negra leader Manu Chao, whose music is simple guitar and lyrics – plain and straightforward. One could be forgiven for thinking that popular music in France is becoming dynastic. The very distinctive M (for Mathieu) is the son of singer Louis Chédid; Arthur H is the progeny of pop-rock musician Jacques Higelin; and Thomas Dutronc is the offspring of 1960s idols *père* Jacques and Françoise Hardy. DJs to note are Étienne de Crécy, who has made quite a noise internationally; Claude Challe, responsible for the Buddha Bar compilations; and Wax Tailor.

Despite its problems (the lead singer, Bertrand Cantat, was imprisoned for the murder of his girlfriend), Noir Désir is *the* sound of French rock; there's talk the band could reform since Cantat's release from jail in 2007. Worth noting are Louise Attack, Mickey 3D and Nosfell, who sings in his very own invented language. It's a long way from the *yéyé* (imitative rock) of the 1960s as sung by Johnny Halliday, otherwise known as 'Johnny National' until he took Belgian nationality for tax reasons.

CINEMA

Parisians go to the cinema on average once a week – the 5pm *séance* (performance) on Sunday is a very popular time. They also take films, especially French films – France is the leading film producer in Europe, making over 200 films a year – very seriously. Parisians always prefer to watch foreign films in their original language with French subtitles.

France's place in film history was firmly ensured when the Lumière brothers from Lyon invented 'moving pictures' and organised the world's first paying public film-screening – a series of two-minute reels – in Paris' Grand Café on the blvd des Capucines (9e) in December 1895.

In the 1920s and 1930s avant-garde directors, such as René Clair, Marcel Carné and the intensely productive Jean Renoir, son of the artist, searched for new forms and subjects.

In the late 1950s a large group of young directors arrived on the scene with a new genre, the so-called *nouvelle vague* (new wave). This group included Jean-Luc Godard, François Truffaut, Claude Chabrol, Eric Rohmer, Jacques Rivette, Louis Malle and Alain Resnais. This disparate group of directors believed in the primacy of the film maker, giving rise to the term *film d'auteur* (literally, 'author's film').

Many films followed, among them Alain Resnais' *Hiroshima Mon Amour* (Hiroshima My Love) and *L'Année Dernière à Marienbad* (Last Year at Marienbad), and Luis Buñuel's *Belle de Jour*. François Truffaut's *Les Quatre Cents Coups* (The 400 Blows) was partly based on his own rebellious adolescence. Jean-Luc Godard made such films as *À Bout de Souffle* (Breathless), *Alphaville* and *Pierrot le Fou*, which showed even less concern for sequence and narrative. The new wave continued until the 1970s, by which time it had lost its experimental edge and appeal.

Of the directors of the 1950s and 1960s who were not part of the new wave school, one of the most notable was Jacques Tati, who made many comic films based around the charming, bumbling figure of Monsieur Hulot and his struggles to adapt to the modern age. The best examples are *Les Vacances de M Hulot* (Mr Hulot's Holiday) and *Mon Oncle* (My Uncle).

The most successful directors of the 1980s and 1990s included Jean-Jacques Beineix, who made *Diva* and *Betty Blue,* Jean-Luc Besson, who shot *Subway* and *The Big Blue,* and Léos Carax *(Boy Meets Girl)*.

Light social comedies *La Vie Est un Long Fleuve Tranquille* (Life is a Long Quiet River) by Étienne Chatiliez, *8 Femmes*, with its all-star cast (including Catherine Deneuve and Isabelle Huppert) by François Ozon and the Marseille comedy *Taxi* have been among the biggest hits in France in recent years.

Matthieu Kassovitz's award-winning *La Haine* (Hate), apparently inspired by American films *Mean Streets, Taxi Driver* and *Do the Right Thing*, examined the prejudice and violence among young French-born Algerians. Alain Resnais' *On Connaît la Chanson* (Same Old Song), based on the life of the late British TV playwright Dennis Potter, received international acclaim and six Césars in 1997.

Other well-regarded directors active today include Bertrand Blier (*Trop Belle pour Toi*; Too Beautiful for You), Cédric Klapisch (*Un Air de Famille*; Family Relations), German-born Dominik Moll (*Harry, un Ami qui Vous Veut du Bien*; With a Friend like Harry), Agnès Jaoul (*Le Gout des Autres*; The Taste of Others), Yves Lavandier (*Oui, Mais…*; Yes, But…), Catherine Breillat (*À Ma Sœur*; Fat Girl) and Abdellatif Kechiche (*La Graine et le Mulet*; The Secret of the Grain), who won his second César in 2008.

Among the most popular and/or biggest-grossing French films at home and abroad in recent years have been Jean-Pierre Jeunet's feel-good *Le Fabuleux Destin d'Amélie Poulain* (Amélie); Christophe Barratier's *Les Choristes* (The Chorus), about a new teacher at a strict boarding school who affects the students' lives through music; *De Battre Mon Cœur s'est Arrêté* (The Beat My Heart Skipped) by Jacques Audiard, a film noir about a violent rent collector turned classical pianist confronting his own life and that of his criminal father; and *Paris, Je T'aime* (Paris, I Love You), a two-hour film made up of 18 short films each set in a different arrondissement. The runaway success story so far this decade has been Olivier Dahan's *La Môme* (La Vie en Rose), starring Marion Cotillard as Édith Piaf. Not only did Cotillard pick up a César, Golden Globe and BAFTA for her efforts, she was the first French woman to win an Oscar for best actress since Simone Signoret was so honoured for *Room at the Top* in 1959. In early 2008 *Bienvenue Chez les Ch'tis* (Welcome to the Ch'tis), a simple film about a postal worker from the south who moves to Picardy in the north and falls for the charm of the locals, broke French box-office records.

top picks

PARIS FILMS

- À Bout de Souffle (Breathless; France, 1959) – Jean-Luc Goddard's first feature is a carefree, fast-paced B&W celebration of Paris – from av des Champs-Élysées to the cafés of the Left Bank.
- Last Tango in Paris (USA, 1972) – in Bernardo Bertolucci's classic, Marlon Brando gives the performance of his career portraying a grief-stricken American in Paris who tries to find salvation in anonymous, sadomasochistic sex.
- La Haine (Hate; France, 1995) – Matthieu Kassovitz's incendiary B&W film examines the racism, social repression and violence among Parisian *beurs* (young French-born Algerians).
- Les Quatre Cents Coups (The 400 Blows; France, 1959) – based on the French idiom *faire les quatre cents coups* (to raise hell), François Truffaut's first film is the semiautobiographical story of a downtrodden and neglected Parisian teenage boy who turns to outward rebellion.
- La Môme (La Vie en Rose; 2007) – biopic so faithful to the person and the time it's as if Édith Piaf – played by the highly honoured (and deservedly so) Marion Cotillard – had just woken up from a long sleep at Père Lachaise cemetery. *Incroyable*.
- Le Fabuleux Destin d'Amélie Poulain (Amelie; France, 2001) – one of the most popular French films internationally in years, Jean-Pierre Jeunet's feel-good story of a winsome young Parisian do-gooder named Amélie takes viewers on a colourful tour of Pigalle, Notre Dame, train stations and, above all, Montmartre.
- Paris, Je T'aime (Paris, I Love You; France, 2006) – an ode to Paris in 18 short films shot in different arrondissements (the 11e and 15e were dropped at the last minute) by different directors, including the Coen Brothers and Gus Van Sant.

THEATRE

France's first important dramatist was Alexandre Hardy, who appeared in Paris in 1597 and published over a relatively short period almost three dozen plays that were enormously popular in their day. Though few of his works have withstood the test of time, Hardy was an innovator who helped bridge the gap between the French theatre of the Middle Ages and Renaissance and that of the 17th century.

During the golden age of French drama the most popular playwright was Molière who, like William Shakespeare, started his career as an actor; Laurent Tirard's 2007 biopic *Molière* is a fictionalised account of his early years. Plays such as *Tartuffe*, a satire on the corruption of the aristocracy, won him the enmity (and a ban) of both the state and the church but are now staples of the classical repertoire. Pierre Corneille and Jean Racine, in contrast, drew their subjects from history and classical mythology. Racine's *Phèdre*, for instance, taken from Euripides, is a story of incest and suicide among the descendants of the Greek gods, while Corneille's tragedy *Horace* is derived from the historian Livy.

Theatre in France didn't really come into its own again until the postwar period of the 20th century with the arrival of two foreigners, both proponents of the so-called Theatre of the Absurd, who wrote in French. Works by Irish-born Samuel Beckett, such as *En Attendant Godot* (Waiting for Godot; 1952), are bleak and point to the existentialist meaninglessness of life but are also richly humorous. The plays of Eugène Ionesco – eg *La Cantatrice Chauve* (The Bald Soprano; 1948) – can be equally dark and satirical but ultimately compassionate.

Plays performed in Paris are – for obvious reasons – performed largely in French but more and more mainstream theatres are projecting English-language subtitles on screens. For information on theatres that host English-speaking troupes and/or stage plays in languages other than French, see p315.

DANCE

Ballet as we know it today originated in Italy but was brought to France in the late 16th century by Catherine de Médici. The first *ballet comique de la reine* (dramatic ballet) was performed at an aristocratic wedding at the Parisian court in 1581. It combined music, dance and poetic recitations (usually in praise of the monarchy) and was performed by male courtiers with women of the court forming the corps de ballet. Louis XIV so enjoyed the spectacles that he danced many leading roles himself at Versailles. In 1661 he founded the Académie Royale de Danse (Royal Dance Academy), from which modern ballet developed.

By the end of the 18th century, choreographers such as Jean-Georges Noverre had become more important than the musicians, poets and the dancers themselves. In the early 19th century, romantic ballets, such as *Giselle* and *Les Sylphides,* were better attended than the opera. For 10 years from 1945 Roland Petit created such innovative ballets as *Turangalila,* with music by Olivier Messiaen, and *Le Jeune Homme et la Mort.* Maurice Béjart shocked his audiences with his *Symphonie pour un Homme Seul* (which was danced in black in 1955), *Le Sacre du Printemps* (The Rite of Spring) and *Le Marteau sans Maître,* with music by Pierre Boulez.

Today French dance seems to be moving in a new, more personal direction with such performers as Maguy Marin, Laurent Hilaire and Aurélie Dupont. Choreographers include the likes of Odile Duboc, Caroline Marcadé, Jean-Claude Gallotta, Jean-François Duroure, Boris Charmatz and, perhaps the most interesting and visible of modern French choreographers, Philippe Decouflé.

ARCHITECTURE

Parisians have never been as intransigent as, say, Londoners in accepting changes to their cityscape, nor as unshocked by the new as New Yorkers appear to be. But then Paris never had as great a fire as London did in 1666, which offered architects a tabula rasa on which to redesign and build a modern city, or the green field that was New York in the late 18th century.

It took disease, clogged streets, an antiquated sewage system, a lack of open spaces and Baron Georges-Eugène Haussmann (p27) to drag Paris out of the Middle Ages into a modern world, and few town planners anywhere in the world have had as great an impact on the city of their birth as he did on his.

Haussmann's 19th-century transformation of Paris was a huge undertaking – Parisians endured years of 'flying dust, noise, and falling plaster and beams', as one contemporary observer wrote; entire areas of the city (eg the labyrinthine Île de la Cité) were razed and hundreds of thousands of (mostly poor) people displaced. Even worse – or better, depending on your outlook – it brought to a head the *vieux* (old) Paris versus *nouveau* (new) Paris, a debate in which writer Victor Hugo played a key role and which continues to this day (p49).

GALLO-ROMAN

Traces of Roman Paris can be seen in the residential foundations and dwellings in the Crypte Archéologique (p106) under the square in front of Notre Dame; in the partially reconstructed Arènes de Lutèce (p109); and in the *frigidarium* (cooling room) and other remains of Roman baths dating from around AD 200 at the Musée National du Moyen Age (p114).

The Musée National du Moyen Age also contains the so-called Pillier des Nautes (Boatsmen's Pillar), one of the most valuable legacies of the Gallo-Roman period. It is a 2.5m-high monument dedicated to Jupiter and was erected by the boatmen's guild during the reign of Tiberius (AD 14–37) on the Île de la Cité. The boat remains the symbol of Paris, and the city's Latin motto is 'Fluctuat Nec Mergitur' (Tosses but Does Not Sink).

MEROVINGIAN & CAROLINGIAN

Although quite a few churches were built in Paris during the Merovingian and Carolingian periods (6th to 10th centuries), very little of them remain.

When the Merovingian ruler Clovis I made Paris his seat in the early 6th century, he established an abbey dedicated to Sts Peter and Paul on the south bank of the Seine. All that remains of this once great abbey (later named in honour of Paris' patron, Sainte Geneviève, and demolished in 1802) is the Tour Clovis (p193), a heavily restored Romanesque tower within the grounds of the prestigious Lycée Henri IV just east of the Panthéon.

Archaeological excavations in the crypt of the 12th-century Basilique de St-Denis (p182) have uncovered extensive tombs from both the Merovingian and Carolingian periods. The oldest of these dates from around AD 570.

ROMANESQUE

A religious revival in the 11th century led to the construction of a large number of *roman* (Romanesque) churches, so-called because their architects adopted many architectural elements (eg vaulting) from Gallo-Roman buildings still standing at the time. Romanesque buildings typically have round arches, heavy walls, few windows that let in very little light, and a lack of ornamentation that borders on the austere.

No civic buildings or churches in Paris are entirely Romanesque in style, but a few have important representative elements. The Église St-Germain des Prés (p115), built in the 11th century on the site of the Merovingian ruler Childeric's 6th-century abbey, has been altered many times over the centuries, but the Romanesque bell tower over the west entrance has changed little since 1000. There are also some decorated capitals (the upper part of the supporting columns) in the nave dating from this time. The choir, apse and truncated bell tower of the Église St-Nicholas des Champs (Map pp92–3), just south of the Musée des Arts et Métiers, are Romanesque dating from about 1130. The Église St-Germain L'Auxerrois (p85) was built in a mixture of Gothic and Renaissance styles between the 13th and 16th centuries on a site used for Christian worship since about AD 500. But the square belfry that rises from next to the south transept arm is Romanesque in style.

GOTHIC

The Gothic style originated in the mid-12th century in northern France, where great wealth attracted the finest architects, engineers and artisans. Gothic structures are characterised by ribbed vaults carved with great precision, pointed arches, slender verticals, chapels (often built or endowed by the wealthy or by guilds), galleries and arcades along the nave and chancel, refined decoration and large stained-glass windows. If you look closely at certain Gothic buildings, however, you'll notice minor asymmetrical elements introduced to avoid monotony.

The world's first Gothic building was the Basilique de St-Denis (p182), which combined various late-Romanesque elements to create a new kind of structural support in which each arch counteracted and complemented the next. Begun in around 1135, the basilica served as a model for many other 12th-century French cathedrals, including Notre Dame de Paris and the cathedral at Chartres.

In the 14th century, the Rayonnant – or Radiant – Gothic style, which was named after the radiating tracery of the rose windows, developed, with interiors becoming even lighter thanks to broader windows and more-translucent stained glass. One of the most influential Rayonnant buildings was Ste-Chapelle (p107), whose stained glass forms a curtain of glazing on the 1st floor. The two transept façades of the Cathédrale de Notre Dame de Paris (p104) and the vaulted Salle des Gens d'Armes (Cavalrymen's Hall) in the Conciergerie (p106), the largest surviving medieval hall in Europe, are other fine examples of the Rayonnant Gothic style.

By the 15th century, decorative extravagance led to what is now called Flamboyant Gothic, so named because the wavy stone carving made the towers appear to be blazing or flaming (*flamboyant*). Beautifully lacy examples of Flamboyant architecture include the Clocher Neuf (New Bell Tower) at Chartres' Cathédrale Notre Dame (p377), the Église St-Séverin (Map pp110–11) and the Tour St-Jacques (p90), a 52m tower which is all that remains of an early-16th-century church. Inside the Église St-Eustache (p89), there's some outstanding Flamboyant Gothic arch work holding up the ceiling of the chancel. Several *hôtels particuliers* (private mansions) were also built in this style, including the Hôtel de Cluny, now the Musée National du Moyen Age (p114) and the Hôtel de Sens (now the Bibliothèque Forney, p190).

RENAISSANCE

The Renaissance, which began in Italy in the early 15th century, set out to realise a 'rebirth' of classical Greek and Roman culture. It had its first impact on France at the end of the 15th century, when Charles VIII began a series of invasions of Italy, returning with some new ideas.

The Early Renaissance style, in which a variety of classical components and decorative motifs (columns, tunnel vaults, round arches, domes etc) were blended with the rich decoration of Flamboyant Gothic, is best exemplified in Paris by the Église St-Eustache (p89) on the Right Bank and Église St-Étienne du Mont (p109) on the Left Bank.

Mannerism, which followed Early Renaissance, was introduced by Italian architects and artists brought to France around 1530 by François I; over the following decades French architects who had studied in Italy took over from their Italian colleagues. In 1546 Pierre Lescot designed the richly decorated southwestern corner of the Cour Carrée of the Musée du Louvre (p80). The Petit Château at the Château de Chantilly (p373) was built about a decade later. The Marais remains the best area for spotting reminders of the Renaissance in Paris proper, with some fine *hôtels particuliers* from this era such as Hôtel Carnavalet, housing part of the Musée Carnavalet (p96) and Hôtel Lamoignon (p190). The Mannerist style lasted until the early 17th century.

BAROQUE

During the baroque period – which lasted from the tail end of the 16th to the late 18th centuries – painting, sculpture and classical architecture were integrated to create structures and interiors of great subtlety, refinement and elegance. With the advent of the baroque, architecture became more pictorial, with the painted ceilings in churches illustrating the Passion of Christ and infinity to the faithful, and palaces invoking the power and order of the state.

Salomon de Brosse, who designed Paris' Palais du Luxembourg (see Jardin du Luxembourg, p119) in 1615, set the stage for two of France's most prominent early baroque architects: François Mansart, designer of the Église Notre Dame du Val-de-Grâce (Map pp110–11), and his young rival Louis Le Vau, the architect of the Château de Vaux-le-Vicomte (p372), which served as a model for Louis XIV's palace at Versailles.

Other fine examples of French baroque are the Église St-Louis en l'Île (p108); the Chapelle de la Sorbonne (p114); the Palais Royal (p88); and the 17th-century Hôtel de Sully (p96), with its inner courtyard decorated with allegorical figures.

Rococo

Rococo, a derivation of late baroque, was popular during the Enlightenment (1700–80). The word comes from the French *rocaille* (loose pebbles), which, together with shells, were used to decorate inside walls and other surfaces. In Paris, rococo was confined almost exclusively to the interiors of private residences and had a minimal impact on churches and civic buildings, which continued to follow the conventional rules of baroque classicism. Rococo interiors, such as the oval rooms of the Hôtel de Rohan-Soubise (see Archives Nationales, p97), were lighter, smoother and airier than their baroque predecessors, and tended to favour pastels over vivid colours.

NEOCLASSICISM

Neoclassical architecture, which emerged in about 1740 and remained popular in Paris until well into the 19th century, had its roots in the renewed interest in classical forms. Although it was, in part, a reaction against baroque and its adjunct, rococo, with emphases on decoration and illusion, neoclassicism was more profoundly a search for order, reason and serenity through the adoption of the forms and conventions of Graeco-Roman antiquity: columns, simple geometric forms and traditional ornamentation.

Among the earliest examples of this style in Paris are the Italianate façade of the Église St-Sulpice (p115), designed in 1733 by Giovanni Servandoni, which took inspiration from Christopher Wren's Cathedral of St Paul in London; and the Petit Trianon at Versailles (p360), designed by Jacques-Ange Gabriel for Louis XV in 1761. The domed building housing the Institut de France (p119) is a masterpiece of early French neoclassical architecture, but France's greatest neoclassical architect of the 18th century was Jacques-Germain Soufflot, who designed the Panthéon (p114).

Neoclassicism really came into its own, however, under Napoleon, who used it extensively for monumental architecture intended to embody the grandeur of imperial France and its capital. Well-known Paris sights designed (though not necessarily completed) under the First Empire (1804–14) include the Arc de Triomphe (p138); the Arc de Triomphe du Carrousel (p85); Église de Ste-Marie Madeleine (p139); the Bourse de Commerce (p90); and the Assemblée Nationale (p127) in the Palais Bourbon. The climax of 19th-century classicism in Paris, however, is thought to be the Palais Garnier (p147), designed by Charles Garnier to house the opera and to showcase the splendour of Napoleon III's France.

top picks

PARIS ARCHITECTURE BOOKS

- Guide de l'Architecture Moderne á Paris/Guide to Modern Architecture in Paris, Hervé Martin (2001) – excellent and very complete guide to all types of architecture; includes walking tours of the city.
- Paris: Architecture & Design, edited by Christian van Uffelen (2004) – a well-illustrated and very useful introduction to Paris' new architecture, inside and out.
- Paris 2000+: New Architecture, Sam Lubell & Axel Sowa (2007) – as new as tomorrow, this richly illustrated coffee-table book focuses on 30 buildings that have gone up since 2000.
- Paris, Grammaire de l'Architecture: XXe-XXIe Siècles, Simon Texier (2007) – contemporaneous with the preceding title, this is a far more serious French-language tome examining late-20th- and early-21st-century structures.
- Paris: A Guide to Recent Architecture, Barbara-Ann Campbell (1997) – dated, with B&W photos, this pocket-size book is for serious aficionados of the subject.

ART NOUVEAU

Art Nouveau, which emerged in Europe and the USA in the second half of the 19th century under various names (Jugendstil, Sezessionstil, Stile Liberty) caught on quickly in Paris, and its influence lasted until about 1910. It was characterised by sinuous curves and flowing, asymmetrical forms reminiscent of creeping vines, water lilies, the patterns on insect wings and the flowering boughs of trees. Influenced by the arrival of exotic *objets d'art* from Japan, its French name came from a Paris gallery that featured works in the 'new art' style.

Paris is still graced by Hector Guimard's Art Nouveau metro entrances (see boxed text, p156). There are some fine Art Nouveau interiors in the Musée d'Orsay (p130); an Art Nouveau glass roof over the Grand Palais (p139); and, on rue Pavée in the Marais, a synagogue designed by Guimard (p91). The city's main department stores, including Le Bon Marché (p212) and Galeries Lafayette (p215), also have elements of this style throughout their interiors.

MODERN

France's best-known 20th-century architect, Charles-Édouard Jeanneret (better known as Le Corbusier), was born in Switzerland but settled in Paris in 1917 at the age of 30. A radical modernist, he tried to adapt buildings to their functions in industrialised society without ignoring the human element. Not everyone thinks he was particularly successful in this endeavour, however.

Most of Le Corbusier's work was done outside Paris though he did design several private residences and the Pavillon Suisse, a dormitory for Swiss students at the Cité Internationale Universitaire (Map pp162–3) in the southeastern 14e bordering the blvd Périphérique. Perhaps most interesting – and frightening – are Le Corbusier's plans for Paris that never left the drawing board. Called Plan Voisin (Neighbour Project; 1925), it envisaged wide boulevards linking the Gare Montparnasse with the Seine and lined with skyscrapers. The project would have required bulldozing much of the Latin Quarter.

One of the best examples of modernist architecture in all of Paris is the Maison de Verre (Map pp128–9; 31 rue St-Guillaume, 7e; M Sèvres Babylone), the exquisite 'Glass House' designed by Pierre Chareau and completed in 1932. It may soon be open for limited tours.

Until 1968, French architects were still being trained almost exclusively at the conformist École de Beaux-Arts, which certainly shows in most of the early structures erected in the sky-scraper district of La Défense (p179). It can also be seen in buildings like the Unesco building (Map pp128–9), erected in 1958 southwest of the École Militaire in the 7e, and the unspeakable, 210m-tall Tour Montparnasse (1973; p123), whose architects, in our opinion, should have been driven in tumbrels to the place de la Concorde and guillotined.

CONTEMPORARY

France owes many of its most attractive and successful contemporary buildings in Paris to the narcissism of its presidents. For centuries France's leaders have sought to immortalise themselves by erecting huge public edifices – known as *grands projets* – in the capital, and the recent past has been no different. The late president Georges Pompidou commissioned the once reviled but now beloved Centre Beaubourg (Renzo Piano and Richard Rogers, 1977), later renamed the Centre Pompidou (p88), in which the architects – in order to keep the exhibition halls as spacious and uncluttered as possible – put the building's insides outside.

Pompidou's successor, Valéry Giscard d'Estaing, was instrumental in transforming the derelict Gare d'Orsay train station into the glorious Musée d'Orsay (p130), a design carried out by the Italian architect Gaeltana Aulenti in 1986. Jacques Chirac's only *grand projet* of 12 years in office was the magnificent Musée du Quai Branly (p134), the first major art gallery to open in Paris since the Centre Pompidou. By contrast, his predecessor François Mitterrand, with his decided preference for the modern, surpassed all of the postwar presidents with a dozen or so monumental projects in Paris costing taxpayers a whopping €4.6 billion.

Since the early 1980s, Paris has seen the construction of such structures as IM Pei's contro-versial Grande Pyramide (1989; see Musée du Louvre, p80), a glass pyramid that serves as the main entrance to the hitherto sacrosanct – and untouchable – Louvre and an architectural *cause célèbre* in the late 1980s; the city's second opera house, the tile-clad Opéra Bastille (1989; p102) designed by Canadian Carlos Ott; the monumental Grande Arche de la Défense (p180) by Danish architect Johan-Otto von Sprekelsen, which opened in 1989; the delightful Conservatoire National Supérieur de Musique et de Danse (1990; p173) and Cité de la Musique (1994; p173), designed by Christian de Portzamparc and serving as a sort of gateway from the city to the whimsi-cal Parc de la Villette; the twinned Grandes Serres (Great Greenhouses) built by Patrick Berger in 1992 at the main entrance to the Parc André Citroën (Map pp166–7); the Ministère de l'Économie, des Finances et de l'Industrie (pp158–9) designed by Paul Chemetov and Borja Huidobro in 1990, with its striking 'pier' over-hanging the Seine in Bercy; and the four glass towers of Dominique Perrault's Bibliothèque Nationale de France (National Library of France; p161), which opened in 1995.

One of the most beautiful and successful of the late-20th-century modern buildings in Paris is the Institut du Monde Arabe (p112), a highly praised structure that opened in 1987

FOR FURTHER INFORMATION

Those wanting to learn more about French architec-ture should visit the new Cité de l'Architecture et du Patrimoine (p134) in the Palais de Chaillot. Contem-porary architecture in the capital is the focus of the permanent exhibition called 'Paris, Visite Guidée' (Paris, a Guided Tour) at the Pavillon de l'Arsenal (Map pp92–3; ☎ 01 42 76 33 97; www.pavillon -arsenal.com; 21 blvd Morland, 4e; admission free; ☑ 10.30am-6.30pm Tue-Sat, 11am-7pm Sun; M Sully Morland), which is the city's town-plan-ning and architectural centre. It also has rotating exhibits.

BUILDING NEW INSPIRATION

For the most part, skyscrapers and other tall buildings are restricted to La Défense (p179), but that doesn't mean other parts of Paris are bereft of interesting and inspired new buildings. Some of our favourites:

1er arrondissement

Immeuble des Bons Enfants (Map p86; 182 rue St-Honoré; M Palais Royal-Musée du Louvre) Home to the Ministère de la Culture et de la Communication (Ministry of Culture & Communication), this inspired structure (Francis Soler and Frédéric Druot, 2004) is actually two separate and disparate buildings 'linked' by a metallic net of what can only be described as tracery that allows in light and also allows the diversity of the existing buildings to be seen.

Marché de St-Honoré (Map pp82–3; place du Marché St-Honoré; M Tuileries or Opéra) This monumental glass hall (Ricardo Bofill, 1996) of offices and shops replaces an unsightly parking garage (now put underground) and evokes the wonderful *passages couverts* (covered shopping arcades) that begin a short distance to the northeast (p188).

7e arrondissement

Musée du Quai Branly (p134) Jean Nouvel's structure of glass, wood and sod takes advantage of its 3-hectare experimental garden designed by Gilles Clément. A wall of the block facing the Seine is a 'vertical garden' (p52) of no fewer than 15,000 plants representing 150 varieties.

9e arrondissement

Hôtel Drouot (p215) We like this zany structure (Jean-Jacques Fernier and André Biro, 1980), a rebuild of the mid-19th-century Hôtel Drouot, for its 1970s retro design.

10e arrondissement

Crèche (Map pp152–3; 8ter rue des Récollets; M Gare de l'Est) This day nursery (Marc Younan, 2002) of wood and resin in the garden of the Couvent des Récollets looks like a jumbled pile of gold- and mustard-coloured building blocks. A central glass atrium functions as a 'village square'.

12e arrondissement

Cinémathèque Française (p157) The former American Centre (Frank Gehry, 1994), from the incomparable American architect of the Guggenheim Museum in Bilbao, is a fascinating building of creamy stone that looks, from some angles, as though it is falling in on itself.

Direction de l'Action Sociale Building (Map pp158–9; 94-96 quai de la Rapée; M Quai de la Rapée) The headquarters of Social Action (Aymeric Zublena, 1991) is unabashed in proclaiming the power of the state, with a huge square within and vast glass-and-metal gates. When the gates close, the square turns into an antechamber worthy of a palace.

13e arrondissement

Passerelle Simone de Beauvoir (p161) This delightful footbridge (Eiffel, 2006), built by the same company responsible for *the* icon, glides across the Seine, linking the 12e and 13e arrondissements, and at night looks like a blade of light.

14e arrondissement

Fondation Cartier pour l'Art Contemporain (p123) Jean Nouvel set to 'conceal' the Cartier Foundation for Contemporary Arts when he designed it in 1993. In some ways the structure (lots of glass and what looks like scaffolding) appears at once both incomplete and invisible. There's a 'vertical garden' (p52) here too.

19e arrondissement

Les Orgues de Flandre (Map pp174–5; 67-107 av de Flandre & 14-24 rue Archereau; M Riquet) As outlandish a structure as you'll find anywhere, these two enormous housing estates are known as 'The Organs of Flanders' due to their resemblance to that musical instrument and their street address. Storeys are stacked at oblique angles and the structures appear to be swaying, though they are firmly anchored at the end of a park south of the blvd Périphérique.

Philharmonie de Paris (Map pp174–5; Parc de la Villette; M Porte de Pantin) The ambitious new home of the Orchestre de Paris, due to open in 2012, will have an auditorium of 2400 'terrace' seats surrounding the orchestra.

and successfully mixes modern and traditional Arab and Western elements. It was designed by Jean Nouvel, France's leading and arguably most talented architect. We can't wait to see his Philharmonie de Paris (opposite).

However, not everything new, different and/or monumental that has appeared in the past two decades has been a government undertaking. The vast majority of the buildings in La Défense (p179), Paris' skyscraper district on the Seine to the west of the city centre, are privately owned and house some 1500 companies, including the head offices of more than a dozen of France's top corporations. Unfortunately, most of the skyscrapers here are impersonal and forgettable 'lipstick tubes' and 'upended shoeboxes', with a few notable exceptions including the Cœur Défense (Défense Heart; 2001), the Tour EDF (2001) and the Tour T1 (2005). But outranking them all in size, beauty and sustainability will be Tour Phare (Lighthouse Tower), a 299m-tall office and retail tower that torques like a human torso and, through awnings that raise and lower when the sun hits them, uses light as a building material. It will be completed in 2012.

ENVIRONMENT & PLANNING

THE LAND

The city of Paris – the capital of both France and the historic Île de France region – covers an area of just under 87 sq km (or 105 sq km if you include the Bois de Boulogne and the Bois de Vincennes). Within central Paris – which Parisians call *intra-muros* (Latin for 'within the walls') – the Right Bank is north of the Seine, while the Left Bank is south of the river.

Paris is a relatively easy city to negotiate. The ring road, known as the Périphérique, makes an irregularly shaped oval containing the entire central area. The Seine cuts an arc across the oval, and the terrain is so flat that the 126m-high Butte de Montmartre (Montmartre Hill) to the north is clearly visible for some distance.

Paris is divided neatly into two by the Seine and also into 20 arrondissements, which spiral clockwise from the centre in a logical progression. City addresses *always* include the number of the arrondissement, as streets with the same name exist in different districts. In this book, arrondissement numbers are given after the street address using the notation generally used by the French: 1er for *premier* (1st), 2e for *deuxième* (2nd), 3e for *troisième* (3rd) and so on. On some signs or commercial maps, you will see the variations 2ème, 3ème etc and sometimes IIe, IIIe etc.

There is almost always a metro station within 500m of wherever you are in Paris so all offices, museums, hotels, restaurants and so on included in this book have the nearest metro or RER (a network of suburban lines) station given immediately after the contact details. Metro stations generally have a *plan du quartier* (map of the neighbourhood) on the wall near the exit(s).

GREEN PARIS

For a densely populated urban centre inhabited for more than two millennia, Paris is a surprisingly healthy and clean city. Thanks mainly to Baron Haussmann (p27), who radically reshaped the city in the second half of the 19th century, a small army of street sweepers brush litter into the gutters from where it is hosed into sewers, and a city ordinance requires residents to have the façades of their buildings cleaned every 10 years.

These days, despite the city's excellent (and cheap) public transport system, Haussmann's wide boulevards are usually choked with traffic, and air pollution is undoubtedly the city's major environmental hazard. But things have improved tremendously on that score: the city leadership, which came to power in coalition with the Green Party, first restricted traffic on some roads at certain times and created lanes only for buses, taxis and bicycles. Then, in 2007, in an unprecedented move for a city its size, Paris launched the

top picks

PARKS & GARDENS

- Parc de La Villette (p172)
- Jardin du Luxembourg (p119)
- Parc des Buttes-Chaumont (p173)
- Parc Floral de Paris (p176)
- Bois de Boulogne (p177)

GROWING UP IN PARIS

The architectural feature *du jour* (currently) in Paris is the vertical garden – called a *mur végétal* (vegetation wall) in French – especially that of Patrick Blanc (www.verticalgardenpatrickblanc.com). His signature works can be found in several locations around Paris but the most famous is the one facing the Seine at the Musée du Quai Branly (p134). Seeming to defy the very laws of gravity, the museum's vertical garden consists of some 15,000 low-light foliage plants from Central Europe, the USA, Japan and China planted on a surface of 800 sq metres. The reason why they don't fall is that they are held in place by a frame of metal, PVC and non-biodegradable felt but no soil.

Other places to view M Blanc's handiwork:

- Centre Commercial des Quatre Temps, **La Défense** (p181)
- Fondation Cartier pour l'Art Contemporain, **14e** (p123)
- Marithé + François Girbaud branch, **6e** (p200)

Vélib' communal bicycle rental programme (p389) with more than 20,500 bicycles available at more than 450 stations. The City of Light (and life for foot-sore Lonely Planet authors) will never be the same.

Though upwards of some 96,500 trees (mostly plane trees and horse chestnuts) line the avenues and boulevards of Paris, the city can often feel excessively built-up. Yet there are more than 455 parks and gardens (with another 87,500 trees) to choose from – some not much bigger than a beach blanket, others the size of a small village. Over the past 15 years, the city government has spent a small fortune transforming vacant lots and derelict industrial land into new parks. Some of the better ones are Parc de Bercy (p157) and the unique Promenade Plantée (p157), the 'planted walkway' above the Viaduc des Arts, both in the 12e; the Jardin de l'Atlantique (p123), behind the Gare Montparnasse, and Parc André Citroën (Map pp166–7) on the banks of the Seine, both in the 15e; Parc de la Villette (p172) and Parc des Buttes-Chaumont (p173), both in the 19e; and Parc de Belleville (p154), 20e. If you'd like a hand in the 'reforestation' of the capital and elsewhere and don't mind spending €5, visit 1 Parisien, 1 Arbre (1 Parisian, 1 Tree; www.1parisien1arbre.com).

In just about every park in Paris, regardless of the size, you'll see a signboard illustrating and explaining the trees, flowers and other plants of the city. Most are rich in birdlife, including magpies, jays, great and blue tits, and even woodpeckers. In winter, seagulls are sometimes seen on the Seine, and a few hardy ducks also brave the river's often swift-flowing waters. Believe it or not, 32 mammals live in the parks of Paris, there are crayfish in the city's canals, and the Seine is teeming with roach, carp, bleak, pike and pike-perch.

If you want to keep Paris clean, leave your car at home and resist the temptation to rent one unless you're touring around the Île de France (p360). Instead, bring or rent a bike (p389), bearing in mind that the Vélib' rental system is more of a way of getting from A to B than a recreational facility; enjoy the city on foot – Paris is an eminently walkable city (see the walking tours in the Neighbourhoods chapter); or use the public transport system, which is cheap and extremely efficient. For further tips on how you can reduce your impact on the environment, contact Les Amis de la Nature (☎ 01 42 85 29 84; www.amisnature-pariscentre.org, in French; 18 rue Victor Massé, 75009) or the World Wildlife Fund France (☎ 01 55 25 84 84; www.wwf.fr, in French; 1 carrefour de Longchamp, 75116).

In theory Parisians can be fined up to €183 for littering (that includes cigarette butts) but we've never heard of anyone having to pay. Don't be nonplussed if you see locals drop paper wrappings or other detritus along the side of the pavement, however; the gutters in every quarter of Paris are washed and swept out daily and Parisians are encouraged to use them if litter bins are not available.

URBAN PLANNING & DEVELOPMENT

In 1967 stringent town-planning regulations in Paris, which had been on the books since Haussmann's time, were relaxed and buildings were allowed to 'soar' to 37m. However, they had to be set back from the road so as not to block the light. But this change allowed the erection of high-rise buildings, which broke up the continuity of many streets. A decade later new restrictions required that buildings again be aligned along the road and that their height be in proportion to the width of the street. In some central areas that means buildings cannot go higher than 18m.

In 2007 Mayor Bertrand Delanoë challenged the law – and Parisians' way of thinking – when he invited a dozen architectural firms from around the world to submit drawings for towers exceeding 100m in three different areas of the city, including Porte de la Chapelle in the 18e and the Masséna-Bruneseau district of the 13e but not the traditional skyscraper district of La Défense. The move was opposed by all opposition parties and, in a municipal survey, 63% of all Parisians.

GOVERNMENT & POLITICS

LOCAL GOVERNMENT

Paris is run by the *maire* (mayor), who is elected by the 163 members of the Conseil de Paris (Council of Paris). They serve terms of six years. The mayor has around 18 *adjoints* (deputy mayors), whose offices are in the Hôtel de Ville (City Hall).

The first mayor of Paris to be elected with real powers was Jacques Chirac in 1977; from 1871 until that year, the mayor was nominated by the national government as the capital was considered a dangerous and revolutionary hotbed. After the 1995 election of Chirac as national president, the Council of Paris elected Jean Tiberi as mayor, a man who was very close to the president and from the same party. In May 2001, Bertrand Delanoë, a socialist with support from the Green Party, became the first openly gay mayor of Paris (and of any European capital). The next election, which should have taken place in 2007, was deferred until March 2008 in deference to the national elections that year. Delanoë handily won re-election to a second term in the second round of voting.

The mayor has many powers, but they do not include control of the police, which is instead handled by the Préfet de Police (Chief of Police), part of the Ministère de l'Intérieur (Ministry of the Interior). Delanoë continues to enjoy widespread popularity, particularly for his efforts to make Paris a more livable city by promoting the use of bicycles and buses, reducing the number of cars on the road and creating a more approachable and responsible city administration.

Paris is a *département* – Ville de Paris; No 75 – as well as a city and the mayor is the head of both. The city is divided into 20 arrondissements and each has its own *maire d'arrondissement* (mayor of the arrondissement) and *conseil d'arrondissement* (council of the arrondissement), who are also elected for six-year terms. They have very limited powers, principally administering local cultural activities and sporting events.

NATIONAL GOVERNMENT

France is a republic with a written constitution adopted by referendum in September 1958 (the so-called Constitution of the Fifth Republic) and adapted 18 times since, most notably in 1962 when a referendum was organised calling for the election of the president by direct universal suffrage; in 1993 when immigration laws were tightened; in 2000 when the president's term was reduced from seven to five years; in 2003 when parliament approved amendments allowing for the devolution of wide powers to the regions and departments; and in 2007 when it banned the death penalty.

As the capital city, Paris is home to almost all the national offices of state, including, of course, the Parlement (Parliament), which is divided into two houses: the Assemblée Nationale (National Assembly) and the Sénat (Senate). The 577 deputies of the National Assembly are directly elected in single-member constituencies for terms lasting five years (next election: 2012). Until September 2004 the rather powerless Senate counted 321 senators, each elected to a nine-year term. Now the term is six years and the number of senators will increase to 346 by 2010 to reflect changes in the France's demographics. Senators are indirectly elected by one half every three years. The president of the republic is directly elected for a term lasting five years and can stand for re-election.

Executive power is shared by the president and the Conseil des Ministres (Council of Ministers), whose members – including the prime minister – are appointed by the president but are responsible to parliament. The president serves as commander-in-chief of the armed forces and theoretically makes all major policy decisions.

MEDIA

The main national daily newspapers are *Le Figaro* (centre-right; aimed at professionals, business-people and the bourgeoisie; www.lefigaro.fr), *Le Monde* (centre-left; popular with professionals and intellectuals; www.lemonde.fr), *France Soir* (right-wing; working and middle class; www .francesoir.fr), *Libération* (left-wing; popular with students and intellectuals; www.liberation.fr) and *L'Humanité* (communist; working-class and intellectuals; www.humanite.fr). The capital's own daily is *Le Parisien* (centre; working class; www.leparisien.fr) and is easy to read if you have basic French. *L'Équipe* (www.lequipe.fr) is a daily devoted exclusively to sport and *Paris Turf* (www.paris-turf.com) to horse racing.

News weeklies with commentary include the comprehensive, left-leaning *Le Nouvel Observateur* (http://tempsreel.nouvelobs.com) and the more conservative *L'Express* (www .lexpress.fr).

For some investigative journalism blended with satire, pick up a copy of *Le Canard Enchaîné* (www.lecanardenchaine.fr) – assuming your French is of a certain level, of course. *Paris Match* (www.parismatch.com) is a gossipy, picture-heavy weekly with a penchant for royalty and film stars; they milked the Sarkozy divorce-and-rebound-remarriage *histoire* (story) for all it was worth – and then some. No group of people in Europe blog as much as the French do – the total at the moment is more than three million and growing – and there is no better way to understand what the French are thinking at the moment than entering the French blogosphere (see p17).

Public radio is grouped under the umbrella of Radio France (www.radiofrance.fr), which broadcasts via a network of dozens of radio stations, of which seven are the most important. These include national stations France Inter (87.8 MHz FM in Paris), the flagship talk station specialising in music, news and entertainment; the very highbrow France Culture (93.5 MHz FM); France Musique (91.7 MHz FM), which broadcasts over 1000 classical-music and jazz concerts each year; Radio Bleu, a network of stations for over-50s listeners; and France Info, a 24-hour news station that broadcasts headlines in French every few minutes and can be heard at 105.5 MHz FM. FIP (105.1 MHz FM) has a wide range of music – from hip-hop and *chanson* to world and rock – while Le Mouv' (92.1 MHz FM) is bubblegum pop.

Radio France Internationale (RFI; www.rfi.fr), France's voice abroad since 1931 and independent of Radio France since 1986, broadcasts in 19 languages (including English) and can be reached in Paris at 738 kHz AM. Arte Radio is a Franco-German web radio station featuring news reports and music.

Among the private radio networks, RTL (104.3 MHz FM) is still the leading general-interest station with over eight million listeners and three stations: RTL 1, RTL 2 and Fun Radio. The droves of FM pop-music stations include Hot Mix Radio, Nostalgie and Chérie FM, most of which follow the phone-in format with wisecracking DJs. Hard-core clubbers turn the dial to Radio Nova at 101.5 MHz FM for the latest on the nightclub scene; Radio FG (98.2 MHz FM) is the station for House, techno, garage and trance; and Paris Jazz (88.2 MHz FM) offers jazz and blues.

By law, radio broadcasters in France have to play at least 40% of their music in French – a law passed to protect French pop from being swamped by English-language imports – and stations can be fined if they don't comply. This helps explain why so many English-language hits are re-recorded in French – not always very successfully.

More than half of France's seven major national terrestrial TV channels (www.francetelevisions.fr) are public: France 2 and France 3 are general-interest stations designed to complement each other: the former focuses on news, entertainment and education, while the latter broadcasts regional programmes and news. France 5 targets its audience with documentaries (eg a daily health programme) and cartoons for the kids. The French/German public channel Arte, which shares with France 5, is a highbrow cultural channel.

The major private stations are the Franco-German TF1, M6 and Canal+. TF1 focuses on entertainment – *télé-réalité* (reality TV) is a big deal here – and sport; with about one-third of all French viewers, it is the most popular station in France. M6 lures a youngish audience with its menu of drama, music and news programmes. Canal+ is a mostly subscription-only channel that shows lots of films, both foreign and French – which isn't surprising, as it's the chief sponsor of the French cinema industry.

FASHION

'Fashion is a way of life,' Yves St Laurent once pronounced, and most Parisians would agree. They live, breathe and consume fashion. After all, to their reckoning, fashion is French – like gastronomy – and the competition from Milan, Tokyo or New York simply doesn't cut the mustard.

But what few Parisians know (or want to admit) is that an Englishman created Parisian *haute couture* (literally 'high sewing') as it exists today. Known as 'the Napoleon of costumers', Charles Frederick Worth (1825–95) arrived in Paris at the age of 20 and revolutionised fashion by banishing the crinoline (stiffened petticoat), lifting hemlines up to the oh-so-shocking ankle length and presenting his creations on live models. The House of Worth stayed in the family for four generations until the 1950s.

Indeed, the British are still key players on the Paris fashion scene today, notably in the form of erstwhile *enfant terrible* and now chief designer for Dior, John Galliano. In 2007, some six decades after house founder Christian Dior (1905–57) revolutionised the postwar fashion scene with his New Look, Galliano, dressed as a matador, hosted a star-studded event (at the Château de Versailles, no less) with top models parading such outfits as a flamenco-inspired, heavily embroidered gown that took some 10 stitchers up to 900 hours to create. Marie-Antoinette would have certainly approved.

Galliano is hardly the only eccentric couturier in Paris; Jean-Paul Gaultier draws his influence from the punk movement, dresses men in skirts and is famous for fitting Madonna into her signature conical bra. But you probably won't encounter women clad in Gaultier (or even Galliano) rubbing shoulders in the metro. Paris style remains quintessentially classic, with Parisian women preferring to play it safe (and sometimes slightly sexy) in monotones. It could be said that today's *parisiennes* are the legitimate daughters of the great Coco Chanel, celebrated creator of the 'little black dress'.

Indeed, nostalgia for Chanel as well as Givenchy, Féraud and other designers from the heyday of Paris fashion in the 1950s have contributed to the big demand for vintage clothing. Twice a year the big auction house Hôtel Drouot (p215) hosts *haute-couture* auctions.

But it's not all about yesterday and looking backward. There are, in fact, several contemporary 'Paris styles' that often relate to certain geographical areas and social classes. The funky streetwear style, heavily inspired by London, can be associated with the trendy shops around rue Étienne Marcel in the Louvre & Les Halles neighbourhood and the Marais. Meanwhile your more upper-crust 'BCBG' *(bon chic bon genre)* girl shops at Le Bon Marché (p212), Max Mara (Map pp140–1; ☎ 01 47 20 61 13; 31 av Montaigne, 8e; Ⓜ Georges V) or Chanel (p214) and rarely ventures outside her preferred districts: the 7e, 8e and 16e. The chic Left Bank *intello* (intellectual) struts her agnès b (p199) and APC (p202) though if she's a bit down on her luck she may discreetly buy used designer clothes at Chercheminippes (p204), an upmarket secondhand boutique in the 6e.

The eastern districts of Oberkampf, Bastille, the area of the 10e around Canal St-Martin and the Batignolles section of Clichy in the 17e tend to be the stomping ground of the *Bobo* (bourgeois bohemian), whose take on style is doused in nostalgia for her voyage to India, Tibet or Senegal and her avowed commitment to free trade and beads. Younger professional *Bobos* frequent Colette (p199), Kabuki Femme (p200) and Isabel Marant (p202). Parisians with Mediterranean roots have a penchant for the more flamboyant Christian Lacroix (p214), whose collections conjure up images of the south in a theatrical and colourful style. The flagship Louis Vuitton (p214) store on the av des Champs-Elysées draws in hordes of overseas shoppers, even on Sundays.

THE SHOW OF SHOWS

The Paris fashion *haute-couture* shows are scheduled in late January for the spring/summer collections and early July for autumn/winter ones. However, most established couturiers present a more affordable *prêt-à-porter* (ready-to-wear) line, and many have abandoned *haute couture* altogether. Prêt-à-porter shows are usually in late January and September. All major shows are ultra-exclusive affairs – even eminent fashion journalists must fight tooth and nail to get a spot on the sidelines. For an overview of Parisian fashion, check out Le Bon Marché (p212), which has an excellent collection of all the big labels and couture designs. For some catwalk action, there's a weekly fashion show at Galeries Lafayette (p215). In some stores you can join mailing lists to receive fashion-show invitations, but you need to be in Paris at the right time to attend.

SPEAKA DA LINGO

Verlan, a kind of French Pig Latin, has been the lingua franca of choice among the *branché* (hip) street-smart of Paris for almost two decades now. It's really just a linguistic sleight of hand, and its very name is illustrative of how it works. *L'envers* means 'reverse' in French, right? Well, twist it around – take the 'vers' and have it precede the 'l'en' and you get *verlan* – more or less. Of course that's the easy bit; shorter words – 'meuf' for *femme* (woman), 'keum' for *mec* (guy), 'teuf' for *fête* (party), 'keuf' for *flic* (cop) and 'auch' for *chaud* (hot; as in cool) are a bit trickier to recognise for the uninitiated.

In recent years the language has started to go mainstream and a few words of verlan – for example *beur* (French-born Algerian) – have entered the lexicography (if not dictionary) of standard French. Of course, the whole idea of verlan was for it to be a secret language – a kind of Cockney rhyming slang – for youths to communicate freely in front of parents, and criminals in front of the police. The next step was obvious: re-verlan words already in the lingo. Thus *beur* becomes *reub* and *keuf* is *feuk*. Fun (that's English verlan for 'enough').

Despite the invasion of 'Made in China' clothes for clones, Parisians never look like fashion victims nor do they go in for anything remotely vulgar or brassy. They stick to a neutral palette: black, grey, beige, brown and white, adding good accessories and great haircuts. They may mix and match designer labels with H&M, making it look like it was all bought on the posh av Montaigne in the 8e. And it is this elegance that attracts visitors from around the globe.

This is a society that coined the expression *lèche-vitrine* (literally 'window-licker') for window-shopping; 'tasting' without buying is an art like any other so don't be shy about just having a look. The fancy couture houses on av Montaigne may seem daunting, as many of their gleaming façades sit behind little fences, giving the impression of luxurious private homes. In most, however, no appointment is necessary and you can simply walk on in. Don't expect overly friendly service but do expect courtesy; after all, how are they to know that behind your jeans-and-sneakers façade you're not hiding a significant trust fund and a penchant for Lagerfeld?

No doubt about it, Parisians take fashion seriously and nowhere is that more obvious than in the new Cité de la Mode et du Design (p161), known as 'Docks en Seine'. The undulating green 'wave' that dances across the front façade is best appreciated from the other side of the river.

LANGUAGE

Respect for the French language is one of the most important aspects of claiming French nationality, and the concept of *la francophonie*, linking the common interests everywhere French is spoken, is supported by both the government and the people. Modern French developed from the *langue d'oïl*, a group of dialects spoken north of the Loire River that grew out of the vernacular Latin used during the late Gallo-Roman period. The *langue d'oïl* – particularly the *francien* dialect spoken in the Île de France encircling Paris – eventually displaced the *langue d'oc*, the dialects spoken in the south of the country.

Standard French is taught and spoken in schools, but its various accents and subdialects are an important source of identity in certain regions. In addition, some languages belonging to peoples long since subjected to French rule have been preserved. These include Flemish in the far north; Alsatian on the German border; Breton, a Celtic tongue, in Brittany; Basque, a language unrelated to any other, in the Basque Country; Catalan, the official language of nearby Andorra and the autonomous Spanish republic of Catalonia, in Roussillon; Provençal in Provence; and Corsican, closely related to Tuscan Italian, on the island of Corsica.

French was *the* international language of culture and diplomacy until WWI, and the French are sensitive to its decline in importance and the hegemony of English, especially since the advent of the internet. It is virtually impossible to separate a French person from his or her language, and it is one of the things they love most about their own culture. Your best bet is always to approach people politely in French, even if the only words you know are *'Pardon, parlez-vous anglais?'* (Excuse me, do you speak English?). Don't worry; they won't bite.

For more on what to say and how to say it *en français*, see p416. Lonely Planet also publishes the more comprehensive *French phrasebook*.

LES QUARTIERS

It is not hyperbole to say that Paris is the world's most beautiful, most romantic city. But it's not an urban museum or a Gallic theme park. Do the sights and ogle at the icons; they're all part of the Paris package. Then jump on the metro or a bus and get off at a place you've never heard of, wander through a *quartier* (neighbourhood) where French mixes easily with Arabic, Bengali or Vietnamese, poke your head into little shops or just lounge on a café terrace and watch the city pass by. More than anything else, Paris is a city to discover.

Pavement dining with style

LOUVRE & LES HALLES

This area forms the very heart of Paris and contains the lion's share of major sights and monuments on the Right Bank. The mammoth Musée du Louvre cannot be missed (in every sense) on any account and the transport hub of Les Halles and surrounds is hard to avoid.

1 Café Marly
Come to this place (p233) not so much for the food (which ain't half-bad) but for the magnificent views of the Louvre and the Grand Pyramid as well as the tier 2 starlets nibbling on radicchio.

2 Centre Pompidou
This somewhat dated cultural centre (p88) boasts the Musée National d'Art Moderne (National Museum of Modern Art), the second-most visited museum in the world after the Louvre (and just before London's Tate Modern).

3 Église St-Eustache
Often overlooked because of its location, this church (p89) contains one of the largest organs in Paris, which can be heard at two different masses on Sunday.

4 Place Vendôme
Home to some of the most fashionable jewellery shops in Paris, this neoclassical square (p87) is where Napoleon married Josephine and where he stands guard from atop the central Colonne Vendôme (Vendôme Column).

5 Palais Royal
With its gardens and galleries, sculptures and history (the French Revolution effectively started at a café here), this former 'Royal Palace' (p88) is a lovely spot on a warm day.

6 Jardin des Tuileries
Part of the 'Banks of the Seine' Unesco World Heritage Site, this riverside garden (p85) contains some lovely sculptures and is a favourite of strollers and joggers.

ST-GERMAIN, ODÉON & LUXEMBOURG

Traditionally an area that attracted artists and writers with its cheap rents and cafés, this *quartier* is now uber-chichi, with sky-high rents and *café crème* prices to prove it. It's also become something of a shopping mecca, with stylish boutiques and shops selling all manner of goods.

❶ Les Éditeurs
This relaxing restaurant (p255), which is full of groaning bookshelves and – unusual in Paris – light attracts writers and hangers-on, especially for Sunday brunch.

❷ Le Petit Zinc
An upmarket restaurant masquerading as a brasserie, this place (p254) is a wonder of Art Nouveau art and detail and the food makes an earnest attempt at competing with it.

❸ Église St-Sulpice
The lovely Italianate façade and neoclassical décor notwithstanding, most people now visit this mostly 18th-century church (p115) because of its connection to (and role in) Dan Brown's bestseller *The Da Vinci Code*.

❹ Les Deux Magots
A café with some of the strongest literary links in Paris, this place (p292) was home away from home for Sartre, Hemingway and André Breton and is now the same for tourists of all nationalities.

❺ Jardin du Luxembourg
One of the best spots in the city for people watching, this large garden (p119) has it all – from beehives and ponies to a museum and the seat of the French Senate.

❻ Église St-Germain des Prés
One of the oldest churches still standing in Paris, this Romanesque structure (p115) can trace its pedigree without going far – the bell tower over the western entrance has hardly changed since AD 990.

MONTMARTRE & PIGALLE

'A village within a city', Montmartre is itself the Paris of legend and the imagination: struggling artists, cancan and cabarets, hookers with hearts of gold and the 2001 film Amélie. *Its dirty sister Pigalle, literally at its feet, is one of the main sex districts of Paris.*

❶ Sacré Cœur

The view from the top of the steps of this very Parisian icon (p168) – which took more than four decades to complete – is said to extend some 30km.

❷ Moulin de la Galette

This windmill (p184), one of two left here, recalls that Montmartre once produced most of the flour for the bakeries 'down in Paris'.

❸ Cimetière de Montmartre

Among the permanent residents in this necropolis (p168), the most famous in Paris after Père Lachaise, are writers, composers, artists, film directors and dancers.

❹ Montmartre Vineyard

The only vineyard extant in central Paris, the Close du Montmartre (p185) still produces an average 850 bottles of wine a year.

❺ Moulin Rouge

The trademark windmill of arguably the most famous cabaret (p303) in Paris dates back only to 1925, a replacement of the 19th-century original, destroyed in a fire.

❻ Place du Tertre

Ground zero of touristy Paris, this crowded square (p168) in the heart of Montmartre is filled with cafés, restaurants and itinerant artists.

MARAIS & BASTILLE

Once Paris' most fashionable residential district and filled with luxurious hôtels particuliers (private mansions), the Marais moonlights as a lively nightlife and shopping district. The gentrification of the Bastille area began with the opening of the landmark Opéra Bastille for the bicentennial of the Revolution and continues apace..

❶ Bofinger
This Art Nouveau brasserie (p238) is an open door to the Paris of the *belle époque*; just make sure to get a seat under the splendid stained-glass cupola.

❷ Place de la Bastille
The site (p101) where once stood the notorious prison stormed at the start of the Revolution is now a busy traffic roundabout with a monument to another revolution – the one that took place in 1830.

❸ Village St-Paul
This redeveloped and very picturesque area (p192) in the southern part of the Marais is effectively a courtyard of antique shops and designer boutiques.

❹ Opéra Bastille
Never as popular as the Palais Garnier, this opera house (p102) has a 2700-seat auditorium with perfect acoustics and some of the most ambitious opera productions in the city.

❺ Chez Marianne
If you're in the mood for Sephardic kosher dishes (falafel, hummus, aubergine 'caviar' etc) this is the place (p243) to come.

❻ Rue Vieille du Temple
This is one of the liveliest streets (p286) in the Marais district for a night out, and has more than a dozen bars lining both sides of the street.

❼ Pâtisseries on Rue des Rosiers
If you're looking for something a bit more gutsy than the usual roundup of French *pâtisseries*, head for the Pletzl and enjoy the scrumptious Jewish and Central European–style breads and pastries, including apple strudel and poppy-seed cakes, available there (p237).

LATIN QUARTER & JARDIN DES PLANTES

The stronghold of Paris' academia since the 13th century, this area takes its name from the lingua franca – Latin – that professors and students once used to converse. The 'green lung' bordering it is filled with museums and even boasts a small menagerie.

❶ Panthéon
Built as a church and completed the year the Revolution broke out, this sublime neoclassical structure (p114) now serves as a mausoleum for *'les grands hommes de l'époque de la liberté française'* (great men of the era of French liberty), though women have been buried here since 1995.

❷ Bouillon Racine
Built as a soup kitchen for workers a few years into the 20th century, this restaurant (p255) is best appreciated for its Art Nouveau splendour. The classically inspired food is good too.

❸ Shakespeare & Company
This bookshop (p208) along the Seine rather successfully recreates the Paris of 50 years ago, when people had the time (and inclination) to discuss weightier issues than the new model of mobile phone.

❹ Place de la Sorbonne
The dominant feature of this little square (p114) is the Chapelle de la Sorbonne, the university's gold-domed church, where the mortal remains of Cardinal Richelieu lie buried.

1 Eiffel Tower
What was once snidely referred to as the 'metal asparagus' has become over 120 years or so the most recognisable and beloved landmark (p131) of Paris.

2 Palais de Chaillot
An Art Deco structure built for the 1937 World Exhibition, the 'palace' (p131) now contains three important museums, and there's a new state-of-the-art aquarium in its shadow.

3 Flame of Liberty Memorial
A replica of the torch held by the Statue of Liberty in New York, this memorial (p135) was put in place by an American newspaper as a symbol of friendship between France and the USA.

4 Parc du Champ de Mars
A large green space at the foot of the Eiffel Tower, the Field of Mars (p134) has always been associated with the French military – the École Militaire (Military Academy) is at its southern end.

EIFFEL TOWER AREA & 16E ARRONDISSEMENT

This is just about the most Parisian area of Paris, with parkland to both the back and front of the city's very icon. Across the Seine is the Palais de Chaillot, with its embarrassment of excellent museums and other sights.

OPÉRA & GRANDS BOULEVARDS

These neighbourhoods are always noisy and frenetic, be it when the faithful are rushing to hear a performance at the Palais Garnier or shoppers are trying to reach les Grands Boulevards' grand magasins (department stores) before closing time.

1 Palais Garnier

A classic example of Second Empire style, Paris' favourite opera house (p147) may not be able to accommodate the numbers that the Opéra Bastille can but is far more intimate.

2 Galeries Lafayette

Galeries Lafayette (p215) is famed for its wide range of fashion labels and the fashion show that takes place at 3pm every Friday.

3 Rue Montorgueil

This street market (p231), with both French and foreign food shops, more or less took over from Les Halles when it moved lock, stock and pig's trotter out of the city in the late 1960s.

ÉTOILE & CHAMPS-ÉLYSÉES

The av des Champs-Élysées, which leads up to the Arc de Triomphe and the enormous roundabout known as place de l'Étoile has both its supporters and its detractors but there is no denying that it is impressively wide and the places on or off it beautiful.

❶ Arc de Triomphe
Beneath this large arch (p138) in the centre of place de l'Étoile lies the body of an unknown soldier from WWI, his fate and that of countless others like him commemorated by a memorial flame burning in perpetuity.

❷ Place de la Concorde
This enormous square (p139), linked to place de l'Étoile by the av des Champs-Élysées, is where most of the guillotining took place during the Reign of Terror.

❸ Avenue des Champs-Élysées
This impressive boulevard (p138) becomes especially alive on New Year's Eve and on a Sunday in late July, when the last stage of the prestigious Tour de France cycling event takes place here.

❹ Église de Ste-Marie Madeleine
The monumental staircase at this church (p139) constructed in the style of a Greek temple affords excellent views down to and across the Seine.

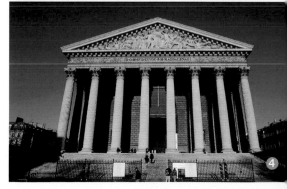

GARE DU NORD, GARE DE L'EST & RÉPUBLIQUE

These neighbourhoods dominated by Paris' two busiest train stations and the enormous place de la République are not without their attractive coins *(corners), especially along the quays of the Canal St-Martin.*

❶ Canal St-Martin
The shaded towpath of this 4.5km-long canal (p151) is a wonderful place for a stroll or a jog in the morning or early evening.

❷ Passage Brady
A little bit of Mumbai or Dhaka in the French capital, this covered passage (p268) is wall-to-wall curry houses offering toned-down but very affordable meals throughout the day.

❸ Place de la République
In the centre of this enormous square (p186), where many political rallies and demonstrations in Paris start and/or end, is a statue of the Republic, erected in 1883.

❹ Porte St-Denis
Like its little sister, Porte St-Martin, two blocks east, this monumental arch (p151) was erected in the 17th century to immortalise military victories during the reign of Louis XIV.

THE ISLANDS

Twins separated at birth, the Île St-Louis has chichi residents with some gourmet shops and posh restaurants to nourish the natives, while Île de la Cité attracts tourists in a big way with its plethora of sights: Notre Dame, Ste-Chapelle, la Conciergerie and so on.

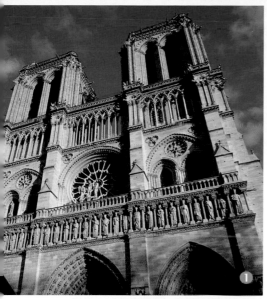

① Cathédrale de Notre Dame de Paris

This masterpiece of Gothic architecture is the most visited site (p104) in Paris, with some 10 million souls crossing its threshold each year.

② Rue St-Louis en l'Île

This arrow-straight thoroughfare (p248) is peppered with fine-food shops, restaurants and boutiques that attract both local residents and visitors.

③ Pont Neuf

The magnificent Pont Neuf (New Bridge; p107) connects Île de la Cité to the Right and Left Banks.

❶ Parc de Belleville
The biggest draw of this park (p154) is its height: at 200m above sea level it's way above the rest of flat Paris and affords excellent, long-reaching views over the city.

❷ Marché Belleville
One of the most colourful in the city, this street market (p231) is nothing short of a trip to Africa and the Middle East.

❸ Cimetière du Père Lachaise
The world's most opulent (and visited) cemetery (p154), this enormous necropolis contains the mortal remains of some 800,000 people – their names read like a Who's Who of French history and the arts.

MÉNILMONTANT & BELLEVILLE

A very ordinary working-class district until the 1990s, Ménilmontant is now a favourite feeding and watering quartier among denizens of the night. Neighbouring Belleville has yet to catch up but it's only a matter of time before it does.

top picks

- **Centre Pompidou** (p88) Architecturally phenomenal and the world's most successful cultural centre.
- **Ste-Chapelle** (p107) Sway with the wall of stained glass as it shimmers in the sun.
- **Musée du Louvre** (p80) View (and view and view again) the world's greatest and most famous works of art.
- **Cité de l'Architecture et du Patrimoine** (p134) Take a tour of the greatest monuments in France.
- **Cathédrale de Notre Dame de Paris** (p104) Ogle at the organ in this grandiose monument to Gothic architecture.
- **Musée Rodin** (p130) Ponder *The Thinker* or re-enact *The Kiss* at the sculptor's home (and garden).
- **Musée de l'Orangerie** (p87) 'Swim' among the fragrant blossoms of Monet's sublime *Water Lilies*.
- **Eiffel Tower** (p131) Climb, circle or just look at the icon that is more Parisian than Paris itself.

Paris is a compact, easily negotiated city. Some 20 arrondissements (city districts) spiral clockwise from the centre and are important locators; their numbers are always included in addresses.

Each of Paris' arrondissements has a distinct personality. The 1er has plenty of sights but few residents, the 5e is studenty, the 7e full of ministries and embassies; the 10e was

> 'Montmartre, the Paris of myth and films, and Pigalle, the naughty red-light district'

traditionally working-class but is now a trendy district in which to live, while the 16e is a bastion of the well-heeled. But the profiles are not always so cut and dried; the lay of the land becomes much clearer to visitors when they see the city as composed of named *quartiers* (quarters or neighbourhoods).

This guide starts on the Right Bank, north of the Seine, in the area around the Louvre and Les Halles, which largely takes in the 1er but also part of the 2e and the westernmost edge of the 4e. Next come the Marais (4e and 3e) and the contiguous Bastille (11e) districts to the east and southeast. The two islands in the Seine – Île de la Cité and Île St-Louis – are on neither the Right nor Left Bank but they do belong to arrondissements – the 1er and 4e, respectively.

We encounter the Left Bank in the Latin Quarter, the traditional centre of learning in Paris, and the leafy Jardin des Plantes to the east of it (both 5e). The 6e, to the west and southwest, is both a frenetic district (St-Germain and Odéon) and tranquil park (Luxembourg). To the south is Montparnasse (14e), once the centre of nightlife. Faubourg St-Germain and Les Invalides to the north in the 7e are important for their sights but also as the locations of many branches of government and embassies. To the west is the Eiffel Tower and, across the Seine on the Right Bank, the posh 16e arrondissement, a district of broad, tree-lined avenues and some excellent museums.

To the east and still on the Right Bank is the 8e, which includes the lion's share of Parisian icons: Étoile, with its landmark Arc de Triomphe, and the wide boulevard known as the Champs-Élysées. At the end of this grand avenue are two very important *places* (squares): Concorde and, to the north, Madeleine. Above the 8e is the multifaceted 17e, with its beautiful, Haussmann-era buildings beyond the Gare St-Lazare and the working-class neighbourhoods of Clichy. To the east is the 9e, where you'll find the city's original Opéra and the Grands Boulevards.

The 10e, hosting both the Gare du Nord and the Gare de l'Est, is the city's rail hub. Below République (3e) and its enormous and chaotic square is the *branché* (trendy) district of Ménilmontant – awash in alternative bars, cafés and restaurants, especially along rue Oberkampf in the northern 11e – and to the east, the solidly working-class neighbourhood of Belleville (20e).

The 12e contains Gare de Lyon to the northwest, the huge square-cum-roundabout called Nation to the east and, to the south, the redeveloped area of Bercy, its old wine-warehouses now turned into a wining-and-dining 'theme park'. Across the Seine is the 13e arrondissement, home to Chinatown and the grandiose Bibliothèque Nationale de France, and currently undergoing massive redevelopment. The 15e arrondissement, the largest and most populous district but arguably, least interesting to tourists, is to the west.

To the north in the 18e is Montmartre, the Paris of myth and films, and Pigalle, the naughty red-light district that today looks pretty tame. La Villette, with its lovely park, canal and cutting-edge museums in the far-flung 19e arrondissement of the northeast, is the last district of major importance *intra-muros*, Latin for 'within the walls' and what Parisians call central Paris. Areas of interest to visitors 'outside the walls' include the Bois de Vincennes and Bois de Boulogne, Paris' 'lungs' and recreational centres to the east and the west respectively; La Défense, the futuristic business and residential district at the northern end of metro line 1; and St-Denis, to the north on metro line 13, which has an important 12th-century cathedral.

In this chapter, the Transport boxed texts provide quick reference for the location of metro and train stations, tram and bus stops, and ferry piers in each district.

LA DÉFENSE (pp179-81)

BOIS DE BOULOGNE & SURROUNDS (pp177-9)

EIFFEL TOWER AREA & 16e ARRONDISSEMENT (pp131-7)

CLICHY & GARE ST-LAZARE (pp143-6)

MONTMARTRE & PIGALLE (pp168-71)

LA VILLETTE (pp172-5)

OPÉRA & GRANDS BOULEVARDS (pp147-50)

GARE DU NORD, GARE DE L'EST & RÉPUBLIQUE (pp151-3)

MÉNILMONTANT & BELLEVILLE (pp154-6)

ÉTOILE & CHAMPS-ELYSÉES (pp138-42)

LOUVRE & LES HALLES (pp80-90)

MARAIS & BASTILLE (pp91-103)

GARE DE LYON, NATION & BERCY (pp157-60)

BOIS DE VINCENNES & SURROUNDS (pp176-7)

FAUBOURG ST-GERMAIN & INVALIDES (pp127-3)

ST-GERMAIN, ODEON & LUXEMBOURG (pp115-21)

THE ISLANDS (pp104-8)

LATIN QUARTER & JARDIN DES PLANTES (pp109-14)

13e ARRONDISSEMENT & CHINATOWN (pp161-4)

15e ARRONDISSEMENT (pp165-7)

MONTPARNASSE (pp122-6)

Seine

Seine

3 km
2 miles

ITINERARY BUILDER

It's easy to see lots of Paris in a very short time; as we point out in Introducing Paris (p2), familiar sights and landmarks seem to leap out at you from every corner. But to really get under the skin of Paris you'll want to look beyond the obvious. This Itinerary Builder should help you find a range of both obvious and slightly more obscure places in eight featured neighbourhoods.

AREA	ACTIVITIES	Sights	Museums & Galleries	Activities
	Louvre & Les Halles	Centre Pompidou (p88)	Musée du Louvre (p80)	Spa Nuxe (p318)
		Église St-Eustache (p89)	Les Arts Décoratifs (p84)	Jardin des Tuileries (p85)
		Passages Couverts (p188)	Musée de l'Orangerie (p87)	Cityrama (p407)
	Marais & Bastille	Place des Vosges (p91)	Musée Picasso (p96)	Vit'Halles Beaubourg (p319)
		Pletzl (p91)	Musée des Arts et Métiers (p97)	Paris à Vélo, C'est Sympa! (p406)
		Cimetière du Père Lachaise (p154)	Maison de Victor Hugo (p91)	Canal Cruises Canauxrama (p406)
	Latin Quarter & Jardin des Plantes	Panthéon (p114)	Institut du Monde Arabe (p112)	Jardin des Plantes (p113)
		Mosquée de Paris (p113)	Musée National d'Histoire Naturelle (p113)	Hammam de la Mosquée de Paris (p318)
		Sorbonne (p114)	Musée National du Moyen Age (p114)	Piscine Pontoise (p323)
	St-Germain, Odéon & Luxembourg	Église St-Sulpice (p115)	Fondation Dubuffet (p119)	Jardin du Luxembourg (p119)
		Église St-Germain des Prés (p115)	Musée National Eugène Delacroix (p121)	
		Institut de France (p119)	Pièce Unique Variations (p210)	
	Étoile & Champs-Élysées	Arc de Triomphe (p138)	Petit Palais (p139)	Spa Harnn & Thann (p318)
		Av des Champs-Élysées (p138)	Palais de la Découverte (p139)	Bateaux-Mouches (p407)
		Place de la Concorde (p139)	Grand Palais (p139)	
	Opéra & Grands Boulevards	Palais Garnier (p147)	Musée National Gustave Moreau (p150)	Paris Story (p405)
		Les Grands Boulevards (p147)	Musée de Parfum (p147)	L'Open Tour (p407)
		Place de l'Opéra (p147)	Musée Grévin (p147)	
	Gare de Lyon, Nation & Bercy	Cinémathèque Française (p157)	Maison Rouge (p157)	Parc de Bercy (p157)
		Viaduc des Arts (p157)	Musée des Arts Forains (p160)	
		Passerelle Simone de Beauvoir (p157)	Maison de Jardinage (p157)	
	Montmartre & Pigalle	Basilique du Sacré Cœur (p168)	Musée de Montmartre (p170)	Petit Train de Montmartre (p170)
		Place du Tertre (p168)	Musée de la Vie Romantique (p171)	Cook'n with Class (p398)
		Cimetière de Montmartre (p168)	Dalí Espace Montmartre (p170)	

HOW TO USE THIS TABLE

The table below allows you to plan a day's worth of activities in any area of the city. Simply select which area you wish to explore, and then mix and match from the corresponding listings to build your day. The first item in each cell represents a well-known highlight of the area, while the other items are more off-the-beaten-track gems.

Eating	Drinking	Shopping
Aux Lyonnais (p234)	Le Fumoir (p285)	Kiliwatch (p200)
Chez la Vieille (p234)	Harry's New York Bar (p285)	E Dehillerin (p201)
Le Vaudeville (p232)	Angélina (p286)	Anna Joliet (p201)
L'Ambassade d'Auvergne (p242)	La Perle (p287)	APC (p202)
Le Petit Marché (p239)	Le Pick-Clops (p288)	CSAO Boutique & Gallery (p206)
Le Temps au Temps (p238)	Le Bistrot du Peintre (p289)	Red Wheelbarrow Bookstore (p202)
Le Coupe-Chou (p250)	Le Verre à Pied (p290)	Pâtisserie Sadaharu Aoki (p209)
L'AOC (p250)	Le Pub St-Hilaire (p291)	Shakespeare & Company (p208)
Le Petit Pontoise (p251)	Le Vieux Chêne (p290)	Magie (p209)
Ze Kitchen Galerie (p255)	Café de Flore (p292)	Ivoire (p209)
Le Mâchon d'Henri (p257)	Le Comptoir des Cannettes (p293)	La Dernier Goutte (p211)
Le Salon d'Hélène (p254)	Le 10 (p292)	Le Dépôt-Vente de Buci (p204)
Bistrot du Sommelier (p261)	Buddha Bar (p294)	Espace IGN (p213)
Graindorge (p262)	Cricketer (p294)	Fromagerie Alléosse (p214)
Ladurée (p234)		Fauchon (p214)
La Boule Rouge (p264)	De La Ville Café (p295)	La Maison du Miel (p215)
Le Roi du Pot au Feu (p265)	O'Sullivan's (p295)	Le Printemps (p215)
Casa Olympe (p264)		Hôtel Drouot (p215)
Sardegna a Tavola (p272)	La Liberté (p297)	Fermob (p216)
Comme Cochons (p273)	La Flèche d'Or (p308)	Marché aux Puces d'Aligre (p216)
Les Amis de Messina (p272)	Chai 33 (p297)	La Maison du Cerf-Volant (p216)
Le Maquis (p279)	Le Dépanneur (p299)	Gaspard de la Butte (p217)
La Table d'Anvers (p278)	Le Progrès (p299)	La Citadelle (p217)
Chez Toinette (p278)	La Fourmi (p298)	

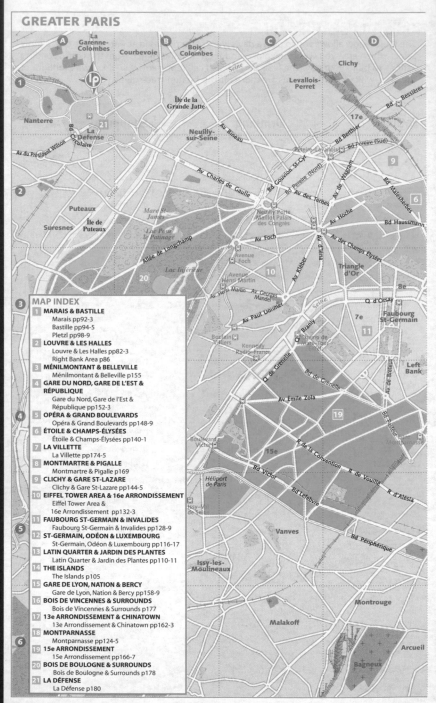

GREATER PARIS

MAP INDEX

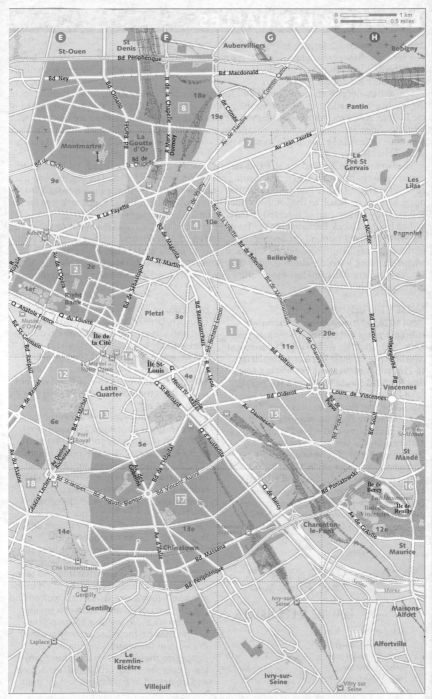

St-Ouen
St Denis
Aubervilliers
Bobigny
E
F
G
H

Bd Ney
Bd Périphérique
Bd Macdonald

Bd Ornano
R de la Chapelle
18e
R de Crimée
Av Corentin Cariou
Pantin

Sacre Cœur
La Goutte d'Or
R Marx Dormoy
19e
Av de Flandre
Le Pré St Gervais
Les Lilas

Montmartre
Bd de la Chapelle
7
Av Jean Jaurès

Bd de Clichy
Q de Valmy

9e
Bd de la Villette
10e
4
Bagnolet

R La Fayette
R de Magenta
Bd de Belleville
Belleville
Bd Mortier

Aube
Av de l'Opéra
2e
Bd St-Martin
3
Bd de Ménilmontant

Royale
2
Bd de Sébastopol
Bd Davout

1er
Right Bank
Pletzl
3e
20e

Q Anatole France
Q du Louvre
Bd Beaumarchais
1
11e
Bd Voltaire

Musée d'Orsay
Île de la Cité
Île St-Louis
Vincennes

Bd St-Germain
Michel Notre Dame
14
R de Lyon

Bd Raspail
12
St-Louis
4e
Bd Diderot
Cours de Vincennes

Latin Quarter
13
Q St-Bernard
Av Daumesnil
15

R de Rennes
Bd St-Michel
Port Royal
5e
Q d'Austerlitz

6e
Bd Auguste Blanqui
Bd de l'Hôpital
Bd Vincent Auriol
Bd Poniatowski
Île de Bercy
16

18
Général Leclerc
Bd St-Jacques
17
Q de Bercy
Île de Reuilly

14e
13e
Av de Graville
12e

Av d'Italie
Chinatown
Bd Masséna
Charenton-le-Pont
St Maurice

Cité Universitaire
Bd Périphérique
Seine
Marne

Gentilly
Ivry-sur-Seine
Maisons-Alfort

Gentilly

Laplace
Alfortville

Le Kremlin-Bicêtre

Villejuif
Ivry-sur-Seine
Vitry sur Seine

0 _____ 1 km
0 _____ 0.5 miles

LOUVRE & LES HALLES

NEIGHBOURHOODS LOUVRE & LES HALLES

Drinking p284; Eating p230; Shopping p198; Sleeping p336

The 1er arrondissement contains some of the most important sights for visitors to Paris. Though it can boast a wild and exciting side, it remains essentially a place where history and culture meet on the banks of the Seine.

Sculptures merge with lawns, pools and fountains, while casual strollers lose themselves in the lovely promenade stretching from the gardens of the Tuileries to the square courtyard of the Louvre. A few metres away, under the arcades of the rue de Rivoli, the pace quickens with bustling shops and chaotic traffic. Parallel to rue de Rivoli, rue St-Honoré runs from place Vendôme to Les Halles, leaving in its wake the Comédie Française and the manicured gardens of the Palais Royal.

The Forum des Halles and rue St-Denis seem kilometres away but are already visible, soliciting unwary passers-by with bright lights, jostling crowds and painted ladies. The mostly pedestrian zone between the Centre Pompidou and the Forum des Halles (with rue Étienne Marcel to the north and rue de Rivoli to the south) is filled with people day and night, just as it was for the 850-odd years when part of it served as Paris' main *halles* (marketplace).

The Bourse (Stock Exchange) is the financial heart of the 2e arrondissement to the north, the Sentier district (around the Sentier metro and rue d'Aboukir and rue de Cléry), the centre of the city's garment trade and the Opéra, its ode to music and dance. From rue de la Paix, where glittering jewellery shops display their wares, to blvd Poissonnière and blvd de Bonne Nouvelle, where stalls and fast-food outlets advertise with garish neon signs, this arrondissement is a real hotchpotch.

MUSÉE DU LOUVRE Map p86

☎ 01 40 20 53 17; www.louvre.fr; permanent collections/permanent collections & temporary exhibits €9/13, after 6pm Wed & Fri €6/11, permanent collections free for under 18yr & after 6pm Fri for 18-25yr, 1st Sun of the month free; ☯ 9am-6pm Mon, Thu, Sat & Sun, to 10pm Wed & Fri; Ⓜ Palais Royal-Musée du Louvre

The vast Palais du Louvre was constructed as a fortress by Philippe-Auguste in the early 13th century and rebuilt in the mid-16th century for use as a royal residence. The Revolutionary Convention turned it into a national museum in 1793.

The paintings, sculptures and artefacts on display in the Louvre Museum have been assembled by French governments over the past five centuries. Among them are works of art and artisanship from all over Europe and collections of Assyrian, Etruscan, Greek, Coptic and Islamic art and antiquities. The Louvre's *raison d'être* is essentially to present Western art from the Middle Ages to about 1848 (at which point the Musée d'Orsay across the river takes over), as well as the works of ancient civilisations that formed the starting point for Western art.

When the museum opened in the late 18th century it contained 2500 paintings and *objets d'art;* today some 35,000 are on display. The 'Grand Louvre' project inaugurated by the late President Mitterrand in 1989 doubled the museum's exhibition space, and new and renovated galleries have opened in recent years devoted to *objets d'art* such as Sèvres porcelain and the crown jewels of Louis XV (Room 66, 1st floor, Apollo Gallery, Denon Wing).

Daunted by the richness and sheer size of the place (the side facing the Seine is 700m long and it is said that it would take nine months to see every piece of art in the museum), locals and visitors alike often find the prospect of an afternoon at a smaller museum far more inviting, meaning the Louvre may be the most actively avoided museum in the world. Eventually, most people do their duty and visit, but many leave overwhelmed, unfulfilled, exhausted and frustrated at having got lost on their

top picks

LOUVRE & LES HALLES

- Musée du Louvre (above)
- Musée de l'Orangerie (p87)
- Centre Pompidou (p88)
- Jardin des Tuileries (p85)
- Église St-Eustache (p89)

way to da Vinci's *La Joconde*, better known as *Mona Lisa* (Room 6, 1st floor, Salle de la Joconde, Denon Wing; see boxed text, p88). Since it takes several serious visits to get anything more than a brief glimpse of the works on offer, your best bet – after checking out a few that you really want to see – is to choose a particular period or section of the Louvre and pretend that the rest is in another museum somewhere across town.

The most famous works from antiquity include the *Seated Scribe* (Room 22, 1st floor, Sully Wing), the *Code of Hammurabi* (Room 3, ground floor, Richelieu Wing) and that armless duo, the *Venus de Milo* (Room 7, ground floor, Denon Wing) and the *Winged Victory of Samothrace* (opposite Room 1, 1st floor, Denon Wing). From the Renaissance, don't miss Michelangelo's *The Dying Slave* (ground floor, Michelangelo Gallery, Denon Wing) and works by Raphael, Botticelli and Titian (1st floor, Denon Wing). French masterpieces of the 19th century include Ingres' *The Turkish Bath* (Room 60, 2nd floor, Sully Wing), Géricault's *The Raft of the Medusa* (Room 77, 1st floor, Denon Wing) and works by Corot, Delacroix and Fragonard (2nd floor, Denon Wing).

The main entrance and ticket windows in the Cour Napoléon are covered by the 21m-high Grande Pyramide, a glass pyramid designed by the Chinese-born American architect IM Pei. You can avoid the queues outside the pyramid or at the Porte des Lions entrance by entering the Louvre complex via the Carrousel du Louvre entrance (Map p86), at 99 rue de Rivoli, or by following the 'Musée du Louvre' exit from the Palais Royal-Musée du Louvre metro station. Buy your tickets in advance from the ticket machines in the Carrousel du Louvre, online or by ringing ☎ 08 92 68 36 22 or 08 25 34 63 46, or from the *billeteries* (ticket offices) of Fnac (p302) for an extra €1.10, and walk straight in without queuing. Tickets are valid for the whole day, so you can come and go as you please. They are also valid for the Musée National Eugène Delacroix (p121) on the same day.

The Louvre is divided into four sections: the Sully, Denon and Richelieu Wings and Hall Napoléon. Sully creates the four sides of the Cour Carrée (literally 'square courtyard') at the eastern end of the complex. Denon stretches along the Seine to the south; Richelieu is the northern wing runing along rue de Rivoli.

TRANSPORT: LOUVRE & LES HALLES

Bus Louvre (rue de Rivoli) for 27 over Pont St-Michel, up blvd St-Michel to Jardin du Luxembourg, rue Claude Bernard (for rue Mouffetard) & Place d'Italie; rue de Rivoli (near Louvre Rivoli metro) for 69 to Invalides, Champ de Mars (Eiffel Tower) and for 72 for place de la Concorde, Grand Palais, Alma Marceau, Bois de Boulogne & Porte de St Cloud; Châtelet for 38 to blvd St-Michel & Jardin du Luxembourg, for 47 to Place Monge (rue Mouffetard), Place d'Italie and 13e (Chinatown), for 67 to Pigalle & for 85 to Barbès & Porte de Clignancourt & Porte de St-Ouen flea markets

Metro & RER Bourse, Châtelet, Châtelet-Les Halles, Concorde, Étienne Marcel, Les Halles, Louvre-Rivoli, Palais Royal-Musée du Louvre, Pont Neuf, Rambuteau, Tuileries

Boat Musée du Louvre Batobus stop (quai du Louvre)

The split-level public area under the Grande Pyramide is known as the Hall Napoléon (9am-10pm Wed-Mon). The hall has an exhibit on the history of the Louvre, a bookshop, restaurant, café, auditoriums for concerts, lectures and films, and CyberLouvre (10am-5.45pm Wed-Mon), an internet research centre with online access to some 35,000 works of art. The centrepiece of the Carrousel du Louvre (p201), the shopping centre that runs underground from the pyramid to the Arc de Triomphe du Carrousel (p85), is the pyramide inversée (inverted glass pyramid), also the work of Pei.

Free English-language maps of the complex (entitled *Louvre Plan/Information*) can be obtained from the circular information desk in the centre of the Hall Napoléon. Excellent publications to guide you if you are doing the Louvre on your own are *Destination Louvre: A Guided Tour* (€7.50), *Louvre: Guide to the Masterpieces* (€8) and the hefty, 475-page *A Guide to the Louvre* (€17). Much more esoteric are the specialist titles *Cats in the Louvre* and the competing *Dogs in the Louvre*, each priced at €15. An attractive and useful memento is the DVD entitled *Louvre: The Visit* (€26). All are available from the museum bookshop.

English-language guided tours (☎ 01 40 20 52 63) lasting 1½ hours depart from the area under the Grande Pyramide, marked *Acceuil des Groupes* (Groups Reception), at 11am, 2pm and (sometimes) 3.45pm

LOUVRE & LES HALLES

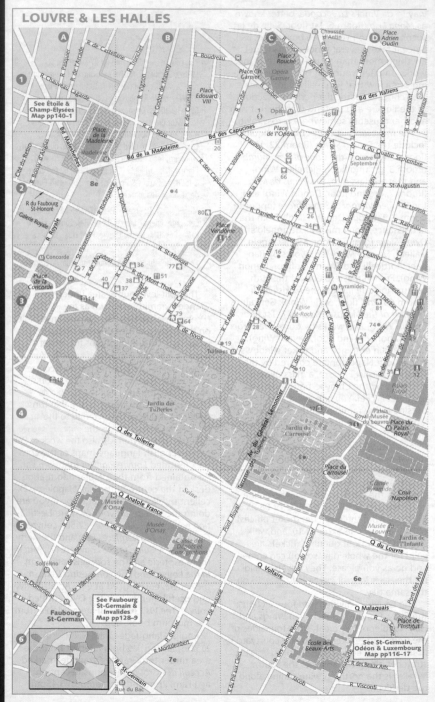

NEIGHBOURHOODS LOUVRE & LES HALLES

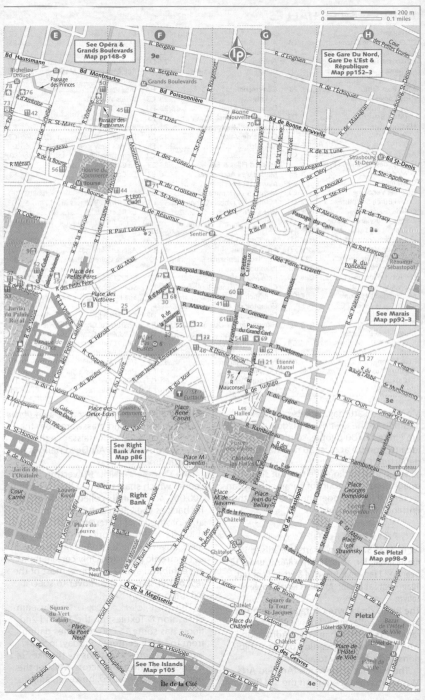

LOUVRE & LES HALLES

Monday to Saturday. Tickets cost €5 in addition to the cost of admission. Groups are limited to 30 people, so it's a good idea to sign up at least 30 minutes before departure time.

Self-paced audioguide tours in six languages, with 1½ hours of commentary, can be rented for €5 under the pyramid at the entrance to each wing.

LES ARTS DÉCORATIFS Map pp82–3

☎ 01 44 55 57 50; www.lesartsdecoratifs.fr; 107 rue de Rivoli, 1er; adult/18-25yr €8/6.50, under 18 free; ☒ 11am-6pm Tue, Wed & Fri, to 9pm Thu, 10am-6pm Sat & Sun; Ⓜ Palais Royal-Musée du Louvre

The Palais du Louvre contains three other museums collectively known as the Decorative Arts in its Rohan Wing. Admission, which may vary depending on the exhibitions, includes entry to all three.

The Musée des Arts Décoratifs (Applied Arts Museum), which begins on the 3rd floor,

displays furniture, jewellery and such *objets d'art* as ceramics and glassware from the Middle Ages and the Renaissance through the Art Nouveau and Art Deco periods to modern times.

The Musée de la Publicité (Advertising Museum), which shares the 3rd floor, has some 100,000 posters in its collection dating as far back as the 13th century, and innumerable promotional materials touting everything from 19th-century elixirs and early radio advertisements to Air France as well as electronic publicity. Only certain items are exhibited at any one time; most of the rest of the space is given over to special exhibitions.

The Musée de la Mode et du Textile (Museum of Fashion & Textiles) on the 1st and 2nd floors has some 16,000 costumes dating from the 16th century to today, including *haute couture* creations by the likes of Chanel and Christian Lacroix. Most of the outfits are warehoused, however, and displayed during regularly scheduled themed exhibitions.

ARC DE TRIOMPHE DU CARROUSEL
Map pp82-3

place du Carrousel, 1er; M Palais Royal-Musée du Louvre
Erected by Napoleon to celebrate his battlefield successes of 1805, this triumphal arch, which is set in the Jardin du Carrousel at the eastern end of the Jardin des Tuileries, was once crowned by the ancient Greek sculpture called *The Horses of St Mark's*, 'borrowed' from the portico of St Mark's Basilica in Venice by Napoleon but returned after his defeat at Waterloo in 1815. The quadriga (the two-wheeled chariot drawn by four horses) that replaced it was added in 1828 and celebrates the return of the Bourbons to the French throne after Napoleon's downfall. The sides of the arch are adorned with depictions of Napoleonic victories and eight pink-marble columns, atop each of which stands a soldier of the emperor's Grande Armée.

ÉGLISE ST-GERMAIN L'AUXERROIS
Map p86

☎ 01 42 60 13 96; 2 place du Louvre, 1er; ☽ 8am-7pm; M Louvre-Rivoli or Pont Neuf
Built between the 13th and 16th centuries in a mixture of Gothic and Renaissance styles and with similar dimensions and ground plans to those of Notre Dame, this once royal parish church stands on a site at the eastern end of the Louvre that has been used for Christian worship since about AD 500. After being mutilated in the 18th century by clergy intent on 'modernisation', and damaged during the Revolution, the church was restored by the Gothic Revivalist architect Eugène Viollet-le-Duc in the mid-19th century. It contains some fine Renaissance stained glass.

LOUVRE DES ANTIQUAIRES
Map p86

☎ 01 42 97 27 27; www.louvre-antiquaires.com; 2 place du Palais Royal; ☽ 11am-7pm Tue-Sun Sep-Jun, to 7pm Tue-Sat Jul & Aug; M Palais Royal-Musée du Louvre
A tourist attraction in itself, this extremely elegant 'mall' houses some 140 antique shops spread over three floors and is filled with *objets d'art*, furniture, clocks, classical antiquities and jewellery. Visit the place as you would the Louvre across the road, bearing in mind that all the stuff here is up for grabs.

JARDIN DES TUILERIES
Map pp82-3

☎ 01 40 20 90 43; ☽ 7am-9pm Apr, May & Sep, 7am-11pm Jun-Aug, 7.30am-7.30pm Oct-Mar; M Tuileries or Concorde
The formal, 28-hectare Tuileries Garden, which begins just west of the Jardin du Carrousel, was laid out in its present form, more or less, in the mid-17th century by André Le Nôtre, who also created the gardens at Vaux-le-Vicomte (p372) and Versailles (p360). The Tuileries soon became the most fashionable spot in Paris for parading about in one's finery; today it is a favourite of joggers and forms part of the Banks of the Seine World Heritage Site as listed by Unesco in 1991. There are some lovely sculptures within the gardens, including Louise Bourgeois' *The Welcoming Hands* (1996), which faces place de la Concorde.

The Voie Triomphale (Triumphal Way), also called the *Axe Historique* (Historic Axis), the western continuation of the Tuileries' east-west axis, follows the av des Champs-Élysées to the Arc de Triomphe and, ultimately, to the Grande Arche in the skyscraper district of La Défense (p179).

THE INS AND OUTS OF PARIS

When a building is put up in a location where they've run out of consecutive street numbers in Paris, a new address is formed by fusing the number of an adjacent building with the notation *bis* (twice), *ter* (thrice) or even *quater* (four times). In essence, the street numbers 17bis and 89ter are the equivalent of 17a and 89b in English.

The *portes cochères* (street doors) of most apartment buildings in Paris can be opened only by *digicode* (entry code), which is usually alphanumeric (eg 26A10) and changed periodically; the days of the concierges, who would vet every caller before allowing them in, are well and truly over.

The doors of many apartments are unmarked: the occupants' names are nowhere in sight and there isn't even an apartment number. To know which door to knock on, you'll usually be given cryptic instructions, such as *cinquième étage, premier à gauche* (5th floor, first on the left) or *troisième étage, droite droite* (3rd floor, turn right twice).

In France (and in this book), the 1st floor is the floor above the *rez-de-chaussée* (ground floor).

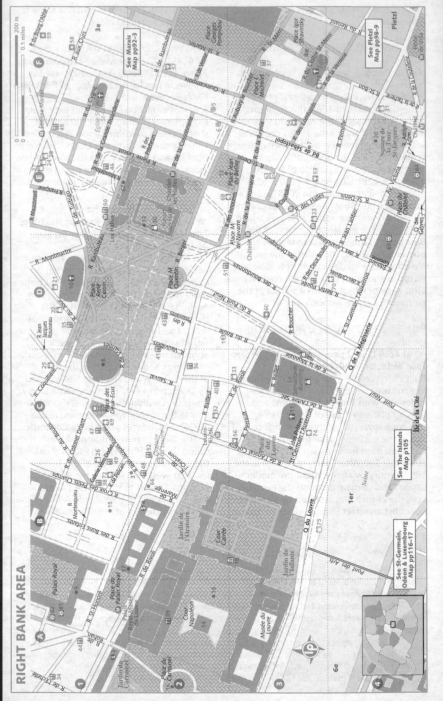

See Marais Map pp92-3

See Pletzl Map pp98-9

See The Islands Map p105

See St-Germain, Odéon & Luxembourg Map pp116-17

Pietzi

Île de la Cité

RIGHT BANK AREA

JEU DE PAUME Map pp82–3

☎ 01 47 03 12 50; www.jeudepaume.org; 1 place de la Concorde, 8e; adult/senior, student & 13-18yr €6/3; ⏱ noon-9pm Tue, to 7pm Wed-Fri, 10am-7pm Sat & Sun; Ⓜ Concorde

The Galerie du Jeu de Paume – Site Concorde (Jeu de Paume National Gallery at Concorde), which stages innovative exhibitions of contemporary art, is housed in an erstwhile *jeu de paume* (real, or royal, tennis court), built in 1861 during the reign of Napoleon III, in the northwestern corner of the Jardin des Tuileries. A branch of the gallery, the Jeu de Paume – Site Sully (p96) in the Hôtel de Sully in the Marais (4e) concentrates on top-notch photography. A joint ticket to both galleries costs €8/4 adult/concession.

MUSÉE DE L'ORANGERIE Map pp82–3

☎ 01 44 77 80 07; www.musee-orangerie.fr; Jardin des Tuileries, 1er; adult/senior, student & 13-18yr €6.50/4.50, 1st Sun of the month free; ⏱ 12.30-7pm Wed, Thu & Sat-Mon, to 9pm Fri; Ⓜ Concorde

This museum in the southwestern corner of the Jardin des Tuileries is, with the Jeu de Paume, all that remains of the once palatial Palais des Tuileries, which was razed during the Paris Commune (p26) in 1871. It exhibits important impressionist works, including an eight-panel series of Monet's *Decorations des Nymphéas* (Water Lilies) in two huge oval rooms purpose-built in 1927 to the artist's specifications, as well as paintings by Cézanne, Matisse, Picasso, Renoir, Sisley, Soutine and Utrillo.

PLACE VENDÔME Map pp82–3

Ⓜ Tuileries or Opéra

This octagonal square, and the arcaded and colonnaded buildings around it, was built between 1687 and 1721. In March 1796, Napoleon married Josephine, Viscountess of Beauharnais, in the building that's at No 3 in the southwest corner. Today, the buildings around the square house the posh Hôtel Ritz Paris (p336) and some of the city's most fashionable boutiques, especially

MONA LISA: THE TRUTH BEHIND THE SMILE

So much has been written – most recently (and most widely read) by Dan Brown in his best-selling novel *The Da Vinci Code* – about the painting the French call *La Joconde* and the Italians *La Gioconda*, yet so little has been known of the lady behind that enigmatic smile. For centuries admirers speculated on everything from the possibility that the subject was mourning the death of a loved one to that she might have been in love – or in bed – with her portraitist.

Mona (actually *monna* in Italian) is a contraction of *madonna*, while Gioconda is the feminine form of the surname Giocondo. With the emergence of several clues in recent years, it is has been established almost certainly that the subject was Lisa Gherardini (1479–1539?), the wife of Florentine merchant Franceso del Giocondo, and that the painting was done between 1503 and 1506 when she was around 25 years old. At the same time, tests done in 2005 with 'emotion recognition' computer software suggest that the smile on 'Madam Lisa' is at least 83% happy. And one other point remains unequivocally certain despite occasional suggestions to the contrary: she was not the lover of Leonardo, who preferred his *Vitruvian Man* to his *Mona*.

jewellery stores – place Vendôme has been synonymous with the bauble trade since the Second Empire of the mid-19th century.

In the centre of the square stands the 43.5m-tall Colonne Vendôme (Vendôme Column) which consists of a stone core wrapped in a 160m-long bronze spiral that's made from hundreds of Austrian and Russian cannons captured by Napoleon at the Battle of Austerlitz in 1805. The 425 bas-reliefs on the spiral celebrate Napoleon's victories between 1805 and 1807. The statue on top depicts Napoleon in classical Roman dress.

PALAIS ROYAL Map pp82–3
place du Palais Royal, 1er; www.monuments -nationaux.fr; M Palais Royal-Musée du Louvre
The Royal Palace, which accommodated a young Louis XIV for a time in the 1640s, lies to the north of place du Palais Royal and the Louvre. Construction was begun in 1624 by Cardinal Richelieu, though most of the present neoclassical complex dates from the latter part of the 18th century. It now contains the governmental Conseil d'État (State Council; Map p86) and is closed to the public.

The colonnaded building facing place André Malraux is the Comédie Française (p315; Map p86), founded in 1680 and the world's oldest national theatre.

Just north of the palace is the Jardin du Palais Royal (Map pp82–3; 01 47 03 92 16; 6 rue de Montpensier, 1er; 7.30am-10pm Apr & May, 7am-11pm Jun-Aug, 7am-9.30pm Sep, 7.30am-8.30pm Oct-Mar), a lovely park surrounded by two arcades. On the eastern side, Galerie de Valois (Map pp82–3) shelters designer fashion

shops, art galleries and jewellers, while Galerie de Montpensier (Map pp82–3) on the western side still has a few old shops remaining.

At the southern end there's a controversial sculpture (Map pp82–3) of black-and-white striped columns of various heights by Daniel Buren. It was started in 1986, interrupted by irate Parisians and finished – following the intervention of the Ministry of Culture and Communication – in 1995. The story (invented by Buren?) goes that if you toss a coin and it lands on one of the columns, your wish will come true.

CABINET DES MÉDAILLES ET MONNAIES Map pp82–3
01 53 79 82 26; www.bnf.fr; 58 rue de Richelieu, 2e; admission free; 1-5.45pm Mon-Fri, 1-4.15pm Sat; M Bourse
Housed in the original home of the Bibliothèque Nationale de France is this enormous hoard of coins, medals and tokens numbering more than 500,000. There's also an important collection of antiques, including items confiscated during the French Revolution from Ste-Chapelle and the abbey at St-Denis, including silverware, jewellery and the so-called Dagobert's Throne, dating from the 7th century, on which French kings were once crowned.

CENTRE POMPIDOU Map pp98–9
01 44 78 12 33; www.centrepompidou.fr; place Georges Pompidou, 4e; M Rambuteau
The Centre National d'Art et de Culture Georges Pompidou (Georges Pompidou National Centre of Art & Culture), also known as the Centre Beaubourg, has

amazed and delighted visitors since it was inaugurated in 1977, not just for its outstanding collection of modern art but for its radical architectural statement (p49).

The Forum du Centre Pompidou (admission free; 11am-10pm Wed-Mon), the open space at ground level, has temporary exhibits and information desks. The 4th and 5th floors of the centre exhibit a fraction of the 50,000-plus works of the Musée National d'Art Moderne (MNAM; National Museum of Modern Art; adult €10-12, senior & 18-25yr €8-10, under 18yr free, 6-9pm Wed free for 18-25yr, 1st Sun of the month free; 11am-9pm Wed-Mon), France's national collection of art dating from 1905 onward, and including the work of the surrealists and cubists as well as pop art and contemporary works.

The huge Bibliothèque Publique d'Information (BPI; ☎ 01 44 78 12 33; www.bpi.fr; noon-10pm Mon & Wed-Fri, 11am-10pm Sat & Sun), entered from rue du Renard, takes up part of the 1st as well as the entire 2nd and 3rd floors of the centre. The 6th floor has two galleries for temporary exhibitions (usually now included in the higher entrance fee) and a restaurant from the trendy Costes stable called Georges (p232), with panoramic views of Paris. There are cinemas (adult/senior & 18-25yr €6/4) and other entertainment venues on the 1st floor and in the basement.

West of the centre, Place Georges Pompidou and the nearby pedestrian streets attract buskers, musicians, jugglers and mime artists, and can be a lot of fun. South of the centre on place Igor Stravinsky, the fanciful mechanical fountains (Map pp98–9) of skeletons, hearts, treble clefs and a big pair of ruby-red lips, created by Jean Tinguely and Niki de St-Phalle, are a positive delight.

The Atelier Brancusi (Map pp98–9; 55 rue Rambuteau, 4e; admission free; 2-6pm Wed-Mon), across place Georges Pompidou to the west of the main building, was designed by Renzo Piano and contains almost 160 examples of the work of Romanian-born sculptor Constantin Brancusi (1876–1957) as well as drawings, paintings and glass photographic plates.

FORUM DES HALLES Map p86
☎ 01 44 76 96 56; www.forum-des-halles.com; 1 rue Pierre Lescaut, 1er; shops 10am-7.30pm; Les Halles or Châtelet les Halles
Les Halles, the city's main wholesale food market, occupied the area just south of

the Église St-Eustache from the early 12th century until 1969, when it was moved lox, stock and lettuce leaf to the southern suburb of Rungis, near Orly. In its place, this unspeakably ugly, four-level, underground shopping centre with 180 shops was constructed in the glass-and-chrome style of the late 1970s; it's slated to be gutted and rebuilt by 2010. Topping the complex on the street level is a popular garden with a rather stunning sculpture by Henri de Miller (1953–99) called *Listen*. In the warmer months, street musicians, fire-eaters and other performers display their talents here, especially at place Jean du Bellay, which is adorned by a multi-tiered Renaissance fountain, the Fontaine des Innocents (1549). It is named after the Cimetière des Innocents, a cemetery formerly on this site from which two million skeletons were disinterred after the Revolution and transferred to the Catacombes (p122).

ÉGLISE ST-EUSTACHE Map p86
☎ 01 42 36 31 05; www.saint-eustache.org in French; 2 impasse St-Eustache, 1er; audioguide €3; 9.30am-7pm Mon-Fri, 10am-7pm Sat, 9am-7.15pm Sun; Les Halles
This majestic church, one of the most beautiful in Paris, is just north of the gardens next to the Forum des Halles. Constructed between 1532 and 1637, St-Eustache is primarily Gothic, though a neoclassical façade was added on the western side in the mid-18th century. Inside, there are some exceptional Flamboyant Gothic arches holding up the ceiling of the chancel, though most of the ornamentation is Renaissance and even classical. Above the western entrance, the gargantuan organ, with 101 stops and 8000 pipes dating from 1854, is used for

MUSEUM CLOSING TIMES

The vast majority of museums in Paris close on Mondays though more than a dozen, including the Louvre, the Centre Pompidou, the Musée Picasso and the Musée National du Moyen Age, are closed on Tuesdays instead. It is also important to remember that all museums and monuments in Paris shut their doors or gates between 30 minutes and an hour before their actual closing times, which are the ones we list in this chapter. Therefore if we say a museum or monument closes at 6pm, for example, don't count on getting in much later than 5pm.

concerts (long a tradition here) and at Sunday Mass (11am and 6.30pm).

BOURSE DE COMMERCE Map p86

☎ 01 55 65 55 65; 2 rue de Viarmes, 1er; admission free; ☽ 9am-6pm Mon-Fri; Ⓜ Les Halles
At one time the city's grain market, the circular Trade Exchange was capped with a copper dome in 1811. The murals running along internal walls below the galleries were painted in 1889 and restored in 1998. They represent French trade and industry through the ages.

TOUR JEAN SANS PEUR Map pp82–3

☎ 01 40 26 20 28; www.tourjeansanspeur.com in French; 20 rue Étienne Marcel, 2e; adult/student & 7-18yr €5/3; ☽ 1.30-6pm Wed-Sun Apr-Oct, 1.30-6pm Wed, Sat & Sun Nov-Mar; Ⓜ Étienne Marcel
The Gothic, 29m-high Tower of John the Fearless was built by the Duke of Bourgogne as part of a splendid mansion in the early 15th century, so he could take refuge from his enemies at the top. It is one of the very few examples of feudal military architecture extant in Paris. Visitors can ascend the 140 steps of the spiral staircase to the turret on top. A guided tour at 3pm costs €8.

TOUR ST-JACQUES Map p86

square de la Tour St-Jacques, 4e; Ⓜ Châtelet
The Flamboyant Gothic, 52m-high St James Tower just north of place du Châtelet is all that remains of the Église St-Jacques la Boucherie, which was built by the powerful butchers guild in 1523 as a starting point for pilgrims setting out for the shrine of St James at Santiago de Compostela in Spain. The church was demolished by the revolutionary Directory in 1797, but the bell tower was spared so it could be used to drop globules of molten lead in the manufacture of shot.

Drinking p286; Eating p237; Shopping p201; Sleeping p337

The Marais, the area of the Right Bank north of Île St-Louis, was exactly what its name in French implies – 'marsh' or 'swamp' – until the 13th century, when it was converted to farmland. In the early 17th century, Henri IV built the place Royale (today's place des Vosges), turning the area into Paris' most fashionable residential district and attracting wealthy aristocrats who then erected their own luxurious private mansions.

When the aristocracy moved out of Paris to Versailles and Faubourg St-Germain during the late 17th and the 18th centuries, the Marais and its town houses passed into the hands of ordinary Parisians. The 110-hectare area was given a major face-lift in the late 1960s and early '70s.

Though the Marais has become a coveted trendy address in recent years, it remains home to a long-established Jewish community. The historic Jewish quarter – the so-called Pletzl – starts in rue des Rosiers, then continues along rue Ste-Croix de la Bretonnerie to rue du Temple, where expensive boutiques sit side-by-side with Jewish bookshops and stores selling religious goods and *cacher* (kosher) grocery shops, butchers, restaurants and takeaway falafel joints. Don't miss the Art Nouveau synagogue (Map pp98–9; 10 rue Pavée, 4e) designed in 1913 by Hector Guimard, who was also responsible for the city's famous metro entrances (see boxed text, p156). You'll also find a lot of gay and lesbian bars and restaurants in this area as well.

After years as a run-down immigrant neighbourhood notorious for its high crime rate, the Bastille area has undergone a fair degree of gentrification, which started with the advent of the Opéra Bastille almost two decades ago. The courtyards and alleyways of the 11e arrondissement used to belong to artisans and labourers; the areas around rue du Faubourg St-Antoine, rue de Charonne and rue de la Roquette buzzed with the sound of cabinet makers, joiners, gilders and the like at work. Today most of that's gone, replaced with artists and their lofts. But the old spirit lives on in some hidden parts of the 11e, and the areas to the east of place de la Bastille in particular retain their lively atmosphere and ethnicity.

HÔTEL DE VILLE Map pp98–9

☎ 39 75; www.paris.fr; place de l'Hôtel de Ville, 4e; M Hôtel de Ville

After having been gutted during the Paris Commune of 1871, Paris' city hall was rebuilt in luxurious neo-Renaissance style from 1874 to 1882. The ornate façade is decorated with 108 statues of noteworthy Parisians. There's a Salon d'Accueil (Reception Hall; 29 rue de Rivoli, 4e; ⏰ 10am-7pm Mon-Sat), which dispenses information and brochures and is used for temporary (and very popular) exhibitions, usually with a Paris theme. Some

exhibits take place in the Salle St-Jean (5 rue Lobau, 4e), which is entered from the eastern side of the building.

PLACE DES VOSGES Map pp98–9

M St-Paul or Bastille

Inaugurated in 1612 as place Royale and thus the oldest square in Paris, Place des Vosges (4e) is an ensemble of 36 symmetrical houses with ground-floor arcades, steep slate roofs and large dormer windows arranged around a large square. Only the earliest houses were built of brick; to save time, the rest were given timber frames and faced with plaster, which was later painted to resemble brick. The square received its present name in 1800 to honour the Vosges *département* (administrative division) for being the first in France to pay its taxes.

The author Victor Hugo lived in an apartment on the 3rd floor of the square's Hôtel de Rohan-Guéménée from 1832 to 1848, moving here a year after the publication of *Notre Dame de Paris* (The Hunchback of Notre Dame); he completed *Ruy Blas* while in residence here. The Maison de Victor Hugo (Map pp92–3; Victor Hugo House; ☎ 01 42 72 10 16; www.musee-hugo.paris.fr; 6 place des Vosges,

MARAS

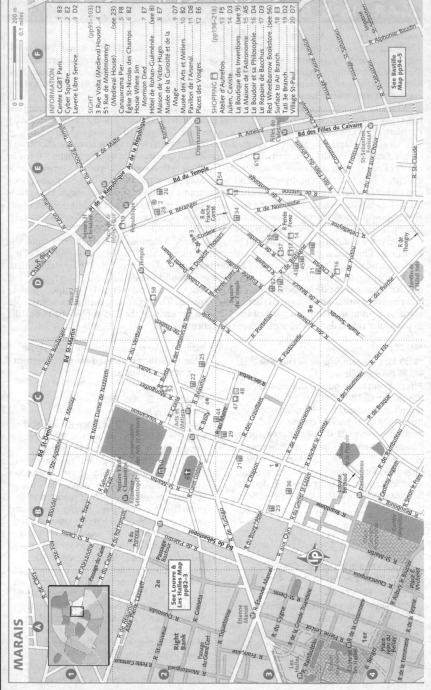

0 ____ 200 m
0 ____ 0.1 miles

INFORMATION	
Centre LGBT Paris.................................1	B3
Cyber Squ@re...2	E2
Laverie Libre Service.............................3	D2

SIGHT	(pp91–103)
3 Rue Volta (Medieval House).............4	C2
51 Rue de Montmorency	
(Medieval House)...........................(see 23)	
Canauxrama Pier...................................5	F8
Église St-Nicolas des Champs............6	B2
House Where Jim	
Morrison Died...............................(see 8)	
Hôtel de Rohan-Guémenée................(see 8)	
Maison de Victor Hugo.......................8	E7
Musée de la Curiosité et de la	
Magie..9	D7
Musée des Arts et Métiers...............10	B2
Pavillon de l'Arsenal.........................11	D8
Places des Vosges.............................12	E6

SHOPPING	(pp198–218)
Atelier d'Autrefois............................13	F5
Julien, Caviste...................................14	D3
La Boutique des Inventions............(see 9)	
La Maison de l'Astronomie..............15	A5
Le Boudoir et sa Philosophie...........16	D4
Le Repaire de Bacchus....................17	D3
Red Wheelbarrow Bookstore..........(see 36)	
Surface to Air Branch.......................18	E3
Tati 3e Branch...................................19	D2
Village St-Paul..................................20	D7

See Bastille
Map pp94–5

See Louvre &
Les Halles Map
pp82–3

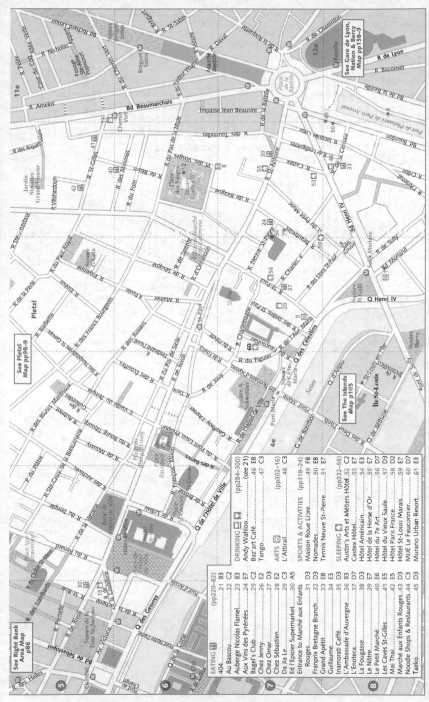

See Gare de Lyon, Nation & Bercy Map pp158-9

See Pletzl Map pp98-9

See Right Bank Area Map p86

See The Islands Map p105

NEIGHBOURHOODS MARAIS & BASTILLE

EATING (pp220–82)
4o4....................................21 B3
Au Bascou..........................22 C2
Auberge Nicolas Flamel.....23 B3
Aux Vins des Pyrénées......24 E7
Bagel's Club........................25 C2
Chez Jenny.........................26 E2
Chez Omar..........................27 D3
Chez Sébastien...................28 E2
Da Jia Le.............................29 C3
Ed l'Épicier Supermarket....30 A5
Entrance to Marché aux Enfants
Rouges..............................31 D3
Franprix Bretagne Branch....32 D3
Grand Apétit.......................33 E8
Guillaume............................34 E3
Inamorati Caffè...................35 D3
L'Ambassade d'Auvergne....36 B3
L'Enoteca............................37 D7
La Fougasse.......................38 D3
Le Nôtre.............................39 E6
Le Petit Marché..................40 E6
Les Caves St-Gilles.............41 E5
Mai Thai.............................42 E5
Marché aux Enfants Rouges.43 D3
Noodle Shops & Restaurants.44 C3
Taeko.................................45 D3

DRINKING (pp284–300)
Andy Wahloo.................(see 21)
Baz'art Café.......................46 E8
Tango.................................47 C3

ARTS (pp302–16)
L'Attirail.............................48 C3

SPORTS & ACTIVITIES (pp318–24)
Maison Roue Libre..............49 F8
Nomades............................50 E8
Tennis Neuve St-Pierre.......51 E7

SLEEPING (pp332–58)
Austin's Arts et Métiers Hôtel.52 C2
Castex Hôtel......................53 E7
Hôtel Américain..................54 E3
Hôtel de la Herse d'Or........55 E3
Hôtel du 7e Art..................56 D7
Hôtel du Vieux Saule...........57 D3
Hôtel Paris France...............58 D2
Hôtel St-Louis Marais..........59 E7
MIJE Le Fauconnier............60 D7
Murano Urban Resort.........61 E3

93

BASTILLE

0 200 m
0 0.1 miles

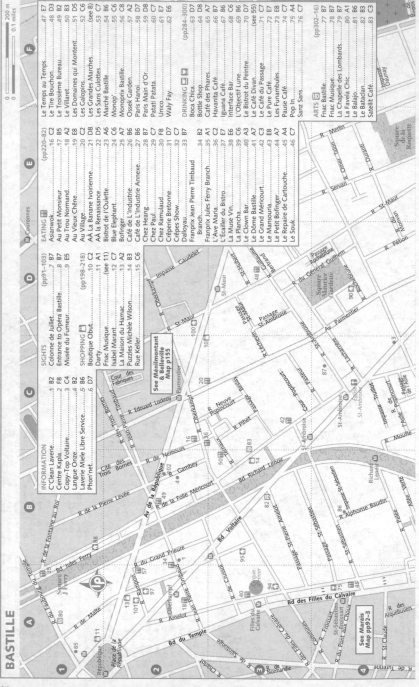

INFORMATION
C'Clean Laverie.....1 B2
Centre Kapla.....2 F8
Copy-Top Voltaire.....3 C4
Langue Onze.....4 B2
Laverie Miele Libre Service.....5 B6
Phon'net.....6 D7

SIGHTS (pp91–103)
Colonne de Juillet.....7 B7
Entrance to Opéra Bastille.....8 B7
Musée du Fumeur.....9 E5

SHOPPING (pp198–218)
Boutique Obut.....10 C2
Darty.....(see 11)
Fnac Musique.....11 A1
Isabel Marant.....12 C7
La Maison du Hamac.....13 A2
Puzzles Michèle Wilson.....14 B3
Rue Keller.....15 C6

EATING (pp220–82)
Asianwok.....16 C2
Au Petit Monsieur.....17 B5
Au Trou Normand.....18 A2
Au Vieux Chêne.....19 E8
Au Village.....20 C2
AA la Banane Ivoirienne.....21 D8
AA la Renaissance.....22 D5
Bistrot de l'Oulette.....23 A6
Blue Elephant.....24 C6
Bofinger.....25 A7
Café de L'Industrie.....26 B6
Café de L'Industrie Annexe.....27 B6
Chez Heang.....28 B7
Chez Paul.....29 C7
Chez Ramulaud.....30 F8
Crêperie Bretonne.....31 D7
Crêpes Show.....32 C7
Dalloyau.....33 B7
Franprix Jean Pierre Timbaud Branch.....34 B2
Franprix Jules Ferry Branch.....35 A1
L'Ave Maria.....36 B7
L'Écailler du Bistro.....37 E7
La Muse Vin.....38 E6
La Plancha.....39 C6
Le Clown Bar.....40 A3
Le Dôme Bastille.....41 A7
Le Grand Méricourt.....42 C3
Le Mansouria.....43 E8
Le Petit Bofinger.....44 A7
Le Repaire de Cartouche.....45 A4
Le souk.....46 C7
Le Temps au Temps.....47 E7
Le Tire Bouchon.....48 D3
Le Troisième Bureau.....49 B2
Le Villaret.....50 B3
Les Domaines qui Montent.....51 D5
Les Galopins.....52 C6
Les Grandes Marches.....(see 8)
Les Sans Culottes.....53 C7
Marché Bastille.....54 B6
Monop'.....55 C6
Monoprix Bastille.....56 C8
Ossek Garden.....57 A2
Paris Hanoi.....58 D7
Paris Main d'Or.....59 D8
Patati Patata.....60 C7
Unico.....61 E7
Waly Fay.....62 E6

DRINKING (pp284–300)
Boca Chica.....63 D7
Bottle Shop.....64 D8
Café des Phares.....65 A7
Havanta Café.....66 B7
Iguana Café.....67 B6
Interface Bar.....68 C6
L'Objectif Lune.....69 B6
Le Bistrot du Peintre.....70 D7
Le Café Divan.....(see 55)
Le Café du Passage.....71 C7
Le Pure Café.....72 E7
Les Funambules.....73 E8
Pause Café.....74 C7
Pop In.....75 A4
Sanz Sans.....76 C7

ARTS (pp302–16)
Fnac Bastille.....77 B7
La Chapelle des Lombards.....78 B7
La Favela Chic.....79 A1
Le Balajo.....80 A1
Le Bataclan.....81 B6
Satellit Café.....82 B3
.....83 C3

See Ménilmontant & Belleville Map p155

See Marais Map pp92–3

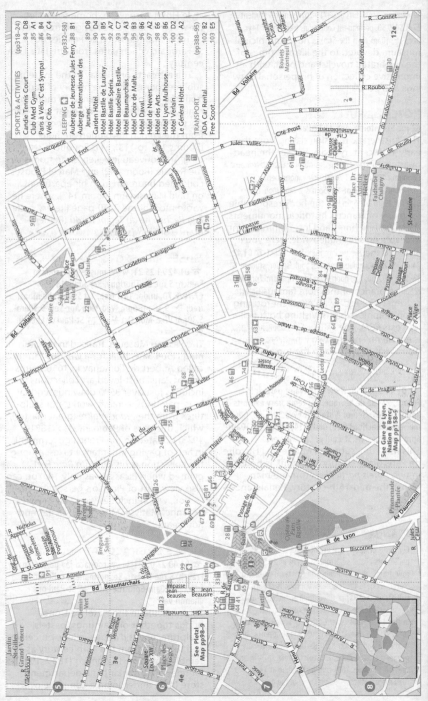

SPORTS & ACTIVITIES	(pp318–24)
Candie Tennis Court	84 D8
Club Med Gym	85 A1
Paris à Vélo, C'est Sympa!	86 B4
Vélo Cito	87 C4

SLEEPING	(pp332–58)
Auberge de Jeunesse Jules Ferry	88 B1
Auberge Internationale des Jeunes	89 D8
Garden Hôtel	90 D4
Hôtel Bastille de Launay	91 B5
Hôtel Bastille Spéria	92 A7
Hôtel Baudelaire Bastille	93 C7
Hôtel Beaumarchais	94 A3
Hôtel Croix de Malte	95 B3
Hôtel Daval	96 B6
Hôtel de Nevers	97 A2
Hôtel des Arts	98 E6
Hôtel Lyon Mulhouse	99 B6
Hôtel Verlain	100 D2
Le Général Hôtel	101 A2

TRANSPORT	(pp388–95)
ADA Car Rental	102 B2
Free Scoot	103 E5

12e

See Gare de Lyon,
Nation & Bercy
Map pp158–9

See Pletzl
Map pp98–9

95

4e; temporary exhibits adult/14-26yr/senior & student €7/3.50/5.50, permanent collections free, under 14yr free; ⊕ 10am-6pm Tue-Sun) is now a municipal museum devoted to the life and times of the celebrated novelist and poet, with an impressive collection of his personal drawings and portraits.

HÔTEL DE SULLY Map pp98–9
62 rue St-Antoine, 4e; M St-Paul
This aristocratic mansion dating from the early 17th century today houses the headquarters of the Centre des Monuments Nationaux (Monum; ☎ 01 44 61 20 00; www.monuments -nationaux.fr; ⊕ 9am-12.45pm & 2-6pm Mon-Thu, 9am-12.45pm & 2-5pm Fri), the body responsible for many of France's historical monuments; there are brochures and lots of information available on sites nationwide. Here you'll also find the Jeu de Paume – Site Sully (☎ 01 42 74 47 75; www.jeudepaume.org; adult/senior, student & 13-18yr €5/2.50; ⊕ noon-7pm Tue-Fri, 10am-7pm Sat & Sun), a branch of the more famous Galerie de Jeu de Paume (p87), with excellent rotating photographic exhibits. Visiting both galleries costs €8/4. The Hôtel de Sully bookshop (p202) is excellent, and the two Renaissance-style courtyards (p193) are worth the trip alone.

MUSÉE CARNAVALET Map pp98–9
☎ 01 44 59 58 58; www.carnavalet.paris.fr in French; 23 rue de Sévigné, 3e; temporary exhibits adult/14-26yr/senior & student €7/3.50/5.50, permanent collections free, under 14yr free; ⊕ 10am-6pm Tue-Sun; M St-Paul or Chemin Vert
This museum, subtitled Musée de l'Histoire de Paris (Paris History Museum), is housed in two *hôtels particuliers* (private mansions): the mid-16th-century, Renaissance-

IF WALLS COULD TALK
Centuries of history are inscribed on the façades and pediments of the 4e arrondissement and in the narrow streets, alleys, porches and courtyards; today the Marais is one of the few neighbourhoods of Paris that still has most of its pre-Revolution architecture intact. These include the house at 3 rue Volta (Map pp92–3) in the 3e arrondissement, parts of which date back to 1292; the one at 51 rue de Montmorency, also in the 3e and dating back to 1407 which is now a restaurant called Auberge Nicolas Flamel (p245); and the half-timbered 16th-century building at 11 and 13 rue François Miron (Map pp98–9) in the 4e.

style Hôtel Carnavalet, home to the letter-writer Madame de Sévigné from 1677 to 1696, and the Hôtel Le Peletier de St-Fargeau, which dates from the late 17th century.

The artefacts on display in the museum's sublime rooms chart the history of Paris from the Gallo-Roman period to modern times. Some of the nation's most important documents, paintings and other objects from the French Revolution are here (Rooms 101 to 113), as is Fouquet's stunning Art Nouveau jewellery shop from the rue Royale (Room 142) and Marcel Proust's cork-lined bedroom from his apartment on blvd Haussmann (Room 147), where he wrote most of the 7350-page literary cycle *À la Recherche du Temps Perdu* (Remembrance of Things Past).

MUSÉE PICASSO Map pp98–9
☎ 01 42 71 25 21; www.musee-picasso.fr in French; 5 rue de Thorigny, 3e; adult/18-25yr €7.70/5.70, under 18yr free, 1st Sun of the month free; ⊕ 9.30am-6pm Wed-Mon Apr-Sep, 9.30am-5.30pm Wed-Mon Oct-Mar; M St-Paul or Chemin Vert
The Picasso Museum, housed in the stunning Hôtel Salé, built for a wealthy farmer called Aubert de Fontenay in 1656, forms one of Paris' best-loved art collections. It includes just over 3500 drawings, engravings, paintings, ceramic works and sculptures from the *grand maître* (great master), which the heirs of Pablo Picasso (1881–1973) donated to the French government in lieu of paying inheritance taxes. Among the collection is his *Girl with Bare Feet*, painted when Picasso was only 14. You can also view part of Picasso's personal art collection, which includes works by Braque, Cézanne, Matisse, Modigliani, Degas and Rousseau.

MUSÉE COGNACQ-JAY Map pp98–9
☎ 01 40 27 07 21; www.cognacq-jay.paris.fr in French; 8 rue Elzévir, 3e; permanent collections free; ⊕ 10am-6pm Tue-Sun; M St-Paul or Chemin Vert
This museum in the Hôtel de Donon brings together oil paintings, pastels, sculpture, *objets d'art,* jewellery, porcelain and furniture from the 18th century assembled by Ernest Cognacq (1839–1928), founder of La Samaritaine department store (now undergoing a complete over-

top picks

MARAIS & BASTILLE

- Place des Vosges (p91)
- Hôtel de Sully (opposite)
- Musée Carnavalet (opposite)
- Musée Picasso (opposite)
- Mémorial de la Shoah (p100)

haul) and his wife Louise Jay. Although Cognacq appreciated little of his collection, boasting to all who would listen that he had never visited the Louvre and was only acquiring collections for the status, the artwork and *objets d'art* give a pretty good idea of upper-class tastes during the Age of Enlightenment.

ARCHIVES NATIONALES Map pp98–9
☎ 01 40 27 60 96; www.archivesnationales.cul ture.gouv.fr in French; 60 rue des Francs Bourgeois, 3e; Ⓜ Rambuteau or St-Paul
France's National Archives are housed in the Soubise wing of the impressive, early-18th-century Hôtel de Rohan-Soubise, which also contains the Musée de l'Histoire de France (Museum of French History; ☎ 01 40 27 62 18; www.archivesnationales.culture.gouv.fr/chan in French; adult/senior & 18-25yr €3/2.30, under 18yr free, 1st Sun of the month free; 🕑 10am-12.30pm & 2-5.30pm Mon & Wed-Fri, 2-5.30pm Sat & Sun; Ⓜ Rambuteau or St-Paul). The museum contains antique furniture and 18th-century paintings but primarily documents – everything from medieval incunabula and letters written by Joan of Arc to the wills of Louis XIV and Napoleon. The ceiling and walls of the interior are extravagantly painted and gilded in the rococo style; look out for the Cabinet des Singes, a simian-filled room painted by Christophe Huet between 1749 and 1752.

MUSÉE DES ARTS ET MÉTIERS
Map pp92–3
☎ 01 53 01 82 00; www.arts-et-metiers.net; 60 rue de Réaumur, 3e; temporary exhibits adult/student & 6-18yr €5.50/3.50, permanent collections free, under 5yr free; 🕑 10am-6pm Tue, Wed & Fri-Sun, to 9.30pm Thu; Ⓜ Arts et Métiers
The Arts & Crafts Museum, the oldest museum of science and technology in Europe, is a must for anyone with an interest in

how things work. Housed in the 18th century priory of St-Martin des Champs, some 3000 instruments, machines and working models from the 18th to 20th centuries are displayed across three floors. Taking pride of place is Foucault's original pendulum, which he introduced to the world in 1855. There are lots of workshops and other activities here for children. An audioguide costs €2.50.

MUSÉE DE LA CHASSE ET DE LA NATURE Map pp98–9
☎ 01 53 01 92 40; www.chassenature.org, in French; Hôtel Guénégaud, 62 rue des Archives, 3e; adult/student & 18-25yr €6/4.50, under 18yr free; 🕑 11am-6pm Tue-Sun; Ⓜ Rambuteau or Hôtel de Ville
The Hunting and Nature Museum may sound like an oxymoron to the politically correct, but in France, where hunting is a very big deal, to show your love for nature is to go out and shoot something – or so it would seem. The delightful Hôtel Guénégaud, dating from 1651 and now open after a two-year renovation, is positively crammed with weapons, paintings, sculpture and *objets d'art* related to hunting and, of course, lots and lots of trophies – horns, antlers, heads.

MUSÉE D'ART ET D'HISTOIRE DU JUDAÏSME Map pp98–9
☎ 01 53 01 86 60; www.mahj.org; 71 rue du Temple, 3e; adult/student & 18-26yr €6.80/4.50 incl audioguide, under 18yr free; 🕑 11am-6pm Mon-Fri, 10am-6pm Sun; Ⓜ Rambuteau
The Museum of the Art & History of Judaism, housed in the sumptuous Hôtel de St-Aignan (1650), traces the evolution of Jewish communities from the Middle Ages to the present, with particular emphasis on the history of the Jews in France but also that of communities in other parts of Europe and North Africa. Highlights include documents relating to the Dreyfus Affair (p26) and works by Chagall, Modigliani and Soutine. Temporary exhibits cost an extra €5.50/4 and a combined ticket is €8.50/6.

MUSÉE DE LA POUPÉE Map pp98–9
☎ 01 42 72 73 11; www.museedelapoupeeparis .com; impasse Berthaud, 3e; adult/aged 3-11yr/senior & 12-25yr €7/3/5, adult €4 10am-1pm Sat & Sun; 🕑 10am-6pm Tue-Sun; Ⓜ Rambuteau
Frightening to some – all those beady eyes and silent screams – the Doll Museum is

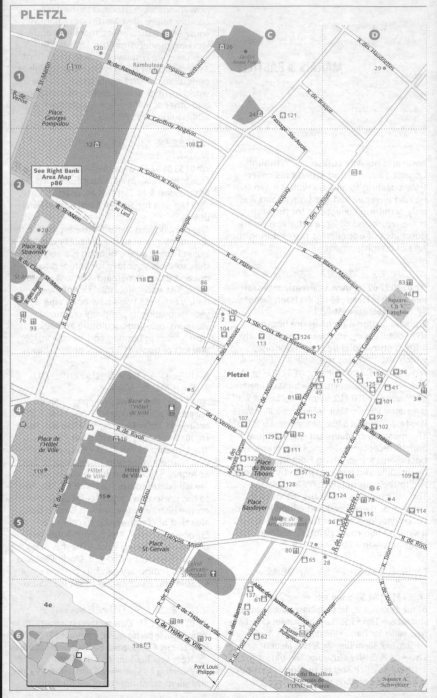

PLETZL

NEIGHBOURHOODS MARAIS & BASTILLE

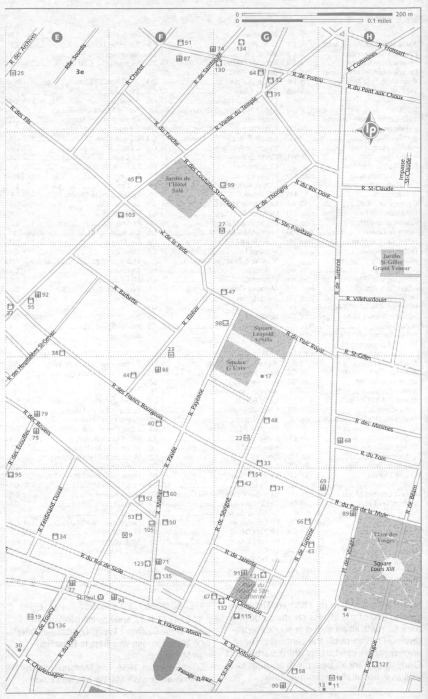

E

F

G

H

R des Archives

R lle Sourdis

3e

25

R Charlot

R de Saintonge

51

74

130

134

R Froissart

R Commines

R de Poitou

64

32

35

R du Pont aux Choux

R des Filk

R du Perche

R Vieille du Temple

Impasse St-Claude

R St-Claude

45

Jardin de l'Hôtel Salé

R des Coutures St-Gervais

99

R de Thorigny

R du Roi Doré

103

27

R de la Perle

R Ste-Anastase

Jardin St-Gilles Grand Veneur

92

55

R Barbette

R Elzévir

47

R de Turenne

R Villehardouin

98

Square Léopold Achille

R du Parc Royal

R St-Gilles

38

23

95

Square G' Caïn

17

44

R des Francs Bourgeois

R Payenne

48

R des Minimes

79

R des Rosiers

75

R des Écouffes

40

22

68

R du Foin

95

R Ferdinand Duval

R Pavée

33

54

42

31

69

52

60

R du Pas de la Mule

89

R de Béarn

53

105

50

66

Place des Vosges

34

9

R de Sévigné

R de Turenne

43

Pl des Vosges

Square Louis XIII

R du Roi de Sicile

123

71

135

R de Jarente

91

131

St-Paul

77

94

67

R d'Ormeson

132

14

19

R de Fourcy

136

115

R François Miron

R St-Antoine

30

R du Prévôt

Passage St-Paul

R St-Paul

58

R de Birague

127

R Charlemagne

90

13

18

11

0   200 m
0   0.1 miles

PLETZL

more for adults than for children. There are around 500 of the lifeless creatures, dating back to 1800, all arranged in scenes representing Paris through the centuries. There are temporary exhibitions (think Barbie and Cindy and 'France's best plush animals') as well as a 'hospital' for antique dolls.

MÉMORIAL DE LA SHOAH Map pp98–9

☎ 01 42 77 44 72; www.memorialdelashoah .org; 17 rue Geoffroy-l'Asnier, 4e; admission free; ⏱ 10am-6pm Sun-Wed & Fri, to 10pm Thu; Ⓜ St-Paul

Established in 1956, the Memorial to the Unknown Jewish Martyr has metamor-

TAKING ON PARIS' MUSEUMS

Warm-up exercises, half-hour breathers, a portable seat, bottled water and an energy-providing snack… It might sound as if you're preparing for a trek in the Alps, but these are some of the recommendations for tackling Paris' more than 100 museums. And with almost three-dozen major ones free of charge on at least one day of the week, the temptation to see more is now greater than ever.

Take the Louvre, for example. Encompassing some 40 sq hectares, the museum has nine enormous departments spread over 60,000 sq metres of gallery space and more than 8 million visitors a year, all elbowing each other to see what they want to see in a limited amount of time. It's hardly surprising that many people feel worn out almost before they've descended into the Cour Napoléon.

To avoid museum fatigue wear comfortable shoes and make use of the cloakrooms. Be aware that standing still and walking slowly promote tiredness; sit down as often as you can. Reflecting on the material and forming associations with it causes information to move from your short- to long-term memory; your experiences will thus amount to more than a series of visual 'bites'.

Tracking and timing studies suggest that museum-goers spend no more than 10 seconds viewing an exhibit and another 10 seconds reading the label as they try to take in as much as they can before succumbing to exhaustion. To avoid this choose a particular period or section to focus on or join a guided tour of the highlights.

phosed into the Memorial of the Holocaust and a documentation centre. The permanent collection and temporary exhibits relate to the Holocaust and the German occupation of parts of France and Paris during WWII; the film clips of contemporary footage and interviews are heart-rending and the displays instructive and easy to follow. The actual memorial to the victims of the Shoah, a Hebrew word meaning 'catastrophe' and synonymous in France with the Holocaust, stands at the entrance, where there is a wall inscribed with the names of 76,000 men, women and children deported from France to Nazi extermination camps. A guided tour (☎ 01 53 01 17 86) in English departs at 3pm on the second Sunday of each month.

MAISON EUROPÉENNE DE LA PHOTOGRAPHIE Map pp98–9

☎ 01 44 78 75 00; www.mep-fr.org; 5-7 rue de Fourcy, 4e; adult/senior & 8-25yr €6/3, under 8 free, 5-7.45pm Wed free; ⏰ 11am-7.45pm Wed-Sun; Ⓜ St-Paul or Pont Marie

The European House of Photography, housed in the overly renovated Hôtel Hénault de Cantorbe (dating from the early 18th century), has cutting-edge temporary exhibits (usually retrospectives on single photographers), as well as an enormous permanent collection on the history of photography and its connections with France. There are frequent showings of short films and documentaries on weekend afternoons. The Japanese garden at the entrance is a delight.

PARIS HISTORIQUE Map pp98–9

☎ 01 48 87 74 31; www.paris-historique.org in French; 44-46 rue François Miron, 4e; admission free; ⏰ 11am-8pm Mon-Sat, 2-7pm Sun; Ⓜ St-Paul

The information centre for the Association for the Conservation and Appreciation of Historic Paris should be on your tick list if you are interested in medieval Paris and, especially, the Marais. It provides information, has a research library, organises exhibitions and leads guided tours (adult/student & child €9/4) of the area at 2pm or 2.30pm daily except Sunday.

MUSÉE DE LA CURIOSITÉ ET DE LA MAGIE Map pp92–3

☎ 01 42 72 13 26; www.museedelamagie.com, in French; 11 rue St-Paul, 4e; adult/3-12yr €9/7; ⏰ 2-7pm Wed, Sat & Sun, 2-7pm daily Easter & Christmas school holidays; Ⓜ St-Paul

The Museum of Curiosity & Magic in the 16th-century caves (cellars) of the house of the Marquis de Sade examines the ancient arts of magic, optical illusion and sleight of hand, with regular magic shows (last one at 6pm) included. But some visitors may feel that the displays – optical illusions and wind-up toys – and very basic magic tricks do not justify the extremely high admission fee. An audioguide costs €3.

PLACE DE LA BASTILLE Map pp94–5

Ⓜ Bastille

The Bastille, built during the 14th century as a fortified royal residence, is the most famous monument in Paris that no longer exists. The notorious prison – the quintessential symbol

IT'S A FREE-FOR-ALL

The permanent collections at 11 of the 15 *musées municipaux* (city museums), run by the Mairie de Paris (www.paris .fr), are free. Temporary exhibitions always incur a separate admission fee.

City museums taking part in this scheme include the following:

Maison de Balzac (p136)	Musée Cognacq-Jay (p96)
Maison de Victor Hugo (p91)	Musée d'Art Moderne de la Ville de Paris (p135)
Musée Atelier Zadkine (p121)	Musée de la Vie Romantique (p171)
Musée Bourdelle (p165)	Musée des Beaux-Arts de la Ville de Paris (Petit
Musée Carnavalet (p96)	Palais; p139)
Musée Cernuschi (p146)	Musée Jean Moulin & Mémorial du Maréchal Leclerc de Hauteclocque et de la Libération de Paris (p123)

At the same time, the *musées nationaux* (national museums) in Paris have reduced rates for those aged over 60 and between 18 and 25, and sometimes for everyone else on one day or part of a day per week (eg Sunday morning). They are always free for those under 18 years of age, and for everyone on the first Sunday of each month (although not always year-round – see the following list). Again, you will have to pay separately for temporary exhibitions.

The museums and monuments in question (and their free-admission days) are:

Arc de Triomphe (p138) **1st Sunday of the month, November to March only.**	Musée Ernest Hébert (p120) **Currently under renovation.**
Basilique de St-Denis (p182) **1st Sunday of the month, November to March only.**	Musée Guimet des Arts Asiatiques (p135)
Château de Vincennes (p176) **1st Sunday of the month, November to May only.**	Musée National d'Art Moderne (Centre Pompidou; p89)
La Conciergerie (p106) **1st Sunday of the month, November to March only.**	Musée National du Moyen Age (Musée de Cluny; p114)
Musée d'Art et d'Histoire (p183)	Musée National Eugène Delacroix (p121)
Musée de l'Assistance Publique-Hôpitaux de Paris (p113)	Musée National Gustave Moreau (p150)
Musée de l'Histoire de France (Archives Nationales; p97)	Musée Picasso (p96)
	Musée Rodin (p130)
Musée de l'Orangerie (p87)	Panthéon (p114) **1st Sunday of the month, November to March only.**
Musée d'Orsay (p130)	Ste-Chapelle (p107) **1st Sunday of the month, November to March only.**
Musée du Louvre (p80)	Tours de Notre Dame (p106) **1st Sunday of the month, November to March only.**
Musée du Quai Branly (p134)	

of royal despotism – was demolished shortly after a mob stormed it on 14 July 1789 and freed a total of just seven prisoners. The site where it once stood, place de la Bastille (11e and 12e), is now a very busy traffic roundabout.

In the centre of the square is the 52m-high Colonne de Juillet (July Column), whose shaft of greenish bronze is topped by a gilded and winged figure of Liberty. It was erected in 1833 as a memorial to those killed in the street battles that accompanied the July Revolution of 1830 – they are

buried in vaults under the column – and was later consecrated as a memorial to the victims of the February Revolution of 1848.

OPÉRA BASTILLE Map pp94–5

☎ 08 92 89 90 90; www.opera-de-paris.fr, in French; 2-6 place de la Bastille, 12e; Ⓜ Bastille
Paris' giant 'second' opera house, designed by the Canadian architect Carlos Ott, was inaugurated on 14 July 1989, the 200th anniversary of the storming of the Bastille. It has three theatres, including the main audi-

torium with 2700 seats. There are 1¼-hour guided tours (☎ 01 40 01 19 70; adult/under 10yr/senior, student & 11-25yr €11/6/9) of the building, which generally depart at around 1.15pm from Monday to Saturday. Tickets go on sale just 10 minutes before departure at the box office (130 rue de Lyon, 12e; ☯ 10.30am-6.30pm Mon-Sat).

MUSÉE DU FUMEUR Map pp94–5

☎ 01 46 59 05 51; www.museedufumeur.net; 7 rue Pache, 11e; adult/concession €4/3; ☯ 2-7pm; Ⓜ Voltaire

The Smoking Museum traces the history of one of mankind's greatest vices: the smoking of tobacco (as well as lots and lots of other substances of various strengths and weaknesses). Hard-core butt-fiends will feel vindicated, though the museum takes an impartial stance, providing (as it states on its website) 'a vantage point for the observation of changing behaviours'. Done up as an old tobacco warehouse, the museum has a wonderful collection of portraits as well as a superb book-and-gift shop.

THE ISLANDS

Eating p248; Shopping p208; Sleeping p342

Paris' twin set of islands could not be more different: with its quaint car-free lanes, legendary ice-cream maker and bijou portfolio of street plaques celebrating famous residents of the past, Île St-Louis is a tourist joy. Its Pandora's box of boutiques lining the only central street might not be worth the trip in itself, but browse and there's no saying what gem you might find – antique spice jars, rose-petal massage oil, a hand-painted glass pharmacy jar from the 1930s…

At the island's western end, the area around Pont St-Louis and Pont Louis-Philippe is one of the city's most romantic spots. On summer days, lovers mingle with cello-playing buskers and teenaged skateboarders. After nightfall, the Seine dances with the watery reflections of street-lights, headlamps, stop signals and the dim glow of curtained windows. Occasionally, tourist boats with super-bright floodlamps cruise by. There's no doubt: you are really in Paris.

Stand on the square in front of Notre Dame on big-brother Île de Cité and there is no doubt where you are: two seconds dodging snap-happy tourists, street sellers pushing €1 Eiffel Tower key rings and backpackers guarding piles of packs while their mates check out the cathedral is a taste of the best and worst of Paris. Sensibly, not very many Parisians live on this island.

ÎLE DE LA CITÉ

The site of the first settlement in Paris (c 3rd century BC) and later the centre of the Roman town of Lutetia (in French, Lutèce), Île de la Cité remained the centre of royal and ecclesiastical power even after the city spread to both banks of the Seine during the Middle Ages. As the institutions on the island grew, so did the island. Buildings on the middle part of the island were demolished and rebuilt during Baron Haussmann's urban renewal scheme of the late 19th century (see p27); the population – considered the poorest in the city – fell from 15,000 in 1860 to 5000 less than a decade later.

The Île de la Cité, mainly in the 4e arrondissement (its western tip is in the 1er) is home to two institutions devoted to maintaining public order: the judiciary (Palais de Justice) and the police (Préfecture de Police).

CATHÉDRALE DE NOTRE DAME DE PARIS Map p105

☎ 01 42 34 56 10; www.cathedraledeparis.com; place du Parvis Notre Dame, 4e; audioguide €5; ⏰ 7.45am-6.45pm, information desk 9.30am-6pm Mon-Fri, 9am-6pm Sat; Ⓜ Cité

This is the heart of Paris – so much so that distances from Paris to every part of metropolitan France are measured from place du Parvis Notre Dame, the square in front of the Cathedral of Our Lady of Paris. A bronze star across the street from the cathedral's main entrance marks the exact location of point zéro des routes de France. Nearby, Charlemagne (742–814), emperor of the Franks, rides his steed under the trees.

Notre Dame, the most visited site in Paris with 10 million people crossing its threshold a year, is not just a masterpiece of French Gothic architecture but has also been the focus of Catholic Paris for seven centuries.

Built on a site occupied by earlier churches – and, a millennium before that, a Gallo-Roman temple perhaps dedicated to the god Mithra (see boxed text, p19) – it was begun in 1163 according to the design of Bishop Maurice de Sully and largely completed by the early 14th century. The cathedral was badly damaged during the Revolution; architect Eugène Emmanuel Viollet-le-Duc carried out extensive renovations between 1845 and 1864. The cathedral is on a very grand scale; the interior alone is 130m long, 48m wide and 35m high and can accommodate more than 6000 worshippers.

Notre Dame is known for its sublime balance, though if you look closely you'll see all sorts of minor asymmetrical elements introduced to avoid monotony, in accordance with standard Gothic practice. These include the slightly different shapes of each

TRANSPORT: THE ISLANDS

Bus Île de la Cité for 47 through the Marais to Gare de l'Est, 21 to Opéra & Gare St-Lazare; Île St Louis for 67 to Jardin des Plantes, Mosquée de Paris & Place d'Italie; 87 through Latin Quarter to Place St-Sulpice, Sèvres Babylone, École Militaire & Champ de Mars

Metro & RER Cité, Pont Marie, Pont Neuf, St-Michel Notre Dame, Sully Morland

Boat Notre Dame Batobus stop (quai Montebello)

THE ISLANDS

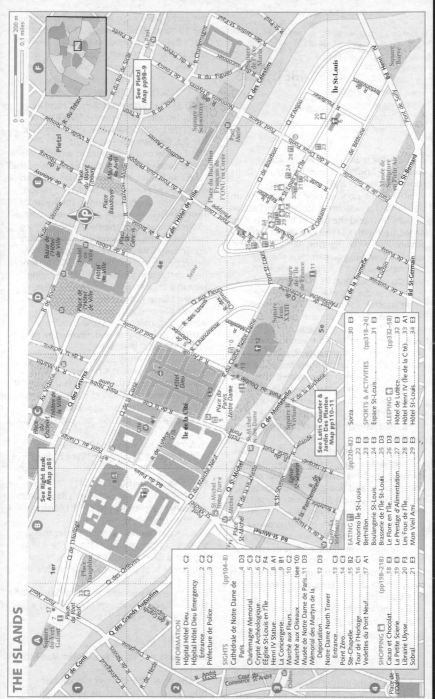

0 — 200 m
0 — 0.1 miles

See Pletzl
Map pp98–9

See Right Bank
Area Map p85

See Latin Quarter &
Jardin Des Plantes
Map pp110–11

Île St-Louis

Île de la Cité

INFORMATION		(pp104–8)
Hôpital Hôtel Dieu................	1	C2
Hôpital Hôtel Dieu Emergency		
Entrance................	2	C2
Préfecture de Police............	3	C2
SIGHTS		
Cathédrale de Notre Dame de		
Paris................	4	D3
Charlemagne Memorial...........	5	C3
Crypte Archéologique............	6	C3
Église St-Louis en l'Île...........	7	F4
Henri IV Statue................	8	A1
La Conciergerie................	9	B1
Marché aux Fleurs...............	10	C2
Marché aux Oiseaux...........	(see 10)	
Musée de Notre Dame de Paris..	11	D3
Mémorial des Martyrs de la		
Déportation................	12	D3
Notre Dame North Tower		
Entrance................	13	C3
Point Zéro................	14	C3
Ste-Chapelle................	15	B2
Tour de l'Horloge...............	16	C1
Vedettes du Pont Neuf..........	17	A1
SHOPPING		(pp198–218)
Cacao et Chocolat..............	18	E3
La Petite Scierie................	19	E3
Librairie Ulysse................	20	F3
Sobral................	21	E3
EATING		(pp220–82)
Amorino Île St-Louis.............	22	E3
Berthillon................	23	E3
Boulangerie St-Louis............	24	E3
Brasserie de l'Île St-Louis........	25	D3
Le Flore en l'Île................	26	D3
Le Prestige d'Alimentation.......	27	E3
Les Fous de l'Île................	28	E3
Mon Vieil Ami................	29	E3
Sorza................	30	E3
SPORTS & ACTIVITIES		(pp318–24)
Espace St-Louis................	31	E3
SLEEPING		(pp332–58)
Hôtel de Lutèce................	32	E3
Hôtel Henri IV (Île de la Cité)...	33	A1
Hôtel St-Louis................	34	E3

top picks

THE ISLANDS

- Cathédrale de Notre Dame de Paris (p104)
- Ste-Chapelle (opposite)
- La Conciergerie (right)
- Pont Neuf (opposite)

of the three main portals, whose statues were once brightly coloured to make them more effective as a *Biblia pauperum* – a 'Bible of the poor' to help the illiterate understand Old Testament stories, the Passion of the Christ and the lives of the saints. One of the best views of Notre Dame is from square Jean XXIII, the little park behind the cathedral, where you can view the forest of ornate flying buttresses that encircle the chancel and support its walls and roof.

Inside, exceptional features include three spectacular rose windows, the most renowned of which are the 10m-wide one over the western façade above the 7800-pipe organ, and the window on the northern side of the transept, which has remained virtually unchanged since the 13th century. The central choir, with its carved wooden stalls and statues representing the Passion of the Christ, is also noteworthy. There are free 1½-hour guided tours (2pm Wed & Thu, 2.30pm Sat) of the cathedral, given in English.

The trésor (treasury; adult/3-12yr €3/1; 9.30am-6pm Mon-Sat, 1-6pm Sun) in the southeastern transept contains artwork, liturgical objects, church plate and first-class relics, some of them of dubious origin. Among these is the Ste-Couronne, the 'Holy Crown', which is purportedly the wreath of thorns placed on Jesus' head before he was crucified, and was brought here in the mid-13th century. It is exhibited between 3pm and 4pm on the first Friday of each month, 3pm to 4pm every Friday during Lent, and 10am to 5pm on Good Friday.

The entrance to the Tours de Notre Dame (Towers of Notre Dame; 01 53 10 07 02; www.monum .fr; rue du Cloître Notre Dame; adult/18-25yr/under 18yr €7.50/4.80/free, 1st Sun of the month Oct-Mar free; 10am-6.30pm Apr-Sep, to 7.30pm Jan-Mar & Oct-Dec) is from the North Tower. Climb the 422 spiralling steps to the top of the western façade, where you'll find yourself face-to-face with

the cathedral's most frightening gargoyles, the 13-tonne bell Emmanuel (all of the cathedral's bells are named) in the South Tower, and, last but not least, a spectacular view of Paris.

LA CONCIERGERIE Map p105

01 53 40 60 97; www.monum.fr; 2 blvd du Palais, 1er; adult/18-25yr/under 18yr €8/6/free, 1st Sun of the month Oct-Mar free; 9.30am-6pm Mar-Oct, 9am-5pm Nov-Feb; M Cité

The Conciergerie was built as a royal palace in the 14th century for the concierge of the Palais de la Cité, but later lost favour with the kings of France and became a prison and torture chamber. During the Reign of Terror (1793–94) it was used to incarcerate alleged enemies of the Revolution before they were brought before the Revolutionary Tribunal, which met next door in the Palais de Justice. Among the 2700 prisoners held in the dungeons here before being sent in tumbrels to the guillotine were Queen Marie-Antoinette (see a reproduction of her cell) and, as the Revolution began to turn on its own, the radicals Danton, Robespierre and, finally, the judges of the Tribunal themselves.

The 14th-century Salle des Gens d'Armes (Cavalrymen's Hall) is a fine example of the Rayonnant Gothic style. It is the largest surviving medieval hall in Europe. The Tour de l'Horloge (Map p105; cnr blvd du Palais & quai de l'Horloge, 1er), built in 1353, has held a public clock aloft since 1370.

A joint ticket with Ste-Chapelle (opposite) costs adult/18-25yr/under 18yr €11.50/9/free.

CRYPTE ARCHÉOLOGIQUE Map p105

01 55 42 50 10; 1 place du Parvis Notre Dame, 4e; adult/14-26yr/under 14yr €3.50/1.60/free; 10am-6pm Tue-Sun; M Cité

The Archaeological Crypt is under the square in front of Notre Dame. The 117m-long and 28m-wide area displays *in situ* the remains of structures built on this site during the Gallo-Roman period, a 4th-century enclosure wall, the foundations of the medieval foundlings hospice and a few of the sewers sunk by Haussman.

MARCHÉ AUX FLEURS Map p105

place Louis Lépin, 4e; 8am-7.30pm Mon-Sat; M Cité

The Île de la Cité's flower market has brightened up this square since 1808. On

Sundays it becomes a Marché aux Oiseaux (bird market; 9am-7pm).

MÉMORIAL DES MARTYRS DE LA DÉPORTATION Map p105
square de l'Île de France, 4e; 10am-noon, 2-7pm Apr-Sep, 10am-noon, 2-5pm Oct-Mar; M St-Michel Notre Dame

The Memorial to the Victims of the Deportation, erected in 1962, is a haunting monument to the 160,000 residents of France – including 76,000 Jews – killed in Nazi concentration camps during WWII. A single barred 'window' separates the bleak, rough concrete courtyard from the waters of the Seine.

The Tomb of the Unknown Deportee is flanked by hundreds of thousands of bits of back-lit glass, and the walls are etched with inscriptions from celebrated writers and poets.

MUSÉE DE NOTRE DAME DE PARIS
Map p105

01 43 25 42 92; 10 rue du Cloître Notre Dame, 4e; adult/3-12yr €3/1.50; 2.30-6pm Wed, Sat & Sun; M Cité

This small museum traces the cathedral's history and life on the Île de la Cité from Gallo-Roman times to today, via scale models, contemporary paintings, engravings and lithographs. An interesting document is a petition signed by Victor Hugo, the artist Ingres and others who sparked the campaign to restore the cathedral.

PONT NEUF p105

M Pont Neuf

The sparkling white stone spans of Paris' oldest bridge, ironically called 'New Bridge', have linked the western end of the Île de la Cité with both river banks since 1607

when Henri IV inaugurated it by crossing the bridge on a white stallion. The occasion is commemorated by an equestrian statue of Henri IV, who was known to his subjects as the Vert Galant ('jolly rogue' or 'dirty old man', depending on your perspective). View the bridge's seven arches, decorated with humorous and grotesque figures of barbers, dentists, pickpockets, loiterers etc, from the river.

Pont Neuf and nearby place Dauphine were used for public exhibitions in the 18th century. In the last century the bridge itself became an *objet d'art* on at least three occasions: in 1963, when School of Paris artist Nonda built, exhibited and lived in a huge Trojan horse of steel and wood on the bridge; in 1984 when the Japanese designer Kenzo covered it with flowers; and in 1985 when the Bulgarian-born 'environmental sculptor' Christo famously wrapped the bridge in beige fabric.

STE-CHAPELLE Map p105

01 53 40 60 97; www.monum.fr; 4 blvd du Palais, 1er; adult/18-25yr/under 18yr €6.50/4.50/free, 1st Sun of the month Oct-Mar free; 9.30am-6pm Mar-Oct, 9am-5pm Nov-Feb; M Cité

The place to visit on a sunny day! Security checks make it long and snail-slow to get into this gemlike Holy Chapel, the most exquisite of Paris' Gothic monuments, tucked away within the walls of the Palais de Justice (Law Courts). But once in, be dazzled by Paris' oldest and finest stained glass – the light on sunny days is extraordinary.

Built in just under three years (compared with nearly 200 for Notre Dame), Ste-Chapelle was consecrated in 1248. The chapel was conceived by Louis IX to house his personal collection of holy relics

SEINE-FUL PURSUITS
The Seine is more than just Paris' dustless highway or the line dividing the Right and Left Banks. The river's award-winning role comes in July and August, when some 5km of its banks are transformed into Paris Plages (p14), 'beaches' with real sand, water fountains and sprays. But the river banks can be just as much fun at the weekend during the rest of the year when the Paris Respire (p320) scheme goes into effect. The banks between the Pont Alexandre III (Map pp140–1) and the Pont d'Austerlitz (Map pp158–9) have been listed as a Unesco World Heritage Site since 1991, but the choicest spots for sunning, picnicking and maybe even a little romancing are the delightful Square du Vert Gallant, 1er (metro Pont Neuf), the little park at the tip of the Île de la Cité named after that rake Henri IV (see above); and the Quai St-Bernard, 5e, just opposite the Jardin des Plantes. Here you'll find the Musée de la Sculpture en Plein Air (Open-Air Sculpture Museum; Map pp110–11; 01 43 26 91 90; square Tino Rossi, 5e; admission free; 24hr; M Quai de la Rapée). A salad beneath a César or a baguette beside a Brancusi is a pretty classy way to see the Seine up close, short of actually getting on it by joining a cruise (see p406).

(including the Holy Crown now kept in the treasury at Notre Dame). The chapel's exterior can be viewed from across the street from the law courts' magnificently gilded 18th-century gate, which faces rue de Lutèce.

A joint ticket with the Conciergerie (p106) costs adult/18-25yr/under 18yr €11.50/9/ free.

ÎLE ST-LOUIS

Downstream from Île de la Cité and entirely in the 4e arrondissement, St-Louis was actually two uninhabited islets called Île Notre Dame

(Our Lady Isle) and Île aux Vaches (Cows Island) in the early 17th century. That was until a building contractor called Christophe Marie and two financiers worked out a deal with Louis XIII to create one island and build two stone bridges to the mainland. In exchange they could subdivide and sell the newly created real estate. This they did with great success, and by 1664 the entire island was covered with fine, airy, grey-stone houses facing the quays and water.

The only sight as such, French Baroque Église St-Louis en l'Île (Map p105; 19bis rue St-Louis en l'Île, 4e; 9am-noon & 3-7pm Tue-Sun; Pont Marie) was built between 1664 and 1726.

LATIN QUARTER & JARDIN DES PLANTES

Drinking p290; Eating p249; Shopping p208; Sleeping p343

There is no better strip to see, smell and taste the Quartier Latin (Latin Quarter), 5e, than rue Mouffetard, a thriving market street that is something of a local mecca with its titillating line-up of patisseries, *fromageries* and fishmongers, interspersed by the odd *droguerie-quincaillerie* (hardware store) – easily spotted by the jumble of laundry baskets, buckets etc piled on the pavement in front. Knowing what's happening is easy here: go into Le Verre à Pied (p290), order *un café* at the bar and the market-stall holders will soon start chatting to you. Or try Cavé La Bourgogne (p291), where old ladies with pet lapdogs gather each day at 10.30am for a coffee and a chinwag.

The centre of Parisian higher education since the Middle Ages, the Latin Quarter is so-called because conversation between students and professors was in Latin until the Revolution. Academia remains a focal point of life – the Sorbonne is here – though its near monopoly on Parisian academic life is not what it was. But bury your nose in one of the quarter's late-opening bookshops, linger in a café, eat cheap in its abundance of budget restaurants or clink drinks during a dozen different happy hours and there will almost certainly be a student or academic affiliated with the Sorbonne sitting next to you.

Come the warmer months, everyone spills over to place St-Michel, place de la Sorbonne and other pigeon-filled squares. Movie buffs watch classics on rue des Écoles, and activists and sympathisers join under the same banner at the Mutualité to chant slogans and fight the good fight. Fancy a *pied à terre* around the corner from the Sorbonne? A 40-sq-metre, contemporary loft-style apartment costs around €430,000.

ARÈNES DE LUTÈCE Map pp110–11

49 rue Monge, 5e; admission free; ☽ 9am-5.30 to 9.30pm Apr-Oct, 8am-5.30 to 9.30pm Nov-Mar; Ⓜ Place Monge

The 2nd-century Roman amphitheatre, Lutetia Arena, once sat around 10,000 people for gladiatorial combats and other events. Found by accident in 1869 when rue Monge was under construction, it's now used by neighbourhood youths for playing football, and by old men for *boules* and *pétanque*.

CENTRE DE LA MER Map pp110–11

☎ 01 44 32 10 90; www.oceano.org, in French; Institut Océanographique; 195 rue St-Jacques, 5e; adult/3-12yr €4.60/2; ☽ 9am-12.30pm & 1.30-6pm Tue-Sun; Ⓜ Luxembourg

France has a long history of success in the field of oceanography (think Jacques Cousteau and, well, Jules Verne), and the Sea Centre cruises through that science, as well as marine biology, via temporary exhibitions, aquariums, scale models and audiovisuals. Kids will love the aquariums and the audiovisuals.

ÉGLISE ST-ÉTIENNE DU MONT
Map pp110–11

☎ 01 43 54 11 79; 1 place Ste-Geneviève, 5e; ☽ 8am-noon & 2-7pm Tue-Sat, 9am-noon & 2.30-7pm Sun; Ⓜ Cardinal Lemoine

The Church of Mount St Stephen, built between 1492 and 1655, contains Paris' only surviving rood screen (1535), separating the chancel from the nave; the others were removed during the late Renaissance because they prevented the faithful assembled in the nave from seeing the priest celebrate Mass. In the nave's southeastern corner, a chapel contains the tomb of Ste Geneviève. A highly decorated reliquary nearby contains all that is left of her earthly remains – a finger bone. Ste Geneviève, patroness of Paris, was born at Nanterre in AD 422 and turned away Attila the Hun from Paris in AD 451.

TRANSPORT: LATIN QUARTER & JARDIN DES PLANTES

Bus Panthéon for 89 to Jardin des Plantes & 13e (Bibliothèque National de France François Mitterrand); blvd St-Michel for 38 to Centre Pompidou, Gare de l'Est & Gare du Nord; rue Gay Lussac for 27 to Île de la Cité, Opéra & Gare St-Lazare

Metro & RER Cardinal Lemoine, Censier Daubenton, Cluny-La Sorbonne, Gare d'Austerlitz, Jussieu, Luxembourg, Maubert Mutualité, Place Monge, St-Michel

Boat Jardin des Plantes Batobus stop (quai St-Bernard)

Train Gare d'Austerlitz

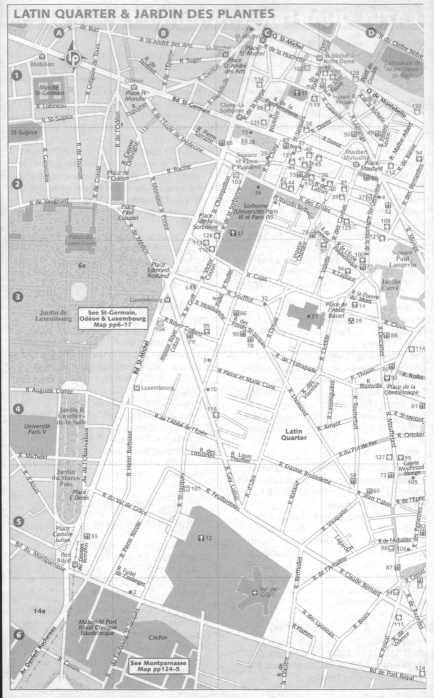

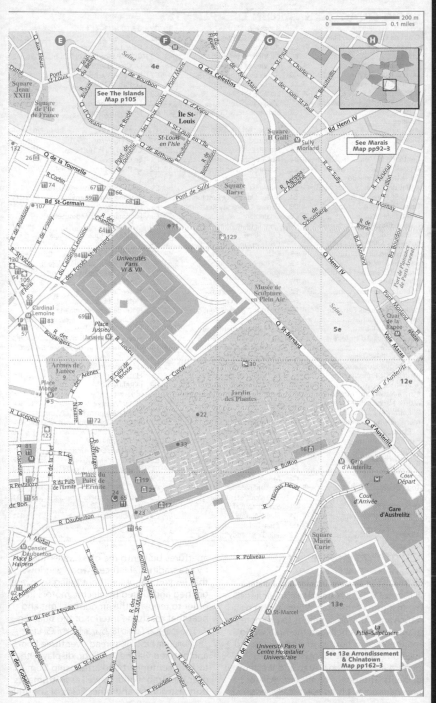

See The Islands
Map p105

See Marais
Map pp92–3

See 13e Arrondissement
& Chinatown
Map pp162–3

LATIN QUARTER & JARDIN DES PLANTES

INSTITUT DU MONDE ARABE
Map pp110–11

☎ 01 40 51 38 38; www.imarabe.org; 1 place Mohammed V, 5e; Ⓜ Cardinal Lemoine or Jussieu
The Institute of the Arab World, set up by France and 20 Arab countries to promote cultural contacts between the Arab world and the West, is housed in a highly praised building (1987) that successfully mixes modern and traditional Arab and Western elements. Thousands of *mushrabiyah* (or *mouche-arabies*, photo-electrically sensitive apertures built into the glass walls), inspired by the traditional latticed-wood windows that let you see out without being seen, are opened and closed by electric motors in order to regulate the amount of light and heat that reach the interior of the building.

The museum (adult/18-25yr/under 18yr €5/4/free; ⏲ 10am-6pm Tue-Sun), spread over three floors and entered via the 7th floor, displays 9th- to 19th-century art and artisanship from all over the Arab world, as well as instruments from astronomy and other fields of scientific endeavour in which Arab technology once led the world. Temporary exhibitions (enter from quai St-Bernard; Map pp110–11) involve a separate fee; combined tickets are available.

JARDIN DES PLANTES Map pp110–11

☎ 01 40 79 56 01, 01 40 79 54 79; 57 rue Cuvier, 5e; 🕒 8am-5.30pm to 8pm (seasonal); Ⓜ Gare d'Austerlitz, Censier Daubenton or Jussieu
Paris' 24-hectare botanical garden, founded in 1626 as a medicinal herb garden for Louis XIII, is idyllic to stroll or jog around. You'll find a rosary, iris garden, the Eden-like Jardin d'Hiver (Winter Garden) or Serres (Greenhouses), renovated in 2008; the Jardin Alpin (Alpine Garden; Sat & Sun admission adult/4-15yr/under 4yr €1/0.50/free; 🕒 8-4.30pm Mon-Fri, 1-5pm Sat & Sun Apr Oct), with 2000 mountainous plants; and the gardens of the École de Botanique, where students of the School of Botany 'practice' and green-fingered Parisians savvy up on horticultural techniques.

During the Prussian siege of Paris in 1870, most of the animals in the Ménagerie du Jardin des Plantes (adult/4-15yr/under 4yr €7/5/free; 🕒 9am-5pm) were eaten by starving Parisians. Though a recreational animal park, the medium-sized zoo dating to 1794 in the northern section of the garden does much research into the reproduction of rare and endangered species.

A two-day combined ticket covering all of the Jardin des Plantes sights, including the park's mightily impressive Grande Galerie de l'Évolution (right), costs €20/15.

MOSQUÉE DE PARIS Map pp110–11

☎ 01 45 35 97 33; www.mosquee-de-paris.org, in French; 2bis place du Puits de l'Ermite, 5e; adult/senior & 7-25yr €3/2; 🕒 9am-noon & 2-6pm Sat-Thu; Ⓜ Censier Daubenton or Place Monge
Paris' central mosque, with its striking 26m-high minaret, was built in 1926 in the ornate Moorish style popular at the time. Visitors must be modestly dressed and remove their shoes at the entrance to the prayer hall. The complex includes a North African–style restaurant (p251) and hammam (p318).

MUSÉE DE L'ASSISTANCE PUBLIQUE-HÔPITAUX DE PARIS Map pp110–11

☎ 01 40 27 50 05; www.aphp.fr/musee, in French; Hôtel de Miramion, 47 quai de la Tournelle, 5e; adult/13-18yr/under 13yr €4/2/free, 1st Sun of the month free; 🕒 10am-6pm Tue-Sun Sep-Jul; Ⓜ Maubert Mutualité
A museum devoted to the history of Parisian hospitals since the Middle Ages may not sound like a crowd-pleaser, but some of the paintings, sculptures, drawings and medical instruments are very evocative of their times.

MUSÉE NATIONAL D'HISTOIRE NATURELLE Map pp110–11

☎ 01 40 79 30 00; www.mnhn.fr; 57 rue Cuvier, 5e; Ⓜ Censier Daubenton or Gare d'Austerlitz
Housed in three buildings on the southern edge of the Jardin des Plantes, the National Museum of Natural History was created in 1793 and became a site of significant scientific research in the 19th century.

A highlight for kids: life-sized elephants, tigers and rhinos play safari in the Grande Galerie de l'Évolution (Map pp110–11; Great Gallery of Evolution; 36 rue Geoffroy St-Hilaire, 5e; adult/4-13yr/under 4yr €8/6/free; 🕒 10am-6pm Wed-Mon), where imaginative exhibits on evolution and humanity's effect on the global ecosystem, including global warming, fill 6000 sq metres. Rare specimens of endangered and extinct species dominate the Salle des Espèces Menacées et des Espèces Disparues (Hall of Threatened and Extinct Species) on level 2, while the Salle de Découverte (Room of Discovery) on level 1 houses interactive exhibits for kids.

Giant natural crystals dance with sunlight in the Galerie de Minéralogie et de Géologie (Mineralogy & Geology Gallery; Map pp110–11; 36 rue Geoffroy St-Hilaire; adult/4-13yr/under 4yr €7/5/free; 🕒 10am-5pm Wed-Mon). Free guided tours (in French) depart the fourth Saturday of the month at 3pm.

Displays on comparative anatomy and palaeontology (the study of fossils) fill the Galerie d'Anatomie Comparée et de Paléontologie (Map

top picks

LATIN QUARTER & JARDINS DES PLANTES

- Musée National du Moyen Age (p114)
- Grande Galerie de l'Évolution (Musée Nationale d'Histoire Naturelle; above)
- Institut du Monde Arabe (opposite)
- Panthéon (p114)
- Centre de la Mer (p109)

pp110–11; 2 rue Buffon; adult/4-13yr/under 4yr €6/4/free; 10am-5pm Wed-Mon). Free guided tours (in French) depart the second Saturday of the month at 3pm.

MUSÉE NATIONAL DU MOYEN AGE
Map pp110–11

☎ 01 53 73 78 00; www.musee-moyenage.fr; 6 place Paul Painlevé, 5e; adult/18-25yr/under 18yr €7.50/5.50/free, 1st Sun of the month free; 9.15am-5.45pm Wed-Mon; Ⓜ Cluny-La Sorbonne or St-Michel

The National Museum of the Middle Ages occupies both a *frigidarium* (cooling room), which holds remains of Gallo-Roman *thermes* (baths) dating from around AD 200, and the 15th-century Hôtel des Abbés de Cluny, Paris' finest example of medieval civil architecture. Inside, spectacular displays include statuary, illuminated manuscripts, weapons, furnishings and *objets d'art* made of gold, ivory and enamel. But nothing compares with *La Dame à la Licorne* (The Lady with the Unicorn), a sublime series of late-15th-century tapestries from the southern Netherlands hung in circular room 13 on the 1st floor. Five of them are devoted to the senses while the sixth is the enigmatic *À Mon Seul Désir* (To My Sole Desire), a reflection on vanity.

Small gardens northeast of the museum, including the Jardin Céleste (Heavenly Garden) and the Jardin d'Amour (Garden of Love), are planted with flowers, herbs and shrubs that appear in masterpieces hanging throughout the museum. To the west the Forêt de la Licorne (Unicorn Forest) is based on the illustrations in the tapestries.

PANTHÉON Map pp110–11

☎ 01 44 32 18 00; www.monum.fr; place du Panthéon, 5e; adult/18-25yr/under 18yr €7.50/4.80/free, 1st Sun of the month Oct-Mar free; 10am-6.30pm Apr-Sep, to 6pm Oct-Mar; Ⓜ Luxembourg

The domed landmark was commissioned by Louis XV around 1750 as an abbey church dedicated to Ste Geneviève in thanksgiving for his recovery from an illness, but due to financial and structural problems it wasn't completed until 1789 – not a good year for church openings in Paris. Two years later the Constituent Assembly turned it into a secular mausoleum and bricked up most of the windows.

The Panthéon is a superb example of 18th-century neoclassicism. It reverted to its religious duties two more times after the Revolution but has played a secular role ever since 1885, when God was evicted in favour of Victor Hugo. Among the crypt's 80 or so permanent residents are Voltaire, Jean-Jacques Rousseau, Louis Braille, Émile Zola and Jean Moulin. The first woman to be interred in the Panthéon was the two-time Nobel Prize–winner Marie Curie (1867–1934), reburied here (along with her husband, Pierre) in 1995.

SORBONNE Map pp110–11
12 rue de la Sorbonne, 5e; Ⓜ Luxembourg or Cluny-La Sorbonne

The *crème de la crème* of academia flock to this distinguished university, one of the world's most famous. Founded in 1253 by Robert de Sorbon, confessor to Louis IX, as a college for 16 impoverished theology students, the Sorbonne soon grew into a powerful body with its own government and laws. Today, it embraces most of the 13 autonomous universities – 35,500-odd students in all – created when the University of Paris was reorganised after the student protests of 1968. Until 2015, when an ambitious, 10-year modernisation programme costing €45 million will be complete, parts of the complex will be under renovation.

Place de la Sorbonne links blvd St-Michel and the Chapelle de la Sorbonne, the university's gold-domed church, built between 1635 and 1642 and currently being restored at a cost of €13.6 million; it should reopen in 2009. The remains of Cardinal Richelieu (1585–1642) lie in a very camp tomb here, with an effigy of a cardinal's hat suspended above it.

ST-GERMAIN, ODÉON & LUXEMBOURG

Drinking p291; Eating p254; Shopping p209; Sleeping p346

From the packed pavement terraces of literary café greats Les Deux Magots (p292) and Café de Flore (p292), where Sartre, de Beauvoir and other postwar Left Bank intellectuals drank, to the pocket-sized studios of lesser-known romantic and Russian cubist artists, this quarter, born out of a 6th-century abbey, oozes panache. Yet weave your way through the shopaholic crowds on blvd St-Germain, past flagship *prêt-à-porter* stores and vast white spaces showcasing interior design, and there's little hint of St-Germain des Prés' legendary bohemia. The arrival of the fashion industry changed all that jazz years ago.

Yet there is a startling cinematic quality to this soulful part of the Left Bank, where Pierre and Jean-Pierre Heckmann restore antique ivory in their 1930s family shop (p209), gourmets talk bread and wine with local legends like Apolliana Poilâne (p223) and Juan Sánchez (p211), and well-dressed ladies take their 1960s cast-offs to vintage dealers on rue de Buci. Artists and writers, students and journalists, actors and musicians cross paths in the shadow of the École Nationale Supérieure des Beaux Arts, the Académie Française and the Odéon-Théâtre de l'Europe.

Despite the passing fashions, village life has survived in this pricey 6e arrondissement (a 200-sq-metre apartment in an elegant 18th-century mansion on the boulevard costs €3.2 million). Stroll past the portfolio of designer boutiques on rue du Cherche Midi, past Patrick Blanc's flamboyant vegetal wall growing inside No 7, past the constant crowd gathered at the foot of guillotined revolutionary leader Georges Danton on Carrefour de l'Odéon, past the heaps of organic veg at the Rue Raspail market and the stalls groaning under the weight of fresh fruit on rue de Seine and watch it leap out at you. *La vie germanopratine* (St-Germain life) is *belle*.

ÉGLISE ST-GERMAIN DES PRÉS

Map pp116–17

☎ 01 55 42 81 33; 3 place St-Germain des Prés, 6e; ⏰ 8am-7pm Mon-Sat, 9am-8pm Sun; Ⓜ St-Germain des Prés

Paris' oldest church still standing, this Romanesque church of St Germanus of the Fields was built in the 11th century on the site of a 6th-century abbey and was the dominant church in Paris until the arrival of Notre Dame. It has been altered many times since, but the Chapelle de St-Symphorien (to the right as you enter) was part of the original abbey and is believed to be the resting place of St Germanus (AD 496–576), the first bishop of Paris. The Merovingian kings were buried here during the 6th and

TRANSPORT: ST-GERMAIN, ODÉON & LUXEMBOURG

Bus blvd St-Germain for 86 to Odéon, Pont Sully (Île St-Louis), Bastille, Ledru Rollin (Marché d'Aligre), place de la Nation & Zoo; rue de Rennes for 96 to place Châtelet, Hôtel de Ville, St-Paul (Marais), rue Oberkampf & rue de Ménilmontant

Metro & RER Luxembourg, Mabillon, Odéon, Pont Neuf, Port Royal, St-Germain des Prés, St-Sulpice

Boat St-Germain des Prés Batobus stop (quai Malaquais)

top picks

ST-GERMAIN, ODÉON & LUXEMBOURG

- Jardin du Luxembourg (p119)
- Église St-Suplice (below)
- Musée National Eugène Delacroix (p121)
- Fondation Dubuffet (p119)

7th centuries, but their tombs disappeared during the Revolution. The bell tower over the western entrance has changed little since 990, although the spire dates only from the 19th century. The vaulted ceiling is a starry sky that seems to float forever upward.

ÉGLISE ST-SULPICE Map pp116–17

☎ 01 46 33 21 78; place St-Sulpice, 6e; ⏰ 7.30am-7.30pm; Ⓜ St-Sulpice

In 1646 work started on the twin-towered Church of St Sulpicius, lined inside with 21 side chapels, and took six architects 150 years to finish. What draws most people is not its lovely Italianate façade with two rows of superimposed columns, nor its neoclassical décor influenced by the Counter-Reformation; rather, this church

ST-GERMAIN, ODÉON & LUXEMBOURG

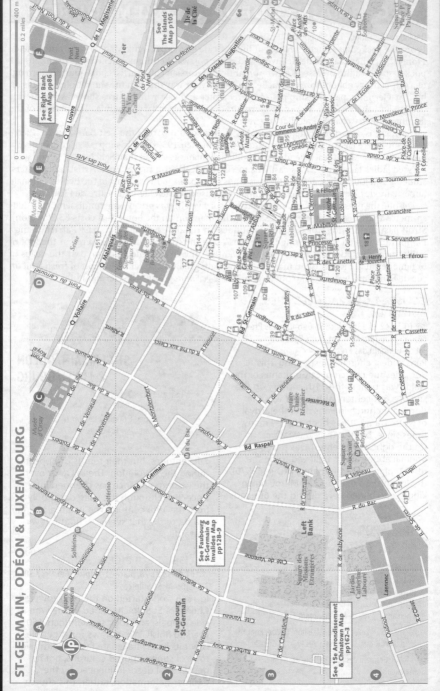

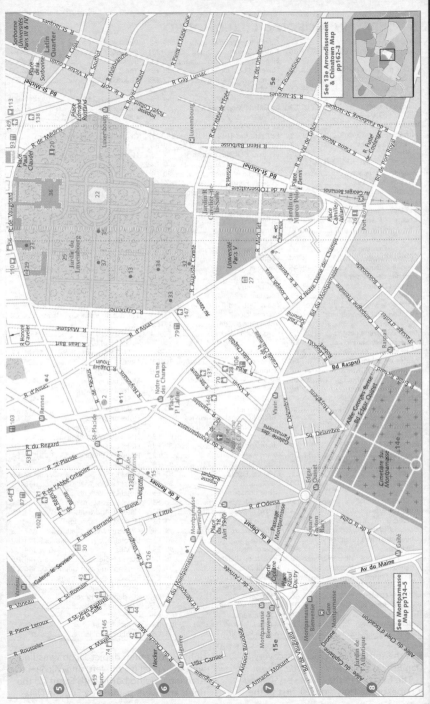

See 13e Arrondissement
& Chinatown Map
pp162–3

See Montparnasse
Map pp124–5

117

ST-GERMAIN, ODÉON & LUXEMBOURG

was the setting for a crucial discovery in
Dan Brown's *The Da Vinci Code*.

The frescoes in the Chapelle des Sts-Anges
(Chapel of the Holy Angels), first to the

right as you enter, depict Jacob wrestling
with the angel (to the left) and Michael the
Archangel doing battle with Satan (to the
right) and were painted by Eugène Dela-

croix between 1855 and 1861. The monumental, 20m-tall organ loft dates from 1781. Listen to it in its full glory during 10.30am Mass on Sunday or the occasional Sunday-afternoon organ concert, which usually starts at 4pm.

FONDATION DUBUFFET Map pp116–17
☎ 01 47 34 12 63; www.dubuffetfondation.com, in French; 137 rue de Sèvres, 6e; adult/under 10yr €4/free; ⏲ 2-6pm Mon-Fri; Ⓜ Duroc
Situated in a lovely 19th-century *hôtel particulier* at the end of a courtyard, the foundation houses the collection of Jean Dubuffet (1901–85), chief of the Art Brut school (a term he himself coined to describe all works of artistic expression not officially recognised). Much of his work is incredibly modern and expressive.

INSTITUT DE FRANCE pp116–17
☎ 01 44 41 44 41; www.institut-de-france.fr; 23 quai de Conti, 6e; Ⓜ Mabillon or Pont Neuf
The French Institute, created in 1795, brought together five of France's academies of arts and sciences. The most famous of these is the Académie Française (French Academy), founded in 1635 by Cardinal Richelieu. Its 40 members, known as the Immortels (Immortals), have the Herculean (some say impossible) task of safeguarding the purity of the French language.

The domed building housing the institute, across the Seine from the Louvre's eastern end, is a masterpiece of French neoclassical architecture. There are 1½-hour tours (adult/18-25yr €8/6) at 3pm one Sunday a month. Contact the Centre des Monuments Nationaux (Centre of National Monuments; ☎ 01 44 54 19 30; www.monum.fr) for schedules or check *Pariscope* or *L'Officiel des Spectacles* (p302) under 'Promenades & Loisirs/Visites Conférences'.

France's oldest public library, the Bibliothèque Mazarine (Mazarine Library; ☎ 01 44 41 44 06; www.bibliotheque-mazarine.fr; ⏲ 10am-6pm Mon-Fri, closed two weeks Aug) founded in 1643, is in the same building. You can visit the bust-lined, late-17th-century reading room or consult the library's collection of 500,000 volumes, using a free, two-day admission pass obtained by leaving your ID at the office to the left of the entrance. An annual membership/10-visit *carnet* to borrow books costs €15/10 and requires two photos.

JARDIN DU LUXEMBOURG Map pp116–17
⏲ 7.30 to 8.15am-5 to 10pm (seasonal);
Ⓜ Luxembourg
Keen to know what the city does on its time off? Then stroll around the formal terraces, chestnut groves and green lawns of this 23-hectare park, where Parisians of all ages flock in all weathers. Be it jogging, practising t'ai chi, gossiping with girlfriends on one of the garden's signature sage-green chairs (fancy one to take home? See p216), reading or romancing, the Jardin du Luxembourg is *the* voyeur's spot to peek on Parisians.

Urban orchards hang heavy with dozens of apple varieties in the southern part of the *jardin* (garden). Bees have produced honey in the nearby Rucher du Luxembourg since the 19th century, don't miss the annual Fête du Miel (Honey Festival), two days of tasting and buying the aviary's sweet harvest in late September in the Pavillon Davioud (55bis rue d'Assas). This ornate pavilion is also the spot where green-fingered Parisians partake in gardening courses with the École d'Horticulture (64 Blvd St-Michel, 6e). For sports-minded souls, there are six tennis courts (p322).

The park is a backdrop to the Palais du Luxembourg, built in the 1620s for Marie de Médici, Henri IV's consort, to assuage her longing for the Pitti Palace in Florence, where she had spent her childhood. Since 1958 the palace has housed the Sénat (Senate, upper house of French parliament; reservations ☎ 01 44 54 19 49; www.senat.fr; rue de Vaugirard, 6e; adult/18-25yr €8/6) which can be visited by guided tour at 10.30am one Saturday per month. East of the palace is the Italianate Fontaine des Médici, an ornate fish pond (1630).

Top spot for sun-soaking – there's always loads of chairs here – is the southern side of the palace's 19th-century, 57m-long Orangery (1834) where lemon and orange trees, palms, grenadiers and oleanders shelter from the cold. A little further is the Musée du Luxembourg (☎ 01 42 34 25 95; www.museedu luxembourg.fr; 19 rue de Vaugirard, 6e; up to adult/10-25yr/under10yr €11/9/free; ⏲ 10.30am-10pm Mon & Fri, 10.30am-7pm Tue-Thu & Sat, to 7pm Sun), housed in two galleries built for the palace to showcase artworks. It hosts very prestigious temporary art exhibitions; admission prices vary. Next door the heavily guarded Hôtel du Petit Luxembourg (rue de Vaugirard, 6e) was the modest 16th-century pad where Marie de Médici lived while Palace du Luxembourg was being built. The president of the Senate has called it home since 1825.

Luxembourg Garden offers all the delights of a Parisian childhood a century ago. At the octagonal Grand Bassin, model sailboats can be rented, and nearby, Shetland ponies take tots for rides. At the pint-sized Théâtre des Marionnettes du Jardin du Luxembourg (☎ 01 43 26 46 47; ticket €4; ☼ 3.15pm Wed, 11am & 3.15pm Sat & Sun, daily during school hols) marionette shows guarantee a giggle, whether you understand French or not. Complete the day with a romp around the kids' playground (adult/child/under 15 months €2.60/1.60/free; ☼ 10am-park close) – the green half is for kids aged seven to 12 years, the blue half for under-sevens – or a summertime waltz on the old-fashioned carousel (merry-go-round).

MUSÉE DE LA MONNAIE DE PARIS
Map pp116–17

☎ 01 40 46 55 35; www.monnaiedeparis.fr; 11 quai de Conti, 6e; adult/under 16yr €5/free; ☼ 11am-5.30pm Tue-Fri, noon-5.30pm Sat & Sun; Ⓜ Pont Neuf

The Parisian Mint Museum traces the history of French coinage from antiquity to the present and displays presses and other minting equipment. There are some excellent audiovisual and other displays, which help to bring to life this otherwise niche subject.

The museum building, the Hôtel de la Monnaie, became the royal mint during the 18th century and is still used by the Ministry of Finance to produce commemorative medals and coins, as well as official weights and measures. One-hour tours of the *ateliers* (workshops) leave at 2.15pm on Wednesday and Friday (€3); advance reservations only.

MUSÉE ERNEST HÉBERT Map pp116–17

☎ 01 42 22 23 82; 85 rue du Cherche Midi, 6e; ☼ 12.30-6pm Mon & Wed-Fri, 2-6pm Sat & Sun; Ⓜ St-Placide

Portrait painter Ernest Hébert (1817–1908) did likenesses of society people of the Second Empire and the *belle époque* and was thus not short of a sou or two. The

IMMORTAL REMAINS

Paris loves to immortalise people from its past with statues and monuments and has done so especially since the mid-19th century. Père Lachaise, Montmartre and Montparnasse Cemeteries are bursting with wonderfully evocative likenesses of heroes and villains, poets and philosophers, and revolutionaries and autocrats, and there's a resident stone or bronze celebrity in even the tiniest park or square. The following is a selection of the larger-than-life characters you might bump into on your way around Paris.

St-Denis, patron saint of France (also known as Dionysius of Paris), introduced Christianity to Paris and was beheaded by the Romans for his pains. You can see him carrying his unfortunate head under his arm on the carved western portal of the Cathédrale de Notre Dame (Map p105).

Ste-Geneviève, the patroness of Paris, was born at Nanterre in AD 422 and turned Attila the Hun away from the city in AD 451. Now she stands, ghostly pale and turning her back on Paris, high above the Pont de la Tournelle (Map p105), just south of Île St Louis in the 5e. Plucky Jeanne d'Arc (Joan of Arc) tried unsuccessfully to wrest Paris from the English almost a millennium later; her gilded likeness now stands in place des Pyramides (Map pp82–3), next to 192 rue de Rivoli, 1er.

Henri IV, known as the Vert Galant ('jolly rogue' or 'dirty old man', depending on your perspective), sits astride his white stallion on the Pont Neuf (Map p105) in the 1er, exactly as he did when he inaugurated the 'New Bridge' in 1607. Charlemagne, emperor of the Franks, rides his steed under the trees in front of Cathédrale de Notre Dame (Map p105), while a poor imitation of the Sun King, Louis XIV, prances in place des Victoires (Map pp82–3) in the 2e. Georges Danton, a leader of the Revolution and later one of its guillotined victims, stands with his head very much intact near the site of his house at carrefour de l'Odéon (Map pp116–17) in the 6e.

Napoleon, horseless and in Roman drag, stands atop the column in place Vendôme (Map pp82–3) in the 1er. The latest addition is a 3.6m-tall bronze of General Charles de Gaulle in full military regalia at the bottom of av des Champs-Élysées (Map pp140–1), ready to march down to the Arc de Triomphe in a liberated Paris on 26 August 1944.

But it's not just people who are immortalised. An illuminated bronze replica of New York's Statue of Liberty (Map pp166–7) faces the Big Apple from a long and narrow artificial island in the Seine. And have a look at the impressive Centaur statue in the centre of carrefour de la Croix Rouge (Map pp116–17) in the 6e, which was sculpted by César Baldaccini. Impossible to miss, the statue of the mythological half-horse, half-man has disproportionate gonads the size of grapefruits. Now that's what we call larger than life.

artist's wonderful 18th-century townhouse and its baubles – not his saccharine, almost cloying portraits – is the draw here, though. The museum was closed for renovations at research time but should be open by the time you read this.

MUSÉE NATIONAL EUGÈNE DELACROIX Map pp116–17

☎ 01 44 41 86 50; www.musee-delacroix.fr; 6 rue de Furstemberg, 6e; adult/under 18yr €5/free, 1st Sun of the month free; ☯ 9.30am-5pm Wed-Mon; Ⓜ Mabillon or St-Germain des Prés

The Eugène Delacroix Museum, in a court-yard off a leafy 'square', was the romantic artist's home and studio when he died in 1863, and contains many of his oils, water-colours, pastels and drawings. If you want to see his major works, such as *Liberty Leading the People,* visit the Musée du Louvre (p80)

or the Musée d'Orsay (p130); here you'll find many of his more intimate works (eg *An Unmade Bed,* 1828) and his paintings of Morocco.

MUSÉE ATELIER ZADKINE Map pp116–17

☎ 01 55 42 77 20; www.zadkine.paris.fr, in French; 100bis rue d'Assas, 6e; admission free; ☯ 10am-6pm Tue-Sun

This museum covers the life and work of Russian cubist sculptor Ossip Zadkine (1890–1967), who arrived in Paris in 1908, and lived and worked in this cottage for almost 40 years. Zadkine produced an enormous catalogue of clay, stone, bronze and wood sculptures: one room displays figures he sculpted in contrasting walnut, pear, ebony, acacia, elm and oak. The oc-casional temporary exhibition commands a token admission fee.

MONTPARNASSE

Drinking p293; Eating p258; Shopping p212; Sleeping p349

Less flamboyant than the Latin Quarter, less hip than Bastille and less audacious than Bercy, the unpretentious 14e arrondissement strikes a better balance than some perhaps: buzzing cafés, brasseries where Picasso and his mates put 1930s Paris to rights, a cemetery with bags of personality (think Sartre, Serge Gainsbourg) and urban grit in the form of a train station and a tall, ugly tower are its modern-day attributes.

Peer long and hard (and long and hard again) at the touristy restaurants and cafés around the unfortunate 1960s Gare Montparnasse complex and glimmers of the area's bohemian past occasionally emerge: after WWI writers, poets and artists of the avant-garde abandoned Montmartre on the Right Bank and crossed the Seine, shifting the centre of Paris' artistic ferment to the area around blvd du Montparnasse. Chagall, Modigliani, Léger, Soutine, Miró, Kandinsky, Stravinsky, Hemingway, Ezra Pound and Cocteau, as well as such political exiles as Lenin and Trotsky, all hung out here, talking endlessly in the cafés and restaurants for which the quarter became famous. It remained a creative hub until the mid-1930s.

Drift south, away from the energising hubbub of the train station area and its neon-lit nightlife, and green spaces unfold in the shape of delightful Parc Montsouris and Cité Universitaire, a lush oasis for students, wedged between parkland and the din of Parisian traffic belting along the ring road encircling Paris.

CATACOMBES Map pp124–5

☎ 01 43 22 47 63; www.catacombes.paris.fr in French; 1 av Colonel Henri Roi-Tanguy, 14e; adult/14-26yr/under 14yr €7/3.50/free; ☼ 10am-5pm Tue-Sun; Ⓜ Denfert Rochereau

Paris' most gruesome and macabre sight: in 1785 it was decided to solve the hygiene and aesthetic problems posed by Paris' overflowing cemeteries by exhuming the bones and storing them in the tunnels of three disused quarries. The Catacombes is one such ossuary, created in 1810. After descending 20m (130 steps) from street level, visitors follow 1.7km of underground corridors in which a mind-boggling amount of bones and skulls of millions of Parisians are neatly packed along each and every wall. During WWII these tunnels were used as a headquarters by the Resistance; so-called *cataphiles* looking for cheap thrills are often caught roaming the tunnels at night (there's a fine of €60).

The route through the Catacombes begins at a small, dark-green *belle époque*-style building in the centre of a grassy area of av Colonel Henri Roi-Tanguy. The exit is at the end of 83 steps on rue Remy Dumoncel (metro Mouton Duvernet), 700m southwest of av Colonel Henri Roi-Tanguy.

CIMETIÈRE DU MONTPARNASSE

Map pp124–5

☎ 01 44 10 86 50; 3 blvd Edgar Quinet, 14e; ☼ 8 or 8.30am-6pm Mon-Sat, 9am-6pm Sun mid-Mar–Oct, 8am or 8.30am-5.30pm Mon-Sat, 9am-5.30pm Sun Nov–mid-Mar; Ⓜ Edgar Quinet or Raspail

Montparnasse Cemetery received its first 'lodger' in 1824. It contains the tombs of

---

STEVE'S TOP PARIS DAY

After an evening of merrymaking at my *bon vivant* friend's *belle époque* apartment near place de la République, as far as I care to/can move my carcass the following morning (usually a Sunday) is to the wonderful Marché Bastille (p231), to stock up on fortifying oysters and foie gras. But I'll need more of a cure than that after all the *mousseux* (sparkling wine) of the previous evening, so I've now set my Navsat for the Spa Harnn & Thann (p318) for a soak and a rubdown. Then I'll slip-slide toward the Musée du Quai Branly (p134) for both its startling Oceanic art and Les Ombres restaurant (p260) in the shadow of the Eiffel Tower, or the Cité de l'Architecture et du Patrimoine (p134) and the adjoining Café de l'Homme (p260), with its arresting views of said *madame*. Still a bit cobwebby, I'll cross the Seine to Ladurée (p234) for a sugar fix (pastel-coloured macaroons will do the trick) and the Champs-Élysées (p138). Some say the broad boulevard is now the height of tack, but I've loved it ever since I was a student and my Moroccan kinda-sorta boyfriend and I stood beneath the Arc de Triomphe (p138) one New Year's Eve shouting *'C'est pour nous! C'est pour nous!'* (It's for us! It's for us!) at the top of our lungs as the cars raced around, blowing their horns and flashing their headlights. Season be damned. I might just do that again right now.

LA POLLUTION CANINE: WATCH YOUR STEP

Every sixth person in France owns a dog, and Parisians are no exception. Problem is, that's a lot of dog dirt – an estimated 150,000 pooches here produce some 16 tonnes of the stuff every day, a lot of which ends up on the streets. The Paris municipality has made some valiant attempts in the past, most notably with the introduction of the *moto-crottes* (motorised pooper-scooters) by then mayor Jacques Chirac in 1982. At one stage, the city was spending up to €11 million each year to keep the city's pavements free of *la pollution canine*, but the machines were abandoned in 2004 as both expensive and ineffective. Plastic-bag dispensers with the words '*J'aime mon chien, je ramasse*' (I love my dog, I pick up) have been placed strategically throughout the city, but the campaign has had less-than-howling success: only 60% of dog owners admit to doing their own scooping. Evidence to this effect takes the form of 'souvenirs' left by recently walked poodles and other breeds, often found smeared along the pavement (www.filthyfrance.com) by daydreaming strollers, one assumes – or guidebook writers absorbed in jotting down something important. And it gets more serious than that: more than 600 people are admitted to hospital each year after slipping on a *crotte*. Until Parisians – and their beloved canines – change their dirty ways, the word on the street remains the same: watch your step.

illustrious personages such as poet Charles Baudelaire, writer Guy de Maupassant, playwright Samuel Beckett, sculptor Constantin Brancusi, painter Chaim Soutine, photographer Man Ray, industrialist André Citroën, Captain Alfred Dreyfus of the infamous affair (see p26), actress Jean Seberg, philosopher Jean-Paul Sartre and his lover, writer Simone de Beauvoir, and the crooner Serge Gainsbourg, whose grave in division No 1 just off av Transversale is a pilgrimage site for fans, who place metro tickets atop his tombstone, a reference to his famous song 'Le Poinçonneur des Lilas' (The Ticket Puncher of Lilas).

FONDATION CARTIER POUR L'ART CONTEMPORAIN Map pp124–5

☎ 01 42 18 56 50; www.fondation.cartier.fr; 261 blvd Raspail, 14e; adult/11-26yr/under 10yr €6.50/4.50/free; ⏰ 11am-10pm Tue, to 8pm Mon & Wed-Sun; Ⓜ Raspail

This stunning contemporary building, designed by Jean Nouvel, is a work of art. It hosts temporary exhibits on contemporary art (from the 1980s till today) in a wide variety of media – from painting and photography to video and fashion.

GARE MONTPARNASSE Map pp124–5

place Raoul Dautry, 14e; Ⓜ Montparnasse Bienvenüe

This sprawling train station, fronted by an ice-skating rink (p321) in winter, has several unusual attractions on its rooftop. The Jardin de l'Atlantique (Atlantic Garden; place des Cinq Martyr du Lycée Buffon, 15e), whose 3.5 hectares of landscaped terraces veil the top of the station, offers a bit of greenery and tranquillity in the heart of a very busy district. The futuristic Observatoire Météorologique

'sculpture' in the centre of the garden measures precipitation, temperature and wind speed.

Next to the garden the small Musée Jean Moulin (☎ 01 40 64 39 44; www.ml-leclerc-moulin .paris.fr, in French; 23 allée de la 2e DB, 15e; temporary exhibitions adult/14-25yr €4/2, permanent collections free; ⏰ 10am-6pm Tue-Sun) is devoted to the WWII German occupation of Paris, with its focus on the Resistance and its leader, Jean Moulin (1899–1943). The attached Mémorial du Maréchal Leclerc de Hauteclocque et de la Libération de Paris shows a panoramic film on the eponymous general (1902–47), who led the Free French units during the war and helped to liberate the city in 1944.

To reach all these attractions, board the bubble lift on the pavement opposite 25 blvd de Vaugirard (15e) and ascend one floor. From there take the escalator and follow the signs to the garden and museums.

TOUR MONTPARNASSE Map pp124–5

☎ 01 45 38 52 56; www.tourmontparnasse56.com; rue de l'Arrivée, 15e; adult/student & 16-20yr/7-15yr/

top picks

MONTPARNASSE

- Catacombes (opposite)
- Tour Montparnasse (view from top only; above)
- Cimetière de Montparnasse (opposite)
- Musée de la Poste (p165)
- Fondation Cartier pour l'Art Contemporain (left)

MONTPARNASSE

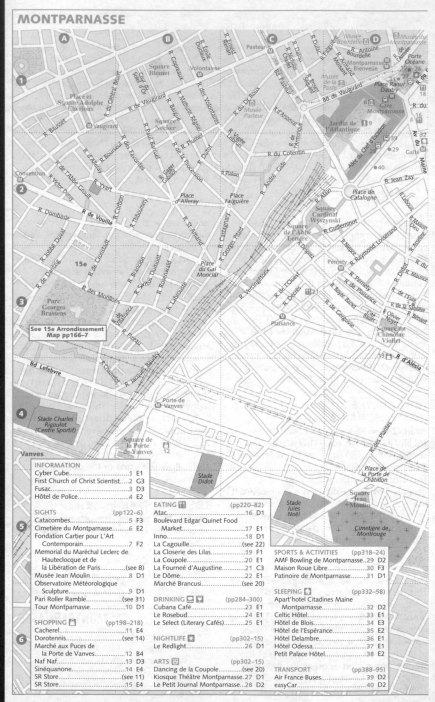

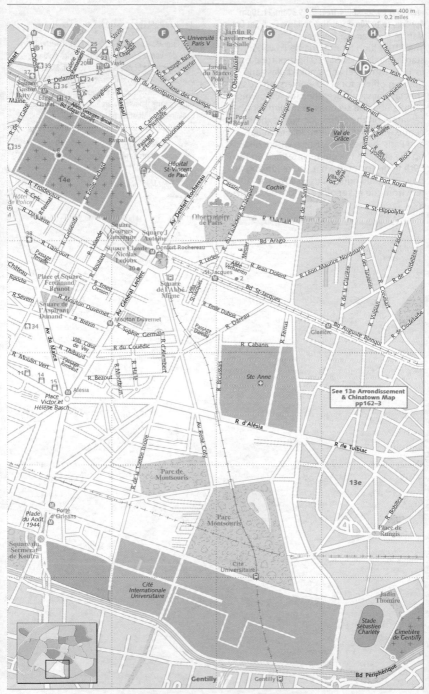

under 7yr €9.50/6.80/4/free; ⏱ 9.30am-11.30pm Apr-Sep, to 10.30pm Sun-Thu, to 11pm Fri & Sat Oct-Mar; Ⓜ Montparnasse Bienvenüe

The 210m-high Montparnasse Tower, a startlingly ugly, oversized lipstick tube built in 1973 with steel and smoked glass and housing offices for 5000 workers, affords spectacular views over the city. A lift whisks visitors up in 38 seconds to the indoor observatory on the 56th floor, with exhibition centre, video clips, multimedia terminals and Paris' highest café. Finish with a hike up the stairs to the open-air terrace on the 59th floor. To know what you're looking at, buy the multilingual *Paris vu d'en haut* guide (€3) from the ticket office before hiking up.

TRANSPORT: MONTPARNASSE

Bus Gare Montparnasse for 91 to Gare d'Austerlitz, Gare de Lyon & Bastille, for 92 to Charles de Gaulle-Étoile, for 94 to Sèvres Babylone (Le Bon Marché); blvd du Montparnasse for 82 to Invalides & Eiffel Tower; rue de Rennes for 95 to St-Germain des Prés, Quai Voltaire, Louvre, Palais Royal, Opéra & Lamarck-Caulaincourt (Montmartre); blvd Raspail (metro stop Vavin) for 68 to via Opéra, Louvre & Musée d'Orsay

Metro Denfert Rochereau, Duroc, Edgar Quinet, Falguière, Montparnasse Bienvenüe, Pasteur, Raspail, St-Placide

Train Gare Montparnasse

FAUBOURG ST-GERMAIN & INVALIDES

Drinking p293; Eating p259; Shopping p212; Sleeping p350

Staid and with no nightlife to speak of, agreed, but this 7e arrondissement – a formal world of exquisite ironwork, flashing gold leaf, Seine-side art galleries and conventional manners – has a timeless beauty and extravagance all of its own. And when it all gets too stiff, take a stroll through pedestrian rue Cler and its bustling street market.

In the 18th century, Faubourg St-Germain, the area between the Seine and rue de Babylone (1km south), was Paris' most fashionable neighbourhood. Elegant mansions ran riot on rue de Lille, rue de Grenelle and rue de Varenne, now an overdose of embassies, cultural centres and government ministries; Hôtel Matignon at 57 rue de Varenne has been the official residence of the French prime minister since the start of the Fifth Republic (1958), and it was to the stylish pad at No 53 that Edith Wharton moved in 1910 to write *Le Temps de l'Innocence* (The Age of Innocence). Play voyeur and peek at dreamy *hôtels particuliers* for sale in the windows of Sotheby's real-estate agent Propriétés Parisiennes (www.proprietesparisiennes.fr) at 7bis rue des St-Pères.

Framing all this Parisian refinement is the Eiffel Tower in the skyline, the gracious curve of the Seine at eye level and, underfoot, the smooth lawns of Les Invalides, where it always feels like Sunday. If you suddenly find yourself leaping on a bike (see p389) and pedalling along the river to watch the kaleidoscope of the National Assembly, the cavernous railway-station shell of the Musée d'Orsay and Quai Voltaire's bijou art galleries flash by, don't be surprised. Just make sure you jump off at 5bis rue Verneuil to see the quarter's finest example of over-the-top extravagance – the house where Parisian singer, sexpot and *provocateur* Serge Gainsbourg lived from 1969 until his death in 1991. Neighbours have long since given up scrubbing off the reappearing graffiti and messages from fans.

ASSEMBLÉE NATIONALE Map pp128–9

☎ 01 40 63 60 00; www.assemblee-nat.fr; 33 quai d'Orsay & 126 rue de l'Université, 7e; Ⓜ Assemblée Nationale or Invalides

The lower house of the French parliament, known as the National Assembly, meets in the 18th-century Palais Bourbon, which fronts the Seine. Tours are available through local deputies, making citizens and residents the only ones eligible. Next door is the Second Empire–style Ministère des Affaires Étrangères (Ministry of Foreign Affairs; ☎ 01 43 17 53 53; 37 quai d'Orsay, 7e), built between 1845 and 1855.

TRANSPORT: FAUBOURG ST-GERMAIN & INVALIDES

Bus Quai d'Orsay for 63 to St-Germain, Odéon, Gare d'Austerlitz & Gare de Lyon, for 83 to Grand Palais, Rond Point des Champs Élysées & rue du Faubourg St-Honoré; Musée d'Orsay for 73 to place de la Concorde, av des Champs-Élysées & La Défense

Metro & RER Assemblée Nationale, École Militaire, Invalides, Musée d'Orsay, Rue du Bac, Solférino, La Tour Maubourg

Boat Musée d'Orsay Batobus stop (quai de Solférino); Paris Canal Croisières pier at quai Anatole France (7e) near the Musée d'Orsay for canal boat to stop Bassin de la Villette (19-21 quai de la Loire)

HÔTEL DES INVALIDES Map pp128–9

Ⓜ Invalides, Varenne or La Tour Maubourg

A 500m long expanse of lawn known as the Esplanade des Invalides separates Faubourg St-Germain from the Eiffel Tower area. At the southern end of the esplanade, laid out between 1704 and 1720, is the final resting place of Napoleon, the man many French people consider to be the nation's greatest hero.

Hôtel des Invalides was built in the 1670s by Louis XIV to provide housing for 4000 *invalides* (disabled war veterans). On 14 July 1789, a mob forced its way into the building and, after fierce fighting, seized 32,000 rifles before heading on to the prison at Bastille and the start of the French Revolution.

North of Hôtel des Invalides' main courtyard, in the so-called Cour d'Honneur, is the Musée de l'Armée (Army Museum; ☎ 01 44 42 38 77; www.invalides.org; 129 rue de Grenelle, 7e; adult/18-25yr/under 18yr €8/6/free; ☼ 10am-6pm Apr-Sep, to 5pm Oct-Mar, closed 1st Mon of the month) – the nation's largest collection on French military history.

South is Église St-Louis des Invalides, once used by soldiers, and Église du Dôme (☼ 10am-7pm mid-Jun–mid-Sep, to 6pm Apr–mid-Jun & Sep, to 5pm mid-Sept–Mar) which, with its sparkling golden dome (1677–1735), is one of the finest religious edifices erected under Louis XIV. It

FAUBOURG ST-GERMAIN & INVALIDES

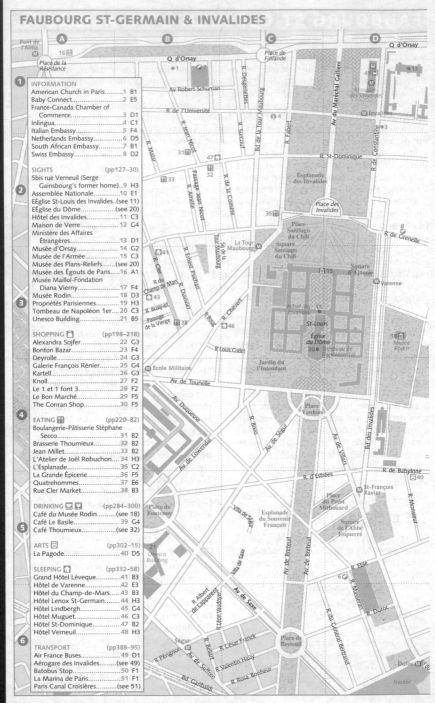

INFORMATION
American Church in Paris.........1 B1
Baby Connect.......................2 E5
France-Canada Chamber of
  Commerce..........................3 D1
Inlingua..............................4 C1
Italian Embassy....................5 F4
Netherlands Embassy............6 D5
South African Embassy...........7 B1
Swiss Embassy.....................8 D2

SIGHTS (pp127–30)
5bis rue Verneuil (Serge
  Gainsbourg's former home)..9 H3
Assemblée Nationale............10 E1
EÉglise St-Louis des Invalides..(see 11)
EÉglise du Dôme................(see 20)
Hôtel des Invalides...............11 C3
Maison de Verre..................12 G4
Ministère des Affaires
  Étrangères........................13 D1
Musée d'Orsay....................14 G2
Musée de l'Armée................15 C3
Musée des Plans-Reliefs......(see 20)
Musée des Égouts de Paris...16 A1
Musée Maillol-Fondation
  Diana Vierny.....................17 F4
Musée Rodin......................18 D3
Propriétés Parisiennes..........19 H3
Tombeau de Napoléon 1er...20 C3
Unesco Building...................21 B5

SHOPPING (pp198–218)
Alexandra Sojfer.................22 G3
Bonton Bazar.....................23 F4
Deyrolle...........................24 G3
Galerie François Rénier........25 G3
Kartell.............................26 G3
Knoll...............................27 F2
Le 1 et 1 font 3..................28 F2
Le Bon Marché...................29 F5
The Conran Shop................30 F5

EATING (pp220–82)
Boulangerie-Pâtisserie Stéphane
  Secco.............................31 B2
Brasserie Thoumieux...........32 B2
Jean Millet........................33 B2
L'Atelier de Joël Robuchon...34 H3
L'Esplanade.......................35 C2
La Grande Épicerie.............36 F5
Quatrehommes....................37 E6
Rue Cler Market.................38 B3

DRINKING (pp284–300)
Café du Musée Rodin.......(see 18)
Café Le Basile....................39 G4
Café Thoumieux..............(see 32)

ARTS (pp302–15)
La Pagode........................40 D5

SLEEPING (pp332–58)
Grand Hôtel Léveque..........41 B3
Hôtel de Varenne...............42 E3
Hôtel du Champ-de-Mars....43 B3
Hôtel Lenox St-Germain......44 H3
Hôtel Lindbergh.................45 G4
Hôtel Muguet....................46 C3
Hôtel St-Dominique............47 B2
Hôtel Verneuil...................48 H3

TRANSPORT (pp388–95)
Air France Buses................49 D1
Aérogare des Invalides......(see 49)
Batobus Stop.....................50 F1
La Marina de Paris.............51 F1
Paris Canal Croisières.......(see 51)

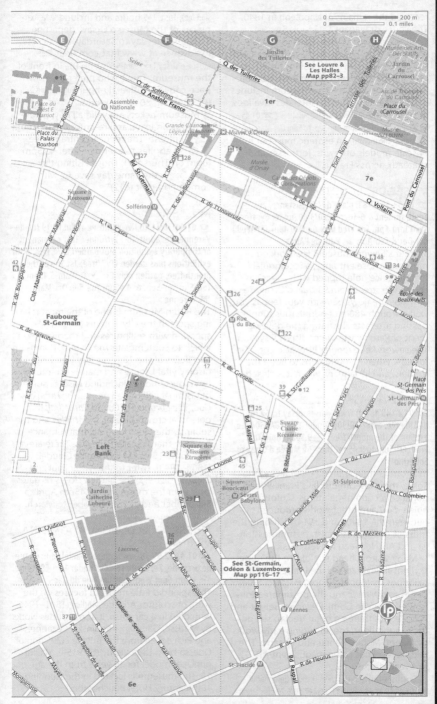

See Louvre &
Les Halles
Map pp82–3

See St-Germain,
Odéon & Luxembourg
Map pp116–17

received the remains of Napoleon in 1840. The very extravagant Tombeau de Napoléon 1er (Napoleon's Tomb; 10am-6pm Apr-Sep, to 5pm Oct-Mar, closed 1st Mon of the month), in the centre of the church, comprises six coffins fitting into one another like a Russian *matryoshka* doll.

Admission to the Army Museum includes entry to all the sights in Hôtel des Invalides, including the Musée des Plans-Reliefs (01 45 51 95 05; 10am-6pm Apr-Sep, to 5pm Oct-Mar, closed 1st Mon of the month), an esoteric museum full of scale models of towns, fortresses and chateaux across France.

MUSÉE DES ÉGOUTS DE PARIS pp128–9
01 53 68 27 81; place de la Résistance, 7e; adult/student & 6-11yr €4.20/3.40, under 6yr free; 11am-5pm Sat-Wed May-Sep, to 4pm Sat-Wed Oct-Dec & Feb-Apr; M Pont de l'Alma
The Paris Sewers Museum is a working museum whose entrance, a rectangular maintenance hole topped with a kiosk, is across the street from 93 quai d'Orsay, 7e. Raw sewage flows beneath your feet as you walk through 480m of odoriferous tunnels, passing artefacts illustrating the development of Paris' waste-water disposal system. The sewers keep regular hours except – God forbid – when rain threatens to flood the tunnels, and in January, when it is closed.

MUSÉE D'ORSAY Map pp128–9
01 40 49 48 14; www.musee-orsay.fr; 62 rue de Lille, 7e; adult/18-30yr/under 18yr €8/5.50/free, 1st Sun of the month free; 9.30am-6pm Tue, Wed, Fri-Sun, to 9.45pm Thu; M Musée d'Orsay or Solférino
In a former train station (1900) facing the Seine, this museum displays France's national collection of paintings, sculptures, *objets d'art* and other works produced between the 1840s and 1914, including the fruits of the impressionist, postimpressionist and Art Nouveau movements.

Many visitors head straight to the upper skylight-lit level to see the impressionist paintings by Monet, Renoir, Pissarro, Sisley, Degas and Manet and the postimpressionist works by Van Gogh, Cézanne, Seurat and Matisse. But there's a great deal to see on the ground floor, too, including early works by Manet, Monet, Renoir and Pissarro. The middle level has some magnificent Art Nouveau rooms.

English-language guided tours (information 01 40 49 48 48; adult/13-17yr €7.50/5.70 plus admis-

sion fee), last 1½ hours and include 'Masterpieces of the Musée d'Orsay', departing 11.30am Tuesday to Saturday. Buy tickets in advance at www.fnac.com or at Kiosque du Musée d'Orsay (9am-5.50pm Tue-Fri), in front of the museum. Those who prefer their own pace can DIY with a 1½-hour audioguide tour (€5) covering 80 major works.

Museum tickets are valid all day, meaning you can leave and re-enter the museum as you please. The reduced entrance fee of €5.50 applies to everyone after 4.15pm (6pm on Thursday). Those visiting the Musée Rodin (below) the same day save €2 with a combined ticket (€12).

MUSÉE RODIN Map pp128–9
01 44 18 61 10; www.musee-rodin.fr; 79 rue de Varenne, 7e; adult/18-25yr/under 18yr permanent or temporary exhibition plus garden €6/4/free, both exhibitions plus garden €9/7/free, 1st Sun of the month free, garden only €1; 9.30am-5.45pm Tue-Sun Apr-Sep, to 4.45pm Tue-Sun Oct-Mar; M Varenne
The Rodin Museum is one of the most relaxing spots in the city, with its garden-speckled with sculptures and shade trees in which to contemplate *The Thinker*. Rooms on two floors of the 18th-century Hôtel Biron display vital bronze and marble sculptures by Auguste Rodin, including casts of some of his most celebrated works: *The Hand of God, The Burghers of Calais, Cathedral*, that perennial crowd-pleaser *The Thinker* and the sublime, the incomparable, that romance-hewn-in-marble called *The Kiss*. There are also some 15 works by Camille Claudel (1864–1943), sister to the writer Paul and Rodin's mistress. The garden closes its gates later than the museum: at 6.45pm April to September and at 5pm October to March.

MUSÉE MAILLOL-FONDATION DINA VIERNY Map pp128–9
01 42 22 59 58; www.museemaillol.com; 61 rue de Grenelle, 7e; adult/16-25yr/under 16yr €8/6/free; 11am-6pm Wed-Mon; M Rue du Bac
This splendid little museum focuses on the work of sculptor Aristide Maillol (1861–1944) who died in a car crash. It also includes works by Matisse, Gauguin, Kandinsky, Cézanne and Picasso, all from the private collection of Odessa-born Dina Vierny (b 1915–), Maillol's principal model for 10 years from the age of 15. The museum is located in the stunning 18th-century Hôtel Bouchardon.

EIFFEL TOWER AREA & 16E ARRONDISSEMENT

Eating p260; Sleeping p351

Paris' very symbol, the Eiffel Tower, is surrounded by open areas on both banks of the Seine, which take in both the 7e and the 16e arrondissements.

On the Right Bank, Passy is among the city's most prestigious neighbourhoods. The wide avenues radiating out from the place du Trocadéro et du 11 November are lined with sober, elegant buildings from the Haussmann era. Luxury boutiques abound, frequented by posh customers who desert the area come nightfall. It's here, on the banks of the Seine, that the architectural curiosity known as the 'Maison Ronde' – the Maison de Radio France – was constructed. Just north, the Maison de Balzac keeps alive the memory of the illustrious author of *Le Père Goriot*. Further north, the ultrabourgeois av Foch thumbs its nose at the restless av de la Grande Armée, teeming with motorbike fanatics. The 16e arrondissement also hosts football meets at the Parc des Princes and, as summer approaches, the thud of tennis balls on clay can be heard at Stade Roland Garros. There are some fabulous cultural institutions here, including the Musée du Quai Branly, Musée Guimet des Arts Asiatiques, Musée d'Art Moderne de la Ville de Paris and the three excellent museums of the Palais de Chaillot. At the same time there are lots and lots of smaller and lesser-known museums on such diverse subjects as wine, crystal and pens.

EIFFEL TOWER pp132–3

☎ 01 44 11 23 23; www.tour-eiffel.fr; 🕓 lifts 9am-midnight mid-Jun–Aug, 9.30am-11pm Sep–mid-Jun; stairs 9am-midnight mid-Jun–Aug, 9.30am-6pm Sep–mid-Jun; Ⓜ Champ de Mars-Tour Eiffel or Bir Hakeim

La Tour Eiffel faced massive opposition from Paris' artistic and literary elite when it was built for the 1889 Exposition Universelle (World Fair), marking the centenary of the Revolution.

The 'metal asparagus', as some Parisians snidely called it, was almost torn down in 1909 but was spared because it proved an ideal platform for the transmitting antennas needed for the newfangled science of radiotelegraphy. It welcomed two million visitors the first year it opened and more than three times that number – 6.9 million in 2007 – make their way to the top each year.

The Eiffel Tower, named after its designer, Gustave Eiffel, is 324m high, including the TV antenna at the tip. This figure can vary by as much as 15cm, however, as the tower's 7300 tonnes of iron, held together by 2.5 million rivets, expand in warm weather and contract when it's cold.

Three levels are open to the public. The lifts (in the east, west and north pillars), which follow a curved trajectory, cost €4.80 to the 1st platform (57m above the ground), €7.80 to the 2nd (115m) and €12 to the 3rd (276m). Children aged three to 11 pay €2.50, €4.30 or €6.70. If you're feeling fit and/or energetic you can avoid the lift queues by taking the stairs (over/under 25yr €4/3.10) in the south pillar as far as the 2nd platform.

TRANSPORT: EIFFEL TOWER AREA & 16E ARRONDISSEMENT

Bus Quai Branly for 82 to Trocadéro (Varsovie), Palais de Chaillot, Porte Maillot, Palais des Congrès & Neuilly; Champ de Mars for 42 to av Montaigne, Madeleine, Opéra (blvd Haussmann) & Gare du Nord & for 69 to Invalides, Musée d'Orsay, Louvre, Châtelet, Marais, Bastille & Gambetta; Trocadéro for 22 to Charles de Gaulle-Étoile, Grands Boulevards, Gare St-Lazare & Opéra

Metro & RER Alma-Marceau, Bir Hakeim, Champ de Mars-Tour Eiffel, École Militaire, Iéna, Kennedy Radio France, Passy, Pont de l'Alma, Porte Dauphine, Trocadéro, Victor Hugo

Boat Eiffel Tower Batobus stop (Port de la Bourdonnais)

PALAIS DE CHAILLOT Map pp132–3

place du Trocadéro et du 11 November, 16e; Ⓜ Trocadéro

The two curved, colonnaded wings of the Palais de Chaillot, built for the 1937 Exposition Universelle held in Paris, and the terrace in between them afford an exceptional panorama of the Jardins du Trocadéro (named after a Spanish stronghold near Cádiz captured by the French in 1823), the Seine and the Eiffel Tower.

EIFFEL TOWER AREA & 16E ARRONDISSEMENT

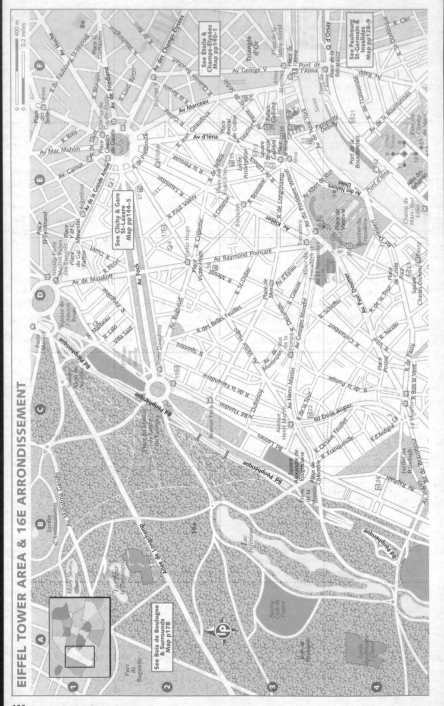

See Étoile & Champs-Élysées Map pp140-1

See Faubourg St-Germain & Invalides Map pp128-9

See Clichy & Gare St-Lazare Map pp144-5

See Bois de Boulogne & Surrounds Map p178

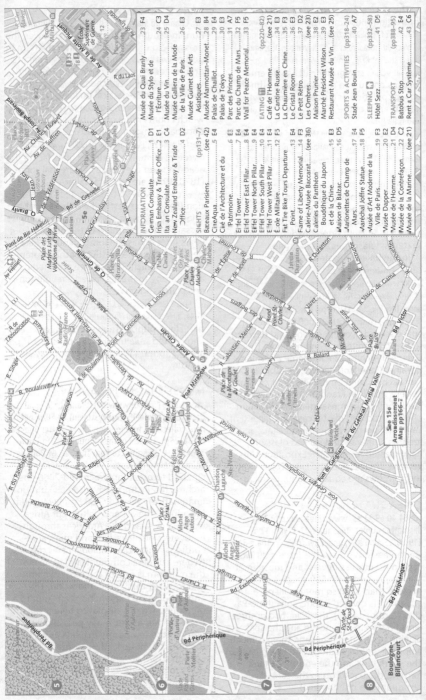

The palace's western wing contains two interesting museums. The Musée de l'Homme (Museum of Mankind; ☎ 01 44 05 72 72; www.mnhn.fr; 17 place du Trocadéro et du 11 November, 16e; adult/4-16yr & student €7/5; 10am-5pm Mon, Wed-Fri, to 6pm Sat & Sun), straight ahead as you enter, focuses on human development, ethnology, population and population growth; it's a branch of the Musée National d'Histoire Naturelle (p113).

The Musée de la Marine (Maritime Museum; ☎ 01 53 65 69 69; www.musee-marine.fr; 17 place du Trocadéro et du 11 November, 16e; adult/student & 18-25yr €6.50/4.50, under 18yr free; 10am-6pm Wed-Mon), to the right of the main entrance, examines France's naval adventures from the 17th century until today and boasts one of the world's finest collections of model ships, as well as ancient figureheads, compasses, sextants, telescopes and paintings.

In the palace's eastern wing is the new Cité de l'Architecture et du Patrimoine (☎ 01 58 51 52 00; www.citechaillot.fr in French; 1 place du Trocadéro et du 11 November, 16; adult/student & 18-25yr €8/5, under 18yr free; 11am-7pm Mon, Wed & Fri-Sun, to 9pm Thu), a mammoth 23,000 sq metres of space spread over three floors and devoted to French architecture and heritage. The Galerie d'Architecture Moderne & Contemporaine (Gallery of Modern and Contemporary Architecture) on the 2nd floor examines current trends in France but the highlight (and core) of the museum is the collection of 350 wood and plaster casts (moulages) of cathedral portals, columns and altars, and replicas of murals and stained glass originally created for the 1878 Exposition Universelle. The views of the Eiffel Tower from the windows are equally monumental.

CINEAQUA Map pp132-3

☎ 01 40 69 23 23; www.cineaqua.com; 2 av des Nations Unies, 16e; adult/13-17yr/3-12yr €19.50/15.50/12.50, under 3yr free; 10am-8pm On the eastern side of the Jardins du Trocadéro is Europe's newest and most ambitious aquarium, with 500 species 'tanked' in more than 3500 sq metres of space. The aquarium is divided into regions (Indo-Pacific, Caribbean etc), there are two or three films related to marine life and the seas playing at any one time, and there is much emphasis on the ecology and green issues. The shark tank and the enormous tank forming the backdrop to the café-restaurant are phenomenal.

PARC DU CHAMP DE MARS Map pp132-3

M Champ de Mars-Tour Eiffel or École Militaire Running southeast from the Eiffel Tower, the grassy Field of Mars (named after the Roman god of war) was originally used as a parade ground for the cadets of the 18th-century École Militaire (Military Academy; Map pp128-9), the vast, French-classical building (1772) at the southeastern end of the park in the 7e, which counts none other than Napoleon Bonaparte among its graduates. The wonderful Wall for Peace memorial (2000; www.wallforpeace.com) of steel and etched glass facing the academy and the statue of Maréchal Joffre (1870-1931) are by Clara Halter.

On 14 July 1790 the Fête de la Fédération (Federation Festival) was held on the Champ de Mars to celebrate the first anniversary of the storming of the Bastille. Four years later it was the scene of the Fête de l'Être-Suprême (Festival of the Supreme Being), at which Robespierre presided over a ceremony that established a revolutionary 'state religion'.

The Marionettes du Champ de Mars (☎ 01 48 56 01 44; allée du Général Margueritte, 7e; M École Militaire) stage puppet shows (€3) in a covered and heated salle (hall) in the park at 3.15pm and 4.15pm on Wednesday, Saturday and Sunday.

MUSÉE DU QUAI BRANLY Map pp132-3

☎ 01 56 61 70 00; www.quaibranly.fr; 37 quai Branly, 7e; adult/18-25yr & student €8.50/6, permanent collections free for under 18yr & after 6pm Sat for 18-25yr, 1st Sun of the month free; 11am-7pm Tue, Wed & Sun, to 9pm Thu-Sat M Pont de l'Alma or Alma-Marceau Opened to great fanfare in mid-2006, the architecturally impressive (see p50) but unimaginatively named Quai Branly Museum introduces the art and cultures of Africa, Oceania, Asia and the Americas through innovative displays, film and musical recordings. With Là où dialoguent les cultures (Where cultures communicate) as its motto, the museum is one of the most dynamic and forward-thinking in the world. The anthropological explanations are kept to a minimum; what is displayed here is meant to be viewed as art. A day pass allowing entry to the temporary exhibits as well as the permanent collection costs adult/concession €13/9.50; an audioguide is €5. And don't miss the views from the 5th-floor restaurant Les Ombres (p260).

top picks

EIFFEL TOWER AREA & 16E ARRONDISSEMENT

- Eiffel Tower (p131)
- Musée du Quai Branly (opposite)
- Cité de l'Architecture et du Patrimoine (p131)
- Musée Guimet des Arts Asiatiques (right)
- CineAqua (opposite)

FLAME OF LIBERTY MEMORIAL
Map pp132-3

Ⓜ Alma-Marceau

This bronze sculpture – a replica of the one topping New York's Statue of Liberty – was placed here in 1987 on the centenary of the launch of the *International Herald Tribune* newspaper, as a symbol of friendship between France and the USA. On 31 August 1997 in the place d'Alma underpass below, Diana, Princess of Wales, was killed in a devastating car accident along with her companion, Dodi Fayed, and their chauffeur, Henri Paul, and the Flame of Liberty became something of a memorial to her, decorated with flowers, photographs, graffiti and personal notes. It was renovated and cleaned in 2002 and, this being the age of short (or no) memories, apart from a bit of sentimental graffiti on a wall nearby there are no longer any reminders of the tragedy that happened so close by and had so much of the Western world in grief at the time.

MUSÉE D'ART MODERNE DE LA VILLE DE PARIS Map pp132-3

☎ 01 53 67 40 00; www.mam.paris.fr in French; 11 av du Président Wilson, 16e; temporary exhibits from adult €5-9, 13-25yr, senior & student €2.50-5.50, permanent collections free, under 13yr free; Ⓨ 10am-6pm Tue, Wed & Fri-Sun, to 10pm Thu; Ⓜ Iéna

The Modern Art Museum of the City of Paris was established in 1961. The museum is housed in what was the Electricity Pavilion at the time of the 1937 Exposition Universelle, and displays works representative of just about every major artistic movement of the 20th and nascent 21st centuries: Fauvism, cubism, Dadaism, surrealism, the School of Paris, expressionism, abstraction-ism and so on. Artists who have works on display include Matisse, Picasso, Braque, Soutine, Modigliani and Chagall.

PALAIS DE TOKYO pp132-3

☎ 01 47 23 38 86; www.palaisdetokyo.com; 13 av du Président Wilson, 16e; adult/senior & 18-26yr €6/4.50, under 18yr free; Ⓨ noon-midnight Tue-Sun; Ⓜ Iéna

The Tokyo Palace, like the Musée d'Art Moderne de la Ville de Paris next door in yet another 1937 Exposition Universelle building, opened in 2002 as a Site de Création Contemporain (Site for Contemporary Arts). It has no permanent collection and plans no exhibitions of a single artist or theme but showcases ephemeral artwork, installations and performances. It's event-driven rather than static and the whole idea is to get the viewer as close to the works of art and the artists as possible.

MUSÉE GALLIERA DE LA MODE DE LA VILLE DE PARIS Map pp132-3

☎ 01 56 52 86 00; www.galliera.paris.fr, in French; 10 av Pierre 1er de Serbie, 16e; adult/14-26yr/ student & senior €7/3.50/5.50, under 14yr free; Ⓨ 10am-6pm Tue-Sun; Ⓜ Iéna

The Fashion Museum of the City of Paris, housed in the 19th-century Palais Galliera, warehouses some 90,000 outfits and accessories – from canes and umbrellas to fans and gloves – from the 18th century to the present day and exhibits them along with items borrowed from collections abroad offering tremendously successful temporary exhibitions. The sumptuous Italianate palace and gardens dating from the mid-19th century are worth a visit in themselves.

MUSÉE GUIMET DES ARTS ASIATIQUES pp132-3

☎ 01 56 52 53 00; www.museeguimet.fr; 6 place d'Iéna, 16e; temporary exhibits adult €6.50-8.50, 18-25, student & senior €4.50-6, permanent collections free, under 18yr free; Ⓨ 10am-6pm Wed-Mon; Ⓜ Iéna

The Guimet Museum of Asiatic Arts is France's foremost repository for Asian art and has sculptures, paintings, *objets d'art* and religious articles from Afghanistan, India, Nepal, Pakistan, Tibet, Cambodia, China, Japan and Korea. Part of the collection, comprising Buddhist paintings and sculptures brought to Paris in 1876 by collector Émile Guimet, is housed in the

Galeries du Panthéon Bouddhique du Japon et de la Chine (Buddhist Pantheon Galleries of Japan & China; ☎ 01 47 23 61 65; 19 av d'Iéna; admission free; ⏰ 10am-6pm Wed-Mon; Ⓜ Iéna) in the scrumptious Hôtel Heidelbach a short distance to the north. Don't miss the wonderful Japanese garden (⏰ 1-5pm Wed-Mon) here.

GALERIE-MUSÉE BACCARAT Map pp132–3
☎ 01 40 22 11 00; www.baccarat.com; 11 place des États-Unis, 16e; adult/student & 18-25yr €5/3.50, under 18yr free; ⏰ 10am-6.30pm Mon, Wed & Sat; Ⓜ Boissière or Kléber
Showcasing 1000 stunning pieces of crystal, many of them custom-made for princes and dictators of desperately poor former colonies, this flashy museum is at home in its striking new rococo-style premises designed by Philippe Starck in the ritzy 16e. It is also home to a superb restaurant called – what else? – Le Cristal Room (p260).

MUSÉE DAPPER Mappp132–3
☎ 01 44 00 91 75; www.dapper.com.fr; 35 rue Paul Valéry, 16e; adult/senior & student €6/3, under 18yr free, last Wed of the month free; ⏰ 11am-7pm Wed-Sun; Ⓜ Victor Hugo
This fantastic museum of sub-Saharan African and Caribbean art collected and exhibited by the nonprofit Dapper Foundation (in a 16th-century hôtel particulier with wonderful 21st-century add-ons) stages a couple of major exhibitions each year. The collection consists mostly of carved wooden figurines and masks, which famously influenced the work of Picasso, Braque and Man Ray. The ever-active auditorium sponsors African and Caribbean cultural events year-round – from concerts and storytelling to films and marionette performances.

MUSÉE DU VIN Map pp132–3
☎ 01 45 25 63 26; www.museeduvinparis.com; rue des Eaux, 5 square Charles Dickens, 16e; adult/student/senior €8.90/7/7.50, under 14yr free; ⏰ 10am-6pm Tue-Sun; Ⓜ Passy
The not-so-comprehensive Wine Museum, headquarters of the prestigious International Federation of Wine Brotherhoods, introduces visitors to the fine art of viticulture with various mock-ups and displays of tools. Admission includes a glass of wine at the end of the visit. Entry is free if you have lunch at the attached Restaurant Musée du Vin (p261).

top picks

FOR CHILDREN
- Cité des Sciences et de l'Industrie (p172)
- Centre Kapla (p396)
- CineAqua (p134)
- Exploradôme (p178)
- Jardin d'Acclimatation (p178)
- Musée des Arts et Métiers (p97)
- Palais de la Découverte (p139)
- Jardin du Luxembourg (p119)

MAISON DE BALZAC Map pp132–3
☎ 01 55 74 41 80; www.balzac.paris.fr, in French; 47 rue Raynouard, 16e; temporary exhibits adult/14-26yr/senior & student €4/2/3, permanent collections free, under 14yr free; ⏰ 10am-6pm Tue-Sun; Ⓜ Passy or Kennedy Radio France
This pretty, three-storey spa house in Passy, about 800m southwest of the Jardins du Trocadéro, is where the realist novelist Honoré de Balzac (1799–1850) lived and worked from 1840 to 1847, editing the entire Comédie Humaine and writing various books. There's lots of memorabilia, letters, prints and portraits and is probably for die-hard Balzac fans only.

MUSÉE DU STYLO ET DE L'ÉCRITURE pp132–3
☎ 06 07 94 13 21; 3 rue Guy de Maupassant, 16e; adult/senior & student €2/1; ⏰ 2-6pm Sun; Ⓜ Av Henri Martin or Rue de la Pompe
The Museum of the Pen and of Penmanship has the most important collection of writing utensils in the world – with pens dating back to the mid-18th century – as well as paper and calligraphy. It can be visited on other days if you phone and book in advance.

MUSÉE DE LA CONTREFAÇON Mappp132–3
☎ 01 56 26 14 00; 16 rue de la Faisanderie, 16e; adult/12-16yr €4/3, under 12yr free; ⏰ 2-5.30pm Tue-Sun; Ⓜ Porte Dauphine
This fascinating museum east of Porte Dauphine is the real thing, dedicated to the not-so-fine art of counterfeiting. Apparently nothing is sacred to the manufacturers of ersatz: banknotes, liqueurs, designer clothing, even Barbie and Ken dolls. What makes this museum, established by the Union des

Fabricants (Manufacturers' Union), so interesting is that it displays the real against the fake and lets you spot the difference. Most of the time it's as plain as the nose (the real, not the plastic one) on your face.

MUSÉE MARMOTTAN-MONET pp132–3

☎ 01 44 96 50 33; www.marmottan.com; 2 rue Louis Boilly, 16e; adult/8-25yr €9/5.50, under 8yr free; ⏱ 11am-9pm Tue, to 6pm Wed-Sun; Ⓜ La Muette

This museum, two blocks east of the Bois de Boulogne between Porte de la Muette and Porte de Passy, has the world's largest collection of works by impressionist painter Claude Monet (1840–1926) – about a hundred – as well as paintings by Gauguin, Sisley, Pissarro, Renoir, Degas, Manet and Berthe Morisot. It also contains an important collection of French, English, Italian and Flemish miniatures from the 13th to the 16th centuries.

ÉTOILE & CHAMPS-ÉLYSÉES

Drinking p294; Eating p261; Shopping p212; Sleeping p352

The 8e arrondissement was born under a lucky star, it would seem. Its avenues radiate from place de l'Étoile – officially place Charles de Gaulle – bathing in the glow of fame. First among them is the av des Champs-Élysées. From the Arc de Triomphe in the northwest to the place de la Concorde in the southeast, this broad boulevard rules supreme. On New Year's Eve and after major sporting victories there's always a huge party here. Like a splendid, regal hostess, the avenue receives its guests, makes them mingle and moves them along. And the guests keep coming. Just a short walk away, the av Montaigne haughtily displays its designer wares. And members of the jet set go shopping along av George V and rue du Faubourg St-Honoré. Here, fashion, art and luxury hotels go hand in hand. Only the finest are on display, as in the neighbourhood's theatres and museums, such as the Grand Palais and Petit Palais.

ARC DE TRIOMPHE Map pp140–1

☎ 01 55 37 73 77; www.monuments-nationaux.fr; viewing platform adult/18-25yr €9/6.50, under 18yr free, 1st Sun of the month Nov-Mar free; ⏰ 10am-11pm Apr-Sep, to 10.30pm Oct-Mar; Ⓜ Charles de Gaulle-Étoile

The Triumphal Arch is 2km northwest of place de la Concorde in the middle of place Charles de Gaulle (aka place de l'Étoile), the world's largest traffic roundabout and the meeting point of 12 avenues (and three arrondissements). It was commissioned in 1806 by Napoleon to commemorate his imperial victories but remained unfinished when he started losing – at first battles and then whole wars. It was finally completed under Louis-Philippe in 1836. Among the armies to march triumphantly through the Arc de Triomphe were the Germans in 1871, the Allies in 1919, the Germans again in 1940 and the Allies again in 1944.

The most famous of the four high-relief panels at the base is to the right, facing the arch from the av des Champs-Élysées side. Entitled *Départ des Volontaires de 1792* (Departure of the Volunteers of 1792) and also known as *La Marseillaise* (France's national anthem), it is the work of François Rude. Higher up, a frieze running around the whole monument depicts hundreds of figures, each one 2m high.

From the viewing platform on top of the arch (50m up via 284 steps and well worth the climb) you can see the dozen broad avenues – many of them named after Napoleonic victories and illustrious generals – radiating towards every compass point. Av de la Grande Armée heads north-west to the skyscraper district of La Défense (p179), where the Grande Arche, a hollow cube measuring 110m on each side, defines the western end of the Grand Axe (the 'Great Axis' linking the Louvre and the Arc de Triomphe). Tickets to the viewing platform of the Arc de Triomphe are sold in the underground passageway that surfaces on the even-numbered side of av des Champs-Élysées. It is the only *sane* way to get to the base of the arch and is *not* linked to nearby metro tunnels.

AVENUE DES CHAMPS-ÉLYSÉES
Map pp140–1

Ⓜ Charles de Gaulle-Étoile, George V, Franklin D Roosevelt or Champs-Élysées Clemenceau

Av des Champs-Élysées (the name refers to the 'Elysian Fields' where happy souls dwelt in the hereafter, according to Greek myth) links place de la Concorde with the Arc de Triomphe. The avenue has symbolised the style and *joie de vivre* of Paris since the mid-19th century and remains a popular tourist destination.

Some 400m north of av des Champs-Élysées is rue du Faubourg St-Honoré (8e), the western extension of rue St-Honoré. It has renowned couture houses, jewellers, antique shops and the 18th-century Palais de l'Élysée (cnr rue du Faubourg St-Honoré & av de Marigny, 8e; Ⓜ Champs-Élysées Clemenceau), which is the official residence of the French president.

TRANSPORT:
ÉTOILE & CHAMPS-ÉLYSÉES

Bus av des Champs-Élysées for 73 to La Défense (west) & Musée d'Orsay (east), for 42 to Grands Boulevards, Opéra & Gare du Nord

Metro Champs-Élysées Clemenceau, Charles De Gaulle-Étoile, Franklin D Roosevelt, George V

Boat Champs-Élysées Batobus stop (Port des Champs-Élysées)

At the bottom of av des Champs-Élysées, on place Clemenceau, is a 3.6m-tall bronze statue of General Charles de Gaulle in full military gear ready to march down the broad avenue to the Arc de Triomphe in a liberated Paris on 26 August 1944.

GRAND PALAIS Map pp140–1

☎ 01 44 13 17 17, reservations 08 92 68 46 94; www.grandpalais.fr, in French; 3 av du Général Eisenhower, 8e; with/without booking adult €11/10, student & 13-25yr €10/8, under 13yr free; ☽ 10am-10pm Fri-Mon & Wed, to 8pm Thu; Ⓜ Champs-Élysées Clemenceau

The 'Great Palace', erected for the 1900 Exposition Universelle, houses the Galeries Nationales du Grand Palais beneath its huge Art Nouveau glass roof. Special exhibitions, among the biggest the city stages, last three or four months. You'll understand just how popular most of the exhibitions here are – and the importance of booking in advance – when you see the queues (especially at the weekend) looping halfway round the building.

PETIT PALAIS Map pp140–1

☎ 01 53 43 40 00; www.petitpalais.paris.fr, in French; av Winston Churchill, 8e; temporary exhibits adult/14-26yr/senior & student €9/4.50/6.50, permanent collections free, under 14yr free; ☽ 10am-6pm Wed-Sun, to 8pm Tue; Ⓜ Champs-Élysées Clemenceau

The 'Little Palace', like the Grand Palais opposite also built for the 1900 Exposition Universelle, is home to the Musée des Beaux-Arts de la Ville de Paris, the Paris municipality's Museum of Fine Arts. It specialises in medieval and Renaissance objets d'art like porcelain and clocks, tapestries, drawings and 19th-century French painting and sculpture.

PALAIS DE LA DÉCOUVERTE Map pp140–1

☎ 01 56 43 20 21; www.palais-decouverte.fr, in French; av Franklin D Roosevelt, 8e; adult/senior, student & 5-18yr €7/4.50, under 5yr free; ☽ 9.30am-6pm Tue-Sat, 10am-7pm Sun; Ⓜ Champs-Élysées Clemenceau

The Palace of Discovery, inaugurated during the 1937 Exposition Universelle and thus the world's first interactive museum, is a fascinating place to take kids thanks to its hands-on exhibits on astronomy, biology, medicine, chemistry, mathematics, computer science, physics and earth sciences. The

top picks

ÉTOILE & CHAMPS-ÉLYSÉES

- Arc de Triomphe (opposite)
- Av des Champs-Élysées (opposite)
- Petit Palais (left)
- Place de la Madeleine (below)
- Place de la Concorde (below)

planetarium (admission €3.50) usually has four shows a day (in French) at 11.30am, 2pm, 3.15pm and 4.30pm; call or consult the website for current schedules.

PLACE DE LA CONCORDE Map pp140–1

Ⓜ Concorde

Place de la Concorde was laid out between 1755 and 1775. The 3300-year-old pink granite obelisk with the gilded top standing in the centre of the square was presented to France in 1831 by Muhammad Ali, viceroy and pasha of Egypt. Weighing 230 tonnes and towering 23m over the cobblestones, it once stood in the Temple of Ramses at Thebes (now Luxor). The eight female statues adorning the four corners of the square represent France's largest cities (at least in the second half of the 18th century).

In 1793, Louis XVI's head was lopped off by a guillotine set up in the northwest corner of the square near the statue representing the city of Brest. During the next two years, another guillotine – this one near the entrance to the Jardin des Tuileries – was used to behead 1343 more people, including Marie-Antoinette and, six months later, the Revolutionary leader Danton. Shortly thereafter, Robespierre lost his head here, too. The square was given its present name after the Reign of Terror in the hope that it would become a place of peace and harmony.

PLACE DE LA MADELEINE Map pp140–1

Ⓜ Madeleine

Ringed by fine-food shops, the place de la Madeleine is 350m north of place de la Concorde, at the end of rue Royale. The square is named after the 19th-century neoclassical church in its centre, the Église de Ste-Marie Madeleine (Church of St Mary Magdalene; ☎ 01 44 51 69 00; www.eglise-lamadeleine.com, in French; place de la

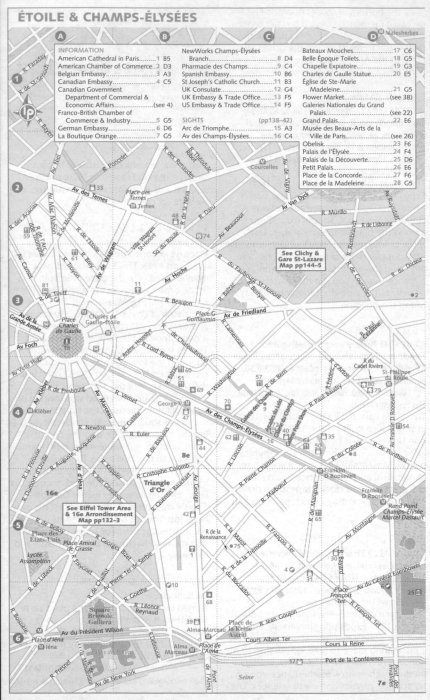

INFORMATION

American Cathedral in Paris........1	B5
American Chamber of Commerce..2	D3
Belgian Embassy........................3	A3
Canadian Embassy......................4	C5
Canadian Government	
Department of Commercial &	
Economic Affairs................(see 4)	
Franco-British Chamber of	
Commerce & Industry............5	G5
German Embassy........................6	D6
La Boutique Orange..................7	G5

NewWorks Champs-Élysées	
Branch................................8	D4
Pharmacie des Champs...............9	C4
Spanish Embassy......................10	B6
St Joseph's Catholic Church.......11	B3
UK Consulate..........................12	G4
UK Embassy & Trade Office.......13	F5
US Embassy & Trade Office.......14	F5

SIGHTS (pp138–42)

Arc de Triomphe......................15	A3
Av des Champs-Élysées.............16	C4

Bateaux Mouches.....................17	C6
Belle Époque Toilets................18	G5
Chapelle Expiatoire.................19	G3
Charles de Gaulle Statue..........20	E5
Église de Ste-Marie	
Madeleine...........................21	G5
Flower Market....................(see 38)	
Galeries Nationales du Grand	
Palais............................(see 22)	
Grand Palais...........................22	E6
Musée des Beaux-Arts de la	
Ville de Paris.................(see 26)	
Obelisk.................................23	F6
Palais de l'Élysée....................24	F4
Palais de la Découverte...........25	D6
Petit Palais............................26	E6
Place de la Concorde................27	F6
Place de la Madeleine..............28	G5

NEIGHBOURHOODS ÉTOILE & CHAMPS-ÉLYSÉES

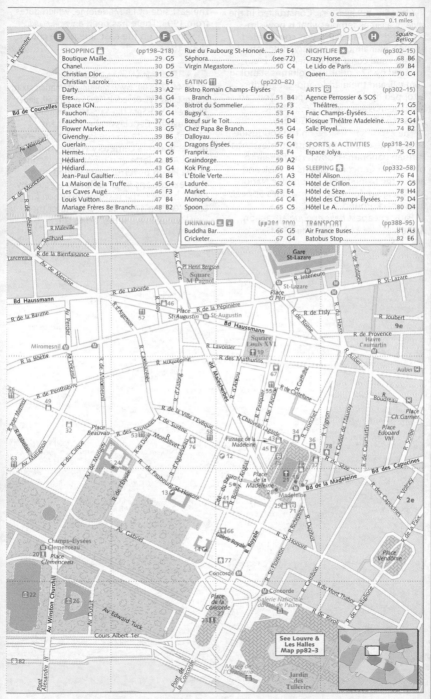

SHOPPING (pp198–218)
Boutique Maille.................29 G5
Chanel................................30 D5
Christian Dior....................31 C5
Christian Lacroix..............32 E4
Darty...................................33 A2
Eres.....................................34 G4
Espace IGN........................35 D4
Fauchon.............................36 G4
Fauchon.............................37 G4
Flower Market...................38 G5
Givenchy............................39 B6
Guerlain.............................40 C4
Hermès...............................41 G5
Hédiard..............................42 B5
Hédiard..............................43 G4
Jean-Paul Gaultier...........44 B4
La Maison de la Truffe.....45 G4
Les Caves Augé.................46 F3
Louis Vuitton....................47 B4
Mariage Frères 8e Branch...48 B2

Rue du Faubourg St-Honoré......49 E4
Séphora...................................(see 72)
Virgin Megastore....................50 C4

EATING (pp220–82)
Bistro Romain Champs-Élysées
  Branch...........................51 B4
Bistrot du Sommelier.......52 F3
Bugsy's..............................53 F4
Bœuf sur le Toit...............54 D4
Chez Papa 8e Branch.......55 G4
Dalloyau............................56 E4
Dragons Élysées...............57 E4
Franprix.............................58 F4
Graindorge........................59 A2
Kok Ping............................60 B4
L'Étoile Verte....................61 C3
Ladurée.............................62 C4
Market...............................63 C4
Monoprix...........................64 C5
Spoon................................65 C5

DRINKING (pp284–300)
Buddha Bar.......................66 G5
Cricketer............................67 G4

NIGHTLIFE (pp302–15)
Crazy Horse......................68 B6
Le Lido de Paris...............69 B4
Queen...............................70 C4

ARTS (pp302–15)
Agence Perrossier & SOS
  Théâtres.........................71 G5
Fnac Champs-Élysées......72 C4
Kiosque Théâtre Madeleine...73 G4
Salle Pleyel......................74 B2

SPORTS & ACTIVITIES (pp318–24)
Espace Joïya....................75 C5

SLEEPING (pp332–58)
Hôtel Alison.....................76 F4
Hôtel de Crillon...............77 G5
Hôtel de Sèze..................78 H4
Hôtel des Champs-Élysées...79 D4
Hôtel Le A........................80 D4

TRANSPORT (pp388–95)
Air France Buses..............81 A3
Batobus Stop....................82 E6

Madeleine, 8e; 9.30am-7pm). Constructed in the style of a Greek temple, what is now simply called 'La Madeleine' was consecrated in 1842 after almost a century of design changes and construction delays. It is surrounded by 52 Corinthian columns standing 20m tall, and the marble-and-gilt interior is topped by three sky-lit cupolas. You can hear the massive organ being played at Mass at 11am and 7pm on Sunday.

The monumental staircase on the south side affords one of the city's most quintessential Parisian panoramas: down rue Royale to place de la Concorde and its obelisk and across the Seine to the Assemblée Nationale. The gold dome of the Invalides appears in the background.

Paris' cheapest *belle époque* attraction is the public toilet (10am-noon & 1-6.15pm) on the east side of La Madeleine, which dates from 1905. There has been a flower market (8am-8pm) on the east side of the church since 1832.

CHAPELLE EXPIATOIRE Map pp140-1

01 44 32 18 00; www.monuments-nationaux.fr; square Louis XVI, 8e; adult/18-25yr €5/3.50, under 18yr free; 1-5pm Thu-Sat; M St-Augustin
The austere, neoclassical Atonement Chapel, opposite 36 rue Pasquier, sits atop the section of a cemetery where Louis XVI, Marie-Antoinette and many other victims of the Reign of Terror were buried after their executions in 1793. It was erected by Louis' brother, the restored Bourbon king Louis XVIII, in 1815. Two years later the royal bones were removed to the Basilique de St-Denis (p182).

CLICHY & GARE ST-LAZARE

Drinking p294; Eating p263; Sleeping p352

This area stretches from the elegant residential districts of the *haute bourgeoisie* (upper middle class) that surround 8.25-hectare Parc de Monceau in the 8e eastward to the Gare St-Lazare, an impressive iron structure built in 1851, and then north to Clichy and the 17e arrondissement.

The 17e is a veritable kaleidoscope of different identies. Its southern neighbourhoods – with their beautiful, Haussmann-era buildings – seem almost like an extension of the 8e and 16e arrondissements, while its northern neighbourhoods assert their working-class, anarchistic identity. The wide av de Wagram, av des Ternes and av de Villiers have both residential and commercial aspects and boast some fine restaurants and shops. A maze of small streets with a pronounced working-class character stretches out around the av de Clichy, a pocket of old Paris that has somehow managed to survive.

The Clichy-Batignolles district to the west of the av de Clichy is a new *quartier* boasting socially integrated housing around a 10-hectare park.

MUSÉE JACQUEMART-ANDRÉ Map pp144–5

☎ 01 45 62 11 59; www.musee-jacquemart-andre
.com; 158 blvd Haussmann, 8e; adult/7-17yr &
student incl audioguide €10/7.30, under 7yr free;
☉ 10am-6pm; Ⓜ Miromesnil

The Jacquemart-André Museum, founded by collector Édouard André and his portrait-ist wife Nélie Jacquemart, is in an opulent mid-19th-century residence on one of Paris' posher avenues. It has furniture, tapestries and enamels, but is most noted for its paintings by Rembrandt and Van Dyck and Italian Renaissance works by Bernini, Botticelli, Carpaccio, Donatello, Mantegna, Tintoretto, Titian and Uccello. Don't miss the Jardin d'Hiver (Winter Garden), with its marble statuary, tropical plants and double-helix marble stair-case. Just off it is the delightful *tumoir* (the erstwhile smoking room) filled with exotic objects collected by Jacquemart during her travels. The salon de thé (tearoom; ☉ 11.45am-5.45pm) is one of the most beautiful in the city.

MUSÉE NISSIM DE CAMONDO Map pp144–5

☎ 01 53 89 06 50; www.lesartsdecoratifs.fr;
63 rue de Monceau, 8e; adult/18-25yr €6/4.50,

under 18yr free; ☉ 10am-5.30pm Wed-Sun;
Ⓜ Monceau or Villiers

The Nissim de Camondo Museum, housed in a sumptuous mansion modelled on the Petit Trianon at Versailles (p360), displays 18th-century furniture, wood panelling, tapestries, porcelain and other *objets d'art* collected by Count Moïse de Camondo, a Sephardic Jewish banker who settled in Paris from Constantinople in the late 19th century. He bequeathed the mansion and his collection to the state on the proviso that it would be a museum named in memory of his son Nissim (1892–1917),

NICOLA'S TOP PARIS DAY

When Matthias sought to convince me a dozen years ago that France was the country we should plump for, he sensibly whisked me to Paris, where we spent a whirlwind week of perfect days...zigzagging around Daniel Buren's zebra columns at the Palais Royal (p88), visiting Musée Picasso (p96) and Musée Rodin (p130), marvelling at that incredible blue at Ste-Chapelle (p107), ogling at the view of La Grande Arche (p180) slotted like a toy brick inside the Arc de Triomphe (p138) from place de la Concorde and the Champs-Élysées, eating ice cream on Île St-Louis (p249) and lounging *forever* in the Jardin du Luxembourg (p119) on those mythical sage-green chairs we then yearned to buy for years: (Fermob (p216) was finally allowed to reproduce the 1923 original – mine's fuschia pink, his, boy-blue). These still are my perfect Parisian days, pebble-dashed with fave-of-the-moment food/drink addresses: Le Coupe-Chou (p250), Le Cristal del Sel (p276), Le Pré Verre (p252), Le Verre à Pied (p290), the Curio Parlor Cocktail Club (p290) and Quatrehommes (p259).

lonelyplanet.com

INFORMATION
Hôtel de Police (Carte de Séjour)..1 G4
Institut Parisien de Langue & de
  Civilisation Françaises............2 F6
Japanese Embassy.....................3 D6
Pharmacie Européenne.............4 H4

SIGHTS (pp143–6)
Musée Cernuschi......................5 F5
Musée des Arts de l'Asie.........(see 5)
Musée Jacquemart-André.........6 E6
Musée Nissim de Camondo.......7 F5
Parc de Monceau.....................8 E5

SHOPPING (pp198–218)
Fromagerie Alléosse..................9 C5

EATING (pp220–82)
Au Bon Coin...........................10 G4
AÀ la Grande Bleue.................11 G2
Bistro des Dames...................(see 26)
Charlot, Roi des Coquillages......12 H4
Joy in Food..........................(see 13)
La Gaieté Cosaque..................13 G4
La Maffiosa di Termoli.............14 H4
La Tête de Goinfre..................15 G3
Marché des Batignolles............16 G5
Rue Poncelet & Rue Bayen
  (Market)............................17 C5

DRINKING (pp284–300)
Bar à Vins du Cinéma
  des Cinéastes......................(see 20)
Le Wepler.............................18 H4
Lush Bar...............................19 H4

ARTS (pp302–16)
Cinéma des Cinéastes..............20 H4
Fnac Étoile............................21 C5
Fnac St-Lazare.......................22 H6

SLEEPING (pp332–58)
Austin's St-Lazare Hôtel............23 H6
Hôtel Aurore Montmartre.........24 H5
Hôtel Britannia.......................25 H6
Hôtel Eldorado.......................26 H4
New Orient Hôtel.....................27 G5

TRANSPORT (pp388–95)
ADA Car Rental.......................28 G5
Buses from Beauvais Airport......29 A5
Parking Pershing.....................30 A5

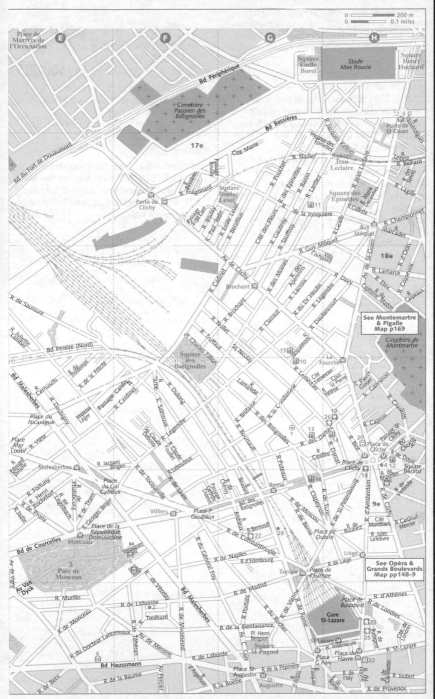

See Montemartre
& Pigalle
Map p169

See Opéra &
Grands Boulevards
Map pp148–9

145

a pilot killed in action during WWI. The museum is run by the same group responsible for the trio of museums in the Rohan Wing of the Palais du Louvre called Les Arts Décoratifs (p84).

MUSÉE CERNUSCHI Map pp144–5

☎ 01 53 96 21 50; www.cernuschi.paris.fr, in French; 7 av Vélasquez, 8e; temporary exhibits adult/14-26yr/student & senior €7/3.50/5.50, permanent collections free, under 14yr free; ☉ 10am-6pm Tue-Sun; Ⓜ Villiers

The Cernuschi Museum, renovated and its exhibition space redefined and enlarged in recent years, houses the city of Paris' Musée des Arts de l'Asie (Asian Arts Museum). In essence it's a collection of ancient Chinese art (funerary statues, bronzes, ceramics)

top picks

SQUARES

- Place des Vosges (p91)
- Place du Marché Ste-Catherine (Map pp98–9)
- Place de la Contrescarpe (p193)
- Rue de Furstemberg (Map pp116–17)
- Village St-Paul (p192)

and some works from Japan assembled during an 1871–73 world tour by the Milan banker and philanthropist Henri Cernuschi (1821–96), who settled in Paris before the unification of Italy.

OPÉRA & GRANDS BOULEVARDS

Drinking p295; Eating p264; Shopping p215; Sleeping p353

Place de l'Opéra, site of Paris' world-famous opera house, abuts the eight contiguous 'Grands Boulevards' (Madeleine, Capucines, Italiens, Montmartre, Poissonnière, Bonne Nouvelle, St-Denis and St-Martin) that stretch from elegant place de la Madeleine in the 8e eastwards to the up-and-coming place de la République (Map pp94–5) in the 3e, a distance of just under 3km. The Grands Boulevards were laid out under Louis XIV in the 17th century on the site of obsolete city walls and served as a centre of café and theatre life through much of the 18th and 19th centuries, reaching the height of fashion during the *belle époque* (p26). North of the western end of the Grands Boulevards is blvd Haussmann (8e and 9e), the heart of the commercial and banking district and known for some of Paris' most famous department stores, including Galeries Lafayette and Le Printemps.

PALAIS GARNIER Map pp148–9
www.operadeparis.fr, in French; place de l'Opéra, 9e; M Opéra
This renowned opera house was designed in 1860 by Charles Garnier to showcase the splendour of Napoleon III's France. Unfortunately, by the time it was completed – 15 years later – the Second Empire was but a distant memory and Napoleon III had been dead for two years. Still, this is one of the most impressive monuments erected in Paris during the 19th century; today it stages ballets, classical music concerts and, of course, opera (p315). If you're not catching a performance here, it can be visited on English-language guided tours (☎ 08 25 05 44 05; http://visites.operadeparis.fr; adult/10-25yr/senior €12/6/10; ⏲ 11.30am & 2.30pm daily Jul & Aug, 11.30am & 2.30pm Wed, Sat & Sun Sep-Jun).

The Palais Garnier also houses the Musée de l'Opéra (☎ 08 92 89 90 90, 01 40 01 24 93; adult/senior, student & 10-25yr €8/5, under 10yr free; ⏲ 10am-5pm Sep-Jun, to 6pm Jul & Aug), which contains three centuries' worth of costumes, backdrops, scores and other memorabilia. Included in the admission to the museum is a self-paced visit to the opera house itself, as long as there's not a daytime rehearsal or matinee scheduled (in which case it closes at 1pm).

MUSÉE DU PARFUM Map pp148–9
☎ 01 47 42 04 56; www.fragonard.com; 9 rue Scribe, 2e; admission free; ⏲ 9am-6pm Mon-Sat, 9.30am-4pm Sun mid-Mar–Oct; M Opéra
The Perfume Museum, run by the *perfumerie* Fragonard (but under extensive renovation when we last visited), is a fragrant collection opposite the Palais Garnier, tracing the history of scent and perfume-making from ancient Egypt (those mum-

mies wouldn't have smelled very nice undoused) to today's designer brands. A short distance to the south is the Théâtre-Musée des Capucines (Map pp02 3; ☎ 01 42 60 37 14; 39 blvd des Capucines, 2e; ⏲ 9am-6pm Mon-Sat; M Opéra), a kind of branch located in an early 20th-century theatre that concentrates largely on bottling (for example, in crystal flasks from Bohemia) and packaging the heady substance. There's a decent short film here and, of course, a shop selling Fragonard scents.

MUSÉE GRÉVIN Map pp148–9
☎ 01 47 70 85 05; www.grevin.com; 10 blvd Montmartre, 9e; adult/6-14yr/under 6yr/senior& student €18.50/11/9.50/16; ⏲ 10am-6.30pm Mon-Fri, to 7pm Sat & Sun; M Grands Boulevards
This large waxworks museum inside the passage Jouffroy boasts an impressive 300 wax figures. They largely look more like caricatures than characters, but where else do you get to see Marilyn Monroe, Charles de Gaulle and Spider Man face to face, or the original death masks of some of the French Revolution leaders? The recently renovated Palais des Mirages (Hall of Mirrors), created for the 1889 Exposition Universelle, dazzles, but the admission fee is positively outrageous and just won't stop a-growin' each year.

MUSÉE DE LA FRANC-MAÇONNERIE
Map pp148–9
☎ 01 45 23 74 07; 16 rue Cadet, 9e; admission €2; ⏲ 2-6pm Tue-Sat; M Cadet or Peletier
This museum, housed in the colossal and quite impressive Grande Orient de France building, provides a brief introduction to the secretive world of Freemasonry, which grew out of medieval stonemasons' guilds of the 16th century. A visit to the museum

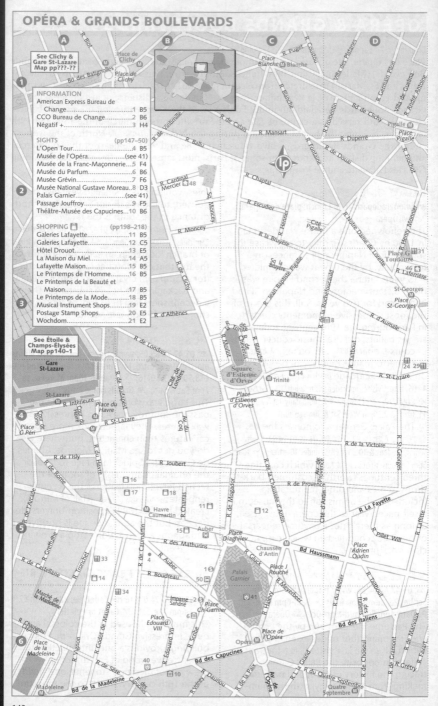

See Clichy &
Gare St-Lazare
Map pp???-??

See Étoile &
Champs-Elysées
Map pp140–1

148

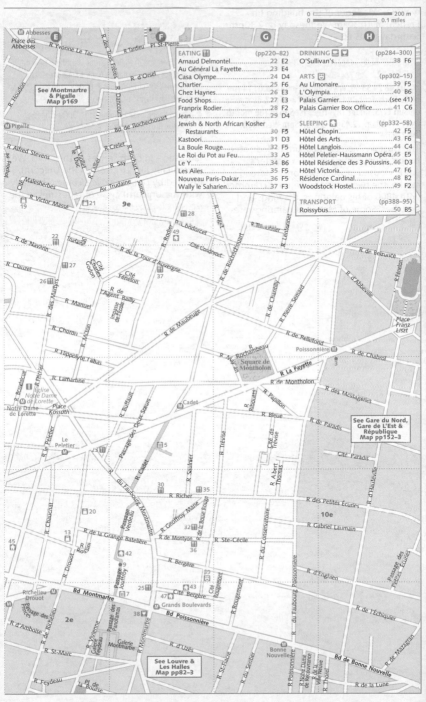

EATING 🍴	(pp220–82)
Arnaud Delmontel	22 E2
Au Général La Fayette	23 E4
Casa Olympe	24 D4
Chartier	25 F6
Chez Haynes	26 E3
Food Shops	27 E3
Franprix Rodier	28 F2
Jean	29 D4
Jewish & North African Kosher	
Restaurants	30 F5
Kastoori	31 D3
La Boule Rouge	32 F5
Le Roi du Pot au Feu	33 F5
Le Y	34 B6
Les Ailes	35 F5
Nouveau Paris-Dakar	36 F5
Wally le Saharien	37 F3

DRINKING 🍷 🍸	(pp284–300)
O'Sullivan's	38 F6

ARTS 🎭	(pp302–15)
Au Limonaire	39 F5
L'Olympia	40 B6
Palais Garnier	(see 41)
Palais Garnier Box Office	41 C6

SLEEPING 🛏	(pp332–58)
Hôtel Chopin	42 F5
Hôtel des Arts	43 F6
Hôtel Langlois	44 C4
Hôtel Peletier-Haussmann Opéra	45 E5
Hôtel Résidence des 3 Poussins	46 D3
Hôtel Victoria	47 F6
Résidence Cardinal	48 B2
Woodstock Hostel	49 F2

TRANSPORT	(pp388–95)
Roissybus	50 B5

NEIGHBOURHOODS OPÉRA & GRANDS BOULEVARDS

with a guided tour of the building (in French) at 10.30am Wednesday or 2.30pm Saturday costs €6.

MUSÉE NATIONAL GUSTAVE MOREAU Map pp148–9

☎ 01 48 74 38 50; www.musee-moreau.fr; 14 rue de La Rochefoucauld, 9e; adult/18-25yr & everyone on Sun €7/5, under 18yr free, 1st Sun of the month free; ⊗ 10am-12.45pm & 2-5.15pm Wed-Mon; Ⓜ Trinité

The Gustave Moreau Museum is dedicated to the eponymous symbolist painter's work. Housed in what was once Moreau's studio, the two-storey museum is crammed with 4800 of his paintings, drawings and sketches. Some of Moreau's paintings are

TRANSPORT: OPÉRA & GRANDS BOULEVARDS

Bus Opéra for 20 to République, Bastille & Gare de Lyon, for 22 to Charles de Gaulle-Étoile, for 29 to place des Victoires, Marais & Bastille, and for 39 to Palais Royal and St-Germain des Prés

Metro Cadet, Grands Boulevards, Opéra, Chaussée d'Antin, Richelieu Drouot

fantastic – in both senses of the word. We particularly like *La Licorne* (The Unicorn), inspired by *La Dame à la Licorne* (The Lady with the Unicorn) cycle of tapestries in the Musée National du Moyen Age (p114).

GARE DU NORD, GARE DE L'EST & RÉPUBLIQUE

Drinking p295; Eating p266; Shopping p215; Sleeping p354

Two sorts of foot traffic give the 10e arrondissement its distinctive feel. The banks of the Canal St-Martin draw leisurely strollers, while travellers part (and are reunited) on the platforms of the Gare du Nord and Gare de l'Est. Outside, the cafés and brasseries do a brisk trade, catering to travellers and locals. Nearby, the blvd de Magenta rushes like a swollen river, the noisy, impatient crowd spreading through the adjoining streets and pouring out onto the place de la République.

The buzzy, working-class area around blvd de Strasbourg and rue du Faubourg St-Denis, especially south of blvd de Magenta, is home to large communities of Indians, Bangladeshis, Pakistanis, West Indians, Africans, Turks and Kurds. Indeed, strolling through passage Brady (p268) is almost like stepping into a back alley in Mumbai or Dhaka.

Canal St-Martin – especially the quai de Jemmapes and the quai de Valmy, with their rows of plane and chestnut trees – seems a world away. Barges appear, pass silently, then vanish behind a lock. Little iron bridges and walkways span the still water. Rundown not so long ago, the canal has a new lease on life, helped in large part by the upmarket restaurants and bistros lining it.

CANAL ST-MARTIN Map pp152–3

M République, Jaurès, Jacques Bonsergent

The tranquil, 4.5km-long St-Martin Canal links the 10e with Parc de la Villette (Map pp174–5) in the 19e via the Bassin de la Villette and Canal de l'Ourcq, and the canal makes its famous dogleg turn in this arrondissement. Its shaded towpaths are a wonderful place for a romantic stroll or a bike ride and take you past nine locks, metal bridges and ordinary Parisian neighbourhoods. Parts of the waterway – built between 1806 and 1825 to link the Seine with the 108km-long Canal de l'Ourcq – are higher than the surrounding land. The best way to see the canal is on tour from a canal boat (p406).

TRANSPORT: GARE DU NORD, GARE DE L'EST & RÉPUBLIQUE

Bus Gare de l'Est for 30 to Barbès, Pigalle, Place Clichy, Parc de Monceau, place des Ternes, place de l'Étoile & Trocadéro, for 31 to Barbès, Château Rouge, 18e arrondissement Mairie, Batignolles & place de l'Étoile, for 32 to Rond Point des Champs Élysées, av Champs-Élysées & Passy, for 39 for Palais Royal, St-Germain, rue de Sèvres & Porte de Versailles, for 47 for Centre Pompidou & Châtelet

Metro & RER Château d'Eau, Gare de l'Est, Gare du Nord, République, Strasbourg St-Denis

Train Gare de l'Est, Gare du Nord

PORTE ST-DENIS & PORTE ST-MARTIN Map pp152–3

cnr rue du Faubourg St-Denis & blvd St-Denis, 10e; **M** Strasbourg St-Denis

St Denis Gate, a 24m-high triumphal arch, was built in 1673 to commemorate Louis XIV's campaign along the Rhine. On the northern side, carvings represent the fall of Maastricht in the same year (note the gilded fleur-de-lys).

Two blocks east is a similar arch, the less impressive, 17m-high Porte St-Martin (St Martin Gate) at the corner of rue du Faubourg St-Martin and blvd St-Denis. It was erected two years after Porte St-Denis to commemorate the capture of Besançon and the Franche-Comté region by Louis XIV's armies.

MUSÉE DE L'ÉVANTAIL Map pp152–3

☎ 01 42 08 90 20; 2 blvd de Strasbourg, 10e; adult/student/senior €6/3/4; ⏱ 2-6pm Mon-Wed; **M** Strasbourg St-Denis

Big fans of this museum, we always find it almost impossible to walk by without checking in on our favourite items screen, folding and brisé (the kind with overlapping struts) fans. Around 900 of the breeze-makers are on display, dating as far back as the mid-18th century. The small museum is housed in what was once a well-known fan manufactory, and its original showroom, dating from 1893, is sublime. It's open every weekday during the school holidays.

GARE DU NORD, GARE DE L'EST & RÉPUBLIQUE

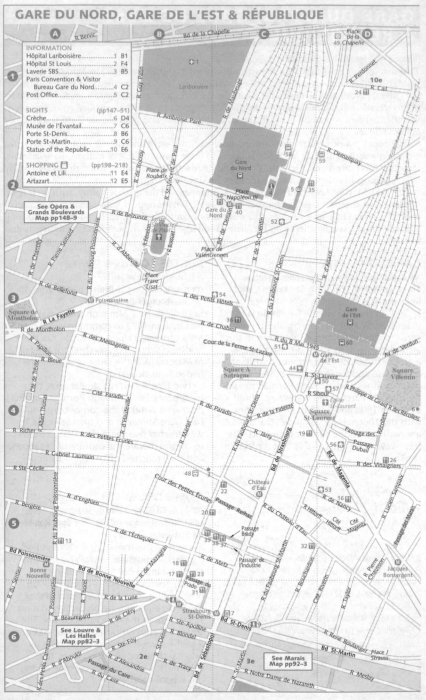

INFORMATION
Hôpital Lariboisière...............1 B1
Hôpital St Louis....................2 F4
Laverie SBS.........................3 B5
Paris Convention & Visitor
  Bureau Gare du Nord.........4 C2
Post Office..........................5 C2

SIGHTS   (pp147–51)
Crèche...............................6 D4
Musée de l'Éventail.............7 C6
Porte St-Denis.....................8 B6
Porte St-Martin...................9 C6
Statue of the Republic........10 E6

SHOPPING   (pp198–218)
Antoine et Lili...................11 E4
Artazart............................12 E5

See Opéra &
Grands Boulevards
Map pp148–9

See Louvre &
Les Halles
Map pp82–3

See Marais
Map pp92–3

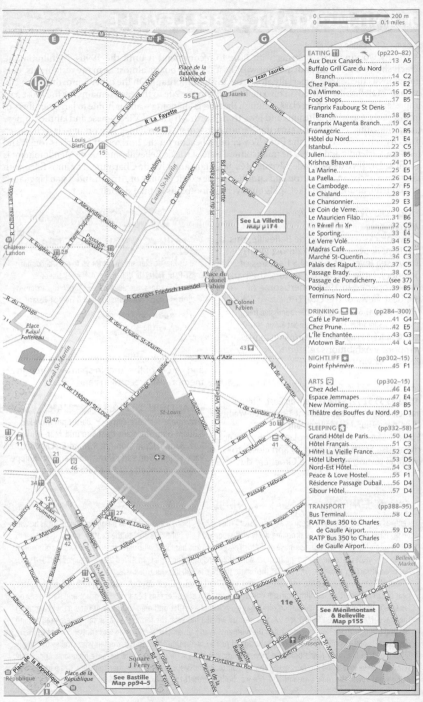

EATING 🍴 (pp220–82)
Aux Deux Canards..............13 A5
Buffalo Grill Gare du Nord
  Branch.........................14 C2
Chez Papa........................15 E2
Da Mimmo........................16 D5
Food Shops.......................17 B5
Franprix Faubourg St Denis
  Branch.........................18 B5
Franprix Magenta Branch......19 C4
Fromagerie.......................20 B5
Hôtel du Nord...................21 E4
Istanbul..........................22 C5
Julien.............................23 B5
Krishna Bhavan..................24 D1
La Marine........................25 E5
La Paella.........................26 D4
Le Cambodge.....................27 F5
Le Chaland.......................28 F3
Le Chansonnier..................29 E3
Le Coin de Verre................30 G4
Le Mauricien Filao...............31 B6
Le Réveil du Xe.................32 C5
Le Sporting......................33 E4
Le Verre Volé....................34 E5
Madras Café.....................35 C2
Marché St-Quentin..............36 C3
Palais des Rajput................37 C5
Passage Brady....................38 C5
Passage de Pondicherry.......(see 37)
Pooja.............................39 B5
Terminus Nord...................40 C2

DRINKING 🍷 🍸 (pp284–300)
Café Le Panier...................41 G4
Chez Prune.......................42 E5
L'Île Enchantée..................43 G3
Motown Bar......................44 C4

NIGHTLIFE 🌃 (pp302–15)
Point Éphémère..................45 F1

ARTS 🎭 (pp302–15)
Chez Adel........................46 E4
Espace Jemmapes................47 E4
New Morning.....................48 B5
Théâtre des Bouffes du Nord.49 D1

SLEEPING 🛏 (pp332–58)
Grand Hôtel de Paris............50 D4
Hôtel Français...................51 C3
Hôtel La Vieille France.........52 C2
Hôtel Liberty....................53 D5
Nord-Est Hôtel..................54 C3
Peace & Love Hostel............55 F1
Résidence Passage Dubail......56 D4
Sibour Hôtel.....................57 D4

TRANSPORT (pp388–95)
Bus Terminal.....................58 C2
RATP Bus 350 to Charles
  de Gaulle Airport.............59 D2
RATP Bus 350 to Charles
  de Gaulle Airport.............60 D3

MÉNILMONTANT & BELLEVILLE

Drinking p296; Eating p269

A solidly working-class *quartier* with little to recommend it until the 1990s, Ménilmontant, which shares the 11e arrondissement with Bastille, now boasts almost as many restaurants, bars and clubs as the Marais, especially along rue de Ménilmontant. On the other hand, the inner-city 'village' of Belleville, centred on blvd de Belleville in the 20e to the east, remains for the most part unpretentious and working class – though that too is changing – and is home to large numbers of immigrants, especially Muslims and Jews from North Africa and Vietnamese and ethnic Chinese from Indochina. For the most part, the 20e arrondissement has retained its working-class character. The city centre is far away, the Eiffel Tower but a beacon on the horizon; this Paris is rough and rebellious, friendly and alive. The multicultural tone of rue de Belleville and rue de Ménilmontant is amplified by blvd de Belleville, blvd de Ménilmontant and blvd de Charonne. The air is filled with the aroma of coriander, saffron and cumin, and the exotic sounds of African and Asian languages. A colourful, abundant market spills out over the footpaths of blvd de Belleville.

PARC DE BELLEVILLE Map p155

Ⓜ Couronnes

A few blocks east of blvd de Belleville, this lovely park occupies a hill almost 200m above sea level, set amid 4.5 hectares of greenery. Little known by visitors, the park (which opened in 1992) offers some of the best views of the city. The Maison de l'Air (☎ 01 43 28 47 63; 27 rue Piat, 20e; admission free; ☽ 1.30-5.30pm Tue-Fri, to 6.30pm Sat & Sun Mar-Oct, to 5.30pm Tue-Sun Nov-Feb; Ⓜ Pyrénées) stages temporary exhibitions related to ecology and the environment.

MUSÉE ÉDITH PIAF Map p155

☎ 01 43 55 52 72; 5 rue Crespin du Gast, 11e; admission free; ☽ by appointment 1-6pm Mon-Wed, 10am-noon Thu; Ⓜ Ménilmontant

Some 1.5km from the birthplace of the iconic chanteuse Édith Piaf (see p311) and closer to her final resting place in the Cimetière du

TRANSPORT: MÉNILMONTANT & BELLEVILLE

Bus Rue de Ménilmontant for 96 to rue Oberkampf, St-Paul, Hôtel de Ville, blvd St-Michel, Odéon & rue de Rennes; rue des Pyrénées for 26 to Parc des Buttes-Chaumont, Gare du Nord & Gare St-Lazare

Metro Belleville, Couronnes, Ménilmontant, Oberkampf, Pyrénées

Père Lachaise, this museum follows the life and career of the 'urchin sparrow' through memorabilia, recordings and video.

CIMETIÈRE DU PÈRE LACHAISE Map p155

www.pere-lachaise.com; ☽ 8am-6pm Mon-Fri, 8.30am-6pm Sat, 9am-6pm Sun mid-Mar–early Nov, 8am-5.30pm Mon-Fri, 8.30am-5.30pm Sat, 9am-5.30pm Sun early Nov–mid-Mar; Ⓜ Philippe Auguste, Gambetta or Père Lachaise

GRAVE CONCERNS AT PÈRE LACHAISE

Camp as a row of tents and as fresh as a daisy, Oscar Wilde (1854–1900) is apparently as flamboyant in death as he was on his hotel deathbed, when he proclaimed 'My wallpaper and I are fighting a duel to the death – one of us has *got* to go.' It seems that the Père Lachaise grave of the Irish playwright and humorist, who was sentenced to two years in prison in 1895 for gross indecency stemming from his homosexual relationship with Lord Alfred 'Bosie' Douglas (1870–1945), has been attracting admirers, who plaster the ornate tomb with indelible lipstick kisses.

But Wilde's tomb is not the only grave concern at Père Lachaise these days. A security guard had to be posted near the grave of rock singer Jim Morrison (1943–71) not long ago after fans began taking drugs and having sex on his tomb. The cemetery's conservation office has even issued a leaflet outlining the rules of conduct when visiting the grave. Meanwhile, up in division 92, a protest by women has seen the removal of a metal fence placed around the grave of one Victor Noir, pseudonym of the journalist Yvan Salman (1848–70), who was shot and killed by Pierre Bonaparte, great-nephew of Napoleon, at the age of just 22. According to legend, a woman who strokes the amply filled crotch of Monsieur Noir's prostrate bronze effigy will enjoy a better sex life or become pregnant. Apparently some would-be lovers and mothers were rubbing a bit too enthusiastically and the larger-than-life-size package was being worn down, the (now dismantled) fence was built to protect the statue.

The world's most visited cemetery, Père Lachaise (named after a confessor of Louis XIV) opened its one-way doors in 1804. Its 69,000 ornate, even ostentatious, tombs of the rich and/or famous form a verdant, 44-hectare sculpture garden. Among the 800,000 people buried here are: the composer Chopin; the playwright Molière; the poet Apollinaire; writers Balzac, Proust, Gertrude Stein and Colette; the actors Simone Signoret, Sarah Bernhardt and Yves Montand; the painters Pissarro, Seurat, Modigliani and Delacroix; the *chanteuse* (singer) Édith Piaf; the dancer Isadora Duncan; and even those immortal 12th-century lovers, Abélard and Héloïse (see p33), whose remains were disinterred and reburied here together in 1817 beneath a neogothic tombstone.

Particularly visited graves are those of Oscar Wilde, interred in Division 89 in 1900, and 1960s rock star Jim Morrison, who died in an flat at 17–19 rue Beautreillis (4e; Map pp92–3) in the Marais in 1971 and is buried in Division 6.

On 27 May 1871, the last of the Communard insurgents, cornered by government forces, fought a hopeless, all-night battle among the tombstones. In the morning, the 147 survivors were lined up against the Mur des Fédérés (Wall of the Federalists), shot and buried where they fell in a mass grave. It is in the southeastern section of the cemetery.

Père Lachaise has five entrances, two of which are on blvd de Ménilmontant. Maps indicating the location of noteworthy graves are available for free from the conservation office (☎ 01 55 25 82 10; 16 rue du Repos, 20e) in the southwestern corner of the cemetery.

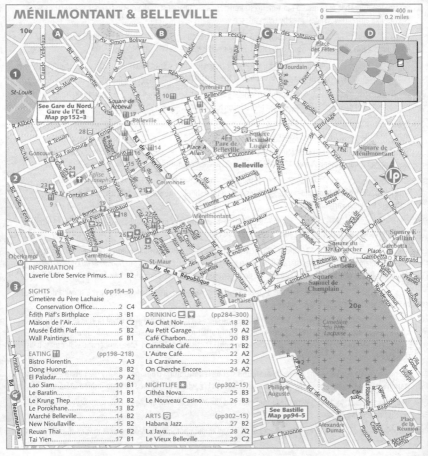

MÉNILMONTANT & BELLEVILLE

		0	400 m
		0	0.2 miles

INFORMATION
Laverie Libre Service Primus.......1 B2

SIGHTS (pp154–5)
Cimetière du Père Lachaise
  Conservation Office...............2 C4
Édith Piaf's Birthplace 3 B1
Maison de l'Air........................4 C2
Musée Édith Piaf.....................5 B2
Wall Paintings.........................6 B1

EATING 🍴 (pp198–218)
Bistro Florentin......................7 A3
Dong Huong..........................8 B2
El Paladar..............................9 A2
Lao Siam..............................10 B1
Le Baratin.............................11 B1
Le Krung Thep......................12 B3
Le Porokhane........................13 B2
Marché Belleville..................14 B2
New Nioullaville....................15 B2
Reuan Thai............................16 B2
Tai Yien................................17 B1

DRINKING 🍷 🍸 (pp284–300)
Au Chat Noir.........................18 B2
Au Petit Garage......................19 A2
Café Charbon.........................20 B3
Cannibale Café.......................21 B2
L'Autre Café...........................22 A2
La Caravane...........................23 A2
On Cherche Encore................24 A2

NIGHTLIFE ⭐ (pp302–15)
Cithéa Nova...........................25 B3
Le Nouveau Casino...............26 B3

ARTS 🎭 (pp302–15)
Habana Jazz...........................27 B2
La Java...................................28 A2
Le Vieux Belleville.................29 C2

See Gare du Nord,
Gare de l'Est
Map pp152–3

See Bastille
Map pp94–5

UNDERGROUND ART

Museums and galleries are not the sole proprietors of art in Paris. Indeed, it is all around you – even in metro stations. Almost half of the 373 stations were given a face-lift to mark the centenary of the world-famous Métropolitain in 2000, and many of them were assigned specific themes, usually relating to the *quartier* or the name of the station (eg Montparnasse Bienvenüe looks at the creation of the metro since it was an engineer named Fulgence Bienvenüe who oversaw the building of the first 91km from 1886). Work has continued apace at even more stations ever since.

Line 14 – the so-called 'Météor' between St-Lazare and Olympiades in the 13e – is a particularly arty one, especially on the way down to the platforms, where art is projected onto the walls at different levels. At varying times, other stations and lines might have temporary exhibitions. In 2008 line 10 made use of a ghost station (Croix Rouge, between Sèvres-Babylone and Mabillon) to tease with pink neon and demure black curtains, promoting an X-rated exhibition on erotic art and pornography at the Bibliothèque Nationale de France.

Though very much 'above ground', the nine works of art that follow the 8km course of tram line T3 (p395) through the 13e, 14e and 15e includes a giant 'Telephone' by Sophie Calle and Frank Gehry and a wonderful 'Skate Park' by Peter Kogler.

The following list is just a sample of the most interesting stations from an artistic perspective. The specific platform is mentioned for those stations served by more than one line.

Abbesses (Map p169; **line 12**) The noodle-like pale-green metalwork and glass canopy of the station entrance is one of the finest examples of the work of Hector Guimard (1867–1942), the celebrated French Art Nouveau architect whose signature style once graced most metro stations. For a complete list of the metro stations that retain *édicules* (shrine-like entranceways) designed by Guimard, see www.parisinconnu.com.

Arts et Métiers (Map pp92–3; **line 11 platform**) The copper panelling, portholes and mechanisms of this station recall Jules Verne, Captain Nemo and collections of the nearby Musée des Arts et Métiers.

Bastille (Map pp94–5; **line 5 platform**) A large ceramic fresco features scenes taken from newspaper engravings published during the Revolution, with illustrations of the destruction of the infamous prison.

Bibliothèque (Map pp162–3; **line 14**) This enormous station – all screens, steel and glass, and the terminus of the high-speed (and driverless) Météor – resembles a hi-tech cathedral.

Bonne Nouvelle (Map pp148–9; **platforms on lines 8 & 9**) The theme here is cinema, presumably because of all the movie theatres along the Grands Boulevards.

Carrefour Pleyel (**line 13**) This station just south of St-Denis (Map p182) and named in honour of composer and piano-maker Ignace Joseph Pleyel (1757–1831) focuses on classical music.

Champs-Élysées Clemenceau (Map pp140–1; **transfer corridor btwn lines 1 & 13**) The elegant frescoes in blue enamelled faïence recall Portuguese *azulejos* tiles and so they should: they were installed as part of a cultural exchange between Paris and Lisbon.

Cluny–La Sorbonne (Map pp110–11; **line 10 platform**) A large ceramic mosaic replicates the signatures of intellectuals, artists and scientists from the Latin Quarter through history.

Concorde (Map pp82–3; **line 12 platform**) On the walls of the station, what look like children's building blocks in white-and-blue ceramic are 45,000 tiles that spell out the text of the *Déclaration des Droits de l'Homme et du Citoyen* (Declaration of the Rights of Man and of the Citizen), the document setting forth the principles of the French Revolution.

Louvre–Rivoli (Map p86; **line 1 platform & corridor**) Statues, bas-reliefs and photographs offer a small taste of what to expect at the Musée du Louvre above ground.

Palais Royal–Musée du Louvre (Map p86) The zany entrance on the place du Palais Royal (a kind of back-to-the-future look at the Guimard entrances), designed by young artist Jean-Michel Othoniel, is made up of two crown-shaped cupolas (one representing the day, the other night) consisting of 800 red, blue, amber and violet glass balls threaded on an aluminium structure.

Parmentier (Map pp94–5; **line 3**) The theme in this station is agricultural crops, particularly the potato – it was the station's namesake, Antoine-Auguste Parmentier (1737–1817), who brought the spud into fashion in France.

Pont Neuf (Map p105; **line 7**) With the former mint and the Musée de la Monnaie de Paris just above it, the focus here is on medals and coins.

Tuileries (Map pp82–3; **line 1**) Huge collages of B&W and colour photographs depict events in Paris since 1900.

GARE DE LYON, NATION & BERCY

Drinking p297; Eating p271; Shopping p216; Sleeping p355

The southern part of the 12e arrondissement is a fairly well-to-do *quartier*, and at the weekend hordes of cyclists and soccer players head for the woods. Walkers can stroll along the Promenade Plantée, a path along the viaduct above av Daumesnil. Within the arches, there are upmarket shops, galleries and cafés. On the other side of the Gare de Lyon, there's the Parc de Bercy, where an orchard, vegetable patch and garden have replaced the old wine market.

Long cut off from the rest of the city but now joined to the Left Bank by the driverless Météor metro line (number 14), the vehicular Pont Charles de Gaulle and the stunning new Passerelle Simone de Beauvoir footbridge linking Parc de Bercy with the Bibliothèque National de France, Bercy has some of Paris' most important new buildings, including Palais Omnisports de Paris-Bercy, serving as both an indoor sports arena and a venue for concerts, ballet and theatre; the giant Ministère de l'Économie, des Finances et de l'Industrie; the stunning Cinémathèque Française and the Docks en Seine (p161), across the river. The development of Bercy Village, a row of former *chais* (wine warehouses) dating from 1877 that now houses bars and restaurants, and the arrival of river barges fitted out with music clubs have given the 12e a new lease on life after dark.

VIADUC DES ARTS Map pp158–9

Ⓜ Gare de Lyon or Daumesnil

The arches beneath this disused railway viaduct running along av Daumesnil south-east of place de la Bastille are a showcase for trendy designers and artisans; if you need your Gobelins tapestry restored, porcelain repainted or the bottom of your antique saucepan re-coppered, this is the place to come. The top of the viaduct forms a leafy, 4.5km-long promenade called the Promenade Plantée (Map pp158–9; Ⓨ 8am-5.45pm to 9.30pm Mon-Fri, 9am 5.45pm to 9.30pm Sat & Sun seasonal), which offers excellent views of the surrounding area. Don't miss the spectacular Art Deco police station (Map pp158–9; 85 av Daumesnil, 12e) at the start of rue de Rambouillet, which is topped with a dozen huge, identical marble torsos.

MAISON ROUGE Map pp158–9

☎ 01 40 01 08 81; www.lamaisonrouge.org; 10 blvd de la Bastille, 12e; adult/student, senior & 13-18yr €6.50/4.50, under 13yr free; Ⓨ 11am-7pm Wed-Sun, to 9pm Thu; Ⓜ Quai de Rapée

Subtitled 'Fondation Antoine de Galbert' after the man who endowed it, this cutting-edge gallery shows contemporary artists and has good access to seldom-seen works from private collections. There's a decent restaurant here and an excellent art book-shop called Bookstorming.

PARC DE BERCY Map pp158–9

rue Paul Belmondo, 12e; Ⓨ 8am-5.45pm to 9.30pm Mon-Fri, 9am-5.45pm to 9.30pm Sat & Sun (seasonal); Ⓜ Bercy or Cour St-Émilion

This park, which links the Palais Omnisports with Bercy Village, is a particularly attractive, 13.5-hectare public garden. On an island in the centre of one of its large ponds is the Pavillon du Lac du Parc de Bercy (☎ 01 53 46 19 34; Ⓨ 10am-6pm Apr-Sep, 11am-5pm Oct-Mar), with temporary exhibitions. The Maison du Jardinage (☎ 01 53 46 19 19; 41 rue Paul Belmondo, 12e; Ⓨ 1.30-5.30pm Tue-Fri, to 6.30pm Sat & Sun Apr-Sep, to 5pm Tue-Sun Oct-Mar) in the centre of the park takes a close look at gardening and the environment, and offers courses.

CINÉMATHÈQUE FRANÇAISE Map pp158–9

☎ 01 71 19 33 33; www.cinemathequefrancaise.com; 51 rue de Bercy, 12e; permanent collection adult/ under 12yr/senior & 12-26yr €5/2.50/4, temporary exhibitions €8/5.50/6.50; Ⓨ noon-7pm Mon, Wed, Fri & Sat, to 10pm Thu, to 8pm Sun; Ⓜ Bercy

This national institution, better known for screening classic French and cutting-edge

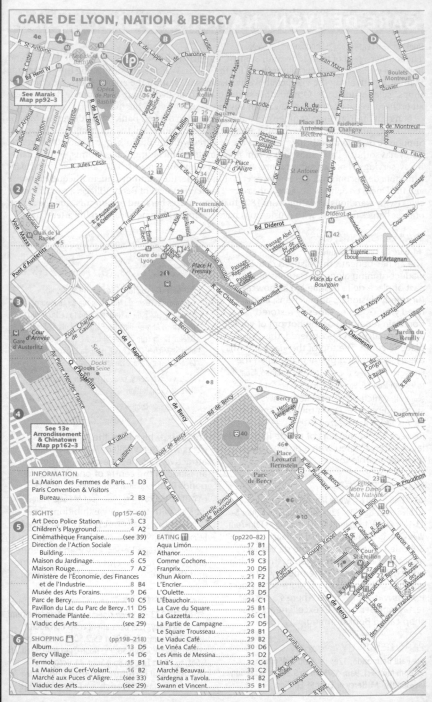

See Marais
Map pp92–3

See 13e
Arrondissement
& Chinatown
Map pp162–3

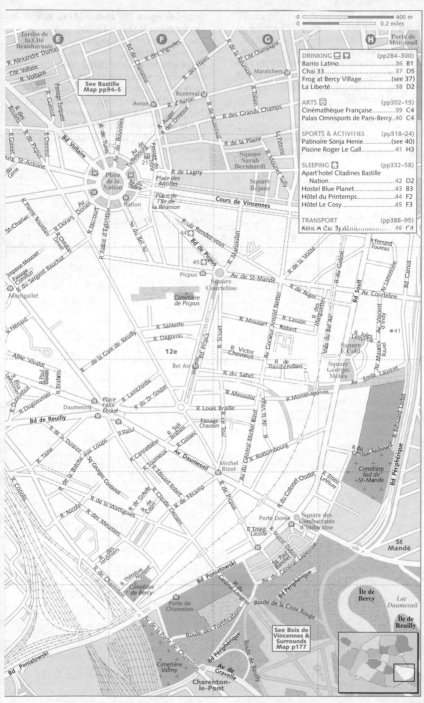

0 — 400 m
0 — 0.2 miles

DRINKING 🍷 🍸 (pp284–300)
Barrio Latino............................36 B1
Chai 33.....................................37 D5
Frog at Bercy Village.............(see 37)
La Liberté..................................38 D2

ARTS 🎭 (pp302–15)
Cinémathèque Française..........39 C4
Palais Omnisports de Paris-Bercy..40 C4

SPORTS & ACTIVITIES (pp318–24)
Patinoire Sonja Henie..............(see 40)
Piscine Roger Le Gall................41 H3

SLEEPING 🛏 (pp332–58)
Apart'hotel Citadines Bastille
  Nation....................................42 D2
Hostel Blue Planet....................43 B3
Hôtel du Printemps...................44 F2
Hôtel Le Cosy...........................45 F3

TRANSPORT (pp388–95)
Rent A Car System....................46 C4

foreign films, is housed in stunning post-modern premises with plenty of exhibition space for its permanent collection and temporary exhibitions. It also houses screening rooms, the Bibliothèque du Film (Film Library) for researchers and an excellent specialist bookshop. Enter from place Leonard Bernstein.

MUSÉE DES ARTS FORAINS Map pp158–9
☎ 01 43 40 16 22, 01 43 40 63 44; www.pavillons -de-bercy.com; Les Pavillons de Bercy, 53 av des Terroirs de France, 12e; adult/child €12.50/4; ☺ by appointment; Ⓜ Cour St-Émilion

The Museum of the Fairground Art, housed in several old wine warehouses in trendy Bercy Village, is a wonderful collection of old amusements from 19th-century funfairs – carousels, organs, stalls etc. Most of the items still work and are pure works of art. The place is usually only rented out for corporate events with minimum numbers but give a call or visit the website and try your luck.

Drinking p297; Eating p274; Sleeping p355

Serious change is afoot in the 13e arrondissement, a once nondescript area south of the Latin Quarter and Jardin des Plantes (5e) that is rapidly becoming the city's new star. Its renaissance was heralded in the 1990s b the controversial Bibliothèque Nationale de France and by the arrival of the high-speed Météor metro line, and is slated not to stop until 2015 (when the 26-year ZAC Paris Rive Gauche redevelopment project – see www.parisrivegauche.com – ends).

A glamorous strip of interior-design shops now fronts riverside Quai de la Gare immediately north of the National Library and MK2 entertainment complex (p314). There's the new river metro (p392). Then there's the swimming pool on the Seine (p323) that floats not quite in the shade of the latest designer bridge to grace the river, the Passerelle Simone de Beauvoir (2006) – across which Right Bank night owls from Bercy hotfoot it to a trio of music venues moored in front of the library. Indeed, Parisian socialites bemoan the fact Bibliothéque is the last stop on the line, but they know this is a great place to be after dark. Once the new library and university buildings for Paris' language and civilisation students open in 2010, there is no saying how many bars will open.

Cutting-edge architecture and design is one face of the 13e, a working-class district that will never lose its feisty spirit and down-to-earth grit. A place proud of its history, it has both a blvd Auguste Blanqui and place Nationale, a pairing propitious to the reconciliation between anarchism and patriotism.

Flit from Chinese restaurant to Vietnamese stall in the capital's Chinatown, the area between av d'Italie and av de Choisy, and you feel you've imperceptibly changed continents. Or trip past the graffiti-covered façade of Les Frigos (www.les-frigos.com; rue des Frigos, 13e), an established artists' squat with several galleries in a 1920s industrial building that used to be a train station for refrigerated wagons, and you could be in Berlin. In the Butte aux Cailles *quartier*, the jewel in this arrondissement's crown, people still sing revolutionary songs from the time of the Paris Commune over chichi cuisine.

BIBLIOTHÈQUE NATIONALE DE FRANCE Map pp162–3

☎ 01 53 79 53 79, 01 53 79 40 41; www.bnf.fr; 11 quai François Mauriac, 13e; temporary exhibitions adult/18-26yr/under 18yr from €7/5/free; ☽ 10am-7pm Tue-Sat, 1-7pm Sun; Ⓜ Bibliothèque

The four glass towers of the €2 billion National Library of France – conceived as a 'wonder of the modern world' – opened in 1995. No expense was spared to carry out a plan that many said defied logic. While books and historical documents are shelved in the sunny, 23-storey and 79m-high towers (shaped like half-open books), patrons sit in artificially lit basement halls built around a 'forest courtyard' of 140 50-year-old pines, trucked in from the countryside. The towers have since been fitted with a complex (and expensive) shutter system and the basement is prone to flooding from the Seine. The national library contains around 12 million tomes stored on some 420km of shelves and can hold 2000 readers and 2000 researchers. Temporary exhibitions (entrance E) revolve around 'the word', focusing on everything from storytelling to bookbinding and French heroes. Using the study library costs €3.30/35

TRANSPORT: 13E ARRONDISSE-MENT & CHINATOWN

Bus Bibliothèque Nationale de France François Mitterrand for 62 through 13e along rue Tolbiac to rue d'Alésia (14e) & rue de la Convention (15e); porte d'Italie for 47 to place d'Italie, rue Monge, quai St Michel, Hôtel de Ville & Gare de l'Est; place d'Italie for 67 to Mosquée de Paris, Jardin des Plantes, Île de St-Louis, Hôtel de Ville & Pigalle; Olympiades & Place d'Italie for 83, to Jardin de Luxembourg, St-Germain & Invalides

Metro & RER Bibliothèque François Mitterrand, Porte de Choisy, Porte d'Italie, Place d'Italie, Tolbiac, Olympiades

per day/year while the research library costs €7/53 for three days/year.

DOCKS EN SEINE Map pp162–3

30 quai d'Austerlitz, 13e; Ⓜ Gare d'Austerlitz
Watch this space! One of Paris' most exciting projects, Docks en Seine is a 20,000-sq-metre riverside warehouse – goods were once brought to it by barge – being

13E ARRONDISSEMENT & CHINATOWN

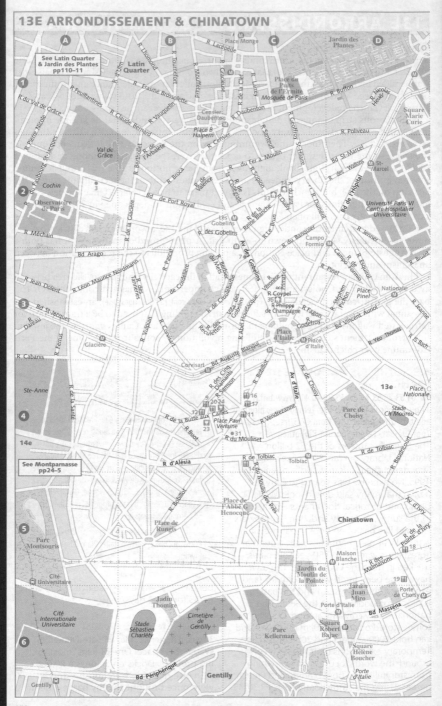

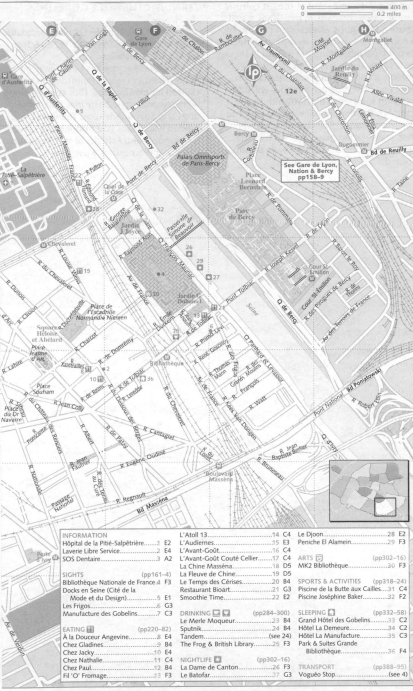

400 m
0.2 miles

transformed into a state-of-the-art cultural centre. Once complete in mid-2008, it will house a few shops, a restaurant etc and be renamed Cité de la Mode et du Design to reflect its principal inhabitant, the Institut Français de la Mode (French Fashion Institute), Paris' fashion school. A panoramic terrace, sun deck and waterside promenades will add jollifying touches to the 1907 industrial complex. For the best view of the startling lime-green 'wave' that dances across its vast, water-facing glass façade, cross the Seine over Pont Charles de Gaulle or hop aboard a Voguéo river metro (p392).

MANUFACTURE DES GOBELINS
Map pp162–3

☎ 01 44 08 52 00; 42 av des Gobelins, 13e; adult/7-25yr/under 7yr €8/6/free; tours ☽ 2pm & 3pm Tue-Thu; Ⓜ Les Gobelins

The Gobelins Factory has been weaving *haute lisse* (high relief) tapestries on specialised looms since the 18th century along with Beauvais-style *basse lisse* (low relief) ones and Savonnerie rugs. The visit, by guided tour, takes you through the *ateliers* (workshops) and exhibits of the thousands carpets and tapestries woven here.

15E ARRONDISSEMENT

Drinking p298; Eating p276; Shopping p217; Sleeping p356

After the war, entire battalions of steelworkers were drawn into the orbit of the 15e arrondissement, clocking in every morning at the Citroën factory or one of the neighbourhood's numerous aeronautical companies. Over the years, the area has become more gentrified and residential. Av de la Motte-Picquet, blvd Pasteur and av Félix Faure are peaceful places – too peaceful for some tastes. For Unesco, the area seemed just right, and not far away the republic's future officers converge on the majestic École Militaire (p134).

But the 15e offers much more than bourgeois homes and institutions. Parisians flock to the shops and restaurants that line rue de la Convention, rue de Vaugirard (the longest street in Paris), rue St-Charles and rue du Commerce. On the quays, the towers of the Centre Beaugrenelle have long since abandoned their monopoly on futurism to the stylish, functional buildings occupied by TV stations Canal+ and France Télévision, and Parisians with their heart in the country can enjoy the Parc André-Citroën, one of the capital's most beautiful open spaces.

MUSÉE BOURDELLE Map pp124–5

☎ 01 49 54 73 73; www.bourdelle.paris.fr in French; 18 rue Antoine Bourdelle, 15e; adult/14-25yr/under 14yr €7/3.50/free; ⏰ 10am-6pm Tue-Sun; Ⓜ Falguière

The Bourdelle Museum contains monumental bronzes in the house and workshop where sculptor Antoine Bourdelle (1861–1929), a pupil of Rodin, lived and worked. The three sculpture gardens are particularly lovely and impart a flavour of *belle époque* and post-WWI Montparnasse. The museum usually has a temporary exhibition going on alongside its permanent collection (free on the rare occasion there's no exhibition).

MUSÉE DE LA POSTE Map pp166–7

☎ 01 42 79 24 24; www.museedelaposte.fr in French; 34 blvd de Vaugirard, 15e; permanent collection adult/under 18yr €5/free, temporary exhibition adult/13-18yr/under 13yr €6.50/5/free; ⏰ 10am-6pm Mon-Sat; Ⓜ Montparnasse Bienvenüe or Pasteur

Think travel and exploration, not stamps, when it comes to the inspired temporary exhibitions hosted at the Postal Museum.

TRANSPORT: 15E ARRONDISSEMENT

Bus Blvd de Grenelle for 80 to Alma-Marceau, av Montaigne, av Matignon, Gare St-Lazare, Place Clichy & Lamarck Caulaincourt; rue de Vaugirard for 89 to Jardin du Luxembourg, Panthéon, Jardin des Plantes, Gare d'Austerliz & Bibliothèque Nationale de France François Mitterrand

Metro Commerce, Convention, Duroc, La Motte-Picquet Grenelle, Vaugirard

The main collection – the history of the French postal service – is spread across several rooms on several floors and is equally impressive. Upon departure, don't miss the shop selling every imaginable French stamp, from Harry Potter designs to romantic red heart-shaped stamps.

MUSÉE DU MONTPARNASSE Map pp166–7

☎ 01 42 22 91 96; www.museedumontparnasse.net; 21 av du Maine, 15e; adult/12-18yr/under 12yr €6/5/free; ⏰ 12.30-7pm Tue Sun; Ⓜ Montparnasse Bienvenüe

Housed in the studio of Russian cubist artist Marie Vassilieff (1884–1957) down a surprisingly leafy alleyway off av du Maine, Montparnasse Museum doesn't have a permanent collection; rather it recalls the great role Montparnasse played during various artistic periods of the 20th century, offered through temporary exhibitions.

MUSÉE PASTEUR Map pp166–7

☎ 01 45 68 82 83; www.pasteur.fr; Institut Pasteur, 25 rue du Docteur Roux, 15e; adult/student €3/1.50; ⏰ 2-5.30pm Mon-Fri Sep-Jul; Ⓜ Pasteur

Housed in the apartment where the famous chemist and bacteriologist spent the last seven years of his life (1888–95), a tour of this museum takes you through Pasteur's private rooms, a hall with such odds and ends as gifts presented to him by heads of state and drawings he did as a young man. After Pasteur's death, the French government wanted to entomb his remains in the Panthéon, but his family, acting in accordance with his wishes, obtained permission to have him buried at his institute. The great savant lies in the basement crypt.

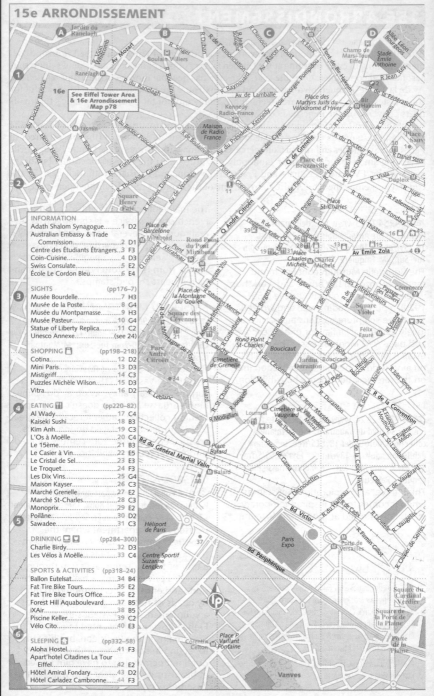

INFORMATION
Adath Shalom Synagogue.........1 D2
Australian Embassy & Trade
 Commission...............................2 D1
Centre des Étudiants Étrangers..3 F3
Coin-Cuisine..................................4 D3
Swiss Consulate............................5 E2
École Le Cordon Bleu...................6 E4

SIGHTS (pp176–7)
Musée Bourdelle............................7 H3
Musée de la Poste.........................8 G4
Musée du Montparnasse................9 H3
Musée Pasteur.............................10 G4
Statue of Liberty Replica.............11 C2
Unesco Annexe.....................(see 24)

SHOPPING (pp198–218)
Cotina...12 D2
Mini Paris....................................13 D3
Mistigriff.....................................14 D2
Puzzles Michèle Wilson...............15 D3
Vitra...16 D2

EATING (pp220–82)
Al Wady.......................................17 C4
Kaiseki Sushi...............................18 B3
Kim Anh......................................19 C3
L'Os à Moëlle..............................20 C4
Le 15ème.....................................21 B3
Le Casier à Vin............................22 E5
Le Cristal de Sel..........................23 E3
Le Troquet..................................24 F3
Les Dix Vins................................25 G4
Maison Kayser.............................26 C3
Marché Grenelle..........................27 E2
Marché St-Charles.......................28 E2
Monoprix.....................................29 E2
Poilâne..30 D2
Sawadee......................................31 C3

DRINKING (pp284–300)
Charlie Birdy...............................32 D3
Les Vélos à Moëlle......................33 C4

SPORTS & ACTIVITIES (pp318–24)
Ballon Eutelsat............................34 B4
Fat Tire Bike Tours......................35 E2
Fat Tire Bike Tours Office............36 E2
Forest Hill Aquaboulevard...........37 B5
iXAir...38 B5
Piscine Keller..............................39 C2
Vélo Cito....................................40 E3

SLEEPING (pp332–58)
Aloha Hostel...............................41 F3
Apart'hotel Citadines La Tour
 Eiffel...42 E2
Hôtel Amiral Fondary..................43 D2
Hôtel Carladez Cambronne........44 F3

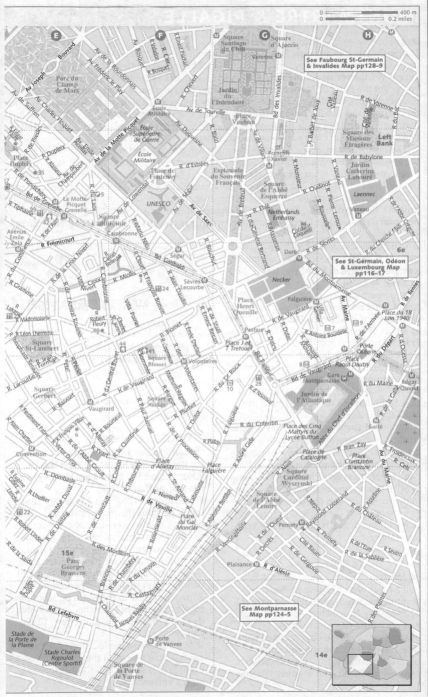

See Faubourg St-Germain & Invalides Map pp128–9

Left Bank

6e

See St-Germain, Odéon & Luxembourg Map pp116–17

See Montparnasse Map pp124–5

14e

MONTMARTRE & PIGALLE

Drinking p298; Eating p277; Shopping p217; Sleeping p357

During the late 19th and early 20th centuries the bohemian lifestyle of Montmartre in the 18e attracted a number of important writers and artists. Although the activity shifted to Montparnasse after WWI, the 18e arrondissement thrives on crowds and a strong sense of community. When you've got the Butte de Montmartre (Montmartre Hill) and Sacré Cœur, what do you expect? Cascading steps, cobblestone streets, small houses with wooden shutters in narrow, quiet lanes; the charm of the *quartier* is immediately apparent. Rue Caulaincourt and av Junot flaunt their bourgeois credentials, while the streets around the square Willette, place des Abbesses and rue Lepic become steeper and narrower, the inhabitants younger and hipper.

The northern part of the 9e arrondissement has a rough-and-ready charm. The lights of the Moulin Rouge dominate blvd de Clichy, and a few blocks southeast is lively, neon-lit place Pigalle, one of Paris' main sex districts. But Pigalle is more than just a sleazy red-light district: the area around blvd de Clichy between Pigalle and Blanche metro stations may be lined with erotica shops and striptease parlours, but there are also plenty of trendy nightspots, clubs and cabarets. South of Pigalle, the district known as Nouvelles Athènes (New Athens), with its beautiful Graeco-Roman architecture and private gardens, has long been favoured by artists.

BASILIQUE DU SACRÉ CŒUR Map p169

☎ 01 53 41 89 00; www.sacre-coeur-montmartre .com; place du Parvis du Sacré Cœur, 18e; ☺ 6am-10.30pm; Ⓜ Anvers

Sacred Heart Basilica, perched at the very top of Butte de Montmartre, was built from contributions pledged by Parisian Catholics as an act of contrition after the humiliating Franco-Prussian War of 1870–71. Construction began in 1876, but the basilica was not consecrated until 1919. In a way, atonement here has never stopped; a perpetual prayer 'cycle' that began at the consecration of the basilica continues round the clock to this day.

Some 234 spiralling steps lead you to the basilica's dome (admission €5; ☺ 9am-7pm Apr-Sep, to 6pm Oct-Mar), which affords one of Paris' most spectacular panoramas; they say you can see for 30km on a clear day. Weighing in at 19 tonnes, the bell called La Savoyarde in the tower above is the largest in France. The chapel-lined crypt, visited in conjunction with the dome, is huge but not very interesting.

PLACE DU TERTRE Map p169

Ⓜ Abbesses

Half a block west of Église St-Pierre de Montmartre, which once formed part of a 12th-century Benedictine abbey, is what was once the main square of the village of Montmartre. These days it's filled with cafés, restaurants, tourists and rather obstinate portrait artists and caricaturists. who will gladly do your likeness. Whether

top picks

MONTMARTRE & PIGALLE

- Basilique du Sacré Cœur (left)
- Place du Tertre (left)
- Musée de la Vie Romantique (p171)
- Cimetière de Montmartre (below)
- Musée de Montmartre (p170)

it looks even remotely like you is another matter.

CIMETIÈRE DE MONTMARTRE Map p169

☺ 8am-6pm Mon-Fri, 8.30am-6pm Sat, 9am-6pm Sun mid-Mar–early Nov, 8am-5.30pm Mon-Fri, 8.30am-5.30pm Sat, 9am-5.30pm Sun early Nov–mid-Mar; Ⓜ Place de Clichy

Established in 1798, this 11-hectare cemetery is perhaps the most celebrated necropolis in Paris after Père Lachaise. It contains the graves of writers Émile Zola, Alexandre Dumas and Stendhal, composers Jacques Offenbach and Hector Berlioz, artist Edgar Degas, film director François Truffaut and dancer Vaslav Nijinsky – among others. The entrance closest to the Butte de Montmartre is at the end of av Rachel, just off blvd de Clichy, or down the stairs from 10 rue Caulaincourt.

Maps showing the location of the tombs are available free from the conservation office (☎ 01 53 42 36 30; 20 av Rachel, 18e) at the cemetery's entrance.

MONTMARTRE & PIGALLE

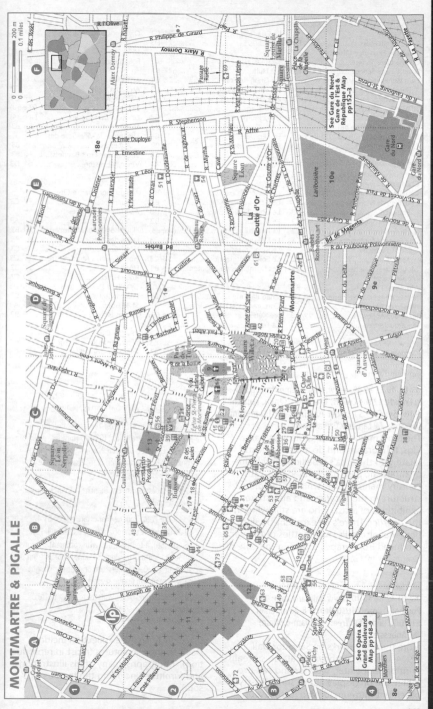

See Gare du Nord, Gare de l'Est & République Map pp152-3

See Opéra & Grand Boulevards Map pp148-9

MONTMARTRE & PIGALLE

MUSÉE DE MONTMARTRE Map p169

☎ 01 49 25 89 39; www.museedemontmartre.fr, in French; 12 rue Cortot, 18e; adult/senior, student & 10-25yr €7/5.50, under 10yr free; ⏱ 11am-6pm Tue-Sun; Ⓜ Lamarck Caulaincourt

The Montmartre Museum displays paintings, lithographs and documents mostly relating to the area's rebellious and bohemian/artistic past. It is located in a 17th-century manor house, which is the oldest structure in the *quartier*, and also stages exhibitions of artists who are still living in the *quartier*. There's an excellent bookshop here that also sells small bottles of the wine produced from grapes grown in the Close du Montmartre (p185).

DALÍ ESPACE MONTMARTRE Map p169

☎ 01 42 64 40 10; www.daliparis.com; 11 rue Poulbot, 18e; adult/student & 8-26yr/senior €10/6/7, under 8yr free; ⏱ 10am-6.30pm; Ⓜ Abbesses

More than 300 works by Salvador Dalí (1904–89), the flamboyant Catalan surrealist printmaker, painter, sculptor and self-promoter, are on display at this surrealist-style basement museum located just west of

TRANSPORT: MONTMARTRE & PIGALLE

Bus 85 bus from Mairie du 18e, stop Muller for Montmartre/Sacré Cœur (10 to 15 minutes' walk!) Bourse, Châtelet; place Pigalle for Montmartrobus through Montmartre from place Pigalle to 18e Mairie on place Jules Joffrin

Metro Abbesses, Anvers, Blanche, Lamarck Caulaincourt, Pigalle

Train The Petit Train de Montmartre (☎ 01 42 62 24 00; www.promotrain.fr; adult/child 3-12yr €5.50/3.50), a tourist 'train' with commentary, runs through Montmartre every 30 minutes or so from 10am or 10.30am to between 6pm and midnight daily, depending on the season

Funicular From square Willette to reach Butte de Montmartre

place du Tertre. The collection includes Dalí's strange sculptures (most in reproduction), lithographs, many of his illustrations and furniture (including the famous 'lips' sofa).

MUSÉE DE LA HALLE ST-PIERRE
Map p169

☎ 01 42 58 72 89; www.hallesaintpierre.org in French; 2 rue Ronsard, 18e; adult/student, senior & under 26yr €7.50/6; ⏱ 10am-6pm daily Sep-Jul, noon-6pm Mon-Fri Aug; Ⓜ Anvers

Founded in 1986, this museum and gallery is in the lovely old covered St Peter's Market across from square Willette and the base of the funicular. It focuses on the primitive and Art Brut schools; there is no permanent collection as such but the museum stages some three temporary exhibitions a year. There's a decent café on site.

MUSÉE DE L'ÉROTISME Map p169

☎ 01 42 58 28 73; www.musee-erotisme.com; 72 blvd de Clichy, 18e; adult/senior & student €8/5; ⏱ 10am-2am; Ⓜ Blanche

The Museum of Erotic Art tries to put some 2000 titillating statuary, stimulating sexual aids and fetishist items from days gone by on a loftier plane, with antique and modern erotic art from four continents spread over seven floors and lots of descriptive information. But most of the punters know why they are here. Still, some of the exhibits are, well, breathtaking, to say the least.

MUSÉE DE LA VIE ROMANTIQUE
Map p169

☎ 01 55 31 95 67; www.vie-romantique.paris.fr, in French; 16 rue Chaptal, 9e; temporary exhibitions adult/14-26yr/student & senior €7/3.50/5.50; permanent collection free, under 14yr free; ⏱ 10am-6pm Tue-Sun; Ⓜ Blanche or St-Georges

One of our favourite small museums in Paris, the Museum of the Romantic Life is in a splendid location at the lovely Hôtel Scheffer-Renan in the centre of the district once known as 'New Athens'. The museum, at the end of a film-worthy cobbled lane, is devoted to the life and work of Amandine Aurore Lucile Dupin Baronne (1804–76) – better known to the world as George Sand – and her intellectual circle of friends and is full of paintings, *objets d'art* and personal effects. Don't miss the tiny but delightful garden.

LA VILLETTE

The Buttes-Chaumont, the Canal de l'Ourcq and the Parc de la Villette, with its wonderful museums and other attractions, create the winning trifecta of the 19e arrondissement. Combining the traditional with the innovative, the old-fashioned with the contemporary, this district makes a virtue of its contradictions. It may not possess the beauty of central Paris, but it is nonetheless full of delightful surprises. An aimless stroll or leisurely bike ride uncovers narrow streets lined with small houses. The Parc des Buttes-Chaumont, with its unusual rocky promontory, attracts local inhabitants at dawn, who run, cycle or do t'ai chi exercises. The quays along the Canal de l'Ourcq have been transformed over the past several years and have become one of the district's main attractions. But the centrepiece is the Parc de la Villette, the former abattoirs of which have made way for a cultural centre (Cité de la Musique), a concert hall (Zénith) and the impressive Cité des Sciences et de l'Industrie and its museums.

PARC DE LA VILLETTE Map pp174–5

☎ 01 04 03 75 75; www.villette.com, in French; Ⓜ Porte de la Villette or Porte de Pantin

This large park in the city's far northeastern corner, which opened in 1993, stretches from the Cité des Sciences et de l'Industrie (below) southwards to the Cité de la Musique (opposite). Divided into two sections by the Canal de l'Ourcq, the park is enlivened by shaded walkways, imaginative street furniture, a series of themed gardens and fanciful, bright-red pavilions known as *folies*. At 35 hectares it is the largest open green space in central Paris and has been called 'the prototype of the urban park of the 21st century'.

Of the 10 themed gardens/playgrounds for kids, the best are the Jardin du Dragon (Dragon Garden), with an enormous dragon slide between the Géode and the nearest bridge, and the Jardin des Dunes (Dunes Garden) and Jardin des Miroirs (Mirror Gardens), which are across Galerie de la Villette (the covered walkway) from the Grande Halle, a wonderful old abattoir of wrought iron and glass now used for concerts, theatre performances, expos and conventions.

CITÉ DES SCIENCES ET DE L'INDUSTRIE Map pp174–5

☎ 01 40 05 80 00, reservations 08 92 69 70 72; www.cite-sciences.fr; 30 av Corentin Cariou, 19e; ☽ 10am-6pm Tue-Sat, to 7pm Sun; Ⓜ Porte de la Villette

The enormous City of Science and Industry, at the northern end of Parc de la Villette, has all sorts of hi-tech exhibits that are particularly well suited for children. You could easily spend a day here with the kids in tow.

Free attractions include the Carrefour Numérique (level -1; ☽ noon-7.45pm Tue, to 6.45pm Wed-Sun) internet centre; Médiathèque (levels 0 & -1; ☽ noon-7.45pm Tue, to 6.45pm Wed-Sun), with multimedia exhibits dealing with childhood, the history of science and health; Cité des Métiers (level -1; ☽ 10am-6pm Tue-Fri, noon-6pm Sat), with information about trades, professions and employment; and a small Aquarium (level -2; ☽ 10am-6pm Tue-Sat, to 7pm Sun).

A free and extremely useful map/brochure (in English) called *The Keys to the Cité* is available from the circular information counter at the main entrance to the complex.

The huge, rather confusingly laid-out Explora (levels 1 & 2; adult/7-25yr €8/6, with Planetarium €11/9, under 7yr free), the heart of the exhibitions at the Cité des Sciences et de l'Industrie, looks at everything from space exploration and automobile technology to genetics and sound. Tickets are valid for a full day and allow you to enter and exit at will.

TRANSPORT: LA VILLETTE

Bus Porte de la Villette for 75 to Buttes-Chaumont, Canal St-Martin, République, Centre Pompidou, Marais, rue des Archives, Hôtel de Ville & Châtelet

Metro Botzaris, Buttes-Chaumont, Porte de Pantin, Porte de la Villette

Boat Canauxrama Bassin de la Villette stop (13 quai de la Loire) for canal boat to Port de Plaisance de Paris-Arsenal (12e) south of place de la Bastille & Paris Canal Croisières stop (19–21 quai de la Loire) for boat to quai Anatole France (7e) near the Musée d'Orsay

The Planétarium (level 1; 11am-4pm Tue-Fri, to 5pm Sat & Sun) has six shows a day on the hour (except at 1pm) on a screen measuring 1000 sq metres. Children under three are not admitted.

The highlight of the Cité des Sciences et de l'Industrie is the brilliant Cité des Enfants (Children's Village; level 0), with imaginative, hands-on demonstrations of basic scientific principles in two sections: for two- to seven-year-olds, and for five- to 12-year-olds. In the first, kids can explore, among other things, the conduct of water (waterproof ponchos provided), a building site and a maze. The second allows children to build toy houses with industrial robots, and stage news broadcasts in a TV studio; this being Paris a very popular and successful exhibition in 2008 was one called Zizi Sexual – love and sex explained to pre-teens. A third section has a special exhibition called Ombres et Lumières (Shadows and Light) devoted largely to the five-to-12 age group.

Visits to Cité des Enfants lasting 1½ hours begin four times a day: at 9.45am, 11.30am, 1.30pm and 3.15pm on Tuesday to Friday and at 10.30am, 12.30pm, 2.30pm and 4.30pm on Saturday and Sunday. Each child (€6) must be accompanied by an adult (maximum two per family). During school holidays, book two or three days in advance by phone or via the internet.

The Cinaxe (01 42 09 85 83, reservations 01 40 05 12 12; admission €5.40, if holding another ticket to Cité des Sciences €4.80; screenings 11am-12.45pm & 2-5pm Tue-Sun), a cinema with hydraulic seating for 60 people, moves in synchronisation with the action on the screen. It's across the walkway from the southwestern side of the Cité des Sciences. Shows begin every 15 minutes.

The Géode (01 40 05 79 99, reservations 08 92 68 45 40; www.lageode.fr in French; 26 av Corentin Cariou; 19e, adult/senior & 3-25yr €9/5.50, 3-D film €11.50/9.50; 10.30am-6.30pm Tue-Sat, to 8.30pm Sun) is a 36m-high sphere with a mirrorlike surface of thousands of polished, stainless-steel triangles, and is one of Paris' architectural calling cards. Inside, high-resolution, 70mm films (45 minutes each) on topics such as virtual reality, special effects and nature are projected onto a 180-degree screen to surround you with the action. Headsets for an English soundtrack are available for free. Reach the Géode via level 0 of the Cité des Sciences et de l'Industrie.

The Argonaute (admission €3, under 7yr free; 10am-5.30pm Tue-Sat, to 7pm Sun), a French Navy submarine commissioned in 1957 and dry-docked in the park in 1989, is just southeast of the Géode. The Argonaute is also accessible from level 0. It's open to children aged three and up.

CITÉ DE LA MUSIQUE Map pp174–5

01 44 84 44 84; www.cite-musique.fr; 221 av Jean Jaurès, 19e; noon-6pm Tue-Sat, 10am-6pm Sun; Porte de Pantin

The City of Music, on the southern edge of Parc de la Villette, is a striking, triangular-shaped concert hall whose mission is to bring nonelitist music from around the world to Paris' multiethnic listeners. (For information on concerts and other musical events, see p310.) Next door is the prestigious Conservatoire National Supérieur de Musique et de Danse (National Higher Conservatory of Music & Dance; 01 40 40 45 45; www.cnsmdp.fr; 209 av Jean Jaurès, 19e; Porte de Pantin), featuring concerts and dance performances.

The Musée de la Musique (Music Museum; 01 44 84 44 84; adult/senior, student & 18-25yr €7/3.40, under 18yr free; noon-6pm Tue-Sat, 10am-6pm Sun) in the Cité de la Musique displays some 900 rare musical instruments (from a warehoused collection of 4500); you can hear many of them being played through the earphones included in the admission cost. The museum's Médiathèque (01 44 84 89 45; noon-6pm Tue-Sat) can answer your music questions via the internet; it has terminals with hundreds of music-related sites.

PARC DES BUTTES-CHAUMONT
Map pp174–5

rue Manin & rue Botzaris, 19e; 7.30am-11pm May-Sep, to 9pm Oct-Apr; Buttes- Chaumont or Botzaris

Encircled by tall apartment blocks, the 25-hectare Buttes-Chaumont Park is the closest thing in Paris to Manhattan's Central Park. The park's forested slopes hide grottoes and artificial waterfalls, and the lake is dominated by a temple-topped island linked to the mainland by two footbridges. Once a quarry and rubbish tip, the park was given its present form by Baron Haussmann in time for the opening of the 1867 Exposition Universelle.

LA VILLETTE

400 m
0.2 miles

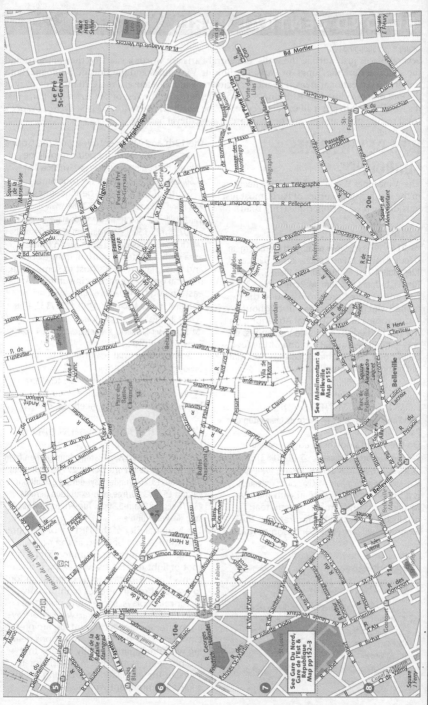

See Ménilmontant &
Belleville
Map p155

See Gare Du Nord,
Gare de l'Est &
République
Map pp152-3

BEYOND CENTRAL PARIS

Eating p281; Shopping p217

Several places just 'outside the walls' of central Paris are worth a visit. To the southeast and the southwest are the 'lungs' of Paris, the Bois de Vincennes and the Bois de Boulogne, both important recreational areas. The modern cityscape of La Défense, a mere 20 minutes away at the end of metro line 1 or RER line A, is so different from the rest of centuries-old Paris that it's worth a visit to put it all in perspective. To the north on metro line 13 is St-Denis, France's royal resting place and the site of an impressive medieval basilica.

BOIS DE VINCENNES & SURROUNDS

The 'Vincennes Wood' embraces 995 hectares in the southeastern corner of Paris, most just outside the blvd Périphérique (ring road).

AQUARIUM TROPICAL Map p177

☎ 01 53 59 58 60; www.palais-portedoree.org, in French; Palais de la Porte Dorée, 293 av Daumesnil, 12e; adult/4-25yr €5.70/4.20; ⊗ 10am-5.15pm Tue-Fri, to 7pm Sat & Sun; Ⓜ Porte Dorée

Fish and sea creatures from around the globe swim in tanks spread throughout a dozen rooms at the Tropical Aquarium, on the western edge of Bois de Vincennes. It was established in 1931 in one of the few buildings left from the Exposition Coloniale of that year; a compelling immigration museum (right) is also here.

BOIS DE VINCENNES Map p177

blvd Poniatowski, 12e; Ⓜ Porte de Charenton or Porte Dorée

On the wood's northern edge, Château de Vincennes (Palace of Vincennes; ☎ 01 48 08 31 20; www .chateau-vincennes.fr; av de Paris, 12e; ⊗ 10am-6pm May-Aug, to 5pm Sep-Apr; Ⓜ Château de Vincennes) is a bona fide royal chateau with massive fortifications and a moat. The chateau grounds can be strolled for free, but the 52m-high dungeon (1369), a prison during

the 17th and 18th centuries, and the Gothic Chapelle Royale (Royal Chapel) can only be visited by guided tour (adult/18-25yr/under 18yr €7.50/4.80/free); call ahead for tour times.

South of the Château de Vincennes is the Parc Floral de Paris (☎ 01 49 57 24 84; www .parcfloraldeparis.com; rte du Champ de Manoeuvre, 12e; adult/7-18yr €3/1.50; ⊗ 9.30am-5pm to 8pm seasonal; Ⓜ Château de Vincennes), a vast green floral area with a butterfly garden, nature library and kids' play areas; it's host to some quite magical open-air concerts in summer. At its eastern edge, the Jardin d'Agronomie Tropicale (Garden of Tropical Agronomy; ☎ 01 43 94 73 33; 45bis av de la Belle Gabrielle; ⊗ 11.30am-5.30pm Sat & Sun; Ⓜ Nogent-sur-Marne) is a vestige of the 1907 Exposition Coloniale.

Some 600 animals call the 15-hectare Parc Zoologique de Paris (☎ 01 44 75 20 10; www.mnhn .fr; 53 av de St-Maurice, 12e; adult/under 4yr €5/free; ⊗ 9am-5pm or 6.30pm seasonal; Ⓜ Porte Dorée), also known as the Zoo de Vincennes, home.

CITÉ NATIONALE DE L'HISTOIRE DE L'IMMIGRATION Map p177

☎ 01 53 59 58 60; www.histoire-immigration.fr, in French; Palais de la Porte Dorée, 293 av Daumesnil, 12e; adult/18-26yr/under 18yr during exhibitions periods €5.50/3.50/free, non-exhibition periods €3/2/free; ⊗ 10am-5.30pm Tue-Fri, to 7pm Sat & Sun; Ⓜ Porte Dorée

The National City of the History of Immigration, in the same building as the Aquarium Tropical (left), is not a museum to visit for a spot of light relief. A heavyweight, it documents the hot-potato topic of immigration to France through a series of informative historical displays, some more objective than others: many of the artworks portraying contemporary immigrant life are pretty emotive – take the video projections dealing with the Algerian family in Paris that has not seen its relatives in Algeria for 16 years, or the installation portraying life in a Parisian immigrant workers' dorm (for

BOIS DE VINCENNES & SURROUNDS

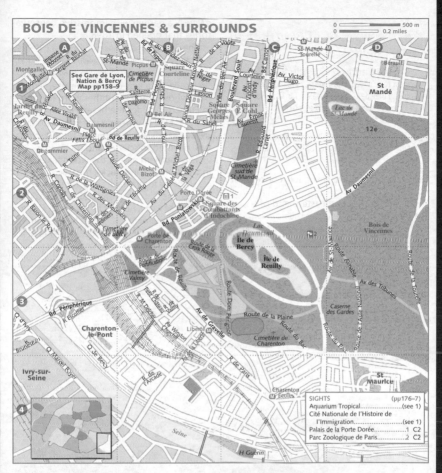

SIGHTS (pp176–7)
Aquarium Tropical..................................(see 1)
Cité Nationale de l'Histoire de
l'Immigration.....................................(see 1)
Palais de la Porte Dorée.....................1 C2
Parc Zoologique de Paris....................2 C2

those interested, www.mahophoto.com has a great photo story on this).

BOIS DE BOULOGNE & SURROUNDS

The 845-hectare Boulogne Wood owes its informal layout to Baron Haussmann, who, inspired by London's Hyde Park, planted 400,000 trees here. Along with various gardens and other sights, the wood has 15km of cycle paths and 28km of bridle paths through 125 hectares of forested land. Be warned that the Bois de Boulogne becomes a distinctly adult playground after dark, especially along the Allée de Longchamp running northeast from the Étang des Réservoirs (Reservoirs Pond), where all kinds of prostitutes cruise for clients.

BOIS DE BOULOGNE Map p178
blvd Maillot, 16e; Ⓜ Porte Maillot or Pont de Neuilly

The wood's enclosed Parc de Bagatelle (☎ 3975; ⏱ 9.30am-5pm to 8pm seasonal), in the northwestern corner, is renowned for its beautiful gardens surrounding the Château de Bagatelle (☎ 01 40 67 97 00; route de Sèvres à Neuilly, 16e; adult/student & 7-18yr €3/1.50, under 7yr free; ⏱ 9am-6pm Apr-Sep, to 5pm Oct-Mar), built in 1775. There are areas dedicated to irises (which bloom in May), roses (June to October) and water lilies (August). The Pré Catalan (Catalan Meadow; ⏱ 9.30am-5-8pm seasonal) to the southeast includes the Jardin Shakespeare, in which plants, flowers and trees mentioned in Shakespeare's plays are cultivated. Exhibitions, flower shows or other events in

177

Bus Porte d'Auteuil for 32 through the 16e arrondissement to av des Champs-Élysées, av Matignon, Trinité & Gare de l'Est; Porte Maillot for 73 to place de l'Étoile, av des Champs-Élysées, place de la Concorde & Musée d'Orsay

Metro & RER Av Foch, Pont de Neuilly, Porte d'Auteuil, Porte Dauphine, Porte Maillot

the park and gardens cost adult/concession €3/1.50.

Located at the southeastern end of the Bois de Boulogne is the Jardin des Serres d'Auteuil (☎ 01 40 71 75 23; av de la Porte d'Auteuil, 16e; ⏰ 9.30am-5pm to 8pm seasonal; Ⓜ Porte d'Auteuil), a garden with impressive conservatories that opened in 1898.

The 20-hectare Jardin d'Acclimatation (☎ 01 40 67 90 82; av du Mahatma Gandhi; adult/3-18yr €2.70/1.35, under 3yr free; ⏰ 10am-7pm Jun-Sep, to 6pm Oct-May; Ⓜ Les Sablons), a kids-oriented amusement park whose name is another word for 'zoo' in French, includes the hi-tech Exploradôme (☎ 01 53 64 90 40; www.exploradome.com, in French; adult/4-18yr €5/3.50, under 4yr free), a tented structure devoted to science and the media.

The southern part of the wood takes in two horse-racing tracks, the Hippodrome de Longchamp for flat races and, for steeplechases, the Hippodrome d'Auteuil, as well as the Stade Roland Garros, home of the French Open tennis tournament (p323). Also here is the Tenniseum-Musée de Roland Garros (☎ 01 47 43 48 48;

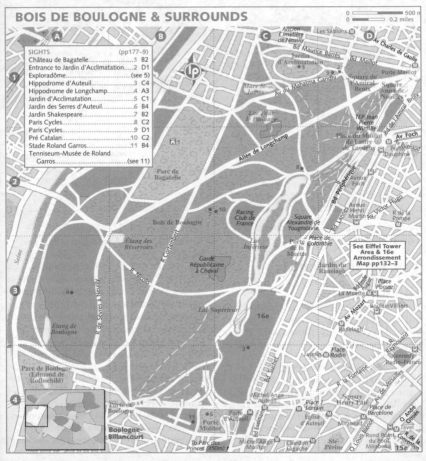

BOIS DE BOULOGNE & SURROUNDS

SIGHTS	(pp177–9)
Château de Bagatelle	1 B2
Entrance to Jardin d'Acclimatation	2 D1
Exploradôme	(see 5)
Hippodrome d'Auteuil	3 C4
Hippodrome de Longchamp	4 A3
Jardin d'Acclimatation	5 C1
Jardin des Serres d'Auteuil	6 B4
Jardin Shakespeare	7 B2
Paris Cycles	8 C2
Paris Cycles	9 D1
Pré Catalan	10 C2
Stade Roland Garros	11 B4
Tenniseum-Musée de Roland Garros	(see 11)

www.rolandgarros.com; 2 av Gordon Bennett, 16e; adult/under 18yr €7.5/4, with stadium visit €15/10; ⏰ 10am-6pm Tue-Sun; Ⓜ Porte d'Auteuil), the world's most extravagant tennis museum, tracing the sport's 500-year history through paintings, sculptures and posters. Visitors to the museum can watch at least 200 hours of play from 1897 till today, including all of the French Open's men's singles matches since 1990 and interviews with all major players. Tours of the stadium take place at 11am in English and at 2.30pm and 4.30pm in French.

Rowing boats (☎ 01 42 88 04 69; per hr €10; ⏰ 10am-6pm mid-Mar–mid-Oct) can be hired at Lac Inférieur (metro Av Henri Martin), the largest of the wood's lakes and ponds. They sometimes open at the weekend in winter. Paris Cycles (☎ 01 47 47 76 50; per hr €5; ⏰ 10am-7pm mid-Apr–mid-Oct) hires out bicycles at two locations in the Bois de Boulogne: on av du Mahatma Gandhi (metro Les Sablons), across from the Porte Sablons entrance to the Jardin d'Acclimatation amusement park, and near the Pavillon Royal (metro Av Foch) at the northern end of Lac Inférieur.

LA DÉFENSE

It was one of the world's most ambitious civil-engineering projects when development of Paris' skyscraper business district, west of the 17e arrondissement, began in the 1950s. Today La Défense counts over 100 buildings, headquarters three-quarters of France's largest 20 corporations and showcases extraordinary monumental art (see p181). By day more than 150,000 city-dwellers – mainly suits and execs – transform the oversized, nocturnal ghost town into a hive of high-flying urban activity; 20,000 people live here.

Architecture buffs will have a field day. First-generation buildings like the Centre des Nouvelles Industries et Technologies (Centre for New Industries & Technologies) – a giant 'pregnant oyster' inaugurated in 1958, extensively rebuilt 30 years

WHAT'S IN A NAME

Skyscraper-camouflaged military installations, subterranean bunkers and a different James Bond gadget embedded in every mirrored window...forget it. There's nothing militaristic about La Défense except its name, derived from a simple sculpture: La Défense de Paris was erected on place de la Défense in 1883 to commemorate the defence of Paris during the Franco-Prussian War of 1870–71.

top picks

BEYOND CENTRAL PARIS

- Basilique de St-Denis (p182)
- Grande Arche de la Défense (p180)
- Musée Marmottan-Monet (p137)
- Stade de France (p183)
- Château de Vincennes (p176)

later and revamped in 2008 as a shopping centre – feel tired. But later generations still excite: the 187m-high Total Coupole (1985) shimmers metallic blue and silver as its rises 48 floors up to the sky. The twin towers of the 161m-tall Cœur Défense (Défense Heart) stand over a light-filled atrium bigger than Notre Dame's nave. Diagonally opposite, the elongated, oval-shaped Tour EDF (2001) – a triumphal solution to a relatively small space and as attractive a steel-and-glass skyscraper as you'll find – almost undulates in the breeze that forever whips across place de la Défense. New for 2008 is Tour T1, a 185m-high sail in glass, and Société General's Tour Granite, which post–September 11 was scaled down from 230m to 183m.

Sky-high future creations throw caution to the wind: the Tour Air 2 (2012), a demolition-reconstruction job of the stubbier 1970s Tour Aurore on place des Reflets will measure 220m; the currently drab Tour AXA (1974) will hit 225m on the height chart and be rechristened Tour CB31 in 2010. American architect Thom Mayne's Tour Phare (2012) will resemble a coiled sheet of woven metal and stand a record-breaking 300m tall, as will the Tour Generali (2012) which should practically tickle the clouds with its cluster of spiky spires. Most ground-breaking of all will be the 300m-tall Tour Signal (2012; www.tour-signal-ladefense .com), a project commissioned as a symbol of the area's third-millennium renaissance.

Reach La Défense by taking metro line 1 to the terminus (La Défense Grande Arche). RER Line A also serves that station; La Défense is in zone 3.

GARDENS & MONUMENTS Map p180
Le Parvis, place de la Défense & Esplanade du Général de Gaulle; Ⓜ **La Défense Grande Arche or Esplanade de la Défense**
The Parvis, place de la Défense and Esplanade du Général de Gaulle – a pleasant 1km walkway – is an open-air contemporary

TRANSPORT: LA DÉFENSE

Bus 73 from Musée d'Orsay, place de la Concorde or Charles de Gaulle-Étoile

Metro Line No 1 to La Défense Grande Arche (terminus)

RER Line A (station: La Défense Grande Arche); if you take the faster RER, remember that La Défense is in zone three and you must pay a supplement (€1.95) if you are carrying a travel pass for zones 1 and 2 only

art gallery. Calder, Miró, Agam, César and Torricini are among the international artists behind the colourful and often surprising sculptures and murals on Voie des Sculptures (Sculptures Way), the Quartier du Parc (Park District) west of the Grande Arche and Jardins de l'Arche, a 2km-long extension of the Axe Historique. Meandering around this skyscraper district in search of these works of art (see opposite) is fun.

GRANDE ARCHE DE LA DÉFENSE
Map p180

☎ 01 49 07 27 27; www.grandearche.com; 1 Parvis de la Défense; adult/6-17yr/under 6yr €9/7.50/free,

family pass €22, ☷ 10am-8pm Apr-Sep, to 7pm Oct-Mar; Ⓜ La Défense Grande Arche

La Défense's draw card is the Grande Arche (Great Arch) – a remarkable, cube-like structure, 110m square, of white Carrara marble, grey granite and glass. It's constructed out of 3600 prefabricated cases, each 2.8m square and 800g in weight, and the entire construction rests on a dozen 30m-tall underground pillars. Scale the cigarettebutt–littered steps to the foot of this incredible arch for free and ponder its meaning as 'a window to the world, a symbol of hope for the future; that all men can meet freely'. Or pay to travel 1.6m per second to the 'roof' on the 35th floor, where temporary art exhibitions hang out alongside scaled models of the arch, a video showing its construction, a ticky-tacky souvenir shop and a soulless restaurant which, incredibly, boasts no view (avoid).

Most interesting is the outlook from the roof terrace over the 8km-long Axe Historique (Historic Axis), begun in 1640 by André Le Nôtre of Versailles fame and stretching from the Louvre's glass pyramid, along av des Champs-Élysées to the Arc de Triomphe, Porte Maillot and finally the Esplanade du

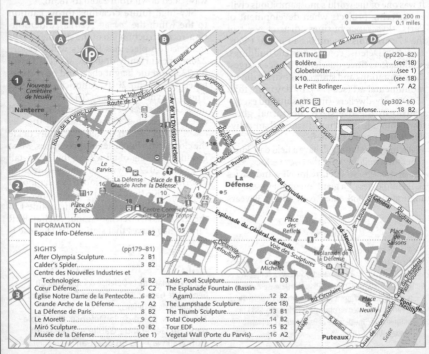

LA DÉFENSE

EATING 🍴	(pp220–82)
Boldère	(see 18)
Globetrotter	(see 1)
K10	(see 18)
Le Petit Bofinger	17 A2

ARTS ▣	(pp302–16)
UGC Ciné Cité de la Défense	18 B2

INFORMATION	
Espace Info-Défense	1 B2

SIGHTS	(pp179–81)
After Olympia Sculpture	2 B1
Calder's Spider	3 B2
Centre des Nouvelles Industries et Technologies	4 B2
Cœur Défense	5 C2
Église Notre Dame de la Pentecôte	6 B2
Grande Arche de la Défense	7 A2
La Défense de Paris	8 B2
Le Moretti	9 C2
Miró Sculpture	10 B2
Musée de la Défense	(see 1)

Takis' Pool Sculpture	11 D3
The Esplanade Fountain (Bassin Agam)	12 B2
The Lampshade Sculpture	(see 18)
The Thumb Sculpture	13 B1
Total Coupole	14 B2
Tour EDF	15 B2
Vegetal Wall (Porte du Parvis)	16 A2

Général de Gaulle. The Grande Arche, home to government and business offices, marks the western end of this axis, although its maker, Danish architect Johan-Otto von Sprekelsen, deliberately placed the arch fractionally out of alignment with the Axe Historique (who wants perfection?!).

ÉGLISE NOTRE DAME DE LA PENTECÔTE Map p180

☎ 01 47 75 83 25; http://catholiques.aladefense .cef.fr, in French; 1 place de la Défense; ☻ 8am-6.30pm Mon-Fri; Ⓜ La Défense Grande Arche
When the crowds of suits gets you down, head for the futuristic Our Lady of the Pentecost Catholic Church and its sublime interior. Check out the flame-shaped pulpit, the image of the Virgin Mary that looks uncannily like the Buddha, and the individual chairs that unfold to create benches.

MUSÉE DE LA DÉFENSE Map p180

☎ 01 47 74 84 24; www.ladefense.fr; 15 place de la Défense; admission free; ☻ 9am-5.15pm Mon-Fri; Ⓜ La Défense Grande Arche
A trip to this space located just below the Espace-Info information centre is a real highlight. Drawings, architectural plans and scale models trace the development of the district from the 17th century to the present day. Especially fascinating are the projects that were never built: the 750m-tall Tour Tourisme TV (1961) by the Polak brothers; Hungarian-born artist Nicholas Schöffer's unspeakable Tour Lumière Cybernetique (1965), a 'Cybernetic Light Tower' that, at 324m, would stand at the same height as the Eiffel Tower; and the Tour sans Fin, a 'Never-Ending Tower' that would be 425m high, but just 39m in diameter. Ouch.

A WORK OF ART

La Défense is not only about architecture. A 12m-high thumb, an antique giant, a chunk of the Berlin Wall and a serpent that snakes underground with kids inside are among the many larger-than-life artworks that loiter between skyscrapers. Grab a copy of the illustrated Guide to Works of Art (€2.50) from La Défense's information office (p411) and hunt for art. Or stroll 'blind' and see what new treasures you find; a few more appear each year.

- The Esplanade Fountain (1975). Also called Bassin Agam or Fontaine Agam after its Palestinian kinetic-art creator, Yaacov Agam, this is actually a colourful, 86m-long pool tiled with Venetian mosaics and pierced by 66 fountains that dance to music at certain times of day (5pm to 7pm Sunday to Friday, to 8.30pm Friday and Saturday). Find it behind the tourist office.
- Calder's Spider (1974). It looks like a spider no one in their right mind would want to meet. Giant-sized and ferocious red, it struts its leggy stuff on place de la Défense.
- Vegetal Wall (2006). A mini version of the vertical garden that blooms on the Musée du Quai Branly (p134), this living wall of green shares the same creator, budding Parisian botanical artist Patrick Blanc. Find it next to the Porte du Parvis entrance of the Centre Commercial des Quatre Temps.
- The Lampshade (2006). Step inside the shopping centre through Porte du Parvis to see this fabulous light-sculpture hanging from the ceiling. Kiko Lopez crafted it from thousands of Swarovski crystals.
- The Thumb (1994). The 12m-tall bronze thumb that gives the thumbs-up on place Carpeaux is not any old thumb. Its maker, Marseille-born César, made it from a cast of his own. Left or right?
- Le Moretti (1990). Candy-striped with myriad reds, blues, yellows (19 colours in total), this industrial, 32m-tall ventilation shaft on place de l'Iris is one of several shafts in La Défense to be transformed as art. Nice-born Taymond Moretti (1931–2005) did it using 672 fibre-glass tubes. Lit at night, it's inspirational.
- Takis' Pool (1987). Plump on that historic axis is this large pool of water studded with 49 multi-coloured lights strung atop spiral metal poles of varying heights. The crystal-clear reflection of the surrounding buildings in the water is a quintessential photo-op.
- The Four Heads (2002). London artist Emily Young, one of several artists whose works mingle with skyscrapers in the Triangle de l'Arche district of La Défense, ranks among Britain's top female sculptors. Masculine stone heads are what you're looking for.
- After Olympia (1986–87) Olympia's Greek temple's ornamental façade is the inspiration behind the 23m-long heap of rusted painted steel on av de la Division Leclerc. The work of English sculptor Anthony Caro, its reflections in the glassy buildings around it are as much a work of art as the work itself.
- Miró figures (1976). Ridiculing the strict symmetry of the surrounding blocks is this comic pair of bright blue, yellow and red figures in front of the Centre Commerical des Quatre Temp. In keeping with the oversized scale of things in La Défense, the Catalan surrealist's figures stand 11m and 12m tall.

ST-DENIS

Today just a suburb north of Paris' 18e arrondissement with a very mixed population, St-Denis was for some 1200 years the burial place of the kings of France. The ornate royal tombs, adorned with some truly remarkable statuary, and the Basilique de St-Denis (the world's first major Gothic structure) containing them are worth a visit and the town is easily accessible by metro in just 20 minutes or so. St-Denis also boasts the Stade de France, the futuristic stadium just south of the Canal de St-Denis where France beat Brazil to win the World Cup at home in 1998.

BASILIQUE DE ST-DENIS Map p182

☎ 01 48 09 83 54; www.monuments-nationaux.fr; 1 rue de la Légion d'Honneur; tombs adult/senior,

student & 18-25yr €6.50/4.50, under 18yr free, 1st Sun of the month Nov-Mar free, basilica admission free; ⏰ 10am-6pm Mon-Sat, noon-6pm Sun Apr-Sep, 10am-5pm Mon-Sat, noon-5pm Sun Oct-Mar; Ⓜ Basilique de St-Denis

St-Denis Basilica was the burial place for all but a handful of France's kings and queens from Dagobert I (r 629–39) to Louis XVIII (r 1814–24), constituting one of Europe's most important collections of funerary sculpture; today the remains of 43 kings and 32 queens repose here. The single-towered basilica, begun around 1136, was the first major structure to be built in the Gothic style, serving as a model for other 12th-century French cathedrals, including the one at Chartres (p377). Features illustrating the transition from Romanesque to Gothic can be seen in the choir and double ambulatory, which

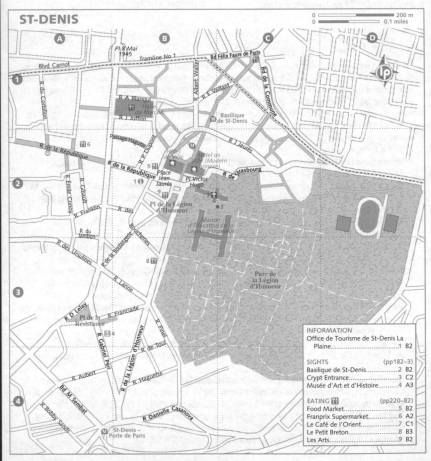

INFORMATION
Office de Tourisme de St-Denis La Plaine.................1 B2

SIGHTS (pp182–3)
Basilique de St-Denis.................2 B2
Crypt Entrance.................3 C2
Musée d'Art et d'Histoire.........4 A3

EATING (pp220–82)
Food Market.................5 B2
Franprix Supermarket.................6 A2
Le Café de l'Orient.................7 C1
Le Petit Breton.................8 B3
Les Arts.................9 B2

182

TRANSPORT: ST-DENIS

Metro Line 13 to Basilique de St-Denis station for the basilica and tourist office, to St-Denis-Porte de Paris station for the Musée d'Art et d'Histoire and the Stade de France (make sure to board a train heading for St-Denis Université, not for Gabriel Péri Asnières-Gennevilliers-Courtilles, as the line splits at La Fourche station)

RER Line B (station: La Plaine-Stade de France) for the Stade de France

Tram Line T1 links Bobigny Pablo Picasso station, the terminus of metro line 5, with Basilique de St-Denis station

are adorned with a number of 12th-century stained-glass windows. The narthex (the portico running along the western end of the basilica) also dates from this period. The nave and transept were built in the 13th century.

During the Revolution and the Reign of Terror, the basilica was devastated; remains from the royal tombs were dumped into two big pits outside the church. The mausoleums were put into storage in Paris, however, and survived. They were brought back in 1816, and the royal bones were reburied in the crypt a year later. Restoration of the structure was begun under Napoleon, but most of the work was carried out by the Gothic Revivalist architect Eugène Viollet-le-Duc from 1858 until his death in 1879. The tombs in the crypt are decorated with life-sized figures of the deceased. Those built before the Renaissance are adorned with *gisants* (recumbent figures). Those made after 1285 were carved from death masks and are thus fairly, well, lifelike; the 14 figures commissioned under Louis IX (St Louis; r 1214–70) are depictions of how earlier rulers *might* have looked. The oldest tombs (from around 1230) are those of Clovis I (d 511) and his son Childebert I (d 558). On no account should you miss the white marble catafalque tomb of Louis XII and Anne of Bretagne that dates from 1597. If you look carefully you'll see graffiti etched on the arms of the seated figures dating from the early 17th century. The Bourbon sepulchral

vault contains the remains of Louis XVI and Marie-Antoinette but not of the king's younger brother Charles X; there's a tomb, but his bones lie in a church in Nova Gorica in Slovenia.

Self-paced 1¼-hour audioguide tours of the basilica and tombs cost €4 (€6.50 for two sharing), available at the crypt ticket kiosk.

MUSÉE D'ART ET D'HISTOIRE Map p182

☎ 01 42 43 05 10; www.musee-saint-denis.fr, in French; 22bis rue Gabriel Péri; adult/student, senior & everyone on Sun €5/3, under 16yr free, 1st Sun of the month free; ☺ 10am-5.30pm Mon, Wed & Fri, to 8pm Thu, 2-6.30pm Sat & Sun; Ⓜ St-Denis-Porte de Paris

To the southwest of the basilica is the Museum of Art and History, housed in a restored Carmelite convent founded in 1625 and later presided over by Louise de France, the youngest daughter of Louis XV. Displays include reconstructions of the Carmelites' cells, an 18th-century apothecary and, in the archaeology section, items found during excavations around the St Denis Basilica. There's a section on modern art, with a collection of work by a local son, the surrealist artist Paul Éluard (1895–1952), as well as an important collection of politically charged posters, cartoons, lithographs and paintings from the 1871 Paris Commune.

STADE DE FRANCE Map p182

☎ 08 92 70 09 00; www.stadefrance.com; rue Francis de Pressensé, ZAC du Cornillon Nord, 93216 St-Denis la Plaine; adult/student & 6-11yr €10/8, family pass €29, under 6yr free; ☺ tours on the hour in French 10am-5pm daily Apr-Aug, 4 to 5 daily Sep-Mar, in English 10.30am & 2.30pm Apr-Aug; Ⓜ St-Denis-Porte de Paris

The 80,000-seat Stadium of France, just south of central St-Denis and in full view from rue Gabriel Péri, was built for the 1998 football World Cup, which France won by miraculously defeating Brazil 3–0. The futuristic and quite beautiful structure, with a roof the size of place de la Concorde, is used for football and rugby matches, major gymnastic events and big-ticket music concerts. It can be visited on guided tours only.

WALKING TOURS

MONTMARTRE ART ATTACK

Montmartre (from the French words *mont* for hill and *martyr*) has been a place of legend ever since St Denis was executed here c AD 250 and began his headless journey on foot to the village north of Paris that still bears his name (p182). In recent times the Montmartre of myth has been resurrected by music, books and especially films such as *Le Fabuleux Destin d'Amélie Poulain* (*Amelie* in English; 2002), which presented the district in various shades of rose, and *Moulin Rouge* (2001), which also made it pretty but gave it a bit more edge.

For centuries Montmartre was a simple country village filled with the *moulins* (mills) that supplied Paris with its flour. But when it was incorporated into the capital in 1860, its picturesque charm and low rents attracted painters and writers – especially after the Communard uprising of 1871 (see p26), which began here. The late 19th and early 20th centuries were Montmartre's heyday, when Toulouse-Lautrec drew his favourite cancan dancers and Picasso and Braque introduced the world to cubism.

After WWI such creative activity shifted to Montparnasse, but Montmartre retained an upbeat ambience that all the tourists in the world still can't spoil. The real attractions here, apart from the great views from the Butte de Montmartre (Montmartre Hill), are the area's little parks and steep, winding cobblestone streets, many of whose houses seem about to be engulfed by creeping vines and ivy.

In English-speaking countries, Montmartre's mystique of unconventionality has been magnified by the supposed notoriety of places like the Moulin Rouge, a nightclub on the edge of the Pigalle district that was founded in 1889 and is known for its scantily clad – ooooh la la! – chorus girls. The garish nightlife that Toulouse-Lautrec loved to portray has spread along blvd de Clichy, and Pigalle has become decidedly sleazy, though really it's pretty tame stuff.

1 Moulin Rouge Begin the walk at the Blanche metro station. Diagonally opposite to the left is the legendary Moulin Rouge (p303) beneath its trademark red windmill.

2 Musée de l'Érotisme Appropriately located to the right is the Musée de l'Érotisme (p171),

an institution that portrays itself as educational rather than titillating. Yeah, right.

3 Café des Deux Moulins Walk up rue Lepic, which is lined with food shops, and halfway up on the left is the Café des Deux Moulins (☎ 01 42 54 90 50; 15 rue Lepic, 18e; 🕑 7am-2am), where our heroine Amélie worked in the eponymous film.

4 Van Gogh's house Follow the curve to the west; Théo Van Gogh owned the house at No 54; his brother, the artist Vincent, stayed with him on the 3rd floor for two years from 1886.

5 Moulin de la Galette Further along rue Lepic are Montmartre's famous twinned windmills. The Moulin de la Galette, the better known, was turned into a popular open-air dance hall in the late 19th century and was immortalised by Pierre-Auguste Renoir in his 1876 tableau *Le Bal du Moulin de La Galette*.

6 Moulin Radet About 100m to the east, at the corner of rue Girardon, is the Moulin Radet. Confusingly, it's now a restaurant called Le Moulin de la Galette.

7 Passe-Muraille statue Crossing through place Marcel Aymé, you'll see a curious statue of a man emerging from a stone wall. It's by the late actor Jean Marais and portrays Dutilleul, the hero of Marcel Aymé's short story *Le Passe-Muraille* (The Walker through Walls), who awakes one fine morning to discover he can do just what he's shown doing here.

8 Cimetière St-Vincent Turn left (north) into rue Girardon, cross through leafy square St-Buisson (Holy Bush) and past the charmingly named Allée des Brouillards (Fog Path) and descend the stairs from place Dalida into rue St-Vincent; on the other side of the wall is Cimetière St-Vincent, final resting place of the great and the good, including Maurice Utrillo (1883–1955), the so-called Painter of Montmartre.

9 Au Lapin Agile Just over rue des Saules is the celebrated cabaret Au Lapin Agile (p311), whose name seems to suggest a nimble rabbit but actually comes from *Le Lapin à Gill,* a mural of

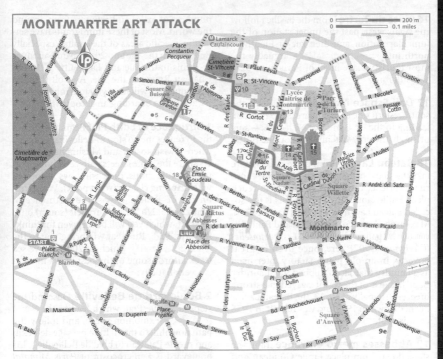

MONTMARTRE ART ATTACK

lonelyplanet.com

NEIGHBOURHOODS WALKING TOURS

WALK FACTS

Start Metro Blanche
End Metro Abbesses
Distance 2.5km
Time Two hours
Fuel stops Il Duca (p278), La Maison Rose (p280)

a rabbit jumping out of a cooking pot by caricaturist André Gill, which can still be seen on the western exterior wall. Among the cabaret's regulars was the poet Guillaume Apollinaire, the great proponent of cubism and futurism, who was killed in combat in 1918.

10 Close du Montmartre Turn right (south) onto rue des Saules. Just opposite is the Close du Montmartre, a small vineyard dating from 1933, whose 2000 vines produce an average of 850 bottles of wine each October (p15). They're auctioned off for charity in the 18e.

11 Musée de Montmartre You can buy sample bottles of the hooch at the Musée de Montmartre (p170), which is on rue Cortot at No 12–14, the first street on the left after the vine-

yard. The museum is housed in Montmartre's oldest building, a manor house built in the 17th century, and one-time home to painters Renoir, Utrillo and Raoul Dufy.

12 Eric Satie's house The celebrated composer lived from 1892 to 1898 in the house at 6 rue Cortot.

13 Water tower At the end of rue Cortot turn right (south) onto rue du Mont Cenis (the attractive water tower just opposite dates from the early 20th century), left onto (tiny) rue de Chevalier de la Barre and then right onto rue du Cardinal Guibert.

14 Église St-Pierre de Montmartre This will lead you past the back of Église St-Pierre de Montmartre. It was built on the site of a Roman temple to Mercury and did time as a 'Temple of Reason' under the Revolution and as a clothing factory during the Commune.

15 Basilique du Sacré Cœur The entrance to the Basilique du Sacré Cœur (p168) and the stunning vista over Paris from the steps and the place du Parvis du Sacré Cœur are just a few paces to the south.

185

16 Place du Tertre From the basilica follow rue Azaïs west, past the upper station of the funicular station, and then rue St-Eleuthère north into place du Tertre (p168) – arguably the most touristy place in all of Paris but buzzy and still fun.

17 Dalí Espace Montmartre Just off the southwestern side of the square is rue Poulbot, leading to the Dalí Espace Montmartre (p170) – surprisingly the only 'art' museum on the Butte.

18 Bateau Lavoir From place du Calvaire take the steps – actually rue du Calvaire – into rue Gabrielle, turning right (west) to reach place Émile Goudeau. At No 11bis is the so-called Bateau Lavoir, where Kees Van Dongen, Max Jacob, Amedeo Modigliani and Pablo Picasso, who painted his seminal *Les Demoiselles d'Avignon* (1907) here, once lived in great poverty, in an old piano factory later used as a laundry that Jacob dubbed the 'Laundry Boat' because of the way it swayed in a strong breeze. Originally at No 13, the Bateau Lavoir burned down in 1970 and was rebuilt in 1978 on this spot.

19 Abbesses metro entrance Take the steps down from place Émile Goudeau and follow rue des Abbesses south into place des Abbesses, where you can't miss the Abbesses metro entrance designed by Hector Guimard (see boxed text, p156).

PARISIAN ROUND-THE-WORLD TOUR

And you thought it was all berets, baguettes and bistros... To be sure, Paris is and will always be *français* – the couturiers will continue to spin their glad rags, the *boulangeries* (bakeries) will churn out those long, crispy loaves and the terrace cafés will remain the places to watch the world go by. But it's a much more international world nowadays, and *Paris Mondial* (World Paris), a diverse, dynamic, multicultural city, vibrates to its rhythms.

France ruled a considerable part of the world until the middle of the 20th century, and today its population includes a large number of immigrants and their descendants from its former colonies and protectorates in Africa, Indochina, the Middle East, India, the Caribbean and the South Pacific. At the same time, France has continued to accept significant numbers of exiles and refugees from around the world. Most of these immigrants have settled in specific areas of the capital, especially Belleville in the 19e and 20e, rue du Faubourg St-Denis in the 10e and La Goutte d'Or and Château Rouge in the 18e. A stroll through these quarters will have you touring the globe without even boarding an aeroplane.

1 Birthplace of Édith Piaf Begin the walk at the Pyrénées metro stop in Belleville, a district where Jewish kosher and Muslim halal butchers share the same streets with cavernous Chinese noodle shops, their windows festooned with dripping *cha siu* (roast pork). Walk west on rue de Belleville, past the birthplace of Édith Piaf at No 72, and turn left (south) onto rue Piat, which you will be forgiven for thinking says 'Piaf'. Rue Piat will bring you to the Parc de Belleville (p154) which, at 200m above sea level, affords some of the best views in what is a very flat city.

2 Boulevard de Belleville Descend the steps at 27 rue Piat, which lead to the Maison de l'Air (p154) exhibition space, and follow the path downhill to the right to passage de Pékin and rue de Pali Kao to blvd de Belleville. This boulevard is a microcosm of *Paris Mondial* and on market mornings (see p231), you might think you've been transported to the Mediterranean, Africa or even Asia. At No 39 is the Mosquée Abou Bakr as Saddiq, just a few doors down from the modern Église Notre Dame Réconciliatrice, a Sri Lankan Christian church at No 57. About 100m up on the right-hand – or Tunisian – side of the street is the Synagogue Michkenot Yaachov at No 118.

3 Rue du Faubourg du Temple Walk north up blvd de Belleville and turn left (west) onto rue du Faubourg du Temple. The walk along rue du Faubourg du Temple to place de la République is a long one and you can take the metro for a couple of stops. But in doing so you'd miss the vibrancy and assorted sights: La Java (p310) at No 105, where Piaf once warbled, and the Épicerie Asie, Antilles, Afrique, which sells goods from three worlds. Once you've crossed the placid Canal St-Martin, the enormous place de la République, where many political rallies and demonstrations in Paris start and/or end, and its statue of the Republic (erected in 1883), pops into view.

4 Boulevard St-Martin Make your way to place de la République's northwest corner and

PARISIAN ROUND-THE-WORLD TOUR

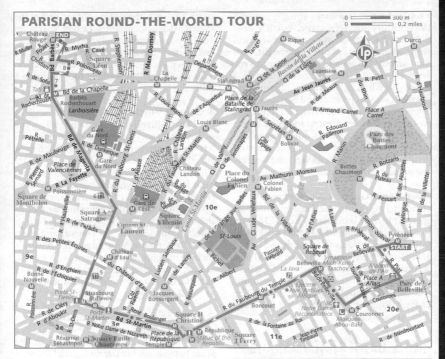

follow blvd St-Martin past the Porte St-Martin and the Porte St-Denis (p151).

5 Passage Brady Turn right (north) and follow rue du Faubourg St-Denis, the main artery linking Tamil Nadu with Turkey. Passage Brady (p268) at No 46, built in 1828 and once housing 100 tiny boutiques, is now a warren of Indian, Pakistani and Bangladeshi cafés and restaurants and the perfect spot for a break and some refuelling. Alternatively you might pop into a Turkish *çay salonu* (tea house) or *döner yemek ve çorba salon* (kebab and soup restaurant), which offer kebabs, soup, *pide* (Turkish pizza, for lack of a better term) and *lahmacun* (thin pitta bread topped with minced meat, tomatoes, onions and fresh parsley) for a cheap and tasty snack.

6 Marché St-Quentin Turn left onto blvd de Magenta and carry on north past the 19th-century Marché St-Quentin (p231) and the Gare du Nord.

7 North African quarter The big pink sign announcing the Tati department store (p217) marks the start of La Goutte d'Or, the North African quarter called the 'Golden Drop' after a white

WALK FACTS

Start **Metro Pyrénées**
End **Metro Château Rouge**
Distance **8km**
Time **3½ hours**
Fuel stop **Istanbul (p268), Passage Brady (p268)**

wine that was produced here in the 19th century. The district is contiguous with African Château Rouge and outside the metro station you'll most likely be presented with the calling cards of various *médiums* (mediums) or *voyants* (fortune tellers) promising to effect the return of your estranged spouse, unrequited love or misspent fortune. From the Barbès Rochechouart metro stop walk north up blvd Barbès past numerous goldsmiths with dazzling window displays. Turn east into rue de la Goutte d'Or, a great souk of a street selling everything from gaudy tea glasses and pointy-toed leather *babouches* (slippers) to belly dancers' costumes. From every direction the sounds of *raï* (a fusion of Algerian folk music and rock) fill the air.

8 Villa Poissonnière A gate at 42 rue de la Goutte d'Or gives way to Villa Poissonnière, a cobbled street that looks straight out of a 19th-century daguerreotype, but it's now locked and a sign warns that trespassers will be prosecuted. Instead carry on straight, turn right on blvd Barbès and right again onto rue des Poissonniers – the 'Street of Fishermen' – where you'll find halal butchers offering special deals on sheep heads and 5kg packets of chicken but no fish. Rue Myrha on your left is the frontier between Central and West Africa and the Maghreb; *rai* music quickly gives way to Cameroonian *bikutsi* (a fusion of ancestral rhythms and fast electric guitars) and Senegalese *mbalax* (drum music).

9 Rue Dejean After crossing over rue Myrha, turn left (west) into rue Dejean, where an open-air market is held from 8am to 1pm on Sundays and 3.30pm to 7.30pm Tuesdays to Saturdays. Here you *will* find fish and lots of it, especially fresh *capitaine* (Nile perch) and *thiof* from Senegal, alongside stalls selling fiery Caribbean Scotch Bonnet chillies, plantains and the ever-popular *dasheen* (taro). The Château Rouge metro station is a few steps to the southwest.

RIGHT BANK TIME PASSAGES

Stepping into the *passages couverts* (covered shopping arcades) of the Right Bank is the simplest way to get a feel for what life was like in early-19th-century Paris. These arcades emerged during a period of relative peace and prosperity under the restored House of Bourbon after Napoleon's fall and the rapid growth of the new industrial classes. In a city without sewers, pavements or sheltered walkways, these arcades allowed shoppers to stroll from boutique to boutique protected from the elements and the filth and noise of the streets.

The *passages* quickly became some of Paris' top attractions – visitors from the provinces made the arcades their first port of call in order to kit themselves out for the capital – and by the mid-19th century Paris counted around 150 of these sumptuously decorated temples to Mammon. As well as shopping, visitors could dine and drink, play billiards, bathe (all the *passages* had public baths), attend the theatre and, at night (the *passages* were open 24 hours a day back then), engage in activities of a carnal nature; the arcades were notorious for attracting prostitutes after dark, and there were rooms available on the 1st floor.

The demise of the *passages* came about for a number of reasons, but the most significant

death knell was the opening of the first of the capital's department stores, Le Bon Marché, in 1852. Today there are only two dozen arcades remaining – mostly in the 1er, 2e and 9e arrondissements – in various states of repair. This is an excellent walking tour to do on a rainy day.

1 Galerie Véro Dodat Begin the walk at the Louvre-Rivoli metro station (1er) on rue de Rivoli; go north along rue du Louvre, turn left (west) onto rue St-Honoré and then right (north) again on rue Jean-Jacques Rousseau. The entrance to the Galerie Véro Dodat, built in 1823 by two well-heeled *charcutiers* (butchers), is at No 19. The arcade retains its 19th-century skylights, ceiling murals, Corinthian columns, tiled floor, gas globe fittings (though now electric, of course) and shop fronts, among the most interesting of which include the Luthier music store, with guitars, violins, banjos and ukuleles, at No 17 and the Marini France stained-glass workshop at No 28.

2 Galeries du Palais Royal The gallery's western exit leads to rue du Bouloi and rue Croix des Petits Champs. Head north on the latter to the corner of rue du Colonel Driant – the massive building ahead of you is the headquarters of the Banque de France – and turn left (west) and walk to rue de Valois. At No 5 is one of the entrances to the Galeries du Palais Royal. Strictly speaking, these galleries are not *passages* as they are arcaded rather than covered, but since they date from 1786 they are considered to be the prototypes of what was to come.

3 Galerie de Montpensier The Café de Foy, from where the Revolution broke out on a warm mid-July day just three years after the galleries opened, once stood on the western side of the Galeries du Palais Royal, at what is today's Galerie de Montpensier. Galerie de Montpensier has several traditional shops, including A Bacqueville at No 6–8, with Légion d'Honneur–style medals and ribbons, and Didier Ludot (p204) at No 20–24, with exquisite antique clothes.

4 Galerie de Valois This *passage* on the eastern side, where Charlotte Corday, Jean-Paul Marat's assassin, once worked in a shop, is more upmarket, with posh galleries and designer shops such as an outlet of Hong Kong–based boutique Joyce at shop No

168–173. Other shops worth a peek include Didier Ludot's La Petite Robe Noire (p204) boutique at No 125 and the *graveur héraldiste* (coat of arms engraver) Guillaumot, which has been printing family coats-of-arms at Nos 151 to 154 since 1785.

5 Passage du Perron The tiny arcade that doglegs from the north of the Galeries du Palais Royal into rue de Beaujolais is passage du Perron; the writer Colette (1873–1954) lived out the last years of her life in a flat above here (9 rue de Beaujolais), from which she wrote *Paris de Ma Fenêtre* (Paris from My Window), her description of the German occupation of Paris.

6 Galerie Vivienne Diagonally opposite from where you exit from Passage du Perron at 4 rue des Petits Champs are the entrances to two of the most stunningly restored *passages* in Paris. Galerie Vivienne, built in 1823 and decorated with bas-reliefs of snakes (signifying prudence), anchors (hope) and beehives (industry), as well as floor mosaics, was (and still is) one of the poshest of the *passages*. As you enter, look to the stairwell to the left at No 13 for its false marble walls; François Eugène Vidocq (1775–1857), master burglar *and* later the chief of detectives in Paris in the early 19th century, lived upstairs. Some shops to check out are Legrand Fille et Fils (p200), which sells wine and wine-related paraphernalia, at No 7–11; Wolff et Descourtis and its silk scarves at No 18; L'Atelir Emilio Robbo, one of the most beautiful flower shops in Paris, at No 29–33; the Librairie Ancienne & Moderne at No 45–46, which Colette frequented; and designer Jean Paul Gaultier's first boutique (main entrance at 6 rue Vivienne, 2e).

7 Galerie Colbert The major draw of the Galerie Colbert, which runs parallel to Galerie Vivienne, is its glass dome and rotunda. Built in 1826 and now part of the University of Paris system, the *passage* served as a car workshop and garage as recently as the early 1980s. Check out the bizarre fresco above the exit to the rue des Petits Champs; it's completely disproportionate. Enter and exit from rue Vivienne.

8 Statue of Sartre From here head south along rue Vivienne – passing the original home of the Bibliothèque Nationale de France (p161) before it moved south, with its curiously bowed statue of Sartre in the courtyard – to rue des Petits Champs and turn right (west).

RIGHT BANK TIME PASSAGES

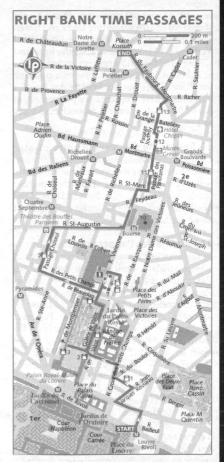

WALK FACTS

Start Metro Louvre-Rivoli
End Metro Le Peletier
Distance 3km
Time Two hours
Fuel stops Baan Boran (p235), Café de l'Époque (p236), Café du Théâtre (p235), Le Véro Dodat (p236)

9 Passage Choiseul At 40 rue des Petits Champs is the entrance to passage Choiseul. Passage Choiseul (1828), some 45m long and containing scores of shops, is more ordinary than many of the other *passages* covered here but is rapidly raising its profile. Discount and secondhand clothing shops (Nos 7–9, 39–41 and 51–53), Asian fast-food shops (for example,

189

Nos 19, 32 and 46) and secondhand book-shops (No 74–76) are getting fewer and fewer. The *passage* has a long literary pedigree: Paul Verlaine (1844–96) drank absinthe here and Céline (1894–1961) grew up in his moth-er's shop at No 62, which now sells costume jewellery. Check out the Théâtre des Bouffes Parisiens, where comedies are performed, at No 61 (the main theatre is around the corner at 4 rue Monsigny, 2e).

10 Bourse de Commerce Leave passage Choiseul at 23 rue St-Augustin and walk east-wards to where the street meets rue du Quatre Septembre. The building across the square is the Bourse de Commerce (p90), built in 1826. Head north and walk up rue Vivienne, and then east along rue St-Marc.

11 Passage des Panoramas The entrance to the mazelike passage des Panoramas is at 10 rue St-Marc. Built in 1800, passage des Panoramas is the oldest covered arcade in Paris and the first to be lit by gas (1817). It was expanded in 1834 with the addition of four other interconnecting *passages:* Feydeau, Montmartre, St-Marc and Variétés. It's a bit faded around the edges now, but keep an eye open for Jean-Paul Belmondo's Théâtre des Variétés at No 17, the erstwhile vaudeville Théâtre d'Offenbach, from where spectators would come out to shop during the interval, and the old engraver Stern at No 47. Exit at 11 blvd Montmartre.

12 Passage Jouffroy Directly across the road, at 10–12 blvd Montmartre, is the en-trance to passage Jouffroy. Passage Jouffroy, the last major *passage* to open in Paris (1846) – and the first to use metal and glass in its sky-lights and to have central heating – remains a personal favourite; no other *passage* offers so much or feels so alive. There are two hotels here, including the Hôtel Chopin (p354), as well as the Musée Grévin (p147) of wax figures. There are also some wonderful boutiques, including the bookshops Librairie du Passage (Nos 39 and 48), with lots of old postcards, and Paul Vulin (No 46–50); M&G Segas (No 34), where Tou-louse-Lautrec bought his walking sticks; Brési-lophile (No 40) filled with colourful rocks and minerals; and Cinedoc (Nos 45–53) with film posters, books and postcards for collectors.

13 Passage Verdeau Leave passage Jouf-froy at 9 rue de la Grange Batelière, cross the road to No 6, and enter passage Verdeau, the last and most modest of this stretch of covered arcades. Verdeau wasn't particularly success-ful because of its 'end-of-the-line' location. Still, there's lots to explore here: Le Cabinet des Curieux (No 12) with weird and curious objects; daguerreotypes at Photo Verdeau (No 14); vintage Tintin and comic books at Librai-rie Roland Buret (No 6); and needlepoint at Le Bonheur des Dames (No 8). The northern exit from passage Verdeau is at 31bis rue du Faubourg Montmartre.

MEDIEVAL MEANDERINGS IN THE MARAIS

Monks and the Knights Templar settled in the Marais as early as the 13th century, which explains the religious nature of many of its street names (eg rue du Temple, rue des Blancs Manteaux). But it wasn't until Henri IV began construction of place Royale (now place des Vosges) in the early 17th century that the ar-istocracy began building the *hôtels particuliers* (private mansions) and *pavillons* (somewhat less-grand houses) so characteristic of the dis-trict. These gold- and cream-coloured brick buildings are among the most beautiful Ren-aissance structures in the city and, because so many were built at more or less the same time, the Marais enjoys an architectural harmony unknown elsewhere in Paris.

The golden age of the Marais' *hôtels par-ticuliers* was the 17th century, though con-struction continued into the first half of the 18th. The removal of the royal court – lock, stock and satin slipper – to Versailles in 1692 sounded the death knell for the Marais, and the mansions passed into the hands of com-moners, who used them as warehouses, mar-kets and shops. The quarter was given a major face-lift in the late 1960s and early '70s, and today many of the *hôtels particuliers* house government offices, libraries and museums.

1 Hôtel d'Aumont Begin the tour at St-Paul metro station on rue François Miron, 4e, fac-ing rue de Rivoli. Walk south on narrow rue du Prévôt to rue Charlemagne, once called rue des Prestres (Street of the Priests). To the right (west) on the corner of rue des Non-nains d'Hyères at 7 rue de Jouy stands the majestic Hôtel d'Aumont, built around 1650 for a financier and one of the most beautiful *hôtels particuliers* in the Marais. It now con-tains offices of the Tribunal Administratif, the body that deals with – *sacré bleu!* – internal

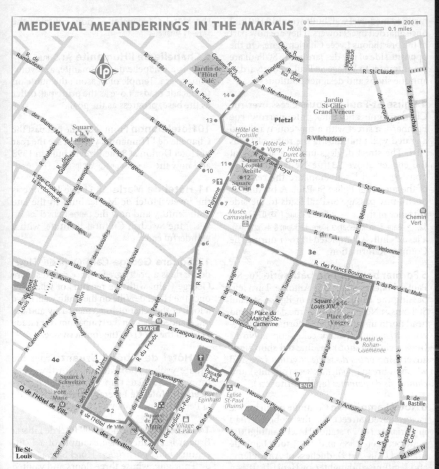

disputes in the bloated and litigious French
civil service.

2 Hôtel de Sens Continue south along
rue des Nonnains d'Hyères, past the Hôtel
d'Aumont's geometrical gardens on the right
and turn left (east) onto rue de l'Hôtel de
Ville. On the left at 1 rue du Figuier is Hôtel
de Sens, the oldest private mansion in the
Marais. Begun around 1475, it was built as
the Paris digs for the powerful archbishops
of Sens, under whose authority Paris fell at
the time. When Paris was made an archbisho-
pric, the Hôtel de Sens was rented out to
coach drivers, fruit sellers, a hatter and even
a jam-maker. It was heavily restored in mock
Gothic style (complete with turrets) in 1911;
today it houses the Bibliothèque Forney (Forney
Library; ☎ 01 42 78 14 60; admission free; ⏰ 1-7.30pm Tue,

Fri & Sat, 10am-7.30pm Wed & Thu) and its temporary
exhibitions.

3 Philippe-Auguste's enceinte Continue
southeast along rue de l'Ave Maria and then
go northeast along rue des Jardins de St-Paul.
The two truncated and crumbling towers
across the basketball courts on the left are all
that remain of Philippe-Auguste's *enceinte*, a

191

fortified medieval wall built around 1190 and once guarded by 39 towers. They are now part of the prestigious Lycée Charlemagne. On the opposite side of rue des Jardins de St-Paul are the entrances to Village St-Paul, a courtyard of antique shops and designer boutiques.

4 Église St-Paul St-Louis Cross over rue Charlemagne and duck into narrow rue Eginhard, a street with a tiny courtyard and a grated well built during the reign of Louis XIII. The street doglegs into rue St-Paul; at the corner above 23 rue Neuve St-Pierre, housing a bed-linen shop, are the remains of the medieval Église St-Paul. A bit further north, tiny passage St-Paul leads to the side entrance of the Église St-Paul St-Louis (☎ 01 42 72 30 32; ⏰ 8am-8pm Mon-Sat, 9.30am-12.30pm & 4-7pm Sun), a Jesuit church completed in 1641 during the Counter-Reformation.

5 Former boulangerie-pâtisserie Rue St-Paul debouches into rue St-Antoine. Turn left, passing the front entrance of Église St-Paul St-Louis at No 99, cross over rue de Rivoli and head north up rue Malher. A former *boulangerie-pâtisserie*, or bakery-cake shop, at No 13 (now a clothes shop) has fine old shop signs advertising *pains de seigle et gruau* (rye and wheaten breads), *gateaux secs* (biscuits) and *chaussons de pommes* (apple turnovers).

6 Hôtel Lamoignon Continue north on rue Pavée (Paved Street), the first cobbled road in Paris. At No 24 stands Hôtel Lamoignon, built between 1585 and 1612 for Diane de France (1538–1619), duchess of Angoulême and legitimised daughter of Henri II. It is a fine example of late Renaissance architecture; note the Corinthian capitals in the courtyard and, above the main gate, the cherubs holding a mirror (symbolising truth) and a snake (for prudence). It now houses the Bibliothèque Historique de la Ville de Paris (☎ 01 44 59 29 40; ⏰ 1-6pm Mon-Fri, 9.30am-6pm Sat).

7 Hôtel Carnavalet Walk north along rue Payenne. The building immediately on the right at No 2 is the back of the mid-16th-century, Renaissance-style Hôtel Carnavalet, built between 1548 and 1654 and home to the letter-writer Madame de Sévigné (1626–96).

8 Hôtel Le Peletier de St-Fargeau Further north is the Hôtel Le Peletier de St-Fargeau, which dates from the late 17th century. With

the Hôtel Carnavalet, it now contains the Musée Carnavalet (p96).

9 Chapelle de l'Humanité At 5 rue Payenne is a Chapelle de l'Humanité, a Revolutionary-era 'Temple of Reason'; the quote on the façade reads: 'Love as the principal, order as the base, progress as the goal'.

10 Hôtel Donon From the grille just past the Chapelle de l'Humanité, you can see the rear of Hôtel Donon at 8 rue Elzévir, built in 1598 and now the Musée Cognacq-Jay (p96).

11 Hôtel de Marle At 11 rue Payenne is the lovely Hôtel de Marle, built in the late 16th century and now the Centre Culturel Suédois (p288), the Swedish Cultural Institute, with a wonderful café.

12 Square George Cain Opposite Hôtel de Marle is a pretty green space called square George Cain, with the remains of what was once the Hôtel de Ville on the south wall. Have a look at the relief of Judgement Day and the one-handed clock on the tympanum (the façade beneath the roof) on the southern side.

13 Hôtel de Libéral Bruant From the square walk a short distance northwest to more spectacular 17th-century *hôtels particuliers*: Hôtel de Libéral Bruant at 1 rue de la Perle is now a gallery.

14 Hôtel Salé Northeast of Hôtel de Libéral Bruant is another prize example of a 17th-century *hôtel particulier*: Hôtel Salé at 5 rue de Thorigny, whose three floors and vaulted cellars house the wonderful Musée Picasso (p96).

15 Rue du Parc Royal Retrace your steps to rue du Parc Royal. Heading east you'll pass three wonderful *hôtels*: Hôtel de Croisille at No 12, Hôtel de Vigny at No 10 and pink-brick Hôtel Duret de Chevry at No 8, the loveliest of the trio. All of these date from about 1620 and now do civic duty as archives and historical libraries.

16 Place des Vosges Walk south down rue de Sévigné and then follow rue des Francs Bourgeois eastwards to the sublime place des Vosges (p91), which has four symmetrical fountains and an 1829 copy of a mounted statue of Louis XIII, originally placed here in 1639. In the southeastern corner at No 6 is Hôtel de Rohan-Guéménée, home to Victor Hugo for

16 years in the first half of the 19th century and now the Maison de Victor Hugo (p91).

17 Hôtel de Sully In the southwestern corner of place des Vosges is the back entrance to Hôtel de Sully (p96), a restored aristocratic mansion at 62 rue St-Antoine built in 1624. Behind the hôtel are two beautifully decorated late Renaissance-style courtyards, both of which are festooned with allegorical reliefs of the seasons and the elements. In the northern courtyard look to the southern side for spring (flowers and a bird in hand) and summer (wheat); in the southern courtyard turn to the northern side for autumn (grapes) and winter, with a symbol representing both the end of the year and the end of life. On the western side of the second courtyard are 'air' on the left and 'fire' on the right. On the eastern side look for 'earth' on the left and 'water' on the right.

LATIN QUARTER LITERARY LOOP

Writers have found their way to Paris ever since that 16th-century hedonist François Rabelais forsook his monastic vows and hightailed it to the capital. The 1920s saw the greatest influx of outsiders, particularly Americans. Many assume it was Paris' reputation for liberal thought and relaxed morals that attracted the likes of Ernest Hemingway, F Scott Fitzgerald, Ezra Pound and so on, but that's just part of the story. Paris was cheap, particularly the Left Bank, and in France, unlike in Prohibition-era America, you could drink alcohol to your heart's (or liver's) content.

1 James Joyce's flat Begin your tour at the Cardinal Lemoine metro station, where rue du Cardinal Lemoine meets rue Monge, 5e. Walk southwest along rue du Cardinal Lemoine, peering down the passageway at No 71, which may or may not be closed off. The Irish writer James Joyce (1882–1941) lived in the courtyard flat at the back marked 'E' when he first arrived in Paris in 1921, and it was here that he finished editing *Ulysses*.

2 Ernest Hemingway's apartment Further south at 74 rue du Cardinal Lemoine is the 3rd-floor apartment where Ernest Hemingway (1899–1961) lived with his first wife Hadley from January 1922 until August 1923. The flat figures prominently in his book of memoirs, *A Moveable Feast*, from which the

quotation on the wall plaque (in French) is taken: 'This is how Paris was in our youth when we were very poor and very happy.' Just below the flat was the Bal au Printemps, a popular *bal musette* (dancing club), which served as the model for the one where Jake Barnes met Brett Ashley in Hemingway's *The Sun Also Rises*. It is now the bookshop Librairie Les Alizés (The Trade Winds; ☎ 01 43 25 20 03; ⊙ 10am-12.30pm & 1.30-9pm Tue-Fri, 10am-12.30pm & 1.30-7pm Mon & Sat, 2-7pm Sun), specialising in new and second-hand books by American writers.

3 Paul Verlaine's garret Hemingway lived on rue du Cardinal Lemoine, but he wrote in a top-floor garret of a hotel round the corner at 39 rue Descartes, the very hotel where the poet Paul Verlaine (1844–96) had died less than three decades before. The plaque, on what is now a restaurant aptly called La Maison de Verlaine, incorrectly states that Hemingway lived here from 1921 to 1925. Japanese historical novelist Kunio Tsuji lived here from 1980 to 1999.

4 Place de la Contrescarpe Rue Descartes runs south into place de la Contrescarpe, now a well-scrubbed square with four Judas trees and a fountain, but once a 'cesspool' (or so Hemingway said), especially the Café des Amateurs at No 2–4, which is now the popular Café Delmas (p290). The Au Nègre Joyeux, above a small supermarket at No 12, which sports a large painting of a jolly black servant and his white master, was another popular music club in the early 20th century.

5 George Orwell's boarding house Rue Mouffetard (from *mofette*, meaning 'skunk') runs south of place de la Contrescarpe. Turn west (right) at the first street on the right (pedestrian rue du Pot de Fer); in 1928 one Eric Blair – better known to the world as George Orwell (1903–50) – stayed in a cheap and dirty boarding house above 6 rue du Pot de Fer called the Hôtel des Trois Moineaux (Hotel of the Three Sparrows) while working as a dishwasher. He wrote all about it and the street, which he called 'rue du Coq d'Or' (Street of the Golden Rooster), in *Down and Out in Paris and London* (1933).

6 Place du Panthéon Turn north (right) onto rue Tournefort (the street where much of Balzac's novel *Père Goriot* takes place) and go left into rue de l'Estrapade. From here follow Hemingway's own directions provided

LATIN QUARTER LITERARY LOOP

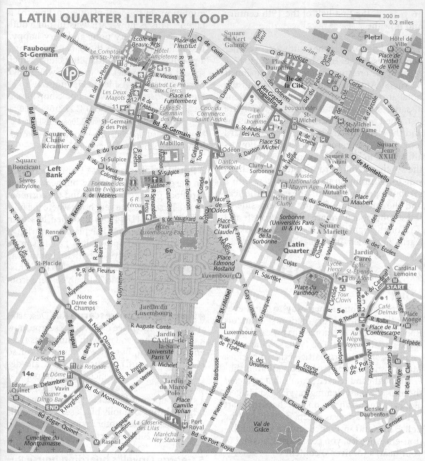

in *A Moveable Feast* as he made his way to a favourite café in place St-Michel. Turn north (right) onto rue Clotilde and walk the length of the street – the eastern side of vast place du Panthéon no less – to the corner of rue Clovis. Just around the corner on rue Clovis is the entrance to the prestigious Lycée Henri IV; cross the road to glimpse the tip of the 13th-century (but heavily restored) Tour Clovis within the school complex; the tower is all that remains of an abbey founded by Clovis I. Opposite is the ancient Église St-Étienne du Mont (p109).

7 Boulevard St-Michel Continue around the northern edge of place du Panthéon and walk west along rue Soufflot, past the bounty of bookshops that line both sides of the street. Turn right onto blvd St-Michel and follow it past Hôtel de Cluny, now the Musée National du

WALK FACTS

Start Metro Cardinal Lemoine
End Former Dingo Bar (Metro Vavin)
Distance 7km
Time Three hours
Fuel stops Les Deux Magots (p292) **or** Café de Flore (p292)

Moyen Age (p114). The cafés on place St-Michel were taken over by tourists decades ago, and Shakespeare & Company (p208) around the corner at 37 rue de la Bûcherie has nothing to do with the real bookshop of that name frequented by Hemingway, but that comes later in the tour.

8 Jack Kerouac's hotel Follow the Seine west along quai des Grands Augustins. Hemingway used to buy books from the *bouquin-istes* (secondhand booksellers), some of whom still line the embankment. To the south, at No 9 of tiny rue Gît le Cœur, is the Relais Hôtel du Vieux Paris, a favourite of poet Allen Ginsberg (1926–97) and Beat writer Jack Kerouac (1922–69) in the 1950s. (There's a not-wholly-substantiated story that when Truman Capote first read Kerouac's stream-of-consciousness *On the Road* he exclaimed, 'That's not writing – that's typewriting!') Ginsberg and Kerouac drank just down the road in a bar called Le Gentilhomme at 28 rue St-André des Arts, now an Irish pub called Corcoran's.

9 Picasso's studio Pablo Picasso (1881–1973) had his studio at 7 rue des Grands Augustins, the street that runs south from quai des Grands Augustins. Picasso lived here from 1936 to 1955 and completed his masterpiece *Guernica* here in 1937 – exactly a century after Balzac's *Le Chef d'Œuvre Inconnu* (The Unknown Masterpiece), set in this *hôtel particulier*, was published.

10 Shakespeare & Company – The Original Walk south to rue St-André des Arts, follow it westwards and then turn south through Cour du Commerce Saint André, a covered passage that empties into blvd St-Germain opposite the statue of Georges Danton. At 12 rue de l'Odéon, the street running south, stood the original Shakespeare & Company bookshop, where founder-owner Sylvia Beach (1887–1962) lent books to Hemingway, and edited, retyped and published *Ulysses* for Joyce in 1922. The bookshop was closed during the occupation when Beach refused to sell her last copy of Joyce's *Finnegan's Wake* to a Nazi officer.

11 Sartre & de Beauvoir's hang-outs Return to blvd St-Germain and walk westwards to the 11th-century Église St-Germain des Prés (p115). Opposite is Les Deux Magots (p292) and beyond it Café de Flore (p292), favourite hang-outs of postwar Left Bank intellectuals such as Jean-Paul Sartre (1905–80) and Simone de Beauvoir (1908–86) and good (though pricey) places to stop for a snack or a drink.

12 Henry Miller's room From place St-Germain des Prés walk north along rue Bonaparte. In spring 1930 Henry Miller (1891–1980) stayed in a 5th-floor mansard room in Hôtel St-Germain des Prés at No 36 and later wrote about the experience in *Letters to Emil* (1989). The philosopher Auguste Comté (1798–1857), the founder of positivism, lived in the same building from 1818 to 1822. A few doors down at No 30 is the Bistrot Le Pré aux Clercs, another Hemingway hang-out.

13 Oscar Wilde's hotel Continue north on rue Bonaparte and turn east onto rue des Beaux-Arts. Walk to No 13 and you'll reach what is now L'Hôtel (p346), the former Hôtel d'Alsace, where Oscar Wilde (b 1854) died of meningitis in 1900. But not before proclaiming, in his typical style, that he and the wallpaper of his room were 'fighting a duel to the death' (see boxed text, p154). The Argentine writer Jorge Luis Borges (1899–1986) also stayed in the same hotel many times in the late 1970s and early '80s.

14 Rue Jacob This street running perpendicular to rue Bonaparte has literary associations from the sublime to the ridiculous. At No 44, Hôtel d'Angleterre (p347) is where Hemingway spent his first night in Paris (in room No 14 on 20 December 1921). A few doors down at No 56, the former Hôtel d'York is of great historic, if not literary, significance – this is where David Hartley, George III's representative, met with Benjamin Franklin, John Adams and John Hay on 3 September 1783 to sign the treaty recognising American independence.

At 52 rue Jacob is a nondescript café called Le Comptoir des Sts-Pères, which under normal circumstances would not deserve a second glance. But this was the fashionable restaurant Michaud's, where Hemingway stood outside watching Joyce and his family dine and, later, when he was on the inside looking out, where a memorable event may – or may not – have taken place. According to Hemingway in his *A Moveable Feast*, the writer F Scott Fitzgerald (1896–1940), concerned about not being able to sexually satisfy his wife, Zelda, asked Hemingway to inspect him in the café's toilet. 'It is not basically a question of the size in repose…' Hemingway advised him, in what could be one of best examples of the 'big lie' in American literary history.

15 Église St-Sulpice Go south on rue des Saints Pères, then east on blvd St-Germain and south on rue Bonaparte. Follow it south past Église St-Sulpice (p115), where a pivotal clue is left and a murder takes place in Dan Brown's *The Da Vinci Code*. It eventually leads to the northwestern corner of the Jardin du

Luxembourg, rue de Vaugirard and the Fontaine des Quatre Évêques (Fountain of the Four Bishops).

16 Gertrude Stein's home After slumming it for a few years in the Latin Quarter, Hemingway and many other members of the so-called Lost Generation moved to this area. In 1925 William Faulkner (1897–1962) spent a few months at 42 rue de Vaugirard in what is now the posh Hôtel Luxembourg Parc. Hemingway spent his last few years in Paris in a rather grand flat at 6 rue Férou, within easy striking (the operative word, as they had fallen out – and big time – by then) distance of 27 rue de Fleurus, where the American novelist Gertrude Stein (1874–1946) first lived with her brother Leo, and then her lifelong companion, Alice B Toklas, for 35 years. Stein entertained such luminaries as Matisse, Picasso, Braque, Gauguin, Pound and of course the young Hemingway and Hadley, who were treated as though they were 'very good, well-mannered and promising children' according to the latter. It's odd to think that this splendid *belle époque* block (1894) was less than 10 years old when Stein first moved here in 1903.

17 Rue Notre Dame des Champs Ezra Pound (1885–1972) lived not far away at 70bis rue Notre Dame des Champs in a flat filled with Japanese paintings and with packing crates posing as furniture, as did Katherine Anne Porter (1890–1980) in the same flat in 1934. Hemingway's first apartment in this part of town was above a sawmill at 113 rue Notre Dames des Champs, now part of the École Alsacienne (Alsatian School) complex. Further east is Le Closerie des Lilas (p258) on blvd du Montparnasse, where Hemingway often met John Dos Passos or just sat alone, contemplating the Maréchal Ney statue in front of it.

18 Literary Cafés Port Royal metro station, where you might end the tour, is just opposite. West of here and clustered around place Pablo Picasso and Vavin metro station is a couple of café-restaurants that have hosted more literary luminaries than any others in the world: Le Dôme (p258) and, as Jake Barnes puts it in *The Sun Also Rises*, 'that new dive, the Select' (p293). Just off blvd Raspail at 10 rue Delambre is the former Dingo Bar, now a restaurant. It was here that Hemingway, the ambitious, middle-class kid from the Midwest, and Fitzgerald, the well-heeled, dissolute Princeton graduate, met for the first time, became friends (of sorts) and went on to change the face of American literature. For at least one of us, the erstwhile Dingo is a church.

top picks

What's your recommendation? www.lonelyplanet.com/paris

When it comes to shopping, Paris naturally has it all: large boulevards lined with international chains, luxury avenues with designer fashion, famous *grands magasins* (department stores) and fabulous *marchés aux puces* (flea markets; p217). But the real charm of Parisian shopping resides in a peripatetic stroll through the side streets, where tiny speciality stores and quirky boutiques selling everything from strawberry-scented Wellington boots to stainless-steel soap holders alternate with cafés, galleries and churches. These shops are what we've focused on in this chapter. Key areas are around the Marais in the 3e and 4e (p201), around St-Germain des Prés in the 6e (p209), and parts of Montmartre and Pigalle in the 9e and 18e (p217).

As in many capital cities, shops are spread out across different neighbourhoods, inspiring very different styles of shopping. If what the French do best – fashion (see p55) – is what you're after, then tread the *haute couture* (high fashion), luxury jewellery and designer perfume boardwalks in the Étoile and Champs-Élysées (p212). For original fashion, both street and vintage (see p204)), the addictive maze of boutique shopping in the Marais and St-Germain will keep you on your toes.

For an overview of Paris fashion, department stores such as Le Bon Marché (p212) in 7e and Galeries Lafayette (p215) and Printemps (p215) in the 9e provide a gentle introduction to what can be a frustratingly intimidating scene; should you not look like a millionaire, trying to raise a smile out of frosty, poker-faced staff in some designer boutiques (or indeed attracting their attention to let you in; most require you to buzz) can be disheartening. Should it be too much for you, personalised shopping tours exist; www.chicshoppingparis.com and www.chicparisi enne.com are two of many.

For a rundown on Paris' main shopping strips and streets specialising in particular products, see p203 and p216.

Shopping in Paris for fine food, wine, tea, books, stationery, art and antiques, and other collectables is particularly rewarding. For gift ideas, see p207.

Opening Hours

Opening hours are generally 10am to 7pm Monday to Saturday. Smaller shops often shut all day on Monday; on other days, their proprietors may close from noon to around 2pm for a long and lazy lunch. Many larger stores hold *nocturnes* (late-night shopping) on Thursday, remaining open until around 10pm. For Sunday shopping, the Champs-Élysées (p212), Montmartre (p217), the Marais (p201) and Bastille (p201) areas are the liveliest.

Winter *soldes* (sales) – during which many shops extend their hours – kick off in mid-January; summer *soldes* start the second week of June.

Consumer Taxes & Bargaining

If you're not an EU resident, you can get a TVA (VAT; sales tax) refund of up to 17%, provided you have spent more than €182 in any one store; see p409. Some larger department stores and 'duty-free' shops give discounts of 10% to foreign passport holders if asked; otherwise bargaining is reserved for flea markets.

LOUVRE & LES HALLES

Though you'll find any number of specialist boutiques selling everything from music boxes to kitchenware here, the 1e and 2e arrondissements are mostly about fashion. Indeed, the Sentier garment district has become a centre for fashion, while rue Étienne Marcel, place des Victoires and rue du Jour (beside the Église St-Eustache; Map p86) offer prominent labels and shoe shops. Nearby rue Montmartre and rue Tiquetonne are known for their streetwear and avant-garde designs. Les Halles itself, once the city's food market, is now a vast underground shopping complex. It's flanked to the east by the sleaze and sports stores of rue St-Denis, and to the south by the chain stores of rue de Rivoli. The easternmost part of the 1e around Palais Royal is far more conservative, with fancy period and label fashion.

BRENTANO'S Map pp82–3   Books
☎ 01 42 61 52 50; www.brentanos.fr; 37 av de l'Opéra, 2e; ☺ 10am-7.30pm Mon-Sat, 1-7pm Sun; Ⓜ Opéra
Situated midway between the Louvre and Palais Garnier, this US-based chain is a

good shop for tracking down American books, including fiction, business and children's titles, as well as magazines.

WH SMITH Map pp82–3 Books
☎ 01 44 77 88 99; www.whsmith.fr; 248 rue de Rivoli, 1er; ⏱ 9am-7.30pm Mon-Sat, 1pm-7.30pm Sun; Ⓜ Concorde

This branch of the British-owned chain counts some 70,000 titles in stock, as well as a good selection of international magazines, DVDs and greetings cards. Oddly, English-speaking staff are thin on the ground here.

AGNÈS B FEMME
Map p86 Clothing & Accessories
☎ 01 45 08 56 56; www.agnesb.com; 6 rue du Jour, 1er; ⏱ 10am-7pm Mon-Fri, to 7.30pm Sat; Ⓜ Les Halles

Style stalwart agnès b excels in extremely durable, comfortable and sometimes quirky clothes. The foundations are excellent; the rest has somewhat lost its cachet of late. On the same street you'll find agnès b homme (Map p86; ☎ 01 42 33 04 13; 3 rue du Jour, 1er) for men and agnès b enfant (Map p86; ☎ 01 40 39 96 88; 2 rue du Jour, 1er) for children.

ANDRÉ Map p86 Clothing & Accessories
☎ 01 53 40 96 84; www.andre.fr, in French; 106 rue de Rivoli, 1er; ⏱ 9.30am-8pm Mon-Sat; Ⓜ Châtelet

This branch of a footwear chain is where ordinary (and still very stylish) Parisians buy their shoes and boots. At the same time each year André invites hot new designers to create new lines of shoes and handbags at affordable prices.

ANTOINE Map pp82–3 Clothing & Accessories
☎ 01 42 96 01 80; www.antoine1745.com; 10 av de l'Opéra, 2e; ⏱ 10am-10pm & 2-4.30pm Mon-Sat; Ⓜ Pyramides

Founded in 1745, Antoine is the place to come if you're in the market for a bespoke cane, umbrella, fan or pair of gloves. It sells both new and vintage items.

BARBARA BUI Map p86 Clothing & Accessories
☎ 01 40 26 43 65; www.barbarabui.com; 23 rue Étienne Marcel, 2e; ⏱ 10.30am-7.30pm Mon-Sat; Ⓜ Étienne Marcel

Franco-Vietnamese Barbara Bui's nearby Kabuki Femme (p200) was an instant success and she went on to open her own shops, known

CLOTHING SIZES

Women's clothing
Aus/UK	8	10	12	14	16	18
Europe	36	38	40	42	44	46
Japan	5	7	9	11	13	15
USA	6	8	10	12	14	16

Women's shoes
Aus/USA	5	6	7	8	9	10
Europe	35	36	37	38	39	40
France only	35	36	38	39	40	42
Japan	22	23	24	25	26	27
UK	3½	4½	5½	6½	7½	8½

Men's clothing
Aus	92	96	100	104	108	112
Europe	46	48	50	52	54	56
Japan	S		M	M		L
UK/USA	35	36	37	38	39	40

Men's shirts (collar sizes)
Aus/Japan	38	39	40	41	42	43
Europe	38	39	40	41	42	43
UK/USA	15	15½	16	16½	17	17½

Men's shoes
Aus/UK	7	8	9	10	11	12
Europe	41	42	43	44½	46	47
Japan	26	27	27½	28	29	30
USA	7½	8½	9½	10½	11½	12½

Measurements approximate only, try before you buy

for their elegant modernism and beautifully cut trousers. There's also a Marais branch (Map pp98–9; ☎ 01 53 01 88 05; 43 rue des Francs Bourgeois, 4e; Ⓜ St-Paul), which keeps the same hours.

BONPOINT Map pp82–3 Clothing & Accessories
☎ 01 40 26 20 90; www.bonpoint.com; 50 rue Étienne Marcel; ⏱ 10am-7pm Mon-Sat; Ⓜ Étienne Marcel

This is a timeless collection of immaculate, classic children's clothes (from newborn to 14 years). It's a longstanding tradition for the chic bébés of Paris to be besuited by their grannies in Bonpoint, but if you're looking to buy into it expect to pay €90 for a pair of perfectly crafted first-time shoes.

COLETTE Map pp82–3 Clothing & Accessories
☎ 01 55 35 33 90; www.colette.fr; 213 rue St-Honoré, 1er; ⏱ 11am-7pm Mon-Sat; Ⓜ Tuileries

Not just an exquisite selection of clothes and accessories, this Japanese-inspired concept store has books, art, music and beauty products. Limited-edition sneakers, candles that smell like sex (so say staff, anyway), cutting-edge clocks – it's worth a look even if you're not buying. Colette's famous sales see huge reductions on the designer stock, including Comme des Garçons, Marc Jacobs and far more. The Water Bar in the basement features still and sparkling waters from around the world.

KABUKI FEMME Map p86   Clothing & Accessories
☎ 01 42 33 55 65; www.barbarabui.com; 25 rue Étienne Marcel, 2e; ✆ 10.30am-7.30pm Mon-Sat; Ⓜ Étienne Marcel
Opened some 20 years ago, this is the shop that brought Barbara Bui to world attention. Her own eponymous store is next door (p199) and you'll find Kabuki Homme (Map p86; ☎ 01 42 33 13 44; 21 rue Étienne Marcel, 2e) for men two doors down. In addition to Bui's own designs you'll find a judicious selection from other brands, including Miu Miu, Prada, Balenciaga and Stella McCartney.

KENZO Map p86   Clothing & Accessories
☎ 01 73 04 20 00; www.kenzo.com; 1 rue du Pont Neuf, 1er; ✆ 11.30am-7.30pm Mon, 11am-7.30pm Tue-Sat; Ⓜ Pont Neuf
While Kenzo himself may have retired from designing almost a decade ago, in recent years Sardinian Antonio Marras has brought a new *joie de vivre* to the label. The Pont Neuf flagship store, which shares the same building as the Philippe Starck–designed Kong (p285), is spread over three floors and is a tantalising temple to fashion and beauty.

KILIWATCH Map pp82-3   Clothing & Accessories
☎ 01 42 21 17 37; www.kiliwatch.fr, in French; 64 rue Tiquetonne, 2e; ✆ 11am-7.30pm Tue-Sat; Ⓜ Étienne Marcel
A Parisian institution, Kiliwatch is always packed with hip guys and gals rummaging through rack after rack of new and used streetwear and designs. There's a startling vintage range including hats and boots, plus art/photography books, eyewear and the latest runners.

MARIA LUISA FEMME
Map pp82-3   Clothing & Accessories
☎ 01 47 03 96 15; 2 rue Cambon, 1er; ✆ 10.30am-7pm Mon-Sat; Ⓜ Concorde
Every fashionista knows this eminent selection of classic and avant-garde designers.

This shop also stocks a range of swimwear. Around the corner you'll find an accessories branch (Map pp82-3; ☎ 01 47 03 48 08; 40 rue Mont Thabor, 1er) and nearby a menswear branch (Map pp82-3; ☎ 01 42 60 89 83; 19bis rue Mont Thabor, 1er).

MARITHÉ & FRANÇOIS GIRBAUD
Map pp82-3   Clothing & Accessories
☎ 01 53 40 74 20; www.girbaud.com; 38 rue Étienne Marcel, 2e; ✆ 11am-7pm Mon, 10am-7pm Tue-Sat; Ⓜ Étienne Marcel
This globetrotting designer couple call themselves 'jeanologists', having devoted themselves to over 30 years of denim. They have four other boutiques including a Marais branch (Map pp98-9; ☎ 01 44 54 99 01; 20 rue Malher, 4e; ✆ 11am-7pm Mon-Sat, 2-7pm Sun; Ⓜ St-Paul) and a St-Germain branch (Map pp116-17; ☎ 01 53 63 53 63; 7 rue Cherche Midi, 6e; ✆ 11.30am-7.30pm Mon, 10.30am-7.30pm Tue-Sat; Ⓜ St-Sulpice) with its own 'vegetation wall' inside (p52).

SURFACE TO AIR
Map p86   Clothing & Accessories
☎ 01 49 27 04 58; www.surface2airparis.com; 46 rue de l'Arbre Sec, 1er; ✆ 12.30pm-7.30pm Mon-Sat; Ⓜ Les Halles
This shop has arty books, accessories, graphic design and very edgy clothing. With an exceedingly up-to-date collection of daring local and international designs, the space also welcomes regular installations and collaborative events with artists. Its Marais branch (Map pp92-3; ☎ 01 44 61 76 27; 68 rue Charlot, 3e; ✆ noon-7.30pm Mon-Sat; Ⓜ Filles du Calvaire) is newer and smaller.

LEGRAND FILLES & FILS
Map pp82-3   Food & Drink
☎ 01 42 60 07 12; www.caves-legrand.com, in French; 7-11 Galerie Vivienne, 1 rue de la Banque, 2e; ✆ 11am-7pm Mon, 10am-7.30pm Tue-Fri, 10am-7pm Sat; Ⓜ Pyramides
This shop in a covered arcade sells not just fine wines but all the accoutrements: corkscrews, tasting glasses, decanters etc. It also has a fancy wine bar and tasting room.

LE REPAIRE DE BACCHUS
Map pp92-3   Food & Drink
☎ 01 48 87 73 68; 40 rue de Bretagne, 3e; ✆ 5-8.30pm Mon, 10am-2pm & 3.30-8.30pm Tue & Wed, 10am-8.30pm Thu-Sat, 10am-1.30pm Sun; Ⓜ Arts et Métiers

'The Den of Bacchus' stocks a good selection of New World wines along with an excellent supply of French vintages, as well as cognacs, Armagnacs and whiskies.

ANNA JOLIET Map pp82–3   Gifts & Souvenirs
☎ 01 42 96 55 13; www.boitesamusique-paris.com, in French; passage du Perron, 9 rue de Beaujolais, 1er; 🕑 10am-7pm Mon-Sat; Ⓜ Pyramides

This wonderful (and tiny) shop at the northern end of the Jardin du Palais Royal specialises in music boxes, both new and old, from Switzerland. Just open the door and see if you aren't tempted in (and/or can recognise the tune).

CANICRÈCHE Map pp82–3   Gifts & Souvenirs
☎ 01 42 71 59 09; www.shopcanicreche.fr, in French; 32 rue de Turbigo, 3e; 🕑 8am-8pm Mon-Sat; Ⓜ Arts et Métiers

And the chic *chiens* (dogs) of Paris? They head for this friendly boutique, which moonlights as a canine hotel, for their collars, toys, bedding and stunning little outfits.

A. SIMON Map pp82–3   Household Goods
☎ 01 42 33 71 65; www.simon-a.com; 48 & 52 rue Montmartre, 2e; 🕑 1.30-6.30pm Mon, 9am-6.30pm Tue-Fri, 9.30am-6.30pm Sat; Ⓜ Étienne Marcel

A more modern kitchenware shop than nearby E Dehillerin (below), a. simon has more pots, pans, mixing bowls and utensils than you thought existed – anyone for a *turbotière* (turbot poacher)? – in two separate shops.

E DEHILLERIN Map p86   Household Goods
☎ 01 42 36 53 13; www.dehillerin.com; 18-20 rue Coquillière, 1er; 🕑 9am-12.30pm & 2-6pm Mon, 9am-6pm Tue-Sat; Ⓜ Les Halles

Founded in 1820, this two-level shop carries an incredible selection of professional-quality *matériel de cuisine* (kitchenware). You're sure to find something you desperately need, such as a *coupe volaille* (poultry scissors) or even a *poêlon escargots* (snail pan), with six or 12 – your choice – holes.

KINDAL Map pp82–3   Household Goods
☎ 01 42 61 75 34; www.kindal.net; 32 av de l'Opéra, 2e; 🕑 10am-6.30pm Mon-Fri, 11am-6pm Sat; Ⓜ Opéra

In the market for something sharp? This *coutellerie* (cutlery shop) sells everything that slices and dices – from table and pocket knives to razors and Japanese swords. We even saw some stunning nail clippers on sale here.

CARROUSEL DU LOUVRE
Map p86   Shopping Centre
☎ 01 43 16 47 10; www.carrouseldulouvre.com; 99 rue de Rivoli, 1er; 🕑 8am-11pm; Ⓜ Palais Royal-Musée du Louvre

Built around IM Pei's inverted glass pyramid beneath the place du Carrousel, this shopping centre contains some three dozen upmarket shops (🕑 10am-8pm daily), more than a dozen restaurants and even the Comédie Française Studio Théâtre (p315).

MARAIS & BASTILLE

The Marais can boast some excellent speciality stores and an ever-expanding fashion presence. Note that the hip young designers are colonising the upper reaches of the 3e towards rue Charlot (Map pp92–3). Meanwhile, rue des Francs Bourgeois and, towards the other side of rue de Rivoli, rue François Mirron in the 4e have well-established boutique shopping for clothing, hats, home furnishings and stationery. Place des Vosges is lined with very high-end art and antique galleries with some amazing sculpture for sale. Over towards the 11e, Bastille has some interesting shops on rue Keller (Map pp94–5; young designers, records and manga/comic book shops) and rue de Charonne (clothes).

GALERIE & ATELIER PUNCINELLO
Map pp98–9   Art & Antiques
☎ 01 42 72 00 60; 16 rue du Parc Royal, 4e; 🕑 2-7pm Tue-Sat; Ⓜ St-Paul

This delightful gallery and workshop stocks masks, shields, spears and other collectables and antiques from Oceania and Southeast Asia. The items coming from the Asmat region of Irian Jaya in Indonesia are particularly fine, though expensive. The workshop can make you a *socle* – a stand or pedestal for your new treasure – to any specification in wood, bronze or plexiglass.

LES MOTS À LA BOUCHE Map pp98–9   Books
☎ 01 42 78 88 30; www.motsbouche.com, in French; 6 rue Ste-Croix de la Bretonnerie, 4e; 🕑 11am-11pm Mon-Sat, 1-9pm Sun; Ⓜ Hôtel de Ville

'On the Tip of the Tongue' is Paris' premier gay bookshop. Most of the left-hand side of the shop on the ground floor is devoted to English-language books, including some guides and novels. If you're feeling naughty, go downstairs.

LIBRAIRIE DE L'HÔTEL DE SULLY
Map pp98–9   Books

☎ 01 44 61 21 75; 62 rue St-Antoine, 4e; ☽ 10am-7pm; Ⓜ St-Paul

This early-17th-century aristocratic mansion housing the Centre des Monuments Nationaux (Monum), the body responsible for many of France's historical monuments, has one of the best bookshops in town for titles related to Paris. From historical texts and biographies to picture books and atlases, it's all here.

RED WHEELBARROW BOOKSTORE
Map pp92–3   Books

☎ 01 48 04 75 08; www.theredwheelbarrow.com; 22 rue St-Paul, 4e; ☽ 10am-7pm Mon-Sat, 2-6pm Sun; Ⓜ St-Paul

This impeccably run English-language bookshop has arguably the best selection of literature and 'serious reading' in Paris, and helpful, well-read staff.

ABOU D'ABI BAZAR
Map pp98–9   Clothing & Accessories

☎ 01 42 77 96 98; www.aboudabibazar.com; 10 rue des Francs Bourgeois, 3e; ☽ 2-7pm Sun & Mon, 10.30am-7.15pm Tue-Sat; Ⓜ St-Paul

This fashionable boutique is a treasure-trove of smart and affordable ready-to-wear pieces from young designers such as Paul & Joe, Isabel Marant, Missoni and Antik Batik. There's also Abou d'Abi 125 (Map pp98–9; ☎ 01 42 71 13 26; 125 rue Vieille du Temple, 3e; Ⓜ Chemin Vert), which keeps the same hours.

ALTERNATIVES
Map pp98–9   Clothing & Accessories

☎ 01 42 78 31 50; 18 rue du Roi de Sicile, 4e; ☽ 1-7pm Tue-Sat; Ⓜ St-Paul

This resale shop stocking mostly men's high-end fashion has great bargains in superb condition. This is an excellent place to pick up Japanese designer-wear at a third of the original price. You can also come across Miu Miu, Prada, Martin Margiela, Comme des Garçons and Rick Owens here on a good day.

APC
Map pp98–9   Clothing & Accessories

☎ 01 42 78 18 02; www.apc.fr; 112 rue Vieille du Temple, 3e; ☽ 11.30am-8pm; Ⓜ Chemin Vert

The hip streetwear of the Atélier de Production et Création (Production and Creation Workshop) is very popular with those young Parisian guys with accidental pop-rock haircuts, white sneakers and jeans falling well below the waist. The focus is on simple lines and straight cuts, though some pieces are more adventurous. It also has women's clothes.

CHERRY CHAU
Map pp98–9   Clothing & Accessories

☎ 01 42 77 12 11; www.cherrychau.com; 30 rue de Sévigné, 4e; ☽ 11am-7.30pm Tue-Sat, 2-7.30pm Sun; Ⓜ St-Paul or Chemin Vert

Long established in Hong Kong, Cherry Chau stocks the eponymous designer's hats, scarves, jewellery and one-of-a-kind coiffes: headbands made from a variety of materials including feathers and beads. The pink-and-white shop is just west of place des Vosges.

EROTOKRITOS
Map pp98–9   Clothing & Accessories

☎ 01 42 78 14 04; www.erotokritos.com; 99 rue Vieille du Temple; ☽ 1-7.30pm Mon, 11am-7.30pm Tue-Sat; Ⓜ Filles du Calvaire

Greek-Cypriot Erotokritos' clothes are chic and colourful, combining and contrasting fabrics with amazing prints. They're also quite affordable, considering the designer's hot reputation. There's also a Les Halles branch (Map pp82–3; ☎ 01 42 21 44 60; 58 rue d'Argout, 2e; Ⓜ Sentier), which keeps the same hours.

ISABEL MARANT
Map pp94–5   Clothing & Accessories

☎ 01 49 29 71 55; 16 rue de Charonne, 11e; ☽ 10.30am-7.30pm Mon-Sat; Ⓜ Bastille

Great cardigans and trousers, interesting accessories, ethnic influences and beautiful fabrics: just a few reasons why Isabel Marant has become the chouchou (darling) of Paris fashion. Bohemian and stylish, these are clothes that people actually look good in.

L'ÉCLAIREUR
Map pp98–9   Clothing & Accessories

☎ 01 48 87 10 22; www.leclaireur.com; 3ter rue des Rosiers, 4e; ☽ 11am-7pm Mon-Sat; Ⓜ St-Paul

You'll find John Galliano and Dries Van Noten rubbing shoulders with objects by Piet Hein Eek and Piero Fornasetti here. Part art space, part lounge and part deconstructionist fashion statement, this collection for women is known for having the next big thing first. Located just down the road is the stunning **Marais branch** (Map pp98–9; ☎ 01 44 54 22 11; 12 rue Malher, 4e; Ⓜ St-Paul) for men's fashion, converted from an old warehouse.

L'HABILLEUR Map pp98–9 Clothing & Accessories
☎ 01 48 87 77 12; 44 rue de Poitou, 3e; 🕐 11am-8pm Mon-Sat; Ⓜ St-Sébastien Froissart
For more than a decade this shop has been known for its discount designer-wear – offering 50% to 70% off original prices. It generally stocks last season's collections – including Plein Sud, Paul & Joe, Giorgio Brato and Belle Rose. The selection of men's clothes is quite extensive.

MAGAZIN Z Map p86 Clothing & Accessories
☎ 01 48 87 68 07; www.z-enfant.com, in French; 39 rue de Rivoli, 4e; 🕐 10am-7pm Mon-Sat; Ⓜ Hôtel de Ville
Just about everyone's getting into the design business these days, so why not Zinédine Zidane, the erstwhile captain of

the French national team? Gratefully ZZ restricts his line to clothing and accessories for kids up to age 14. No if, ands or (head) buts about it…

SHINE Map pp98–9 Clothing & Accessories
☎ 01 48 05 80 10; 15 rue de Poitou, 3e; 🕐 11am-7pm Tue-Sat, 2-5pm Sun; Ⓜ Filles du Calvaire
Another limited but discerning collection of designer stuff in the trendsetting 3e. Young women's clothing and some excellent shoes and handbags have been astutely selected, with plenty of Marc Jacobs, See by Chloé, K by Karl Lagerfeld and the current jewellery fetish, Bijoux de Sophie.

FRAGONARD Map pp98–9 Cosmetics & Perfume
☎ 01 44 78 01 32; www.fragonard.com; 51 rue des Francs Bourgeois, 4e; 🕐 10.30am-7.30pm Mon-Sat, 12-7pm Sun; Ⓜ St-Paul
This Parisian perfume maker has alluring natural scents in elegant bottles as well as candles, essential oils and soaps. In addition to the splendid smells, it has a small, expensive and very tasteful selection of clothing, hand-stitched linen tablecloths and napkins as well as jewellery. There's also a **St-Germain branch** (Map pp116–17; ☎ 01 42 84 12 12; 196 blvd St-Germain, 6e; Ⓜ St-Germain des Prés) and Fragonard runs the **Musée du Parfum** (see p147), which has its own shop.

L'ARTISAN PARFUMEUR
Map pp98–9 Cosmetics & Perfume
☎ 01 48 04 55 66; www.artisanparfumeur.com; 32 rue du Bourg Tibourg, 4e; 🕐 10.30am-7.30pm Mon-Sat; Ⓜ St-Paul
This artisan has been making exquisite original scents and candles for decades. The products are expensive but of very high quality and attractively packaged. There are a half-dozen other outlets across town, as well as stands at the Galeries Lafayette and Printemps department stores.

BAZAR DE L'HÔTEL DE VILLE
Map pp98–9 Department Store
☎ 01 42 74 90 00; www.bhv.fr, in French; 14 rue du Temple, 4e; 🕐 9.30am-7.30pm Mon, Tue, Thu & Fri, to 9pm Wed, to 8pm Sat; Ⓜ Hôtel de Ville
Recently renovated, expanded and dragged kicking and screaming into the 21st century, BHV is still pretty much a straightforward (though now flashier) department

top picks

SHOPPING STRIPS

- Av Montaigne, av Georges V & rue du Faubourg St-Honoré, 8e (p214) Historic *haute couture* (high fashion).
- Place de la Madeleine, 8e (p212) Gourmet fine-food shops.
- Rue de Rivoli, 1er & Les Halles, 2e (p198) & av des Champs-Élysées, 8e (p212) Major, super-sized chain stores like Gap, H&M and Zara.
- Blvd Haussmann & around, 9e (p215) Department stores.
- Rue Charlot & beyond, 3e (p201) Hip young designers – in fashion and art – in the northern Marais.
- Place des Vosges, 4e (p201) Art and antique galleries with particularly amazing sculpture.
- Carré Rive Gauche, 6e (p212) A group of 120 fine art and antique galleries, clustered along quai Voltaire, rue de l'Université, rue des St-Pères & rue du Bac in this 'Left-Bank Square'.
- Rue Mazarine & rue de Seine, 6e (p210) Fabulous contemporary art and design galleries.
- Rue d'Alésia, 14e (p204) Factory outlet clothing stores for men, women and kids.

DRESS FOR LESS

When I shop secondhand in Paris I don't want to rummage through sloppy piles of someone else's has-beens. That's fine in my own village hall, but not in Paris.

First stop on my carefully researched list of designer outlets was Mistigriff (Map pp166–7; www.mistigriff.fr; 83-53 rue St-Charles, 15e; M St-Charles), a shop that got rave reports online. But in the flesh its neon-lit façade screamed 'tack', the security guard was snarling and the heaps of strings spilling onto the floor just didn't ooze the elegance I'd set my heart on.

One peg up but still cut from the same soulless cloth was Mouton à Cinq Pattes (Map pp116–17; ☎ 01 45 48 86 26; 8 & 18 rue St-Placide, 6e; M Sèvres Babylone), two shops with a €1 trough of bargains as window display. But its tightly packed rows of clothes oozed choice and at €119 the Jean-Paul Gaultier bustiers (sorry, no conical cups) were a snip of the Triangle d'Or (p214) price tag.

A pleasant surprise was La Clef des Marques (☎ 01 45 49 31 00; 122-126 blvd Raspail, 6e; M Vavin), despite its hackles-raising door policy: surrender your handbag in exchange for a ticket or keep it and be searched later. I swallowed my pride and left an hour later with a last-season Emilio Pucci ski top (€50), classic Ralph Lauren jumper (€80) and a note in my diary to bring my husband here for business suits next time. Its extensive designer lingerie (loads of Calvin Klein), children's fashion (Le Petit Bateau, Diesel, Ralph Lauren) and sportswear sections were equally impressive.

I could have spent all day browsing les bonnes affaires – a mix of last-season leftovers at half the price and the current season's collection costing 10% to 15% less – on Rue d'Alésia, 14e (Map pp124–5; M Alésia). Fascinating was the rail of prototypes of this summer's frocks in Cacherel at No 114. There was only one of each design and each a taille unique (one size), but at €90 what a find. Exiting the metro station, walk west along rue d'Alésia to uncover its line-up of outlets, including Sonia Rykiel in the SR Store at Nos 64 and 112, Sinéquanone and Dorotennis at No 74, and Naf Naf at No 143.

My foray in current designer secondhand was short and sweet: Parisian pioneer of dépôt-vente in 1970, Chercheminippes (Map pp116–17; www.chercheminippes.com; 102, 109-11 & 124 rue du Cherche Midi, 6e; M Vaneau) in St-Germain des Prés was everything I could dream of in the shape of five beautifully presented boutiques on one street, each specialising in a different genre (haute couture, kids, menswear etc) and perfectly ordered by size and designer. There were even changing rooms.

The single biggest draw of shopping for vintage in Paris is not the promise of Parisian chic but price. Secondhand haute couture from previous decades costs 20% to 30% less in Paris than London, says Lawrence Carlier at Le Dépôt-Vente de Buci (Map pp116–17; ☎ 01 46 34 28 28; 4 rue Bourbon le Château, 6e; M Mabillion). She stocks hand-me-downs brought in from well-off ladies in the 6e arrondissement, returning anything that hasn't sold after three months. 'My vintage is mainly from the 1960s, very à la mode again', she adds, as I mentally calculate if my bank account can handle pea-green cowboy boots, a Chanel jacket and an A-line skirt smothered in sequins. This stylish 'boutique of curiosities' with black wooden façade and a hip wine shop as neighbour is right up my alley – as is Madame Auguet's Ragtime (Map pp116–17; ☎ 01 56 24 00 36; 23 rue de l'Échaude, 6e; M Mabillion) selling vêtements anciens from 1870 to 1970, and elegant L'Embellie (Map pp116–17; ☎ 01 45 48 29 82; 2 rue du Regard, 6e; M Sèvres Babylone). Count €100 to €1500 for a designer dress at all three. For old-fashioned accessories like gentlemen's pocket watches, ladies' hats and walking canes, browse Aspasie & Mathieu (Map pp110–11; 10 rue des Carmes, 5e; M Maubert Mutualité) in the Latin Quarter.

Paris being Paris, there's secondhand…and secondhand: in the rag trade since 1975, collector Didier Ludot not only sells the city's finest couture creations of yesteryear in his exclusive twinset of boutiques Didier Ludot (Map pp82–3; ☎ 01 42 96 06 56; www.didierludot.com; 20 & 24 Galerie de Montpensier, 1er; M Palais Royal-Musée du Louvre), he also hosts fashion exhibitions in the neighbouring galleries of the Palais Royal, and has published a book portraying the evolution of the little black dress, brilliantly brought to life in his boutique that sells just that, La Petite Robe Noire (☎ 01 40 15 01 04; 125 Galerie de Valois, 1er). Shop mannequins modelled a 1960s Chanel and 2006 Lanvin the day we were there.

Prize for innovation goes to Andrea Crews (Map pp82–3; ☎ 01 45 26 36 68; www.andreacrews.com; 10 rue Frochot, 9e; M Pigalle), a creative collective that added a whole new dimension to my quest to dress for less. Using everything from discarded clothing to electrical fittings and household bric-a-brac, the team chops, sews, recycles and reinvents to create the most extraordinary new fashion not everyone (few?) would wear. 'Sustainable secondhand' is its motto.

Nicola Williams

store – apart from its huge hardware/DIY department in the basement, with every possible type of hammer, power tool, nail, plug or hinge you could ask for.

À L'OLIVIER Map pp98–9   Food & Drink
☎ 01 48 04 86 59; www.alolivier.com; 23 rue de Rivoli, 4e; ⏰ 2-7pm Mon, 9.30am-7pm Tue-Sat; Ⓜ St-Paul

'At the Olive Tree' has been *the* place for oil, from olive and walnut to soy and sesame, since 1822. It also offers olive oil tastings and olive-oil beauty products, as well as good vinegars, jams and honeys.

JULIEN, CAVISTE Map pp92–3   Food & Drink
☎ 01 42 72 00 94; 50 rue Charlot, 3e; ⏰ 9.30am-1.30pm & 3.30-8.30pm Tue-Fri, 9.30am-8pm Sat; Ⓜ Filles du Calvaire

This independent wine store on hip rue Charlot focuses on small, independent producers and organic wines. There's a unique selection of Rhône, Languedoc and Loire vintages and exceptional champagnes. The enthusiastic merchant Julien will locate, explain (and wax lyrical about) the wine for you, whatever your budget.

LE PALAIS DES THÉS Map pp98–9   Food & Drink
☎ 01 48 87 80 60; www.palaisdesthes.com; 64 rue Vieille du Temple, 3e; ⏰ 10am-8pm Mon-Sat; Ⓜ Hôtel de Ville or St-Paul

The 'Palace of Teas' is not as well established as Mariage Frères (right), but the selection is as large and the surroundings much more 21st-century. There are three other outlets in Paris, including the 6e branch (Map pp116–17; ☎ 01 42 22 03 98; 61 rue du Cherche Midi, 6e; Ⓜ Rennes), which keeps the same hours.

LES RUCHERS DU ROY
Map pp98–9   Food & Drink
☎ 01 42 72 02 96; www.lesruchersduroy.com, in French; 37 rue du Roi de Sicile, 4e; ⏰ 11am-8pm Mon-Sat, 2-8pm Sun; Ⓜ St-Paul

'The King's Apiaries' sells honey and apiarian products fit for a monarch – especially its pure royal jelly, a substance secreted by worker bees and fed to future queen bees. It sells dozens of types of honey, including those made from one single type of flower (*miels monofloraux*), honeys made from a number of blossoms (*miels polyfloraux*) and various regional honeys (*miels des régions*).

MARIAGE FRÈRES
Map pp98–9   Food & Drink
☎ 01 42 72 28 11; www.mariagefreres.com; 30 & 35 rue du Bourg Tibourg, 4e; ⏰ shop 10.30am-7.30pm, tearooms noon-7pm; Ⓜ Hôtel de Ville

Founded in 1854, this is Paris' first and arguably its finest teashop. Choose from more than 500 varieties of tea sourced from some 35 countries. In addition, Mariage Frères has two other outlets: the 6e branch (Map pp116–17; ☎ 01 40 51 82 50; 13 rue des Grands Augustins; Ⓜ Odéon) and the 8e branch (Map pp140–1; ☎ 01 46 22 18 54; 260 rue Faubourg Saint Honoré, 8e; Ⓜ Ternes)

PRODUITS DES MONASTÈRES
Map pp98–9   Food & Drink
☎ 01 48 04 39 05; 10 rue des Barres, 4e; ⏰ 9.30am-noon & 2.30-8pm Tue-Fri, 10am-noon & 2.30-6.30pm Sat, 12.15-1pm Sun (just after church service); Ⓜ Hôtel de Ville or Pont Marie

This shop on an ancient cobbled street just down from Église St-Gervais-St-Protais sells jams, biscuits, cakes, muesli, honey, herbal teas and other comestibles made at Benedictine and Trappist monasteries in Jerusalem. For linens, candles, sandals and ceramics sourced from the same places, go around the corner to Monastica (Map pp98–9; ☎ 01 48 87 85 13; 11 rue du Pont Louis-Philippe, 4e; ⏰ 10am-6pm Tue-Fri, 10am-noon & 1.15-6.30pm Sat).

2 MILLE & 1 NUITS
Map pp98–9   Gifts & Souvenirs
☎ 01 48 87 07 07; http://2001nuits.free.fr; 13 rue des Francs Bourgeois, 4e; ⏰ 11am-7.30pm; Ⓜ Chemin Vert or St-Paul

The large '2001 Nights' shop at the end of a courtyard just off rue des Francs Bourgeois has colourful gifts and decorative items with an Oriental (read: 'Arabian Nights') slant. Some of the stuff for sale – a silver cup with a handle made from antelope horn, for example – is just this side of kitsch, but it's all good fun.

ATELIER D'AUTREFOIS
Map pp92–3   Gifts & Souvenirs
☎ 01 42 77 35 56; 61 blvd Beaumarchais, 3e; ⏰ 10am-5.30pm; Ⓜ Chemin Vert

This treasure chest of a shop stocks exquisite music boxes – both new and antique – and will repair any that are ailing. It's a shop that will attract both collectors and souvenir hunters.

BOUTIQUE PARIS-MUSÉES

Map pp98–9   Gifts & Souvenirs

☎ 01 42 74 13 02; 29 rue des Francs Bourgeois, 4e; 2-7pm Mon, 11am-1pm & 2-7pm Tue-Sat, noon-7.30pm Sun; Ⓜ St-Paul or Chemin Vert

This boutique stocks museum reproductions, especially of art and sculpture on exhibit at museums run by the City of Paris, such as the Musée Carnavalet (p96) and the Musée d'Art Moderne de la Ville de Paris (p135).

CSAO BOUTIQUE & GALLERY

Map pp98–9   Gifts & Souvenirs

☎ 01 42 71 33 17, 01 42 77 66 42; www.csao.fr, in French; 9 & 9bis rue Elzévir, 3e; 11am-7pm Tue-Fri, to 7.30pm Sat; Ⓜ St-Paul or Chemin Vert

This wonderful shop and gallery, owned and operated by the charitable Compagnie du Sénégal et de l'Afrique de l'Ouest (CSAO; Senegal and West Africa Company), distributes the work of African craftspeople and artists. Many of the colourful fabrics and weavings are exquisite. Included are items handmade from recycled handbags, aluminium cans and tomato paste tins.

LA BOUTIQUE DES INVENTIONS

Map pp92–3   Gifts & Souvenirs

☎ 01 42 71 44 19; www.la-boutique-des-inventions.com; Village St-Paul, 13 rue St-Paul, 4e; 11am-7pm Wed-Sun; Ⓜ St-Paul

This unique shop in the heart of Village St-Paul, a delightful little shopping square with antique shops, galleries and boutiques, is a forum for inventors and their inventions. Be the first on the block to own a shaker that sprinkles its own salt, a pepper grinder that twists itself or a miraculous filter that turns water into wine. Lots of wacky designs, too.

EXPECTANT FASHION

The French do it well. Chic shops include Formes (Map pp116–17; ☎ 01 45 49 09 80; 5 rue du Vieux Colombier, 6e; Ⓜ St-Germain des Prés), with its classic but contemporary cuts sold elsewhere in Europe, too; the youthful with a dash of rock 'n' roll 1 et 1 font 3 (Map pp128–9; ☎ 01 40 62 92 15; www.1et1font3.com; 3 rue de Solférino, 7e; Ⓜ Solferino); and maternity fashion designer Véronique Delachaux (Map pp116–17; ☎ 01 42 22 53 30; www.veroniquedelachaux.com; 55 blvd Raspail, 6e; Ⓜ Rennes).

LA CHARRUE ET LES ÉTOILES

Map pp98–9   Gifts & Souvenirs

☎ 01 48 87 39 07; 19 rue des Francs Bourgeois, 4e; 11am-7pm; Ⓜ St-Paul or Chemin Vert

Presumably named after Sean O'Casey's 1926 play (though the Irish connection is lost on us), 'The Plough and Stars' may look like just another gift shop but stocks an usual collection of figurines modelled after celebrated works of art (eg Vertumnus by Arcimboldo) and miniature soldiers.

L'AGENDA MODERN

Map pp98–9   Gifts & Souvenirs

☎ 01 44 54 59 20; 42 rue de Sévigné, 3e; 9.30am-4.30pm Mon-Fri; Ⓜ St-Paul

Subtitled 'The Shop of Days', this boutique sells handmade diaries beautifully bound in natural or dyed alligator or calves' leather. And, fear not, they're bilingual, so the Monday-morning blues will not become les blues de lundi.

LE BOUDOIR ET SA PHILOSOPHIE

Map pp92–3   Gifts & Souvenirs

☎ 01 48 04 89 79; www.leboudoiretsaphilosophie.fr, in French; 18 rue Charlot, 3e; 2-7pm Tue-Sat; Ⓜ Filles du Calvaire

Like a 19th-century powder room bursting at the seams, this kitschy boudoir's philosophy is one of parlour games, floral prints and silky nightgowns. Overflowing with all sorts of things from soaps to carnival masks, it's great for finding that esoteric, nonfunctional gift.

MÉLODIES GRAPHIQUES

Map pp98–9   Gifts & Souvenirs

☎ 01 42 74 57 68; 10 rue du Pont Louis-Philippe, 4e; 2-7pm Mon, 11am-7pm Tue-Sat; Ⓜ Pont Marie

Here you'll find all sorts of items made from exquisite Florentine papier à cuve (paper hand-decorated with marbled designs). There are several other fine stationery shops along the same street.

BOUTIQUE OBUT Map pp94–5   Hobby Items

☎ 01 47 00 91 38; www.laboulebout.com; 60 av de la République, 11e; 10am-noon & 12.30-6.30pm Tue-Sat; Ⓜ Parmentier

This is the Parisian mecca for fans of pétanque or the similar (though more formal) game of boules, a form of bowls played with heavy steel balls wherever a bit of flat and shady ground can be found. It will kit you out with all the equipment necessary to get a game going and even has team uniforms.

LA MAISON DE L'ASTRONOMIE

Map pp92–3   Hobby Items

☎ 01 42 77 99 55; 33-35 rue de Rivoli, 4e; ⏰ 10.30am-6.40pm Tue-Sat; Ⓜ Hôtel de Ville

If you've ever had the inclination to gaze at the stars, visit this large shop just west of the Hôtel de Ville. The 1st floor is positively crammed with telescopes, some of which can run into the tens of thousands of euros. It also stocks astronomical books, periodicals, sky maps, binoculars and globes.

BAINS PLUS Map pp98–9   Household Goods

☎ 01 48 87 83 07; www.parismarais.com/shopping-guide/bains-plus-spa; 51 rue des Francs Bourgeois, 3e; ⏰ 2-7pm Sun & Mon, 11am-7.30pm Tue-Sat; Ⓜ Hôtel de Ville

A bathroom supplier for the 21st century and true to its name, 'Baths Plus' stocks luxurious robes and gowns, soaps and oils, shaving brushes and mirrors.

LA MAISON DU HAMAC

Map pp94–5   Household Goods

☎ 01 47 00 66 00; www.lamaisonduhamac.com; 57 rue de Malte, 11e ⏰ 10.30am-7pm Tue-Sat; Ⓜ République

'The House of the Hammock' specialises in just that – a movable bed you string between two trees and rock till you drop. Choose anything from a brightly coloured net specimen from Brazil, Colombia or Nicaragua, or one shrouded in mosquito netting for napping by the water.

SIC AMOR Map pp98–9   Jewellery

☎ 01 42 76 02 37; 20 rue du Pont Louis-Philippe, 4e; ⏰ 11am-7pm Mon-Sat; Ⓜ Pont Marie

This shop sells contemporary jewellery by local designers from a shop located opposite the erstwhile headquarters of the all-but-moribund Partie Communiste Française, which is now reborn as the Galerie PCF.

FNAC MUSIQUE Map pp94–5   Music

☎ 08 25 02 00 20; www.fnac.com, in French; 4 place de la Bastille, 12e; Ⓜ Bastille; ⏰ 10am-8pm Mon-Sat

Fnac's flagship music store at Bastille has one of the largest collections of local and international music in Paris.

top picks

GIFT IDEAS

- Perfume and scented candles from Guerlain (p213), L'Artisan Parfumeur (p203) or Fragonard (p203).
- Fine food and wine from Fauchon (p214), À l'Olivier (p205), Hédiard (p214), La Maison du Miel (p215) or Boutique Maille (p214).
- Beautiful stationery from Mélodies Graphiques (opposite) or L'Agenda Modern (opposite).
- Tea from Le Palais des Thés (p205) or Mariage Frères (p205).
- A music box from Anna Joliet (p201), African blankets from CSAO Boutique & Gallery (opposite), something for the kitchen from E Dehillerin (p201), a hammock from La Maison du Hamac (left) or a kite from La Maison du Cerf-Volant (p216).

L'OURS DU MARAIS Map pp98–9   Toys

☎ 01 42 77 60 43; www.oursdumarais.com; 18 rue Pavée, 4e; ⏰ 11.30am-7.30pm Tue-Sat, 2-7.30pm Sun; Ⓜ St-Paul

'The Marais Bear' doesn't focus on Smoky or Yogi but on Teddy – there are more versions of the popular cuddly toy in this crowded little boutique than you could fill a den with.

PUZZLES MICHÈLE WILSON

Map pp94–5   Toys

☎ 01 47 00 12 27; www.pmw.fr; 39 rue de la Folie Méricourt, 11e; ⏰ 10am-6pm Tue-Thu, to 7pm Fri & Sat; Ⓜ St-Ambroise

Puzzleurs and *puzzleuses* will love the selection of hand-cut wooden jigsaw puzzles available in this shop. Ranging in size (and degree of difficulty) from 80 to 900 pieces, the puzzles depict for the most part major works of art – everything from Delacroix and Millet to the impressionists. The ones of medieval stained glass and 18th-century fans are particularly fine. There's also a 15e branch (Map pp166–7; ☎ 01 45 75 35 28; 97 av Émile Zola, 15e; ⏰ 9am-7pm Mon-Fri, 10am-7pm Sat; Ⓜ Charles Michels)

TUMBLEWEED Map pp98–9   Toys

☎ 01 42 78 06 10; www.tumbleweedparis.com; 19 rue de Turenne, 4e; ⏰ 11am-7pm Mon-Sat, 2-7pm Sun; Ⓜ St-Paul or Chemin Vert

This gorgeous little shop, which specialises in *l'artisanat d'art ludique* (crafts of the playing art), stocks wonderful handmade wooden toys, some of which look too nice

top picks

BOOKSHOPS

- Abbey Bookshop (right)
- Librairie Ulysse (below)
- Red Wheelbarrow Bookstore (p202)
- Shakespeare & Company (right)
- Tea & Tattered Pages (p210)
- Village Voice (p210)

to play with. The brain teasers and puzzles for adults are exquisitely made; we especially love the Japanese 'spin' and 'secret' boxes that defy entry.

VERT D'ABSINTHE Map pp98–9   Drink
☎ 01 42 71 69 73; 11 rue d'Ormesson, 4e; ☻ noon-7pm Tue-Sat; Ⓜ St-Paul

Fans of the *fée verte* (green fairy), as absinthe was known during the Belle Époque, will think they've died and gone to heaven here. Not only can you buy bottles of the best-quality hooch here but all the paraphernalia as well: glasses, water jogs and tiny spoons for the all-important sugar cube.

THE ISLANDS

LIBRAIRIE ULYSSE Map p105   Books
☎ 01 43 25 17 35; www.ulysse.fr; 26 rue St-Louis en l'Île, 4e; ☻ 2-8pm Tue-Fri; Ⓜ Pont Marie

A delightful shop full of travel guides, maps and sage advice from well-travelled staff. The 20,000 back issues of *National Geographic* are not to be sniffed at.

LA PETITE SCIERIE Map p105   Food
☎ 01 55 42 14 88; 60 rue St-Louis en l'Île, 4e; ☻ 11am-8pm; Ⓜ Pont Marie

This little hole-in-the-wall sells every permutation of duck edibles with the emphasis – *naturellement* – on foie gras. The products come direct from the farm with no intermediary involved, so you can be assured of the highest quality.

SOBRAL Map p105   Jewellery
☎ 01 43 25 17 35; 26 rue St-Louis en l'Île, 4e; ☻ 11am-7.30pm Mon-Sat, to 7pm Sun; Ⓜ Pont Marie

Brighten up your life with a bangle, pendant, pair of earrings or other costume

jewellery pieces made from recycled resin by Brazilian jeweller, Carlos Sobral. Yes, he makes toilet seats and Eiffel Towers, too.

LATIN QUARTER & JARDIN DES PLANTES

ABBEY BOOKSHOP Map pp110–11   Books
☎ 01 46 33 16 24; www.abbeybookshop.net; 29 rue de la Parcheminerie, 5e; ☻ 10am-7pm Mon-Sat; Ⓜ Cluny-La Sorbonne

This mellow, Canadian-owned bookshop is known for its free tea and coffee (sweetened with maple syrup) sipped over new and secondhand books, fiction and nonfiction.

LIBRAIRIE EYROLLES Map pp110–11   Books
☎ 01 44 41 11 72; www.eyrolles.com, in French; 61 blvd St-Germain, 5e; ☻ 9.30am-7.30pm Mon-Sat; Ⓜ Maubert Mutualité

Art, design, architecture, dictionaries and kids' books are the mainstay of this large bookshop with titles in English and bags of browsing space. For maps, guides and travel lit hop two doors over to its Librairie de Voyage (Map pp110–11; ☎ 01 46 34 82 75; 63 blvd St-Germain, 5e; ☻ 10.30am-7.30pm Mon, 9.30am-7.30pm Tue-Fri, 9.30am-8pm Sat; Ⓜ Maubert Mutualité).

SHAKESPEARE & COMPANY
Map pp110–11   Books
☎ 01 43 26 96 50; 37 rue de la Bûcherie, 5e; ☻ 10am-11pm Mon-Sat, 11am-11pm Sun; Ⓜ St-Michel

Paris' most famous English-language bookshop sells new and used books and is a charm to browse (grab a read and sink into one of the two cinema chairs near the stairs out back); the staff's picks are worth noting and there's a dusty old library on the 1st floor. This isn't the original Shakespeare & Company owned by Sylvia Beach, who published James Joyce's *Ulysses;* that was closed down by the Nazis.

ALBUM Map pp110–11   Comics
☎ 01 43 25 85 19; 8 rue Dante, 5e; ☻ 10am-8pm Mon-Sat, noon-7pm Sun; Ⓜ Maubert Mutualité

The ultimate in adult fantasy: *bandes dessinées* (comic books) – *huge* in France – is the speciality here. For graphic novels or comic characters modelled in plastic or incorporated in a grown-up designer toy or gadget, nip to its other nearby branch (Map

pp110–11; ☎ 01 53 10 00 60; 67 blvd St-Germain, 5e;
Ⓜ Maubert Mutualité).

PÂTISSERIE SADAHARU AOKI
Map pp110–11   Food

☎ 01 45 35 36 80; www.sadaharuaoki.com;
56 blvd du Port-Royal, 5e; ⏰ 9am-7pm Tue-Sat,
10am-6pm Sun; Ⓜ Port-Royal
'Exquisite' fails to describe the creations
of one of Paris' top pastry chefs, Tokyo-
born Sadaharu Aoki. Too beautiful to eat,
his gourmet works include 'eye-shadow'
palettes, boxes of 72 different flavoured
macaroons and green-tea chocolate.

MAGIE Map pp110–11   Hobby Items

☎ 01 43 54 13 63; www.mayette.com; 8 rue des
Carmes, 5e; ⏰ 1-8pm Mon-Sat; Ⓜ Maubert
Mutualité
One of a kind, this 19th-century magic
shop (1808) is said to be the world's oldest.
In the hands of world-famous magic pro
Dominique Duvivier since 1991, professional and hobbyist magicians flock here
to discuss king sandwiches, reverse assem-
blies, false cuts and other card tricks with
him and his daughter, Alexandra. Should
you want to learn the tricks of the trade,
Duvivier has magic courses up his sleeve.

AU VIEUX CAMPEUR
Map pp110–11   Outdoor Gear, Books

☎ 01 53 10 48 48; www.auvieuxcampeur.fr, in
French; 48 rue des Écoles, 5e; ⏰ 11am-8pm Mon-
Wed & Fri, to 9pm Thu, 10am-8pm Sat; Ⓜ Maubert
Mutualité or Cluny La Sorbonne
This sporting-gear chain runs 26 shops in
the Latin Quarter, each selling equipment
for a specific outdoor activity. Find camping gear at 6 rue Thénard; clothing for *le
froid urbain* (city cold) at 50 rue des Écoles
and 3 rue de Latran; and Paris's most complete range of maps and guides at 2 rue de
Latran (Map pp110–11).

ST-GERMAIN, ODÉON & LUXEMBOURG

Bijou art galleries, florists, antique stores,
designer furnishings, stylish vintage clothes
(see p204), moderately priced fashion…the
northern wedge of the 6e between Église St-
Germain des Prés and the Seine is a dream
to mooch. Left Bank fashion in the shape of

midrange boutiques (Ventilo, Cacharel, Penny
Black, Vanessa Bruno, Joseph etc) where middle-class French women buy clothes goes down
rue Bonaparte and rue St-Suplice and continues with chain stores on rue de Rennes.

For children's fashion, walk the length of
rue Vavin, 6e (metro Vavin), avoiding, if you
have the kids in tow, chocolate-maker Jean-Paul
Hévin (Map pp116–17) at No 3, who sells chocolate
stiletto shoes and 15cm-tall chocolate Eiffel
Towers. If it's smelly wellies that tickle your
kid's fancy go to Boatilus (Map pp116–17; 18 rue du
Dragon, 6e; Ⓜ St-Germain des Prés).

Don't miss the old-fashioned boutiques selling music boxes, carousels and globes in the
Cour du Commerce St-André, an enchanting glass-
covered passageway built in 1735 to link a pair
of Jeu de Paume (old-style tennis) courts.

IVOIRE Map pp116–17   Art & Antiques
☎ 01 43 54 71 09; 57 rue Bonaparte, 6e;
Ⓜ St-Germain des Prés
This family-run business dating to 1913 is
a two-man team comprising father Pierre
Heckmann (in his mid-80s) and son Jean-
Pierre (apprenticed at age 14 and not far off
retirement himself). Sculpting and restoring ivory, bone and nacre is their trade and
their art is extraordinary. The workshop
interior, last refitted in 1937, is original.

VOYAGEURS & CURIEUX
Map pp116–17   Art & Antiques
☎ 01 43 26 14 58; 2 rue Visconti, 6e; ⏰ 2-7pm
Tue-Sat; Ⓜ St-Germain des Prés
Jean-Édouard Carlier's primitive art shop
looks and feels like an 18th-century cabinet
of curiosities collected from around the
world: chalices made from coconut shells,
unusual feathers and beads, and odd masks.

GALERIE HÉLÈNE PORÉE
Map pp116–17   Art, Jewellery
☎ 01 43 54 17 00; 1 rue de l'Odéon, 6e; ⏰ 11am-
1pm & 2-7pm Tue-Sat; Ⓜ Odéon
Exquisite ceramics, glassware and jewellery
is showcased at this thoroughly modern art
gallery, host to six or seven shows a year.

LIBRAIRIE LE MONITEUR Map pp116–17 Books
☎ 01 44 41 15 75; www.librairiedumoniteur.com;
7 place de l'Odéon, 6e; ⏰ 10am-7pm Mon-Sat;
Ⓜ Odéon
This specialist bookshop sports books relating to design, architecture and urbanism,

including the annual French–English *Paris Design Guide* published by bilingual design mag *Intramuros*.

TASCHEN Map pp116–17 — Books
☎ 01 40 52 79 22; 2 rue du Buci, 6e; ⏰ 11am-8pm Sun-Wed, to midnight Thu & Fri; Ⓜ Odéon
Illustrated books on art, design, architecture, fashion and urban culture is what this innovative book publisher is about. Equally striking is its shop design by Philippe Starck. Bargain buys begging to be browsed fill stands on the pavement outside.

TEA & TATTERED PAGES
Map pp116–17 — Books
☎ 01 40 65 94 35; 24 rue Mayet, 6e; ⏰ 11am-7pm Mon-Sat, noon-6pm Sun; Ⓜ Duroc
More than 15,000 volumes are squeezed onto two floors at this secondhand English-language bookshop with tearoom.

VILLAGE VOICE Map pp116–17 — Books
☎ 01 46 33 36 47; www.villagevoicebookshop.com; 6 rue Princesse, 6e; ⏰ 2-8pm Mon, 10am-8pm Tue-Sat, 2-6pm Sun; Ⓜ Mabillon
With an excellent selection of contemporary North American fiction and European literature, lots of readings and helpful staff, the Village Voice is a favourite.

SHU UEMURA Map pp116–17 — Cosmetics
☎ 01 45 48 02 55; 176 blvd St-Germain, 6e; ⏰ 11am-8pm Sun-Wed, to midnight Thu & Fri; Ⓜ Odéon
Curly fake eyelashes, lime-marmalade lip gloss (yep, it's green), 71 shades of lipstick and badger-hair make-up brushes: this Japanese cosmetic boutique founded by the Hollywood make-up guru who painted Shirley Maclaine's face in the film *My Geisha* (1962) is extraordinary. Treat yourself to a 1½-hour lesson (€150) at its make-up school.

HUILERIE J LEBLANC ET FILS
Map pp116–17 — Food
☎ 01 46 34 61 55; www.huile-leblanc.com; 6 rue Jacob, 6e; ⏰ 11am-7pm Tue-Sat; Ⓜ St-Germain des Près
The Leblanc family has made the smoothest of culinary oils (almonds, pistachios, sesame seeds, pine kernels, peanuts etc) at its stone mill in Burgundy since 1878. Taste and buy.

top picks

LEFT-BANK GALLERIES

Meandering rue Mazarine and surrounding rue Jacques Callot, rue de l'Echaudé and rue de Seine are a feast for the soul with their vibrant art and design galleries.

- **Galerie Downtown** (Map pp116–17; ☎ 01 46 33 82 41; www.galeriedowntown.com; 33 rue de Seine, 6e) Designer furniture has been this gallery's exclusive forté for 25 years.
- **Galerie Loevenbruck** (Map pp116–17; ☎ 01 53 10 85 68; www.loevenbruck.com; 40 rue de Seine, 6e) Larger-than-life pop art.
- **Galerie Onega** (Map pp116–17; ☎ 01 40 46 81 25; 60 rue Mazarine, 6e) Street art and graffiti – a bold statement indeed.
- **La Galerie Moderne** (Map pp116–17; ☎ 01 46 33 13 59; www.lagaleriemoderne.com; 52 rue Mazarine, 6e) Original designer furniture and lights from the 1950s, '60s and '70s.
- **Pièce Unique Variations** (Map pp116–17; ☎ 01 43 26 85 93; www.galeriepieceunique.com; 26-28 rue Mazarine & 4 rue Jacques Callot, 6e) Permanent collection of works and installations by contemporary artists; its single-room gallery on rue Jacques Callot showcases one (usually very large) piece especially created for this *pièce unique* (unique room), illuminated until 2am.

PIERRE HERMÉ Map pp116–17 — Food
☎ 01 43 54 47 77; www.pierreherme.com; 72 rue Bonaparte, 6e; ⏰ 10am-7pm Sun-Fri, to 7.30pm Sat; Ⓜ Odéon or Luxembourg
It's the size of chocolate box, but once in your tastebuds will go wild. Pierre Hermé is one of Paris' top *chocolatiers* and his two boutiques are a veritable feast of perfectly presented petits fours, cakes, chocolate, nougats, macaroons and jam. The second branch (☎ 01 47 83 89 96; 185 rue Vaugirard, 15e; ⏰ 10am-7pm Tue-Sat; Ⓜ Pasteur) is located in the 15 arrondissement.

CACAO ET CHOCOLAT Map pp116–17 — Food & Drink
☎ 01 46 33 77 63; www.cacaoetchocolat.com; 29 rue du Buci, 6e; ⏰ 10.30am-7.30pm Mon-Sat, 11am-7pm Sun; Ⓜ Mabillon
You haven't tasted chocolate till you've had a hot chocolate (€3.50) spiced with cinnamon, ginger or cayenne pepper at this exotic shop showcasing cocoa beans in every guise. Citrus, spice and chilli are among the

flavoured bars to buy here or at its outlets in the Marais (Map pp98–9; ☎ 01 42 71 50 06; 36 rue Vieille du Temple, 4e; 🕙 11am-7.30pm; Ⓜ St-Paul) and on Île St-Louis (☎ 01 46 33 33 33; 63 rue St-Louis en l'Île, 4e; 🕙 10.30am-7.30pm; 🕙 Pont Marie).

LA BOUTIQUE DU CRÉATEUR DE JEUX Map pp116–17 Games
☎ 08 75 97 69 63; www.laboutiqueducreateur dejeux.com, in French; 40 rue St-Jacques, 6e; 🕙 11am-7pm Tue-Sat; Ⓜ Cluny La Sorbonne
Another gem, this one sells brand-new board and card games created in the last couple of years in France (many are bilingual French–English). Its *jeux de mesure* are made-to-measure, limited editions often focusing on a social issue such as alcohol abuse, immigrant equality etc.

ROUGE & NOIR Map pp116–17 Games
☎ 01 43 26 05 77; www.rouge-et-noir.fr; 26 rue Vavin, 6e; 🕙 10am-7pm Mon-Sat; Ⓜ Vavin
Trivial Pursuit Paris, Rubik's cubes, juggling balls, backgammon, chess, tarot and playing cards… This small family-run boutique specialising in traditional and not-so-traditional games promises bags of fun.

AU PLAT D'ÉTAIN Map pp116–17 Hobby Items
☎ 01 43 54 32 06; http://auplatdetain.com, in French; 16 rue Guisarde, 6e; 🕙 11am-12.30pm & 2-7pm Tue-Sat; Ⓜ Odéon
People do collect tin (*étain*) and lead soldiers, as this fascinating boutique crammed with nail-sized, hand-painted military soldiers, drummers, musicians, snipers and cavaliers attests. In business since 1775, the shop itself is practically a collectable.

LA MAISON DE POUPÉE
Map pp116–17 Hobby Items
☎ 01 46 33 74 05, 06 09 65 58 68; 40 rue de Vaugirard, 6e; 🕙 10am-7pm Mon-Sat; Ⓜ Odéon & Luxembourg
Poupées anciennes (antique dolls) is what this enchanting boutique opposite the residence of the French Senate's president sells.

FLAMANT HOME INTERIORS
Map pp116–17 Home & Garden
☎ 01 56 81 12 40; 8 place de Furstenberg & 8 rue de l'Abaze, 6e; 🕙 noon-7pm Mon, 10.30am-7pm Tue-Sat; Ⓜ Mabillon
Silverware, curtains, cutlery, tableware, linens and other quality home furnishings:

This maze of a concept store with two entrances is the place where moneyed Parisians shop for the home.

LES BEAUX DRAPS DE JEANINE CROS
Map pp116–17 Home Interiors
☎ 01 45 48 00 67; 11 rue d'Assas, 6e; 🕙 10am-7pm Mon-Sat; Ⓜ Rennes
Restoring old fabrics is the highly specialist trade of passionate seamstress Jeanine Cros ,and this old-style boudoir – a Pandora's box of fabric – is draped with layer after layer of exquisite old linen, materials tinted with natural pigments etc.

ODIMEX PARIS Map pp116–17 Home Interiors
☎ 01 46 33 98 96; 17 Rue de l'Odéon, 6e; 🕙 10.30am-6.30pm Mon-Sat; Ⓜ Odéon
Teapots in all their guises: there are little ones, big ones, sophisticated, comic and very expensive ones. Some of the Japanese teapots are particularly beautiful

LE PETIT BATEAU Map pp116–17 Kids
☎ 01 45 49 48 38; www.petit-bateau.fr; 81 rue de Sèvres, 7e; Ⓜ Sèvres Babylone
This much-loved French brand, now global, has been kicking around since 1893, when it first started making the soft, cotton children's underwear for which it's famed. A staple of any French family, Le Petit Bateau is substantially cheaper to buy in France than elsewhere. Its flagship store is at 116 av des Champs-Elsyée, 8e.

HAPART Map pp116–17 Toys, Antiques
☎ 01 56 24 94 34; 72 rue Mazarine, 6e; 🕙 2-7pm Tue-Sun; Ⓜ Odéon
A lovely one to idle in, this collector's delight the size of a pocket handkerchief recalls lost childhoods with its romantic collection of old and antique toys.

LA DERNIER GOUTTE Map pp116–17 Wine
☎ 01 43 29 11 62; 6 rue du Bourbon le Château, 6e; 🕙 10.30am-1.30pm & 3-8.30pm Mon-Fri, 10am-8.30pm Sat, 11am-7pm Sun; Ⓜ Mabillon
'The Last Drop' is the lovechild of sommelier Juan Sánchez, the American behind the extraordinary wine list to grace Fish La Boissonerie (p257). His tiny wine shop is packed with exciting French *vins de propriétaires* (estate-bottled wines) made by small independent producers. Saturday evening ushers in a talk and tasting.

MONTPARNASSE

There might be just one *raison d'être* to shop in the 14e arrondissement, but it's bargain-packed.

MARCHÉ AUX PUCES DE LA PORTE DE VANVES Map pp124–5 Flea Market

av Georges Lafenestre & av Marc Sangnier, 14e; ☎ 7am-6pm or later Sat & Sun; Ⓜ Porte de Vanves
The Porte de Vanves flea market is the smallest and, some say, friendliest of the lot. Av Georges Lafenestre has lots of 'curios' that don't quite qualify as antiques. Av Marc Sangnier is lined with stalls of new clothes, shoes, handbags and household items for sale.

FAUBOURG ST-GERMAIN & INVALIDES

In the more austere 7e arrondissement, the style of St-Germain des Prés continues along the western half of blvd St-Germain and rue du Bac – two streets with a stylish collection of contemporary furniture, kitchen and design shops (including the Conran Shop, Kartell, and Paris' biggest shop window in the shape of Knoll at No 268).

The fashion show congregates on rue de Grenelle, spilling across from place St-Sulpice in the neighbouring 6e (p209). By the water, the exclusive Carré Rive Gauche (www.carrerivegauche.com; Ⓜ Rue du Bac or Solférino) portfolio of 120 art and antiques galleries sits square on quai Voltaire and the trio of parallel streets south.

ALEXANDRA SOJFER Map pp128–9 Accessories

☎ 01 42 22 17 02; www.alexandrasojfer.fr; 218 blvd St-Germain, 7e; ☎ 9.30am-7pm; Ⓜ Rue du Bac
Become Parisian chic with a frivolous, frilly, fantastical or frightfully fashionable umbrella *(parapluie),* parasol or walking cane, handcrafted by Alexandra Sojfer at this *parapluie*-packed St-Germain boutique, in the trade since 1834.

GALERIE FRANÇOIS RÉNIER
Map pp128–9 Accessories

☎ 01 45 49 26 88; www.unjourunsac.com; 27 blvd Raspail, 7e; ☎ 10am-7pm Mon-Sat; Ⓜ Sèvres Babylone
Un jour un sac (a bag a day) is the philosophy of handbag designer François Renier, who creates bags in paper, fabric or leather

and leaves her customer to pick which handles to attach. Buy a couple to mix 'n' match at home.

LE BON MARCHÉ Map pp128–9 Department Store

☎ 01 44 39 80 00; www.bonmarche.fr; 24 rue de Sèvres, 7e; ☎ 9.30am-7pm Mon-Wed & Fri, 10am-9pm Thu, 9.30am-8pm Sat; Ⓜ Sèvres Babylone
Built by Gustave Eiffel as Paris' first department store in 1852, Le Bon Marché (which translates as 'good market' but also means 'bargain') is less frenetic than its rivals across the river, but no less chic. It has excellent men's and women's fashion collections, and a designer *'snack chic'* café on the 1st floor. But the icing on the cake is its glorious food hall, La Grande Épicerie de Paris (Map pp128–9; 26 rue de Sèvres; Ⓜ Sèvres Babylone), which sells, among other edibles, vodka-flavoured lollipops with detoxified ants inside and fist-sized Himalayan salt crystals to grate over food.

DEYROLLE Map pp128–9 Home & Garden

☎ 01 42 22 30 07; 46 rue du Bac, 7e; ☎ 10am-1pm & 2-7pm Mon, 10am-7pm Tue-Sat; Ⓜ Rue du Bac
This shop, born in 1831, has to be seen to be believed. Be it a stuffed white stork, baby chick, butterfly or tiger you want to hang in your home, you can buy one here. A quick chat with a member of staff confirmed that Deyrolle stocks every animal species legally allowed. Buy rare and unusual seeds (including many old types of tomato), gardening tools and accessories on the ground floor.

BONTON BAZAR Map pp128–9 Kids

☎ 01 42 22 77 69; www.bonton.fr; 122 rue du Bac, 7e; ☎ 10am-7pm Mon-Sat; Ⓜ Sèvres Babylone
This ode to childhood is an old-fashioned delight. It sells a mix of clothes, toys, kids' chopsticks (handy for families dining out a lot in Paris), kitchen and bathroomwares (polka-dotted cutlery, black rubber ducks with fishing rods), bedroom decorations, pedal-powered metal cars and so on.

ÉTOILE & CHAMPS-ÉLYSÉES

The av des Champs-Élysées is lined with super-sized chain stores; the luxury fashion houses for which the area is famous and which make for such wonderful window-shopping are mostly situated along av Montaigne (with

PATRICIA WELLS – ONLY THE BEST

The only American considered to have truly captured the soul of French cuisine, writer, cookery teacher and author of *The Food Lover's Guide to Paris* Patricia Wells (www.patriciawells.com) has lived, cooked and shopped in Paris since 1980. 'Only the best' is the label on the fresh fish, meat, cheese, breads and other market produce that guests at her St-Germain des Prés cooking studio use in class. So just where does she shop? Nicola Williams finds out.

What is it that makes Paris so wonderful for culinary shopping? The tradition, the quality, the quantity, the atmosphere and physical beauty!

Where do you buy your weekly groceries? All over: The Sunday organic market (blvd Raspail, 7e; M Rennes) at Rennes; Poilâne (p223) for bread; Quatrehommes (p259) for cheese; Poissonnerie du Bac (69 rue du Bac, 7e; M Rue du Bac) for fish; also the President Wilson market (p231).

And for that extra-special gourmet meal? I shop regularly at Le Bon Marché's La Grande Épicerie (opposite) because it is right down the street from me. But for special meals I always order things in advance and go from shop to shop. That is the fun of Paris and of France.

Favourite markets & and top tips? I love the dried fruits and nuts at the Sunday Rennes market, *all* the fish stands at the President Wilson market, the Planet Fruits and Daguerre Marée stands at the Rue Poncelet market (p231). If you live in Paris, become a *client fidèle* so they reach in the back and give you the best stuff. If you only go once in a while, just smile and be friendly.

Your top specialist addresses? Poilâne and Kayser (bread; p223); Maison du Chocolat (19 rue de Sèvres, 6e) and Pierre Hermé (chocolate and cakes; p210); La Dernière Goutte (wine; p211).

A creative idea for a culinary souvenir from Paris? Fragonard (p203), the perfume maker, has a great shop on blvd St-Germain. They have a changing litany of *great things for the home*, such as fabulous vases with an Eiffel Tower theme, lovely embroidered napkins with a fish or vegetable theme, great little spoons with a cake or pastry theme. Nothing is very expensive and the offerings change every few months, so you have to pounce when you find something you love. The gift wrapping in gorgeous Fragonard bags is worth it alone!
Interviewed by Nicola Williams

the mammoth Louis Vuitton store on the corner) and the equally prestigious av Georges V. For more, see the boxed text, p214.

If the big fashion houses reign mainly on the other side of the Champs-Élysées, the class and couture continues along in the 8e rue du Faubourg St-Honoré and its eastern extension, rue St-Honoré in the 1e, where designer shops – and designer shoppers – abound. This area is also home to the grand gourmet food stores of place de la Madeleine and the luxury jewellery of place Vendôme.

ESPACE IGN Map pp140–1   Books
☎ 01 43 98 80 00; www.ign.fr; 107 rue La Boétie, 8e; ✆ noon-6.30pm Mon, 11am-7pm Tue-Fri, to 6.30pm Sat; M Franklin D Roosevelt
This is the place to find a full selection of Institut Géographique National (IGN) maps, as well as atlases, globes, walking maps, city plans, compasses, satellite images, historic maps and guidebooks.

ERES Map pp140–1   Clothing & Accessories
☎ 01 47 42 28 82; www.eres.fr; 2 rue Tronchet, 8e; ✆ 10am-7pm Mon-Sat; M Madeleine
You will pay an arm and a leg for a swimsuit here, but anyone who has despaired at

buying bathers in the past will understand why these have become a must-have item for those in the know. The stunning swimmers are cut to suit all shapes and sizes, with bikini tops and bottoms sold separately. It also stocks magnificent lingerie.

GUERLAIN Map pp140–1   Cosmetics & Perfume
☎ 01 45 62 52 57; www.guerlain.com; 68 av des Champs-Élysées, 8e; ✆ 10am-7.30pm Mon-Sat, 3-7pm Sun; M Franklin D Roosevelt
Guerlain is Paris' most famous *parfumerie*, and its shop, dating from 1912, is one of the most beautiful in the city. With its shimmering mirror and marble Art Deco interior, it's a reminder of the former glory of the Champs-Élysées.

SÉPHORA Map pp140–1   Cosmetics & Perfume
☎ 01 53 93 22 50; www.sephora.com; 70-72 av des Champs-Élysées, 8e; ✆ 10am-midnight; M Franklin D Roosevelt
Séphora's flagship store features over 12,000 fragrances and cosmetics for your sampling pleasure. You can spend hours in here and will invariably come out with bags of stuff (and maybe a headache from all the scent in the air).

SHOPPING ÉTOILE & CHAMPS-ÉLYSÉES

BOUTIQUE MAILLE Map pp140–1 Food & Drink

☎ 01 40 15 06 00; www.maille.com; 6 place de la Madeleine, 8e; ☯ 10am-7pm Mon-Sat; Ⓜ Madeleine

The mustard specialist has premade items, but can also prepare an unimaginable 30 different varieties for you, designed to accompany your cuisine, such as the type with chestnuts and pink bay to accompany game or poultry, or garlic and lemon to go with fowl. There is a range of exclusive vinegars too, and the cruets to hold them.

FAUCHON Map pp140–1 Food & Drink

☎ 01 70 39 38 00; www.fauchon.fr, in French; 26 & 30 place de la Madeleine, 8e; ☯ 8.30am-7pm Mon-Sat; Ⓜ Madeleine

Paris' most famous caterer has a half-dozen departments in two buildings selling the most incredibly mouthwatering delicacies, from pâté de foie gras and truffles to confitures (jams).

FROMAGERIE ALLÉOSSE
Map p144–5 Food & Drink

☎ 01 46 22 50 45; www.alleosse.com; 13 rue Poncelet, 17e; ☯ 9.30am-1pm & 4-7pm Tue-Thu, 9am-1pm & 3.30-7pm Fri & Sat, 9am-1pm Sun; Ⓜ Ternes

To our minds, this is the best cheese shop in Paris and worth a trip across town. Cheeses are sold as they should be – grouped in five main categories: fromage de chèvre (goat's milk cheese), fromage à pâte persillée (veined or blue cheese), fromage à pâte molle (soft cheese), fromage à pâte demi-dure (semi-hard cheese) and fromage à pâte dure (hard cheese). Ask for advice.

HÉDIARD Map pp140–1 Food & Drink

☎ 01 43 12 88 88; www.hediard.fr; 21 place de la Madeleine, 8e; ☯ 9am-9pm Mon-Sat; Ⓜ Madeleine

This famous luxury food shop established in 1854 consists of two adjacent sections selling prepared dishes, teas, coffees, jams, wines, pastries, fruits, vegetables and so on, as well as a popular restaurant (☎ 01 43 12 88 99; ☯ 8.30am-9pm Mon-Fri, to 10pm Sat), where tea is served from 3pm to 6pm. There's a George V branch (Map pp140–1; ☎ 01 47 20 44 44; 31 av George V, 8e; Ⓜ George V) open Sundays.

LA MAISON DE LA TRUFFE
Map pp140–1 Food & Drink

☎ 01 42 65 53 22; www.maison-de-la-truffe.com, in French; 19 place de la Madeleine, 8e; ☯ 10am-10pm Mon-Sat; Ⓜ Madeleine

'The House of Truffles' is the place for tasting these fine fungi – French black from late October to March, Alba white (over €200 per 100g) from mid-October to December. There's a restaurant attached where you can sample dishes.

LES CAVES AUGÉ Map pp140–1 Food & Drink

☎ 01 45 22 16 97; 116 blvd Haussmann, 8e; ☯ 1-7.30pm Mon, 9am-7.30pm Tue-Sat; Ⓜ St-Augustin

---

HISTORIC HAUTE COUTURE

A stroll around the legendary Triangle d'Or (av Montaigne and av Georges V) and along rue du Faubourg St-Honoré, all in the 8e, constitutes the walk of fame of top French fashion. Rubbing shoulders with the world's top international designers are Paris' most influential French fashion houses (Map pp140–1; Ⓜ Georges V):

- Chanel (Map pp140–1; ☎ 01 47 23 74 12; www.chanel.com; 42 av Montaigne, 8e) Box jackets and little black dresses, chic ever since their first appearance in the 1920s.
- Christian Dior (Map pp140–1; ☎ 01 40 73 73 73; www.dior.com; 30 av Montaigne, 8e) Post-WWII, Dior's creations dictated style, re-establishing Paris as the world fashion capital.
- Christian Lacroix (Map pp140–1; ☎ 01 42 68 79 04; www.christianlacroix.com; 73 rue Faubourg St-Honoré, 8e) Taffeta and lace flirt with denim and knits in this designer's theatrical combinations.
- Givenchy (Map pp140–1; ☎ 01 44 31 51 09; www.givenchy.com; 3 av Georges V, 8e) The first to present a luxurious collection of women's prêt à porter (ready to wear).
- Hermès (Map pp140–1; ☎ 01 40 17 47 17; www.hermes.com; 24 rue du Faubourg St-Honoré, 8e) Founded in 1837 by a saddle-maker, Hermès' famous scarves are the fashion accessory.
- Jean-Paul Gaultier (Map pp140–1; ☎ 01 44 43 00 44; www.jeanpaulgaultier.com; 44 av George V, 8e) A shy kid from the Paris suburbs, JPG morphed into the enfant terrible of the fashion world with his granny's corsets, men dressed in skirts and Madonna's conical bra.
- Louis Vuitton (Map pp140–1; ☎ 01 53 57 52 00; www.vuitton.com; 101 av des Champs-Élysées, 8e) Take home a Real McCoy canvas bag with the 'LV' monogram.

Founded in 1850, this *marchand de vin* (wine shop) should be your first choice if you trust the taste of Marcel Proust, who was a regular customer. It's now under the stewardship of knowledgeable sommelier Marc Sibard.

VIRGIN MEGASTORE Map pp140–1 *Music, Books*
☎ 01 49 53 50 00; 52-60 av des Champs-Élysées, 8e; ☉ 10am-midnight Mon-Sat, noon-midnight Sun; Ⓜ Franklin D Roosevelt
This French-owned version of the huge British music and bookshop chain has the largest music collection in Paris, as well as English-language books.

OPÉRA & GRANDS BOULEVARDS

The area around Opéra and the Grands Boulevards is where you'll find Paris' most popular *grands magasins*, around which are clustered branches of all the major French and international chain stores. If here in December, check out the fabulous Christmas shows in the department store windows and the sales in January and July.

HÔTEL DROUOT Map pp148–9 *Art & Antiques*
☎ 01 48 00 20 20; www.drouot.com; 7-9 rue Drouot, 9e; ☉ sales 2-6pm; Ⓜ Richelieu Drouot
Paris' most established auction house has been selling fine lots for more than a century. The bidding is in rapid-fire French (also now available on the website) and a 10% to 15% commission is charged on top of the purchase price. Viewings (always a vicarious pleasure) are usually from 11am to 6pm the day before and from 10.30am to 11.30am the morning of the auction. Further details can be found in the weekly *Gazette de l'Hôtel Drouot* (www.gazette-drouot.com; €3.40), available at the auction house and selected newsstands on Friday as well as on the main Hôtel Drouot website.

WOCHDOM Map pp148–9 *Clothing & Accessories*
☎ 01 53 21 09 72; www.wochdom.com; 72 rue Condorcet, 18e; ☉ 12-8pm Mon-Sat; Ⓜ Pigalle
Cool in a slightly creepy way, this self-consciously chic, retro seconds store is painstakingly selected 'design vintage' and shoes, mostly from the '70s. Staff are helpful and full of ideas.

GALERIES LAFAYETTE *Department Store*
Map pp148–9
☎ 01 42 82 36 40; www.galerieslafayette.com; 40 blvd Haussmann, 9e; ☉ 9.30am-7.30pm Mon-Wed, Fri & Sat, to 9pm Thu; Ⓜ Auber or Chaussée d'Antin
A vast *grand magasin* in two adjacent buildings, Galeries Lafayette features over 75,000 brand-name items and a wide range of fashion labels. In the annexe linked by a covered footbridge over rue de Mogador you'll find menswear, the world's largest lingerie department and Lafayette Gourmet (☉ 9.30am-8.30pm Mon-Wed, Fri & Sat, 9am-9pm Thu). There's a fine view from the rooftop restaurant. A fashion show (bookings ☎ 01 42 82 30 25) takes place at 3pm Friday. The 10,000-sq metre Lafayette Maison (Map pp148–9; 35 blvd Haussmann, 9e; Ⓜ Auber or Chaussée d'Antin) has four floors with each dedicated to a particular room in the house.

LE PRINTEMPS Map pp148–9 *Department Store*
☎ 01 42 82 57 87; www.printemps.com; 64 blvd Haussmann, 9e; ☉ 9.35am-7pm Mon-Wed, Fri & Sat, to 10pm Thu; Ⓜ Havre Caumartin
This is actually three separate stores – Le Printemps de la Mode (women's fashion), Le Printemps de l'Homme (for men) and Le Printemps de la Beauté et Maison (for beauty and household goods) – offering a staggering display of perfume, cosmetics and accessories, as well as established and up-and-coming designer wear.

LA MAISON DU MIEL Map pp148–9 *Food & Drink*
☎ 01 47 42 26 70; www.maisondumiel.com; 24 rue Vignon, 9e; ☉ 9.30am-7pm Mon-Sat; Ⓜ Madeleine
In this sticky, very sweet business since 1898, 'The Honey House' stocks over 50 kinds of honey, with such flavours as Corsican chestnut flower, Turkish pine and Tasmanian leatherwood.

GARE DU NORD, GARE DE L'EST & RÉPUBLIQUE

These areas are not especially known for their shops, but there are a couple of specialist boutiques worth going the extra mile for, and workaday department stores and electronics retailers ready to supply you with the toothbrushes and adaptors you left at home.

ARTAZART Map pp152–3   Books

☎ 01 40 40 24 00; www.artazart.com; 83 quai de Valmy, 10e; ☟ 10.30am-7.30pm Mon-Fri, 2-8pm Sat & Sun; Ⓜ République or Gare de l'Est
Hard by the Canal St-Martin, Artazart is the leading design bookshop in Paris and, along with design and source books, stocks directories, DVDs and CDs in French, English and other languages. Staff are knowledgeable and helpful.

ANTOINE ET LILI
Map pp152–3   Clothing, Household Goods

☎ 01 40 37 41 55; www.antoineetlili.com; 95 quai de Valmy, 10e; ☟ 10.30am-7pm Mon, to 7.30pm Tue-Fri, 10am-8pm Sat, 12.30-7.30pm Sun; Ⓜ République or Gare de l'Est
Do not – repeat, *do not* – enter this huge shop, spread through three townhouses facing the Canal St-Martin, with a hangover. The décor (shocking pink, chartreuse, blinding yellow) will have you begging for mercy. All the colours of the rainbow and all the patterns in the world congregate in this wonderful Parisian institution with designer clothing and hip home decorations. It also has a Marais store (Map pp98–9; ☎ 01 42 72 26 60; 51 rue des Francs Bourgeois, 3e; Ⓜ St-Paul), which keeps the same hours.

DARTY Map pp94–5   Electronics

☎ 08 21 08 20 82; www.darty.com, in French; 1 av de la République, 11e; ☟ 10am-7.30pm Mon-Sat; Ⓜ République
The best place to seek out adaptors and other electrical goods is the Bazar de l'Hôtel de Ville (BHV; p203) department store or any branch of the electronics chain Darty, including this outlet at République. There's also a Ternes branch (Map pp140–1; ☎ 0821 08 20 82; 8 av des Ternes, 17e; ☟ 10am-7.30pm Mon-Sat).

GARE DE LYON, NATION & BERCY

The upmarket boutiques of Bercy have transformed the 12e and are always packed with shoppers. Elsewhere in the 12e, the area near the Viaduc des Arts (Map pp158–9) has discerning furniture, antiques and art. The flea market at place d'Aligre is a must.

ALBUM Map pp158–9   Books, Hobby Items

☎ 01 53 33 87 88; www.album.fr, in French; 46 Cour St-Émilion, 12e; ☟ 11am-9pm; Ⓜ Cour St-Émilion
Album specialises in *bandes dessinées*, which have an enormous following in France, with everything from Tintin and Babar to erotic comics and the latest Japanese manga. There are seven more outlets in Paris, including a Latin Quarter branch (p208).

MARCHÉ AUX PUCES D'ALIGRE
Map pp158–9   Flea Market

place d'Aligre & rue d'Aligre, 12e; ☟ 7.30am-1.30pm Tue-Sun; Ⓜ Ledru Rollin
Smaller but more central (and, punters say, more trustworthy) than Paris' other flea markets (opposite), this is one of the best places to rummage through boxes of clothes and accessories worn decades ago by those fashionable (and not-so-fashionable) Parisians, as well as their bric-a-brac.

FERMOB Map pp158–9   Furniture

☎ 01 43 07 17 15; www.fermob.com; 81-83 av Ledru-Rollin, 12e; ☟ 10am-7pm Mon-Sat; Ⓜ Ledru Rollin
If you want to create the 'Jardin du Luxembourg look' in your own backyard or garden, head for Fermob. It makes French park–style benches and folding chairs in a range of yummy colours – from carrot and vanilla to sage and aubergine.

LA MAISON DU CERF-VOLANT
Map pp158–9   Gifts & Souvenirs

☎ 01 44 68 00 75; www.lamaisonducerfvolant .com; 7 rue de Prague, 12e; ☟ 11am-7pm Tue-Sat; Ⓜ Ledru Rollin

top picks

SPECIALITY STREETS

- Rue de Paradis, 10e (Map pp152–3; Ⓜ Château d'Eau) Crystal, glass and tableware.
- Rue Drouot, 9e (Map pp148–9; Ⓜ Richelieu Drouot) Collectable postage stamps.
- Rue du Pont Louis-Philippe, 4e (Map pp98–9; Ⓜ Pont Marie) Stationery and fine paper.
- Rue Keller, 11e (Map pp94–5; Ⓜ Ledru Rollin) Comic books, mangas, DVDs.
- Rue Martel, 10e (Map pp152–3; Ⓜ Château d'Eau) Sewing machines.
- Rue Victor Massé, 9e (Map p169; Ⓜ Pigalle) Musical instruments.

'The Kite House' has just that – kites in every conceivable size, shape, colour and design, and kits with which to make them. You'll also find quite a nice collection of boomerangs, should you be in the market for one.

15E ARRONDISSEMENT

Hardly a frantic shopping district, but it is privy to a clutch of specialist addresses.

CODINA Map pp166–7   Food
☎ 01 45 75 00 08; www.codina.net; 24 rue Violet, 15e; ⏱ 2.30-7pm Tue & Wed, 10am-1pm & 2.30-7pm Thu-Sat; Ⓜ Av Émile Zola
Organic oils (pumpkin seed oil, avocado oil, daisy oil, carrot, cashew and cherry) are made at this sky-blue atelier. Be it your hair or health you need to boost, Codina has something to suit.

MINI PARIS Map pp166–7   Hobby Items
☎ 01 56 77 00 00; www.miniparis.fr, in French; 91-93 av Émile Zola, 15e; ⏱ 8.30am-7pm Mon-Fri; Ⓜ Charles Michels or Av Émile Zola
Tricky to take a Mini Cooper home, yes, but this showroom is a must – not only for the gorgeous, top-of-the-range convertibles It showcases, but for its interior design. Buy a pedal-powered version of the peppy little cult car for your kid or simply enjoy the glam experience it promises.

VITRA Map pp166–7   Home Interiors
☎ 01 56 77 07 77; www.vitra.com; 40 rue Violet, 15e; ⏱ 9am-6pm Mon-Thu, to 5pm Fri; Ⓜ Charles Michels or Av Émile Zola
The classics from the history of furniture design can be ogled at in this crisp, white space in life-size or miniature form. Go to the back of this inspiring showroom to fully appreciate its own industrial, glass-roofed design.

MONTMARTRE & PIGALLE

The area of the 9e and 18e along rue des Martyrs and climbing up rue des Abbesses from metro Pigalle constitutes a good stroll for the patient shopper who wants to enjoy the scenery. You'll find little designer-clothing shops and a mixed bag of secondhand fashion depots, vintage clothing and records, not to mention some excellent, typically Parisian bakeries and food stores. The rest of the 18e, especially around the less-than-salubrious Goutte d'Or area (rue Myrha and rue de la Goutte d'Or) has cheap fabrics, cut-price fashion, young designers and assorted frippery. Around metro Barbès Rochechouart and blvd Magenta it's working-class, bargain-basement shopping: take a detour from the glamorous avenues and see how the other half lives.

GASPARD DE LA BUTTE
Map p169   Clothing & Accessories
☎ 01 42 55 99 40; www.gasparddelabutte.com, in French; 10bis rue Yvonne le Tac, 18e; ⏱ 11am-7.30pm Tue-Sun; Ⓜ Pigalle
This shop specialises in women's and children's wear, all locally made with beautiful cottons as well as colourful felts for the infants' clothing. It's very 'Montmartre' in style – you could imagine Amélie Poulain shopping here.

LA CITADELLE Map p169   Clothing & Accessories
☎ 01 42 52 21 56; 1 rue des Trois Frères, 18e; ⏱ 11am-8pm Mon-Sat, to 7pm Sun; Ⓜ Abbesses
This designer discount shop hidden away in Montmartre has some real finds from new French, Italian and Japanese designers. Look out for labels like Les Chemins Blancs and Yoshi Kondo.

TATI Map p169   Department Store
☎ 01 55 29 52 20; www.tati.fr, in French; 4 blvd Rochechouart, 18e; ⏱ 10am-7pm Mon-Fri, 9.15-7pm Sat; Ⓜ Barbès Rochechouart
With its war cry of les plus bas prix (the lowest prices) – and quality to match, some would say – Tati has been Paris' great working-class department store for more than half a century. Don't be surprised to see trendy Parisians fighting for bargains hidden in the crammed bins and piled onto tables. There's a smaller 3e branch (Map pp92–3; ☎ 01 48 87 72 81; 172-174 rue du Temple, 3e; ⏱ 9.30-7.30pm Mon-Fri, 10am-7pm Sat; Ⓜ Temple or République) as well.

BEYOND CENTRAL PARIS

Don't expect to find unusual little boutiques selling all sorts of ephemera beyond central Paris. Instead, head out beyond the blvd Périphérique for the capital's wonderful flea markets.

MARCHÉ AUX PUCES DE MONTREUIL
off Map pp158–9   Flea Market

av du Professeur André Lemière, 20e; 8am-7.30pm Sat-Mon; Porte de Montreuil
Established in the 19th century, the Montreuil flea market is known for its quality secondhand clothes and designer seconds. The 500-odd stalls also sell engravings, jewellery, linen, crockery, old furniture and appliances.

MARCHÉ AUX PUCES DE ST-OUEN
Map p169   Flea Market

www.parispuces.com; rue des Rosiers, av Michelet, rue Voltaire, rue Paul Bert & rue Jean-Henri Fabre, 18e; 9am-6pm Sat, 10am-6pm Sun, 11am-5pm Mon; Porte de Clignancourt
This vast flea market, founded in the late 19th century and said to be Europe's largest, has more than 2500 stalls grouped into 10 marchés (market areas), each with its own speciality (eg Marché Serpette and Marché Biron for antiques, Marché Malik for secondhand clothing, the enormous Marché Vernaison for antiques etc). There are miles of modern clothing and 'freelance' stalls selling anything from batteries and rusty tools to stolen mobile phones.

LA VALLÉE VILLAGE   Shopping Centre
01 60 42 35 00; www.lavalleevillage.com; 3 cours de la Garonne, Serris; 10am-8pm Mon-Sat May-Sep, to 7pm Mon-Sat Oct-Apr, 11am-7pm Sun
This shopping centre within the Disneyland Resort (p384), 30km east of Paris, contains some 75 big-name outlets (Christian Lacroix, Kenzo, Versace et al) offering discounts on last season's clothing, accessories and tableware. From Paris, take RER line A4 (€5.60, 30 to 35 minutes) to the Val d'Europe station. Alternatively, Cityrama (p407) runs a coach (€19 return) from 4 place des Pyramides, 1er (metro Tuileries) three times weekly, departing at 10.15am and returning at 4pm; book in advance.

EATING

top picks

French cuisine is the West's most important and influential style of cooking. With the arguable exception of the Chinese, no other cuisine can compare to French for freshness of ingredients, reliance on natural flavours and the use of refined, often very complex cooking methods. Add to that the typical Parisian's passion for anything connected with the table and you will soon realise what everyone else here already knows: you are in a gourmet's paradise.

The very word 'cuisine', of course, is French in origin – the English 'cooking style' just cannot handle all the nuances – while 'French' conjures up a sophisticated, cultured people who know their arts, including gastronomy. While there is only some truth to that notion (not *every* Parisian is a walking *Larousse Gastronomique,* the seminal encyclopaedia of French gastronomy), eating well is still of prime importance to most people here, and they continue to spend an inordinate amount of time thinking about, talking about and consuming food.

Do not think for a moment, though, that this national obsession with things culinary and a familiarity with the complexities of *haute cuisine* (high cuisine) means that eating out or dining in a private home here has to be a ceremonious or even formal occasion, one full of pitfalls for the uninitiated. Indeed, approach food and wine with half the enthusiasm that the Parisians themselves do, and you will be warmly received, tutored, encouraged and well fed.

HISTORY

Up to the Middle Ages, dining – at least for the wealthier classes and at court in Paris – essentially meant sitting around a large table, sawing off hunks of meat with small knives. Peasants and the urban poor subsisted on bread or dumplings made of rye flour and whatever *companaticum* (Latin for 'that which goes with bread') was available in the cauldron forever stewing over the hearth. Even by the time the first French-language cookbook was published by Charles V's head chef, Guillaume Tirel (or Taillevent), in about 1375, menus consisted almost entirely of 'soups' (or 'sops'), pieces of bread boiled in a thickened stock, and meat and poultry heavy with the taste of herbs and spices, including new ones like ginger, cinnamon and cloves.

The 16th century was a watershed for French cuisine. When Catherine de Médici, consort to Henri II, arrived in Paris from Florence in 1533, she brought with her a team of chefs and pastry cooks adept in the subtleties of Italian Renaissance cooking. They introduced such delicacies as aspics, truffles, *quenelles* (dumplings), artichokes, macaroons and puddings to the French court. Catherine's cousin, Marie de Médici, brought even more chefs to Paris when she married Henri IV in 1600. The French cooks, increasingly aware of their rising social status, took the Italians' recipes and sophisticated cooking styles on board, and the rest – to the eternal gratitude of epicures everywhere – is history.

France and its capital enjoyed an era of order and prosperity under Henri IV, who famously wished all of his subjects to have a *poule au pot* (chicken in the pot) every Sunday. Later in the 17th century, the sweet tooth of Louis XIV launched the custom of eating desserts, once reserved for feast days and other celebrations, at the end of a meal.

The most decisive influence on French cuisine at this time, however, was the work of

SMOKE-FREE PARIS

And they said it could never happen in the capital of a country where more people smoke (and eat more saturated fats and exercise less) than almost anyone else in the developed world. On 1 January 2008 France expanded a year-old ban on smoking in public places (schools, hospitals, offices etc) to include all bars, restaurants, night clubs, and even – *sacré bleu!* – sacrosanct cafés. It's true that, unlike their London equivalents, café and bar owners here have the option of installing a hermetically sealed smoking room covering up to 20% of the café's surface area, though no food or drink can be served within. And hotel guestrooms – not the lobby or other public spaces – are a separate matter, something that has caused no end of confusion even in the industry (see p332). But one thing is clear: a fag with that *café crème* or Armagnac is no longer an option (at least indoors). Those of you who still engage in the retro habit of smoking tobacco have two choices: stub out or step out. And, boy, can the rest of us now breathe easy.

chef François-Pierre de la Varenne (1618–78), who learned his trade in Marie de Médici's kitchens. La Varenne's cookbook, *Le Cuisinier François* (1651), was a gastronomic landmark for many reasons. It was the first to give instructions for preparing vegetables; it introduced soups in the modern sense, with the 'soup' being more important than the sops it contained; and it discarded bread and breadcrumbs as thickening agents in favour of *roux*, a much more versatile mixture of flour and fat. Most importantly, La Varenne downplayed the use of spices, preferring to serve meat in its natural juices sharpened with vinegar or lemon juice. A basic tenet of French cuisine was thus born – to enhance the natural flavours of food in cooking and not to disguise it with heavy seasonings.

The 18th century, the so-called Grand Siècle (Great Century) of reason, brought little enlightenment to the French table apart from dishes and sauces named after lords and other royalty by their sycophantic chefs. This was the century when newfangled foodstuffs from the New World – tomatoes, corn, beans, red pepper and especially the potato so integral today in French cuisine – gained currency, and when the fork became a standard part of the table setting. Most important was the new trend to serve dishes in a logical order rather than heaping them in a pyramid on the table all at the same time (see p222).

This century also saw the birth of the restaurant as we know it today. In 1765 one Monsieur A Boulanger opened a small business in rue Bailleul in the 1er, just off rue de Rivoli, selling soups, broths and, later, that old crowd-pleaser, sheep's trotters in a white sauce. Above the door he hung a sign to advertise these *restaurants* (restoratives). Hostelries and inns did exist at the time, but they only served guests set meals at set times and prices from the *table d'hôte* (host's table), and cafés only offered drinks. Monsieur Boulanger's restaurant is thought to have been the first public place where diners could order a meal from a menu that offered a choice of dishes.

During the French Revolution and the ensuing Reign of Terror, the ovens in the kitchens of the great aristocratic households went cold, and their chefs were driven in tumbrels to the guillotine. But a new avenue soon opened to those who managed to escape execution: employment in the kitchens of the hundreds of restaurants opening to the public in Paris. By 1804 Paris counted some 500 eateries. A typical menu at that time included 12 soups, two dozen hors d'oeuvre, between 12 and 30 dishes of beef, veal, mutton, fowl and game, 24 fish dishes, 12 types of *pâtisserie* (pastries) and 50 desserts.

The first and most important of these new chefs was Marie-Antoine Carême (1784–1833), who set out to establish 'order and taste' in French gastronomy and became personal chef to such luminaries as French statesman Talleyrand, England's Prince Regent and Tsar Alexander I. But to most English speakers, the name Georges-August Escoffier (1846–1935) is more synonymous with *haute cuisine*. Escoffier, nicknamed 'the king of chefs and the chef of kings', was a reformer who simplified or discarded decorations and garnishes, shortened menus and streamlined food preparation in kitchens, having taken his cue from Prosper Montagné, one of the great French chefs of all time and author of *Larousse Gastronomique*.

The most important development in French gastronomy in the 20th century was the arrival of *nouvelle cuisine* (new cuisine), a reaction against Escoffier's *grande cuisine* (great cuisine). This low-fat style of cooking eliminated many sauces in favour of stock reductions, prepared dishes in such a way as to emphasise the inherent textures and colours of the ingredients, and served them artistically on large plates. *Nouvelle cuisine* made a big splash in the diet-conscious 1970s and '80s, when it was also known as *cuisine minceur* (lean cuisine), and its proponents, including chefs Paul Bocuse, Jean and Pierre Troisgros and Michel Guérard, became the new saints of the grazing faithful from Paris to Perth.

By the turn of the millennium, however, this revolutionary new style of cooking had fallen out of favour and new genres and styles were being developed and explored. First came the concept of *fooding*, formed by combining the English words 'food' and 'feeling' and used to describe the art of appreciating not only the contents of your plate but also what's going on around you – ambience, décor, 'scene'. Before long it was the word in the mouths of *branché* (trendy) Parisians and within a year an annual Semaine du Fooding (Fooding Week) was established. Fooding guide books were written, a fooding dictionary published and *Le Nouvel Observateur* started calling its annual restaurant review 'Le Guide Fooding'.

But this 'fusion confusion' just wasn't enough and within a few more years journalists at the now defunct lifestyle magazine *Zurban* were again slicing and dicing words. Their new creation was the term *bistronomie*,

EATING IN ORDER

At a traditional French meal – be it lunch starting at around 1pm or dinner at about 8.30pm – courses are served as follows:

- Apéritif – a predinner drink
- Hors d'œuvre – appetisers; cold and/or warm snacks served before the start of the meal
- Entrée – first course or starter
- Plat principal – main course
- Salade – salad, usually a relatively simple green one with vinaigrette dressing
- Fromage – cheese
- Dessert – pudding
- Fruit – sometimes served in place of dessert
- Café – coffee, almost always drunk black
- Digestif – digestive; an after-dinner drink

a neologism combining 'bistro' and 'gastronomy' to describe a new phenomenon that was taking Paris by storm. 'A group of us were meeting to determine the prizes for Fooding Week,' said research editor Sébastien Demorand. 'We wanted a word to describe a restaurant that combined the conviviality and relaxation of a *bistrot* with the cuisine of a 'grand restaurant'.' Today the neo-bistro, usually a small, relatively informal venue serving outstanding cuisine under the tutelage of a talented (and often 'name') chef, is the biggest growth industry in Paris. As they say in French: *Plus ça change, plus c'est la même chose* (the more things change, the more they stay the same).

CELEBRATING WITH FOOD

It may sound facile but food itself makes people here celebrated. There are birthdays and engagements and weddings and christenings and, like everywhere, special holidays, usually based in religion.

One tradition that is very much alive is *Le Jour des Rois* (Day of the Kings), which falls on 6 January and marks the feast of the Épiphanie (Epiphany), when the Three Wise Men called on the Infant Jesus. A *galette des rois* (literally 'kings' cake'; a puff pastry tart with frangipane cream), which has a little dried bean (or a porcelain figurine) hidden inside and is topped with a gold paper crown, is placed on the table. The youngest person in the room goes under the table and calls out which member of the party should get each slice. The person who gets the bean is named king or queen, dons the crown and chooses his or her consort. This tradition is popular not just among families but also at offices and dinner parties.

At Chandeleur (Candlemas, marking the Feast of the Purification of the Virgin Mary) on 2 February, family and friends gather together in their kitchens to make *crêpes de la Chandeleur* (sweet Candlemas pancakes).

Pâques (Easter) is marked as elsewhere with *œufs au chocolat* (chocolate eggs) – here filled with candy fish and chickens – and there is always an egg hunt for the kids. The traditional meal at Easter lunch is *agneau* (lamb) or *jambon de Pâques* (Easter ham).

After the *dinde aux marrons* (turkey stuffed with chestnuts) eaten at lunch on Noël (Christmas), a *bûche de Noël*, a 'Yule log' of chocolate and cream or ice cream, is served.

ETIQUETTE

French people do not eat in the clatter/clutter style of the Chinese or with the exuberance and sheer gusto of, say, the Italians. A meal is an artistic and sensual delight to most people here, something to be savoured and enjoyed with a certain amount of style and savoir-vivre. That said, it is easy to cause offence at a French table, and manners here have more to do with common sense than learned behaviour. Still, there are subtle differences in the way French people handle themselves while eating that are worth pointing out.

A French table will be set for all courses at restaurants (not always at home), with two forks, two knives and a large spoon for soup or dessert. When diners finish each course, they cross their knife and fork (not lay them side by side) face down on the plate to be cleared away. If there's only one knife and fork at your setting, you should place the cutlery back on the table after each course.

At a dinner party courses may not be served in the order to which you are accustomed; salad may follow the main course, for example, and cheese *always* precedes dessert (see left). A separate plate for bread may or may not be provided. If it is missing, rest the slice on the edge of the main plate or on the tablecloth itself. It is quite acceptable – in fact, encouraged – to sop up sauces and juices with slices of bread, though some people use a fork instead of their hands to do so.

You will not be expected to know the intricacies of how to cut different types of cheese but at least try to remember the basic rules (see opposite). If there are wine glasses of varying sizes at each place setting, the larger one (or ones) will be for red wine (and water), the smaller one for white wine. In general it's better to wait for the host to pour the wine rather than helping yourself, but this depends on your relationship and the tone of the evening. Tasting the wine in restaurants and pouring it at home have traditionally been male tasks, but these days many women will happily serve and more enlightened *sommeliers* (wine waiters) will ask which one of a mixed couple would like to try the wine.

STAPLES & SPECIALITIES

Every nation or culture has its own staples dictated by climate, geography and tradition. French cuisine has long stood apart for its great use of a variety of foods – beef, lamb, pork, poultry, fish and shellfish, cereals, vegetables and legumes – but its three most important staples are bread, cheese and *charcuterie* (cured, smoked or processed meat – usually pork – products). And as for regional specialities, well, *tout est possible* (the sky's the limit).

Staples

The complete list of French staples might include everything from cereals, grains and pulses to jams and honeys but we'll restrict ourselves to the 'holy trinity' of the French kitchen.

BREAD

Nothing is more French than *pain* (bread). More than 80% of all French people eat it at every meal, and it comes in infinite varieties, some 80 at last count.

All bakeries have *baguettes* (and the somewhat similar *flûtes*), which are long, thin and crusty loaves weighing 250g, and wider loaves of what are simply called *pains*. A *pain*, which weighs 400g, is softer on the inside and has a less crispy crust than a baguette. Both types are at their best if eaten within four hours of baking; if you're not very hungry, ask for a half a loaf: a *demi baguette* or a *demi pain*. A *ficelle* is a thinner, crustier 200g version of a baguette – not unlike a very thick breadstick, really.

Bread has experienced a renaissance here in recent years, and most bakeries also carry heavier, more expensive breads made with all sorts of grains and cereals; you will also find loaves studded with nuts, raisins or herbs. These heavier breads keep much longer than baguettes and standard white-flour breads.

top picks

BAKERIES

- Au Levain du Marais (Map pp98–9; ☎ 01 42 78 07 31; 32 rue de Turenne, 3e; 6.30am-1pm & 3.30-7.30pm Tue-Sat; M Chemin Vert)
- Arnaud Delmontel (Map pp148–9; ☎ 01 48 78 29 33; www.arnaud-delmontel.com, in French; 39 rue des Martyrs, 9e; 7am-8.30pm Mon & Wed-Sat, to 2.30pm Sun; M St-Georges)
- Boulangerie Eric Kayser (Map pp110–11; ☎ 01 44 07 01 42; www.maison-kayser.com, in French; 8 rue Monge, 5e; 7am-8.30pm Wed-Mon; M Maubert Mutualité)
- Boulangerie-Pâtisserie Stéphane Secco (Map pp128–9; ☎ 01 43 17 35 20; 20 rue Jean Nicot, 7e; 8.30am-8.30pm Tue-Sat; M La Tour Maubourg)
- La Fournée d'Augustine (Map pp124–5; ☎ 01 45 43 42 45; 96 rue Raymond-Losserand, 14e; 7.30am-8pm Mon-Sat; M Pernety)
- Poilâne (www.poilane.fr) 6e branch (Map pp116–17; ☎ 01 45 48 42 59; 8 rue du Cherche Midi, 6e; 7.15am-8.15pm Mon Sat; M Sèvres Babylone); 15e branch (Map pp166–7; ☎ 01 45 79 11 49; 49 blvd de Grenelle; M Dupleix)

Bread is baked at various times during the day, so it's available fresh as early as 6am and also in the afternoon. Most bakeries close for one day a week but you'll always find one open in the neighbourhood – even on Sunday morning.

CHEESE

Charles de Gaulle, expostulating on the inability of anyone to unite the French on a single issue after WWII, famously grumbled: 'You cannot easily unite a country that has 265 kinds of cheese.' The general's comments are well out of date; today France counts upwards of 500 varieties of *fromage* (cheese) made of cow's, goat's or ewe's milk. Bear in mind, though, that there are just five basic types (see boxed text, p224), which can be raw, pasteurised or *petit-lait* ('little milk'; the whey left over after the milk fats and solids have been curdled with rennet, an enzyme derived from the stomach of a calf or young goat).

When cutting cheese at the table, remember that a small circular cheese such as a

THE FIVE BASIC CHEESE TYPES

The choice on offer at a *fromagerie* (cheese shop) can be overwhelming, but *fromagers* (cheese merchants) always allow you to sample what's on offer before you buy, and are usually very generous with their guidance and pairing advice. The following list divides French cheeses into five main groups – as they are usually divided in a *fromagerie* – and recommends several types to try.

Fromage à pâte demi-dure 'Semi-hard cheese' means uncooked, pressed cheese. Among the finest are Tomme de Savoie, made from either raw or pasteurised cow's milk; Cantal, a cow's milk cheese from Auvergne that tastes something like cheddar; Saint Nectaire, a strong-smelling pressed cheese that has both a strong and complex taste; and Ossau-Iraty, a ewe's milk cheese made in the Basque Country.

Fromage à pâte dure 'Hard cheese' is always cooked and pressed in France. Among the most popular are: Beaufort, a grainy cow's milk cheese with a slightly fruity taste from Rhône-Alpes; Comté, a cheese made with raw cow's milk in Franche-Comté; Emmental, a cow's milk cheese made all over France; and Mimolette, an Edam-like bright orange cheese from Lille that can be aged for up to 36 months.

Fromage à pâte molle 'Soft cheese' is moulded or rind-washed. Camembert, a classic moulded cheese from Normandy that for many is synonymous with 'French cheese', and the refined Brie de Meaux are both made from raw cow's milk; Munster from Alsace, mild Chaource and strong-smelling Langres from Champagne, and the odorous Époisses de Bourgogne are rind-washed, fine-textured cheeses.

Fromage à pâte persillée 'Marbled' or 'blue cheese' is so called because the veins often resemble *persille* (parsley). Roquefort is a ewe's milk veined cheese that is to many the king of French cheeses. Fourme d'Ambert is a very mild cow's milk cheese from Rhône-Alpes. Bleu du Haut Jura (also called Bleu de Gex) is a mild, blue-veined mountain cheese.

Fromage de chèvre 'Goat's milk cheese' is usually creamy and both sweet and a little salty when fresh, but hardens and gets much saltier as it matures. Among the best varieties are: Sainte Maure de Touraine, a creamy, mild cheese from the Loire region; Crottin de Chavignol, a classic though saltier variety from Burgundy; Cabécou de Rocamadour from Midi-Pyrénées, often served warm with salad or marinated in oil and rosemary; and Saint Marcellin, a soft white cheese from Lyon.

Camembert is cut in wedges like a pie. If a larger cheese (eg a Brie) has been bought already sliced into a wedge shape, cut from the tip to the rind; cutting off the top is just not on. Slice cheeses whose middle is the best part (eg blue or veined cheeses) in such a way as to take your fair share of the rind. A flat piece of semi-hard cheese like Emmental is usually just cut horizontally in hunks.

Wine and cheese are often a match made in heaven. It's a matter of taste, but in general, strong, pungent cheeses require a young, full-bodied red or a sweet wine, while soft cheeses with a refined flavour call for more quality and age in the wine. Some classic pairings include: Alsatian Gewürztraminer and Munster; Côtes du Rhone red with Roquefort; Côte d'Or (Burgundy) red and Brie or Camembert; and mature Bordeaux with Emmental or Cantal. Even Champagne can get into the act; drink it with Chaource, a mild cheese that smells of mushrooms.

CHARCUTERIE

Traditionally *charcuterie* is made only from pork, though a number of other meats – from beef and veal to chicken and goose – are now used in making sausages, blood puddings, hams, and other cured and salted meats. Pâtés, terrines and *rillettes* are essentially *charcuterie* and are prepared in many different ways.

The difference between a pâté and a terrine is academic: a pâté is removed from its container and sliced before it is served or sold, while a terrine is sliced while still in the container. *Rillettes,* on the other hand, is potted meat (pork, goose, duck or rabbit) or fish that is not ground, chopped or sliced but shredded, seasoned, mixed with fat and spread cold, like pâté, over bread or toast.

While every region in France produces standard *charcuterie* favourites as well as its own specialities, Alsace, Lyon and the Auvergne produce the best sausages, and Périgord and the north of France, some of the most popular pâtés. Some very popular types of *charcuterie* are *andouillette* (soft raw sausage made from the pig's small intestines that is grilled and eaten with onions and potatoes), *boudin noir* (blood sausage or pudding made with pig's blood, onions and spices, and usually eaten hot with stewed apples and potatoes), *jambon* (ham, either smoked or salt-cured), *saucisse* (usually a small fresh sausage that is boiled or grilled before eating), *saucisson* (usually a large salami eaten cold) and *saucisson sec* (air-dried salami).

Regional Specialities

As the culinary centre of the most aggressively gastronomic country in the world, Paris has more 'generic French', regional and ethnic restaurants, gourmet food shops and markets than any other place in France. Generally speaking, *la cuisine parisienne* (Parisian cuisine) is a poor relation of that extended family known as *la cuisine des provinces* (provincial cuisine), and today very few dishes are associated with the capital as such.

The cuisines of Paris and the Île de France surrounding the capital are basically indistinguishable from the cooking of France in general. Dishes associated with these regions are few – *vol-au-vent*, a light pastry shell filled with chicken or fish in a creamy sauce; *potage Saint-Germain*, a thick green pea soup; *gâteau Paris-Brest*, a ring-shaped cake filled with *praline* (butter cream) and topped with flaked almonds and icing sugar; and the humble onion soup and pig's trotters described so intimately in Ernest Hemingway's *The Sun Also Rises*. Deep-fried potatoes (*frites*) and other dishes such as *steak-frites* have always been a Parisian speciality. Today very few dishes are associated with the capital as such, though certain side dishes bear the names of some of its suburbs. See boxed text, (below).

The surfeit of other cuisines available in Paris – from Lyonnais and Corsican to Vietnamese and Moroccan – is another story, and will have you spoilt for choice and begging for more.

Diverse though it may be, French cuisine is typified by certain regions, most notably by Normandy, Burgundy, Périgord, Lyon and, to a lesser extent, Alsace, Provence and the Loire region and, still further down the 'influential regions' list, the Auvergne, Languedoc, the Basque Country and Corsica. The first four types of regional cuisine can be found in restaurants throughout Paris, while Alsatian *choucroute* (sauerkraut with sausage and other prepared meats) is the dish of choice at the capital's many brasseries. *La cuisine provençale* (Provence cooking) can be somewhat elusive in Paris, though many seafood restaurants claim to do an authentic *bouillabaisse* (fish soup). Cuisine of the Loire region has made more contributions to what can generically be called French food than any other. Dishes from the last five regions appear on menus from time to time while certain food products can be bought from speciality shops.

WHERE TO EAT

There are a vast number of cateries in Paris where you can get breakfast or brunch, a full lunch or dinner, and a snack between meals. Most have defined roles, though some definitions are less strict nowadays and some have even become blurred.

Auberge

In the provinces, an *auberge* (inn), which may also appear as an *auberge de campagne* or *auberge du terroir* (country inn), is just that: a restaurant serving traditional country fare attached to a rural inn or small hotel. If you see the word attached to an eatery in Paris, they're just being cute.

Bar

A *bar* or *bar américain* (cocktail bar) is an establishment dedicated to drinking and usually serves only sandwiches or snacks. A *bar à vins* is a wine bar, which may or may not serve full meals at lunch and dinner. A *bar à huîtres* is an oyster bar.

SAVOURING THE SUBURBS

The *maraîchers* (market gardeners) of the Île de France encircling Paris traditionally supplied the capital with fresh produce. Today, while the Île de France is less important agriculturally and encompasses the eight *départements* that make up the urbanised Région Parisienne (Parisian Region), the green and gentle 'Island of France' has clung to many of the products it knows best.

A list of fruits and vegetables from the region reads like a map of the RER: *asperges d'Argenteuil* (Argenteuil asparagus), *carottes de Crécy* (Crécy carrots), *cerises de Montmorency* (Montmorency cherries), *fraises de Palaiseau* (Palaiseau strawberries), *pétales de roses de Provins* (Provins rose petals, used to make jam), *tomates de Montlhéry* (Montlhéry tomatoes), *champignons de Paris* (Paris mushrooms, grown *for* – not *in* – the capital) and so on. A dish served *à la parisienne* (in the Parisian style) is a combination of vegetables along with potato balls that have been sautéed in butter, glazed in meat drippings and sprinkled with parsley.

Bistro

A bistro (sometimes written *bistrot*) is not clearly defined in Paris. It can be simply a pub or bar serving snacks and light pub meals, or a fully fledged restaurant.

Brasserie

Unlike the vast majority of restaurants in Paris, brasseries – which can look very much like cafés – serve full meals from morning till 11pm or even later. The featured dishes almost always include *choucroute* and sausages because the brasserie, which actually means 'brewery' in French, originated in Alsace. Most Parisians go to a brasserie as much for the lively atmosphere and the convenience as for the food.

Buffet

A *buffet* (or *buvette*) is a kiosk usually found at train stations and airports selling drinks, filled baguettes and snacks.

Café

Cafés are an important focal point for social life in Paris, and sitting in a café to read, write, talk with friends or just daydream is an integral part of many people's daily life here. Many Parisians see café-sitting – like shopping at outdoor markets – as a way of keeping in touch with their neighbourhood and maximising their chances of running into friends and acquaintances.

The main focus here, of course, is coffee, and only basic food is available at most cafés. Common options include a baguette filled with Camembert or pâté with *cornichons* (gherkins), a *croque-monsieur* (grilled ham and cheese sandwich) or a *croque-madame* (a croque-monsieur topped with a fried egg).

Three factors determine how much you'll pay in a café: where the café is located, where you are sitting within the café, and what time of day it is. Progressively more expensive tariffs apply at the *comptoir* or *zinc* (counter or bar), in the *salle* (inside seating area) and on the *terrasse* (pavement terrace), the best vantage point from which to see and be seen. A café on a major boulevard, such as blvd du Montparnasse or the av des Champs-Élysées, will charge considerably more than a place that fronts a quiet side street in the 3e. The price of drinks usually goes up after 8pm.

Ordering a cup of coffee (or anything else, for that matter) earns you the right to occupy the seat for as long as you like. You will never feel pressured to order something else.

You usually run a tab at a café and pay the *addition* (bill or check) right before you leave. However, if your waiter is going off duty, you may be asked to settle at the end of his or her shift.

Caféteria

Paris has several chains of *cafétérias* (cafeteria restaurants), including Flunch, that offer a decent and cheap (menus €6.50 to €8) selection of dishes that you can see before ordering, a factor that can make life easier if you're travelling with kids.

Crêperie

Crêperies (sometimes seen as *galetteries*) specialise in *crêpes*, ultrathin pancakes cooked on a flat surface and then folded or rolled over a filling. Sometimes the word *crêpe* is used to refer only to sweet crepes made with *farine de froment* (wheat flour), whereas a savoury crepe, more accurately a *galette*, is made with *farine de sarrasin* (buckwheat flour), and filled with cheese, mushrooms, eggs and the like.

Restaurant

The restaurant comes in many guises and price ranges in Paris – from ultrabudget *restaurants universitaires* (canteens or refectories, p229) to three-star Michelin *restaurants gastronomiques* (gourmet restaurants).

An important distinction between a brasserie and a restaurant is that while the former serves food throughout the day, a restaurant is usually open only for lunch and dinner. Almost all restaurants close for at least 1½ days (ie a full day and either one lunch or dinner period) each week, and this schedule is usually posted on the front door. Chain restaurants are usually open throughout the day, seven days a week.

Restaurants generally also post a *carte* (menu) outside, so you can decide before going in whether the selection and prices are to your liking and/or budget. Most offer at least one fixed-price, multicourse meal known in French as a *menu, menu à prix fixe* or *menu du jour* (daily menu). A *menu* (not to be confused with a *carte*) almost always costs much less than ordering à la carte.

When you order a three-course *menu*, you usually get to choose an entrée, such as salad, pâté or soup; a main dish (several meat, poultry or fish dishes, including the *plat du jour,* or 'the daily special', are generally on offer); and one or more final courses (usually cheese or dessert). In some places, you may also be able to order a *formule,* which allows you to pick two of three courses – an entrée and a main course, say, or a main course and a dessert.

Boissons (drinks), including wine, cost extra unless the menu says *boisson comprise* (drink included), in which case you may get a beer or a glass of mineral water. If the *menu* says *vin compris* (wine included), you'll probably be served a 25cL *pichet* (jug) of house red or white. The waiter will always ask if you would like coffee to end the meal, but this will almost always cost extra.

Restaurant meals in Paris are almost always served with bread, which is never accompanied by butter.

Restaurant Libre-Service

A *restaurant libre-service* is a self-service restaurant not unlike a *cafétéria.*

Restaurant Rapide

A *restaurant rapide* is a fast-food place, be it imported (eg McDonald's) or home grown ones such as Quick.

Restaurant Universitaire

The University of Paris system has some 14 *restaurants universitaires* (canteens or refectories) and 20 *cafétérias* subsidised by the Ministry of Education and operated by the Centre Régional des Œuvres Universitaires et Scolaires, better known as CROUS (p229). They serve very cheap meals (typically under €2.80 for local and visiting students and €6.60 for nonstudents).

Salon de Thé

A *salon de thé* (tearoom) is a trendy, somewhat pricey establishment that offers quiches, salads, cakes, tarts, pies and pastries, in addition, of course, to black and herbal teas.

VEGETARIANS & VEGANS

Vegetarians and vegans make up a small minority in a society where *viande* (meat) once also meant 'food', and they are not very well catered for; specialised vegetarian restaurants are few and far between. In fact, the vegetarian establishments that do exist in Paris often look more like laid-back cafés than restaurants. On the bright side, more and more restaurants are offering vegetarian choices on their set menus and *produits biologiques* (organic products) are all the rage nowadays, even among carnivores. Other options include *saladeries,* casual restaurants that serve a long list of *salades composées* (mixed salads).

Many restaurants now have at least a couple of vegetarian dishes on the menu, though it may be one of the starters/first courses. Unfortunately, very few set menus include vegetarian options. Sometimes the only way for vegetarians to assemble a real meal is by ordering one or more side dishes.

Strict vegetarians and vegans should note that most French cheeses are made with rennet, an enzyme derived from the stomach of a calf or young goat, and that some red wines (especially Bordeaux) are clarified with the albumin of egg whites.

The trade of *produits sans chimiques* (products without additives) or *produits biologiques,* usually abbreviated to *bio* is carefully government-regulated and very much on the increase in France.

PRACTICALITIES
Breakfast

What the French call *petit déjeuner* is not every Anglo-Saxon's cup of tea. For many, a croissant with butter and jam and a cup of milky coffee do not a breakfast make. Masters of the kitchen throughout the rest of the day, French chefs don't seem up to it in the morning. But there's method to their meanness; the whole idea is not to fill up – *petit déjeuner* means 'little lunch', and the real *déjeuner* (lunch) is just around the corner!

In the Continental style, people here traditionally start the day with a bread roll or a bit of baguette left over from the night before, eaten with butter and jam and followed by a *café au lait* (coffee with lots of hot milk), a small black coffee or even a hot chocolate. Some people also eat cereal, toast, fruit and even yoghurt in the morning – something they never did in the past. Commuters will often eschew breakfast at home altogether, opting for a quick coffee and a sweet roll at a train station kiosk or at their desk in the office.

Contrary to what many foreigners think, Parisians do not eat croissants every day but usually reserve these for a treat at the weekend, when they may also choose *brioches* (small roll or cake sometimes flavoured with nuts, currants or candied fruits), *pains au chocolat* (chocolate-filled brioche) or other *viennoiserie* (baked goods).

Lunch & Dinner

Many Parisians still consider *déjeuner* (lunch) to be the main meal of the day. Restaurants generally serve it between noon and 2.30pm (or 3pm) and *dîner* (dinner or supper) from 7.30pm to sometime between 10pm and midnight. With the exception of brasseries, cafés and fast-food places, very few restaurants are open between lunch and dinner. The vast majority of restaurants close on Sunday; in August, when most Parisians flee for the beaches or the mountains, many restaurateurs lock up and leave town along with their customers.

As the pace of life is as hectic here as it is elsewhere in the industrialised world nowadays, the two-hour midday meal has become increasingly rare, at least during the week. Dinner, however, is still turned into an elaborate affair whenever time and finances permit. A fully fledged traditional French meal at home is an awesome event, often comprising six distinct *plats* (courses; see p222). They are always served with wine – red, white or rosé, depending on what you're eating. A meal in a restaurant almost never consists of more than three courses: the *entrée* (starter or first course), the *plat principal* (main course) and dessert or cheese.

Snacks

Though Parisians may snack or eat between meals, they do not seem to go in for street food; hot dogs stands and noodle carts are nowhere to be seen and eating in public is considered somewhat *anglo-saxon* (English or American) and thus rude. You may encounter a crepe-maker on a busy street corner in Bastille, Marais or the Latin Quarter, or someone selling roasted *châtaignes* (chestnuts) in autumn and winter, but generally people will duck into a café for *un truc à grignoter* (something to nibble on) or a patisserie for a slice of something sweet to be eaten on the trot.

Opening Hours

Restaurants generally open from noon to 2.30pm or 3pm for lunch and from 7pm or 7.30pm to between 10pm and midnight for dinner. Only brasseries serve full meals continuously throughout the day (usually from

11am or noon to as late as 1am). National and local laws require that restaurants close for 1½ days a week and that employees work no more than 35 hours a week (though exceptions can be made). That means most eateries will be shut for a full day and (usually) an afternoon. Be advised that the vast majority of restaurants in Paris close on Sunday – there's a distressing tendency for many to shut down for the entire weekend. Supermarkets are generally open from 8.30am or 9am to 8pm Monday to Saturday, with a few open Sunday (9am to 12.30pm or 1pm). Due to the quirkiness of restaurant opening hours, we have listed them under each review.

How Much?

When it comes to eating out in Paris, the question 'How much?' is like asking 'How long is a piece of string?' It all depends… A three-course dinner *menu* (fixed-price meal with two or three courses) can be had for as little as €12 at budget places, and one-plate *plats du jour* (daily specials) at lunch are sometimes available for under €10. On the other hand, three courses for lunch at Le Grand Véfour (p232) overlooking the Jardin du Palais Royal will set you back €88, and dinner is more than three times that amount.

In general, however, you should be able to enjoy a substantial sit-down lunch for under around €12/€20 at a budget/medium-priced restaurant and an excellent three-course dinner with wine for around €35.

Lower-priced good-value *menus* that are available at lunch only (and usually just on weekdays) are noted as such throughout the chapter. Generally, higher-priced *menus* are available at dinner.

Booking Tables

It is always advisable to book in advance at midrange restaurants and absolutely mandatory at top-end ones. If you do arrive at a restaurant without a reservation, you will be treated more seriously if you state the number of *couverts* (covers) required upon entry rather than referring to the number of places. If you're a party of two, ask *Avez-vous deux couverts?*

Paying the Bill & Tipping

With the exception of cafeterias, service restaurants and the like, most eateries in Paris take credit cards, though there is usually a minimum charge of €20. A hand-held ma-

CHEAP EATS

Along with the less-expensive places listed at the end of each neighbourhood in this chapter, French chain and university restaurants offer excellent value for those counting their euros.

Fast-Food & Chain Restaurants

American fast-food chains have busy branches all over Paris, as does the local hamburger chain Quick (www.quick .fr in French). In addition, a number of local chain restaurants have outlets around Paris with standard menus. They are definitely a cut above fast-food outlets and can be good value in areas such as the av des Champs-Élysées, where restaurants tend to be overpriced.

Bistro Romain (www.bistroromain.fr in French; starters €4.90-17.10, pasta €13.30-16.40, mains €14.30-19.40, menu €12.50-33.60; 🕙 11am-midnight Sun-Thu, to 1am Fri & Sat) This ever-popular Italian-ish bistro-restaurant chain, which has some 14 branches in Paris proper and another nine in the *banlieues* (suburbs), is a surprisingly upmarket place for its price category, and service is always pleasant and efficient. The Champs-Élysées branch (Map 140–1; ☎ 01 43 59 93 31; 122 av des Champs-Élysées, 8e; Ⓜ George V), one of a pair along the city's most famous thoroughfare, is a stone's throw from place Charles de Gaulle and the Arc de Triomphe.

Buffalo Grill (www.buffalo-grill.fr; starters €4.20-10, mains €9.70-20.20, menu from €9.10; 🕙 11am-11pm Sun-Thu, to midnight Fri & Sat) This successful chain has nine branches in Paris, including the Gare du Nord branch (Map pp152–3; ☎ 01 40 16 47 81; 9 blvd de Denain, 10e; Ⓜ Gare du Nord). Not surprisingly, the emphasis here is on grills and steak – everything from Canadian bison burgers (€10.50) to a huge *entrecôte* cowboy steak (€17.60).

Hippopotamus (www.hippopotamus.fr in French; starters €4.80-9.90, mains €11.50-24.50, menu €15.50-29.50; 🕙 11.45am-12.30am Sun-Thu, to 1am Fri & Sat) This spreading chain, which has 20 branches in Paris proper, specialises in solid, steak-based meals. Three of the outlets here stay open to 5am daily, including Opéra branch (Map pp82–3; ☎ 01 47 42 75 70; 1 blvd des Capucines, 2e; Ⓜ Opéra).

Léon de Bruxelles (www.leon-de-bruxelles.com in French; starters €5.30-9.90, mains €10.50-16, menu €11.20-15.90; 🕙 11.45am 11pm) At Léon the focus is on one thing and one thing only: *moules* (mussels). Meal size bowls of the meaty bivalves, served with chips and bread, start at about €10.50 and are exceptionally good value, especially at lunch. There are 9 Léons in Paris, including the Les Halles branch (Map p86; ☎ 01 42 36 18 50; 120 rue Rambu-teau, 1er; Ⓜ Châtelet-Les Halles).

University Canteens

Stodgy but filling *cafétéria* food is available in copious quantities at Paris' 14 *restaurants universitaires* (student res-taurants). Another 20 cafeterias (sometimes in the same building) serve drinks, snacks and lighter meals from 8am to between 3pm and 6pm on weekdays. Tickets for three-course meals at Paris' university restaurants are €2.80 for local students with a French university or college ID card and visiting students with an ISIC or youth card and €6.60 for guests accompanied by a CROUS cardholder.

Centre Régional des Œuvres Universitaires et Scolaires (CROUS; ☎ 01 40 51 36 00; www.crous-paris.fr in French) restaurants (usually called *restos U*) have variable hours that change according to university holiday schedules and weekend rotational agreements, check the schedule posted outside any of the following or the CROUS website for current times. The only one open all year and on Sunday (for brunch) is Bullier.

Branches include Bullier (Map pp110–11; ☎ 01 40 51 37 85; 39 av Georges Bernanos, 5e; 🕙 11.30am-2pm & 6.30-8pm daily; Ⓜ Port Royal); Censier (Map pp110–11; ☎ 01 45 35 41 24; 31 rue Geoffroy St-Hilaire, 5e; 🕙 11am-2.30pm Mon-Fri; Ⓜ Censier Daubenton or Jussieu); Châtelet (Map pp110–11; ☎ 01 43 31 51 66; 10 rue Jean Calvin, 5e; 🕙 11.30am-2pm Mon-Fri; Ⓜ Censier Daubenton); Mabillon (Map pp116–17; ☎ 01 43 25 66 23; 3 rue Mabillon, 6e; 🕙 11.30am-2.30pm & 6-8pm; Ⓜ Mabillon); and Mazet (Map pp116–17; ☎ 01 46 34 23 83; 5 rue André Mazet, 6e; 🕙 11.30am-2pm Mon-Fri; Ⓜ Odéon).

chine used to verify your credit card and payment is brought to the table, where the transaction takes place; if your card has a chip (*puce* in French) you will almost surely require a PIN number. Always check your bill before paying: small 'mistakes' do happen from time to time in Paris.

Many French people traditionally felt that 'going Dutch' (ie splitting the bill) at restau-rants was an uncivilised custom, and in general the person who did the inviting would do the paying. That may still happen but nowadays close friends and colleagues will usually share the cost equally. They never calculate it down to the last euro and centime, however.

French law requires that restaurant and café bills include the service charge, which is usually between 12% and 15%. But a word of warning is in order. *Service compris* (service included, sometimes abbreviated as 'sc' at the bottom of the bill) means that the service charge is built into the price of each dish; *service non-compris* (service not included) or *service en sus* (service in addition) means that the service charge is calculated after the food and/or drink you've consumed has been added up. In either case you pay only the total of the bill so a *pourboire* (tip) on top of that is neither necessary nor expected in most cases. However, many Parisians will leave a few coins on the table in a restaurant, unless the service was particularly bad. They rarely tip in cafés and bars when they've just had a coffee or a drink, however.

Self-Catering

Most people in Paris buy a good part of their food from a series of small neighbourhood shops, each with its own speciality, though as everywhere more and more people are relying on supermarkets and hypermarkets these days. Having to go to four shops and stand in four queues to fill the fridge (or assemble a picnic) may seem rather a waste of time, but the whole ritual is an important part of the way many Parisians live their daily lives. And as each *commerçant* (shopkeeper) specialises in purveying only one type of food, he or she can almost always provide all sorts of useful tips: which round of Camembert is ripe, which wine will complement a certain food, which type of pot to cook rabbit in and so on. In any case, most products for sale at *charcuteries* (delicatessens), *pâtisseries* (pastry shops) and *traiteurs* (caterers) or *charcuteries-traiteurs* (delicatessens/caterers) are clearly marked and labelled.

As these stores are geared to people buying small quantities of fresh food each day, it's perfectly acceptable to purchase only meal-size amounts: a few *tranches* (slices) of meat to make a sandwich, perhaps, or a *petit bout* (small hunk) of sausage. You can also request just enough for *une/deux personne(s)* (one/two persons). If you want a bit more, ask for *encore un petit peu*, and if you are being given too much, say *'C'est trop'*.

Fresh bread is baked and sold at *boulangeries;* mouth-watering pastries are available at *pâtisseries;* a *fromagerie* can supply you with cheese that is *fait* (ripe) to the exact degree that you request; a *charcuterie* offers sliced meat, pâtés and so on; and fresh fruit and vegetables are sold at *épiceries* (greengrocers), supermarkets and open-air markets.

A *boucherie* is a general butcher, but for specialised poultry you have to go to a *marchand de volaille*. A *boucherie chevaline*, easily identifiable by the gilded horse's head above the entrance, sells horse meat, which some people prefer to beef or mutton. Fresh fish and seafood are available from a *poissonnerie*.

Neighbourhood markets are equally a part of life here. If on a Saturday morning you notice throngs of basket-toting people passing you by with great determination, and others, laden down with bags, going the opposite direction in a more relaxed pace, then by all means follow the crowds, as you have stumbled upon the most Parisian of weekend pastimes: shopping at the *marché alimentaire* (food market). Bear in mind, though, that when buying fruit and vegetables, you should not touch the produce unless invited to do so. Indicate to the shopkeeper what you want and he or she will choose for you.

The city's *marchés découverts* (open-air markets) – some 70 of which pop up in public squares around the city two or three times a week – are usually open from about 7am or 8am to 2pm or 3pm, depending on the time of year. The dozen or so *marchés couverts* (covered markets) keep more regular hours: 8am to 1pm and 3.30pm or 4pm to 7pm or 7.30pm from Tuesday to Saturday and till lunch time on Sunday. Completing the picture are numerous independent *rues commerçantes*, pedestrian streets where the shops set up outdoor stalls. To find out when there's a market near you, check out the list opposite, enquire at your hotel or hostel or ask anyone who lives in the neighbourhood. Also, self-catering details are included at the end of neighbourhood sections in this chapter.

LOUVRE & LES HALLES

The area between Forum des Halles (1er) and the Centre Pompidou (4e) is filled with a number of trendy restaurants, but most of them cater mostly to tourists and few of them are especially good. Streets lined with places to eat include rue des Lombards, the narrow streets to the north and east of Forum des

TO MARKET, TO MARKET

The following is a list of Paris markets selected according to the variety of their produce, their ethnicity and the neigh-bourhood. They are *la crème de la crème* of what's on offer in Paris.

Marché aux Enfants Rouges (Map pp92–3; 39 rue de Bretagne, 3e; ☺ 9am-2pm & 4-8pm Tue-Thu, 9am-8pm Fri & Sat, 9am-2pm Sun; Ⓜ Filles du Calvaire) This covered market south of place de la République has ethnic (Italian, Japanese etc) stalls as well as French ones.

Marché Bastille (Map pp94–5; blvd Richard Lenoir, 11e; ☺ 7am-2.30pm Tue & Sun; Ⓜ Bastille or Richard Lenoir) Stretching as far north as the Richard Lenoir metro station, this is arguably the best open-air market in Paris, with a fair number of ethnic food stalls now in attendance.

Marché des Batignolles (Map pp144–5; blvd des Batignolles btwn rue des Batignolles & rue Puteaux, 8e & 17e; ☺ 9am-2pm Sat; Ⓜ Place de Clichy or Rome) This was the first of Paris' *marchés biologiques* (organic markets).

Marché Beauvau (Map pp158–9; place d'Aligre, 12e; ☺ 8am-1pm & 4-7.30pm Tue-Sat, 8am-1pm Sun; Ⓜ Ledru Rollin) This covered market remains a colourful Arab and North African enclave not far from Bastille.

Marché Belleville (Map p155; blvd de Belleville btwn rue Jean-Pierre Timbaud & rue du Faubourg du Temple, 11e & 20e; ☺ 7am-2.30pm Tue & Fri, Ⓜ Belleville or Couronne) This market offers a fascinating (and easy) entry into the large, vibrant ethnic communities of the *quartiers de l'est* (eastern neighbourhoods), home to African, Middle Eastern and Asian immigrants as well as artists and students.

Marché Brancusi (Map pp174–5; place Constantin Brancusi, 14e; ☺ 9am-2pm Sat; Ⓜ Vavin) This weekly open-air market specialises in organic produce.

Marché Grenelle (Map pp166–7; blvd de Grenelle btwn rue de Lourmel & rue du Commerce, 15e; ☺ 7am-2.30pm Wed & Sun; Ⓜ La Motte-Picquet Grenelle) Arranged below an elevated railway and surrounded by stately Hauss-mann boulevards and Art Nouveau apartment blocks, the Grenelle market attracts a posh clientele.

Marché Maubert (Map pp110–11; place Maubert, 5e; ☺ 7am-2.30pm Tue, Thu & Sat; Ⓜ Maubert Mutualité) This market, spread over a small triangle of intersecting streets, reigns over St-Germain des Prés, the poshest part of the bohemian 5e.

Marché Monge (Map pp110–11; place Monge, 5e; ☺ 7am-2pm Wed, Fri & Sun; Ⓜ Place Monge) This is one of the better open-air neighbourhood markets on the Left Bank.

Marché Président Wilson (Map pp132–3; av du Président Wilson btwn rue Debrousse & place d'Iéna, 16e; ☺ 7am-2.30pm Wed & Sat; Ⓜ Iéna or Alma Marceau) This upscale market attracts a well-heeled crowd from the 16e.

Marché Raspail (Map pp116–17; blvd Raspail btwn rue de Rennes & rue du Cherche Midi, 6e; ☺ 7am-2.30pm Tue & Sun; Ⓜ Rennes) This traditional open-air market north of Rennes metro station features organic produce on Sunday.

Marché St-Charles (Map pp166–7; rue St-Charles btwn rue de Javel & rond-point St-Charles, 15e; ☺ 7am-2.30pm Tue & Fri; Ⓜ Charles Michels) This market may appear somewhat far-flung off in the western 15e, but shoppers will go any distance for its quality produce, including organic goods.

Marché St-Quentin (Map pp152–3; 85bis blvd de Magenta, 10e; ☺ 8am-1pm & 3.30-7.30pm Tue-Sat, 8am-1pm Sun; Ⓜ Gare de l'Est) This iron-and-glass covered market, built in 1866, is a maze of corridors lined mostly with gourmet and upmarket food stalls.

Rue Cler (Map pp128–9; rue Cler, 7e; ☺ 7am or 8am-7pm or 7.30pm Tue-Sat, 8am-noon Sun; Ⓜ École Militaire) This commercial street in the 7e is a breath of fresh air in a sometimes stuffy *quartier* and can almost feel like a party at the weekend when the whole neighbourhood turns out en masse.

Rue Montorgueil (Map pp82–3; rue Montorgueil btwn rue de Turbigo & rue Réaumur, 2e; ☺ 8am-7.30pm Tue-Sat, to noon Sun; Ⓜ Les Halles or Sentier) This rue commerçante is the closest market to Paris' 700-year-old wholesale market, Les Halles, which was moved from this area to Rungis in 1969.

Rue Mouffetard (Map pp110–11; rue Mouffetard around rue de l'Arbalète, 5e; ☺ 8am-7.30pm Tue-Sat, 8am-noon Sun; Ⓜ Censier Daubenton) Rue Mouffetard is the city's most photogenic commercial market street and it's the place where Parisians send tourists (travellers go to Marché Bastille).

Rue Poncelet & Rue Bayen (Map pp144–5; rue Poncelet & rue Bayen, 17e; ☺ 9am-1pm & 4-7.30pm Tue-Sat, 8am-1pm Sun; Ⓜ Ternes) This *rue commerçante* caters to the flush denizens of the 16e and 17e arrondissements.

Halles and pedestrian-only rue Montorgueil, a market street that's probably your best bet for something quick. In addition, there are several worthwhile places in the *passages couverts* (covered shopping arcades; p188).

Those in search of Asian food flock to rue Ste-Anne and other streets of Paris' so-called Japantown, which is just west of the Jardin du Palais Royal. There are also some good-value restaurants serving other Asian cuisines in the area.

LE GRAND VÉFOUR Map pp82–3 French €€€
☎ 01 42 96 56 27; www.grand-vefour.com; 17 rue de Beaujolais, 1er; starters €79-92, mains €85-102, menus €88 (lunch only) & €268; ☽ lunch Mon-Fri, dinner to 9.30pm Mon-Thu; Ⓜ Pyramides
This 18th-century jewel on the northern edge of the Jardin du Palais Royal has been a dining favourite of the Parisian elite since 1784; just look at who gets their names ascribed to each table – from Napoleon to Victor Hugo and Colette (who lived next door). The food is tiptop; expect a voyage of discovery in one of the most beautiful restaurants in the world.

GEORGES Map pp98–9 International €€€
☎ 01 44 78 47 99; www.centrepompidou.fr; 6th fl, Centre Pompidou, place Georges Pompidou, 4e; starters €20, mains €40; ☽ lunch & dinner to 1am Wed-Mon; Ⓜ Rambuteau
Encased in aluminium sheeting with modular arctic-white seats, the Pompidou Centre's hyperindustrial dining room offers pretty predictable and expensive Coste food – most people go for the tuna tartare or avocado and crab salad (€20 to €22) or the steak with the Asianesque name Le Tigre qui Pleure (The Crying Tiger). But this place is really all about the stunning views over Paris' rooftops, especially from its terrace.

LE VAUDEVILLE
Map pp82–3 French, Brasserie €€€
☎ 01 40 20 04 62; www.vaudevilleparis.com; 29 rue Vivienne, 2e; starters €8.50-17.50, mains €18-39, menus €24 & €31; ☽ lunch & dinner to 1am; Ⓜ Bourse
This stunning brasserie opposite the stock exchange is to Art Deco what the Bouillon Racine (p255) is to Art Nouveau. OK, the food – steaks, fish, oysters – might be something of an afterthought, but at least you can be guaranteed a certain standard. Come

for the fabulous décor – engraved glass, extravagant lighting, domed ceiling and intricate ironwork – designed in the 1920s by the Solvet brothers, who also did La Coupole (p258).

AUX CRUS DE BOURGOGNE Map pp82–3 French, Bistro €€€
☎ 01 42 33 48 24; 3 rue Bachaumont, 2e; starters €7-25, mains €13.50-38, menu €29; ☽ lunch & dinner to 11pm Mon-Fri; Ⓜ Les Halles or Sentier
A favourite of André Malraux, this bistro dating back to 1900 on a pedestrian street just off busy rue Montorgueil has a penchant for fish and seafood – especially lobster (half a lobster with mayonnaise is €25). As its name implies, Burgundy is the wine of choice. A real plus in the warmer months is the open terrace, which allows you to enjoy your crustaceans without a side order of exhaust fumes.

AU DAUPHIN Map p86 French, Basque €€€
☎ 01 42 60 40 11; 167 rue St-Honoré, 1er; menus €20 & €27 (lunch only), €38; ☽ lunch & dinner to 10.15pm; Ⓜ Palais Royal-Musée du Louvre
The force behind this unassuming bistro facing place André Malraux and Palais Royal is two pedigreed chefs from Biarritz (on the southwest coast) who have brought the flavours of the Basque country and the coastal Landes region to Paris. There are two hard-to-choose routes through the menu – the first being jars of wonderful rustic starters such as *lapereau à la grand-mère* (young rabbit in mushroom cream sauce), *rillettes* (shredded potted meat) and foie gras, to be shared with excellent bread, while the other offers combinations of classic Spanish *parrillada* (mixed grill).

AU PIED DE COCHON
Map p86 French, Brasserie €€€
☎ 01 40 13 77 00; www.pieddecochon.com; 6 rue Coquillère, 1er; starters €7.90-18.50, mains €16.50-35, 2-/3-course menus €19.50/24; ☽ 24hr; Ⓜ Les Halles
This venerable establishment, which once satisfied the appetites of both market porters and theatre-goers with its onion soup and *pieds de cochon* (pig's feet or trotters), has become more uniformly upmarket and touristy since Les Halles was moved to the suburbs, but it still opens round the clock seven days a week. Generous breakfasts are a snip at €11.50.

CAFÉ MODERNE Map pp82–3   French €€€
☎ 01 53 40 84 10; www.cafemoderne.fr; 40 rue
Notre Dames des Victoires, 2e; 2-/3-course menus
€28/34; ⌚ lunch Mon-Fri, dinner to 11pm Mon-Sat;
Ⓜ Bourse

Located just opposite the Bourse, the 'Modern Café' feels more New York than Paris
but so much the better for that. The food
on offer is contemporary rather than classic
bistro; the fish dishes are particularly recommended, as is the wonderful *millefeuille* of
pastry, cream and fresh fruit.

L'ARDOISE Map pp82–3   French, Bistro €€€
☎ 01 42 96 28 18; www.lardoise-paris.com; 28 rue
du Mont Thabor, 1er; menu €33; ⌚ lunch Tue-Sat,
dinner to 11pm Tue-Sun; Ⓜ Concorde or Tuileries

This is a lovely little bistro with no menu
as such (*ardoise* means 'blackboard', which
is all there is), but who cares? The food –
hare in black pepper and beef fillet with
morels, prepared dextrously by chef Pierre
Jay (ex-Tour d'Argent) – is superb and the
three-course *prix fixe* (set menu) offers
good value. L'Ardoise is bound to attract a
fair number of tourists due to its location,
but generally they too are on a culinary
quest.

CAFÉ MARLY Map p86   French, Café €€€
☎ 01 46 26 06 60; cour Napoléon du Louvre, 93
rue de Rivoli, 1er; starters €8-25, mains €19-31;
⌚ 8am-2am; Ⓜ Palais Royal-Musée du Louvre

This classic venue facing the Louvre's inner
courtyard serves contemporary French
fare throughout the day under the palace
colonnades. The views of the glass pyramid
are priceless – if you don't know you're in
Paris now, you never will – and depending
on how *au courant* (familiar) you are with
French starlets and people who appear in
Match, you should get an eyeful. Decent
pastas are €17 to €24 while sandwiches and
snacks are from €12 to €20.

DROUANT Map pp82–3   French €€€
☎ 01 42 65 15 16; www.drouant.com; 16-18
place Gaillon, 2e; starters €20, mains €30; menus
€42 (lunch only), €40 & €52; ⌚ lunch & dinner to
midnight; Ⓜ Quatre September

If you're something of a literary groupie,
you've just got to make your way to the
restaurant where they award the Prix Goncourt, France's equivalent of the Booker or
Pulitzer. Of course you might also come for
the food, prepared by Alsatian chef Antoine

Westerman, who cut his teeth at the Mon Vieil
Ami (p248). Food comes bite-sized and in lots
of four; think tapas and get ready to share.

MACÉO Map pp82–3   International €€€
☎ 01 42 97 53 85; www.maceorestaurant.com;
15 rue des Petits Champs, 1er; starters €11-18,
mains €26-30, menus €30 (lunch only), €37 &
€46; ⌚ lunch Mon-Fri, dinner to 11pm Mon-Sat;
Ⓜ Pyramides

From the people who brought us Willi's Wine
Bar (p236) comes this very upper-crust restaurant housed in a former brothel with Second
Empire décor; it's one of the most attractive
dining rooms in Paris. The cuisine is innovative and there is a very sophisticated (and
very unusual) vegetarian menu.

LE GRAND COLBERT
Map pp82–3   French €€€
☎ 01 42 86 87 88; www.legrandcolbert.fr; 2-4 rue
Vivienne, 2e; starters €10-21.50, mains €19.50-30,
menus €32 (lunch only) & €39; ⌚ noon-3am;
Ⓜ Pyramides

This former workers' *cafétéria* transformed
into a *fin de siècle* showcase is more relaxed
than many similarly restored restaurants
and a convenient spot for lunch if visiting
Galerie Vivienne and Galerie Colbert or
cruising the streets late at night (last orders:
1am). Don't expect gastronomic miracles,
but portions are big and service is friendly.

JOE ALLEN Map p86   American €€€
☎ 01 42 36 70 13; www.joeallenrestaurant.com;
30 rue Pierre Lescot, 1er; starters €7.50-10.30,
mains €15.50-26, menus €13.90 (lunch only), €18 &
€22.50; ⌚ noon-1am; Ⓜ Étienne Marcel

An institution in Paris since 1972, Joe Allen
is a little bit of New York in Paris, with a
great atmosphere and a good selection
of Californian wines. There's an excellent
brunch (€19.50 to €23.50) from noon to 4pm
at the weekend, where many can be seen
slumped over a Bloody Mary and trying to
make sense of the night – or was that the

SWEET MEMORIES

Parisians love *sucreries* (sweet things) and fruit and, judging from the eye-catching and saliva-inducing window displays at pastry shops throughout the city, they can't get enough of either in combination. The following are some of our favourite *pâtisseries* in Paris, but be warned: the list is *not* comprehensive. For a more complete rundown, consult the informative (and mouth-wateringly attractive) *The Pâtisseries of Paris* by Jamie Cahill.

Dalloyau (Map pp94–5; ☎ 01 48 87 89 88; www.dalloyau.fr; 3 blvd Beaumarchais, 4e; ⏱ 9am-9pm; Ⓜ Bastille) Specialities include *pain aux raisins* (raisin bread), *millefeuille* (pastry layered with cream) and *tarte au citron* (lemon tart). There's also a 8e branch (Map pp140–1; ☎ 01 42 99 90 00; 101 rue du Faubourg St-Honoré, 8e; ⏱ 8.30am-9pm; Ⓜ St-Philippe du Roule).

Florence Finkelsztajn (Map pp98–9; ☎ 01 48 87 92 85; 24 rue des Écouffes, 4e; ⏱ 10am-7pm Thu-Tue; Ⓜ St-Paul) Dating back to 1932, this pâtisserie has scrumptious Jewish and Central European–style breads and pastries, including apple strudel and poppy-seed cakes.

Gérard Mulot (Map pp116–17; ☎ 01 43 26 85 77; www.gerard-mulot.com in French; 76 rue de Seine, 6e; ⏱ 9.30am-8.30pm Thu-Tue; Ⓜ Odéon or Mabillon) Specialities include various fruit tarts (peach, lemon, apple), *tarte normande* (apple cake) and *mabillon* (caramel mousse with apricot conserves).

Jean Millet (Map pp128–9; ☎ 01 45 51 49 80; 103 rue St-Dominique, 7e; ⏱ 9am-7pm Mon-Sat, 8am-1pm Sun; Ⓜ École Militaire) Specialities include *délice au chocolat praliné* (a heavenly almond and chocolate concoction) and *bavarois d'abricots* (a cold, moulded mousse dessert of cream and apricot fruit purée).

La Fougasse (Map pp92–3; ☎ 01 42 72 36 80; 25 rue de Bretagne, 3e; ⏱ 7am-8pm Tue-Sat, 7am-2pm Sun; Ⓜ Filles du Calvaire) Come here for the scrumptious *marrons glacés* (candied chestnuts) & *tarte aux abricots* (apricot tart).

Ladurée (Map pp140–1; ☎ 01 40 75 08 75; www.laduree.fr in French; 75 av des Champs-Élysées, 8e; ⏱ 7.30am-11pm Mon-Fri, 8.30-midnight Sat & Sun; Ⓜ George V) Specialities include *macarons au chocolat* (chocolate macaroons) and *macarons à la pistache* (pistachio macaroons).

Le Nôtre (Map pp92–3; ☎ 01 53 01 91 91; www.lenotre.fr in French; 10 rue St-Antoine, 4e; ⏱ 9am-9.30pm; Ⓜ Bastille) This branch of the famous *traiteur* chain at the corner of rue des Tournelles has some of the most delectable pastries and chocolate in Paris. There are a dozen other outlets sprinkled across the capital.

Stohrer (Map pp82–3; ☎ 01 42 33 38 20; www.stohrer.fr in French; 51 rue Montorgueil, 2e; ⏱ 7.30am-8.30pm; Ⓜ Les Halles or Sentier) Specialities include *galette des rois* (kings' cake; puff pastry with frangipane cream) and *marrons glacées* (candied chestnuts).

morning? – before. The food is simple but finely prepared; the ribs (€17) are particularly recommended and some people think Joe Allen serves the best hamburgers in town.

AUX LYONNAIS Map pp82–3   French, Lyonnais €€€
☎ 01 42 96 65 04; www.alainducasse.fr; 32 rue St-Marc, 2e; starters €11-14, mains €21-25, menu €30; ⏱ lunch Tue-Fri, dinner to 11pm Tue-Sat; Ⓜ Richelieu Drouot
This is where Alain Ducasse (who's got three Michelin stars at his restaurant over at the Plaza Athénée) and his followers 'slum' it. The venue is an Art Nouveau masterpiece that feels more real than movie set and the food is restructured Lyonnais classics on the short, seasonal menu; any item based on *cochon* (pig) comes with an ironclad guarantee to satisfy and everything goes well with Beaujolais. Two complaints: there are too

many covers in the small space and service is rushed and impersonal.

CHEZ LA VIEILLE Map p86   French €€€
☎ 01 42 60 15 78; 1 rue Bailleul, 1er; starters €15-21, mains €18-25, menu €23 (lunch only); ⏱ lunch Mon-Fri, dinner to 9.45pm Mon, Tue, Thu & Fri; Ⓜ Louvre-Rivoli
This favourite little restaurant on the corner of rue de l'Arbre à Sec, 'At the Old Lady's' is on two floors, but don't expect a slot on the more rustic ground floor; that's reserved for regulars. The small menu reflects the size of the place but is universally sublime. Try the excellent *terrine maison* and *poitrine de veau confit* (veal breast confit; €21).

L'ÉPI D'OR Map p86   French, Bistro €€
☎ 01 42 36 38 12; 25 rue Jean-Jacques Rousseau, 1er; starters €6.50-16, mains €18-24, 2-/3-course

menus €19/23; ☺ lunch Mon-Fri, dinner to
11.30pm Mon-Sat; Ⓜ Louvre-Rivoli
'The Golden Sword' has been an institution since the *belle époque,* when it would
open at 10pm to serve the *'forts des halles',*
the brutes who stacked the *'devils',* huge
bags of potatoes and cabbage, all night
at the old Marché des Halles. Today it's
an oh-so-Parisian bistro with 1940s décor
and well-prepared, classic dishes – *gigot
d'agneau* (leg of lamb) cooked for seven
hours, *magret de canard* (sliced duck
breast) – to a surprisingly well-heeled
crowd. The *menus* are available at lunch
and till 9pm only.

RESTAURANT DU THÉÂTRE
Map pp82–3   French, Bistro €€
☎ 01 42 97 59 46; 36 rue de Montpensier, 1er;
starters €9.50-16, mains €16-22, menus €30 & €38;
☺ lunch & dinner to 8.30pm Tue-Fri, to 10pm Sat;
Ⓜ Pyramides
This civilised bistro and wine bar facing the
Jardin du Palais Royal is next door to the
little-known Théâtre du Palais Royal. It's
a convenient spot if visiting the *passages
couverts* around Palais Royal or even the
Louvre and is best entered via 67 Galerie de
Montpensier. The *plat du jour* is €17.

COMPTOIR DE LA GASTRONOMIE
Map pp82–3   French €€
☎ 01 42 33 31 32; www.comptoir-gastronomie
.com, in French; 34 rue Montmartre, 1er; starters
€7-14, mains €16-22; ☺ 11am-11pm Mon-Sat,
noon-4pm; Ⓜ Les Halles
This striking Art Nouveau establishment,
here since 1894, has an elegant dining room
where dishes are constructed around delicacies such as foie gras, truffles and caviar. The
adjoining *épicerie fine* (specialist grocer; ☺ 6am-
11pm Mon-Sat, to 4pm Sun) stocks a scrumptious
array of gourmet goods to take home.

CAFÉ BEAUBOURG
Map p86   French, International €€
☎ 01 48 87 63 96; 100 rue St-Martin, 4e; starters
€8-14, mains €15-22; ☺ 8am-1am Sun-Wed, to
2am Thu-Sat; Ⓜ Châtelet-Les Halles
This upbeat minimalist café across from
the Centre Pompidou has been drawing
a well-heeled crowd for breakfast and
brunch (from €13 to €24) on its terrace for
over 20 years now. Bonus: there's always
free entertainment on the *parvis* (large
square) just opposite.

LE PETIT MÂCHON
Map p86   French, Lyonnais €€
☎ 01 42 60 08 06; 158 rue St-Honoré, 1er; starters
€7-12.50, mains €14-22; ☺ lunch & dinner to 11pm
Tue-Sun; Ⓜ Palais Royal-Musée du Louvre
Close to the Louvre, this upbeat bistro
serves some of the best Lyons-inspired
specialities in town and the welcome is
always warm. It takes its name from a
Burgundian variety of *galette des rois* (kings'
cake), a puff pastry filled with frangipane
cream that is eaten at Epiphany (Twelfth
night; p222).

DJAKARTA BALI Map p86   Indonesian €€
☎ 01 45 08 83 11; www.djakarta-bali.com;
9 rue Vauvilliers, 1er; starters €10.50-14.50, mains
€11-22; ☺ dinner to 11pm Tue-Sun; Ⓜ Louvre
Rivoli
OK, it might look like Hollywood's idea of
an Indonesian restaurant with all those
Balinese handicrafts adorning the walls, but
this is the real thing, run by the progeny
of an Indonesian diplomat exiled when
President Sukarno was overthrown in 1967.
If you think you can handle it, order one of
four *rijstafels* (Dutch for 'rice table'), priced
from €20 to €45: they are feasts of between
seven and 10 courses that just won't stop
coming. Those with nut allergies beware:
peanuts seem to appear in one form or
another in most dishes.

LE TAMBOUR Map pp82–3   French, Bistro €€
☎ 01 42 33 06 90; 41 rue Montmartre, 2e; starters
€7-17, mains €13-20; ☺ lunch Tue-Sat, dinner to
1.30am Sun & Mon, to 3.30am Tue-Sat; Ⓜ Étienne
Marcel or Sentier
'The Drummer' is a Paris mecca for night
owls, with generously long hours and
friendly service. It attracts a mixed and
somewhat boisterous crowd. You'll enjoy
the recycled street furniture, straightforward
cuisine and the cocky staff. The café-bar is
open noon to 6am Tuesday to Saturday and
6pm to 6am Sunday and Monday.

BAAN BORAN Map pp82–3   Thai €€
☎ 01 40 15 90 45; www.baan-boran.com, in
French; 43 rue de Montpensier, 1er; starters €8-18,
mains €12-20; ☺ lunch Mon-Fri, dinner to 11pm
Mon-Sat; Ⓜ Palais Royal-Musée du Louvre or
Pyramides
The fare at this eatery, just opposite the
Théâtre du Palais Royal, is provincial Thai
and about as authentic as you'll find in this

top picks

PLACES FOR BRUNCH

- Joe Allen (p233)
- Scoop (right)
- Le Café qui Parle (p278)
- Le Chéri-Bibi (p278)
- Le Sporting (p267)
- Le Viaduc Café (p272)
- Alef-Bet (p249)
- Le Baba Bourgeois (p251)

part of Paris. It makes a convenient stop before or after touring the Louvre. There are several vegetarian dishes, priced between €8 and €10. If you just want something quick and on the trot, visit Baan Boran à Emporter (Map p86; ☎ 01 40 13 96 70; 103 rue St-Honoré, 1er; dishes €4-6.50, menu €8.90; 11am-8pm Mon-Sat; Châtelet or Pont Neuf), which has takeaway service and counter seating.

LE LOUP BLANC Map pp82–3 International €€€
☎ 01 40 13 08 35; www.loup-blanc.com; 42 rue Tiquetonne, 2e; veg dishes €12.50-14.50, mains €13.50-19.50; dinner to midnight Sun-Thu, to 12.30am Fri, to 1am Sat, brunch 11am-4.30pm Sun; Étienne Marcel
Some inventive and inexpensive dishes are on offer at 'The White Wolf': meat and fish marinated with herbs and spices (eg cardamom, star anise, marjoram) and then grilled. For accompaniments, you can choose from up to four vegetables and grains, according to your appetite and the season: red lentils, quinoa (a South American grain), creamed corn with peppers (a must) or carrots with cumin. We like the chicken with rosemary and savoury pork with tangerine and Macassar fillets of duck. It's a popular place for brunch on Sunday (€19.50)

WILLI'S WINE BAR Map pp82–3 French, Bistro €€€
☎ 01 42 61 05 09; www.williswinebar.com; 13 rue des Petits Champs, 1er; starters €9, mains €18, menus €19 & €25 (lunch only), €32 & €34; lunch & dinner to 11pm Mon-Sat; Bourse
This civilised and very convivial wine bar-cum-bistro was opened in 1980 by British expats who introduced the wine-bar concept to Paris. The food by chef François Yon is still excellent, the wines (especially Côtes

du Rhône) well chosen and Willi's legendary status lives on – and deservedly so.

CAFÉ DE L'ÉPOQUE Map p86 French, Café €€
☎ 01 42 33 40 70; 12 rue Croix des Petits Champs, 1er; starters €5.50-14, mains €15-18; lunch daily, dinner to midnight Mon-Sat; Louvre-Rivoli
A lovely old relic of the belle époque when the passages couverts were the places to shop, this café full of old mirrors, banquettes and a heated terrace is a popular location for period films. It can be entered from the covered passage itself or the terrace facing rue du Bouloi.

L'ARBRE À CANNELLE
Map pp82–3 French, Tearoom €€
☎ 01 45 08 55 87; 57 passage des Panoramas, 2e; dishes €7-17.80; 11.30am-6.30pm Mon-Sat; Grands Boulevards
The 'Cinnamon Tree' is a lovely tearoom with tartes salées (savoury pies; from €7), excellent salads (€7 to €9.80), great plats du jour (€12) and red-fruit crumble for dessert. The original 19th-century décor is worth a visit in itself; seating is on the ground and 1st floors.

SAVEURS VÉGÉT'HALLES
Map p86 Vegetarian €€
☎ 01 40 41 93 95; 41 rue des Bourdonnais, 1er; starters & salads €4.80-9.80, mains €11.20-17.20, menus €9.80 & 12.50 (lunch only), €15.30; lunch & dinner to 10.30pm Mon-Sat; Châtelet
Occupying the former premises of another vegetarian restaurant, La Victoire Suprême du Cœur (p245), this vegan eatery is egg-free and offers quite a few mock-meat dishes, such as poulet végétal aux champignons ('chicken' with mushrooms) and escalope de seitan (wheat gluten 'escalope'). No alcohol is served.

SCOOP Map p86 International €€
☎ 01 42 60 31 84; www.scoopcafe.com, in French; 154 rue St-Honoré, 1er; dishes €10.90-16.90; 11am-7pm; Louvre-Rivoli
This erstwhile American-style ice-cream parlour has been making quite a splash for its excellent wraps, burgers, tarts and soups and central, very fashionable location. The upstairs lounge is made for a tête-à-tête, and Sunday brunch (11.30am to 4pm) includes pancakes with maple syrup.

LE VÉRO DODAT Map p86 French €€
☎ 01 45 08 92 06; 1st fl, 19 Galerie Véro Dodat, 2 rue du Bouloi, 1er; mains €13.50, menu €16.50;

EATING LOUVRE & LES HALLES

lunch & dinner to 10.30pm Tue-Sat; M Louvre-Rivoli

This friendly little place in the heart of the Véro Dodat passage *couvert* has seating both downstairs and upstairs. At lunchtime it's especially popular with workers from the nearby Bourse de la Commerce, who come for the reasonably priced *plats du jour*.

KUNITORAYA Map pp82–3   Japanese €€

☎ 01 47 03 33 65; www.kunitoraya.com, in French; 39 rue Ste-Anne, 1er; dishes €8.50-15, menu €12.50 (lunch only); ⏰ 11.30am-10pm; M Pyramides
With seating on two floors, this simple and intimate place has a wide and excellent range of Japanese shop-made noodle dishes and set lunches and dinners. If headed here, aim to arrive before 1pm for lunch or before 8pm for dinner to beat the crowds.

HIGUMA Map p00   Japanese €€

☎ 01 58 62 49 22; 163 rue St-Honoré, 1er; mains €7-12.50, menus €10 & €11.50; ⏰ lunch & dinner to 11.30pm; M Palais Royal-Musée du Louvre
This authentic, no-nonsense Japanese noodle shop offers great value, particularly for its location opposite the Comédie Française. We love the *gyoza* (dumplings) and the fried noodles with pork and vegetables.

SELF-CATERING

Rue Montorgueil (p231), one of the busiest and best-stocked *rues commerçantes* (commercial streets, not unlike open-air markets) in Paris, is north of Les Halles.

There are several supermarkets around Forum des Halles. Other options are Franprix Les Halles branch (Map p86; 35 rue Berger, 1er; ⏰ 8.30am-9.50pm Mon-Sat; M Châtelet) and Franprix Châtelet branch (Map p86; 16 rue Bertin Poirée, 1er; ⏰ 8.30am-8pm Mon-Sat; M Châtelet).

MARAIS & BASTILLE

The Marais, filled with small restaurants of every imaginable type, is one of Paris' premier neighbourhoods for eating out. Make sure to book ahead at the weekend.

Towards République there's a decent selection of ethnic places. If you're after authentic Chinese food but can't be bothered going to the larger Chinatown in the 13e (see p274), check out the small noodle shops and restaurants along rue Au Maire, 3e (Map pp92–3). The kosher and kosher-style restaurants along rue des Rosiers (Map pp98–9), the so-called Pletzl area, serve specialities from North Africa, Central Europe and Israel. Be aware: many are closed on Friday evening, Saturday and Jewish holidays. Takeaway falafel and *shwarma* (kebabs) are available at several places along the street.

Bastille is another area chock-a-block with restaurants, some of which have added a star or two to their epaulets in recent years. Narrow rue de Lappe and rue de la Roquette (11e), just east of place de la Bastille, may not be as hip as they were a dozen years ago, but they remain popular streets for nightlife and attract a young, alternative crowd.

BEL CANTO Map pp98–9   French €€€

☎ 01 42 78 30 18; www.lebelcanto.com; 72 quai de l'Hôtel de Ville, 4e; menu €72; ⏰ dinner to midnight; M Hôtel de Ville or Pont Marie
If London, New York and even Budapest can have one – a restaurant where the waiters sing (arias) for their supper – why can't Paris have one too? So if you fancy Rossini with your roast, Verdi with your veg and Puccini with your pud, this place and its *dîners lyriques* is the place for you.

LE DÔME DU MARAIS Map pp98–9   French €€€

☎ 01 42 74 54 17; 53bis rue des Francs Bourgeois, 4e; starters €17-33, mains €25-35, 2-/3-course menus €19/25 (lunch only), dinner menu €36; ⏰ lunch & dinner to 11pm Tue-Sat; M Rambuteau
This place serves classic French dishes such as *joues de bœuf* (beef cheeks) as well as hare and lighter fare – often shellfish and fish. The location is sublime: a pre-Revolution building and former auction room with a glassed-in courtyard just down from the Archives Nationales. The octagonal-shaped dining room is a knockout.

LE VILLARET Map pp94–5   French €€€

☎ 01 43 57 89 76; 13 rue Ternaux, 11e; starters €8.50-20, mains €18-35, menu €23 & €28 (lunch only); ⏰ lunch Mon-Fri, dinner to 11.30pm Mon-Sat; M Parmentier
An excellent neighbourhood bistro serving very rich food, Le Villaret has diners coming from across Paris to sample the house specialities. The *velouté de cèpes à la mousse de foie gras* (cep mushroom soup with foie-gras mousse) and the *gigot d'agneau de Lozère rôti et son gratin de topinambours* (roast lamb with Jerusalem artichoke gratin) are all recommended, but only the

chef knows what will be available as he changes the menu daily. Tasting menus start at €50.

L'ÉCAILLER DU BISTROT

Map pp94–5   French, Seafood €€€

☎ 01 43 72 76 77; 22 rue Paul Bert, 11e; starters €10-22, mains €18-35, menu €16 (lunch only); ◷ lunch & dinner to 11.30pm Tue-Sat; Ⓜ Faidherbe Chaligny

Oyster lovers should make a beeline for 'The Bistro Shucker', a neighbourhood resto done up in nautical kitsch that serves up to a dozen varieties of fresh bivalves, freshly shucked and accompanied by a little lemon juice. Other delights are platters of seafood for between one and four people (€34 to €130), a half-dozen *oursins* (sea urchins; €14), minute-cooked tuna steak with sesame oil and the extravagant lobster *menu* (€45).

BOFINGER Map pp94–5   French, Brasserie €€€

☎ 01 42 72 87 82; www.bofingerparis.com; 5-7 rue de la Bastille, 4e; starters €8-18.50, mains €15.50-31.50, menus €24 (lunch only) & €31.50; ◷ lunch & dinner to 12.30am daily; Ⓜ Bastille

Founded in 1864, Bofinger is reputedly the oldest brasserie in Paris, though its polished Art Nouveau brass, glass and mirrors throughout suggest a redecoration a few decades later. As at most Parisian brasseries, specialities include Alsatian-inspired dishes such as *choucroute* (sauerkraut with assorted meats; €18 to €20), and seafood dishes (€24.50 to €49). There's a budget *menu* of €23.90 available after 11pm. Ask for a seat downstairs, under the *coupole* (stained-glass dome); it's the prettiest part of the restaurant. Just opposite is Le Petit Bofinger (☎ 01 42 72 05 23; 6 rue de la Bastille, 4e; starters €7.60-15.70, mains €15.30-26, menus with wine €20.50 & €29; ◷ lunch & dinner to 12.30am daily; Ⓜ Bastille), the brasserie's less brash (and cheaper) little sister.

LE DÔME BASTILLE

Map pp94–5   French, Seafood €€€

☎ 01 48 04 88 44; 2 rue de la Bastille, 4e; starters €9.50-15, mains €21-31; ◷ lunch & dinner to 11pm; Ⓜ Bastille

This lovely restaurant, little sister to the more established Dôme (p258) in Montparnasse and awash in pale yellows, specialises in superbly prepared fish and seafood dishes. The blackboard menu changes daily. Wines are a uniform (and affordable) €22.50 per bottle.

LE TEMPS AU TEMPS Map pp94–5   French €€€

☎ 01 43 79 63 40; 3 rue Paul Bert, 11e; menu €30; ◷ lunch & dinner to 10.30pm Tue-Sat; Ⓜ Faidherbe Chaligny

This tiny little place with about 10 tables has a very exciting three-course menu that changes daily; some of the dishes have been inspired by the *cuisine récréative* (entertaining cuisine) of the great Catalan chef Ferran Adria. Come here for lunch; you're much more likely to get a seat.

LE REPAIRE DE CARTOUCHE

Map pp94–5   French €€€

☎ 01 47 00 25 86; 8 blvd des Filles du Calvaire & 99 rue Amelot, 11e; starters €10-14, mains €18-30, menus €14 & €26 (lunch only); ◷ lunch & dinner to 11pm Tue-Sat; Ⓜ St-Sébastien Froissart

With entrances at both front and back, 'Cartouche's Den' – a reference to the 18th-century Parisian 'Robin Hood' Louis-Dominique Cartouche – looks to the past and the future. It's an old-fashioned place that takes a very modern, innovative approach to French food under the direction of Norman chef Rodolphe Paquin. As its name implies and the rifle on the wall underscores, it focuses on meat and game (poached?) though there are some excellent fish and shellfish dishes on the menu.

INAMORATI CAFFÈ Map pp92–3   Italian €€€

☎ 01 48 04 88 28; 57 rue Charlot, 3e; mains €16-30, menus €15 (lunch only), €25 & with wine €30; ◷ lunch & dinner to midnight daily; Ⓜ Temple or République

This long and narrow storefront space filled with tables covered in checked tablecloths attracts a loyal and local clientele who love the authentic (and ample) dishes, prepared by partners Salvatore and Rocco. The mammoth salads and risotto are excellent choices but we usually go for something in a *marmite* (cooking pot), be it homemade cheese-stuffed ravioli with meatballs or the fisherman's stew of shellfish.

LES GRANDES MARCHES

Map pp94–5   French, Brasserie €€€

☎ 01 43 43 90 32; 6 place de la Bastille, 12e; starters €8.50-13, mains €15-29; ◷ noon-midnight; Ⓜ Bastille

This futuristic modern brasserie next to the 'Great Steps' of the Opéra Bastille was designed by Elisabeth and Christian Portzamparc for the Flo group. The result has been disappointing – both in décor and food served – but it has a convenient (and much coveted) location. If you do find yourself here on Sunday, check out the jazz brunch (€24) from noon to 4pm. The bar stays open till 4am daily.

UNICO Map pp94–5 Argentian €€€

☎ 01 43 67 68 08; www.resto-unico.com, in French; 15 rue Paul Bert, 11e; starters €6.50-11, mains €20-26, menu €19 (lunch only); ☷ lunch & dinner to 11pm Tue-Sat; Ⓜ Faidherbe Chaligny
This very trendy, very orange Argentine *parillada* (steakhouse) has taken over an old butcher and put a modern (well, sort of 1970s, but it works) spin on it. This place is all about meat – especially the barbecued *entrecôte* (rib steak) with chunky *frites* (chips). Good wine selection.

MA BOURGOGNE
Map pp98–9 French, Bistro €€€

☎ 01 42 78 44 64; 19 place des Vosges, 4e; starters €8-20, mains €18-26, menu €32; ☷ noon-1am daily; Ⓜ St-Paul
With its terrace under the arcades of the place des Vosges looking onto what is arguably the most beautiful square in Paris, this is a wonderful place to have lunch or just a drink. The *plats du jour* are good value at €14 to €25 when you consider the location. Specialities include *andouillette* (sausage made of pork/veal tripe) and charcuterie from the Auvergne region.

CHEZ OMAR Map pp92–3 North African €€€

☎ 01 42 72 36 26; 47 rue de Bretagne, 3e; couscous & tajines €12-22, grills €12-26; ☷ lunch Mon-Sat, dinner to 11.30pm daily; Ⓜ Arts et Métiers
Once a favourite of celebrity types, Chez Omar doesn't seem to attract the very rich or particularly famous these days, but the quality of the couscous remains top-notch, judging from the crowds. Apart from the food and the serving staff, don't expect anything else to be North African at Chez Omar: it looks almost exactly like the corner street café it was a quarter of a century ago.

LES DOMAINES QUI MONTENT
Map pp94–5 French, Wine €€€

☎ 01 43 56 89 15; www.lesdomainesquimontent. com, in French; 136 blvd Voltaire, 11; menus €14.50 & €25.50; ☷ lunch Mon-Sat daily; Ⓜ Voltaire
What better way to enjoy wine with a meal than at a wine merchant's establishment

amid shelves and cartons of bottles? The optimistically named 'Estates on the Rise' serves a *table d'hôtes* – a set meal with little or no choice – at lunchtime of a cheese and charcuterie or a *plat du jour*. These can be paired expertly with any of the wine around you and expert advice is included in the price! There are several other Domaines qui Montent, including a Montmartre branch (Map p169; ☎ 01 42 64 18 91; 42 rue Véron, 18e; ☷ lunch Mon-Sat daily; Ⓜ Abbesses or Blanche).

MANSOURIA
Map pp94–5 North African, Moroccan €€€

☎ 01 43 71 00 16; 11 rue Faidherbe, 11e; starters €8-16, mains €17-25, menu €30, with wine €46; ☷ lunch Wed-Sat, dinner to 11pm Mon-Sat; Ⓜ Faidherbe Chaligny
This is an especially attractive Moroccan restaurant that serves excellent milk-fed steamed lamb, if not the best *kascsou* (couscous) and *touagin (tajine)* in town. Someone in your group should definitely order the *mourouzia*, lamb simmered in a complex combination of some 27 spices and served with a honey sauce.

LE PETIT MARCHÉ
Map pp92–3 French, Café €€€

☎ 01 42 72 06 67; 9 rue de Béarn, 3e; starters €8-11, mains €15-25, menu €14 (lunch only); ☷ lunch & dinner to midnight daily; Ⓜ Chemin Vert
This great little bistro just up from the place des Vosges fills up at lunch and then again in the evening with a mixed crowd who come to enjoy the hearty cooking and friendly service. The salad starters are popular, as are the *brochette d'agneau aux épices doux* (spicy lamb brochette). The open kitchen also offers a fair few vegetarian choices.

AUX VINS DES PYRÉNÉES
Map pp92–3 French €€€

☎ 01 42 72 64 94; 25 rue Beautreillis, 4e; starters €7.50-13, mains €14-25, menu €13.50 (lunch only); ☷ lunch Sun-Fri, dinner to 11.30pm; Ⓜ St-Paul or Bastille
Located in a former wine warehouse a couple of doors down from the house where rock singer Jim Morrison of the Doors died in 1971 (No 17–19), this is a good place to enjoy a unpretentious French meal with a lot of wine. The place has been able to retain its old-world charm and it's not surprising that a crowd of *bobo* ('bohemian

EATING MARAIS & BASTILLE

bourgeois') locals, a few *showbiz parisien* types among them, have set up headquarters here. The fish, meat and game dishes are all equally good, but worth a special mention is the foie gras and the top-notch *pavé de rumsteak* (thick rump steak). The wine list offers a wide choice of celebrated and little-known estate wines.

CHEZ JENNY Map pp92–3   French, Alsatian €€
☎ 01 44 54 39 00; www.chezjenny.com; 39 blvd du Temple, 3e; starters €5.90-17.50, mains €17.50-24.50, menus €19.50 & €23.50; ☷ noon-midnight Sun-Thu, to 1am Fri & Sat; Ⓜ République
This cavernous brasserie dating from 1932 serves a huge *choucroute garnie* and excellent *baeckeoffe* (€22.50), an Alsatian stew made of meat and several types of vegetables, but we suspect that most people visit to admire the stunning marquetry of Alsatian scenes by Charles Spindler on the 1st floor. A quick and tasty lunch at Chez Jenny is *flammekuche* (€14.50), an Alsatian-style tart made with cream, onion, bacon and cheese.

BISTROT DE L'OULETTE
Map pp94–5   French €€
☎ 01 42 71 43 33; www.l-oulette.com; 38 rue des Tournelles, 4e; starters €11-14, mains €19-24, 2-/3-course menus €12/17 (lunch only) & €26/34; ☷ lunch Mon-Fri, dinner to 11pm Mon-Thu, to midnight Fri & Sat; Ⓜ Bastille or Chemin Vert
A younger cousin of the chic L'Oulette (p271) in Bercy, this *bistrot* bustles by day and night with a mix of locals and tourists who are here for the capable southwestern provincial cooking. Duck features heavily – try the *foie gras de canard* (€17) or the *magret de canard* (fillet of duck breast; €19). Wines include almost a dozen from the southwest.

AU PETIT MONSIEUR
Map pp94–5   French, Bistro €€
☎ 01 43 55 54 04; 50 rue Amelot, 11e; starters €10-20, mains €18-24, menus €11-22 (lunch only) & €35; ☷ lunch Tue-Fri, dinner to 10.30pm Mon-Sat; Ⓜ St-Sébastien Froissart
We're still out to lunch, as it were, on this new avatar of the much missed C'Amelot, but 'At the Little Guy' looks like it might win some hearts with starters like *risotto aux deux artichaux, caviar de tomates confites* (risotto with two types of artichokes with glazed tomato) and mains like *mille-feuille de rouget et sa ratatouillle* (red mullet in flaky pastry with Mediterranean vegetable 'stew'). The atmosphere is less staid than C'Amelot was too.

PITCHI POÏ
Map pp98–9   Eastern European, Jewish €€
☎ 01 42 77 46 15; www.pitchipoi.com; 9 place du Marché Ste-Catherine & 7 rue Caron, 4e; dishes €16-24, menu €23; ☷ lunch & dinner to 11pm daily; Ⓜ St-Paul
This convivial Eastern-European Jewish restaurant on one of Paris' most picturesque squares serves traditional dishes such as *tchoulent* (cholent; slowly simmered meat with beans and vegetables) at lunch and dinner and lighter fare such as smoked salmon and chopped chicken liver at its Sunday buffet (€27; noon to 5pm).

À LA RENAISSANCE
Map pp94–5   French, Café €€€
☎ 01 43 79 83 09; 87 rue de la Roquette, 11e; starters €8.50-14.50, mains €16-24; ☷ lunch & dinner to 11.30pm daily; Ⓜ Voltaire
This large, café-like *bistro de quartier* has a huge bar (open 8am to 2am) with large plate-glass windows looking onto the street. Food is reliable if unadventurous – herring fillets on a bed of warm potatoes, mackerel *rillettes,* steak tartare and that all-time favourite, *œufs à la coq aux tartines* (soft-boiled eggs with toast). Sunday brunch is €25.

404 Map pp92–3   North African, Moroccan €€
☎ 01 42 74 57 81; 69 rue des Gravilliers, 3e; starters €7-9, couscous & tajines €14-24, menus €17 (lunch only) & €21 (brunch); ☷ lunch Mon-Fri, dinner to midnight daily, brunch 10am-4pm Sat & Sun; Ⓜ Arts et Métiers
As comfortable a Maghreb (North African) caravanserai as you'll find in Paris, the 404 not only has excellent couscous and *tajines* but superb grills (€12 to €22) and pigeon *pastillas*. The *brunch berbère* (Berber brunch) is available at the weekend. You'll just love the One Thousand and One Nights décor with real antiques and curios, but the tables are set too close to one another.

L'AUTOBUS IMPÉRIAL
Map p86   French €€
☎ 01 42 36 00 18; www.autobus-imperial.fr, in French; 14 rue Mondétour, 1er; mains €14-23.50; menus €16.50-23.50 (lunch only), €28-43; ☷ lunch & dinner to 2am Mon-Sat; Ⓜ Les Halles

This wonderful find just north of the unspeakable Forum des Halles shopping centre boasts a vintage Belle Époque dining room beneath a wonderful glass dome. It's elegant and the food traditional; try *salade de filets de caille braisés au vinaigre de truffle noire* (quail salad with black truffle vinegar) and the *Parmentier de jambon confit* (ham confit in mashed potatoes).

AU VIEUX CHÊNE Map pp94–5   French €€
☎ 01 43 71 67 69; 7 rue du Dahomey, 11e; starters €10-16, mains €18.50-23, menus €13 (lunch only) & €29; ☽ lunch & dinner to 10.30pm Mon-Sat; M Faidherbe Chaligny

Along a quiet side street in a neighbourhood full of traditional woodworking studios, 'At the Old Oak' bistro offers an excellent seasonal menu and some well-chosen wines. The surrounds are fabulous and very retro. Three of the cast-iron columns holding the place up are registered monuments.

CHEZ RAMULAUD Map pp94–5   French €€
☎ 01 43 72 23 29; 269 rue du Faubourg St-Antoine, 11e; starters €9-13, mains €18-23, menus €15-17 (lunch only) & €29; ☽ lunch Mon-Fri, dinner to 11pm Mon-Sat; M Faidherbe Chaligny

With its peaceful, retro atmosphere, this enormous establishment is reminiscent of established provincial restaurants. The blackboard offerings are not overly adventurous but they are comforting and substantial – daily soups, terrine, *œufs cocotte aux champignons de saison* (coddled eggs with seasonal mushrooms). For mains, the fish dishes are usually winners. The plat du jour is good value at €10.

L'ALIVI Map pp98–9   French, Corsican €€€
☎ 01 48 87 90 20; www.restaurant-alivi.com, in French; 27 rue du Roi de Sicile, 4e; starters €9-16, mains €15-23, menus €17 & €23 (lunch only), €25 & €29; ☽ lunch & dinner to 11.30pm daily; M St-Paul

The ingredients at this rather fashionable Corsican restaurant are always fresh and refined, with *brocciu* cheese, charcuterie and basil featuring strongly on the menu. Try *starzapreti* (*brocciu* and spinach quenelles) and the unrivalled *cabri braisé au rosmarin* (kid braised with rosemary) with a Leccia wine to fully experience the pleasures of what the French call *l'île de beauté* (the beautiful island).

top picks

FOOD STREETS

- Av de Choisy, av d'Ivry and rue Baudricourt (p274) have a plethora of Chinese and Southeast Asian eateries.
- Blvd de Belleville (p269) is the place for Middle Eastern and Pakistani food and kosher couscous.
- Passage Brady (p266), a covered arcade, is the place for Indian, Pakistani and Bangladeshi dishes.
- Rue Cadet, rue Richer and rue Geoffroy Marie (p264) all have restaurants serving Sephardic Jewish kosher food, including couscous.
- Rue Montorgueil (p231), a pedestrians-only market street, is one of the best places around for something quick to eat.
- Rue Mouffetard (p231) is not just a food market but an excellent street to find ethnic and French restaurants in the budget category.
- Rue Rosiers (p237) in the Marais is the best place to find Ashkenazic Jewish kosher food.

LE TRUMILOU Map pp98–9   French, Bistro €€
☎ 01 42 77 63 98; 84 quai de l'Hôtel de Ville, 4e; starters €4.50-13, mains €15-22, menu €16.50 & €19.50; ☽ lunch & dinner to 11pm daily; M Hôtel de Ville

This no-frills bistro just round the corner from the Hôtel de Ville and facing the posh Île de St-Louis square is a Parisian institution *in situ* for over a century. If you're looking for an authentic menu from the early 20th century and prices (well, almost) to match, you won't do better than this. The *confit aux pruneaux* (duck with prunes) and the *ris de veau grand-mère* (veal sweetbreads in mushroom cream sauce) are particularly good.

CHEZ PAUL Map pp94–5   French, Bistro €€
☎ 01 47 00 34 57; 13 rue de Charonne, 11e; starters €4.80-17.50, mains €14.50-22; ☽ lunch & dinner to 12.30am daily; M Ledru Rollin

When they put up a 'French restaurant' film set in Hollywood, this ever-expanding bistro is what it must look like. An extremely popular bistro, it has traditional French main courses handwritten on a yellowing menu and brusque service – Paris in true form! Stick with the simplest of dishes – the steak or foie gras with lentils – and make sure you've booked ahead.

L'AMBASSADE D'AUVERGNE

Map pp92–3   French, Auvergne €€

☎ 01 42 72 31 22; www.ambassade-auvergne
.com; 22 rue du Grenier St-Lazare, 3e; starters
€8-16, mains €14-22, menu €20 (lunch only) & €28;
🕐 lunch & dinner to 10pm daily; Ⓜ Rambuteau
The 'Auvergne Embassy' is the place to
head if you are a truly hungry carnivore.
This century-old restaurant offers traditional dishes from the Auvergne such as
salade tiède de lentilles vertes du Puy (warm
salad of green Puy lentils; €9), a great
lead-up to the house speciality: *saucisse
de Parlan à l'aligot* (Auvergne-style pork
sausage served with a potato and cheese
purée; €14).

LE RÉCONFORT

Map pp98–9   French €€

☎ 01 49 96 09 60; 37 rue de Poitou, 3e; starters
€7-10, mains €17-21, menus €17 & €22 (lunch only);
🕐 lunch Mon-Fri, dinner to 11pm daily; Ⓜ St-
Sébastien Froissart
Unusual for a restaurant in the Marais, 'The
Comfort' has generous space between
tables and is quiet enough to chat without
yelling. The kitchen produces very tasty
and inventive dishes, including homemade
foie gras. For mains, consider king prawns
in an aromatic citrus and coconut sauce or
souris d'agneau rotie (roast lamb shank). The
plat du jour at lunch is €12.

LE SOUK

Map pp94–5   North African €€

☎ 01 49 29 05 08; www.lesoukfr.com, in French;
1 rue Keller, 11e; starters €7.50-13, mains €16-21;
menus €20 & €27; 🕐 lunch & dinner to 11.30pm
Tue-Sat; Ⓜ Ledru Rollin
We like coming here almost as much for
the décor as the food – from the clay pots
overflowing with spices on the outside to
the exuberant (but never kitsch) Moroccan
interior. And the food? As authentic as the
decoration, notably the duck *tajine* and
vegetarian couscous. Be warned: mains
are enormous, so this might have to be a
one-dish meal.

LE TROISIÈME BUREAU

Map pp94–5   French, Bistro €€

☎ 01 43 55 87 65; 74 rue de la Folie Méricourt,
11e; starters €7.50-11.50, mains €15.50-21, menus
€11.50 & €13.50 (lunch only); 🕐 lunch & dinner to
midnight daily; Ⓜ Oberkampf
An interesting clientele frequents this pub-
cum-bistro, where you can read, listen to
music, do a little work on the laptop, tickle

the ivories on the funky old piano and
enjoy Sunday brunch (€15.50) from noon
to 4pm. There are one-plate specials for
between €9.80 and €13.50.

BLUE ELEPHANT Map pp94–5   Thai €€

☎ 01 47 00 42 00; www.blueelephant.com/paris;
43-45 rue de la Roquette, 11e; starters €13.50-18,
mains €14.80-21, menus €42 & €52; 🕐 lunch Sun-
Fri, dinner to midnight daily; Ⓜ Bastille
This is Paris' most famous upmarket Thai
restaurant and part of an international
chain, with a dozen branches in cities
round the world from Brussels to Beirut.
Although it has become a little too successful for its own good (it also sells its own
branded knick-knacks and gift items), the
indoor tropical rainforest and well-prepared
spicy dishes (look for the one, two or three
elephant symbols on the menu) are still
worth the inflated prices. Sunday buffet
(noon to 3pm) is good value at €39.

L'ENOTECA Map pp92–3   Italian €€

☎ 01 42 78 91 44; 25 rue Charles V, 4e; starters
€10-14, mains €18-20, menu €14 (lunch only)
& €30-43; 🕐 lunch & dinner to 11.30pm daily;
Ⓜ Sully Morland or Pont Marie
'The Vinotheque', a *trattoria* in the historic Village St-Paul quarter of the Marais,
serves *haute cuisine à l'italienne,* and
there's an excellent list of Italian wines
by the glass (€3.50 to €12). It's no secret
that this is one of the few Italian wine
bars in Paris to take its vino seriously, so
book ahead. Pasta dishes (€13 to €23) are
good, as is the generous *tavola antipasti*
(antipasto buffet table). The *cocotte du jour*
(casserole of the day; €13) is served with a
glass of wine.

LES SANS CULOTTES

Map pp94–5   French, Bistro €€

☎ 01 48 05 42 92; www.lessansculottesfr.com, in
French; 27 rue de Lappe, 11e; starters €9-15, mains
€14-20, menus €18 & €23; 🕐 lunch & dinner to
11pm Tue-Sun; Ⓜ Bastille
You wouldn't cross Paris to eat at Sans Culottes – the place takes its name from the
working-class 'men without breeches' who
fought in the French Revolution – but in
a neighbourhood that has become somewhat trendy in recent years it's a comforting reminder of the past. The interior, with
frosted glass, huge zinc bar, ornate ceilings and wooden floors, positively glows

in the evening. The range of food is un-
even, though relatively low-priced; service
is friendly and attentive. The set *menus*
include wine.

LES GALOPINS Map pp94–5   French, Bistro €€
☎ 01 47 00 45 35; www.lesgalopins.com; 24 rue
des Taillandiers, 11e; starters €6.50-10.50, mains
€13.50-20, menus €14.50 & €17.50 (lunch only);
☽ lunch Mon-Fri, dinner to 11pm Mon-Thu, to
11.30pm Fri & Sat; Ⓜ Bastille or Voltaire
The décor of this cute neighbourhood
bistro is simple, the meals are straightforward and in the best tradition of French
cuisine, with offerings such as *raviolis de
pétoncles* (queen scallops ravioli), *confit de
canard laqué au sirop d'érable* (duck confit
cooked with maple syrup) and *compotée
d'agneau aux aubergines* (lamb and aubergine ragout). It's not a secret find, so it can
feel like a bit of a factory at lunch or on a
weekend night.

CHEZ MARIANNE
Map pp98–9   Jewish, Kosher €€
☎ 01 42 72 18 86; 2 rue des Hospitalières
St-Gervais, 4e; dishes €3-20; ☽ noon-midnight
daily; Ⓜ St-Paul
This is a Sephardic kosher alternative to the
Ashkenazi fare usually available at Pletzl eateries. Platters containing four to 10 different meze (such as falafel, hummus, purées
of aubergine and chickpeas) cost from €12
to €26. The takeaway window sells falafel
in pita for €4.50 and there's also an excellent bakery attached. Chez Marianne's set
menus include a number of vegetarian
options.

PARIS MAIN D'OR
Map pp94–5   French, Corsican €€
☎ 01 44 68 04 68; 133 rue du Faubourg St-Antoine,
11e; starters €6.50-16.10, mains €13-19.50, menu
€12; ☽ lunch & dinner to 11pm Mon-Sat; Ⓜ Ledru
Rollin
The unprepossessing, cafélike 'Paris Golden
Hand' serves authentic Corsican dishes – a
surprisingly elusive cuisine in Paris. *Sturza
preti* (spinach and fine *brocciu* cheese; €8)
and traditional omelette with *brocciu* and
jambon sec (dried ham, matured for two
years) are some of the appetisers on the
menu. For mains, favourites include the
tian de veau aux olives (veal ragout) and the
caprettu arrustini (roast kid). Pasta dishes
come in at about €10.50.

LE GRAND MÉRICOURT
Map pp94–5   French €€
☎ 01 43 38 94 04; 22 rue de la Folie Méricourt,
11e; starters €12, mains €19, menus €14 (lunch
only), €17 & €35; ☽ lunch Tue-Fri, dinner to
10.30pm Mon-Sat; Ⓜ St-Ambroise
Young chef Gregory Merten Antonelli offers
his version of *'la cuisine créative'* (basically
traditional French that is light on oils and
fat and heavy on seasonal produce) in a
very English, almost fussy (floral wallpaper,
wooden floors, starched tablecloths and napkins) place just a stone's throw from trendy
rue Oberkampf. Try the *sanglier en pâté à la
liqueur d'orange* (boar pâté flavoured with orange liqueur) and the *joue de bœuf fondante
au muscat* (beef cheek with sweet wine).

LES CAVES ST-GILLES Map pp92–3   Spanish €€
☎ 01 48 87 22 62; 4 rue St-Gilles, 3e; tapas €5.30-
22, mains €15.50-19; ☽ lunch & dinner to 11.30pm
daily; Ⓜ Chemin Vert
This Spanish wine bar a short distance
northeast of place des Vosges is the most
authentic place on the Right Bank for tapas,
paella (at the weekend only; €19), *zarzuela*
(Spanish bouillabaisse; €16.50) and sangria
(€28 for 1.4cL). If you don't believe us, just
ask the Spanish expats who arrive here in
droves. We like the bowls of complimentary
olives provided on tables and at the bar.

GUILLAUME Map pp92–3   Modern French €€
☎ 01 44 54 20 60; 32 rue de Picardie, 3e; starters
€8-14.50, mains €15-19; ☽ lunch Mon-Fri, dinner
to 11pm Mon-Sat daily; Ⓜ Temple or République
Some of the starters at this sophisticated
venue near place de la République make
an ideal light lunch – try the tomato Tatin
and the *samoussa d'escargots* (samosa with
snails) – and there's a two-course *formule* (set
menu) for €15.50. You can eat either in the
front bar or in the spacious dinning room
behind. There's a lovely art gallery on the
1st floor and, if you're a group (something
unusual in Paris), there's a huge round table
available for seating at least a dozen people.

CAFÉ DE L'INDUSTRIE
Map pp94–5   French, Café €€
☎ 01 47 00 13 53; 16 & 17 rue St-Sabin, 11e; starters €5.10-6.90, mains €8.90-19; ☽ 9.30am-2am
daily; Ⓜ Bastille
This popular café-restaurant with neocolo-
nial décor has two locations directly opposite one another. It's a pleasant space and

the perfect spot to meet a friend instead of at one of the crowded cafés or bars in Bastille. Food is competitively priced but not always up to scratch; to avoid disappointment stick with the simple entrées or just graze off the fabulous dessert table (€4 to €5.90).

CAFFÉ BOBOLI Map p98-9 Italian €€
☎ 01 42 77 89 27; www.caffeboboli.com; 13 rue du Roi de Sicile, 4e; starters €10-13, mains €14-18.50; ☺ lunch Tue-Sun, dinner to 11pm Mon-Sat; Ⓜ St-Paul
Affordable Italian fare in the heart of the Marais? Not as preposterous a notion as you might think with the advent of this small restaurant run by two young Florentines. The food is very wholesome and based on vegetables, cheese and charcuterie like Parma ham and beef carpaccio. On the walls are original paintings and photographs that are changed every three months.

LE PETIT PICARD Map pp98-9 French €€
☎ 01 42 78 54 03; 42 rue Ste-Croix de la Bretonnerie, 4e; starters €7-16, mains €12.50-18.50, menus €15 (lunch only), €18 & €29; ☺ lunch Tue-Fri, dinner to 11.30pm Tue-Sun; Ⓜ Hôtel de Ville
This popular little restaurant in the centre of the Marais serves traditional French cuisine (try the generous menu traditionel at €29). Despite its name, the only dish from Picardy (unless you count salade picarde) that we could spot on the menu was flamiche aux poireaux, a Flemish-style leek pie. The place is always packed, so book well in advance.

LA MUSE VIN Map pp94-5 French, Wine €€
☎ 01 40 09 93 05; 101 rue de Charonne; starters €8, mains €18, menus €9.50 & with wine €15.50 (lunch only), €25 & €30; ☺ lunch Mon-Fri, dinner to 11pm Mon-Sat; Ⓜ Charonne
Primarily a wine bar and bottle shop, the very pink (or is that rosé?) 'Wine Muse' also does food both day (plat du jour €11) and night and its offerings go well beyond plates of cold meats and cheese. In fact, the evening menu changes every three weeks. It takes its wines very seriously, though, so keep that foremost in your mind.

OSSEK GARDEN Map pp94-5 Korean €€
☎ 01 48 07 16 35; 14 rue Rampon, 11e; starters €5-14, barbecue €16-18, menus €9.50 & €12.50 (lunch only), €16.50-30; ☺ lunch & dinner to 11pm daily; Ⓜ Oberkampf
Things Korean – especially films – seem to be taking the world by storm these days and Paris is no exception. This place not far from place de la République has excellent barbecues on offer, but we particularly like the bibimbab (€12 to €18), rice served in a sizzling pot topped with thinly sliced beef (or other meat) and cooked with preserved vegetables, then bound by a raw egg and flavoured with chilli-laced soy paste. Staff, in traditional Korean dress, are welcoming.

LE CLOWN BAR Map pp94-5 French, Bistro €€
☎ 01 43 55 87 35; 114 rue Amelot, 11e; starters €7.50-10.50, mains €15-18, menu €15/18 (weekday/weekend lunch only) & €25; ☺ lunch & dinner to 1am Mon-Sat; Ⓜ Filles du Calvaire
A wonderful wine-bar-cum-bistro next to the Cirque d'Hiver (Map pp94-5), the Clown Bar is like a museum with its painted ceilings, mosaics on the wall, lovely zinc bar and circus memorabilia that touches on one of our favourite themes of all time: the evil clown. The food is simple and unpretentious traditional French; the charcuterie platter (€10.50) is substantial and goes well with a half-bottle of Brouilly, while the Parmentier de boudin à la normande (black pudding Parmentier with apple) is deservedly one of the restaurant's most popular dishes.

LE TIRE BOUCHON Map pp94-5 French €€
☎ 01 47 00 43 50; 5 rue Guillaume Bertrand, 11e; starters €7-19, mains €15-18, menus €12 (lunch only), €17 & €25; ☺ lunch Mon-Fri, dinner to 11pm Mon-Sat; Ⓜ St-Maur
This mock old-style bistro close to the flashy rue Oberkampf has a dozen tables with gingham tablecloths arranged around a polished wooden bar. Add a few old photographs of the quartier, a touch of greenery and some decent bottles of wine and voilà: 'The Corkscrew'. The cassoulet confit (casserole or stew with beans and meat) and millefeuille de dorade (sea bream in flaky pastry) will tickle your taste buds. Expect friendly, attentive service but book well in advance.

ROBERT ET LOUISE Map pp98-9 French €€
☎ 01 42 78 55 89; 64 rue Vieille du Temple, 3e; starters €6-13, mains €12-18, menu €12 (lunch only); ☺ lunch & dinner to 10.30pm Tue-Sun; Ⓜ St-Sébastien Froissart

EATING MARAIS & BASTILLE

This 'country inn', complete with its red gingham curtains, offers delightful, simple and inexpensive French food, including *côte de bœuf* (side of beef; €40), which is cooked on an open fire and prepared by the original owners' daughter and her husband. If you arrive early, choose to sit at the farmhouse table, right next to the fireplace. It's a jolly, truly Rabelaisian evening. The *plat du jour* is a snip at €12.50

CHEZ NÉNESSE Map pp98–9   French, Bistro €€
☎ 01 42 78 46 49; 17 rue de Saintonge, 3e; starters €4-16, mains €10-18; ☯ lunch & dinner to 10.30pm Mon-Fri; Ⓜ Filles du Calvaire
The atmosphere at this bistro is very 'old Parisian café' and unpretentious, the dishes made with fresh, high-quality ingredients such as *salade de canard au vinaigre d'hydromel* (duck salad with honey vinegar) and *fricassée de volaille aux morilles* (poultry fricassee with morel mushrooms). The lunchtime starters are €4 and *plats du jour* are €10 to €12.

CHEZ HEANG Map pp94–5   Korean €€
☎ 01 48 07 80 98; 5 rue de la Roquette, 11e; barbecue €8.50-17.50, menus €9 (lunch only) & €11-23; ☯ lunch & dinner to midnight daily; Ⓜ Bastille
Also known as 'Barbecue de Seoul', this tiny place is where you cook your food on a grill in the middle of your table. The *fondue maison*, a kind of spicy hotpot in which you dip and cook your food, costs €25 per person (minimum two).

AU BASCOU Map pp92–3   French, Basque €€
☎ 01 42 72 69 25; 38 rue Réaumur, 3e; starters €9, mains €17, menu €19 (lunch only); ☯ lunch & dinner to 10.30pm Mon-Fri; Ⓜ Arts et Métiers
This is a popular eatery serving such classic Basque dishes as *pipérade* (peppers, onions, tomatoes and ham cooked with scrambled eggs), *axoa* (ragout of ground veal with a sauce of pimento and peppers) and Bayonne ham in all its guises. Round off the meal with a piece of Ardi Gasna *brebis,* (a ewe's milk cheese), or a slice of *gâteau basque,* a relatively simple layer cake filled with cream and cherry jam.

LA VICTOIRE SUPRÊME DU CŒUR
Map pp98–9   Vegetarian €€
☎ 01 40 41 95 03; www.vscoeur.com; 27-31 rue du Bourg Tibourg, 4e; starters & salads €4-10,

mains €14-17, menus €10.50-13.50; ☯ lunch & dinner to 10.30pm Mon-Sat, brunch 11am-5pm Sun; Ⓜ Châtelet
This Indian-inspired vegan restaurant is a welcome addition to the hubbub of the Marais. Food is actually quite good; avoid the mock-meat dishes like the devilish-sounding *seitan* (wheat gluten) 'steak' and go for a *thalli*, a sampling tray of Indian goodies for €15. For drinks try the mango lassi or spiced tea. Weekend brunch is €21. No meat, no alcohol, no guilt.

AUBERGE NICOLAS FLAMEL
Map pp92–3   French €€
☎ 01 42 71 77 78; www.auberge-nicolas-flamel .fr, in French; 51 rue de Montmorency, 3e; starters €9.50, mains €16.50; menus €18.50 (lunch only), €31 & €45 ☯ lunch & dinner to 11pm Mon-Sat; Ⓜ Rambuteau or Arts et Métiers
A visit to this charming restaurant, with its higgledy-piggledy rooms on two floors, is not so much about the food but the location: this was once the residence of celebrated alchemist and writer Flamel (1330–1417) and is the oldest building extant in Paris. Expect dishes that are correct but not earth-moving – duck foie gras, lamb cooked in a *tajine* and so on. There are wine tastings (€12) in the atmospheric (read: spooky) cellar.

À LA BANANE IVOIRIENNE
Map pp94–5   African, Côte d'Ivoire €€
☎ 01 43 70 49 90; http://alabanane.ivoirienne .club.fr; 10 rue de la Forge Royale, 11e; starters €5-7.50, mains €10-16.50, menu with wine €28; ☯ dinner to midnight Tue-Sat; Ⓜ Ledru Rollin
West African specialities (including a generous vegetarian platter; €12) are served in a relaxed and friendly setting, with lots of West African gewgaws on display. There's live African music in the cellar restaurant starting at 10pm on Fridays.

AU VILLAGE Map pp94–5   African, Senegalese €€
☎ 01 43 57 18 95; 86 av Parmentier, 11e; starters €5.50-8, mains €11-16; ☯ dinner to midnight Sun-Thu, to 1am Fri & Sat; Ⓜ Parmentier
Newcomers to African cuisine can choose from a range of classic Senegalese dishes such as *aloko* (fried plantain bananas with red sauce; €5.50), followed by the delicious, lightly spiced fish or chicken *yassa* (€12) or the hearty beef *mafé* (€11). For dessert, check out the amazing *thiakry* (semolina

and cream cheese salad; €5.50). The *plat du jour* is usually €13. The atmosphere is warm, friendly and a bit hip and the décor is delightful. You'll think you're in a Senegalese village, especially when the *kora* music starts.

MAI THAI Map pp92–3 Thai €€
☎ 01 42 72 18 77; www.maithai.fr, in French; 24bis rue St-Gilles, 3e; starters €8-11, mains €13-15, menus €13.50 (lunch only); ☺ lunch & dinner to 11pm daily; Ⓜ Chemin Vert
This rather stylish place, done up in warm tones of orange, red and yellow with Buddha figures, the *sine qua non* of Thai restaurants, throughout, has gained a loyal following in recent years and you should book in advance for dinner. Among *les classiques de la cuisine du Siam* (classics of the cuisine of Siam) on offer is chicken cooked with sacred basil and the usual spicy Thai sausages.

LE PETIT DAKAR
Map pp98–9 African, Senegalese €€
☎ 01 44 59 34 74; 6 rue Elzévir, 3e; starters €7, mains €13-15, menu €15 (lunch only); ☺ lunch Tue-Sat, dinner to 11pm Tue-Sun; Ⓜ St-Paul
Some people think this is the most authentic Senegalese restaurant in Paris, and with the CSAO Boutique & Gallery (p206) up the road, it does feel like a little bit of Africa has fallen onto a quiet Marais street.

WALY FAY Map pp94–5 African, Creole €€
☎ 01 40 24 17 79; 6 rue Godefroy Cavaignac, 11e; starters €6-8, mains €10-15; ☺ dinner to midnight Mon-Sat, brunch noon-5pm Sun; Ⓜ Charonne
This easygoing 'loungin' restaurant' attracts a rather hip crowd for the African food with a West Indian twist served to the sounds of soul and jazz. For starters, the *pepe* (fish soup) is deliciously smooth and highly spiced. For mains, the *tiéboudienne* (rice, fish and vegetables) and fish *n'dole* are recommended by the staff, but try instead the copious *mafé* (beef simmered in peanut sauce) served with rice and *aloko* (fried plantain bananas). The distressed walls and low lighting add warmth to the surrounds.

AU TROU NORMAND Map pp94–5 French €€
☎ 01 48 05 80 23; 9 rue Jean-Pierre Timbaud, 11e; starters €6-9.50, mains €8.50-14.50. menus €12.50

& €15 (lunch only); ☺ lunch & dinner to 11.30pm Sun-Thu, to midnight Fri & Sat; Ⓜ Oberkampf
Even under a younger and more dynamic team, 'The Norman Hole' remains the bargain-basement *cafétéria* of the 11e arrondissement. In keeping with the surrounds, the dishes served are simple and portions fairly generous. There are dozens of starters to choose from; main courses include *confit de canard* (duck confit) *brandade de morue* (cod puréed with potatoes) and various cuts of beef (tournedos, steak tartare etc) served with chips made on the premises.

TAEKO Map pp92–3 Japanese €€
☎ 01 48 04 34 59; 39 rue de Bretagne, 3e; menus €8.90-12.50; ☺ 9am-8pm Tue-Sat, to 2pm Sun; Ⓜ Marais
Just about the last thing you would expect to find in the Marché des Enfants Rouges (p231), one of the oldest markets in Paris, is this mom-and-pop Japanese eatery. There's sushi and sashimi and salmon tartar to start and delightful warm dishes like codfish balls and chicken cooked with soy sauce. Sit at the communal table near the entrance – if there's room!

BREAKFAST IN AMERICA
Map pp98–9 American, Deli €€
☎ 01 42 72 40 21; www. breakfast-in-america .com; 4 rue Malher, 4e; meals €6.50-12; ☺ 8.30am-11.30pm daily; Ⓜ St-Paul
This American-style diner, complete with red banquettes and Formica surfaces, is as authentic as you'll find outside the US of A. Breakfast, served all day and with free coffee refills, starts at €6.50, and there are generous burgers, chicken wings and fish and chips (€7.95 to €11.50). There's also a Latin Quarter branch (Map pp110–11; ☎ 01 43 54 50 28; 17 rue des Écoles, 5e; Ⓜ Cardinal Lemoine) open the same hours.

BAGEL STORE Map pp98–9 American, Kosher €€
☎ 01 44 78 06 05; 31 rue de Turenne, 3e; dishes €3.60-11.50; ☺ 9am-7pm Sun-Thu, 9am-3, to 7pm Fri (depending on season); Ⓜ Chemin Vert
This small place just up from the Marais is a great spot if you want something *sur le pouce* (literally 'on the thumb', meaning on the run). There are soups, salads, plates of *charcuterie* and, of course, its signature bagels with a more than a dozen different fillings.

GRAND APPÉTIT Map pp92–3 Vegetarian €€

☎ 01 40 27 04 95; 9 rue de la Cerisaie, 4e; soups €3-4, dishes €5-11; ⏰ lunch Mon-Fri, dinner to 9pm Mon-Wed; Ⓜ Bastille or Sully Morland

Set back from Bastille in a small, quiet street, this place offers light fare such as miso soup and cereals plus strength-building *bols garnis* (bowls of rice and mixed vegetables) and *assiettes* (platters) for those with a *grand appétit* (big appetite). The menu features delicious, filling dishes served with 100% organic cereals, raw and cooked vegetables and seaweed. Next door there's an excellent organic and macrobiotic grocery store (⏰ 9.30am-7.30pm Mon-Thu, to 4pm Fri).

LA PERLA Map pp98–9 Mexican €€

☎ 01 42 77 59 40; 26 rue François Miron, 4e; starters €6.10-9.10, mains €8.50-10.70, menu €9.90 (lunch only); ⏰ lunch & dinner to midnight daily; Ⓜ St-Paul or Hôtel de Ville

A Californian-style Mexican bar and restaurant with excellent guacamole (€7), nachos (from €6.10) and quesadillas (€6.10 to €7.50), 'The Pearl' is best known as the 'kingdom of tequila', with some 60 varieties on the shelf. Knock it back neat with salt and lemon or disguised in a margarita (€8.80 to €12). The bar is open from noon to 2am daily.

PARIS HANOI Map pp94–5 Vietnamese €

☎ 01 47 00 47 59; 74 rue de Charonne, 11e; starters €3.50-8, mains €8.50-10.50; ⏰ lunch & dinner to 10.30pm daily; Ⓜ Charonne

This upbeat, very yellow restaurant is an excellent place to come for *pho* (soup noodles, usually with beef) and shrimp noodles. Judging from the clientele, the local Vietnamese community thinks so, too.

CRÊPES SHOW Map pp94–5 French, Breton €

☎ 01 47 00 36 46; 51 rue de Lappe, 11e; crepes & galettes €3-9.80, menu €8.90 (lunch only); ⏰ lunch Mon-Fri, dinner to 1am Sun-Thu, to 2am Fri & Sat; Ⓜ Ledru Rollin

This unpretentious little restaurant specialises in sweet crepes (€3 to €7.60) and savoury buckwheat *galettes* (pancakes; €3.10 to €9.20). OK, they may not be the most authentic in town, but the location is convenient and the welcome, warm. There are lots of vegetarian choices, including great salads from around €5.

CHEZ SÉBASTIEN Map pp92–3 Turkish €

☎ 01 42 78 58 62; 22 passage Vendôme, 3e; dishes €4.80-8.90; ⏰ 11.30am-8pm Mon-Sat; Ⓜ République

This simple little Turkish café on two levels in a scruffy *passage* south of place de la République is just the ticket if you're looking for something cheap, filling and tasty to eat 'on the thumb' as the French say. Try any of the meze or the kebabs, especially the Iskender kebab, lamb slices served with *pide* bread and yogurt.

CRÊPERIE BRETONNE

Map pp94–5 French, Breton €

☎ 01 43 55 62 29; 67 rue de Charonne, 12e; starters €3.70-7.60, crepes & galettes €2.40-8.50; ⏰ lunch Mon-Fri, dinner to 11.30pm Mon-Sat; Ⓜ Charonne

Head here if you fancy savoury buckwheat *galettes* – try the ham, cheese and egg *complète* – or a sweet crepe and wash it down with dry *cidre de Rance* (Rance cider; €6.20 for 50cL) served in a teacup (as is traditional). The Breton paraphernalia and B&W photos will keep you occupied if there's a lull in the chatter.

L'AS DE FELAFEL Map pp98–9 Jewish, Kosher €

☎ 01 48 87 63 60; 34 rue des Rosiers, 4e; dishes €5-7; ⏰ noon-midnight Sun-Thu, to 5pm Fri; Ⓜ St-Paul

This has always been our favourite place for those deep-fried balls of chickpeas and herbs (€5 takeaway, €6.50 sit down). It's always packed, particularly at weekday lunch, so avoid that time if possible.

PATATI PATATA Map pp94–5 International, Café €

☎ 01 48 05 94 90; 51 rue de Lappe, 11e; dishes €4.90-6.80, menu €7.50; ⏰ 11.30am-3am Mon-Sat; Ⓜ Bastille or Ledru Rollin

If you're looking for something cheap and filling at almost any time of the day, visit this simple little caff with Formica tables that dispenses *pommes de terre au four* (baked or jacket potatoes) with toppings to the appreciative masses of Bastille.

ALSO RECOMMENDED

Bagel's Club (Map pp92–3; ☎ 01 40 29 00 91; 24 rue Réaumur, 3e; bagels & sandwiches €5-7.50, salads €7-10; ⏰ 8.30am-6pm Mon-Fri; Ⓜ Arts et Métiers). This place in the northern Marais serves *glatt kosher* sandwiches, bagels and snacks under the supervision of the Paris Beth Din.

Da Jia Le (Map pp92–3; ☎ 01 48 87 02 46; 37 rue au Maire, 3e; dishes €3-16, menu €7.50; ☺ lunch & dinner to 10.30am; Ⓜ Arts et Métiers). Don't cross town to eat noodles or dumplings here but if you're in the neighbourhood of Paris' original Chinatown and need an Asian fix, the 'Big Happy House' will oblige nicely and put a smile on your face.

La Plancha (Map pp94–5; ☎ 01 48 05 20 30; 34 rue Keller, 11e; tapas €8, mains €9-16; ☺ dinner to 1.30am Tue-Sat; Ⓜ Bastille) This tiny Spanish-Basque bodega (note the pelota baskets and bullfighting photos) serves up the best tapas in the neighbourhood till the wee hours.

Le Coude Fou (Map pp98–9; ☎ 01 42 77 15 16; www .lecoudefou.com, in French; 12 rue du Bourg Tibourg, 4e; starters €8-12, mains €16.50-18.50, menus €16.50 & €19.50; ☺ lunch Mon-Sat, dinner to midnight daily; Ⓜ Hôtel de Ville) Long-term fixture in the heart of the Marais serves cuisine traditionelle in a convivial bistro decorated with murals celebrating wine and the good life.

SELF-CATERING

Markets in the Marais and Bastille area include the incomparable (and open-air) Marché Bastille (p231).

There are a number of food shops and Asian delicatessens on the odd-numbered side of rue St-Antoine, 4e (Map pp98–9; Ⓜ St-Paul), as well as several supermarkets. Closer to Bastille there are lots of food shops along rue de la Roquette (Map pp94–5; Ⓜ Voltaire or Bastille) towards place Léon Blum.

Supermarkets include: Ed l'Épicier (Map pp92–3; 80 rue de Rivoli, 4e; 9am-8pm Mon-Sat; Ⓜ Hôtel de Ville), Franprix Marais (Map pp98–9; 135 rue St-Antoine, 4e; ☺ 9am-9pm Mon-Sat; Ⓜ St-Paul), Franprix Bretagne branch (Map pp92–3; 49 rue de Bretagne, 3e; ☺ 8.30am-9pm Tue-Sat, 9am-2pm Sun; Ⓜ Arts et Métiers), Franprix (Map pp98–9; 87 rue de la Verrerie, 4e; ☺ 9.30am-9pm Mon-Sat; Ⓜ Hôtel de Ville), Monoprix (Map pp98–9; basement, 71 rue St-Antoine, 4e; ☺ 9am-9pm Mon-Sat, to 8pm Sun; Ⓜ St-Paul), Monoprix Bastille branch (Map pp94–5; 97 rue du Faubourg St-Antoine, 11e; ☺ 9am-9.45pm Mon-Sat; Ⓜ Ledru Rollin), Supermarché G20 (Map pp98–9; 81-83 rue de la Verrerie, 4e; ☺ 8.30am-8.30pm; Ⓜ Hôtel de Ville), Supermarché G20 Bastille (Map pp98–9; 115 rue St-Antoine, 4e; ☺ 9am-8.30pm Mon-Sat; Ⓜ St-Paul), and the late-opening Monop' (Map pp94–5; 62-64 rue de la Roquette, 11e; ☺ 9am-midnight Mon-Sat; Ⓜ Voltaire).

THE ISLANDS

Famed more for its ice cream than dining options, Île St-Louis is a pricey place to eat, although there are a couple of fine places worth a brunch or lunchtime munch with,

depending on which you choose, some great street entertainment (see p303) thrown in for free. As for Île de la Cité, forget it – eating spots are almost nonexistent.

MON VIEIL AMI
Map p105   French, Alsatian €€€
☎ 01 40 46 01 35; 69 rue St-Louis en l'Île, 4e; menus €15 (lunch only) & €41; ☺ lunch Wed-Sun, dinner to 10.15pm Tue-Sun; Ⓜ Pont Marie
You're treated like an old friend – thus the name – from the minute you enter this sleek black bistro in one of Paris' most sought-after neighbourhoods. The pâté in pastry crust is a fabulous starter and any of the Alsatian mains are worth exploring. The chocolate tart is the pick of the desserts.

SORZA Map p105   International €€€
☎ 01 43 54 78 62; www.restaurant-sorza.fr, in French; 51 rue St-Louis en l'Île, 4e; starters €11-15, mains €16-40, 2-/3-course menu incl wine €18/22; ☺ noon-10.30pm daily; Ⓜ Pont Marie
It's all very trendy at this black-and-red cube where a buoyant crowd dines well any time of day. Its weekend brunches (€18) ooze health-conscious ingredients, as does its stylish Italianate cuisine. We ate an octopus salad, followed by foie gras risotto and French-baked panettone with caramelised pears. Should hunger not have struck yet, enjoy a drink at the flashy orange neon bar.

BRASSERIE DE L'ÎLE ST-LOUIS
Map p105   French, Brasserie €€
☎ 01 43 54 02 59; 55 quai de Bourbon, 4e; starters €10-15, mains €17.50; ☺ 6pm-1am Thu, noon-midnight Fri-Tue; Ⓜ Pont Marie
Founded in 1870, this riverside brasserie enjoys a spectacular location on the Seine just across the footbridge (prime busking spot) between Île de St-Louis and Île de la Cité. Feast on old faithfuls like choucroute garnie (sauerkraut with meat), jarret (veal shank), cassoulet and onglet de bœuf (prime rib of beef) or simply revel in the riverside location over a coffee/beer/Berthillon ice cream (opposite).

LES FOUS DE L'ÎLE
Map p105   French, Tearoom €€
☎ 01 43 25 76 67; 33 rue des Deux Ponts, 4e; starters €6.50-9, mains €14, menu €15 (lunch), €19 & €25; ☺ noon-11pm Tue-Sat, to 7pm Sun; Ⓜ Pont Marie

Innovative café-style dishes served from an open kitchen into a relaxed but arty setting ensure this friendly, down-to-earth *salon de thé* and restaurant is always busy. Dining is around old wooden tables and there's loads to look at, not least some cutting-edge photography and art shows when it moonlights as exhibition space. Our favourite meal: stuffed mussels with caramelised almonds, followed by roast lamb in a rosemary sauce.

LE FLORE EN L'ÎLE
Map p105   French, Tearoom €€

☎ 01 43 29 88 27; 42 quai d'Orléans, 4e; snacks €8, lunch €14; ⏰ 8am-1am daily; Ⓜ Pont Marie
A tourist crowd piles into this excellent people-watching spot for several very good reasons – its simple coffee 'n' croissant breakfast and Full Monty bacon 'n' egg brunch (€21); its club sandwich–style lunches (€14); its afternoon crepes (€8); its Berthillon ice-cream shakes and sundaes (from €9.80 to €15); and its prime views of the buskers on Pont St-Louis. Look for the long queue in front of its Berthillon takeaway ice-cream counter.

BERTHILLON Map p105   Ice Cream €

☎ 01 43 54 31 61; 31 rue St-Louis en l'Île, 4e; ice creams €2.10-5.40; ⏰ 10am-8pm Wed-Sun; Ⓜ Pont Marie
Berthillon is to ice cream what Château Lafite Rothschild is to wine and Valhrona is to chocolate. And with among 70 flavours to choose from, you'll be spoilt for choice. While the fruit flavours (eg cassis) produced by this celebrated *glacier* (ice-cream maker) are renowned, the chocolate, coffee, *marrons glacés* (candied chestnuts), Agenaise (Armagnac and prunes), *noisette* (hazelnut) and *nougat au miel* (honey nougat) are richer. The takeaway counter of this café has one/two/three/four small scoops for €2.10/3.20/4.30/5.40.

SELF-CATERING

On Île de St-Louis, there are a couple of *fromageries* on rue St-Louis en l'Île, 4e, as well as small supermarket Le Prestige d'Alimentation (Map p105; 67 rue St-Louis en l'Île, 4e; ⏰ 8am-10pm Wed-Mon) and Boulangerie St-Louis (Map p105; 80 rue St-Louis en l'Île, 4e) which sells well-filled sandwiches, quiche slices and cheese-topped hot dogs in baguettes to take away.

LATIN QUARTER & JARDIN DES PLANTES

From cheap-eat student haunts to chandelier-lit palaces loaded with history, the 5e arrondissement has something to suit every budget and culinary taste. Rue Mouffetard is famed for its food market and food shops, while its side streets, especially pedestrian rue du Pot au Fer, cook up some fine budget dining.

A tourist-busy concentration of ethnic restaurants is squeezed into the maze of narrow streets, a duck and a dive from Notre Dame across the Seine, between rue St-Jacques, blvd St-Germain and blvd St-Michel: Rue Bouterbie alone cooks up Georgian, Tunisian, Japanese and south American; rue Xavier Privas, rue St-Steven and rue de la Huchette heave with budget restaurants flouncing €15 *menus*.

LA TOUR D'ARGENT
Map pp110–11   French, Classical €€€

☎ 01 43 54 23 31; www.latourdargent.com; 15 quai de la Tournelle, 5e; menu lunch €70, dinner à la carte around €250; ⏰ lunch Wed-Sun, dinner to 9pm Tue-Sun; Ⓜ Cardinal Lemoine or Pont Marie
A much-vaunted riverside address, the Silver Tower is famous – for its *caneton* (duckling), Michelin stars that come and go, rooftop garden with Notre Dame view and fabulous history harking back to 1582. Its wine cellar is one of Paris' best, dining is dressy and exceedingly fine. Should you fail to snag a table (reserve eight to 10 days ahead for lunch, three weeks ahead for dinner), pop into its boutique opposite to buy an edible, oenological or silver souvenir that says 'quack' to take home.

ALEF-BET Map pp110–11   Jewish, Kosher €€€

☎ 01 40 18 17 22; www.alef-bet.biz, in French; 25 rue Galande, 5e; cooking course with meal €45-55; ⏰ 10am-8pm or 11pm daily; Ⓜ Maubert Mutualité
A tricky one to categorise, this bold red-and-white food space named after the first two letters of the Hebrew alphabet is a kosher café and cooking-school-cum-*épicerie*. The essential principle sees a cultured crowd mingle in an open kitchen for a one-to three-hour cooking course, after which they share the fruits of their labour around a beautifully laid table. Be it lunch, brunch, dinner, a Friday-night Shabbat or thematic

evening soirée, Alef-Bet screams design and innovation. The café sells fruit cocktails and light snacks; the shop sells designer kitchen utensils and gadgets; and the cooking sessions sell out like hot cakes – book in advance online. Opening hours vary, depending on what course is on.

L'AOC Map pp110–11   French, Classical €€€
☎ 01 43 54 22 52; www.restoaoc.com; 14 rue des Fosses St-Bernard, 5e; meals around €35; 🕑 lunch & dinner to 11.30pm Tue-Sat; Ⓜ Cardinal Lemoine
'Bistrot carnivore' is the strapline of this tasty little number concocted around France's most respected culinary products. The concept here is AOC (appellation d'origine contrôlée), meaning everything has been reared or made according to strict guidelines designed to protect a product unique to a particular village, town or area. The result? Only the best! Rare is the chance to taste porc noir de Bigorre, a type of black piggie bred in the Pyrénées.

LES VIGNES DU PANTHÉON
Map pp110–11   French, Southwest €€€
☎ 01 43 54 80 81; 4 rue des Fossés St-Jacques, 5e; starters €8-15, mains €18-35, menus €30 & €35; 🕑 lunch Mon-Fri, dinner to 10pm Mon-Sat; Ⓜ Luxembourg
Stroll but a few paces down the hill from the Panthéon to find this charming bistro, owned and managed by a husband-and-wife team who dish up an appealing cocktail of southwest-inspired cuisine with the accompaniment of fine wine. Old-fashioned wood panelling in the front room, exposed stone out back and the flicker of candles ensure a certain romance in the air.

MAVROMMÁTIS Map pp110–11   Greek €€€
☎ 01 43 31 17 17; www.mavrommatis.fr; 42 rue Daubenton, 5e; starters €12-18, mains €20-30, menus lunch €28 & €35, dinner €42 & €68; 🕑 lunch & dinner to 11pm Tue-Sat; Ⓜ Censier Daubenton
Sea-blue window frames and olive trees in giant terracotta pots whisk gourmet punters off to the Med at this well-established Greek restaurant. One bite into a tarama-drenched toast, aubergine fumée (smoked aubergine), salade grecque (tomatoes, lettuce, peppers and feta) or crépines d'agneau sur lit de tomates, courgettes et pommes de terre (lamb tripe with tomatoes, courgette and potatoes) and those inauthentic Greek takeaway joints on rue de la Huchette and

streets like rue St-Séverin are instantly put to shame. Reserve in advance.

PERRAUDIN Map pp110–11   French €€€
☎ 01 46 33 15 75; www.restaurant-perraudin .com, in French; 157 rue St-Jacques, 5e; starters €10-20, mains €15-30, menus lunch/dinner €19/29; 🕑 lunch & dinner to 11.30pm Mon-Fri; Ⓜ Luxembourg
Perraudin is a traditional French restaurant with embroidered handkerchief lampshades. If that doesn't put you off, launch yourself into this blast to the past with classics such as bœuf bourguignon (beef marinated and cooked in red wine with mushrooms, onions, carrots and bacon), gigot d'agneau (leg of lamb), confit de canard or flamiche (leek pie from northern France). Prices are reasonable (the plat du jour at lunchtime costs €12) and the place has atmosphere, even if it is a tad on the shabby side.

THE TEA CADDY Map pp110–11   Tearoom €€€
☎ 01 43 54 15 56; 14 rue St-Julien le Pauvre, 5e; set brunch/lunch €26/28; 🕑 11am-6pm Wed-Mon; Ⓜ St-Michel Notre Dame
Arguably the most English of the 'English' tearooms in Paris, this institution, founded in 1928, is a fine place to break for lunch or tea and a Devon scone with double cream and jam after a tour of nearby Notre Dame, Ste-Chapelle or the Conciergerie.

CHEZ RENÉ Map pp110–11   French, Bistro €€€
☎ 01 43 54 30 23; 14 blvd St-Germain, 5e; starters €10-15, mains €18-26; 🕑 lunch & dinner to 11pm Tue-Sat; Ⓜ Cardinal Lemoine or Maubert Mutualité
Proud owner of one of blvd St-Germain's busiest pavement terraces, Chez René has been an institution since the 1950s. Perfect for punters seeking no surprises, cuisine is quintessentially bistro: Think pot au feu (beef stew), coq au vin (chicken cooked in wine), rognons de veau (calf kidneys) etc accompanied by your pick of garnitures (fries, boiled potatoes, fresh spinach or other veg of the season etc) and sauces (béchamel, béarnaise, bourgognoise etc). A classic.

LE COUPE-CHOU
Map PP110–11   French, Romantic €€€
☎ 01 46 33 68 69; www.lecoupechou.com, in French; 9 & 11 rue de Lanneau, 5e; starters €12.50-15.50, mains €19-25, menu lunch €19, dinner

€26.50; ⊗ lunch & dinner to 11.30pm Mon-Sat, dinner to 11.30pm Sun; Ⓜ Maubert Mutualité
Well hidden but well known among Paris expats, this maze of candle-lit rooms snaking through a vine-clad 17th-century townhouse is overwhelmingly romantic. Ceilings are beamed, furnishings are antique, and background classical music mingles with the intimate chatter of diners. Le Coupe-Chou, incidentally, has nothing to do with cabbage *(chou)*; rather it's named after the barber's razor once wielded with a deft hand in one of its seven rooms. As in the days when Marlene Dietrich et al dined here, advanced reservations are all essential.

LE PETIT PONTOISE
Map pp110–11   French, Bistro €€€
☎ 01 43 29 25 20; 9 rue de Pontoise, 5e; starters €8-13.50, mains €15-25; ⊗ lunch & dinner to 10.30pm daily; Ⓜ Maubert Mutualité
Plop yourself down at a wooden table, note the lace curtains hiding you from the world, and pig out on fantastic old-fashioned classics like *rognons de veau à l'ancienne* (calf kidneys), *boudin campagnard* (black pudding) and sweet apple purée or roast quail with dates at this great bistro. Dishes might seem simple, but you'll leave pledging to return.

LA MOSQUÉE DE PARIS
Map pp110–11   North African €€€
☎ 01 43 31 38 20; www.la-mosquee.com; 39 rue Geoffroy St-Hilaire, 5e; mains €13.50-25; ⊗ lunch & dinner to 10.30pm daily; Ⓜ Censier Daubenton or Place Monge
Dig into one of 11 types of couscous (from €13 to €25), two hands' worth of *tajines* (from €15.50 to €17) or a meaty grill (€14.50) at this authentic restaurant tucked within the walls of the city's central mosque (p113). Feeling decadent? Plump for a peppermint tea (€2) and a calorie-loaded *pâtisserie orientale* (€2) between trees and chirping birds in the North African–style tearoom (⊗ 9am-11.30pm) or, better still, a *formule orientale* (€58) which includes a body scrub, 10-minute massage and lounge in the *hammam* (Turkish bath) as well as lunch, mint tea and sweet pastry.

CHEZ LÉNA ET MIMILLE
Map pp110–11   French €€
☎ 01 47 07 72 47; www.chezlenaetmimile.fr; 32 rue Tournefort, 5e; plat du jour €9.50, mains

€20, menus €28 & €55; ⊗ lunch Tue-Fri, dinner to 11pm Tue-Sat; Ⓜ Censier Daubenton
One of Paris's *bonnes tables* with a fabulous terrace, this intimate restaurant peeps down on a tiny park with fountain and comical equestrian statue. Its notably varied and choice-loaded menu, moreover, allows diners to decide just how fine or otherwise the experience will be. Fancy a simple plate of finely sliced Iberian salami over a lazy glass of wine? Or you want the whole multiple-course hog? Then the *Menu Note à Note* (€55), finely tuned to the culinary principles of molecular gastronomy (know what that is?), is an exquisite choice.

MOISSONIER Map pp110–11   French, Lyonnais €€
☎ 01 43 29 87 65; 28 rue des Fossés St-Bernard, 5e; starters €7-13, mains €20, menu €24; ⊗ lunch & dinner to 9.30pm Tue-Sat; Ⓜ Cardinal Lemoine
It's Lyon, not Paris, that French gourmets venerate as the French food capital (they have a point). Indeed, take one bite of a big fat *andouillette* (pig-intestine sausage), *tablier de sapeur* (breaded, fried stomach), traditional *quenelles* (fish-flavoured dumplings) or *boudin noir aux pommes* (black pudding with apples) and you'll realise why. A perfect reflection of one of France's most unforgettable regional cuisines, Moissonier is worth the wait. Look for the elegant oyster-grey façade opposite the university.

LE BABA BOURGEOIS
Map pp110–11   French, Trendy €€
☎ 01 44 07 46 75; http://lebababourgeois.com, in French; 5 quai de la Tournelle, 5e; mains €15-20; ⊗ lunch & dinner to 10.30pm Wed-Sat, 11.30am-5pm Sun; Ⓜ Cardinal Lemoine or Pont Marie
It's all very trendy, le BB. Bang-slap on the Seine with a pavement terrace facing Notre Dame, this contemporary eating and drinking space is a former architect's studio. Its interior screams 1970s Italian design and the menu – imaginative *tartines* (open sandwiches), *terrines, tartes salées* (savoury tarts) and salads – makes for a simple stylish bite any time. Sunday ushers in a splendid all-day buffet brunch, *à volonté* (all you can eat).

FOUNTI AGADIR Map pp110–1   Moroccan €€
☎ 01 43 37 85 10; www.fountiagadir.com, in French; 117 rue Monge, 5e; starters €8-10, mains

€11.50-20; menu lunch €12.50, dinner €36; 🕙 lunch & dinner to 11.30pm daily; Ⓜ Censier Daubenton

The décor is as richly coloured as the delicious couscous (€11.50 to €16), *tajines* (€13.50 to €15) and pastillas (around €8) cooked up in this busy Moroccan kitchen. The best on the Left Bank, some say. Dinner menus are for parties of 10 or more; otherwise, it's simply à la carte.

AL DAR Map pp110–11 Lebanese €€
☎ 01 43 25 17 15; 8-10 rue Frédéric Sauton, 5e; starters €6.50-10, mains €10-20; 🕙 lunch & dinner to midnight daily; Ⓜ Maubert Mutualité

This is a popular, award-winning Lebanese restaurant with a terrace open in the warmer months. For those pressed for time, an excellent delicatessen (🕙 7.30am-midnight) selling meze, mini pizzas, sandwiches and other cheap eats to munch on the move is attached.

LE BUISSON ARDENT
Map pp110–11 French, Bistro €€
☎ 01 43 54 93 02; www.lebuissonardent.fr, in French; 25 rue Jussieu, 5e; mains €19, menus lunch €14 & €19, dinner €31; 🕙 lunch & dinner to 10pm Mon-Fri, dinner to 10pm Sat; Ⓜ Jussieu

Stéphane Mauduit (gastronomy-mad chef) and his childhood, wine-mad mate, Jean-Thomas Lopez, head the team at this pocket-sized *bistrot gastronomique* where a local set flocks for lunch. In true bistro fashion, tables are jammed tightly together and the cuisine is traditional with an inventive kick. Think cheese-stuffed courgette, minestrone soup with pan-fried langoustine tails or scallops with a chicory fondue and sweet pepper 'n' anchovy *coulis*.

MAYJU Map pp110–11 World, Tearoom €€
☎ 01 44 07 13 29; 36 rue des boulangers, 5e; 2-/3-course menu lunch €14/18; 🕙 noon-5pm & 7-10pm Mon-Sat; Ⓜ Cardinal Lemoine

Wedged between the Sorbonne and Paris University, Mayju is a Zen retreat in a frenetic part of Paris. Pink and black are clearly the favourite colours of the interior designer – love the gargantuan pink rose, darling – whose modish mezzanine area oozes style. Pick from four starters, four *plats* (mains) alongside four savoury *tartes* (€6) and no guessing how many desserts. '*Saveurs du monde*' (world flavours) is the culinary theme.

LE PRÉ VERRE Map pp110–11 French, Bistro €€
☎ 01 43 54 59 47; 25 rue Thénard, 5e; starters €6, mains €17, 2-/3-course menu €13/27.50; 🕙 lunch & dinner Tue-Sat; Ⓜ Maubert Mutualité

Noisy, busy and buzzing, this jovial bistro run by the Delacourcelle brothers plunges diners into the heart of a Parisian's Paris. At lunchtime join the flock and go for the fabulous-value *formule dejeuner* (€13) – the day we were there it had curried chickpea soup, guinea-fowl thigh spiced with ginger on a bed of red and green cabbage, a glass of wine and loads of ultra-crusty, ultra-chewy baguette (the best). Desserts mix Asian spices with traditional French equally well. Philippe cooks but is constantly in and out the kitchen, throwing around his charm, while Marc is the man behind the interesting wine list, which features France's small independent *vignerons* (wine producers).

SAVANNAH CAFÉ
Map pp110–11 World, Bistro €€
☎ 01 43 29 45 77; www.savannahcafe.fr; 27 rue Descartes, 5e; starters €7-16, mains €13-15; 🕙 dinner to 11pm Mon-Sat; Ⓜ Cardinal Lemoine

The food at this hip little bistro is as eclectic as its retro, carnival-like decorations and choice of world music. Tabouli mixes with tortellini as does hummus with mozzarella and *fromage blanc* (cream cheese) with baklava. Can't decide? Kick off with the mixed plate of starters that flit from Italy to Lebanon to India.

BOUTIQUE CENSIER
Map pp110–11 Greek, Delicatessen €€
☎ 01 45 35 96 50; 47 rue Censier, 5e; mains €10-15; 🕙 9am-7.30pm Mon-Sat; Ⓜ Censier Daubenton

Pocket-sized and scarcely big enough to swing a shopping basket – but who cares when the food is so delicious? The self-catering arm of Mavrommátis (p250), this *traiteur* (delicatessen-caterer) is *the* pit-stop for a discerning lunchtime crowd who don't have hours to dine but still want to dine well. Most takeaway dishes are just like those served in its big-brother restaurant.

LES CINQ SAVEURS D'ANANDA
Map pp110–11 Organic €€
☎ 01 43 29 58 54; 72 rue du Cardinal Lemoine, 5e; plats du jour €13.90 & €14.90, menu

€26.90; ☺ lunch & dinner to 10.30pm Tue-Sun;
Ⓜ Cardinal Lemoine
Set back from place de la Contrescarpe,
this bright semi-vegetarian – it serves fish –
restaurant is much-loved by health-food
lovers. Ingredients are fresh and 100% bio.
Décor is simple, refined and stylish.

MACHU PICCHU
Map pp110–11   South American €€
☎ 01 43 26 13 13; 9 rue Royer Collard, 5e; starters €6.50-8.20, mains €8.50-14.90, menu lunch
€10.50; ☺ lunch & dinner to 10.30pm Mon-Fri;
Ⓜ Luxembourg
Students adore this place, named after the
lost city of the Incas in Peru. But doesn't
Peruvian food mean guinea-pig fricassee?
No. This hidey-hole, going strong since the
1980s, serves excellent meat and seafood
dishes as well as a bargain-basement lunch
menu and *plats du jour* (€6). No credit cards.

LE JARDIN DES PÂTES
Map pp110–11   Organic €€
☎ 01 43 31 50 71; 4 rue Lacépède, 5e; mains
€9.50-14; ☺ lunch & dinner to 11pm daily;
Ⓜ Place Monge
A crisp white-and-green façade handily
placed next to a Vélib' station flags the
Pasta Garden, a simple, smart 100% *bio*
(organic) place where pasta comes in every
guise imaginable – barley, buckwheat,
rye, wheat, rice, chestnut and so on. Our
favourite: *pâtes de chataignes* (chestnut
pasta) with duck breast, nutmeg, crème
fraîche and mushrooms. If you're in the
13e arrondissement nip into its second branch
(Map pp162–3; ☎ 01 45 35 93 67; 33 blvd Arago, 13e;
☺ lunch & dinner to 11pm Mon-Sat; Ⓜ Les Gobelins).

LES PIPOS Map pp110–11   French, Wine Bar €€
☎ 01 43 54 11 40; www.les-pipos.com, in French;
2 rue de l'École Polytechnique, 5e; plats du jour
€11.80-13.50; ☺ 8am-2am Mon-Sat; Ⓜ Maubert
Mutualité
A feast for the eyes and the senses, this *bar
à vins* is constantly propped up by a couple
of regulars over 60. Bistro tables wear red
and white, and are so close you risk dis-
turbing the entire house should you need
the loo midway through your meal. Its
charcuteries de terroir (regional cold meats
and sausages) is mouth-watering, as is its
cheese board, which includes all the gourmet names (bleu d'Auvergne, St-Félicien,
St-Marcellin etc). Indeed, take one glance

at the titles on the bookshelf (feel free to
browse) and you'll realise Les Pipos' overtly
casual, laidback scene is a guise for feasting
on the finer things in a French foodie's life.

KOOTCHI Map pp110–11   Afghan €€
☎ 01 44 07 20 56; 40 rue du Cardinal Lemoine,
5e; mains €12, menus lunch €9.50 & €12.50, dinner
€15.50; ☺ lunch & dinner to 10.30pm Mon-Sat;
Ⓜ Cardinal Lemoine
A menagerie of carpets, traditional instruments and other jumble lend this Afghan
restaurant a definite Central-Asian caravanserai air. The welcome is warm and the
food, warming. Specialities include *qhaboli
palawo* (veal stew with nuts and spices);
dogh, a drink not unlike salted Indian lassi;
and traditional *halwa* (a type of sweet
cake) perfumed with rose and cardamom.
Vegetarians keen to spice up their culinary
life should plump for *borani palawo* (spicy
vegetable stew) as a main course.

AUX CÉRISES DE LUTÈCE
Map pp110–11   Tearoom €
☎ 01 43 31 67 51; 86 rue Monge, 5e; mains €10;
☺ 11am-6.30pm Tue-Sat; Ⓜ Place Monge
A feast for the eyes and tastebuds, this cosy
eating space, heaped with colourful tea
pots, jugs and jumble, is the type of place
that would wear flowery wellies. As much
café and tearoom as lunchtime restaurant,
it serves breakfast all day (from €8 to €14)
alongside salads, quiches and *tartines*. Market mornings see punters clawing for the
trio of tables on the pavement out front.

TASHI DELEK Map pp110–11   Tibetan €
☎ 01 43 26 55 55; 4 rue des Fossés St-Jacques, 5e;
soups & bowls €4-6.80, mains €6.90-9.80, menus
lunch €10.50, dinner €20; ☺ lunch & dinner to
11pm Mon-Sat; Ⓜ Luxembourg
Gourmet it might not be; cheap, tasty and
inexpensive, it is. Tickle the tastebuds with
a *tsampa* (vegetable and barley soup),
followed by delicious *daril seu* (meatballs
with garlic, ginger and rice) or *tselmok*
(cheese and vegetable ravioli). Then wash
the whole lot down with traditional or
salted-butter tea. Don't forget to say 'tashi
delek' upon entering – it means 'bonjour'
in Tibetan.

SUSHI WASABI Map pp110–11   Japanese €
☎ 01 44 07 06 88; 86 blvd St-Germain, 5e; menu
lunch €7, 12 piece sushi €9.50, 14-piece sushi-maki

€8; 🕑 11.30am-10.30pm daily; Ⓜ Maubert Mutualité

It's hardly five star, but for the price who cares? This cheap and cheerful Japanese *traiteur* serves pre-prepared sushi, maki, futo maki etc and a good choice of hot meals to a quick-eat crowd. Jugs of water and condiments are readily placed on each long, shared table, sushi platters include a bowl of miso, and there's free tea or coffee to finish. Dishes to take away.

LE FOYER DU VIETNAM
Map pp110–11   Vietnamese €

☎ 01 45 35 32 54; 80 rue Monge, 5e; starters €3-6, mains €6-8.50, menus €8.20 & €12.20; 🕑 lunch & dinner to 10pm Mon-Sat; Ⓜ Place Monge

The 'Vietnam Club', with its self-proclaimed *ambiance familiale* (family atmosphere), might be nothing more than a long room with peeling walls and tables covered in oilcloths and plastic flowers, but everyone flocks here to feast on its hearty house specialities, 'Saigon' or 'Hanoi' soup (noodles, soya beans and pork flavoured with lemon grass, coriander and chives) included. Dishes come in medium or large portions and the price/quality ratio is astonishing. Students can fill up for €7.

SELF-CATERING

Shop with Parisians at a trio of lively outdoor food markets, framed (as with every market), by some lovely food shops: Place Maubert (p231), rue Mouffetard (p231) and Place Monge (p231). Supermarkets in the area include:

Champion (Map pp110–11; 34 rue Monge, 5e; Ⓜ Cardinal Lemoine)

Ed (Map pp110–11; 37 rue Lacépède, 5e; Ⓜ Place Monge)

Le Marché Franprix (Map pp110–11; 82 rue Mouffetard, 5e; Ⓜ Place Monge)

Monoprix (Map pp110–11; 24 blvd St-Michel, 5e; 🕑 9am-midnight Mon-Sat)

ST-GERMAIN, ODÉON & LUXEMBOURG

There's far more to this fabled pocket of Paris – effectively the 6e arrondissement – than the literary cafés (see p291) of Sartre and de Beauvoir or the prime picnicking turf of the Jardin de Luxembourg. Rue St-André des Arts and its continuation, rue du Buci, are lined with places to drink and dine as lightly or lavishly as your heart/wallet desires, as is the stretch between Église St-Sulpice and Église St-Germain des Prés (especially rue des Canettes, rue Princesse and rue Guisarde). Quintessential Parisian bistros and brasseries abound in this busy neck of the Left Bank, but if contemporary design à la Terence Conran is more your style, restaurant Alcazar (p292) is the smart choice.

LE SALON D'HÉLÈNE
Map pp116–17   French, Contemporary €€€

☎ 01 42 22 00 11; www.helenedarroze.com; 4 rue d'Assas, 6e; menu lunch €35/45, dinner €88; 🕑 lunch & dinner to 10.15pm Tue-Sat; Ⓜ Sèvres Babylone

While culinary star and media darling Hélène Darroze has a fine-dining Michelin-starred restaurant (called La Salle à Manger) upstairs, this more casual 'salon' is far more fun. The best way to experience her wonderful creations come dusk is to persuade your table to each order the tapas-sized tasting menu (€88). Five courses come in matched pairs, each dish with descriptions longer than this review. Lunch *menus* include a choice of two/three tapas with one/two glasses of wine.

LE PETIT ZINC Map pp116–17   French, Brasserie €€€

☎ 01 42 86 61 00; www.petit-zinc.com, in French; 11 rue St-Benoît, 6e; starters €8.50-19.50, mains €17.50-38, menu €35; 🕑 noon-2am daily; Ⓜ St-Germain des Prés

Not a 'little bar' but a wonderful, large brasserie serving mountains of fresh seafood, traditional French cuisine and regional specialities from the southwest in true Art Nouveau splendour. The term brasserie is used loosely here; you'll feel more like you're in a starred restaurant, so book ahead and dress accordingly.

SENSING Map pp116–17   French, Contemporary €€€

☎ 01 43 27 08 80; www.restaurantsensing.com; 19 rue Bréa, 6e; starters €21-24, mains €32-37, menu lunch €25, dinner €95; 🕑 dinner to 10.30pm Mon, lunch & dinner to 10.30pm Tue-Sat; Ⓜ Vavin

Don't worry about arriving at this elegant address with a hair out of place or smudged lipstick – a quick preen in the mirrored door upon entering will sort it out. The swanky 'affordable-bistro' creation of Michelin-starred celebrity chef Guy Martin, Sensing is one of those try-hard New York–type places

top picks

ST-GERMAIN LUNCH SPOTS

- Ze Kitchen Galerie (below)
- Huîterie Regis (p256)
- Le Mâchon d'Henri (p257)
- Mamie Gâteaux (p256)
- Le Jacobine (p257)

with an interior design so cutting edge it seriously distracts from the food (oddly, glance quickly from the outside and you could easily mistake it for a luxury jewellery shop, although another review I read mentioned a hairdresser's…). 'Snacking' is the trendy name for pre-dinner nibbles.

LES BOUQUINISTES

Map pp116–17   French, Contemporary €€€

☎ 01 43 25 45 94; 53 quai des Grands Augustins, 6e; starters €12-17.50. mains €27.50-31, 2-/3-course menus lunch €25/28; ☺ lunch & dinner to 11pm Mon-Thu, lunch & dinner to 11.30pm Fri, dinner to 11.30pm Sat; Ⓜ St-Michel

This stylish eating space courtesy of Guy Savoy sits across from Notre Dame and the Seine-side booksellers. Modern but elegant décor aside, its menu lures gourmets with tantalising dishes such as Brittany crab ravioli with lobster and fennel in a lemongrass juice, veal shank or a spiced duck filet. Don't torture yourself over which dessert to pick – the dessert for two (€20) features a tiny tasty morsel of each.

ZE KITCHEN GALERIE

Map pp116–17   Fusion €€€

☎ 01 44 32 00 32; 4 rue des Grands Augustins, 6e; starters €15, mains €28, 2-/3-course menu lunch €29/39; ☺ lunch & dinner to 11pm Mon-Fri, dinner to 11.30pm Sat; Ⓜ St-Michel

William Ledeuil's passion for Southeast Asian travel oozes out of the feisty dishes he creates in his Michelin single-starred glass-box kitchen, which hosts three to five different art exhibitions a year. The menu is a vibrant feast of broths loaded with Thai herbs and coconut milk, meat and fish cooked à la plancha and inventive desserts like sweet chestnut-and-vanilla soup. Service is speedy and lunch *menus* include a glass of wine and coffee.

BOUILLON RACINE

Map pp116–17   French, Classical €€€

☎ 01 44 32 15 60; 3 rue Racine, 6e; starters €7.50-14.50, mains €15.50-28, menus €14.90 (lunch) & €29; ☺ lunch & dinner to 11pm daily; Ⓜ Cluny La Sorbonne

We've never seen anything quite like this 'soup kitchen', built in 1906 to feed market workers. A gorgeous Art Nouveau palace with mirrored walls, floral motifs and ceramic tiling, the interior is a positive delight. Oh, and the food? Wholly classic inspired by age-old recipes such as roast snails, *caille confite* (preserved quail) and lamb shank with liquorice. Finish off your foray in gastronomic history with an old-fashioned sherbet.

CHEZ ALLARD   Map pp116–17   French, Bistro €€€

☎ 01 43 26 48 23; 41 rue St-André des Arts, 6e; starters €8-20, mains €25, 2-/3-course menu €25/34; ☺ lunch & dinner to 11.30pm Mon-Sat; Ⓜ St-Michel

A definite Left Bank favourite is this charming bistro where the staff couldn't be kinder or more professional – even during its enormously busy lunchtime. And the food is superb. Try a dozen snails, some *cuisses de grenouilles* (frogs' legs) or *un poulet de Bresse* (France's most legendary chicken, from Burgundy) for two. Enter from 1 rue de l'Éperon.

YEN   Map pp116–17   Japanese €€€

☎ 01 45 44 11 18; 22 rue St-Benoît, 6e; mains €20-25, menu lunch €30, dinner €55; ☺ lunch & dinner to 10.30pm Mon-Sat; Ⓜ St-Germain des Prés

This Japanese place – the last word in minimalism with its light wood and charcoal-grey slate floor – is a favourite of resident Japanese and knowledgeable Parisians. It has a flair for *soba* (Japanese noodles) and tempura and you shouldn't leave without trying the aubergine in miso. Unusual for Paris, Yen serves and sells *bento* boxes at lunchtime.

LES ÉDITEURS   Map pp116–17   French, Café €€€

☎ 01 43 26 67 76; 4 Carrefour de l'Odéon, 6e; starters €10-18, mains €17.50-25; ☺ 8am-2am daily; Ⓜ Odéon

This place goes to great lengths to describe itself as café, restaurant, library, bar and *salon de thé*, but for us it's a place to eat and/or people-watch. It is intended for writers – there are more than 5000 books on hand and it's done up to feel like a slightly faded and dingy library – but it has floor-to-ceiling windows through which you can watch the Germanopratin (yes, there is an adjective for St-Germain des Prés) goings-on. Its daily breakfasts/Sunday brunch are a snip at €8.50 to €12/25.50.

L'ARBUCI Map pp116–17 French, Brasserie €€€

☎ 01 44 32 16 00; 25 rue du Buci, 6e; starters €7-18, mains €16-25; ☯ noon-midnight daily; Ⓜ Mabillon

A popular choice for breakfast or brunch, this airy lounge bar with big, street-facing windows buzzes. Its décor is a contemporary take on traditional brasserie-style and the easygoing menu caters to all tastes, including those whose buds go wild over bottomless plates of oysters. Prime real estate, the packed tables on the pavement terrace in front see you vying for foot space with passing pedestrians. Live jazz in the basement on Fridays and Saturdays.

BRASSERIE LIPP

Map pp116–17 French, Brasserie €€€

☎ 01 45 48 53 91; www.brasserie-lipp.fr/page3 .html; 151 blvd St-Germain, 6e; starters €10-15, mains €15.50-25; ☯ noon-2am daily; Ⓜ St-Germain des Prés

Politicians rub shoulders with intellectu-als, while waiters in black waistcoats, bow ties and long white aprons serve brasserie favourites like *choucroute garnie* and *jarret de porc aux lentilles* (pork knuckle with len-tils) at this celebrated wood-panelled café, opened by Léonard Lipp in 1880.

HUÎTERIE REGIS Map pp116–17 Oyster Bar €€

☎ 01 44 41 10 07; 3 rue de Montfaucon, 6e; dozen oysters & glass wine €22.50; ☯ 11am-midnight Tue-Sun mid-Sep–mid-Jul; Ⓜ Mabillon

Hip, trendy, tiny and white, this is *the* spot for revelling in oysters on crisp winter days. They come only by the dozen, along with fresh bread and butter, but wash them down with a glass of chilled Muscadet and *voilà*, one perfect lunch for €22.50! Two tables loiter on the pavement outside; otherwise it's all inside.

POLIDOR Map pp116–17 French €€€

☎ 01 43 26 95 34; http://restaurantpolidor.info, in French; 41 rue Monsieur le Prince, 6e; start-ers €4.50-17, mains €11-22, menus €22 & €32; ☯ lunch & dinner to 12.30am Mon-Sat, to 11pm Sun; Ⓜ Odéon

A meal at this quintessentially Parisian *crèmerie-restaurant* is like a trip to Victor

Hugo's Paris: the restaurant and its décor date from 1845 and everyone knows about it (read: touristy). Still, *menus* of tasty, family-style French cuisine ensure a never-ending stream of punters eager to sample *bœuf bourguignon* (€11), *blanquette de veau à l'ancienne* (veal in white sauce; €15) and the most famous *tarte Tatin* (€8) in Paris! Expect to wait.

FOGÓN ST-JULIEN Map pp116–17 Spanish €€

☎ 01 43 54 31 33; 45 quai des Grands Augustins, 6e; mains €20, menus €35 & €45; ☯ lunch Sat & Sun, dinner to midnight Tue-Sun; Ⓜ St-Michel

Enter *España*: Fogón St-Julien the best Spanish restaurant in Paris, many say. Indeed, its menu tours Spain with a feast of a *menu tapas* (€45) but goes well beyond tapas, too, with excellent paellas (vegetable, rabbit, chicken, seafood; €18) and other tasty mains like *arroz negro* (rice blackened with squid ink & laced with shrimps & cuttlefish).

MAMIE GÂTEAUX Map pp116–17 Tearoom €

☎ 01 42 22 32 15; www.mamie-gateaux.com, in French; 66-70 rue du Cherche-Midi, 6e; lunch €10-15; ☯ 11.30am-6pm Tue-Sat; Ⓜ St-Placide & Sèvres-Babylone

A perfect light-lunch spot after a taxing morning savouring the stylish boutiques around nearby Le Bon Marché (p212), this retro tearoom with lace curtains and a *brocante* (second-hand) décor positively heaves at lunchtime. Funnily enough for this hot shopping area, the clientele is predomi-nantly female and chatty as the electrifying buzz of happy shoppers chomping into homemade quiches, savoury cakes, tarts and salads testifies. For us, the ratatouille-and-mozzarella tart is the icing on the cake.

CHEZ LES FILLES Map pp116–17 Tearoom €

☎ 01 45 48 61 54; 64 rue du Cherche-Midi, 6e; lunch €10-15; ☯ 11.30am-4.30pm Mon-Sat, 12.30-5.30pm Sat; Ⓜ St-Placide or Sèvres-Babylone

If Mamie Gâteaux is full, try this other female-filled hot spot which – unlike its grandmotherly neighbour – transports an eager lunch crowd into the land of the Orient. Salads, *tajines*, savoury tarts and a fantastic value *plat du jour* (€13) make for a colourful lunch. Midafternoon, refresh parched souls with a *pâtisserie orientale* and cup of sweet mint tea.

LA JACOBINE Map pp116–17 — Tearoom €

☎ 01 46 34 15 95; 59-61 rue St-André des Arts, 6e; lunch €10-15; ⏰ 11.30am-11.30pm daily; Ⓜ Odéon

What a sweet find! An oldy-worldy hybrid tearoom and busy lunch spot, La Jacobine is packed to the rafters by noon with punters keen to fill up on homemade tarts, giant-sized salads and crêpes. Its lovely location inside Cour du Commerce St-André, a glass-covered passageway built in 1735 to link two Jeu de Paume (old-style tennis) courts, makes it all the more romantic.

INDONESIA Map pp116–17 — Indonesian €€

☎ 01 43 25 70 22; 12 rue de Vaugirard, 6e; mains €9-15, menus lunch €11.50 & €12.50, dinner €18-25; ⏰ lunch Mon-Fri, dinner to 10.30pm daily; Ⓜ Luxembourg

One of a couple of Indonesian restaurants in Paris, this well-established eatery, around for more than 25 years, has all the old favourites, from an elaborate, nine-dish *rijstafel* (rice with side dishes) to *lumpia* (a type of spring roll), *rendang* (spicy beef or chicken curry) and *gado-gado* (vegetable salad with spicy peanut sauce; €6). Numerous *menus* are available at lunch and dinner. Traditional décor, incense and the gentle rhythm of the gamelan orchestra create a convincing atmosphere. Balinese dancers dance some Friday evenings.

FISH LA BOISSONNERIE
Map pp116–17 — Seafood €€

☎ 01 43 54 34 69; 69 rue de Seine, 6e; starters €7, mains €14, menu lunch €21.50; ⏰ lunch & dinner to 10.45pm Tue-Sun; Ⓜ Mabillon

A hybrid of a Mediterranean place run by a New Zealander (of Cosi fame; p257) and an American, with its rustic communal seating and bonhomie, Fish has surely taken its cue from London, where such places have been a mainstay for several years. The wine selection is excellent – it's almost as much a wine bar as a restaurant – and the wonderful old mosaic on the front façade is a delight.

LE MÂCHON D'HENRI Map pp116–17 French €€

☎ 01 43 29 08 70; 8 rue Guisarde, 6e; starters €6-8, mains €12-14; ⏰ lunch & dinner until 11.30pm daily; Ⓜ St-Sulpice or Mabillon

What with the gaggle of hungry customers constantly waiting for a seat and the extraordinary proximity of the 10 marble-topped tables, this is one busy, tiny bistro. But the staff, seemingly exclusively male and over a certain age, are smile and charm personified. And the menu, crammed with feisty French staples like *boudin noir aux pommes* (black pudding with apples) from Lyon, *saucisse de Morteau* (a type of sausage) and lentils from the Jura or tripe cooked Caen-style, guarantees you'll leave absolutely stuffed.

COSI Map pp116–17 — Sandwich Bar €

☎ 01 46 33 35 36; 54 rue de Seine, 6e; sandwich menus €9-11; ⏰ noon-11pm daily; Ⓜ Odéon

An institution in the 6th for a quick cheap eat in or out, Cosi could easily run for Paris' most imaginative sandwich maker: with sandwich names like Stonker, Tom Dooley and Naked Willi, how could you expect otherwise? Classical music playing in the background and homemade Italian bread, still warm from the oven, only adds to Cosi's natural sex appeal which, incidentally, is of New Zealand origin.

BAR À SOUPES ET QUENELLES
GIRAUDET Map pp116–17 — French, Lyonnais €€

☎ 01 43 25 44 44; www.giraudet.fr, in French; 5 rue Princesse, 6e; lunch around €10; ⏰ 10am-5pm Mon, 10am-5pm & 7-11.30pm Tue-Fri, 10am-11.30pm Sat; Ⓜ Mabillon

This soup-and-dumpling bar is a perfect spot in shop-busy St-Germain to rest legs on a bar stool and tuck into a light 'n' tasty lunch. Soups are thick, creamy, seasonal, organic and packed with unusual combinations – pear and litchi, chestnut or cardoon perhaps? But it is the typical Lyonnais *quenelles* (pike-perch dumplings) topped with a sauce of your choice that steal the show. Buy some to eat at home afterwards from the nearby Boutique Giraudet (☎ 01 43 25 23 00; 16 rue Mabillon, 6e; ⏰ 2.30-7.30pm Mon, 10am-1pm & 1.30-7.30pm Tue-Sat; Ⓜ Mabillon).

AMORINO Map pp116–17 — Ice Cream €

☎ 01 43 26 57 46; 4 rue de Buci, 6e; 1/2/3 scoops €3/4/5; ⏰ noon-midnight daily; Ⓜ St-Germain des Prés

Though not such dedicated *lécheurs* (lickers) as some, we're told that Berthillon (p248) has serious competition and Amorino's homemade ice cream (yogurt, caramel, kiwi, strawberry etc) is, in fact, better. It has no less than 10 others branches in Paris, including Amorino Luxembourg (Map pp116–17; ☎ 01 42 22 66 86; 4 rue Vavin, 6e; Ⓜ Vavin) and Amorino Île St-Louis (Map p105; ☎ 01 44 07 48 08; 47 rue St-Louis en l'Île, 4e; Ⓜ Pont Marie).

SELF-CATERING

Food shops cluster on rue de Seine and rue de Buci, while the covered Marché St-Germain (Map p116–17; 4-8 rue Lobineau, 6e; ⏰ 8.30am-1pm & 4-7.30pm Tue-Sat, 8.30am-1pm Sun; Ⓜ Mabillon), just north of the eastern end of Église St-Sulpice, has a huge array of fine fresh produce and prepared food.

Should black pudding turn you on, Charcuterie Charles (☎ 01 43 54 25 19; 10 rue Dauphiné, 6e; ⏰ 9am-2pm & 4-8pm Mon-Sat) is your man. One of Paris' few and most respected *boudiniers* (sausage makers), Charles Claude is famed for his 18 different types of *boudins* – black, white, spiced, laced with truffles or chestnuts or shallots.

If you are looking for a supermarket, Champion (Map p116–17; 79 rue de Seine, 6e; ⏰ 1-9pm Mon, 8.40am-9pm Tue-Sat, 9am-1pm Sun; Ⓜ Mabillon) should meet your needs.

MONTPARNASSE

Since the 1920s, the area around blvd du Montparnasse has been one of the city's premier avenues for enjoying Parisian café life, though younger Parisians deem the place somewhat *démodé* and touristy these days. Glam it's not. But it does boast a handful of legendary brasseries and cafés which warrant a culinary visit. Made famous by writers (see p193) and artists like Picasso, Dalí and Cocteau between the wars, these same cafés attracted exiles such as Lenin and Trotsky before the Russian Revolution.

LE DÔME   Map pp124–5   French, Seafood €€€
☎ 01 43 35 25 81, 01 43 35 23 95; 108 blvd du Montparnasse, 14e; starters €12.50-25, mains €29-60; ⏰ lunch & dinner to 23.30pm daily; Ⓜ Vavin
An Art Deco extravaganza dating from the 1930s, Le Dôme is a monumental place for a meal, with a restaurant and *poissonnerie* where the emphasis, of course, is on the freshest of oysters, shellfish and fish dishes such as *sole meunière* (sole sautéed in butter and garnished with lemon and parsley). Stick with the basics at this historical venue and leave fussier dishes to the 'fooding' upstarts.

LA CLOSERIE DES LILAS
Map pp124–5   French, Brasserie €€€
☎ 01 40 51 34 50; www.closeriedeslilas.fr; 171 blvd du Montparnasse, 6e; restaurant/brasserie starters €30-50, €11-20, mains €40-50, €22-27,

menu lunch €45; ⏰ restaurant lunch & dinner to 11.30pm, brasserie noon-1am, bar 11-1.30am; Ⓜ Port Royal
As anyone who has read Hemingway will know, what is now the American Bar at the 'Lilac Enclosure' is where Papa did a lot of writing, drinking and oyster slurping; brass plaques tell you exactly where he and other luminaries such as Picasso, Apollinaire, Man Ray, Jean-Paul Sartre and Samuel Beckett stood or sat (or fell) and whiled away the hours. The place is split into bar, chic restaurant and more lovable (and cheaper) brasserie with hedged-in pavement terrace.

LA COUPOLE
Map pp124–5   French, Brasserie €€€
☎ 01 43 20 14 20; 102 blvd du Montparnasse, 14e; starters €6.50-20, mains €12.50-35, menus 24.50 (lunch) & €31.50; ⏰ 8am-1am Sun-Thu, to 1.30am Fri & Sat; Ⓜ Vavin
The famous mural-covered columns (painted by such artists as Brancusi and Chagall), dark wood panelling and soft lighting have hardly changed an iota since the days of Sartre, Soutine, Man Ray, the dancer Josephine Baker and other regulars. The reason for visiting this enormous, 450-seat brasserie, designed by the Solvet brothers and opened in 1927, is more history than gastronomy. You can book for lunch, but you'll have to queue for dinner; though there's always breakfast. The more expensive *menus* are available until 6pm and after 10.30pm.

LA CAGOUILLE
Map pp124–5   French, Seafood €€€
☎ 01 43 22 09 01; www.la-cagouille.fr; 10 place Constantin Brancusi, 14e; starters €11-15, mains €18-33, 2-/3-course menu €26/42; ⏰ lunch & dinner to 10.30pm daily; Ⓜ Vavin
Chef Gérard Allemandou, one of the best seafood cooks (and cookery book writers) in Paris, gets rave reviews for his fish and shellfish dishes at this café-restaurant opposite 23 rue de l'Ouest. The *menus* here are exceptionally good value.

SELF-CATERING

Opposite the Tour Montparnasse is the open-air Blvd Edgar Quinet food market (Map pp124–5; blvd Edgar Quinet; ⏰ 7am-2pm Wed & Sat; Ⓜ Edgar Quinet or Montparnasse Bienvenüe). Or shop organic at nearby Marché Raspail (p232) or Marché Brancusi (p231).

Convenient supermarkets:

Atac (Map pp124–5; 55 av du Maine, 14e; 9am-10pm Mon-Sat; M Gaîté)

Inno (Map pp124–5; 29-31 rue du Départ, 14e; 9am-9.50pm Mon-Fri, to 8.50pm Sat; M Montparnasse Bienvenüe)

FAUBOURG ST-GERMAIN & INVALIDES

Wedged between the tourist hotspot of the Eiffel Tower area and the chic boutiques and literary cafés of St-Germain des Prés, this district – effectively the entire 7e arrondissement – is something of a culinary no-man's land. That said, Parisians flock here like bees to a honey pot to shop at the Harrods food hall of Paris (p212) that sits on its southern fringe, while a couple of highly prized addresses ensure the diplomats and political bods working at the many government ministries and embassies here (not to mention the National Assembly) can schmooze in style. Off the corporate credit card, stroll pedestrian rue Cler and its surrounding streets.

L'ATELIER DE JOËL ROBUCHON
Map pp128–9 International €€€

☎ 0 826 101 219; www.restaurants-joel-robuchon .com; 5 rue de Montalembert, 7e; starters €20-45, mains €27-58, menu €110; lunch & dinner to midnight daily; M Rue du Bac
It's a mean feat to snag a seat at this celebrity-chef address, which accepts reservations only between 11am and 11.30am the day you want to dine or at precisely 6.30pm for dinner. Once in, you'll realise what all the fuss is about. Diners are taken on a mind-blowing culinary tour of the finer things in French gastronomy, lobster, sardines, foie gras and milk-fed lamb included. And with accolades like 'chef of the century' and 'world's best restaurant' under Joël Robuchon's belt, you know it'll be good. Dining is stool-style around a U-shaped black lacquer bar and the décor – bamboo in glass vases and the like – throws in a touch of Japan.

L'ESPLANADE Map pp128–9 Fusion €€€

☎ 01 47 05 38 80; 52 rue Fabert, 7e; meals around €50; lunch & dinner to 12.30am daily; M La Tour Maubourg
An address to impress (so dress to impress), Café de l'Esplanade might well be one of those chic, hobnobbing society places to be seen in between business deals – it is of the same Costes brothers ilk as Café Marly (p233), Georges (p232) et al, much loved by politicians and journalists. (In the Sarkozy-Cécilia soap opera, this was where the pair made public their reconciliation before splitting again.) But take one look at the astonishing view and you'll understand why. This is, after all, the only café-restaurant on the magnificent Esplanade des Invalides. No menus – just à la carte until half past midnight.

BRASSERIE THOUMIEUX
Map pp128–9 French, Brasserie €€€

☎ 01 47 05 49 75; www.thoumieux.com, in French; 79 rue St-Dominique, 7e; starters €10, mains €25, menus €15 (lunch only) & €35; lunch & dinner to 11pm daily; M La Tour Maubourg
Chef Christian Beguet has been here since 1979 – and that's just the tip of the iceberg. Founded in 1923, Thoumieux is an old-school institution just south of the Seine, loved by politicians and tourists alike. Duck thighs, veal, snails…the menu is typical brasserie and the service, silky smooth. It has 10 rooms up top should you need to crash.

LA GRANDE ÉPICERIE
Map pp128–9 Wok & Sandwich Bar €€

☎ 01 46 39 81 00; www.lagrandeepicerie.fr; 26 rue de Sèvres, 7e; sandwich menus €9-11; 8.30am-9pm Mon-Sat; M Sèvres Babylone
Join the hordes of workers from the offices in this area for a quick tasty lunch at the Espace Pic Nic, in the ground-floor food hall of stylish Le Bon Marché department store (p212). Hover around the bar over a wok-cooked hot dish (€8.05), a design-your-own sandwich (pick the bread type and fillings yourself; €5.38), a self-designed salad (€6.75) or an 11-piece sushi plate (€11.60). Pay marginally less to take the same away, or build your own gourmet picnic from the food hall.

SELF-CATERING

Just west of Invalides spills an open-air food market six days a week on Rue Cler (p231). Or there's the finest of fine food halls La Grande Épicerie (see above).

A fromagerie to die for, Quatrehommes (Map pp128–9; ☎ 01 47 34 33 45; 62 rue de Sèvres, 6e; 8.45am-1pm & 4-7.45pm Tue-Thu, 8.45am-7.45pm Fri & Sat;

M Vanneau) sells the best of every French cheese, many with an original take (eg Epoisses boxed in chestnut leaves, Mont d'Or flavoured with black truffles, spiced honey and Roquefort bread etc). The smell alone as you enter is heavenly.

EIFFEL TOWER AREA & 16E ARRONDISSEMENT

The 16e arrondissement is perhaps the most chichi and snobby part of Paris, the kind of area where a waiter will ask a fluent though non-native speaker of French whether they would like *la carte en anglais* (English menu). It's not everyone's *tasse de thé* (cup of tea), but a couple of its ethnic restaurants are worth a visit.

MAISON PRUNIER Map pp132-3 French €€€
☎ 01 44 17 35 85; www.prunier.com; 16 av Victor Hugo, 16e; starters €15-49, mains €29-69, menu €59 (lunch only); ☀ lunch Tue-Sat, dinner to 11pm Mon-Sat; M Charles de Gaulle-Étoile
A venerable restaurant founded in 1925, Prunier is as famed for its Art Deco interior as for its own brand of caviar, fish and seafood dishes and dozens of vodkas. Definitely a place for celebrations and the experience of it all; a *menu caviar* will set you back €155.

LE CRISTAL ROOM Map pp132-3 French €€€
☎ 01 40 22 11 10; www.baccarat.com; 11 place des États-Unis, 16e; mains €25-43, menus €59 (lunch only) & €92; ☀ lunch & dinner to 10pm Mon-Sat; M Iéna
Located on the first floor of the Galerie-Musée Baccarat (p136), this stunner of a venue features interiors conceived by the over-employed Philippe Starck: mirrors, crystal and even a black chandelier. The menu by Thierry Burlot is excellent but expensive. Note that you will need to book well in advance.

LES OMBRES Map pp132-3 French €€€
☎ 01 47 53 68 00; www.lesombres-restaurant .com; 27 quai Branly, 7e; starters €21-23, mains €33-36; menus €38 (lunch only) & €95; ☀ lunch & dinner to 11pm Fri & Sat; M Pont de l'Alma or Alma-Marceau
Paris not only gained a new museum in the Musée du Quai Branly (p134) but also this

glass-enclosed rooftop restaurant on the museum's 5th floor. Named 'The Shadows' for the patterns cast by the Eiffel Tower's webbed ironwork, the dramatic views are complemented by Arnaud Busquet's elegant creations, such as pan-seared tuna with sesame seeds and onion rings, or lamb with zucchini ravioli and ginger-bread.

CAFÉ DE L'HOMME
Map pp132-3 International €€€
☎ 01 44 05 30 15; www.restaurant-cafedel homme.com; 17 place du Trocadéro, 16e; starters €15-24, mains €18-35; ☀ lunch & dinner to 11.30pm daily; M George V
You probably wouldn't cross town for the food at the Café de L'Homme, the new restaurant sharing the same wing of the Palais de Chaillot as the Musée de l'Homme and the Musée de la Marine (p134); it's over-priced and designed for the beautiful people who are flocking here at the moment. But you would travel for the view; virtually any spot at any table is a front-row seat before the Eiffel Tower. This is why you came to Paris.

LA CANTINE RUSSE
Map pp132-3 Russian €€€
☎ 01 47 20 56 12; 26 av de New York, 16e; starters €8.90-23, mains €15.50-24.90, menus €15 & €25; ☀ lunch & dinner to midnight Mon-Sat; M Alma Marceau
Established for the overwhelmingly Russian students at the prestigious Conservatoire Rachmaninov in 1923, this 'canteen' is still going strong more than eight decades later. At communal tables you can savour herrings served with blinis, aubergine 'caviar', chicken Kiev, beef Stroganov, *chachliks* (marinated lamb kebabs) and, to complete the tableau, *vatrouchka* (cream cheese cake).

LE PETIT RÉTRO Map pp132-3 French €€
☎ 01 44 05 06 05; www.petitretro.fr; 5 rue Mesnil, 16e; starters €7-16, mains €15-22, menus €21.90 & €24.90 (lunch only), €29.50 & €34.50; ☀ lunch & dinner to 10.30pm Mon-Fri; M Victor Hugo
From the gorgeous 'Petit Rétro' embla-zoned on the zinc bar to the Art Nouveau folk tiles, this is a handsome space and one that serves up hearty dishes year-round. With dishes such as *rognons de*

veau poêles (potted veal kidneys) and *choucroute maison* as house specials, it's hearty, heart-warming stuff. They've expanded in recent years, making the seating less cramped.

LA CHAUMIÈRE EN CHINE
Map pp132–3   Chinese €€

☎ 01 47 20 85 56; 26 av Pierre 1er de Serbie, 16e; starters €6.50-9, mains €8-18, menus lunch €12, dinner €17 & €22; ⏰ lunch & dinner to 10.30pm Mon-Sat; Ⓜ Alma Marceau

Parisians in the know would warn you against eating in ethnic restaurants outside ethnic *quartiers,* but the Chinese embassy just down the road from this place makes it a notable exception to that rule. The largely Chinese clientele favour the *crevettes au sel de cinq parfums* (prawns in five spice salt), the *canard aux champignons noirs* (duck with black mushrooms) and the dim sum.

RESTAURANT MUSÉE DU VIN
Map pp132–3   French €€

☎ 01 45 25 63 26; www.museeduvinparis.com; 5 square Charles Dickens (rue des Eaux), 16e; starters €7.50-17, mains €13-16, menus €23, €34 (with champagne) & €58 (with wine); ⏰ lunch to 3pm Tue-Sat; Ⓜ Passy

Where else to enjoy a wine-paired set menu than at the restaurant of the Musée du Vin (p136)? What's more, a meal here allows you to look at the exhibits for free. Try the *terrine de canard en gelée forestière* (duck terrine in aspic with berries) followed by the *petit salé aux lentilles* (lean salt pork with lentils).

SELF-CATERING

The open-air Marché Prèsident Wilson (p231) is convenient to the neighbourhood.

ÉTOILE & CHAMPS-ÉLYSÉES

The 8e arrondissement seems to have been born under a lucky star. Its broad avenues radiate from place Charles de Gaulle – also known as place de l'Étoile or simply Étoile – and among them is the celebrated av des Champs-Élysées; from the Arc de Triomphe to the place de la Concorde, the 'Elysian Fields' rules unchallenged. With very few exceptions, eateries lining this touristy thoroughfare offer little value for money, but those in surrounding areas can be excellent and well-worth seeking out.

SPOON
Map pp140–1   Fusion €€€

☎ 01 40 76 34 44; www.spoon-restaurants.com; 14 rue de Marignan, 8e; starters €16-20, mains €20-47, menu €47 (lunch only) & €89; ⏰ lunch & dinner to 11pm Mon-Fri; Ⓜ Franklin D Roosevelt

Diners at this Ducasse/Starck-inspired, recently renovated venue are invited to mix and match their own main courses and sauces – pan-seared red mullet, say, with a choice of barbecue, lemon or sesame sauces or duckling with peppers, lemon-parsley butter or crushed olives. It has an excellent selection of New World and non-French European wines.

MARKET
Map pp140–1   French €€€

☎ 01 56 43 40 90; 15 av Matignon, 8e; starters €12-27, mains €26-42, menu €34 & €45 (lunch only); ⏰ lunch Mon-Fri, brunch noon-4.30pm Sat & Sun, dinner to 11.30; Ⓜ Franklin D Roosevelt

Jean-Georges Vongerichten's very swish restaurant focuses on fresh market produce delivered with signature eclectic combinations and Asian leanings. While it's less formal than his accolade-adorned restaurants in the US and China, it's still a refined experience with lunch attracting a business crowd and dinner a somewhat sexier proposition. It's a place for everyone; breakfast is served from 8am to 11am during the week.

BISTROT DU SOMMELIER
Map pp140–1   French €€€

☎ 01 42 65 24 85; www.bistrotdusommelier.com; 97 blvd Haussmann, 8e; starters €14-25, mains €22-32, lunch menus €32 & €39, with wine €42 & €54; ⏰ lunch & dinner to 10.30pm Mon-Fri; Ⓜ St-Augustin

This is the place to choose if you are as serious about wine as you are about food. The whole point of this attractive eatery is to match wine with food, and owner Philippe Faure-Brac, one of the world's foremost sommeliers (see p279), is at hand to help. The best way to sample his wine-food pairings is on Friday, when a three-course tasting lunch with wine is €45 and a five-course dinner with wine is €70e. The food, prepared by chef Jean-André Lallican, is hearty bistro fare and, surprisingly, not all the wines are French.

top picks

LATE-NIGHT BITES

- Chez Papa (p267)
- Julien (p266)
- Le Clown Bar (p244)
- Le Grand Colbert (p233)
- Le Vaudeville (p232)
- Terminus Nord (p266)
- Le Petit Zinc (p254)
- Les Pipos (p253)
- Brasserie Lipp (p256)
- La Coupole (p258)

GRAINDORGE Map pp140–1   Belgian €€€

☎ 01 47 54 00 28; 15 rue de l'Arc de Triomphe, 17e; starters €12-16, mains €22-30, menu €34; ☽ lunch Mon-Fri, dinner to 11pm Mon-Sat; Ⓜ Charles de Gaulle-Étoile

The name of this stylish restaurant, with its soft lighting, burgundy chairs and banquettes and Art Deco touches, means 'barleycorn' – it alludes to the great breweries of Flanders (check out the list of beers on offer). The signature dish is *potjevleesch* (€12), four kinds of meat cooked slowly together and served in aspic, though you'll find plenty of other dishes that hint at the Low Countries, including *waterzooi de homard* (lobster poached with shredded vegetables and served in a creamy broth) and *bintje farcie de morue en brandade* (potatoes stuffed with cod purée).

BŒUF SUR LE TOIT

Map pp140–1   French €€€

☎ 01 53 93 65 55; www.boeufsurletoit.com; 34 rue du Colisée, 8e; mains €19.90 & €29.90; ☽ lunch & dinner to 1am daily; Ⓜ St-Philippe du Roule or Franklin D. Roosevelt

Part of the Flo stable of restaurants, the 'Ox on the Roof' is yet another museum-quality brasserie that allows you so easily to recall the Paris of the 1920s and 30s. Oysters and other seafood dishes are paramount here, but it's best to stick with the set menus, which offer *bon rapport qualité prix* (value for money).

KOK PING Map pp140–1   Thai, Chinese €€

☎ 01 42 25 28 85; www.kokping.com, in French; 4 rue Balzac, 8e; starters €9-12, mains €15-23;

menus €22 (lunch only) & €35; ☽ lunch Sun-Fri, dinner to 11.30 daily; Ⓜ George V

A very upscale Asian restaurant in a posh part of town, Kok Ping serves classic and very refined Chinese and Thai food to a predominantly business crowd at lunch. But come evening, the place lets its hair down, turning far less formal and becoming almost cosy. There's a lot of choices for vegetarians with almost 10 meatless mains on offer.

DRAGONS ÉLYSÉES

Map pp140–1   Chinese, Thai €€

☎ 01 42 89 85 10; 11 rue de Berri, 8e; starters €8-12, mains €15-22; menus €13.50 (lunch only) & €40; ☽ lunch & dinner to 11.30pm daily; Ⓜ George V

This mostly Chinese restaurant is a novelty. Below the tables and chairs perched on different levels and scattered about a large dining room is a glass floor beneath which various types of goldfish cavort. If you enjoy watching your dinner in action, than this is the place for you.

L'ÉTOILE VERTE Map pp140–1   French €€

☎ 01 43 80 69 34; www.etoile-verte.fr, in French; 13 rue Brey, 17e; starters €9-13, mains €13-22, menu €14 (lunch only), dinner €18 & €25 (with wine); ☽ lunch Mon-Fri, dinner to 11pm daily; Ⓜ Charles de Gaulle-Étoile

Founded in 1951, the 'Green Star' is where all the old French classics remain: the onion soup, the snails, the rabbit. When one of us was a student in Paris (back when the glaziers were still installing the stained glass at Ste-Chapelle) this was the place for both Esperanto speakers (a green star is their symbol) and students on a splurge. That may have changed, but the lunch *menu* is still a great deal for this neighbourhood.

BUGSY'S Map pp140–1   American €€

☎ 01 42 68 18 44; 15 rue Montlivet, 8e; salads €12-13.50, mains €11-18.50; ☽ lunch & dinner to 11pm daily; Ⓜ Madeleine

This immensely popular place – it's heaving at lunchtime, especially with expats – is done up to resemble a Prohibition-era Chicago speakeasy from the 1920s. Food is the please-everyone easy option: Tex-Mex, salads, ploughman's lunches, burgers (€12 to €13.50) and the intriguing *entrecôte irlandaise* (Irish rib steak). The huge bar keeps going till 1am daily.

SELF-CATERING

Rue Poncelet and rue Bayen have some excellent food shops, including the incomparable Fromagerie Alléosse (p214). The huge Monoprix (Map pp140–1; 62 av des Champs-Élysées, 8e; 9am-midnight Mon-Sat; M Franklin D Roosevelt) at the corner of rue la Boétie has a big supermarket section in the basement, and there's a Franprix (Map pp140–1; 12 rue de Surène, 8e; 8.30am-8pm Mon-Sat; M Madeleine) near place de la Madeleine.

CLICHY & GARE ST-LAZARE

Unlike their neighbour to the west, these areas are not gentrified in the least. Indeed, heading east in the 8e arrondissement, by the time you reach Gare St-Lazare, the shops and architecture have changed and another journey has begun. Around place de Clichy and the eponymous avenue leading north and south from it, a maze of small streets with a pronounced working-class character stretches out, a pocket of old Paris that has survived. These are happy hunting grounds for ethnic eateries and restaurants with character.

CHARLOT, ROI DES COQUILLAGES
Map pp144–5   French, Seafood €€€
☎ 01 53 20 48 00; www.charlot-paris.com, in French; 12 place de Clichy, 9e; starters €10.50-29, mains €19.50-39, menus €20 & €26 (lunch only); lunch & dinner to midnight Sun-Wed, to 1am Thu-Sat; M Place de Clichy
'Charlot, the King of Shellfish' is an Art Deco palace that some Parisians think is the best place in town for no-nonsense seafood. The seafood platters and oysters are why everyone is here, but don't ignore the wonderful fish soup and mains, such as grilled sardines, sole meunière and bouillabaisse (€38).

BISTRO DES DAMES
Map pp144–5   French €€
☎ 01 45 22 13 42; 18 rue des Dames, 17e; starters €6.50-14, mains €13-22; lunch & dinner to 11.30pm; M Place de Clichy
This charming little bistro will appeal to lovers of simple, authentic cuisine, such as hearty salads, tortillas and glorious charcuterie platters of pâté de campagne and paper-thin Serrano ham. The dining room,

which looks out onto the street, is lovely, but during those humid Parisian summers it's the cool and tranquillity of the small back garden that pulls in the punters.

LA GAIETÉ COSAQUE
Map pp144–5   Russian €€
☎ 01 44 70 06 07; 6 rue Truffaut, 17e; starters €1.90-19.50, mains €16-20.50, menus €9.50 & €11 (lunch only), €23 & €27; lunch & dinner to 11.45pm Mon-Sat; M Place de Clichy or Rome
This bistro-like restaurant with the oxymoronic name (Cossack Cheerfulness indeed!) is the place for zakouski (Russian hors d'oeuvres), typically drunk with ice-cold vodka. Among the stand-outs are salades de choux blancs aux baies roses (a coleslaw-like salad with bay leaves), the various herring dishes and aubergine 'caviar'. Hearty mains include chachlyik (lamb kebab; €19) and koulbiaka (pie filled with fish, rice, veg and boiled eggs; €20.50).

À LA GRANDE BLEUE
Map pp144–5   North African, Berber €€
☎ 01 42 28 04 26; 4 rue Lantiez, 17e; starters €4.50-7.50, mains €10-18.50, menu €10.90 (lunch only); lunch Mon-Fri, dinner to 10.30pm Mon-Sat; M Brochant or Guy Moquet
You'll find unusual barley couscous (€11.80 to €18.50) prepared in the style of the Berbers (Kabyles) of eastern Algeria, as well as the usual semolina variety (€10 to €17.50), tajines (€13 to €23) and savoury-sweet pastilla au poulet (chicken pastilla; €18.50). The rare crêpes berbères (Berber crepes; €8.50 to €11.50) require a minimum of four people. We love the blue and yellow décor, the art on the walls and warm welcome.

LA TÊTE DE GOINFRE
Map pp144–5   French, Café €€
☎ 01 42 29 89 80; 16 rue Jacquemont, 18e; starters €4-7.50, mains €13-17; lunch & dinner to 10.30pm Mon-Sat; M La Fourche
This funny place, whose name translates as 'Glutton Head', has a piggy theme, and cute little figurines pepper the joint. As for the joints and other comestibles on the plate, it's (mostly) pork – from the charcuterie to munch on while you wait for a table to the l'os à moëlle (marrow bone) and confit de porc (pork confit). It's a lively place, always packed and an evening to experience. Just go with a carnivore.

AU BON COIN Map pp144–5 French, Café €€

☎ 01 58 60 28 72; 52 rue Lemercier, 17e; starters €6-9.50, mains €11-17; ☽ lunch Mon-Fri, dinner to 11.30pm Tue-Fri; Ⓜ La Fourche
There's nothing particularly spectacular about this café up from place de Clichy that moonlights as a restaurant four nights a week. In fact, it's crowded and rather noisy. But if you are looking for solid café food and a quintessential Parisian eating experience, look no further than 'At the Right Corner'.

JOY IN FOOD Map pp144–5 Vegetarian €€

☎ 01 43 87 96 79; 2 rue Truffaut, 17e; starters €5, mains €10, menus €13 & €16; ☽ lunch Mon-Fri; Ⓜ Place de Clichy
This cosy little place just northwest of the place de Clichy serves homemade vegetarian dishes including omelettes and savoury tarte. The plat du jour might be couscous or vegetarian gratin and the huge desserts (apple crumble, chocolate cake) are legendary.

LA MAFFIOSA DI TERMOLI
Map pp144–5 Italian, Pizzeria €

☎ 01 55 30 01 83; 19 rue des Dames, 17e; pizzas & pasta €7.50-9.90; ☽ lunch Mon-Sat, dinner to 11pm; Ⓜ Place de Clichy
This place has more than 40 pizzas that are too good to ignore, as well as decent garlic bread with or without Parma ham. It does a thriving takeaway business, too.

SELF-CATERING
Marché Batignolles-Clichy (p231) is excellent for *produits biologiques* (organic food products).

OPÉRA & GRANDS BOULEVARDS
The neon-lit blvd Montmartre and nearby sections of rue du Faubourg Montmartre (neither of which are anywhere near the neighbourhood of Montmartre in the 18e, by the way) form one of the Right Bank's most animated café and dining districts. This area also has a couple of French restaurants that could almost be declared national monuments. A short distance to the north there's a large selection of Jewish and North African kosher restaurants along rue Richer, rue Cadet and rue Geoffroy Marie, 9e, south of metro Cadet.

top picks

DINING ROOMS WITH A VIEW
- Les Ombres (p260)
- Café de l'Homme (p260)
- Georges (p232)
- Café Beaubourg (p235)
- Café Marly (p233)
- Le Grand Véfour (p232)
- Ma Bourgogne (p239)
- L'Esplanade (p259)

JEAN Map pp148–9 French €€€

☎ 01 48 78 62 73; www.restaurantjean.fr; 8 rue St-Lazare, 9e; starters €16-21, mains €36-41, menu €37 (lunch only); ☽ lunch Mon-Fri, dinner to 10.30pm Mon-Sat; Ⓜ Notre Dame de Lorette
This stylish gourmet restaurant manages to balance just the right amounts of sophistication and genuine warmth. Dark-red banquette seats liven up the large, quiet dining room. A sample meal might include *fricassée de langoustines* (scampi) served with a julienne of vegetables, *magret de canard rôti au miel et ses navets et échalotes confites* (honey-roasted fillet of duck breast served with preserved turnips and shallots) and a modern version of profiteroles – a scoop of vanilla ice cream between two crunchy, chocolate-coated meringues. There are multicourse tasting menus available at €60 and €75.

CASA OLYMPE Map pp148–9 French €€€

☎ 01 42 85 26 01; 48 rue St-Georges, 9e; menus €31 (lunch only) & €40; ☽ lunch & dinner to 11pm Mon-Fri; Ⓜ St-Georges
This very smart (if somewhat sombre) restaurant run by Dominique Versini, the first female chef in France to be awarded a Michelin star, serves excellent and rather inventive dishes served in surprisingly ample sizes. We loved our pot of warming winter vegetables with bacon followed by a veal chop cooked with bay leaf and *pleurotte* mushrooms. The artwork on the walls was done by the chef-owner's mother.

LA BOULE ROUGE
Map pp148–9 Jewish, Kosher €€€

☎ 01 47 70 43 90; 1 rue de la Boule Rouge, 9e; starters €6-17.50, mains €16-28.50; menu €25

& €35; ⏲ lunch & dinner to midnight Mon-Sat;
Ⓜ Cadet or Grands Boulevards
Though this Tunisian stalwart has been *in situ* for three decades, 'The Red Ball' has been getting a lot of press – good, bad or otherwise – only since Monsieur Sarkozy was spotted dining here. It's a lovely space, with a wonderful caravan mural on the ceiling and photos of politicians and celebs on the walls. Some of the couscous dishes served here – mince with okra, spinach, spicy chicken with corn – are unusual and the three-course *menu* includes an excellent array of *kemia* (vegetarian meze) plus a drink.

LES AILES Map pp148–9 Jewish, Kosher €€€
☎ 01 47 70 62 53; www.lesailes.fr, in French; 34 rue Richer, 9e; starters €10-18.50, mains €17-26; ⏲ lunch & dinner to 11.30pm daily; Ⓜ Cadet
With a delicatessen and bakery attached, 'Wings' is a kosher North African (Sephardic) place that has superb couscous with meat or fish (€17 to €22) and grills as well as light meals of salad and pasta (€11 to €23). Don't even consider a starter; you'll be inundated with little plates of salad, olives etc before you can say *shalom*. Sabbath meals (pre-ordered and prepaid) are also available.

WALLY LE SAHARIEN
Map pp148–9 North African €€€
☎ 01 42 85 51 90; 36 rue Rodier, 9e; starters €6.50-8.50, mains €17.50-23.50, menus €15 & €19 (lunch only), €39; ⏲ lunch & dinner to 10.30pm Tue-Sat; Ⓜ St-Georges or Cadet
This is several cuts above most Maghreb restaurants in Paris, offering couscous in its pure Saharan form – without stock or vegetables, just a finely cooked grain served with a delicious sauce – and excellent *tajines*. It's somewhat pricey for North African but you won't walk away hungry.

LE ROI DU POT AU FEU
Map pp148–9 French €€
☎ 01 47 42 37 10; 34 rue Vignon, 9e; starters €5-7, mains €17-20, menus €24 & €29; ⏲ noon-10.30pm Mon-Sat; Ⓜ Havre Caumartin
The typical Parisian bistro atmosphere, '30s décor and checked tablecloths all add to the charm of 'The King of Hotpots', and we always go back when we're in Paris. What you really want to come here for is a genuine pot-au-feu, a stockpot of beef, aromatic root vegetables and herbs stewed together, with the stock served as an entree and the meat and vegetables as the main course. Other offerings – the chef's terrine, leeks *à la vinaigrette*, *hachis Parmentier* (chopped beef with potatoes), crème caramel, *tarte Tatin* or chocolate mousse, and the complimentary *cornichons* at the start – are equally traditional fare but less noteworthy. You drink from an open bottle of wine and pay for what you've consumed. No reservations accepted.

AU GÉNÉRAL LA FAYETTE
Map pp148–9 French, Brasserie €€
☎ 01 47 70 59 08; 52 rue La Fayette, 9e; starters €5.20-9.50, mains €16-20; ⏲ 10am-4am daily; Ⓜ Le Peletier
With its all-day menu, archetypal *belle époque* décor and special beers on offer, this is an excellent stop if you're hungry outside normal restaurant hours. Stick to the classics, though, like the hearty onion soup (€6.50) and crisp *confit de canard* (preserved duck leg cooked very slowly in its own fat; €16) with tasty potatoes, and you can't go wrong. For something lighter go for one of the generous *grandes salades* (€4.50 to €13.50).

LE Y Map pp148–9 Greek €€
☎ 01 42 68 08 51; 24 rue Godot de Mauroy, 9e; menu €13.50 (lunch only) & €16; ⏲ lunch Mon-Sat, dinner to midnight Tue-Sat; Ⓜ Havre Caumartin
Don't expect very much from the Y (pronounced 'ee grec' in French) except traditional, family-style Greek cooking and a warm welcome. The lunch *menu* is available until 8pm. The mezzanine area is a pleasant place to sit and there are occasional art and photographic exhibits here.

NOUVEAU PARIS-DAKAR
Map pp148–9 African, Senegalese €€
☎ 01 42 46 12 30; 11 rue de Montyon, 9e; starters €6.90, mains €12.50-16, menus €9.90 (lunch only), €24 & €32; ⏲ lunch Mon-Thu, Sat & Sun, dinner to 1am daily; Ⓜ Grands Boulevards
This is a little bit of Senegal in Paris, with Mamadou still reigning as the 'King of Dakar' despite the new location. Specialities here include *yassa* (chicken or fish marinated in lime juice and onion sauce; €12.50) and *mafé Cap Vert* (lamb in peanut sauce; €12.50). There's live African music most nights.

CHEZ HAYNES
Map pp148–9   American, Southern €€

☎ 01 48 78 40 63; 3 rue Clauzel, 9e; starters €7, mains €8-16; ☽ dinner to midnight Tue-Sat; Ⓜ St-Georges

A legendary, funky hang-out set up by an African American ex-GI in 1947, Haynes dishes up such soul food as shrimp gumbo, fried chicken, barbecued ribs and cornbread. There's usually a crowd for the blues, dance and performance art sessions on Fridays and Saturdays from 8.30pm or 9pm (€5) and jamming from 11pm to midnight.

CHARTIER Map pp148–9   French, Bistro €€

☎ 01 47 70 86 29; www.restaurant-chartier .com; 7 rue du Faubourg Montmartre, 9e; starters €2.20-12.40, mains €6.50-16, menu with wine €20; ☽ lunch & dinner to 10pm daily; Ⓜ Grands Boulevards

Chartier, which started life as a *bouillon,* or soup kitchen, in 1896, is a real gem that is justifiably famous for its 330-seat *belle époque* dining room. With a 50cL *pitchet* (pitcher) of wine for €3.60, you should spend no more than €15/20 for two/three courses per person. The menu changes (well, alters) daily, but don't expect gourmet. Reservations are not accepted so count on joining a queue at busy times. Single diners will have to share a table.

KASTOORI Map pp148–9   Indian, Pakistani €€

☎ 01 44 53 06 10; 4 place Gustave Toudouze, 9e; starters €3-6, mains €9-12; menus €8 (lunch only), €10 & €15; ☽ lunch & dinner to 11.30pm; Ⓜ St-Georges

This eatery just a stone's throw from place Pigalle is a delight in summer, with its large

top picks

BUDGET FRENCH

- Au Trou Normand (p246)
- Chartier (above)
- Le Chaland (p268)
- Le Trumilou (p241)
- L'Encrier (p273)
- Robert et Louise (p244)
- Chez Gladines (p275)
- Bar à Soupe et Quenelles Giarudet (p257)

terrace looking onto a quiet, leafy square. The excellent value set *menus* include three generous courses; if you just want one dish go for the excellent vegetable biryani.

SELF-CATERING

Conveniently located is the Franprix Rodier (Map pp148–9; 52 rue Rodier, 9e; ☽ 9am-9pm Mon-Sat; Ⓜ St-Georges or Cadet), south of square d'Anvers. Both av de l'Opéra and rue de Richelieu have several supermarkets, including a large one in Monoprix (Map pp82–3; 21 av de l'Opéra, 2e; ☽ 9am-10pm Mon-Fri, to 9pm Sat; Ⓜ Pyramides).

GARE DU NORD, GARE DE L'EST & RÉPUBLIQUE

These areas offer all types of food but most notably Indian and Pakistani, which can be elusive in Paris. There's a cluster of brasseries and bistros around the Gare du Nord. They're decent options for a first (or final) meal in the City of Light.

JULIEN Map pp152–3   French, Brasserie €€€

☎ 01 47 70 12 06; www.julienparis.com; 16 rue du Faubourg St-Denis, 10e; starters €6.90-17, mains €16.70-39, menus €21.50 & €28.50 (lunch only), €21.90-31.50; ☽ lunch & dinner to 1am daily; Ⓜ Strasbourg St-Denis

Located in the less-than-salubrious neighbourhood of St-Denis, Julien offers food that you wouldn't cross town for. But – *mon Dieu!* – the décor and the atmosphere: it's an Art Nouveau extravaganza perpetually in motion and a real step back in time. Service is always excellent here, and you'll feel welcome at any time of day.

TERMINUS NORD
Map pp152–3   French, Brasserie €€€

☎ 01 42 85 05 15; www.terminusnord.com; 23 rue de Dunkerque, 10e; starters €7.80-19, mains €14.50-38.50, menus €24.50 & €31.50; ☽ 8am-1am daily; Ⓜ Gare du Nord

'The North Terminus' is a brasserie with a copper bar, waiters in white uniforms, brass fixtures and mirrored walls that look as they did when it opened in 1925. Breakfast (from €8) is available from 8am to 11am, and full meals are served continuously from 11am to 1am. It's a museum-quality time piece and an excellent place for a final meal before returning to London.

LA PAELLA Map pp152–3   Spanish €€€
☎ 01 46 07 28 89; www.restaurantlapaella.com, in French; 50 rue des Vinaigriers, 11e; starters €6.10-12, mains €15-28, menus €12.50 (lunch only) & €27; ☻ lunch & dinner to 11pm daily; Ⓜ Jacques Bonsergent
This homely place, which almost feels like a buzzy café (especially on weekend nights), specialises in Spain's most famous culinary export – though it does a mean *zarzuela de pescado* (Spanish 'bouillabaisse'; €25) as well. The paella is cooked to order so count on at least a 30-minute wait and don't overdo the tapas.

CHEZ PAPA Map pp152–3   French, Southwest €€€
☎ 01 42 09 53 87; www.chezpapa.fr, in French; 206 rue La Fayette, 10e; starters & salads €8.20-14.10, mains €14.10-27.20, menus €15.35 & €19.95; ☻ 11am-1am daily; Ⓜ Louis Blanc
Chez Papa serves all sorts of specialities of the southwest, including cassoulet (€17.80), *pipérade* (€15.35) and *garbure* (€18.55), but most diners are here for the famous *salade Boyarde*, an enormous bowl filled with lettuce, tomato, sautéed potatoes, two types of cheese and ham – all for the princely sum of €8.20 (or €9.10 if you want two fried eggs thrown in). There's a Grands Boulevards branch (Map pp82–3; ☎ 01 40 13 07 31; 153 rue Montmartre, 2e; Ⓜ Grands Boulevards) and a 8e branch (Map pp140–1) ☎ 01 42 65 43 68; rue de l'Arcade, 8e; Ⓜ Havre Caumartin), which open noon to midnight Sunday to Thursday and till 1am at the weekend.

DA MIMMO Map pp152–3   Italian €€€
☎ 01 42 06 44 47; 39 blvd de Magenta, 10e; starters €7-22, mains €19-26; ☻ lunch & dinner to 11.30pm Tue-Sat; Ⓜ Jacques Bonsergent
Neither the less-than-salubrious neighbourhood nor the relatively high prices are enough to keep fans away from this delightful *trattoria* with its authentic Neapolitan cuisine. Naples is, of course, the birthplace of pizza (€11.50 to €20); try one with rocket and forget about pizzas of the past.

AUX DEUX CANARDS
Map pp152–3   French €€€
☎ 01 47 70 03 23; www.lesdeuxcanards.com, in French; 8 rue du Faubourg Poissonnière, 10e; start-

ers €5-14.50, mains €16-25, menu €20 (lunch only); ☻ lunch Tue-Fri, dinner to 10.15pm Mon-Sat; Ⓜ Bonne Nouvelle
The tradition at this long-established inn-like place is that you ring first (is this a speakeasy or what?) before you are allowed entry. The name of the restaurant – 'At the Two Ducks' – reflects much of the menu (there's everything from foie gras to *à l'orange*), but you'll find starters as diverse as mussels with leek and a salad of Jerusalem artichoke and sheep's cheese. The host is a true, err, ham and performs to an appreciative, mostly English-speaking audience.

HÔTEL DU NORD Map pp152–3   French €€
☎ 01 40 40 78 78; www.hoteldunord.org; 102 quai de Jenmapes, 10e; starters €7-14.50, mains €15-22; menu €13.50 (lunch only); ☻ lunch & dinner to midnight; Ⓜ Jacques Bonsergent
The setting for the eponymous 1938 film starring Louis Jouvet and Arletty, the dining room and bar at this vintage venue by the Canal St-Martin feel as if they were stuck in a time warp with their Art Deco posters, zinc counter and old piano. The food is *correct* if not mind-blowing; stick with basics like the jumbo hamburger (€16) and its trimmings and you'll be fine. The *plat du jour* is usually €10.

LE SPORTING Map pp152–3   International €€
☎ 01 46 07 02 00; www.lesporting.com; 3 rue des Récollets, 10e; starters €7-14, mains €14-20, menus €9.90 & €14 (lunch only) €24 & €32; ☻ lunch & dinner to 11.30pm daily; Ⓜ Gare de l'Est
This is one of the more sophisticated café-restaurants along the Canal St-Martin and the minimalist décor – all browns and ash greys and bare wooden floors – suggests an up-to-the-moment bar or club in London. Brunch on Sunday (noon to 4pm) is when Le Sporting is at its busiest.

LA MARINE Map pp152–3   French €€
☎ 01 42 39 69 81; 55bis quai de Valmy, 10e; starters €7-20, mains €14-17.50, menu weekday/weekend lunch €13/16; ☻ lunch & dinner to 11.30pm daily; Ⓜ République
This large, airy bistro overlooking Canal St-Martin is a favourite, especially in the warmer months, among *les branchés du quartier* (neighbourhood trendies), who nibble on dishes like *millefeuille de rouget à la vinaigrette* (mullet in layered pastry with

vinaigrette) and *brick de poisson à la crème océane* (fish fritter with seafood sauce).

LE CHANSONNIER Map pp152–3   French €€

☎ 01 42 09 40 58; www.lechansonnier.com, in French; 14 rue Eugène Varlin, 10e; starters €8.20, mains €17, menus €11.50 (lunch only) & €24; ⏰ lunch Mon-Fri, dinner to 11pm Mon-Sat; Ⓜ Château Landon or Louis Blanc

Now under new management, 'The Singer' (named after the 19th-century Lyonnais socialist singer-songwriter Pierre Dupont) doesn't quite offer the same value for money that it once did but it could still be a film set, with its curved zinc bar and Art Nouveau mouldings. The food remains very substantial; try the *noix St-Jacques provençal* (scallops in herbed tomato sauce), bouillabaisse or *daube de sanglier* (boar stew) as a main course.

LE COIN DE VERRE Map pp152–3   French €€

☎ 01 42 45 31 82; 38 rue de Sambre et Meuse, 10e; dishes €10-15; ⏰ dinner to midnight Mon-Sat; Ⓜ Belleville or Colonel Fabien

This bistro, where you must ring to gain entry, is full of retro character with its dark yellow walls, old posters and fireplace. The speciality here is charcuterie, cheese and, of course, wine; try the generous *assiette de cochonnailles* (pork platter; €10.50) and, if you can manage it, the *clafoutis maison* (€4), which is fruit covered with a thick batter and baked until puffy.

ISTANBUL Map pp152–3   Turkish €€

☎ 01 48 00 98 10; 66 rue du Faubourg St-Denis, 10e; starters €4-8.50, mains €11-15; ⏰ lunch & dinner to 11pm Sun-Thu, to 11.30 Fri & Sat; Ⓜ Château d'Eau

Our new favourite Turkish restaurant in the heart of Turkey Town serves all our favourites – Iskender kebab (lamb slices served with pide bread and yogurt), *imam bayildi* ('the imam fainted'; an eggplant dish) – and the combination meze platter (€8.50) is a meal in itself. What friendly and generous staff: the baklava, fruit slices and mint tea kept coming after we had settled the bill!

LE RÉVEIL DU XE Map pp152–3   French €€

☎ 01 42 41 77 59; 35 rue du Château d'Eau, 10e; starters €4.20-9.80, mains €9.90-15; ⏰ lunch Mon-Sat, dinner to 11pm Mon-Fri; Ⓜ Chateau d'Eau

'The Awakening of the 10th Arrondissement', taking its name from a left-wing

newspaper of the late 19th century, is an authentic and historic wine bistro, where hearty and flavoursome family cooking is served in a friendly atmosphere. Try the Périgord-style chicken with truffles or the *pied de cochon farci* (stuffed pig's trotter).

PASSAGE BRADY
Map pp152–3   Indian, Pakistani €€

46 rue du Faubourg St-Denis & 33 blvd de Strasbourg, 10e; mains €5-14.50; ⏰ lunch & dinner to 11pm; Ⓜ Château d'Eau

Joining rue du Faubourg St-Denis and blvd de Strasbourg in the 10e, this old-style covered arcade could easily be in Calcutta. Its incredibly cheap Indian, Pakistani and Bangladeshi cafés offer among the best-value lunches in Paris (meat curry, rice and a tiny salad €5 to €9.50, chicken or lamb biryani €10.50 to €14.50, thalis €7 to €9.50). Dinner *menus* are from €12.50 to €24 but it must be said that most of the eateries here offer subcontinental food *à la française*. There are lots of places to choose from, but the pick of the crop are Palais des Rajpout (☎ 01 42 46 23 75; 64-66 passage Brady), Passage de Pondicherry (☎ 01 53 34 63 10; 84 passage Brady) and Pooja (☎ 01 48 24 00 83; 91 passage Brady).

LE CHALAND Map pp152–3   French, Café €€

☎ 01 40 05 18 68; 163 quai de Valmy, 10e; starters €7, mains €13-14, menu lunch €11.50; ⏰ lunch & dinner to 11.30pm Mon-Fri, to 2am Sat & Sun; Ⓜ Louis Blanc

'The Barge' is a pleasant *café du quartier* serving rock-solid favourites like *blanquette de veau* and *tartes salées* (savoury pies) with the occasional leap into the 21st century with gigantic salads. It's one of the more approachable (and affordable) eateries on the canal and you're offered a kir (white wine with cassis) as an apéritif. The *plat du jour* is €9.50

LE VERRE VOLÉ Map pp152–3   French €€

☎ 01 48 03 17 34; 67 rue de Lancry, 10e; starters €5-8.60, mains €11-11.50; ⏰ lunch & dinner to 11pm; Ⓜ Jacques Bonsergent

The tiny 'Stolen Glass' – a wine shop with a few tables – is just about the most perfect wine-bar-cum-restaurant in Paris, with excellent wines from southeastern France (€18 to €54 a bottle) and expert advice. Unpretentious and hearty *plats du jour* are excellent.

MADRAS CAFÉ Map pp152–3   Indian €€

☎ 01 42 05 29 56; 180 rue du Faubourg St-Denis, 10e; starters €2.50-13.50, mains €6-11, menus €6.50 (lunch only), €9.50 & €15; ⊗ lunch & dinner to 11.30pm; Ⓜ Gare du Nord

You wouldn't cross town to eat at this simple restaurant with specialities from both northern and southern India – the one-dish thalis (€7) are good – but if you've just arrived at or are just about to leave from the Gare du Nord and need a curry fix, this café is right around the corner.

LE CAMBODGE Map pp152–3   Cambodian €

☎ 01 44 84 37 70; www.lecambodge.fr, in French; 10 av Richerand, 10e; dishes €5-10; ⊗ lunch & dinner to 11.30pm Mon-Sat; Ⓜ Goncourt

Hidden in a quiet street between the gargantuan Hôpital St-Louis and Canal St-Martin, this favourite spot among students serves enormous rouleaux de printemps (spring rolls; €5) and the ever-popular pique-nique Angkorien ('Angkor picnic' of rice vermicelli and sautéed beef, which you wrap up in lettuce leaves; €10). The food tastes homemade (if not especially authentic) and the vegetarian platters (€7 to €8.50) are especially good.

KRISHNA BHAVAN
Map pp152–3   Indian, Vegetarian €

☎ 01 42 05 78 43; 2 rue Cail, 10e; dishes €1.50-7.50, menu €10.50; ⊗ lunch & dinner to 11pm Tue-Sun; Ⓜ La Chapelle

This is about as authentic an Indian vegetarian canteen as you'll find in an area that is rapidly overtaking Faubourg St-Denis as Paris' Little India. If in doubt as to what to order, ask for a thali (€7.50), a circular steel tray with samosas, dosas and other wrapped goodies. And wash it all down with a yoghurt-based lassi, which comes in five flavours, including mango and rose.

LE MAURICIEN FILAO
Map pp152–3   Mauritian, Creole €

☎ 01 48 24 17 17; 9 passage du Prado, 10e; dishes €6-6.50; ⊗ lunch & dinner to 10pm Mon-Sat; Ⓜ Strasbourg St-Denis

This hole-in-the-wall canteen in passage du Prado, a derelict covered arcade accessible from 12 rue du Faubourg St-Denis and 18–20 blvd St-Denis, serves cheap but tasty Mauritian dishes such as spicy rougaille de poisson (a Creole dish of fish cooked with onions, garlic, ginger, chilli and coriander)

and cari poissons aux lentilles (curried fish with lentils). Only certain dishes from the main menu are available daily, though.

SELF-CATERING

Two covered markets in this area are the Marché aux Enfants Rouges and the more extravagant Marché St-Quentin. For details, see p231.

Rue du Faubourg St-Denis, 10e, which links blvd St-Denis and blvd de Magenta, is one of the cheapest places to buy food, especially fruit and vegetables; the shops at Nos 23, 27–29 and 41–43 are laden with produce. The street has a distinctively Middle Eastern air, and quite a few of the groceries offer Turkish, North African and subcontinental specialities. Many of the food shops, including the fromagerie at No 54, are open Tuesday to Saturday and until noon on Sunday.

Supermarkets convenient to this area include Franprix St-Denis branch (Map pp152–3; 7-9 rue des Petites Écuries,10e; ⊗ 9am-8.20pm Mon-Sat; Ⓜ Château d'Eau) and Franprix Magenta branch (Map pp152–3; 57 blvd de Magenta, 10e; ⊗ 9am-8pm Mon-Sat; Ⓜ Gare de l'Est).

MÉNILMONTANT & BELLEVILLE

In the northern part of the 11e and into the 19e and 20e arrondissements, rue Oberkampf and its extension, rue de Ménilmontant, are popular with diners and denizens of the night, though rue Jean-Pierre Timbaud, running parallel to the north, has been stolen some of their glory in the past decade or so. Rue de Belleville and the streets running off it are dotted with Chinese, Southeast Asian and a few Middle Eastern places; blvd de Belleville has some kosher couscous restaurants, most of which are closed on Saturday.

LAO SIAM Map p155   Thai €€

☎ 01 40 40 09 68; 49 rue de Belleville, 19e; starters €7-10.30, mains €7.50-22; ⊗ lunch & dinner to 11.30pm; Ⓜ Belleville

This Thai-Chinese place, with neon lights and spartan décor, looks like any other Asian restaurant in Belleville. Though we've heard some complaints about its authenticity, Lao Siam must be doing something right because it's always packed. There are more than 120 dishes on the menu – from the classic beef and duck with coconut milk and bamboo to the more unusual *tourteau à la diable* (spicy devilled crab).

EL PALADAR Map p155 — Cuban €€

☎ 01 43 57 42 70; 26bis rue de la Fontaine au Roi, 11e; starters €4-6, mains €14-21, menus €12 & €14 (lunch only); ☽ lunch & dinner to midnight; Ⓜ Goncourt

While the name of this place suggests the restaurants run from private homes in today's cash-strapped Havana, the food and sheer exuberance recalls the Cuba of the 1950s, when everything was plentiful. It's a convivial, graffiti-covered place with super *caipirinhas* (€6) – cocktails made from a sugarcane-based alcohol, lime juice and sugarcane syrup – and such authentic dishes as *pescado guisado* (fried fish), *pollo piopio* (chicken cooked with citrus) and *yuca con mojo* (manioc with onions and garlic).

LE KRUNG THEP Map p155 — Thai €€€

☎ 01 43 66 83 74; 93 rue Julien Lacroix, 20e; starters €8-12, mains €8-20; ☽ lunch Sat & Sun, dinner to 11pm; Ⓜ Pyrénées

Krung Thep, which means 'Bangkok' in Thai, is a small – some might say cramped – and kitsch place with all our favourite dishes (and then some – there are dozens and dozens of dishes on the menu): green curries, *tom kha goong* (spicy soup with prawns; €20) and fish steamed in banana leaves (€18). The steamed shrimp ravioli and curried crab will hit the spot. There is also a generous number of vegetarian dishes (€8 to €10).

NEW NIOULLAVILLE Map p155 — Chinese €€

☎ 01 40 21 96 18; www.nioullaville.fr, in French; 32 rue de l'Orillon, 11e; starters €4.90-7.50, mains €9.80-19.50, menus €7-14; ☽ lunch & dinner to 1am daily; Ⓜ Belleville or Goncourt

This cavernous, 400-seat place tries to please all of the people all of the time. As a result the food is a bit of a mishmash – dim sum sits next to beef satay, as do scallops with black bean alongside Singapore noodles, though whether they do so comfortably is another matter. Order carefully and you should get some authenticity. Rice and noodle dishes are between €6.10 and €9.90.

LE BARATIN Map p155 — French, Bistro €€

☎ 01 43 49 39 70; 3 rue Jouye-Rouve, 20e; starters €8-10, mains €15-18, menu €14 (lunch only); ☽ lunch Tue-Fri, dinner to midnight Tue-Sat; Ⓜ Pyrénées or Belleville

Baratin (chatter) rhymes with *bar à vin* (wine bar) in French and this animated place just a step away from the lively Belleville quarter does both awfully well. In addition it offers some of the best (and very affordable) French food in the 20e on its ever-changing blackboard. The wine selection (by the glass or carafe) is excellent; most are between €21 and €30 a bottle.

REUAN THAI Map p155 — Thai €€

☎ 01 43 55 15 82; 36 rue de l'Orillon, 11e; starters €5-13, mains €8-18, menu €8 (lunch only); ☽ lunch & dinner to 10.30pm daily; Ⓜ Belleville

This fragrant place offers some of the most authentic Thai food in Paris and has all your favourite Thai dishes, including soups. About a half-dozen of the choices are vegetarian. Décor is on the kitsch side, but we weren't here for the figurines and the bolsters piled up almost to the ceiling.

BISTRO FLORENTIN Map p155 — Italian €€

☎ 01 43 55 57 00; 40 rue Jean-Pierre Timbaud, 11e; starters €8.50-15, mains €14-17, menu €13 (lunch only); ☽ lunch Mon-Fri, dinner to 11pm Mon-Sat; Ⓜ Parmentier

Expect excellent Italian fare amidst cosy surroundings: grilled, finely seasoned aubergine for starters, tiramisu as light as a feather for dessert and, between those two courses, a wide choice of mains and pastas (€12 to €17). The *penne à la crème d'artichauts* (penne with cream and artichokes; €13) is superb as is the *ravioli à la ricotta et aux épinards, sauce aux champignons* (spinach and cheese ravioli with a mushroom sauce). Pizzas are €8 to €13.

top picks

VEGETARIAN RESTAURANTS

- Au Grain de Folie (p281)
- Grand Appétit (p247)
- Joy in Food (p264)
- Krishna Bhavan (p269)
- La Victoire Auprême du Cœur (p245)
- Saveurs Végét'halles (p236)
- Boldère (p281)

ASIANWOK Map pp94–5   Asian €€

☎ 01 43 57 63 24; 63 rue Oberkampf, 11e; dishes €13.80-15.20, menu €18.50; ☼ lunch & dinner to 10pm Mon-Sat; Ⓜ Parmentier

We can't get enough of the wonderful stir-fries, big salads and ample platters served at this pan-Asian eatery that has opened recently in an vintage bar-café along trendy rue Oberkampf. The welcome from the young Asian staff is always warm and the two-course *formule* (available any time) a snip at €18.50.

L'AVE MARIA Map pp94–5   Fusion €€

☎ 01 47 00 61 73; 1 rue Jacquard, 11e; dishes €12-15; ☼ dinner to midnight daily; Ⓜ Parmentier

This chic and colourful canteen combines the flavours of the southern hemisphere and creates hearty, hybrid and harmonious dishes. You might be treated to West African *mafé de poulet fermier* (farm chicken simmered in peanut sauce) or the Amazonian fish and chips, which is of no mean size. Tropical fruit, unknown wild grasses, and heavenly vegetation provide a lush garnish and an extra touch of exoticism. The music livens up towards midnight and on to 1 or 2am.

LE POROKHANE Map p155   African, Senegalese €€

☎ 01 40 21 86 74; www.leporokhane.com, in French; 3 rue Moret, 11e; menu €15; ☼ dinner to 2am daily; Ⓜ Ménilmontant or Parmentier

A large dining room in hues of ochre and terracotta, this cheapie is a popular meeting place for Senegalese artists. The clientele has *un peu tendance show-biz*, we're told – and live *kora* (a traditional string instrument) music is not unusual at the weekend. Try the *tiéboudienne*, *yassa* or *mafé*.

TAI YIEN Map p155   Chinese €€

☎ 01 42 41 44 16; 5 rue de Belleville, 19e; starters €3.90-6.40, mains €7.90-11.40; ☼ lunch & dinner to midnight daily; Ⓜ Belleville

This is usually where we eat when we are looking for a fix of rice or noodles, especially late in the evening. It's a Hong Kong–style 'steam restaurant' and the real McCoy: it's hard to imagine better *char siu* (barbecued pork) in this part of Paris.

DONG HUONG Map p155   Vietnamese €

☎ 01 43 38 29 42; 14 rue Louis Bonnet; dishes €5.50-9.50; ☼ lunch & dinner to 10pm Wed-Mon; Ⓜ Belleville

Despite a name that sounds like a Spanish Lothario, this no-frills Vietnamese noodle- shop-cum-restaurant serves up great bowls of *pho* to rooms full of appreciative regulars. The fact that the regulars are all Asian (and mainly Vietnamese) and the food comes out so fast is a testament to its authenticity and freshness.

SELF-CATERING

Supermarkets close to these two areas include Franprix Jean-Pierre Timbaud branch (Map pp94–5; 23 rue Jean-Pierre Timbaud, 11e; ☼ 8.30am-9pm Mon-Sat, 9am-1.30pm Sun; Ⓜ Oberkampf) and Franprix Jules Ferry branch (Map pp94–5; 28 blvd Jules Ferry, 11e; ☼ 8.30am-9pm Tue-Sun; Ⓜ République or Goncourt). Marché Belleville (p231) is one of the most exotic markets in Paris.

GARE DE LYON, NATION & BERCY

The waterfront southwest of Gare de Lyon has got a new lease on life in recent years. The development of the old wine warehouses in Bercy Village (p157) attract winers and diners till the wee hours. There are loads of decent restaurants on the roads fanning out from huge place de la Nation.

L'OULETTE Map pp158–9   French, Southwest €€€

☎ 01 40 02 02 12; www.l-oulette.com; 15 place Lachambeaudie, 12e; starters €16-30, mains €26-39, menus €45, with wine €51; ☼ lunch & dinner to 10.15pm Mon-Fri; Ⓜ Cour St-Émilion

A distant relative of the Bistrot de l'Oulette (p240) near Bastille, this is a lovely (and pricey) restaurant with a terrace overlooking a pretty church in a rather dreary neighbourhood. Owner-chef Marcel Baudis' *menu du saison* (seasonal menu) might include *soupe de poisson à la crème de coquillages au safran* (fish soup with saffron cream) and *la chartreuse de queue de bœuf braisée aux poivrons* (ox tail braised with leeks).

LA GAZZETTA Map pp158–9   French €€€

☎ 01 43 47 47 05; www.lagazzetta.fr; 29 rue de Cotte, 12e; starters €10-17, mains €20-26, menus €14 (lunch only) €34 & €45; ☼ lunch Tue-Sat, dinner to 11pm Mon-Sat; Ⓜ Ledru Rollin

A distant relative of the now defunct (and much missed China Club) this contemporary French bistro is as comfortable producing dishes like scallops with cress and milk-fed lamb confit as it is mini anchovy pizzas. The lunchtime menu is excellent value and the welcome especially warm.

LE SQUARE TROUSSEAU
Map pp158–9   French €€€
☎ 01 43 43 06 00; 1 rue Antoine Vollon, 12e; starters €7-12, mains €19-26, menus €21 & €25 (lunch only); ☾ lunch & dinner to 11.30pm Tue-Sat; Ⓜ Ledru Rollin
This vintage (c 1900) bistro with etched glass, zinc bar and polished wood panelling is comfortable rather than trendy and attracts a jolly, mixed clientele. Most people come to enjoy the lovely terrace overlooking a small park. Next door is the less-formal La Cave du Square (menus €12-20; ☾ lunch & dinner to 11.30pm Tue-Sat), where you can have two- or three-course meals or even pick up that bottle of Touraine you enjoyed so much over lunch next door.

LES AMIS DE MESSINA
Map pp158–9   Italian, Sicilian €€€
☎ 01 43 67 96 01; 204 rue du Faubourg St-Antoine, 12e; starters €8.50-13.90, mains €17.50-24.90; ☾ lunch Mon-Fri, dinner to 11.30pm Mon-Sat; Ⓜ Faidherbe Chaligny
The décor of this wonderful little neighbourhood trattoria is stylish, with clean lines, an open kitchen and the inevitable Italian football pennant. For starters, try the tortino di melanzane (eggplant casserole) or share a mixed antipasto (€19.80). For mains, the escalope farcie aux oignons, jambon et fromage (veal escalope stuffed with onions, ham and cheese) is a huge hit, or go for any of the exquisite Sicilian pastas (€13.50 to €16.50).

L'ÉBAUCHOIR
Map pp158–9   French €€
☎ 01 43 42 49 31; 43-45 rue de Cîteaux, 12e; starters €8-15, mains €17-23; menus €11.50 & €13.50 (lunch only) & €24; ☾ lunch Tue-Sat, dinner to 11pm Mon-Sat; Ⓜ Faidherbe Chaligny
This convivial, one-time workers' eatery attracts a loyal clientele who mix with an 'outside' crowd who have discovered it (and clearly forced up the prices). The usual menu of bistro food is well prepared and dishes such as marinated herrings, crème de lentilles au Beaufort (creamed lentils with Beaufort cheese) and foie de veau au miel (veal liver with honey sauce) keep customers coming back.

SARDEGNA A TAVOLA
Map pp158–9   Italian, Sardinian €€
☎ 01 44 75 03 28; 1 rue de Cotte, 12e; starters & pasta €10-26, mains €16-22; ☾ lunch Tue-Sat, dinner to 11pm Mon-Sat; Ⓜ Ledru Rollin
'Sardinia at the Table' claims it will introduce you to 'les saveurs, les couleurs et les odeurs de la Méditerranée' (the flavours, colours and fragrances of the Mediterranean) and you barely have to walk though the door for the last two. But stick around for the flavours and you won't be disappointed. Try the poêlon (pot) of mixed seafood cooked with parsley, tomatoes and garlic and the distinctly Sardinian spaghetti with bottarga (cured mullet roe) cooked with oil, garlic, parsley and red pepper flakes.

ATHANOR Map pp158–9   Romanian €€
☎ 01 43 43 49 15; 4 rue Crozatier, 12e; starters €8-12, mains €15-21, menu €23; ☾ lunch & dinner to 11.30pm Tue-Sat; Ⓜ Reuilly Diderot
It's not easy to get a fix of Romanian cuisine in Paris, but Athanor can provide. The décor (puppets, red curtains, old carpets) is theatrical in the extreme; grab a vodka and tune in to the baroque music. Try the grilled blinis with tarama (fish-roe dip) and herrings in cream. Seasoned soup of freshwater river fish (€12) is the speciality of the house, though you mustn't miss the sarmale (stuffed cabbage or grape leaves), the national dish.

LE VIADUC CAFÉ
Map pp158–9   International, Café €€€
☎ 01 44 74 70 70; 43 av Daumesnil, 12e; starters €7.50-16, mains €14-20, menu €15.50 (lunch only) & €20.50; ☾ 9am-2am; Ⓜ Gare de Lyon
This New York–style café-bar with a terrace in one of the glassed-in arches of the Viaduc des Arts (p157) is an excellent spot to while away the early hours and enjoy brunch (€26), with live jazz from noon to 4pm on Sundays from mid-June to mid-September. Plats du jours are excellent value at €12/15 by day/night.

LE VINÉA CAFÉ Map pp158–9   French, Café €€
☎ 01 44 74 09 09; 26-28 cour St-Émilion, 12e; starters €4.50-14.50, mains €10.90-20, menus €14.50 & €18 (lunch only); ☾ 9am-2am Sun-Thu, to 4am Fri & Sat; Ⓜ Cour St-Émilion
The anchor tenant – or so it would seem – of the cour St-Émilion, this is a delightful wine bar-restaurant with a lovely terrace to the back facing place des Vins de France.

There's live music some nights and a popular brunch (€23) from noon to 4pm on Sunday.

L'ENCRIER Map pp158–9 French, Bistro €€
☎ 01 44 68 08 16; www.enoteca.fr, in French; 55 rue Traversière, 12e; starters €5.50-11, mains €10-19, menus €14 (lunch only) & €19-33; ✆ lunch Mon-Fri, dinner to 11pm Mon-Sat; Ⓜ Ledru Rollin or Gare de Lyon
Always heaving but especially at lunch, 'The Inkwell' attracts punters with its classic salmon *assiette de foie gras* and less-common dishes like *cervelle des canuts* (a herbed cheese from Lyons). To follow, try the *bar entier grillé* (whole grilled bass) or delicate *joues de cochon aux épices* (pig's cheeks with spices). A variety of set *menus*, an open kitchen, exposed beams and a large picture window make this a winner.

SWANN ET VINCENT Map pp158–9 Italian €€
☎ 01 43 43 49 40; 7 rue St-Nicolas, 12e; starters €6.50-12, mains €13-18, menu €15.90 (lunch only); ✆ lunch & dinner to 11.45pm; Ⓜ Ledru Rollin
If you're visiting this fine restaurant, ask for a table in the front room, which will hopefully be awash with sunlight. Unpretentious French staff can help you select from the huge blackboard, where at least two of the starters, pastas and main dishes change every day. Go slow on the complimentary basket of olive-and-sweet-herb bread, though; you need to leave room for the tiramisu (€6.50). And, if you must know, Swann and Vincent, whose larger-than-life portraits face you through the front window opposite at No 14, are the children of the owner.

KHUN AKORN Map pp158–9 Thai €€
☎ 01 43 56 20 03; 8 av de Taillebourg, 11e; starters €10-14, mains €15-17; ✆ lunch & dinner to 11pm Tue-Sun; Ⓜ Nation
This Thai eatery near place de la Nation is an oasis of sophistication and good taste – in every sense. Among the traditional dishes, the *tom yum,* and the beef and chicken satays with scrumptious peanut sauce are outstanding. More innovative offerings include *fruits de mer grillés sauce barbecue maison* (grilled seafood with barbecue sauce) and the *larmes du tigre* ('tears of the tiger'; grilled fillet of beef marinated in honey and herbs). In fine weather, try the terrace upstairs.

COMME COCHONS Map pp158–9 French €€
☎ 01 43 42 43 36; 135 rue de Charenton, 12e; starters €7-14, mains €14-17, menus €12 & €15 (lunch only); ✆ lunch & dinner to 11pm; Ⓜ Gare de Lyon
You may not be attracted by the name but the excellent traditional dishes and the sunny terrace at 'Like Pigs' will undoubtedly change your mind. This bistro is like a page out of the past – only the contemporary paintings on the wall by local artists will keep you in the present. Among the specialities are potted *pleurotte* mushrooms with foie gras and *l'os a moëlle fleur de sel* (marrow bone with sea salt). There's live jazz on Thursday evening.

AGUA LIMÓN Map pp158–9 Spanish €€
☎ 01 43 44 92 24; 12 rue Théophile Roussel, 12e; tapas €5.50-15; menus €13 (lunch only); ✆ lunch & dinner Tue-Sat; Ⓜ Ledru Rollin
Considered by some to have the best tapas in Paris, 'Lemon Water' is an attractive bar-restaurant within easy walking distance of Bastille. Go for the *boquerones* (whitebait) in vinegar, the octopus Catalan-style and the excellent *patatas bravas*. There's decent selection of Spanish wines, including Riojas.

LA PARTIE DE CAMPAGNE
Map pp158–9 French €€
☎ 01 43 40 44 11; 36 cour St-Émilion, 12e; dishes €10.90-13.50; ✆ 8am-2am daily; Ⓜ Cour St-Émilion
Located in one of the old *chais* (wine warehouses) of Bercy, 'The Country Outing' serves some of the best food in the area. Business people and strollers from the Jardin de Bercy sit cheek by jowl at a large communal table set up at the back of the room, and order from a menu that includes soups, *tartines* and pies. It's also a great place for breakfast, and the inviting terrace is open in the warmer months.

LINA'S Map pp158–9 Sandwich Bar €
☎ 01 43 40 42 42; www.linascafe.fr; 102 rue de Bercy, 12e; soups & salads €4.50-6.10, sandwiches €3.90-6.90 ✆ 8.30am-4.30pm Mon-Sat; Ⓜ Bercy)
This branch of a popular chain of lunch spots across Paris (some 17 outlets so far) has upmarket sandwiches, salads and soups. Other outlets include Opéra branch (Map pp148–9; ☎ 01 42 46 02 06; 30 blvd des Italiens, 9e; Ⓜ Richelieu Drouot) and La Défense (Map p180; ✆ 01 46 92 28 47; parvis de la Défense; Ⓜ La Défense).

SELF-CATERING

West of Parc de Bercy there's a Franprix (Map pp158–9; 3 rue Baron le Roy, 12e; 8.30am-8.30pm Tue-Sun; M Cour St-Émilion) that's open on Sundays.

13E ARRONDISSEMENT & CHINATOWN

With the Simone de Beauvoir footbridge (p161) making Bercy (p157) footsteps away from the 13e, foodies are hot-footing it to Paris' Chinatown in search of authentic Asian food: Av de Choisy, av d'Ivry and rue Baudricourt are the streets to try.

North around the Bibliothèque Nationale de France and MK2 entertainment complex (p313), stretching north along av Pierre Mendès to Gare d'Austerlitz, is the land of opportunity where a new cutting-edge dining or drinking venue seems to open every day. Westwards is Butte aux Cailles, a gritty, real-life 'village' within Paris, likewise chock-a-block with interesting, fun-guaranteed addresses.

To penetrate the absolute heart of this unexpectedly varied neighbourhood, consider an alternative evening of culinary and artistic entertainment at L'Atoll 13 (Map pp162–3; www.atoll13.org, in French; 175ter rue Tolbiac, 13e; M Bibliothèque François Mitterand), an artists' squat symbolic host to concerts, bands, happenings and – each Tuesday evening – an atmospheric *repas de quartier*.

CHEZ JACKY Map pp162–3 French €€€
01 45 83 71 55; www.chezjacky.fr, in French; 109 rue du Dessous des Berges, 13e; starters & mains €20-29, menu €35, with wine €45; lunch & dinner to 10.30pm Mon-Fri; M Bibliothèque
In the shadow of the national library, Chez Jacky is a serious, traditional restaurant with thoughtful service and a nice, old-fashioned provincial atmosphere. The brothers in charge know how to find good regional produce and present it with great panache, even if originality isn't their cardinal virtue.

CHEZ NATHALIE
Map pp162–3 French, Contemporary €€
01 45 80 20 42; 41 rue Vandrezanne, 13e; starters €10-15, mains €15-24; lunch & dinner to 11pm daily; M Corvisart or Place d'Italie
Refreshingly different with summertime tables on car-quiet rue Vandrezanne, this pocket-sized dining spot is a lovely spot to dine *tête à tête*. A transparent Kartell chair and potted bamboos stand outside, and inside black lacquered tables ooze modernity. On the menu, traditional French fuses with world food in the guise of a pressed artichoke heart with foie gras, wild boar with celery puree, squid pan-fried with chilli and so on.

CHEZ PAUL Map pp162–3 French €€
01 45 89 22 11; 22 rue de la Butte aux Cailles, 13e; starters €9.50-12, mains €16-21; lunch & dinner to midnight daily; M Corvisart or Place d'Italie
Paul's pad is a classic in Butte aux Cailles. Soak up the relaxed, chatty feel and indulge in Frencher-than-French dishes cooked to perfection. Despite its name *gras double* (double fat) is not fatty; rather, it's belly pan-fried with garlic and parsley, as the friendly note on the menu thoughtfully explains.

LE TEMPS DES CÉRISES
Map pp162–3 French €€
01 45 89 69 48; 18-20 rue de la Butte aux Cailles, 13e; starters €8-10, mains €10-21, menus lunch/dinner €14.50/22.50; lunch Mon-Fri, dinner to 11.30pm Mon-Fri, to midnight Sat; M Corvisart or Place d'Italie
There's no beating about the bush at 'The Time of Cherries' (ie 'days of wine and roses' to English speakers), an easygoing restaurant run by a workers' cooperative for three decades. Switch off your mobile (lest there be hell to pay) before entering, plonk yourself down at a table and while away several hours munching on faithfully solid fare in a quintessentially Parisian atmosphere. Buy their *coton-bio* T-shirt upon departure.

RESTAURANT BIOART
Map pp162–3 Organic €€
01 45 85 66 88; www.restaurantbioart.fr; 1 quai François Mauriac, 13e; starters €8, mains €18; lunch Mon, lunch & dinner to 11.30pm Tue-Fri, dinner to 11.30pm Sat; M Bibliothèque
Split across two floors, this Seine-side eating space with neon lighting and glass windows is 100% *bio*. Less formal snacks, salads (€10) and bowls of pasta ' n' risotto (€10) make up the ground-floor café menu, while the *risotto au cognac à la crème* is typical of the more formal fare served upstairs. Savouring '*un plaisir naturel*' (a natural pleasure) is the hip but laidback mood here.

L'AVANT GOÛT Map pp162–3   French, Bistro €€

☎ 01 53 80 24 00; www.lavantgout.com, in
French; 26 rue Bobillot, 13e; starters €10, mains
€16.50, menus lunch/dinner €14/31; ☸ lunch &
dinner to 10.45pm Tue-Sat; Ⓜ Place d'Italie
A prototype of the Parisian 'neo-bistro', the
'Foretaste' has chef Christophe Beaufront
serving some of the most inventive modern
cuisine around. The place gets noisy, tables
count little more than a dozen, and service
is stern. But the food is different and divine.
Advance reservations are vital but, should
you not get in, its wine shop, Côte Cellier
(☎ 01 45 81 14 06; 37 rue Bobillot, 13e; ☸ noon-8pm
Tue-Fri, 10.30am-12.30pm & 3.30-8.30pm Sat), opposite, sells dishes to take away.

À LA DOUCEUR ANGEVINE

Map pp162–3   French €€

☎ 01 45 83 32 30; 1 rue Xaintrailles, 13e; starters
€8-10, mains €10-15; ☸ 8.30am-4.30pm Mon-
Wed, 8.30am-4.30pm & 7.45-10.30pm Thu & Fri;
Ⓜ Bibliothèque
A typical bistro de quartier, À la Douceur
Angevine is the place in the 13e to jostle
with locals. Its name, penned in a poem by
16th-century French poet Joachim du Bellay, celebrates the sweetness of gastronomy
and viticulture from Anjou, land of kings,
chateaux and Rabelais, west of Paris in the
Loire Valley. In spring, when a dozen lucky
diners can dine on the terrace outside, it
bumps up its opening hours to three evenings a week. It closes for three weeks in
August.

LA FLEUVE DE CHINE

Map pp162–3   Chinese €€

☎ 01 45 82 06 88; 15 av de Choisy, 13e; starters
€3.50-10, mains €7-15; ☸ lunch & dinner to 11pm
Fri-Wed; Ⓜ Porte de Choisy
Here you'll find the most authentic Cantonese and Hakka food in Paris and, as is typical, both the surroundings and the service
are forgettable. Go for the superb dishes
cooked in clay pots. La Fleuve de Chine can
also be reached through the Tour Bergame
housing estate at 130 blvd Masséna.

LA CHINE MASSÉNA Map pp162–3 Chinese €€

☎ 01 45 83 98 88; 18 av de Choisy, 13e; soups &
starters €4.10-11, mains €6.50-14; ☸ lunch & dinner to 11pm daily; Ⓜ Porte de Choisy
This enormous restaurant specialising in
Cantonese and Chiu Chow cuisine is a real
favourite in Chinatown; to ensure it would

have good joss for the coming year we fed
the dragon lettuce at the last Lunar New
Year celebrations. The dim sum here is
especially good and women still go around
the dining area with trolleys calling out
their wares.

L'AUDIERNES

Map pp162–3   French, Brasserie €€

☎ 01 44 24 86 23; 22 rue Louise Weiss, 13e; starters €4.30-11.50, mains €11.50-12.50, menu €13;
☸ lunch Mon-Sat; Ⓜ Chevaleret
In an annexe of the Department of the
Economy & Finance, this brasserie-bar serves
well-prepared and traditional French dishes
to demanding civil servants. The contemporary décor gives the place a lively feel; the
menu is good (although hardly original),
featuring such dishes as tartare hâché (steak
tartar), faux-filet (beef sirloin) and a range of
main-course salads. There's also a lovely terrace where you can sit on sunny days.

CHEZ GLADINES

Map pp162–3   French, Basque €€

☎ 01 45 80 70 10; 30 rue des Cinq Diamants,
13e; starters €5-10, mains €8.50-11.50; ☸ lunch
& dinner to midnight Sun-Tue, to 1am Wed-Sat;
Ⓜ Corvisart
Enormous 'meal-in-a-metal-bowl' salads
(€6.80-9) and potato platters guaranteed to
reap change from a €10 note is the prime
draw of this down-to-earth Basque bistro in
Buttes aux Cailles. It buzzes with students
and spend-thrift diners under 30, and is
always a hoot. Traditional Basque specialities (€9.50-11) to munch on atop red-
and-checked cloth tables include pipérade
and poulet basque (chicken cooked with
tomatoes, onions, peppers and white wine).
Arrive early to grab a pew.

SMOOTHIE TIME

Map pp162–3   Juice & Salad Bar €

☎ 01 45 83 98 88; www.smoothie-time.com, in
French; 22 av Pierre Mendès France, 13e; salads
€6.40-8.90, bagels €3.50-6.60, menu breakfast
€8.90, lunch €8.50 & 11.50; ☸ 8.30am-7.30pm
Mon-Fri; Ⓜ Gare d'Austerlitz
This pristine space polka-dotted with
trendy lime-green and shocking-pink
furnishings is a look good/feel good type
of hangout. Juices, smoothies, salads and
filled bagels are categorised on the menu
according to their muscle-, energy-, beauty-
or veggie-power. All very trendy.

FIL 'O' FROMAGE Map pp162–3   French, Cheese €

☎ 01 53 79 13 35; www.filofromage.com; 12 rue Neuve Tolbiac, 13e; sandwiches €4.50-7, menus €14.50-15.50; ⏰ 10am-7.30pm Mon-Wed, to 10.30pm Thu-Sat; Ⓜ Bibliothèque

This new *fromagerie* offering lunches and light meals throughout the day six days a week is godsend in an area that is not overly endowed with places to eat, especially budget ones. Everything here involves cheese, including the *assiette froide* (cold plate) of three cheese, three cold meats and salad and the *poêlons* (pots) of warm cheese.

SELF-CATERING

Wines selected by and dishes created by top Parisian chef Christophe Beaufront are sold to take home at L'Avant-Goût Coté Cellier (Map pp162–3; ☎ 01 53 81 14 06; www.lavantgout.com, in French; 37 rue Bobillot, 13e; ⏰ noon-8pm Tue-Fri, 10.30am-1.30pm & 3.30-8.30pm Sat; Ⓜ Place d'Italie). Don't miss his signature dish, *pot au feu au cochon aux épices* (spicy pork stew).

15E ARRONDISSEMENT

With its dearth of food shops and twin-set of quintessential café-cum-bars on seemingly every pair of street corners, this is one arrondissement where you know real Parisians really live. Solidly down to earth and stoically free of any trendy concept dining, the 15e cooks up fabulously simple bistro fare. Rue de la Convention, rue de Vaugirard, rue St-Charles, rue du Commerce and those south of blvd de Grenelle are key streets.

Near the water, two culinary innovators add an element of surprise: Japanese nouvelle-cuisine chef Hisayuki Takeuchi's Saturday-afternoon École du Sushi at Kaiseki Sushi (Map pp166–7; ☎ 01 45 54 48 60; www.kaiseki.com; 7bis rue André Lefevbre, 15e; Ⓜ Javel) is *the* place in Paris to learn how to make sushi; Cyril Lignac, something of a Jamie Oliver with his televised chef-training and school canteen projects, cooks up *cuisine attitude* at Le 15ème (☎ 01 45 54 43 43; www.cyrillig nac.com; 14 rue Cauchy, 15e; menu lunch €40, dinner €105; ⏰ lunch & dinner to 10pm Mon-Fri, dinner Sat; Ⓜ Javel), aptly placed on the ground floor of an apartment block.

KIM ANH Map pp166–7   Vietnamese €€€

☎ 01 45 79 40 96; 49 av Émile Zola, 15e; starters €13-15, mains €22-42, menu €37; ⏰ dinner to 10.30pm daily; Ⓜ Charles Michels

A travel guide hotspot situated across the road from Sawadee, this place is the antithesis of the typically Parisian canteen-style Vietnamese restaurant. Kim Anh greets its customers with tapestries, white tablecloths, fresh flowers and extraordinarily fresh and flavoursome food, all elaborately presented. The *émincé de bœuf à la citronnelle* (beef with lemon grass) is a skilful combination of flavours, but the true sensation is the caramelised langoustine.

L'OS À MOËLLE Map pp166–7   French, Bistro €€€

☎ 01 45 57 27 27; 3 rue Vasco de Gama, 15e; menus lunch €17 & €30, dinner €36; ⏰ lunch & dinner to 11.30pm Tue-Fri, dinner to midnight Sat; Ⓜ Lourmel

Marrowbone chef Thierry Faucher (ex-Hotel Crillon) makes no bones about his outstanding cuisine wholly inspired by 'the market, the season and the humour of the moment'. His six-course sampling menus are among the most affordable in town, embracing delicacies like scallops with coriander, sea bass in cumin butter or half a quail with endives and chestnuts, while his chocolate *quenelle* (dumpling) with saffron cream is award-winning. Should you fail to snag a table, try his wine bar (p298) opposite.

SAWADEE Map pp166–7   Thai €€€

☎ 01 45 77 68 90; 53 av Émile Zola, 15e; menu lunch €14.50, dinner €20, €25, €28 & €32; ⏰ lunch & dinner to 10.30pm Mon-Sat; Ⓜ Charles Michels

For 20 years this well-known restaurant has been bidding *sawadee* (welcome) to Thai-food lovers – and is in most guidebooks to prove it. The décor is rather impersonal, but the sophisticated cuisine more than makes up for it. Twist your tongue around prawn or chicken soup flavoured with lemon grass, spicy beef salad (a real treat), satay sticks (chicken, beef, lamb and pork) with peanut sauce and other classic dishes of Siam.

LE CRISTAL DE SEL Map pp166–7   French €€

☎ 01 42 50 35 29; www.lecristaldesel.fr, in French; 13 rue Mademoiselle, 15e; starters €10-17, mains €16-24; ⏰ lunch & dinner to 10pm Tue-Sat; Ⓜ Commerce

The raved-about stage of young rising chef Karl Lopez, this modern bistro has a distinct kitchen feel with its small brightly-lit white walls, white-painted beams and gaggle of busy chefs behind the bar. The only decorative feature is a candle-lit crystal of rose-tinted salt on each table – a sure sign that food is what The Salt Crystal is all about. Lopez's *tarte à la bergamote fraîche meringuée* (lemon meringue pie) – divine – has to be the zestiest in Paris. Reservations essential.

LE CASIER À VIN
Map pp166–7   French, Bistro €€
☎ 01 45 57 27 27; lecasieravin@noos.fr; 53 rue Olivier de Serres, 15e; starters €7-10.50, mains €13.80-19.50; ⏱ lunch & dinner to 10.30pm Mon-Fri, dinner to 10.30pm Sat; Ⓜ Convention
The bottle-lined walls, ham-cutting machine, wood-slat blinds and tatty mustard façade promise great things. Indeed, this much-loved bistro is a dining staple in most 15e Parisians' daily lives. Titillate your tastebuds with a signature *assiette de dégustation* (tasting platter; €12.50) of *fromage* (cheese) or *charcuterie* (cold cuts), or go for a classic like *pot au feu de canard* (duck stew) or *tartare de bœuf* (steak tartare). After the main course, sweeten your tastebuds with a bowl of *riz au lait à l'ancienne* (old-fashioned rice pudding) and leave in love with the place.

AL WADY
Map pp166–7   Lebanese €€
☎ 01 45 58 57 18; 153 rue de Lourmel, 15e; starters €10, mains €14.50-18, lunch menus €12 & €14.50; ⏱ lunch & dinner to 10.30pm Mon-Fri, dinner to 10.30pm Sat; Ⓜ Lourmel
It's not so much the decor as the incredibly warm welcome complemented by a cuisine well above average that has made this Lebanese restaurant much-loved over the years. Around for a couple of decades, Parisians flock here to gorge on meal-sized platters of mixed hot and cold *mezzes*, grilled meats and unbeatable-value lunchtime *menus*. Among the handful of Al Wady specialities is *moutabal,* a typical Lebanese aubergine dip spiced with walnut and pomegranate.

ALSO RECOMMENDED
Le Troquet (Map pp166–7; ☎ 01 45 66 89 00; 21 rue François Bonvin, 15e; 2-/3-course menu lunch €24/28, dinner €30 & €40; ⏱ lunch & dinner to 11.30pm Tue-Sat; Ⓜ Sèvres Lecourbe) 'Ordinary' things cooked with a spin by Basque chef Christian Etchebest.

Les Dix Vins (Map pp166–7; ☎ 01 43 20 91 77; 57 rue Falguière, 15e; menu lunch €20, dinner €24; ⏱ lunch & dinner to 11pm Mon-Fri, dinner to 11pm Sat; Ⓜ Pasteur) Excellent value and good service at this tiny restaurant devoted to Bacchus; only *menus*.

SELF-CATERING
The 15e has two markets, Marché Grenelle and Marché St-Charles (p231), and ample supermarkets including Monoprix (Map pp166–7; 2 rue du Commerce, 15e; ⏱ 9am-10pm Mon-Sat; Ⓜ La Motte Picquet-Grenelle). If all you seek for lunch is a well-filled bread roll (from €3.60 to €4.70) or salad and a fruit tart (from €5 to €8.50) to take away or eaten at bar-stool seating, bakery Maison Kayser (Map pp166–7; 49 rue Linois, 15e; ⏱ 7am-8.30pm Mon-Sat; Ⓜ Charles Michels) is the best deal around.

MONTMARTRE & PIGALLE
The 18e arrondissement, where you'll find Montmartre and the northern boundary of Pigalle, thrives on crowds and little else. When you've got Sacré Coeur, place du Tertre and its portrait artists and Paris literally at your feet, who needs decent restaurants? But that's not to say that everything is a write-off in this well trodden tourist area. You just have to pick and choose a bit more carefully than elsewhere in Paris. The restaurants along rue des Trois Frères, for example, are generally a much better bet than their touristy counterparts in and around place du Tertre.

À LA CLOCHE D'OR
Map p169   French €€€
☎ 01 48 74 48 88; www.alaclochedor.com, in French; 3 rue Mansart, 9e; starters €7.50-10, mains €18-33; menus €18.50 (lunch only), €29 & €33; ⏱ lunch Mon-Fri, dinner to 5am Mon-Sat; Ⓜ Blanche or Pigalle
This place, at the foot of the Butte Montmartre since 1928 and once the property of actress Jeanne Moreau's parents, is the antithesis of trendy. Decorated in 'old bistro' style with photos of stars of stage (mostly) and screen (some) plastering the walls, 'The Gold Bell' serves up favourites like steak tartare (its signature dish), massive steaks and fish of the day. Order the baked Camembert and, in winter, sit by the fire.

CAFÉ BURQ Map p169 French €€€

☎ 01 42 52 81 27; 6 rue Burq, 18e; menus €15 & €19 (lunch only), €26 & €30; 🕒 lunch & dinner to 2am Tue-Sat; M Abbesses

This convivial, retro bistro in the heart of Montmartre is always buzzing; make sure you book ahead – especially at the weekend. Don't come for the décor or the space, though; both are nonexistent. Instead visit for the unfussy but well-prepared dishes like baked Camembert and lamb shoulder.

LA MASCOTTE Map p169 French, Seafood €€€

☎ 01 46 06 28 15; www.la-mascotte-montmartre .com; 52 rue des Abbesses, 18e; starters €8.50-11.50, mains €19-25, menu €19.50 (lunch only) & €35; 🕒 lunch & dinner to midnight daily; M Abbesses

La Mascotte is a small, unassuming spot much frequented by regulars who can't get enough of its seafood and regional cuisine. In winter, don't hesitate to sample the wide variety of seafood, especially the shellfish. In summer sit on the terrace and savour the delicious *fricassée de pétoncles* (fricassee of queen scallops). Meat lovers won't be disappointed with various regional delicacies, including Auvergne sausage and Troyes *andouillette* (veal tripe sausage).

LE CHÉRI-BIBI Map p169 French €€

☎ 01 42 54 88 96; 15 rue André del Sarte, 18e; menus €19 & €24; 🕒 dinner to 11.30pm Tue-Sat, brunch Sun; M Barbès Rochechouart

Taking its name from the series of detective novels by Gaston Leroux (1868–1927), this odd little place can be found (with some difficulty, it must be said) on a grotty street on the 'other' (read: wrong) side of the Butte de Montmartre and when you arrive you won't even know it as there is no sign outside. Just look for the thick black drapes in the shopfront window and enter what feels like the 1950s, with its postwar décor and excellent 'family' cooking (try the *boeuf bourguignon*).

IL DUCA Map p169 Italian €€

☎ 01 46 06 71 98; 26 rue Yvonne le Tac, 18e; starters €9-14, mains €15-23.50, menu €13 (lunch only) & €24; 🕒 lunch & dinner to 11.30pm daily; M Abbesses

This intimate little Italian restaurant has good, straightforward food, including homemade pastas (€11 to €13). The selec-

tion of Italian wine and cheese is phenomenal; themed weeks, with various regions and types of produce, are scheduled throughout the year.

CHEZ PLUMEAU Map p169 French €€

☎ 01 46 06 26 29; 4 place du Calvaire, 18e; starters €9.8-17, mains €17-20.50, menu €16 (lunch only); 🕒 lunch & dinner to midnight daily Apr-Oct, lunch & dinner to 11pm Thu-Mon Nov-Mar; M Abbesses

Once the popular Auberge du Coucou restaurant and cabaret, today's 'Feather Duster' caters mainly to tourists fresh from having their portraits done on place du Tertre. But for a tourist haunt it's not too bad and the back terrace is great on a warm spring or summer afternoon. Plats du jour are a snip at around €15.

CHEZ TOINETTE Map p169 French €€

☎ 01 42 54 44 36; 20 rue Germain Pilon, 18e; starters €6-9, mains €15-20; 🕒 dinner to 11.15pm Tue-Sat; M Abbesses

The atmosphere of this convivial restaurant is rivalled only by its fine cuisine. In the heart of one of the capital's most touristy neighbourhoods, Chez Toinette has kept alive the tradition of old Montmartre with its simplicity and culinary expertise. Game lovers won't be disappointed; *perdreau* (partridge), *biche* (doe), *chevreuil* (roebuck) and the famous *filet de canard à la sauge et au miel* (fillet of duck with sage and honey) are the house specialities and go well with a glass of Bordeaux.

LE CAFÉ QUI PARLE Map p169 French €€

☎ 01 46 06 06 88; 24 rue Caulaincourt, 18e; starters €7-14, mains €13.50-20; menus €12.50 & €17; 🕒 lunch & dinner to 11pm Thu-Tue; M Lamarck Caulaincourt or Blanche

The talking café is a fine example of where modern-day eateries are headed in Paris. It offers inventive, reasonably priced dishes prepared by owner-chef Damian Moeuf and cuisine amid comfortable surroundings. We love the art on the walls and the ancient safes down below (the building was once a bank), but not as much as we do their brunch (€15), served from 10am on Saturdays and Sundays.

LA TABLE D'ANVERS Map p169 French €€

☎ 01 48 78 35 21; 2 place d'Anvers, 9e; starters €11, mains €19, menus €17.90 & €23.90 (lunch

PHILIPPE FAURE-BRAC

The much decorated Philippe Faure-Brac – he was named Best Sommelier in France in 1988 and Best Sommelier in the World four years later – owns and operates the highly successful Bistrot du Sommelier (p261), produces his own label (a Côtes du Rhône Villages called Domaine Duseigneur) and has written a half-dozen books on the subject of wine and on wine and food pairing, including *Exquisite Matches* (Éditions EPA, 2005).

Bring me a bottle of... Red from the Rhône Valley – a Châteauneuf-du-Pape, maybe – or a good quality Riesling from Alsace.

Let's cut to the chase. Is there life beyond French wines? Yes, of course, but understand that my references are French. Parisians are very keen on so-called New World wines and we list bottles from three-dozen different countries on our card, including one from Kent (Chapel Down 2006 Bacchus). The best sauvignon outside France is made in New Zealand, shiraz from Australia is especially good and the best malbec is from Argentina.

I'm going to have a glass of red wine with the chicken and my friend wants white with the lamb. OK with you? The *code de couleur* does not have to be rigid. What you drink is really a matter of taste; at the end of the day a good wine is a good wine. The question you have to ask yourself is: 'What is the dominant characteristic of the food?' Cream sauces can go well with red wine, for example shellfish with champagne and certain cheeses (Chaource, Comté) with rosé.

Then what should I have with my Mexican chilli and my (even spicier) Thai tom yum gung? These two cuisines are especially difficult to pair with wines. Try a white or, even better, a rosé. Avoid reds, particularly complex ones.

About wine whiners... What do you do when someone claims a wine is corked and you know it isn't? We always smell it first, which tells us whether the wine is off. But one can make mistakes, and the customer is always right. Of course we will change it even if we don't believe it is corked.

It's a kind of snobbery, isn't it? It's not easy to stay a wine snob for long. A blind taste test is a great equaliser. Wine snobs don't tend to come here. Instead we get guests who are particularly knowledgeable about wine. If they're not French, they're often Belgian or English.

Interviewed by Steve Fallon

only) & €34; lunch Tue-Fri, dinner to 11pm Mon-Sat; M Anvers
Just far enough off the Montmartre tourist track to keep the tourist hordes away, this local favourite overlooking a stylish and grassy square offers contemporary French cuisine with Mediterranean (and especially Provençale) influences. The lunch *menus* are particularly good value.

ISAAN Map p169 Thai €€
01 42 80 09 72; 1 rue de Calais, 9e; starters €5-8, mains €10-19; menus €10.90 (lunch only), €14.90 & €16.90; lunch Mon-Fri, dinner to 11pm daily; M Blanche
The name of this friendly little eatery just south of Montmartre refers to Thailand's Northeast, which produces the spiciest dishes in the realm. While we can't say the dishes blew our tops off, they were certainly authentic. Go for the basics: chicken green curry and *pat tai* noodles.

LE MAQUIS Map p169 French €€
01 42 59 76 07; 69 rue Caulaincourt, 18e; starters €10, mains €18, menus €15 (lunch only),

€22 & €33; lunch & dinner to 10pm Tue-Sat; M Lamarck Caulaincourt
If you're in Montmartre and despairing over the choice of eateries (overpriced with poor service), give the Butte the boot and head the short distance north to rue Caulaincourt and this typical bistro with *cuisine traditionelle* (traditional cooking). The name refers to the neighbourhood and not the French Resistance or the herbal underbrush of Corsica. The set lunch includes a 25cL *pichet* of wine.

LE REFUGE DES FONDUS
Map p169 French, Savoie €€
01 42 55 22 65; www.lerefugedesfondus.com, in French; 17 rue des Trois Frères, 18e; menu €17; dinner to 2am daily; M Abbesses or Anvers
This odd place has been a Montmartre favourite for nigh on four decades. The single *menu* provides an aperitif, hors d'oeuvre, red wine (or beer or soft drink) in a *biberon* (baby bottle) and a good quantity of either *fondue savoyarde* (melted cheese) or *fondue bourguignonne* (meat fondue). The last sitting is at midnight.

EATING MONTMARTRE & PIGALLE

LE MONO Map p169
African, Togolese €€

☎ 01 46 06 99 20; 40 rue Véron, 18e; starters
€5-15, mains €9-17; ⏰ dinner to 1am Thu-Tue;
Ⓜ Abbesses or Blanche

Le Mono, run by a cheery Togolese family,
offers West African specialities, including
lélé (flat, steamed cakes of white beans and
shrimp; €6.50), *azidessi* (beef or chicken
with peanut sauce; €11), *gbekui* (goulash
with spinach, onions, beef, fish and shrimp;
€13) and *djenkoumé* (grilled chicken with
semolina noodles; €12). The rum-based
punches are an excellent prelude.

AU PETIT BUDAPEST
Map p169
Hungarian €€

☎ 01 46 06 10 34; 96 rue des Martyrs, 18e; starters €7.50-9.50, mains €14.50-16.50, menu €18.50;
⏰ dinner to midnight Mon-Sat; Ⓜ Abbesses

With old etchings and the requisite Gypsy
music, this little eatery does a reasonable
job of recreating the atmosphere of a late-
19th-century Hungarian *csárda* (traditional
inn). From the chicken paprika to the
crepe à la Hortobagy (crepe with meat and
crème fraîche; €9.50), these are refined
versions of popular Hungarian dishes. For
dessert try the ever-rich *Gundel palacsinta*
(flambéed pancake with chocolate and
nuts).

LA MAISON ROSE Map p169
French €€

☎ 01 42 57 66 75; 2 rue de l'Abreuvoir, 18e; starters €7.20-13, mains €14.50-16.50, menu €16.50;
⏰ lunch & dinner to 10.30pm daily Mar-Oct, lunch
Thu-Mon, dinner to 9pm Mon, Thu-Sun Nov-Feb;
Ⓜ Lamarck Caulaincourt

Looking for the quintessential Montmartre
bistro in a house that was the subject of

top picks

ASIAN RICE & NOODLES

- Asianwok (p271)
- Higuma (p237)
- Isaan (p279)
- Ossek Garden (p244)
- Paris Hanoi (p247)
- Tai Yien (p271)
- Le Foyer du Vietnam (p254)
- La Chine Masséna (p275)
- La Fleuve de Chine (p275)

a lithograph by Maurice Utrillo? Head for
the tiny 'Pink House' located just north of
the Place du Tertre. It's not so much about
food here but rather location, location,
location.

LE RELAIS GASCON
Map p169
French, Southwest €€

☎ 01 42 58 58 22; 6 rue des Abbesses, 18e; starters
€6-11, mains €10.50-16, menus €8 (lunch only),
€15 & €23.50; ⏰ lunch & dinner to midnight daily;
Ⓜ Abbesses

Situated just a short stroll from the place
des Abbesses, the Relais Gascon has a
relaxed atmosphere and authentic regional cuisine at very reasonable prices.
The *salades géantes* (giant salads, a house
speciality) and the *confit de canard* (duck
confit) will satisfy big eaters, while the
traditional Basque *cassoulet* and *tartiflette*
are equally tasty and filling. After, try the
traditional *gâteau basque* (a simple layer
cake filled with cream and cherry jam) or a
crème brûlée.

AUX NÉGOCIANTS Map p169
French €€

☎ 01 46 06 15 11; 27 rue Lambert, 18e; starters
€6.20-12, mains €13.80-15.50; ⏰ lunch & dinner to
10.30pm Mon-Fri; Ⓜ Château Rouge

This old-style wine bar and bistro is far
enough from the madding crowds of Montmartre to attract a faithful local clientele.
Patés, terrines, traditional mains like *bœuf
bourguinon*, and wine paid for according to
consumption – it all feels like the Paris of
the 1950s (or even earlier).

L'ÉPICERIE Map p169
Italian €€

☎ 01 48 78 07 50; 51 rue des Martyrs, 9e;
salads €6-10, dishes €9-13; ⏰ 9am-10pm daily;
Ⓜ Pigalle

An excellent place for lunch is this Italian
grocer and caterer, which has a large array
of cold and hot dishes as well as salads
available. You can eat *in situ* in what looks
and feels more like café than a shop, or
take it with you for a picnic.

LE SOLEIL GOURMAND
Map p169
French, Mediterranean €€

☎ 01 42 51 00 50; 10 rue Ravignan, 18e; dishes
€8.50-12.50; ⏰ lunch & dinner to 11pm Tue-Sun;
Ⓜ Abbesses

This cheery boutique and restaurant exudes
the south of France with its warm décor
and simple dishes like salads, savoury tarts

and baked *bricks* (stuffed fritters). Treat yourself to the *tarte aux tomates confites* (glazed tomato tart) or the *(tarte aux oignons, poivrons, raisins et pignons grillés* (tart with onion, green peppers, grapes and grilled pine nuts) and any of the wonderful ice creams. The *plat du jour* is priced between €10.50 and €12.50.

AU GRAIN DE FOLIE
Map p169   Vegetarian €€

☎ 01 42 58 15 57; 24 rue de la Vieuville, 18e; dishes €10-12, menus €14 & €16; ☽ lunch Tue-Sun, dinner to 11pm Tue-Sat; Ⓜ Abbesses
This hole-in-the-wall macrobiotic and organic eatery run by a woman from Cambridge and in business for over 25 years has excellent vegetarian pâté and vegan quiche. There are also lots of good dippy things like hummus and guacamole.

SELF-CATERING
Towards place Pigalle there are lots of groceries, many of them open until late at night; try the side streets leading off blvd de Clichy (eg rue Lepic). Heading south from blvd de Clichy, rue des Martyrs, 9e, is lined with food shops almost all the way to the Notre Dame de Lorette metro station. Supermarkets in the area include 8 à Huit (Map p169; 24 rue Lepic, 18e; ☽ 8.30am-10.30pm Mon-Sat; Ⓜ Abbesses) and Ed l'Épicier (Map p169; 6 blvd de Clichy, 18e; ☽ 9am-9pm Mon-Sat; Ⓜ Pigalle).

BEYOND CENTRAL PARIS
LA DÉFENSE
Quick eats to stave off pangs between business meetings and soulless but pricey woo-that-client places form the backbone of La Défense's dining scene: The 3rd floor of the Centre Commercial des Quatre Temps (☎ 01 47 73 54 44; www.les4temps.com, in French; 15 Parvis de la Défense; ☽ 9am-10pm Mon-Fri, 8.30am-10pm Sat) alone is loaded with places to eat quickly, be it pizza or pancakes, Häagen-Dazs ice cream, Starbucks coffee, soup 'n' juice or stylish Japanese.

GLOBETROTTER Map p180   Island Cuisine €€€

☎ 01 55 91 96 96; 16 place de la Défense; starters €8-23, mains €15-30; ☽ lunch Mon-Fri; Ⓜ La Défense Grande Arche

La Défense's *gens d'affaires* (businesspeople) come to this tropical restaurant to embark on a culinary tour of the world through various islands. Think swordfish carpaccio with Caribbean pineapple or duck breast with dried fruit. Tables on the wooden-deck terrace face La Grande Arche and those inside woo diners with first-row seats at the Bassin Agam (p181). Shoebox-shaped, this must be the stubbiest building in La Défense!

LE PETIT BOFINGER
Map p180   French, Brasserie €€€

☎ 01 46 92 46 46; 1 place du Dôme; menu €20.50 & €25; ☽ lunch & dinner until 11pm daily; Ⓜ La Défense Grande Arche
It's easy to find this glassed-in dining room. Just head to the cinematic glass dome of a building, immediately on your left/right as you walk up/down the steps of the Grande Arche. The fare is typical bistro, bolstered by a good-value *formule bistro* (€21.80) which invites its overwhelmingly business clientele to network over *saucisses de Strasbourg* and *choucroute* (sauerkraut).

BOLDÈRE Map p180   Vegetarian €€

☎ 01 47 73 54 44; 15 Parvis de la Défense; salads €8-15; ☽ 9am-1am Mon-Fri; Ⓜ La Défense Grande Arche
The hottest address on the block, this *bar à legumes* on the 3rd floor of Les Quatre Temps has done a roaring trade since its debut in late 2007. Health-conscious punters build their salad from a hundred and one different ingredients or plump for one of four different homemade soups. Interior décor is contemporary, the mood, chic-casual and the cuisine, 100% vegetarian. An invigorating shot of country air in a wholly urban landscape.

K10 Map p180   Japanese €

☎ 01 47 44 92 52, 15 Parvis de la Défense; dishes €2.20-5.80; ☽ noon-10.30pm daily; Ⓜ La Défense Grande Arche
Dishes are colour-coded at this quick, bright, modern eating joint, tagged as the 'rolling fusion-food experience', also on Les Quatre Temps' 3rd floor. Sit down on a bar stool or bright table, and take your pick from the mouth-watering array of rolls, yakitori (Japanese brochettes), sashimi, maki and sushi dishes that glide silently past on a conveyor belt. White dishes cost the least, orange the most.

ST-DENIS

There are a number of restaurants in the modern shopping area around the Basilique de St-Denis metro station.

LES ARTS Map p182   North African, French €€

☎ 01 42 43 22 40; 6 rue de la Boulangerie; starters €6-7, mains €11-18, menu €18; ☷ lunch & dinner to 10.30pm Tue-Sun; Ⓜ Basilique de St-Denis
This central restaurant has mostly Maghreb cuisine (couscous, *tajines* etc; €11 to €16), with a few traditional French dishes as well, and comes recommended by local people. It's just opposite the basilica.

LE PETIT BRETON

Map p182   French, Breton €€
☎ 01 48 20 11 58; 18 rue de la Légion d'Honneur; menus €11 & €14; ☷ 10am-3pm Mon-Fri, 11.30am-3.30pm Sat; Ⓜ St-Denis Porte de Paris
'The Little Breton' is a decent spot for a lunch of traditional French fare (don't expect *galettes* or crepes despite the name). The plat du jour is a bargain-basement €8.

LE CAFÉ DE L'ORIENT

Map p182   Tearoom €
☎ 01 48 20 30 83; 8 blvd de la Commune de Paris; teas €3-8, cocktails €5-6; ☷ noon-midnight; Ⓜ Basilique de St-Denis
If you fancy some North African mint tea and pastries or a cocktail, this is a comfortable Moroccan café with overstuffed cushions and Moroccan décor northeast of the basilica. They also do heartier dishes such as couscous and *tajines*.

Self-Catering

The large, multi-ethnic food market (Map p182; place Jean Jaurès; ☷ 8am-2pm Tue, Fri & Sun; Ⓜ Basilique de St-Denis) is opposite the tourist office. Halle du Marché, the large covered market a short stroll to the northwest, is known for its selection of spices.

Franprix (Map p182; 34 rue de la République; ☷ 9am-8pm Mon, 8.30am-8pm Tue-Sat, 8.30am-1.30pm Sun; Ⓜ Basilique de St-Denis) is in the centre of town near the post office.

top picks

- Le Fumoir (p285)
- La Perle (p287)
- Le Bistrot du Peintre (p289)
- On Cherche Encore (p296)
- Bar à Vins du Cinéma des Cinéastes (p294)
- Stolly's (p289)
- Café Chéri(e) (p295)
- Le Verre à Pied (p290)
- Le 10 (p292)
- Les Vélos à Moëlle (p298)

Yearning for a chilled venue where you don't need a gold-plated credit card or membership to the local anarchists' association to feel at ease? Don't despair: there's far more to the Parisian drinking scene than chic, design-driven lounge bars brimming with beautiful people, or tatty, dime-a-dozen *tabacs* (bar-tobacconists) with thin-haired regulars propping up the bar.

Drinking in Paris as salt-of-the-earth Parisians do means: savouring wafer-thin slices of *saucisson* (sausage) over a glass of sauvignon on a terrace at sundown; quaffing an early-evening apéritif in the same literary café as Sartre and Simone once did; dancing on tables to bossa nova beats; hovering at a zinc counter with local winos; indulging in a spot of *dégustation* (tasting; see boxed text, p299); sipping martinis on a dark leather couch while listening to live jazz; sipping *gyokuro* in a trendy Japanese *salon de thé* (tearoom).

In a country where eating and drinking are as inseparable as cheese and wine, it's inevitable that the line between bars, cafés and bistros is blurred at best (no, you haven't drunk too much). Practically every place serves food of some description, but those featured in this chapter are favoured, first and foremost, as happening places to drink – be it alcohol, coffee or tea.

The distinct lack of any hardcore clubbing circuit in the French capital, moreover, only serves to spice up Paris' drinking scene still further; what might appear as a simple café at 5pm can morph quite comfortably to DJ bar and pounding dance floor as the night rolls on.

PRACTICALITIES

Drinking in Paris essentially means paying the rent for the space you take up. So it costs more sitting at tables than standing at the counter, more on a fancy square than a backstreet, more in the 8e than in the 18e. Come 10pm many cafés apply a pricier *tarif de nuit* (night rate).

A glass of wine starts at €3 or €4, a cocktail costs €7 to €15 and a *demi* (half-pint) of beer is €3 to €5. In clubs and chic bars, prices are easily double this. To hunt down the place with the cheapest drinks, just follow the trail of students. Most venues have a 'happy hour' with reduced-price drinks from around 5pm to 9pm.

Closing time tends to be 2am, though some bars have later licences. See p304 for clubbing spots and p307 for live music venues – great places to drink, too.

Since 1 January 2008, the Parisian drinking scene has been smoke-free – kind of. Following the blanket smoking-in-public-places ban (see p220), smokers have simply moved from inside to out, socialising on the street in front of bars instead or lighting up on packed pavement terraces which, heated and plastic-covered during the colder months, are smokier than ever!

LOUVRE & LES HALLES

Some great bars skirt the no-man's-land of Les Halles, but be prudent and avoid crossing the garden above the Forum des Halles at night. Rue des Lombards is celebrated for its jazz venues (p309), while sophisticated bars are grouped towards the Louvre and Palais Royal. The Étienne Marcel area, especially along rue Tiquetonne and rue Montorgueil, has a fine selection of hip cafés. This area is right next to the happening bars of rue Montmartre, which are listed on p298.

FOOTSIE Map pp82–3   Bar
☎ 01 42 60 07 20; 10-12 rue Daunou, 2e; ☽ 6pm-2am Mon-Thu, to 4am Fri & Sat; Ⓜ Opéra
In this place – otherwise known as the FTSE (the London Stock Exchange) – drink prices

---

top picks

FOR COCKTAILS

Feeling fancy? Flit into urban high life for a taste of Paris at its most chic:

- Buddha Bar (p294)
- Hemingway Bar (opposite)
- Kong (opposite)
- Le Fumoir (opposite)
- Alcazar (p292)
- Le Rosebud (p293)
- Harry's New York Bar (opposite)
- Ice Kube (p300)

are floated like stocks, with prices changing according to demand; when certain drinks are purchased they then cost more, while others drop in price. It's a successful gimmick and the gorgeous wood-panelled bar attracts besuited brokers and way-too-young girls batting their eyelashes throughout the night.

LE CAFÉ NOIR Map pp82–3 — Bar
☎ 01 40 39 07 36; 65 rue Montmartre, 2e; ☽ 8am-2am Mon-Fri, 4pm-2am Sat; Ⓜ Sentier
An excellent, dependable bar on the edge of the Sentier garment district, 'The Black Café' is, in fact, predominantly red, and one of those bars you decide to turn into a regular haunt. It's always packed, with a mix of French and Anglo imbibers attracted by the friendly and very hip ambience.

LE CŒUR FOU Map pp82–3 — Bar
☎ 01 42 33 91 33; 55 rue Montmartre, 2e; ☽ 5pm-2am; Ⓜ Étienne Marcel
'The Crazy Heart' is hip without attaining that too-cool-by-half pretentiousness that reigns in the Étienne Marcel environs. It's a tiny, gallery-like bar with little candles nestled in whitewashed walls, a dapper late-20s crowd that doesn't keep to itself, and art exhibitions that rotate every two weeks.

L'IMPRÉVU Map p86 — Bar
☎ 01 42 78 23 50; 9 rue Quincampoix, 4e; ☽ 1pm-2am Sun, noon-2am Tue-Sat; Ⓜ Rambuteau
'The Unexpected' is just that – something of an oasis in the busy Les Halles area. It's a relatively inexpensive and gay friendly bar, with mismatched furniture and a relaxed charm. The bar is quite large but the different rooms and corners mean you'll soon find your niche. It's popular with students.

CAFÉ DES INITIÉS Map p86 — Café
☎ 01 42 33 78 29; 3 place des Deux Écus, 1er; ☽ 8am-2am; Ⓜ Louvre-Rivoli
This modern-design café almost on rue du Louvre is popular with journalists and communications types. While not a late-night venue, it has a pleasant terrace and is great for evening drinks, coffees and light meals (*plats du jour* – daily specials – around €14.50). Slick service, nondeafening music and good food attract a trendy 30-something mix of suits and hooded tops.

HARRY'S NEW YORK BAR
Map pp82–3 — Cocktail Bar
☎ 01 42 61 71 14; 5 rue Daunou, 2e; ☽ 10.30am-4am; Ⓜ Opéra
One of the most popular American-style bars in the prewar years (when there were several dozen in Paris), Harry's once welcomed such habitués as writers F Scott Fitzgerald and Ernest Hemingway, who no doubt sampled the bar's unique cocktail and creation: the Bloody Mary. The Cuban mahogany interior dates from the mid-19th century and was brought over from a Manhattan bar in 1911. There's a basement piano bar and, for the peckish, old-school hot dogs and tasty club sandwiches. The advertisement for Harry's that occasionally appears in the *International Herald Tribune* still reads 'Tell the Taxi Driver Sank Roo Doe Noo' and is copyrighted.

HEMINGWAY BAR Map pp82–3 — Cocktail Bar
☎ 01 43 16 30 50; Hôtel Ritz Paris, 15 place Vendôme, 1er; ☽ 6.30pm-2am; Ⓜ Madeleine
This epic bar, nestled in the finery and grandeur of the Ritz, is a paean to Papa and is where he imbibed after making a name for himself. Legend has it that during the liberation of Paris, Hemingway himself was put in charge of the bar – complete with machine gun. Fabulous décor, outstanding cocktails (from €22) and expert bar staff.

KONG Map p86 — Cocktail Bar
☎ 01 40 39 09 00; 5th fl, 1 rue du Pont Neuf, 1er; ☽ 10.30am-2am Sun-Thurs, to 3am Fri & Sat; Ⓜ Pont Neuf
This Philippe Starck–designed bar is carefully perched upon the Kenzo building. The concept is kind of postmodern Japanese, a cradle for new-generation wannabes who trail their Vuitton handbags along the bar and snap their fingers for more bottles of champagne. The cocktails are around €13, not bad for a place this pretentious, and DJs playing hip-hop Thursday to Saturday somehow get everyone dancing on the tables. Happy hour is 6pm to 8pm. Dress up: no running shoes.

LE FUMOIR Map p86 — Cocktail Bar
☎ 01 42 92 00 24; 6 rue de l'Amiral de Coligny, 1er; ☽ 11am-2am; Ⓜ Louvre-Rivoli
This colonial-style bar-restaurant opposite the eastern flank of the Louvre is a fine place to sip top-notch gin from quality

glassware while nibbling on olives; during happy hour (6pm to 8pm) the cocktails, usually €8.50 to €11, drop to €6. There's a buoyant, corporate crowd on weekday evenings. The restaurant is popular for late breakfast during the week and brunch on Sundays; try to get a seat in the 'library'.

CAFÉ OZ Map p86 Pub
☎ 01 40 39 00 18; 18 rue St-Denis, 1er; ⏰ 5pm-3am Sun-Thu, to 6am Fri, 1pm-6am Sat; Ⓜ Châtelet

A militantly Aussie pub at the bottom of sleazy rue St-Denis, Oz is authentic – from its wood-and-ochre décor to its strong commitment to maximising your drink intake. Convivial bordering on raucous, it's popular with Anglos but the French love it too. The place is packed on Friday and Saturday nights, when it heats up with DJs and dancing. Happy hour is 6pm to 8pm. There's also a smaller and more chilled branch in Pigalle (Map p169; ☎ 01 40 16 11 16; 1 rue de Bruxelles, 9e; ⏰ 5pm-2am Sun-Wed, to 4am Thurs, to 10am Fri & Sat; Ⓜ Blanche) and Happy Hour is from 6pm to 9pm.

ANGÉLINA Map pp82–3 Tea Room
☎ 01 42 60 82 00; 226 rue de Rivoli, 1er; ⏰ 9am-5pm; Ⓜ Tuileries

Take a break from the long trek along the Tuileries gardens and line up for a table at Angélina, along with the lunching ladies, their posturing poodles and half the stu-

dents from Waseda University. This beautiful, high-ceilinged tearoom has exquisite furnishings, mirrored walls and fabulous fluffy cakes. More importantly, it serves the best and most wonderfully sickening 'African' hot chocolate in the history of time (€6.20), served with a pot of whipped cream. It's a positive meal replacement and is said to be the best hot chocolate in Paris.

MARAIS & BASTILLE

The Marais is an excellent spot to go out for drinks. It's a fascinating mix of gay-friendly (and gay-only) café society and bourgeois arty spots, with an interesting sprinkling of eclectic bars and relatively raucous pubs. Bastille has become increasingly *démodé* (unfashionable) and even crass over the years, but it invariably draws a crowd, particularly to heaving rue de Lappe. Things get quieter – and better – as you go further up rue de la Roquette and rue de Charonne. Rue Keller has some good cafés and a decent gay bar (see p327).

AU PETIT FER À CHEVAL Map pp98–9 Bar
☎ 01 42 72 47 47; 30 rue Vieille du Temple, 4e; ⏰ 9am-2am; Ⓜ Hôtel de Ville or St-Paul

The original (1903) horseshoe-shaped zinc bar leaves little room for much else, but nobody seems to mind at this genial place. It overflows with friendly regulars enjoying a drink or a sandwich (simple meals are served from noon to 1am). The stainless-steel toilets are straight out of a Flash Gordon film.

BOCA CHICA Map pp94–5 Bar
☎ 01 43 57 93 13; 58 rue de Charonne, 11e; ⏰ 4pm-1am Mon-Thu, to 4am Fri & Sat; Ⓜ Ledru Rollin

This enormous, colourfully decorated place attracts a salsa-lovin' crowd that isn't shy about getting up to dance. When the multilevel bar areas and terrace are not hosting salsa soirees you'll find DJs, flamenco artists and '80s theme nights. The extensive tapas selection is unsatisfying; stick to the sangria. Happy hour is 4pm to 8pm.

HAVANITA CAFÉ Map pp94–5 Bar
☎ 01 43 55 96 42; 11 rue de Lappe, 11e; ⏰ 5pm-2am Sun-Thu, to 4am Fri & Sat; Ⓜ Bastille

Flashy Cuban style every inch of the way, from the *mojitos* (Cuban cocktails created with rum, mint and limes) to the main

top picks

BAR-HOPPING STREETS

- Rue Princesse & rue des Canettes, 6e (p291) Student, sports 'n' tapas bars and pubs.
- Rue Oberkampf & rue Jean-Pierre Timbaud, 11e (right) Hip bars, bohemian hang-outs and atmospheric cafés.
- Rue de la Roquette, rue Keller & rue de Lappe, 11e (right) Whatever you fancy; Bastille has the lot.
- Rue Montmartre, 2e (p284) Modern, slick bars and pubs.
- Canal St-Martin, 10e (p295) Heady summer nights in casual canal-side cafés.
- Rue Vieille du Temple & surrounding streets, 4e (right) Marais cocktail of gay bars and chic cafés.

courses to the murals on the walls. This attractive but commercial bar-restaurant has stood the test of time on the increasingly lurid rue de Lappe, thanks to its always reliably festive atmosphere.

IGUANA CAFÉ Map pp94–5 Bar
☎ 01 40 21 39 99; 15 rue de la Roquette, 11e; ⏲ 3pm-5am; Ⓜ Bastille

A contemporary, two-level, backlit café-pub whose clientele is slipping progressively from 30-somethings to early-20s punters. It's the best of a mediocre bunch and we love the red, black and silver décor on two levels. It has the advantage of closing late – or would that be early? – every night, and there's a DJ at the weekend, with themed nights twice a month.

LA CHAISE AU PLAFOND Map pp98–9 Bar
☎ 01 42 76 03 22; 10 Rue du Trésor, 4e; ⏲ 9.30am-2am; Ⓜ Hôtel de Ville or St-Paul

'The Chair on the Ceiling' is a peaceful, warm place, with wooden tables outside on a terrace giving onto tranquil passage du Trésor. It's a real oasis from the frenzy of the Marais and worth knowing about in summer.

LA PERLE Map pp98–9 Bar
☎ 01 42 72 69 93; 78 rue Vieille du Temple, 3e; ⏲ 6am-2am Mon-Fri, 8am-2am Sat & Sun; Ⓜ St-Paul or Chemin Vert

This is where *bobos* (bohemian bourgeois) come to slum it over *un rouge* (glass of red wine) until the DJ arrives and things liven up. We like the (for real) distressed look of the place and the locomotive over the bar.

LE CAFÉ DIVAN Map pp94–5 Bar
☎ 01 48 05 72 36; 60 rue de la Roquette, 11e; ⏲ 8am-2am; Ⓜ Bastille

Although a touch sombre, the Divan bar-restaurant scores a mention for three reasons. First, its long copper bar with stools: highly suitable for that moody apéritif or *Le Monde*–scrutinising coffee break. Second, a local clientele that's older and considerably less hysterical than the usual rue de Lappe lot. And, finally, it opens onto a little passage – great on a warm evening.

LES ÉTAGES Map pp98–9 Bar
☎ 01 42 78 72 00; 35 rue Vieille du Temple, 4e; ⏲ 5pm-2am; Ⓜ Hôtel de Ville or St-Paul

Students and expats find 'The Storeys' (all three of them) a viable alternative to the standard Marais fare, and happily appropriate the upgraded lounge rooms upstairs. Before 9.30pm certain cocktails are €4.50 (instead of the usual €8).

LES FUNAMBULES Map pp94–5 Bar
☎ 01 43 70 83 70; 12 rue Faidherbe, 11e; ⏲ 8am-2am Mon-Sat, noon-midnight Sun; Ⓜ Faidherbe Chaligny

Like so many small cafés in east Paris, 'The Tightrope Walkers' has been transformed into a fashionable bar. While the original architecture provides character, nowadays the terrace is crammed with beautiful people on warm summer evenings. The rest of the year customers take shelter inside under the stunning coffered ceiling with chandelier and bird cages and enjoy a cocktail at the bar or a snack in the back room.

L'ÉTOILE MANQUANTE Map pp98–9 Bar
☎ 01 42 72 48 34; 34 rue Vieille du Temple, 4e; ⏲ 8am-2am; Ⓜ Hôtel de Ville or St-Paul

A long, elegant room with a long, elegant wine and cocktail list, 'The Missing Star' takes standard café-bar décor up a slight notch with modern art, metal frames and fittings, clustered mirrors and dim lighting. There are light meals but it's not a restaurant as such.

L'OBJECTIF LUNE Map pp94–5 Bar
☎ 01 48 06 46 05; 19 rue de la Roquette, 11e; ⏲ 6pm-5am; Ⓜ Bastille

This perennial favourite (the name comes from a Tintin story) in Bastille attracts punters with its 'Maxi Happy Hours' – 6pm to 9pm and 9pm to 1.30am, when pints are €3 and €4 respectively – and its Cuban-themed and DJ nights, when it works itself up to a fever pitch.

MIXER BAR Map pp98–9 Bar
☎ 01 48 87 55 44; 23 rue Ste-Croix de la Bretonnerie, 4e; ⏲ 7pm-2am; Ⓜ Hôtel de Ville

This bright and colourful club has regular party nights and chill-out sessions. Blended up in this hedonistic mix are an animated gay crowd, a happy sprinkling of enlightened heteros, and three different DJs each night, spinning techno, electro and house.

POP IN Map pp94–5   Bar

☎ 01 48 05 56 11; 105 rue Amelot, 11e;
🕑 6.30pm-1.30am Tue-Sun; Ⓜ St-Sébastien
Froissart
All skinny jeans and cultivated pop-rock
nonchalance, the Pop In somehow got
itself on the in-crowd map but maintains
a relaxed regulars' vibe. It's popular with
expats and Parisian students starting out
the evening, and the drinks are reasonably
priced.

SANZ SANS Map pp94–5   Bar

☎ 01 44 75 78 78; 49 rue du Faubourg St-Antoine,
11e; 🕑 9am-2am Sun-Thu, to 5am Fri & Sat;
Ⓜ Bastille
A little cheesy, a lot sleazy, this lively bar
clad in red velvet and zebra stripes continues to hold out as a busy drinking venue
on the Bastille beat. DJs play a very mixed
bag of music, mostly electronic or funk and
soul, and the crowd is similarly unpredicta-
ble. It's always good fun. There's a €5 cover
charge at the weekend.

LE PICK-CLOPS Map pp98–9   Bar, Café

☎ 01 40 29 02 18; 16 rue Vieille du Temple, 4e;
🕑 7am-2am Mon-Sat, 8am-2am Sun; Ⓜ Hôtel de
Ville or St-Paul
This buzzy bar-café – all shades of blue and
lit by neon – has Formica tables, ancient
bar stools and plenty of mirrors. Attracting
a friendly flow of locals and passers-by, it's
a great place for morning or afternoon coffee, or that last drink alone or with friends.
Great rum punch served with copious
amounts of peanuts.

BAZ'ART CAFÉ Map pp92–3   Café

☎ 01 42 78 62 23; 36 blvd Henri IV, 4e;
🕑 7.30am-2am; Ⓜ Bastille
This café, whose name sounds suspiciously
like 'bizarre' in English, is just southwest of
Bastille but could be a million miles away
from the hoopla usually associated with
that *quartier* (neighbourhood). It's a grown-
up, stylish place with friendly service and
good-value food.

CAFÉ DES PHARES Map pp94–5   Café

☎ 01 42 72 04 70; 7 place de la Bastille, 4e;
🕑 7.30am-3am Sun-Thu, to 4am Fri & Sat;
Ⓜ Bastille
'The Beacons Café' is best known as the
city's original *philocafé* (philosophers' café),

established by the late philosopher and
Sorbonne professor Marc Sautet (1947–98)
in 1992. If you feel like debating such topics
as 'What is a fact?' and 'Can people communicate?', head for this place at 11am on
Sunday. It sounds posey in the extreme and
it is, but – hey! – this is Paris.

CENTRE CULTUREL SUÉDOIS
Map pp98–9   Café

☎ 01 44 78 80 20; 11 rue Payenne, 3e; 🕑 noon-
6pm Tue-Sun; Ⓜ Chemin Vert
Housed in the beautiful Hôtel de Marle, a
16th-century mansion, this gorgeous café
in the Swedish Cultural Centre hosts a variety of exhibitions, concerts and debates,
with rich resources on Swedish history and
culture. But what we're interested in here
are the delicious soups, sandwiches and
cakes and the tables outside in the tranquil
paved courtyard.

L'APPARTEMENT CAFÉ Map pp98–9   Café

☎ 01 48 87 12 22; 18 rue des Coutures St-Gervais,
3e; 🕑 noon-2am Mon-Sat, 12.30pm-midnight Sun;
Ⓜ St-Sébastien Froissart
This place is a tasteful haven tucked behind the Musée Picasso and at a merciful
distance from the Marais, madding crowds.
It's a bit like a private living room, with
wood panelling, leather sofas, scattered
parlour games, dog-eared books – and
Parisians languidly studying their 'lounch'
(their word, not ours) and (on Sunday till
4pm) their brunch – or is that 'brounch'?
– menus.

LE PURE CAFÉ Map pp94–5   Café

☎ 01 43 71 47 22; 14 rue Jean Macé, 11e; 🕑 7am-
2am Mon-Fri, 8am-2am Sat, 10am-midnight Sun;
Ⓜ Charonne
This old café, which should be declared
a national monument (if it already hasn't
been), moonlights as a restaurant with a
modern kitchen and some dishes that veer
toward 'world' food (mains €16.50 to €20).
But we like it as it was intended to be,
especially over a *grand crème* (large white
coffee) and the papers on Sunday morning.

PAUSE CAFÉ Map pp94–5   Café

☎ 01 48 06 80 33; 41 rue de Charonne, 11e;
🕑 7.30am-2am Mon-Sat, 9am-8.30pm Sun;
Ⓜ Ledru Rollin
Principally a restaurant with *plats du jour* for
around €12, this attractive café with lots of

windows remains a firmly popular destination for drinks, meals, coffee or brunch. Well situated a little away from the fray of Bastille, its generous terrace (covered and heated in winter) fills up with fashionable locals and the almost famous.

ANDY WAHLOO Map pp92–3 — Cocktail Bar
☎ 01 42 71 20 38; 69 rue des Gravilliers, 3e; ⏱ 5pm-2am Tue-Sat; Ⓜ Arts et Métiers
Casablanca meets pop-artist Andy Warhol in this cool, multicoloured cocktail lounge hidden away just north of the Centre Georges Pompidou. Its clever name means 'I have nothing' in Arabic. The acid colours, sweet cocktails, pushy staff and loud house music may be a bit too much for some palates, but it's a lively, spirited little bar that most will enjoy. There are great olives as well as promising meze plates. Happy hour is 5pm to 8pm. Enter through the courtyard.

BOTTLE SHOP Map pp94–5 — Pub
☎ 01 43 14 28 04; 5 rue Trousseau, 11e; ⏱ 11.30am-2am; Ⓜ Ledru Rollin
A popular lunch café by day, this great little local has a lively pub feeling in the evenings. There's a welcoming mix of regular expats and travellers – at least half the friendly banter going on is in English. Happy hour is 5pm to 8pm.

LIZARD LOUNGE Map pp98–9 — Pub
☎ 01 42 72 81 34; 18 rue du Bourg Tibourg, 4e; ⏱ noon-2pm; Ⓜ Hôtel de Ville or St-Paul
A quality outpost of Anglo-Saxon attitude in the heart of the Marais, this relaxed pub has beer on tap, cocktails and food (think

top picks

FOR TEA

Salons de thé – English, Japanese or North African – are increasingly chic in Paris.

- Kilàli, 6e (p293)
- Mamie Gâteaux, 6e (p256)
- La Jacobine, 6e (p257)
- La Mosquée de Paris, 5e (p251)
- The Tea Caddy, 5e (p250)
- Angélina, 1er (p286)
- Le Loir dans la Théière, 4e (right)

club sandwiches and burgers). Young expats with clutch purses file straight downstairs to the cellar, complete with stone walls, a DJ, and magnanimous little corners in which to schmooze.

PURE MALT Map pp98–9 — Pub
☎ 01 42 76 03 77; 4 rue Caron, 4e; ⏱ 5pm-2am; Ⓜ St-Paul
A little Scottish pub-bar just south of the lovely place du Marché Ste-Catherine, the Pure Malt is for the whisky connoisseur. More than 150 types of whisky are on hand to try at €7 to €17 a glass. It concentrates mainly on single malts, though there's beer available for €5 or €6 a pint. It's a great place for watching sport and there's a DJ on Friday and Saturday evenings.

STOLLY'S Map pp98–9 — Pub
☎ 01 42 76 06 76; 16 rue de la Cloche Percée, 4e; ⏱ 4.30pm-2am; Ⓜ Hôtel de Ville or St-Paul
This itty-bitty Anglophone pub on a tiny street just above rue de Rivoli is always crowded, particularly during the 4.30pm to 8pm happy hour, when all cocktails and a pint of cheap *blonde* (that's the house lager – not the Monroe lookalike propping up the bar) cost €5. When big football matches are on and you're looking forward to a quiet drink, go elsewhere.

LE LOIR DANS LA THÉIÈRE
Map pp98–9 — Tea Room
☎ 01 42 72 90 61; 3 rue des Rosiers, 4e; ⏱ 9.30am-7pm; Ⓜ St-Paul
The cutesily named 'Dormouse in the Teapot' is a wonderful old space filled with retro toys, comfy couches and scenes of *Through the Looking Glass* on the walls. It serves up to a dozen different types of tea, excellent sandwiches and desserts like apple crumble (€8.50 to €12), and brunch at the weekend. Best time to find a table is about 4pm.

LE BISTROT DU PEINTRE
Map pp94–5 — Wine Bar
☎ 01 47 00 34 39; 116 av Ledru-Rollin, 11e; ⏱ 8am-2am; Ⓜ Bastille
This lovely *belle époque* bistro and wine bar should really count more as a restaurant than a drinking place; after all, the food is great. But the 1902 Art Nouveau bar, elegant terrace and spot-on service put this place on our apéritif A-list – and that of local artists, *bobos* and local celebs.

LE CAFÉ DU PASSAGE Map pp94–5   Wine Bar

☎ 01 49 29 97 64; 12 rue de Charonne, 11e;
🕑 6pm-2am; Ⓜ Ledru Rollin

This is the destination of choice for willing wine buffs, who relax in armchairs while sampling vintages from the excellent range on offer. Le Café du Passage has hundreds of wines available, including many by the glass (from €5.80). Whisky aficionados are also catered for and won't be disappointed by the selection of single malts. It's a warm, cosy place and gourmet snacks and light meals (€6 to €17) are available.

LATIN QUARTER & JARDIN DES PLANTES

Rive Gauche romantics, well-heeled café society types and students by the gallon drink in the 5e arrondissement, where old-but-good recipes, nostalgic formulas and a flurry of early-evening happy hours ensure a quintessential Parisian soiree. It's all good fun here, though nothing ground-breaking.

LE CROCODILE Map pp110–11   Bar

☎ 01 43 54 32 37; 6 rue Royer Collard, 5e;
🕑 10pm-6am Mon-Sat; Ⓜ Luxembourg

This bar with racing-green wooden shutters has been dispensing cocktails (more than 200 on the list) since 1966. Apparently the '70s were 'epic' in this bar, and the dream kicks on well into the wee hours of the new century. Arrive late for a truly eclectic crowd including lots of students, and an atmosphere that can go from quiet tippling to raucous revelry.

LE PIANO VACHE Map pp110–11   Bar

☎ 01 46 33 75 03; 8 rue Laplace, 5e; 🕑 noon-2am Mon-Fri, 9pm-2am Sat & Sun; Ⓜ Maubert Mutualité

Down the hill from the Panthéon, this bar is covered in old posters above old couches and is drenched in 1970s and '80s rock ambience. Effortlessly underground and a real student fave, bands and DJs play mainly rock, plus some goth, reggae and pop.

LE VIEUX CHÊNE Map pp110–11   Bar

☎ 01 43 37 71 51; 69 rue Mouffetard, 5e; 🕑 4pm-2am Sun-Thu, to 5am Fri & Sat; Ⓜ Place Monge

This rue Mouffetard institution is reckoned to be Paris' oldest bar. Indeed, a revolution-

ary circle met here in 1848 and it was a popular *bal musette* (dancing club) in the late 19th and early 20th centuries. Today it's popular with students, and hosts jazz on weekends.

L'URGENCE BAR Map pp116–17   Bar

☎ 01 43 26 45 69; www.urgencebar.com, in French; 45 rue Monsieur le Prince, 6e; 🕑 9pm-4am Tue-Sat; Ⓜ Luxembourg

Just south of the École de Médecine is located this medical-themed 'emergency room'. Here are the future doctors of France, busy imbibing luridly coloured liquor from babies' bottles and test tubes, loosening their stethoscopes and pointing to the 'X-ray art' – making comments like '*mais non! Clarisse, that's so not the tibia!*'. Even if you don't understand French, its website gives a good sense of the vibe here.

CURIO PARLOR COCKTAIL CLUB

Map pp110–11   Bar, Club

☎ 06 11 22 29 79; 16 rue des Bernardins, 5e;
🕑 6pm-2am Sun-Thu, 6pm-4am Fri & Sat;
Ⓜ Maubert Mutualité

This new place, run by the same group who run the Experimental Cocktail Club, opened in mid 2008. It is a bar-cum-club on the weekends, with a good mixture of soul thrown in for good measure. The aim is to see a return to the inter-war *années folles* (crazy years) of 1920s Paris, London and New York.

CAFÉ DELMAS Map pp110–11   Café

☎ 01 43 26 51 26; 2 place de la Contrescarpe, 5e;
🕑 8am-2am Sun-Thu, to 4am Fri & Sat;
Ⓜ Cardinal Lemoine

Enviably situated on tree-studded place de la Contrescarpe, the Delmas is a hot spot for chilling over *un café*/cappuccino (€2.70/5.80) or all-day breakfast (€11). Sit comfortably beneath overhead heaters outside to soak up the street atmosphere or snuggle up between books in the library-style interior – awash with students from the nearby universities. Should you need the loo, Jacqueline is for women, Jacques for men.

LE VERRE À PIED Map pp110–11   Café

☎ 01 43 31 15 72; 118bis rue Mouffetard, 5e; lunch menus €13.50; 🕑 8am-9pm Tue-Sat, to 4pm Sun; Ⓜ Censier Daubenton

This *café-tabac* is a pearl of a place where little has changed since 1870. Its nicotine-hued mirrored wall, moulded cornices and original bar make it part of a dying breed, but the place oozes the charm, glamour and romance of an old Paris everyone loves. Stall holders from the rue Mouffetard market yo-yo in 'n' out, contemporary photography and art adorns one wall. Lunch is a busy, lively affair, and live music quickens the pulse a couple of evenings a week.

CAVE LA BOURGOGNE
Map pp110–11   Café, Wine Bar
☎ 01 47 07 82 80; 144 rue Mouffetard, 5e; 🕙 9am-10.30pm; Ⓜ Censier Daubenton
Prime spot for lapping up rue Mouffetard's contagious 'saunter-all-day' spirit, this neighbourhood hang-out sits on square St-Médard, one of the Latin Quarter's loveliest squares: think flower-bedecked fountain, centuries-old church and tastebud-titillating market stalls spilling across one side. Inside, old ladies and their pet dogs meet for coffee around dark wood tables alongside a local wine-sipping set. In summer everything spills outside.

LE PUB ST-HILAIRE Map pp110–11   Pub
www.pubsthilaire.com; 2 rue Valette, 5e; 🕙 11am-2am Mon-Thu, to 4am Fri, 4pm-4am Sat, 3pm-midnight Sun; Ⓜ Maubert Mutualité
'Buzzing' fails to do justice to the pulsating vibe inside this student-loved pub. Generous happy hours last several hours and a trio of pool tables, board games, music on two floors and various gimmicks to rev up the party crowd (a metre of cocktails, 'be your own barman' etc) keep the place packed. Pay €3.50/5.50/10 for a *demi/pinte/litre* of *bière pression* (draught beer).

LE VIOLON DINGUE Map pp110–11   Pub
☎ 01 43 25 79 93; 46 rue de la Montagne Ste-Geneviève, 5e; 🕙 8pm-4.30am Tue-Sat; Ⓜ Maubert Mutualité
A loud, lively bar adopted by revolving generations of students, the 'Crazy Violin' attracts lots of young English-speakers with big-screen sports shown upstairs and the flirty 'Dingue Lounge' downstairs. The name 'Crazy Violin' is a pun on the expression *le violon d'Ingres*, meaning 'hobby' in

French, because the celebrated painter Jean-Auguste-Dominique Ingres used to fiddle in his spare time.

ST-GERMAIN, ODÉON & LUXEMBOURG

While much of the 6e is sleepy and snobby, Carrefour de l'Odéon has a cluster of lively bars, cafés and restaurants. Rue de Buci, rue St-André des Arts and rue de l'Odéon enjoy a fair slice of night action with their arty cafés and busy pubs, while place St-Germain des Prés buzzes with the pavement terraces of St-Germain's beloved literary cafés. The local and international student hordes pile into the bars and pubs on atmospheric '*rue de la soif*' (street of thirst), aka rue Princesse and rue des Canettes.

LE ZÉRO DE CONDUITE Map pp116–17   Bar
☎ 01 46 34 26 35; www.zerodeconduite.fr, in French; 14 rue Jacob, 6e; 🕙 8.30pm-1.30am Tue-Thu, 6pm-2am Fri & Sat; Ⓜ Odéon
Originality if nothing else ensures that this bijou drinking hole, in the house where Richard Wagner lived briefly in the 1840s, gets a mention. Serving cocktails in *biberons* (baby bottles) and throwing *concours de grimaces* (face-pulling competitions), it goes all out to rekindle your infancy. Bizarre, yes, but obviously some enjoy sucking vodka and banana liqueur shaken with grenadine and orange juice through a teat. Board games, dice, cards

top picks

DRINKS 'TIL DAWN

Serious night owls wanting to drink 'til dawn (most bars shut at 2am) should try these top picks; some open late only on weekends.

- Café Charbon, 11e (p296)
- Café Oz, 1er (p286)
- Cubana Café, 6e (p293)
- Harry's New York Bar, 2e (p285)
- Highlander, 6e (p292)
- Iguana Café, 11e (p287)
- Le Crocodile, 5e (opposite)
- Le Tambour, 2e (p235)
- Le Violon Dingue, 5e (left)

and Trivial Pursuit complete the playful scene.

CAFÉ DE FLORE Map pp116–17   Café
☎ 01 45 48 55 26; 172 blvd St-Germain, 6e; ⌚ 7.30am-1.30am; Ⓜ St-Germain des Prés
The red upholstered benches, mirrors and marble walls at this Art Deco landmark haven't changed much since the days when Jean-Paul Sartre, Simone de Beauvoir, Albert Camus and Pablo Picasso wagged their chins here. Its busy terrace draws in lunching ladies, posh business-folk and foreigners in search of the past.

LA PALETTE Map pp116–17   Café
☎ 01 43 26 68 15; 43 rue de Seine, 6e; ⌚ 8am-2am Mon-Sat; Ⓜ Mabillon
In the heart of gallery land (see boxed text, p210), this *fin-de-siècle* café and erstwhile stomping ground of Paul Cézanne and Georges Braque attracts a grown-up set of fashion people and local art dealers. Its summer terrace is beautiful.

LES DEUX MAGOTS Map pp116–17   Café
☎ 01 45 48 55 25; 170 blvd St-Germain, 6e; ⌚ 7am-1am; Ⓜ St-Germain des Prés
This erstwhile literary haunt dates from 1914 and is known as the favoured hang-out of Sartre, Hemingway and André Breton. Its name refers to the two *magots* (grotesque figurines) of Chinese dignitaries at the entrance. It's touristy, but just once you can give in to the nostalgia and sit on this inimitable terrace where passing celebrities, retiring philosophers and remnants of noblesse sip its famous shop-made hot chocolate, served in porcelain jugs.

ALCAZAR Map pp116–17   Cocktail Bar
☎ 01 53 10 19 99; www.alcazar.fr; 62 rue Mazarine, 6e; ⌚ noon-3pm & 7pm-2am; Ⓜ Odéon
Also known as 'La Mezzanine', this hip bar inside Alcazar has got Conran's name all over it. Narcissistic but alluring, it's a modern white-and-glass mezzanine overlooking the restaurant with fancy cocktails, *nouvelle cuisine* dinners and a fashionable supper-club clientele. Wednesday to Saturday, DJs 'pass records' in the corner – this place is famous for its excellent trip-hop/house/lounge music compilations. Next door is Conran's club Le Wagg (p306). Flyers for all three are posted at www.blogalcazar.fr.

HIGHLANDER Map pp116–17   Pub
☎ 01 43 26 54 20; 8 rue de Nevers, 6e; ⌚ 5pm-5am Mon-Fri, noon-5am Sat; Ⓜ Odéon
Establishing a kind of love/hate relationship with its regulars, the jubilant Highlander scrapes up the after-hours remains of the Left Bank pub crowd. This mainly means French students, Anglophone lassies, rugby players, hobos and combinations thereof, all intent on drinking until dawn. Downstairs from the Scottish pub is a quasi dance floor, moved more by Long Island iced teas served in pint glasses than any kind of rhythm.

LE 10 Map pp116–17   Pub
☎ 01 43 26 66 83; 10 rue de l'Odéon, 6e; ⌚ 5.30pm-2am; Ⓜ Odéon
A local institution, this cellar pub groans with students, smoky ambience and cheap sangria. Posters adorn the walls and an eclectic selection emerges from the jukebox – everything from jazz and the Doors to *chanson française* ('French song'; traditional musical genre where lyrics are paramount). It's the ideal spot for plotting the next revolution or conquering a lonely heart.

LITTLE TEMPLE BAR Map pp116–17   Pub
☎ 01 43 26 79 95; www.littletemplebar.fr; 12 rue Princesse, 6e; ⌚ 5pm-2am Mon-Fri, noon-2am Sat & Sun; Ⓜ Mabillon
Sports fans pile in to this Irish bar, where football and rugby matches are screened live. It can get heated depending on who's playing/winning, and the place practically vibrates with noise. But that's all part of the vibe. Happy hour (5pm to 8pm, Monday to Friday) whittles a pint down to €5.

O'NEIL Map pp116–17   Pub
☎ 01 46 33 36 66; 20 rue des Canettes, 6e; ⌚ noon-2am; Ⓜ Mabillon
This micro brasserie brews its own: Taste all four with a *palatte en dégustation* (€5.90) or pick the colour to suit your – *blonde* (blond), *blanche* (white), *brune* (brown) or *ambrée* (amber) – poured straight from the barrel. Weekday 'Happy Hour' (6pm to 8pm) spells good-value drinking, as does O'Neil's mighty 1.8L pitchers of beer (€16/20 before/after 6pm). Beer cocktails (€4 to €9.60) and *les chasse-bières* (beer chasers; €7.50) are its unusual specialities.

KILÀLI Map pp116–17   Tearoom
☎ 01 43 25 65 64; 3-5 rue des Quatre Vents, 6e;
☽ noon-10pm Tue-Sat, 1-9pm Sun; Ⓜ Odéon
Style personified, this Japanese tearoom-cum-art gallery is a peaceful oasis amid shops. Finesse, nobility and other elevated adjectives describe the different green teas served in pottery teapots with matching *yunomi* (goblets). Ask for a refill of water when you've drained the pot.

LE COMPTOIR DES CANNETTES
Map pp116–17   Wine Bar
☎ 01 43 26 79 15; 11 rue des Canettes, 6e;
☽ noon-2am Tue-Sat, closed Aug; Ⓜ Mabillon
In the biz since 1952, a faithful local following pours into this cellar, a stuffy, atmospheric tribute to downtrodden romanticism complete with red tablecloths, melting candles and nostalgic photos of musicians. The wine is cheap, the regulars incorrigible and on a good night the whole thing spills up the stairs and onto the street.

MONTPARNASSE
The scene here is far from rocking, but the pace is not slow thanks to the comings and goings of the train station and a trio of legendary cafés-cum-bars-cum-neighbourhood hang-outs.

LE SELECT Map pp124–5   Café
☎ 01 42 22 65 27; 99 blvd du Montparnasse, 6e;
☽ 7.30am-2.30am; Ⓜ Vavin
Along with La Coupole (p258) and Le Dôme (p258), this café is a Montparnasse institution that has changed little since 1923. Students congregate in the early evening; regulars take over as the night wears on. *Tartines* made with Poilâne bread (see p223) are a speciality.

CUBANA CAFÉ Map pp124–5   Cocktail Bar
☎ 01 40 46 80 81; 47 rue Vavin, 6e; ☽ 11am-3am
Sun-Wed, to 5am Thu-Sat; Ⓜ Vavin
This is the perfect place for cocktails and tapas, be it a single dish (€3.70 to €7.10) or a mixed platter (€16) shared among friends, before carrying on to nearby La Coupole (p310). A post-work crowd sinks into the comfy leather armchairs and flops beneath oil paintings of daily life in Cuba.

LE ROSEBUD Map pp124–5   Cocktail Bar
☎ 01 43 35 38 54; 11bis rue Delambre, 14e;
☽ 7pm-2am; Ⓜ Edgar Quinet or Vavin

Like the sleigh of that name in *Citizen Kane,* Rosebud harkens to the past. In this case it's to the time of the Montparnos (painters and writers who frequented Montparnasse during the neighbourhood's golden years of the early 20th century). Enjoy an expertly mixed champagne cocktail or whisky sour amid the quiet elegance of polished wood and aged leather.

FAUBOURG ST-GERMAIN & INVALIDES
An undisputable day rather than night venue, with government ministries and embassies outweighing drinking venues hands-down, the 7e arrondissement does have a redeeming feature for socialites, in the shape of three very lovely cafés.

CAFÉ DU MUSÉE RODIN Map pp128–9   Café
☎ 01 44 18 61 10; 77 rue de Varenne, 7e;
☽ 9.30am-6.45pm Tue-Sun Apr-Sep, to 5pm Tue-Sun Oct-Mar; Ⓜ Varenne
A serene beauty pervades the garden of the Musée Rodin (p130), with the great master's sculptures popping up among the roses and lime trees that line the pathways. If the weather is fine you can have a drink and a snack at one of the tables hidden behind the trees (garden admission €1).

CAFÉ LE BASILE Map pp128–9   Café
☎ 01 42 22 59 46; 34 rue de Grenelle, 7e; ☽ 7am-9pm Mon-Sat; Ⓜ Rue du Bac
Don't bother looking for a name above this hip student café, framed by expensive designer fashion shops – there isn't one. Well-worn Formica tables, petrol-blue banquettes and a fine collection of 1950s lights and lampshades keep the sleek crowd out, the retro crowd in. A fabulous find for a chocolate or beer, light lunch or flop between lectures.

CAFÉ THOUMIEUX Map pp128–9   Café
☎ 01 45 51 50 40; 4 rue de la Comète, 7e; ☽ noon-2am Mon-Fri, 5pm-2am Sat; Ⓜ La Tour Maubourg
The trendy tapas annexe of Brasserie Thoumieux (p259) is always full of well-heeled young people who seem to enjoy the Iberian ambience. Tapas and San Miguel beer set the scene, but perfumed vodka is the house speciality, with no fewer than 40 different

types (including chocolate, fig, watermelon and mint tea) to pick from.

ÉTOILE & CHAMPS-ÉLYSÉES

The av des Champs-Élysées is still a popular place for drinking but the vast majority of venues are terribly expensive and tend to be either tacky tourist traps or exceedingly pretentious lounges. A few nondescript but less flashy pubs can be found in the side streets to the north and south.

The chic quarters around Concorde are not great for finding a classic Parisian café or happening drinking hole, but there are some very memorable, glamorous venues with fantastic décor and, often, a rich history. While not on most Parisians' regular outing list, they definitely merit at least one visit. Most of the fancy hotels along rue de Rivoli have very classy bars and lounges.

BUDDHA BAR Map pp140–1 — Cocktail Bar
☎ 01 53 05 90 00; 8-12 rue Boissy d'Anglas, 8e;
🕑 noon-2am Sun-Thu, 4pm-3am Fri & Sat;
Ⓜ Concorde
Although moving in and out of A-list status as the fickle übercrowd comes and goes, Buddha Bar has made a name for itself with its Zen lounge music CDs and remains a hit – especially with tourists. The décor is simply spectacular, with a two-storey golden Buddha, millions of candles, inti-

top picks

CAFÉ TERRACES

Languish lazily on a café terrace like a Parisian and watch the capital enjoy life over an early-evening apéritif at:

- Café Beaubourg, 3e (p235)
- Café Delmas, 5e (p290)
- Chez Prune, 10e (opposite)
- De la Ville Café, 10e (opposite)
- Le Bistrot du Peintre, 11e (p289)
- Café Le Panier, 10e (p296)
- Le Sancerre, 18e (p299)
- Café des Initiés, 1er (p285)
- Les Funambules, 11e (p287)
- Chai 33, 12e (p297)

mate corners and supremely attitudinous staff. Go for the cocktails (from €16) and Asian-inspired bar snacks.

CRICKETER Map pp140–1 — Pub
☎ 01 40 07 01 45; 41 rue des Mathurins, 8e;
🕑 noon-2am; Ⓜ Madeleine or Havre Caumartin
This self-proclaimed 'English sports pub' can stake a claim to authenticity – it was transported lock, stock and barrel from Ipswich. It's not a happening venue at night, but with Newcastle Brown on tap, salt 'n' vinegar chips, Brit tabloids, three big screens and quiz night every Tuesday it is as close to Old Blighty as you'll find on this side of the Channel.

CLICHY & GARE ST-LAZARE

The neighbourhood around place de Clichy, traditionally the centre of the 'have-not' half of the otherwise very well-heeled 17e, has come into its own in recent years with the development of nearby (and *très bobo*) Batignolles. Rue des Dames is a particularly rewarding street when in search of a libation or a laugh. There's also an excellent wine bar and one of our favourite big terrace cafés here.

LUSH BAR Map p144–5 — Bar
☎ 01 43 87 49 46; 16 rue des Dames, 17e;
🕑 5pm-2am; Ⓜ Place de Clichy
This Clichy post has made a name for itself with a relaxed-but-hip local following and Anglo expats. It has excellent cocktails including killer white Russians, as well as wines and, in true English (or Irish – there are photos of the Emerald Isle on the walls) style, affordable beers. DJs often play on weekends.

BAR À VINS DU CINÉMA DES CINÉASTES Map pp144–5 — Wine Bar
☎ 01 53 42 40 34; 7 av de Clichy, 17e; 🕑 5.30pm-midnight Tue-Sun; Ⓜ Place de Clichy
This excellent wine bar is seldom filled to capacity, presumably because most people are downstairs, watching a film at the Cinéma des Cinéastes (p313). The selection of wines by the glass, 'pot' (a Lyon-inspired carafe measuring 46cL) or bottle is excellent, there is a brief but well-considered menu and the first Sunday of each month hosts a music night starting at 6pm.

LE WEPLER Map pp144–5   Café

☎ 01 45 22 53 24; 14 Place de Clichy, 18e;
⏰ 8am-1am; Ⓜ Place de Clichy

Though this large café-brasserie founded in 1892 is celebrated for its oysters, we go across the road to Charlot, Roi des Coquillages (p263) for our bivalves and to the Wepler to sit in the large covered terrace and enjoy the hubbub and scenery of Place de Clichy. Great people-watching; friendly service.

OPÉRA & GRANDS BOULEVARDS

At times Haussmann's windswept boulevards can be traffic-clogged and as a result feel unwelcoming, but some excellent bars stand out along the main axes and in the side streets. There are some interesting bars near the Bourse (stock exchange) and Opéra, catering mainly to the trader/corporate crowds. Another nocturnal niche is rue Montmartre in the Sentier district, with a few trendy bars and clubs.

O'SULLIVAN'S Map pp148–9   Pub

☎ 01 40 26 73 41; 1 blvd Montmartre, 2o;
⏰ 10am-5am Sun-Thu, to 7am Fri & Sat;
Ⓜ Grands Boulevards

From the outside this looks like just another supermarket-chain Irish pub, but O'Sullivan's is so much more. It's hugely popular thanks to its prominent location and friendly vibe. The spacious surrounds are always packed for big sporting events, plus concerts (jazz, rock, pop, Irish music) on Thursdays and DJs at the weekend. Different available areas such as the 1st floor and the outdoor terrace mean you can (almost) always find a tranquil place to chat.

GARE DU NORD, GARE DE L'EST & RÉPUBLIQUE

Canal St-Martin offers a trendy bohemian atmosphere and wonderful summer nights (and days) in casual canal-side cafés. The proliferation of bars and cafés in the 10e is gradually joining up this area with Belleville and Ménilmontant (see p296). There are also a few decent bars around Gare du Nord and Gare de l'Est.

DE LA VILLE CAFÉ Map pp152–3   Bar

☎ 01 48 24 48 09; 34 blvd de Bonne Nouvelle, 10e;
⏰ 11am-2.30am; Ⓜ Bonne Nouvelle

Another success story from the founders of Café Charbon (p296), this grand erstwhile brothel has an alluring, slightly confused mix of restored history (original mosaic tiles, distressed walls) and modern design. Between the high-ceilinged restaurant, the extensive terrace and the bar/lounge areas, you're sure to find your niche somewhere. DJs play most nights, making it a quality 'before' venue for the nearby Rex Club (p306).

MOTOWN BAR Map pp152–3   Bar

☎ 01 46 07 09 79; 81-83 blvd de Strasbourg, 10e;
⏰ closed 1am-6pm Tue & Wed; Ⓜ Gare de l'Est

This *almost* 24-hour place – it's open continuously except for two early-morning gaps at the start of the week – is the venue of choice in the wee hours when you have a thirst and a few bob but, alas, no friends. You can drink at almost any time of day, and eat (mains €7.50 to €11.50) until 11pm, live singers croon on certain nights. There's a warm and festive feel, and the staff and the patrons are friendly.

CAFÉ CHÉRI(E) Map pp174–5   Bar, Café

☎ 01 42 02 02 05; 44 blvd de la Villette, 19e;
⏰ 8am-2am; Ⓜ Belleville

Very reminiscent of Belleville before all the changes, this successful bar-café has a lively, gritty, art-chic crowd and electro DJs Thursday to Saturday. An imaginative, colourful bar with its signature red lighting, infamous *mojitos* and *caiparinhas* and commitment to quality tunes, it's become everyone's *chéri(e)* (darling) and the first port of call on a night out in this part of town.

CHEZ PRUNE Map pp152–3   Bar, Café

☎ 01 42 41 30 47; 71 quai de Valmy, 10e; ⏰ 8am-2am Mon-Sat, 10am-2am Sun; Ⓜ République

This Soho-boho café put Canal St-Martin on the map. It's a classic Parisian bar-café, nicely rough around the edges, with good vibes – a terrace opposite the Canal St-Martin open in summer and a cosy atmosphere in winter. Brunch on Sundays (noon to 4pm) is popular.

L'ÎLE ENCHANTÉE Map pp152–3   Bar, Café
☎ 01 42 01 67 99; 65 blvd de la Villette, 19e;
🕑 8am-2am Mon-Fri, 6pm-2am Sat & Sun;
Ⓜ Belleville

In a similar vein to Café Chéri(e) (p295), this 'Enchanted Island' in Belleville has become a popular stop-off for the before-clubbing crowd. With its colourful façade, huge windows and large, modern interior, it's a relaxed restaurant and terrace by day that turns electric at nightfall from Thursday to Saturday, with quality DJs mixing most evenings.

CAFÉ LE PANIER Map pp152–3   Café
☎ 01 42 01 38 18; 32 place Ste-Marthe, 10e;
🕑 11am-2am Tue-Sun May-Sep, 4pm-2am Mon-Sat & 10am-2am Sun Oct-Apr; Ⓜ Belleville

Out in the western flanks of Belleville, it's easy to miss the rue Ste-Marthe, filled with colourful restaurants and bars exerting a dilapidated, funky charm. At the top, literally and figuratively, is this splendid and convivial café, a bit of Marseille in Paris, with an enormous terrace on sheltered place Ste-Marthe. It's brilliant for warm afternoons, casual meals (mains €9.50 to €16.50) and an extended apéritif.

MÉNILMONTANT & BELLEVILLE

Rue Oberkampf is the essential hub of the Ménilmontant bar crawl, springing from a few cafés to being the epicentre of a vibrant, rapidly expanding bar scene. But as Oberkampf commercialises, the arty/edgy crowd has been moving steadily outwards, through cosmopolitan Belleville and towards La Villette (see p172).

AU PETIT GARAGE Map p155   Bar
☎ 01 48 07 08 12; 63 rue Jean-Pierre-Timbaud, 11e; 🕑 6pm-2am; Ⓜ Parmentier.

Just about the last 'neighbourhood' bar in the *quartier,* the 'Little Garage' attracts local custom (think grease monkeys and others with cleaner hands) with its rock 'n' roll, laid-back staff and rough-and-ready décor. Definitely worth a visit.

CANNIBALE CAFÉ Map p155   Bar
☎ 01 49 20 95 59; 93 rue Jean-Pierre Timbaud, 11e; 🕑 8am-2am Mon-Fri, 9am-2am Sat & Sun;
Ⓜ Couronnes

In fact 'Cannibal Café' couldn't be more welcoming, with its grand rococo-style bar topped with worn zinc, decrepit mirrors, peeling mouldings, wood panelling, Formica tables and red leatherette bench seats. It's a laid-back, almost frayed alternative to the groovy pubs and bars of rue Oberkampf and the perfect place to linger over a coffee or grab a quick beer at the bar. There's an extensive menu with popular breakfasts (€9 to €12), and brunch (served between noon and 4pm on the weekend) is €18. Oh, and the name of this place isn't suggesting that you bring condiments if you miss the mealtimes; it comes from a Dada manifesto and a painting by Goya.

LA CARAVANE Map p155   Bar
☎ 01 49 23 01 86; 35 rue de la Fontaine au Roi, 11e; 🕑 11am-2am Mon-Fri, 5pm-2am Sat & Sun;
Ⓜ Goncourt

This funky, animated bar is a little jewel tucked away between République and Oberkampf; look for the tiny campervan above the door. The bar is surrounded by colourful kitsch furnishings and the people around it and behind it are amiable and relaxed. The kitchen was into a rather odd hybrid cuisine – Thai noodles, Indian bhajis, *chèvre chaud* – the last time we looked. Stick with the reasonably priced drinks.

CAFÉ CHARBON Map p155   Bar, Café
☎ 01 43 57 55 13; 109 rue Oberkampf, 11e;
🕑 9am-2am Sun-Thu, to 4am Fri & Sat;
Ⓜ Parmentier

With its postindustrial *belle époque* ambience, the Charbon was the first of the hip cafés and bars to catch on in Ménilmontant. Now it's somewhat a victim of its own success, but it's always crowded and worth heading to for the distressed décor with high ceilings, chandeliers and perched DJ booth. The food (mains €11 to €18) is good; it's a popular spot for brunch between noon and 3pm on Sundays.

ON CHERCHE ENCORE Map p155   Bar, Café
☎ 01 49 20 79 56; 2 rue des Goncourt, 11e;
🕑 11am-4pm Mon, to 2am Tue-Fri, noon-2am Sat;
Ⓜ Goncourt

This relaxed, modern, loft-style bar-café with the less-than-inspired name of 'We're Still Looking', is trying to do it all and succeeding. It's committed to serving quality food and wines at reasonable prices; the Saturday brunch from noon to 4pm is one of the best around. It is also intent on providing quality tunes (electro, house and funk) from Thursday to Saturday, which leads to some quality mingling. The corner terrace is positioned for all-afternoon sun and is worth pouncing on.

AU CHAT NOIR Map p155   Café
☎ 01 48 06 98 22; 76 rue Jean-Pierre Timbaud, 10e; ⏰ 10am-2am Sun-Thu, 11am-2am Fri & Sat; Ⓜ Parmentier

Slightly removed from the overexcitement of Oberkampf and with a slightly older crowd, this attractive corner café with high ceilings and a long, wooden bar is a happening but relaxed drinking space at night. It's also a great café in which to hang out or read during the day. Downstairs is more animated, with occasional live concerts.

L'AUTRE CAFÉ Map p155   Café
☎ 01 40 21 03 07; 62 rue Jean-Pierre Timbaud, 11e; ⏰ 8am-2am; Ⓜ Parmentier

A young mixed crowd of locals, artists and party-goers remains faithful to this quality café with its long bar, spacious seating areas, relaxed environment, reasonable prices and exhibition openings. It's a great place to do a little work, and there is a small lounge upstairs.

GARE DE LYON, NATION & BERCY

Once a desert when it came to drinking and carousing, Bercy is an increasingly happening place that draws in crowds for its cinemas and wine bars, though it's a somewhat artificially created scene. Gare de Lyon and Nation are close to drinking spots in Bastille (p286), and to the eastern side of the 11e (opposite).

BARRIO LATINO Map pp158–9   Bar
☎ 01 55 78 84 75; 46-48 rue du Faubourg St-Antoine, 11e; ⏰ 11am-2am Sun-Thu, to 3am Fri & Sat; Ⓜ Bastille

Still squeezing the salsa theme for all that it's worth, this enormous bar-restaurant with serious dancing – distantly related to Buddha Bar (p294) – is spread over three highly impressive floors. It attracts Latinos, Latino

wannabes and Latino wannahaves. The delicious *mojitos* go down a treat.

LA LIBERTÉ Map pp158–9   Bar
☎ 01 43 72 11 18; 196 rue de Faubourg St-Antoine, 12e; ⏰ 9am-2am Mon-Fri, 11am-2am Sat & Sun; Ⓜ Faidherbe-Chaligny

A delightfully messy bar infused with the spirit of the '68 revolution, 'The Liberty' does simple meals and wine by day, and is a heaving mix of regulars and drop-ins, raspy-voiced arguments and glasses going clink by night. It's the kind of place where *bobos*, artists and old rockers find their common point: a passionate love of drink and talk.

CHAI 33 Map pp158–9   Wine Bar
☎ 01 53 44 01 01; 33 cour St-Émilion, 12e; ⏰ noon-midnight Sun & Mon, to 1am Tue-Thu, to 2am Fri & Sat; Ⓜ Cour St-Émilion

The converted wine warehouses in Bercy Village house a variety of restaurants and bars, including this enormous wine-oriented concept space with a restaurant, lounge, tasting room and shop. Wine, both French and foreign, is divided into six colour-coded categories: purple is 'fruity and intense', green is 'light and spirited', yellow is 'dry and soft' etc. There are cocktails and decent food here, too, as well as two terraces.

LE VINÉA CAFÉ Map pp158–9   Wine Bar
☎ 01 44 74 09 09; 26-28 cour St-Émilion, 12e; ⏰ 9am-2am Sun-Thu, to 4am Fri & Sat; Ⓜ Cour St-Émilion

The anchor tenant – or so it would seem – of the cour St-Émilion, this is a delightful wine bar/restaurant with a lovely terrace to the back facing place des Vins de France. There's live music some nights and a popular brunch (€23) from noon to 4pm on Sundays.

13E ARRONDISSEMENT & CHINATOWN

While Chinatown isn't a hopping spot for bars, the area around the Butte aux Cailles, a kind of molehill southwest of Place d'Italie, has some good options. It is a pretty area that is popular with students and local residents: places in this area tend to have diehard regulars.

SPUTNIK Map pp162–3   Bar
☎ 01 45 65 19 82; 14 rue de la Butte aux Cailles, 13e; ⏲ 2pm-2am Mon-Sat, 4pm-midnight Sun; Ⓜ Corvisart or Place d'Italie
This large bar with wi-fi zone and a dozen machines to surf is far more than an internet café. With its buzzing pavement terrace on one of Paris' hippest streets, Sputnik is a place to be seen. Students love it, particularly between 6pm and 8pm during happy hour.

THE FROG & BRITISH LIBRARY
Map pp162–3   Pub
☎ 01 45 84 34 26; 114 av de France, 13e; mains €13.50, lunch menus €14; ⏲ 7.30am-2am Mon-Fri, noon-2am Sat & Sun; Ⓜ Bibliothèque
A hybrid English pub/French brasserie, this spacious drinking venue around the corner from the Bibliothèque Nationale is propped up by French students who flock here between library visits for apple pie and custard, weekend brunches, potato wedges and cheese nachos washed down with a pint (€4.50). The pick of the drinks list is the six beers brewed on the premises: Dark de Triomphe, Inseine, Parislytic and so on. Pints are €6 or €4.50 at happy hour (6pm to 8pm Monday to Friday). Free wi-fi, live bands, groove and soul DJs, themed party nights. The enormous Frog at Bercy Village (Map pp158–9; ☎ 01 43 40 70 71; 25 cour St-Émilion, 12e; ⏲ noon-2am; Ⓜ Cour St-Émilion) is just across the river.

TANDEM Map pp162–3   Wine Bar
☎ 01 45 80 38 39; 10 rue de la Butte aux Cailles, 13e; starters €7-8.50, mains €13.50-20; ⏲ noon-2.30pm & 7.30-11pm Tue-Sat; Ⓜ Corvisart or Place d'Italie
If wine's your love, make a beeline for this overwhelmingly old-fashioned bar à vins crammed with regulars. The lovechild of two brothers with a fierce oenological passion, Tandem homes in on 'boutique' (vins de propriétés) and organic wines as well as those produced by new vignerons (winemakers). A traditional bistro menu compliments the wine list.

ALSO RECOMMENDED
Friendly and convivial, Le Merle Moqueur (Map pp162–3; 11 rue de la Butte aux Cailles, 13e; ⏲ 5pm-2am; Ⓜ Corvisart) stocks the largest selection of rum punches we've seen.

15E ARRONDISSEMENT
It's hardly buzzing, but as with every quartier it has a clutch of faithfuls propped up by die-hard regulars.

CHARLIE BIRDY Map pp166–7   Bar
☎ 01 48 28 06 06; www.charliebirdy.com, in French; 1 place Étienne Pernet, 15e; ⏲ 5pm-2am; Ⓜ Commerce
Love it or hate it, this lounge bar – one of three Parisian Charlie Birdies – is the place to sit back, relax and savour a well-earned apéritif after a hard day's work. Décor is modern; the place splits into part bar, part red-brick-walled restaurant; and live gospel 'n' soul makes weekend brunch (€17.50) an upbeat affair.

LES VÉLOS À MOËLLE Map pp166–7   Wine Bar
☎ 01 45 57 28 28; rue Vasco de Gama, 15e; ⏲ noon-3pm & 7.30-10.30pm Tue-Sat, noon-4pm & 7.30-10.30pm Sun; Ⓜ Lourmel
Geared as much towards energetic cyclists as wine lovers who are happy to loll at the bar, this wine bar rents out bikes equipped with gourmet picnic hampers (€32). Warming the cockles with a vin chaud (mulled wine) and chunk of pain d'épice (honey spiced bread) around a wine-barrel-turned-table on the pavement outside is a winter delight. Should hunger pains strike, its lunchtime formule à buffet (€22.50) is excellent value.

MONTMARTRE & PIGALLE
Crowded around the hill side of Montmartre you'll find an utterly eclectic selection of places to drink. This area offers a strange medley of tourist-trap chanson bars at Sacré Cœur, sleazy sex-shop venues at Pigalle, African outposts at Château Rouge and picturesque Parisian spots around Abbesses.

LA FOURMI Map p169   Bar
☎ 01 42 64 70 35; 74 rue des Martyrs, 18e; ⏲ 8am-2am Mon-Thu, to 4am Fri & Sat, 10am-2am Sun; Ⓜ Pigalle
A Pigalle stayer, 'The Ant' hits the mark with its lively yet unpretentious atmosphere. The décor is hip but not overwhelming, the zinc bar is long and inviting and the people are laid-back. The music is mostly rock – qual-

CAPITAL WINE TASTING

Sorting the good wines from the inferior ones when it comes to serious wine-tasting in Paris is no mean feat. Dozens of courses exist, but few come recommended.

One man in the capital who really knows his stuff is sommelier Juan Sánchez, who holds talks and *dégustations* (tastings) most Saturday evenings with independent French wine growers he buys from at his wine shop La Dernier Goutte (p211) in St-Germain des Prés. Le Pré Verre (p252) and Tandem (opposite) are informal, atmospheric places to taste interesting wines by small producers over a meal.

Oenophiles aspiring to headier heights should aim for one of the sporadic tastings held in Paris' oldest wine shop, Caves Augé (Map pp140–1; ☎ 01 45 22 16 97; 116 blvd Haussmann, 8e; Ⓜ St-Augustin), in business since 1850. On the same street, one of the world's foremost sommeliers, Philippe Faure-Brac, pairs food and wine to perfection for a price at Bistrot du Sommelier (p261). Cellar tastings with wine growers pre-empt Friday's brilliantly matched three-/five-course lunch/dinner (€45/70).

To learn how to sort the wheat from the chaff, embark on a wine-tasting course at the highly esteemed Centre de Dégustation Jacques Vivet (Map pp116–17; ☎ 01 43 25 96 30, 06 07 28 61 85; 48 rue de Vaugirard, 6e; Ⓜ Luxembourg), opposite Jardin de Luxembourg. As well as one-day tasting courses (€194) and introductory wine courses (in English and French), it runs advanced *cours d'oeonologie* (in French only) focusing on several wines from one appellation or grape variety.

ity, well-known tunes that get you going while leaving space in the airways for the rise and fall of unbridled conversation. If you're hungry, its *plat du jour* costs €9.

LE DÉPANNEUR Map p169   Bar
☎ 01 44 53 03 78; 27 rue Pierre Fontaine, 9e; ⏲ 10am-2am Mon-Thu, 24hr Fri-Sun; Ⓜ Blanche
'The Repairman', an American diner-cum-bar with postmodern frills and almost 24-hour service, has plenty of tequila and fancy cocktails (€7.50). There are DJs after 11pm from Thursday to Saturday. After 3am or 4am at the weekend most clients have just come out of the clubs. Be on guard.

LE SANCERRE Map p169   Bar
☎ 01 42 58 08 20; 35 rue des Abbesses, 18e; ⏲ 7am-2am; Ⓜ Abbesses
Le Sancerre is a popular, rather brash bistro-cum-bar that's often crowded to capacity in the evening, especially on Saturdays. Scruffy yet attractive with its classic bistro décor and hip local mood, it has a prized terrace that gets the late morning sun. It serves bistro food and breakfasts from 11.30am to 11.30pm. Happy hour is 5.30pm to 8pm.

OLYMPIC CAFÉ Map p169   Bar
☎ 01 42 52 29 93; 20 rue Léon, 18e; ⏲ 7pm-2am Tue-Sat; Ⓜ Château Rouge
This community bar in the Goutte d'Or neighbourhood is full of surprises. From plays and film screenings to concerts of Guinean *griot,* Balkan folk, Cameroon hip-hop and so on in the basement (tickets €5 to €7), this is a breeding ground for creative young people bursting with original ideas. The monthly program available at the bar also includes events (tickets adult/concession €15/10) at the Lavoir Moderne Parisien (Map p169; ☎ 01 42 52 09 14; 35 rue Léon, 18e), another springboard for young talent down the road.

CHÀO BÀ CAFÉ Map p169   Café
☎ 01 46 06 72 90; 22 blvd de Clichy, 18e; ⏲ 8.30am-2am Sun-Wed, to 4am Thu, to 5am Fri & Sat; Ⓜ Pigalle
This comfortable café-restaurant on two levels is decorated in colonial Oriental style with huge plants, ceiling fans and bamboo chairs. It serves great cocktails (from €9.50) in goldfish-bowl-sized glasses, and somewhat bland Franco-Vietnamese fusion food. And BTW: *chào bà* means *bonjour madame* in Vietnamese.

LE PROGRÈS Map p169   Café
☎ 01 42 64 07 37; 7 rue des Trois Frères, 18e; ⏲ 9am-2am; Ⓜ Abbesses
A real live *café du quartier* perched in the heart of Abbesses, 'The Progress' occupies a corner site with huge windows and simple seating and attracts a relaxed mix of local artists, shop staff, writers and hangers-on. It's great for convivial evenings, with DJs and bands some nights, but, it's also a good place to come for inexpensive meals and daytime coffees.

ICE KUBE Map p169 — Cocktail Bar

☎ 01 42 05 20 00; 1-5 passage Ruelle, 18e; ☼ 7pm-1.30am Wed-Sat, 2-11pm Sun; Ⓜ La Chapelle

Every city worth its, err, salt, has got to have an ice bar nowadays, and this *temple de glace* (ice temple) on the first floor of the *très boutique* Kube Hôtel (p357) is the French capital's first. The temperature is still set at -20°C, there are down jackets on loan and the bar is a shimmering block of carved ice. But the rules have changed. It's no longer all the vodka you can dispatch in 30 min-utes for €38, but a far less cool four vodka cocktails for the same.

CORCORAN'S CLICHY Map p169 — Pub

☎ 01 42 23 00 30; 110 blvd de Clichy, 18e; ☼ 11.30am-5am; Ⓜ Blanche

OK, so it's just another Irish pub… But with the entrance to the Cimetière de Montmartre (p168) just paces away, Corcoran's is a great place to stop off on your way to/from paying obeisance to Zola or Stendhal. And it's at the start of a quiet cul-de-sac.

NIGHTLIFE & THE ARTS

top picks

What's your recommendation? www.lonelyplanet.com/paris

A night out in Paris can mean anything from swilling champagne on the Champs-Elysées to opening unmarked doorways in search of a new club in the *banlieues* (suburbs) or dancing on tables till dawn in a mad-loud DJ bar (see p284). From jazz cellar to comic theatre, garage beat to go-go dancer, world-class art gallery to avant-garde artist squat, this is *the* capital of savoir-vivre, with spectacular entertainment to suit every budget, every taste.

The French capital holds a firm place on the touring circuit of the world's finest artists and boasts dozens of historic and/or legendary concert venues: seeing a performance here is a treat. French and international opera, ballet and theatre companies (not to mention cabaret's incorrigible cancan dancers) take to the stage in a clutch of venues of mythical proportion – the Palais Garnier, Comédie Française and the Moulin Rouge included. Away from the bright lights and media glare, a flurry of young, passionate, highly creative musicians, theatre aficionados and artists make the city's fascinating fringe art scene what it is.

The film-lover's ultimate city, Paris provides the best seat in the house to catch new flicks, avant-garde cinema and priceless classics. Its inhabitants are film fetishists *par excellence*, with wonderful movie theatres – 1930s Chinese pagoda to Seine-side cutting-edge shoebox – to prove it.

So go out. Delve into the Parisian night.

Information & Listings

'Theatre', 'Kids', 'Outings & Leisure', 'Cinema', 'Restaurants', 'Festivals', 'Music', 'The Arts' and 'Paris by Nights' are the key headings in the index of *Pariscope* (€0.40), the capital's primary weekly listings guide published every Wednesday. Its 230-odd pages – B&W with the odd splash of colour – are almost too packed with information, but everything you need to know about what's on and happening is there. Many find Paris' other weekly listings bible, *L'Officiel des Spectacles* (€0.35), also out on Wednesday, easier to handle. Buy both (in French only) at any newsstand.

Rock, jazz, world and *chanson* (song) are among the many genres covered by *Les Inrockuptibles* (www.lesinrocks.com, in French; €3), a national music mag with a strong Paris focus and great soiree and concert listings.

Of the surfeit of various French-language freebies, easy to pick up on the street and great for a gander between metro stops, *A nous Paris* (www.anous.fr/paris, in French) is among the most informed and posts its contents online; click 'Lieux Branchés' (Trendsetters) to find in-vogue bars, clubs and restaurants of the moment. Pocket-sized booklet *LYLO* (short for *Les Yeux, Les Oreilles*, meaning 'eyes and ears'), freely available at bars and cafés, is a fortnightly lowdown on the live music, concert and clubbing scene and runs an information line (☎ 0 892 68 59 56; www.lylo.fr, in French). Flyers, schedules and programmes for cultural events float around the ticket office areas in Fnac (below).

Electronic links finely tuned to the music, clubbing, theatre scene etc right now are listed in the respective sections of this chapter.

Tickets & Reservations

Buy tickets for concerts, theatre performances and other cultural events at *billeteries* (ticket offices) in Fnac (rhymes with 'snack') and Virgin Megastore. Both accept reservations by phone and the internet, and most credit cards. Tickets can't usually be returned or exchanged unless a performance is cancelled.

Some Fnac (☎ 0 892 68 36 22; www.fnacspectacles .com, in French) outlets:

Bastille (Map pp94–5; ☎ 01 43 42 04 04; 4 place de la Bastille, 12e; ☼ 10am-8pm Mon-Sat; Ⓜ Bastille)

Champs-Élysées (Map pp140–1; ☎ 01 53 53 64 64; 74 av des Champs-Élysées, 8e; ☼ 10am-midnight Mon-Sat, noon-midnight Sun; Ⓜ Franklin D Roosevelt)

Étoile (Map pp144–5; ☎ 01 44 09 18 00; 26-30 av des Ternes, 17e; ☼ 10am-7.30pm Mon-Sat; Ⓜ Ternes)

Forum des Halles (Map p86; ☎ 01 40 41 40 00; Forum des Halles shopping centre, level 3, 1-7 rue Pierre Lescot, 1er; ☼ 10am-7pm Mon-Sat; Ⓜ Châtelet Les Halles)

DIGITAL DISCOUNT TICKETING

- www.billetreduc.com
- www.ticketac.com
- www.webguichet.com

Montparnasse (Map pp116–17; ☎ 01 49 54 30 00; 136 rue de Rennes, 6e; ☺ 10am-7pm Mon-Sat; Ⓜ St-Placide)

St-Lazare (Map pp144–5; ☎ 01 55 31 20 00; 109 rue St-Lazare, 9e; ☺ 10am-7.30pm Mon-Wed & Sat, to 8.30pm Thu & Fri; Ⓜ St-Lazare).

Virgin Megastore (☎ 08 25 12 91 39; www.virginmega .fr, in French) branches:

Barbès (Map p169; ☎ 01 56 55 53 70; 15 blvd Barbès, 18e; ☺ 10am-9pm Mon-Sat; Ⓜ Barbès Rochechouart)

Champs-Élysées (Map pp140–1; ☎ 01 49 53 50 00; 52-60 av des Champs-Élysées, 8e; ☺ 10am-midnight Mon-Sat, noon-midnight Sun; Ⓜ Franklin D Roosevelt)

Galerie du Carrousel du Louvre (Map p86; ☎ 01 44 50 03 10; 99 rue de Rivoli, 1er; ☺ 10am-8pm Mon & Tue, to 9pm Wed-Sun; Ⓜ Palais Royal Musée du Louvre)

Gare Montparnasse (Map pp124–5; place Raoul Dautry, 14e; ☺ 7am-8.30pm Mon-Thu, to 9pm Fri, 8am-8pm Sat; Ⓜ Montparnasse Bienvenüe)

Other ticketing box offices:

Agence Marivaux (Map pp82–3; ☎ 01 42 97 46 70; 7 rue de Marivaux, 2e; ☺ 11.30am-7.30pm Mon-Fri, noon-4pm Sat; Ⓜ Richelieu Drouot) Paris' oldest ticket agency, just opposite the Opéra Comique.

Agence Perrossier & SOS Théâtres (Map pp140–1; ☎ 01 42 60 58 31, 01 44 77 88 55; www.agencedetheatres-deparis.fr; 6 place de la Madeleine, 8e; ☺ 10am-7pm Mon-Sat; Ⓜ Madeleine)

Discount Tickets

Come the day of a performance, snag a half-price ticket for the ballet, theatre, opera etc at discount-ticket outlet Kiosque Théâtre Madeleine (Map pp140–1; opp 15 place de la Madeleine, 8e; ☺ 12.30-8pm Tue-Sat, to 4pm Sun; Ⓜ Madeleine) or Kiosque Théâtre Montparnasse (Map pp124–5; Parvis Montparnasse, 15e; ☺ 12.30-8pm Tue-Sat, to 4pm Sun; Ⓜ Montparnasse Bienvenüe).

CABARET

Parisians don't tend to watch the city's risqué cabaret revues – tourists do. Times and prices for the dazzling, pseudo-bohemian productions starring women in two beads and a feather (or was that two feathers and a bead?) vary: shows often begin at 7pm or 7.30pm, 8.30pm or 9pm, or 11pm, and some venues have matinées and additional evening shows at the weekend. Tickets cost anything from €65 to €120 per person (€140 to €400 with swish dinner and champagne). All venues sell tickets online.

top picks

FREE SHOWS

Paris' eclectic gaggle of clowns, acrobats, Rollerbladers, buskers and other street entertainers can be highly entertaining and costs substantially less than a theatre ticket (€1 in the hat is a sweet gesture). Our favourite spots for a good show:

- Place Georges Pompidou, 4e (Map p86) The huge square in front of the Centre Pompidou.
- Place Jean du Bellay, 1er (Map p86) Musicians and fire-eaters near the Fontaine des Innocents.
- Pont St-Louis, 4e (Map p105) The bridge linking Paris' two islands.
- Pont au Double, 4e (Map p105) The pedestrian bridge linking Notre Dame with the Left Bank.
- Palais de Tokyo (p135) & Musée d'Art Moderne de la Ville de Paris, 16e (p135) Venue of choice for the city's most acrobatic inline skaters.
- Parc de la Villette, 19e (p172) African drummers at the weekend.
- Metro (Map p2) Any time on any line – even when you're not in the mood.

CRAZY HORSE Map pp140–1

☎ 01 47 23 32 32; www.lecrazyhorseparis.com; 12 av George V, 8e; Ⓜ Alma Marceau

This popular cabaret, whose dressing (or, rather, undressing) rooms were featured in Woody Allen's film *What's New Pussycat?* (1965), now promotes fine art – abstract 1960s patterns as they appear superimposed on the female nude form.

LE LIDO DE PARIS Map pp140–1

☎ 01 40 76 56 10; www.lido.fr; 116bis av des Champs-Élysées, 8e; Ⓜ George V

Founded at the close of WWII, this gets top marks for its sets and the lavish costumes of its 70 artistes, including the famed Bluebell Girls and now the Lido Boy Dancers.

MOULIN ROUGE Map p169

☎ 01 53 09 82 82; www.moulinrouge.fr; 82 blvd de Clichy, 18e; Ⓜ Blanche

Ooh la la… What is probably Paris' most celebrated cabaret was founded in 1889 and its dancers appeared in the celebrated posters by Toulouse-Lautrec. It sits under its trademark red windmill (actually a 1925 replica of the 19th-century original) and attracts viewers and voyeurs by the busload.

CLUBBING

Paris is *not* London, Berlin or New York when it comes to clubbing, and hardcore clubbers from other European capitals might be surprised by the pick of Paris clubs. Lacking a mainstream scene, clubbing here tends to be underground and extremely mobile, making blogs, forums and websites (see boxed text, below) the savviest means of keeping apace with what's happening (loads of clubs/events are on MySpace). The best DJs and their followings have short stints in a certain venue before moving on, and the scene's hippest *soirées clubbing* (clubbing events) float between a clutch of venues – including the city's many dance-driven bars (see p284).

But the beat is strong. Electronic music is of particularly high quality in Paris' clubs, with some excellent local house and techno. Funk and groove have given the whimsical predominance of dark minimal sounds a good pounding, and the Latin scene is huge; salsa dancing and Latino music nights pack out plenty of clubs. R 'n' B and hip-hop pickings are decent, if less represented than in, say, London.

Club admission costs anything from €5 to €20 and often includes a drink; admission is usually cheaper before 1am and men can't always get in unaccompanied by a woman. Drink prices start at around €6 for a beer and €8 for amixed drink or cocktail, but often cost more.

CITHÉA NOVA Map p155

☎ 01 40 21 70 95; www.citheanova.com, in French; 112 rue Oberkampf, 11e; admission free; ⏲ 9am-5am Sun-Thu, 10pm-6am Fri & Sat; Ⓜ Parmentier or Ménilmontant

Beefing up the kitchen (it does all meals and brunch at the weekend from 11am

---

to 4pm) and sticking 'new' at the end of your name doesn't always work when times are hard, But these guys have done it and what was a pub-meets-concert-hall with quality bands is now a stylish resto-bar with same. Concerts usually run from 10.30pm, with DJs from 1am on Wednesday to Saturday.

FOLIE'S PIGALLE Map p169

☎ 01 48 78 55 25; www.folies-pigalle.com; 11 place Pigalle, 9e; admission €7-20; ⏲ midnight-dawn Mon-Thu, to noon Fri & Sat, 6pm-dawn; Ⓜ Pigalle

Folie's Pigalle is a heaving place with a mixed gay and straight crowd that is great for cruising from the balcony above the dance floor. There are theme nights and concerts (usually at 2am) throughout the week. Sunday evening is the 'Original Gay Tea Party', followed by the after 'La Grande Soirée Trans', Paris' only transsexual theme night, with R 'n' B, dance, techno and house. It's Latino night on Monday.

LA DAME DE CANTON Map pp162–3

☎ 01 53 61 08 49, 06 10 41 02 29; www.dame canton.com, in French; opp 11 quai François Mauriac, 13e; admission incl 1 drink €10; ⏲ 7pm-2am Tue-Thu, to dawn Fri & Sat; Ⓜ Quai de la Gare or Bibliothèque

This floating *boîte* (club) aboard a three-masted Chinese junk with a couple of world voyages under its belt is moored opposite the Bibliothèque Nationale de France. Called *Cabaret Pirate* and *Guinguette Pirate* in previous lives, it re-adopted its maiden name – 'The Lady from Canton' – in 2008 to mark its 30th birthday. Concerts (8.30pm) range from pop and indie to electro, hip-hop, reggae and rock; afterwards, DJs keep the young crowd moving.

LA FAVELA CHIC Map pp94–5

☎ 01 40 21 38 14; www.favelachic.com, in French; 18 rue du Faubourg du Temple, 10e; admission free-€10; ⏲ 8pm-2am Tue-Thu, to 4am Fri & Sat; Ⓜ République

It starts as a chic, convivial restaurant (open for lunch and dinner to 11pm) and gives way to *caipirinha*- and *mojito*-fuelled bumping, grinding, flirting and dancing – mostly on the long tables. The music is traditionally bossa nova, samba, *baile* (dance) funk and Brazilian pop, and it can get very crowded and hot.

DIGITAL CLUBBING

Track tomorrow's hot 'n' happening *soirée* with these finger-on-the-pulse Parisian nightlife links (in French).

- www.gogoparis.com (in English)
- www.lemonsound.com
- www.novaplanet.com
- www.parisbouge.com
- www.parissi.com
- www.radiofg.com
- www.tribudenuit.com

CLUBBING IN PARIS: BEFORE, AFTER & D'AFTER

Seasoned Parisian clubbers, who tend to have a finely tuned sense of the absurd, split their night into three parts. First, *la before* – drinks in a bar that has a DJ playing (loads listed in the Drinking chapter, p284). Second, they head to a club for *la soirée*, which rarely kicks off before 1am or 2am. When the party continues (or begins) at around 5am and goes until midday, it's the third in the trio – *l'after*. Invariably, though, given the lack of any clear-cut distinction between Parisian bars and clubs, the before and after can easily blend into one without any real 'during'. *'After d'afters'*, meanwhile, kicks off in bars and clubs on Sunday afternoons and evenings, with a mix of strung-out hardcore clubbers pressing on amid less-mad socialites out for a party that doesn't take place in the middle of the night.

LE BALAJO Map pp94–5

☎ 01 47 00 07 87; www.balajo.fr, in French; 9 rue de Lappe, 11e; admission €12-18; ☉ 10pm-2am Tue & Thu, 9pm-2am Wed, 11pm-5am Fri & Sat, 3-7.30pm Sun; Ⓜ Bastille

A mainstay of Parisian nightlife since 1936, this ancient ballroom is devoted to salsa classes and Latino music during the week. Weekends see DJs spinning a very mixed bag of rock, disco, funk, R 'n' B and house. While a bit lower-shelf these days, it scores a mention for its historical value and its old-fashioned *musette* (accordion music) gigs on Sundays: waltz, tango and cha-cha for aficionados of retro tea-dancing.

LE BATOFAR Map pp162–3

☎ 01 53 16 70 30; www.batofar.org, in French; opp 11 quai François Mauriac, 13e; admission free-€15; ☉ 9pm-midnight Mon & Tue, to 4am or later Wed-Sun; Ⓜ Quai de la Gare or Bibliothèque

This incongruous, much-loved, red-metal tugboat has a rooftop bar that's great in summer, while the club underneath provides memorable underwater acoustics between its metal walls and portholes. Le Batofar is known for its edgy, experimental music policy and live performances, mostly electro-oriented but also incorporating hip-hop, new wave, rock, punk or jazz. Sometimes it doesn't open till 10pm.

LE DIVAN DU MONDE Map p169

☎ 01 42 52 02 46; www.divandumonde.com; 75 rue des Martyrs, 18e; admission free-€12; ☉ 7pm-3am Tue-Thu, to 6am Fri & Sat; Ⓜ Pigalle

Take some cinematographic events, Gypsy gatherings, *nouvelles chansons françaises* (new French songs). Add in soul/funk fiestas, air-guitar face-offs and rock parties of the Arctic Monkeys/Killers/Libertines persuasion and stir with an Amy Winehouse swizzle stick. You may now be getting some idea of the inventive, open-minded approach at this excellent cross-cultural venue in Pigalle.

LE DJOON Map pp162–3

☎ 01 45 70 83 49; www.djoon.fr, in French; 22-24 blvd Vincent Auriol, 13e; admission €5-20; ☉ 7pm-midnight Thu, 11.30pm-5am or 6am Fri & Sat, 6pm-midnight Sun; Ⓜ Quai de la Gare

Something of a new kid on the block in an area becoming increasingly known for its cutting-edge venues, this urbanite, New York–inspired loft club and restaurant is rapidly carving out a name for itself as a super-stylish weekend venue for soul, funk, deep house, garage and disco, courtesy of different visiting DJs. Thursday and Sunday evenings are tamer but still 100% DJ-fed dance. Look for the striking glass-and-steel façade.

LE NOUVEAU CASINO Map p155

☎ 01 43 57 57 40; www.nouveaucasino.net, in French; 109 rue Oberkampf, 11e; club admission €5-10, concerts €15-22; ☉ 7.30pm or midnight to 2am or 5am Tue-Sun; Ⓜ Parmentier

This club/concert annexe of the Café Charbon (p296) has a name for itself amid the bars of Oberkampf with its live music concerts (Tuesday to Thursday and Sunday) and top club nights such as Jockey Club at the weekend. Electro, pop, deep House, rock – the programme is eclectic, underground and always up to the minute.

LE REDLIGHT Map pp124–5

☎ 01 42 79 94 53; www.enfer.fr, in French; 34 rue du Départ, 14e; admission €12-20; ☉ 11pm or midnight to 5am or 6am Sat & Sun; Ⓜ Montparnasse Bienvenüe

It seems that this underground (literally) venue beneath Tour Montparnasse, fittingly called *l'enfer* (hell) in a previous life, will never perish. Up there among Paris' busiest house, techno and electro clubs, its podiums get packed out with a young, dance-mad crowd well past dawn. French Kiss 'after' parties often kick off at 6am. Huge and laser-lit, its hours vary depending on

top picks

CLUBS

- Point Éphemère (right)
- Le Rex Club (below)
- Social Club (opposite)
- Les Bains Douches (right)
- Le Batofar (p305)
- Le Slow Club (below)

NIGHTLIFE & THE ARTS CLUBBING

the *soirée* – see its website for flyers – and admission is often half-price before 1am.

LE REX CLUB Map pp82–3
☎ 01 42 36 10 96; www.rexclub.com, in French; 5 blvd Poissonnière, 2e; admission free–€15; 11.30pm–6am Wed-Sat; M Bonne Nouvelle
The Rex reigns majestic in the house and techno scene, always has and probably always will. The new(ish) sound system is impeccable but getting in is more a question of lining up than looking right. Friday nights are a techno institution in Paris; after all, this is the old stomping ground of pioneer Laurent Garnier.

LE SLOW CLUB Map p86
☎ 01 42 33 84 30; 130 rue de Rivoli, 1er; admission €9–13; 10pm-3am Tue & Thu, to 4am Fri-Sun; M Châtelet
Unpretentious dance and jazz club (concerts from 10pm at the weekend) housed in a deep cellar once used to ripen bananas imported from the Caribbean. It attracts a very mixed-age crowd and is as much an institution as a club. The music varies from night to night but includes jazz, boogie, bebop, swing and reggae.

LE WAGG Map pp116–17
☎ 01 55 42 22 00; www.wagg.fr, in French; 62 rue Mazarine, 6e; admission incl 1 drink Fri & Sat €12, Sun €12, before/after midnight Thu free/€10; 11pm-6am Thu-Sat, 3pm-midnight Sun; M Odéon
The Wagg is a UK-style Conran club (associated with the popular Fabric in London), beautifully dressed in slick fixtures and contemporary design, but with a somewhat stifled vibe. Last time we looked it had been taken over by the salsa craze – indeed, it opens early on Sunday to host a two-hour salsa class followed by *une soirée*

100% cubaine. Find event flyers posted on the blog (www.blogalcazar.fr) of the neighbouring Conran restaurant.

LES BAINS DOUCHES Map pp82–3
☎ 01 48 87 01 80; www.lesbainsdouches.net, in French; 7 rue du Bourg l'Abbé, 3e; admission €20; 11pm-5am Wed-Sun; M Étienne Marcel
Housed in a refitted old Turkish *hammam*, this darling of the 1990s has returned with a vengeance and is as elegant a place as you're going to find in the Marais. Once famous for its glamorous clientele and impassable door complete with blocking limo, it has sought to shake off its inaccessible image with a new mix of theme nights, Sunday morning 'afters' and gay soirees.

PENICHE EL ALAMEIN Map pp162–3
☎ 01 45 86 41 60; http://elalamein.free.fr, in French; opp 11 quai François Mauriac, 13e; admission €8; 7pm-2am Sep-Jun; M Quai de la Gare or Bibliothèque
The third in the trendy trio afloat opposite the library, this deep-purple boat is strung with terracotta pots of flowers from head to toe, making it a lovely spot on the Seine to sip away summer evenings. Sit amid flowering tulips and enjoy live bands from 9pm; flyers are stuck on the lamppost in front. Its sound – less hectic than its next-door neighbours, hence the older crowd – embraces jazz, world and Piaf-style *chansons françaises* (French songs) of 1930s Paris.

POINT ÉPHEMÈRE Map pp152–3
☎ 01 40 34 02 48; www.pointephemere.org; 200 quai de Valmy, 10e; admission free–€14; 10am-2pm; M Louis Blanc
A relatively new arrival by the Canal St-Martin, with some of the best electronic music nights in town. Once this self-proclaimed 'centre for dynamic artists' gets in gear, *'on y danse, on danse'* (you'll dance your arse off). Just try to get there before everyone pours out of the surrounding canal-side bars and café-bars at 2am.

QUEEN Map pp140–1
☎ 01 53 89 08 90; www.queen.fr; 102 av des Champs-Élysées, 8e; admission €15-20; 11pm-Sun-Thu, midnight-8am Fri & Sat; M George V
Once the king (as it were) of gay discos in Paris, Le Queen now reigns supreme with a very mixed crowd, though it still has a mostly gay Disco Queen on Monday. While

right on the Champs-Élysées, it's not as difficult to get into as it used to be – and not nearly as inaccessible as most of the nearby clubs. There's a festive atmosphere and mix of music with lots of house and electro.

SOCIAL CLUB Map pp82–3

☎ 01 40 28 05 55; www.myspace.com/parissoc ialclub; 142 rue Montmartre, 2e; admission free-€20; ⏰ 11pm-3am Wed & Sun, to 6am Thu-Sat; Ⓜ Grands Boulevards

Known as the Triptyque till the end of 2007, this vast and very popular club is set up in three stonewalled underground rooms and fills somewhat of a gap in inner-city clubbing. Musically it's on to it, with a serious sound system offering electro, hip-hop and funk, as well as jazz and live acts.

COMEDY

Surprising to some perhaps, Parisians do like to laugh, and the capital is not short of comedy clubs, where comedians such as Bourvil, Fernandel, Bernard Blier, Louis de Funès, Francis Blanche, Jean Poiret, Michel Serrault, Smaïn and the duo Elie Kakou and Guy Bedos have enjoyed enormous popularity over the years. The 'one-man show' (say it with a French accent) is increasingly popular, while English-language comedy is a growing scene.

An outfit called Laughing & Music Matters (☎ 01 53 19 98 88; www.anythingmatters.com; adult/student €20/15), with no fixed address, presents some of the best English-language laugh-fests in town, with both local and imported talent (last seen: Jools Holland from the UK). It usually puts on shows at La Java (p310) but also at Espace Jemmapes (Map pp152–3; ☎ 01 48 03 33 22; www.jemmapes .com, in French; 116 quai de Jemmapes, 10e; Ⓜ République). See the website for details.

POINT VIRGULE Map pp98–9

☎ 01 42 78 67 03; www.lepointvirgule.com, in French; 7 rue Ste-Croix de la Bretonnerie, 4e; 1/2/3 shows adult €17/29/36, per show student except Sat €13; Ⓜ Hôtel de Ville

This tiny and convivial comedy spot in the Marais has been going strong for well over five decades. It offers café-theatre at its best – stand-up comics, performance artists, musical acts. The quality is variable, but it's great fun and the place has a reputation for discovering new talent. There are three or four shows daily, usually at 7pm, 8pm, 9.15pm and 10.15pm.

MUSIC

Music thrives in cosmopolitan Paris, a first-class stage for classical music and big-name rock, pop and independent acts, not to mention world-renowned jazz. A musical culture deeply influenced by rich immigration, vibrant subcultures and an open-minded public make it a fervent breeding ground for experimental music: Paris-bred world music, especially from Africa and South America, is renowned. As with the hybrid drinking–clubbing scene, bars (p284) are as much a space to revel in these sounds as specific music venues.

Festivals for just about every music genre going ensure that everyone gets to listen in; to check what's on, see p302 and p12. Street music is a constant in this busker-merry city (p303), summer adding a soul-stirring string of open-air concerts along the Seine and in city parks to the year-round hum of accordion players on the metro and amateur opera singers around the Centre Pompidou.

And should classical music be your love, don't forget Paris' beautiful churches – wonderful places to listen to organ music – in addition to the theatres and concert halls listed in this chapter: the magnificent Sunday-afternoon concerts in the Église St-Sulpice (p115) are nothing short of earth-shattering.

ROCK, POP & INDIE

With several venues in and around the city regularly hosting international performers, it can be easier to see big-name Anglophone acts in Paris than in their home countries. Palais Omnisports de Paris-Bercy (Map pp158–9; ☎ 08 92 39 01 00, 01 40 02 60 60; www.bercy.fr, in French; 8 blvd de Bercy, 12e; Ⓜ Bercy); Stade de France (Map p182; ☎ 08 92 70 09 00; www.stadefrance.com, in French; rue Francis de Pressensé, ZAC du Cornillon Nord, St-Denis La Plaine; Ⓜ St-Denis-Porte de Paris); and Le Zénith (Map pp174–5; ☎ 08 90 71 02 07, 01 55 80 09 38; www.le-zenith.com, in French; 211 av Jean Jaurès, 19e; Ⓜ Porte de Pantin) in Parc de la Villette are the largest (and most impersonal) venues. But it's is the smaller concert halls with real history and charm that most fans favour.

LA CIGALE Map p169

☎ 01 49 25 89 99; www.lacigale.fr; 120 blvd de Rochechouart, 18e; admission €25-60; Ⓜ Anvers or Pigalle

Now classed as a historical monument, this music hall dates from 1887 but was redecorated 100 years later by Philippe Starck.

Having welcomed artists from Jean Cocteau to Sheryl Crow, today it prides itself on its avant-garde programme, with rock and jazz concerts by French and international acts.

LA FLÈCHE D'OR off Map pp94–5
☎ 01 44 64 01 02; www.flechedor.fr, in French; 102bis rue de Bagnolet, 20e; admission free; ⏰ 8pm-2am Mon-Thu, to 6am Fri & Sat, noon-2am Sun; Ⓜ Alexandre Dumas or Gambetta

Just over 1km northeast of place de la Nation, this music bar has a striking setup in a former railway station on the outer edge of central Paris. It attracts a young, arty and alternative crowd; this could very well be Berlin and it's best known for its DJ nights and concerts. Reggae, house/electro and rock feature; 'The Golden Arrow' has a solid reputation for promoting young talent.

LE BATACLAN Map pp94–5
☎ 01 43 14 00 30; www.bataclan.fr, in French; 50 blvd Voltaire, 11e; admission €20-45; Ⓜ Oberkampf or St-Ambroise

Built in 1864 and Maurice Chevalier's debut venue in 1910, this excellent little concert hall draws French (eg Les Têtes Raides) and international rock and pop legends. Recently renovated and now a symphony of lively reds, yellows and green, the Bataclan also masquerades as a theatre and dance hall.

L'ÉLYSÉE-MONTMARTRE Map p169
☎ 01 44 92 45 47; www.elyseemontmartre.com; 72 blvd de Rochechouart, 18e; admission €15-45; Ⓜ Anvers

A huge old music hall with a great sound system, L'Élysée-Montmartre is one of the better venues in Paris for one-off rock and indie concerts (Hush Puppies, Morgan Heritage, Sabotage, Skatalites). It opens for concerts at 6.30pm and hosts club events and big-name DJs at 11.30pm on Fridays and Saturdays.

L'OLYMPIA Map pp148–9
☎ 08 92 68 33 68; www.olympiahall.com; 28 blvd des Capucines, 9e; admission €35-110; Ⓜ Opéra

The Olympia was opened by the founder of the Moulin Rouge in 1888 and is said to be the oldest concert hall in Paris. It's an atmospheric venue of manageable size, with a sloping floor. It has hosted all the big names over the years, from Johnny Halliday to Jimi Hendrix. This is the hallowed venue of one of Édith Piaf's last performances, and what

Jeff Buckley considered his best ever concert, the seminal *Live at l'Olympia* in 1995.

CLASSICAL

The city hosts dozens of orchestral, organ and chamber-music concerts each week. In addition to the theatres and concert halls listed here, Paris' beautiful churches have much-celebrated organs and can be wonderful places to hear music. Many concerts don't keep to any fixed schedule, but are simply advertised on posters around town. Admission fees vary, but usually cost from €20 for adults and half that for students.

CONSERVATOIRE NATIONAL SUPÉRIEUR DE MUSIQUE ET DE DANSE Map pp174–5
☎ 01 40 40 46 47; www.cnsmdp.fr; 209 av Jean Jaurès, 19e; ⏰ box office noon-6pm Tue-Sat, 10am-6pm Sun, to 8pm on day of performance; Ⓜ Porte de Pantin

Students at France's National Higher Conservatory of Music and Dance put on free orchestra concerts and recitals several times a week, in the afternoon or evening; check its website for the monthly schedule.

SALLE PLEYEL Map pp140–1
☎ 01 42 56 13 13; www.sallepleyel.fr; 252 rue du Faubourg St-Honoré, 8e; tickets €10-85; ⏰ box office noon-7pm Mon-Sat, to 8pm on day of performance; Ⓜ Ternes

This highly regarded hall dating from the 1920s hosts many of Paris' finest classical music recitals and concerts, including those by the celebrated Orchestre de Paris (www.orchestredeparis.com, in French). It has recently emerged from a protracted renovation and now looks (and sounds) even more *magnifique*.

THÉÂTRE DU CHÂTELET Map p86
☎ 01 40 28 28 40; www.chatelet-theatre.com, in French; 1 place du Châtelet, 1er; concert tickets €10-60, opera €10-90, ballet €10-55; ⏰ box office 11am-7pm, no performances Jul & Aug; Ⓜ Châtelet

This central venue hosts concerts as well as operas, ballets, theatre, and musical performances. Tickets go on sale at the box office 14 days before the performance date. Subject to availability, anyone under 26 or over 65 can get reduced-price tickets from 15 minutes before curtain time. The Sunday concerts at 11am (adult/under 26yr €23/12) are a popular fixture.

DIGITAL MUSIC

Tune into the latest sounds and the concerts they spawn with these useful sites (in French). Most listed on p304 also cover the music scene.

- www.france-techno.fr
- www.paris.fr (click 'Culture')
- www.figaroscope.fr (click 'Musiques')

JAZZ & BLUES

Paris became Europe's most important jazz centre after WWII and, niche as the style has since become, the city's best clubs and cellars still lure international stars – as does the wonderful Paris Jazz Festival (www.parcfloraldeparis.com or www.paris.fr) that sets the Parc Floral buzzing each year in June and July. Big-name talent is likewise on the billing at Banlieues Bleues (Suburban Blues; www.banlieuesbleues.org), a jazz festival held in March and early April in St-Denis and other Parisian suburbs.

Download podcasts, tunes, concert information and all that jazz to listen to on your iPod from Paris' soothing jazz radio station, TFS (89.9 MHz FM; www.tsfjazz.com).

CAFÉ UNIVERSEL Map pp110–11

☎ 01 43 25 74 20; www.café-universel.com; 267 rue St-Jacques, 5e; admission free; ⏰ 9.30pm-2am Mon-Sat; Ⓜ Port Royal
Café Universel hosts a brilliant array of live concerts with everything from bebop and Latin sounds to vocal jazz sessions. Plenty of freedom is given to young producers and artists, and its convivial relaxed atmosphere attracts a mix of students and jazz lovers.

CAVEAU DE LA HUCHETTE Map pp110–11

☎ 01 43 26 65 05; www.caveaudelahuchette.fr; 5 rue de la Huchette, 5e; admission Sun-Thu €11, Fri & Sat €13; ⏰ 9.30pm-2.30am Sun-Wed, to 4am Thu-Sat; Ⓜ St-Michel
Housed in a medieval caveau (cellar) used as a courtroom and torture chamber during the Revolution, this club is where virtually all the jazz greats have played since the end of WWII. It's touristy, but the atmosphere can be more electric than at the more serious jazz clubs. Sessions start at 10pm.

HABANA JAZZ Map p155

☎ 01 43 38 14 92; www.habanajazzparis.com, in French; 9 rue Moret, 11e; ⏰ 8pm-1am Wed-Sun; Ⓜ St-Maur

New jazz supper club on the Ménilmontant/Bastille border that evokes the music and atmosphere of postwar Cuba, with emphasis on viola jazz. Tapas are €5.50, Cuban dishes, €12 to €17 and there are a couple of menus (fixed-price meal with two or three courses) at €30 and €35.

LE BAISER SALÉ Map p86

☎ 01 42 33 37 71; www.lebaisersale.com, in French; 58 rue des Lombards, 1er; admission free-€20; ⏰ 5pm-6am; Ⓜ Châtelet
One of several jazz clubs located on this street, the salle de jazz (jazz room) on its 1st floor has concerts of jazz, Afro and Latin jazz and jazz fusion. Combining big names and unknown artists, it is known for its relaxed vibe and has a gift for discovering new talents. Music starts at 7pm and again at 10pm.

LE PETIT JOURNAL ST-MICHEL
Map pp110–11

☎ 01 43 26 28 59; www.petitjournalsaintmichel.com, in French; 71 blvd St-Michel, 5e; admission incl 1 drink adult €17-20, admission incl 1 drink student €11-15; ⏰ 6pm-2am Mon-Sat; Ⓜ Luxembourg
Classic jazz concerts kick off at 9.15pm in the atmospheric downstairs cellar – think St-Germain des Prés in the 1930s – of this sophisticated jazz venue opposite the Jardin du Luxembourg. Everything from Dixieland and vocals to big band and swing sets toes tapping, and Monday-night jam sessions are free. Dinner (menus €48 and €53) is served at 8pm, should you wish to make a meal of it.

Concerts at St-Michel's sister club near Gare de Montparnasse, Le Petit Journal Montparnasse (Map p124–5; ☎ 01 43 21 56 70; www.petitjournal-montparnasse.com; 13 rue Commandant Mouchotte, 14e; admission adult/student €25/15; ⏰ 8pm-2am Mon-Sat), start at 10pm, and a traditional French dinner (€60) can be enjoyed beforehand.

NEW MORNING Map pp152–3

☎ 01 45 23 51 41; www.newmorning.com, in French; 7-9 rue des Petites Écuries, 10e; admission €15-21; ⏰ 8pm-2am; Ⓜ Château d'Eau
New Morning is a highly regarded auditorium with excellent acoustics that hosts big-name jazz concerts as well as blues, rock, funk, salsa, Afro-Cuban and Brazilian music. Concerts take place three to seven nights a week at 9pm, with the second set ending at about 1am. Tickets can usually be purchased at the door.

SUNSET & SUNSIDE Map p86

☎ 01 40 26 46 60; www.sunset-sunside.com; 60 rue des Lombards, 1er; admission free-€25; ⏰ 8pm-4am; Ⓜ Châtelet

Two venues in one at this trendy, well-respected club. The Sunset downstairs has electric jazz and fusion concerts beginning at 10pm. It leans towards world music and sometimes runs salsa sessions during the week. The Sunside picks things up upstairs with jazz acoustics and concerts at 9pm.

WORLD & LATINO

Sono mondiale (world music) is a big deal in Paris, where everything – from Algerian *raï* and other North African music to Senegalese *mbalax* and West Indian *zouk* – goes at clubs. Latino music, especially Cuban salsa, has been overwhelmingly popular over the past decade or so. Many concert and clubbing venues (p304) listed have salsa classes; look for dancing along the Seine in summer.

CITÉ DE LA MUSIQUE Map pp174-5

☎ 01 44 84 44 84; www.cite-musique.fr; 221 av Jean Jaurès, 19e; tickets €8-38; ⏰ box office noon-6pm Tue-Sat, 10am-6pm Sun, to 8pm on day of performance; Ⓜ Porte de Pantin

At the Parc de la Villette, every imaginable type of music and dance, from Western classical to North African and Japanese, is hosted at this venue's oval-shaped, 1200-seat main auditorium. Concerts are in the little Amphithéâtre du Musée de la Musique. Get tickets from the glassed-in box office opposite the main auditorium and next to the Fontaine aux Lions.

DANCING DE LA COUPOLE Map pp124-5

☎ 01 43 27 56 00; 102 blvd du Montparnasse, 14e; admission €12-16; ⏰ 9.30pm-3am Thu, 11.30pm-5.30am Fri, 10am-5pm Sat; Ⓜ Vavin

Above the restaurant of the same name, this established club is famed for its salsa nights, which were credited with single-handedly passing Latin fever to most of Paris. Salsa and Latino nights still take place, but the venue also hosts other kinds of music like *zouk*, reggae, funk and garage.

LA CHAPELLE DES LOMBARDS
Map pp94-5

☎ 01 43 57 24 24; 19 rue de Lappe, 11e; admission free-€19; ⏰ 11pm-6am Tue-Sun; Ⓜ Bastille

This perennially popular Bastille dance club

has happening Latino DJs and reggae, funk and Afro jazz concerts – in a word, a bit of everything. Concerts usually take place at 8pm on Thursday, Friday and Saturday.

LA JAVA Map p155

☎ 01 42 02 20 52; www.la-java.fr; 105 rue du Faubourg du Temple, 10e; admission €5-24; ⏰ 7.30pm-3am Tue-Thu, 11pm-6am Fri & Sat; Ⓜ Goncourt

Built in 1922, this is the dance hall where Édith Piaf got her first break, and it now reverberates to the sound of live salsa and other Latino music. Live concerts of the world music variety usually take place during the week at 8pm or 9pm. Afterwards a festive crowd gets dancing to electro, house, disco and Latino DJs.

L'ATTIRAIL Map pp92-3

☎ 01 42 72 44 42; www.lattirail.com, in French; 9 rue au Maire, 3e; admission free; ⏰ 10.30am-1.30am Mon-Sat, 3pm-1.30am Sun; Ⓜ Arts et Métiers

There are free concerts of *chansons françaises* and world music (Hungarian and Balkan Gypsy music, Irish folk, *klezmer*, southern Italian folk) almost daily at 9.30pm at this cosmopolitan enclave next door to the popular club Tango (p328). Manic but friendly customers crowd the Formica bar, with its cheap *pots* (460mL bottle) of wine and friendly staff.

SATELLIT CAFÉ Map pp94-5

☎ 01 47 00 48 87; www.satellit-café.com; 44 rue de la Folie Méricourt, 11e; admission €5-10; ⏰ 8pm-3am Tue-Thu, 10pm-dawn Fri & Sat, 4pm-3am Sun; Ⓜ Oberkampf

A great venue for world music, and not as painfully trendy as some others in Paris. Come here to hear everything from blues and flamenco to reggae and bossa nova. Concerts usually take place at 9pm. Salsa nights with dancing lessons take place every 1st and 3rd Friday at 8.30pm; Sunday is Latino night.

FRENCH CHANSONS

Think of French music and accordions or *chansonniers* (cabaret singers) like Édith Piaf, Jacques Brel, Georges Brassens and Léo Ferré float through the air. But though you may stumble upon buskers performing *chansons françaises* or playing *musette* (accordion music) in the markets, it is harder than you'd imagine to catch traditional French music in a more formal setting. Try the venues listed here to hear it in traditional and modern forms.

Keep an eye open for the reopening of the long-overdue Théâtre des Trois Baudets (Map p169; http://troisbaudets.com; 2 rue Coustou, 18e; Blanche), a mecca for *chansonniers* and their fans for almost 50 years till it closed in 1996.

AU LAPIN AGILE Map p169

☎ 01 46 06 85 87; www.au-lapin-agile.com; 22 rue des Saules, 18e; adult €24, student except Sat €17; 9pm-2am Tue-Sun; M Lamarck Caulaincourt
This rustic cabaret venue was favoured by artists and intellectuals in the early 20th century and *chansons* are still performed here. The four-hour show starts at 9.30pm and includes singing and poetry. Some love it, others feel it's a bit of a trap. Admission includes one drink (€6 or €7 subsequently). It's named after *Le lapin à Gill*, a mural of a rabbit jumping out of a cooking pot by caricaturist André Gill, which can still be seen on the western exterior wall.

AU LIMONAIRE Map pp148–9

☎ 01 45 23 33 33; http://limonaire.free.fr; 18 cité Bergère, 9e; admission free; 7pm-midnight Mon, 6pm-midnight Tue-Sun; M Grands Boulevards
This little wine bar, tucked far away from the big commercial cabarets off rue Bergère, is one of the best places to listen to traditional French *chansons* and other traditional vocals. The singers (who change regularly) perform on the small stage every night; the fun begins at 7pm on Sunday, 8.30pm on Monday and at 10pm Tuesday to Saturday. It's free entry, and simple meals are served for between €8.50 and €11.

CHEZ ADEL Map pp152–3

☎ 01 42 08 24 61; 10 rue de la Grange aux Belles, 10e; admission free; noon-2am Tue-Sun; M Jacques Bonsergent
Chez Adel is a truly Parisian concept: Syrian hosts with guest *chansonniers* (as well as Gypsy, folk and world music singers) performing most nights to a mixed and enthusiastic crowd. Mains cost from €7.50. The

NIGHTLIFE & THE ARTS MUSIC

ÉDITH PIAF: URCHIN SPARROW

Like her American contemporary Judy Garland, Édith Piaf was not just a singer but a tragic and stoic figure whom the nation took to its heart yet never leting go.

She was born Édith Giovanna Gassion to a street acrobat and a singer in the working-class district of Belleville in 1915. Spending her childhood with an alcoholic grandmother who neglected her, and a stint with her father's family, who ran a local brothel in Normandy, Piaf's beginnings were far from fortunate. On tour with her father at the age of nine, by 15 she had left home to sing alone in the streets of Paris. It was her first employer, Louis Leplée, who dubbed her *la môme piaf* (urchin sparrow) and introduced her to the cabarets of the capital.

When Leplée was murdered in 1935 Piaf faced the streets again, but along came Raymond Asso, an ex–French Legionnaire who became her Pygmalion. He forced her to break with her pimp and hustler friends, put her in her signature black dress and was the inspiration for her first big hit, *'Mon legionnaire'* ('My Legionnaire') in 1937. When she signed a contract with what is now La Java (opposite), one of the most famous Parisian music halls of the time, her career skyrocketed.

This frail woman, who sang about street life, drugs, unrequited love, violence, death and whores, seemed to embody all the miseries of the world, yet sang in a husky, powerful voice with no self-pity. Her tumultuous love life earned her the reputation as *une dévoreuse d'hommes* (a man-eater); in fact she launched the careers of several of her lovers, including Yves Montand and Charles Aznavour. When one of her lovers, world middleweight boxing champion Marcel Cerdan, died suddenly in a plane crash, Piaf insisted that the show go on – and fainted on stage in the middle of *'L'Hymne à l'amour'* ('Hymn to Love'), a song inspired by her late lover.

After suffering injuries in a car accident in 1951, Piaf began drinking heavily and became addicted to morphine. Despite her rapidly declining health she continued to take the world stage, including New York's Carnegie Hall in 1956, and recorded some of her biggest hits such as *'Je ne regrette rien'* ('I regret nothing') and *'Milord'* ('My Lord'). In 1962, frail and once again penniless, Piaf married a 20-year-old hairdresser called Théophanis Lamboukas (aka Théo Sarapo), recorded the duet *'À quoi ça sert l'amour?'* ('What Use Is Love?') with him and left Paris for the south of France, where she died the following year. Some two million people attended her funeral in Paris, and the grave of the beloved and much missed Urchin Sparrow at Père Lachaise Cemetery is still visited and decorated by thousands of loyal fans each year. And interest in her life and work lives on: the 2007 biopic La Môme (p43) was an international success and won several major awards including an Academy Award for Marion Cotillard, who played Piaf.

PARIS VIBES

Tariq Krim, charismatic founder and CEO of Netvibes.com, is among a clutch of young innovators credited with making the internet what it is. Be it tracking the future in digital space or the next best bar in his city, he is a Parisian in tune with the vibe. He has clubbed with Paris' finest first-generation electronic-music DJs, his music taste is eclectic and as work increasingly takes him around the world, he is enjoying a new weekend affair with his city. So where does he go on Saturday night? He opened his address book to Nicola Williams at Netvibes' sunlit loft offices in the 2e, around the corner from the Rex Club.

You go out a lot, right? I'm not very often here anymore (always travelling with Netvibes), and when I am it's for fun; it's interesting because now I'm experiencing Paris at the weekend. I'm very loyal to lots of places. I grew up in the Marais and spent almost all my life there and the Bastille. The 11e is my all-time favourite neighbourhood: I'm very much this side of the Seine, but you know the story... If I have to go to St-Germain I don't know where to go.

Your ideal night out? Two kinds: when you have no voice because you have to yell over the music and places where you can actually talk.

Perfect lose-your-voice places? Chez Janou (☎ 01 42 72 28 41; www.chezjanou.com; 2 rue Roger Verlomme, 3e; Ⓜ Chemin Vert), one of my favourite restaurants in France, period. It's been there for 10 years and is an institution, the canteen of people like John Malkovich. I call it little New York now because so many people speak English there these days. Or Café de l'Industrie (☎ 01 47 00 13 53; 17 rue St-Sabin, 11e; Ⓜ Breguet Sabin); that's a loud place. Then drinks at L'Aréa (☎ 01 42 72 96 50; 10 rue Tournelles, 4e; Ⓜ Bastille), a Lebanese-Brazilian restaurant with lots of music. The owner, Édouard, is an amazing guy, super nice, and knows where to send you next, which clubs... I used to go to the Rex (p306). Now there's the Social Club (p307).

For something quieter? Two Italian restaurants: There is one I love – it could be the perfect date restaurant: Swann et Vincent (p273; ☎ 01 43 43 49 40; 7 rue St-Nicolas, 12e; Ⓜ Ledru-Rollin). And there's Le Rusti (☎ 01 42 72 02 51; 8 rue des Tournelles, 4e; Ⓜ Bastille): small, very trendy, lots of beautiful people.

part-Parisian, part-Eastern décor of this simple bistro looks better as the owners' punch goes down. Music starts at 7pm weekdays and at 4pm on Saturday and Sunday.

CHEZ LOUISETTE Map p169

☎ 01 40 12 10 14; Marché aux Puces de St-Ouen; ☷ noon-6pm Sat-Mon; Ⓜ Porte de Clignancourt
Here since 1967, this little bistro is a highlight of any visit to Paris' largest flea market (p217). Market-goers crowd around little tables to eat lunch (mains €15 to €20) and hear old-time *chanteuses* and *chanteurs* (they change regularly) belt out numbers by Piaf and other classic French singers, accompanied by accordion music; you might even get to see an inspired diner jump up to dance *la guingette* (the jig) in the aisles.

LE VIEUX BELLEVILLE Map p155

☎ 01 44 62 92 66; www.le-vieux-belleville.com; 12 rue des Envierges, 20e; admission free; ☷ performances at 8.30pm Tue, Thu & Fri; Ⓜ Pyrénées
This old-fashioned bistro at the top of Parc de Belleville is an atmospheric venue for performances of *chansons* featuring accordions and an organ grinder three times a week. It's a lively favourite with locals,

though, so booking ahead is advised. 'The Old Belleville' serves classic bistro food (open for lunch Monday to Saturday and dinner Tuesday to Saturday).

DANCE

The Ballet de l'Opéra National de Paris (www.opera-de-paris.fr, in French) performs at both the Palais Garnier (p315) and the Opéra Bastille (p314). Other important venues for both classical and modern dance are the Théâtre du Châtelet and those listed here.

LE REGARD DU CYGNE Map pp174–5

☎ 01 43 58 55 93; www.leregarducygne.com, in French; 210 rue de Belleville, 20e; admission €5-13; Ⓜ Place des Fêtes
Le Regard du Cygne prides itself on being an independent, alternative performance space. Situated in the creative 20e, this is where many of Paris' young and daring talents in movement, music and theatre congregate to perform. If you're in the mood for some innovative and experimental modern dance, performance or participation, this is the place to come. The box office is open one hour before performances.

Then I go for a cocktail. Le Fumoir (p285) has the best collection of vodka martinis and is very quiet, especially the last room at the back. I love the idea of a vintage club with armchairs, a library full of books and international magazines, and people drinking very nice cocktails. The décor is also amazing: Art Deco – lost in New York after Prohibition.

The other place I go is a new place called The Experimental Cocktail Club (☎ 01 45 08 88 09; www.myspace .com/experimentalcocktailclub; 37 rue St-Saveur, 2e; ☺ 6pm-2am Sun-Thu, to even later Fri & Sat; Ⓜ Reaumur Sébastopol), so successful they're opening another (p290). A similar concept to Milk & Honey – amazing cocktails, people super-nice and it's small.

Another, already known by a bunch of people, but one I love is L'Étoile Manquante (p287; ☎ 01 42 72 48 34; www.cafeine.com; 34 rue du Vieille du Temple, 4e; Ⓜ Hôtel de Ville or St-Paul Café).

For an aperitif? Definitely The Experimental Cocktail Club or Le Fumoir.

Best neighbourhood bar? Le Fée Verte (☎ 01 43 72 31 24; 108 rue de la Roquette, 11e; Ⓜ Voltaire): I started Netvibes here three years ago – imagine the perfect dream bar with wi-fi; it was one of the first. I love the idea of being in contact with the world and saying 'Can I have another cappuccino, please?'!

For live music? La Scène Bastille (☎ 01 48 06 50 70; www.scenebastille.com; 2bis rue des Taillandiers, 11e; ☺ 7.30pm-6am Mon-Sat; Ⓜ Bastille) and Le Batofar (p305), far from everything (it's the last stop) but one of the most interesting places, different types of music and lots of style.

Best concept bar? There are very few. On Elizabeth St in New York every bar is a whole experience, has an entire design. Here in Paris you still have the *vieux bistro* type, but you don't see the concept bar, or when you do see it, it's on the Champs-Elysées and tries too hard to be trendy.

A new address? L'Orange Mécanique (☎ 09 54 43 55 02; www.myspace.com/lorangemecanique; 72 rue Jean-Pierre Timbaud, 11e; Ⓜ Parmentier) – not crowded, interesting music and a fun décor.

Nightlife philosophy? You can be in the best place by yourself or the worst place with your friends; I would always go for the second.

Interviewed by Nicola Williams

THÉÂTRE DE LA VILLE Map p86

☎ 01 42 74 22 77; www.theatredelaville-paris .com, in French; 2 place du Châtelet, 4e; adult €1/-23, student & under 28yr €12-13.50; ☺ box office 11am-7pm Mon, to 8pm Tue-Sat; Ⓜ Châtelet

While the Théâtre de la Ville also hosts theatre and music, it's most celebrated for its contemporary dance productions by such noted choreographers as Merce Cunningham, Angelin Preljocaj and Maguy Marin. Depending on availability, students and those under 28 can buy up to two tickets for €12 or €13.50 each on the day of the performance. There are no performances in July and August. Its sister venue, the Théâtre de la Ville-Salle Abbesses (Map p169; ☎ 01 42 74 22 77; 31 rue des Abbesses, 18e; Ⓜ Abbesses) stages even more avant-garde productions.

FILM

Both *Pariscope* and *L'Officiel des Spectacles* (p302) list the full crop of Paris' cinematic pickings and screening times, though going to the cinema in Paris is not cheap: expect to pay up to €10 for a first-run film. Students, under 18s and over 60s get discounted tickets (usually just under €6) every night except Friday, and all day Saturday and on Sunday matinées.

Wednesday yields discounts for everyone. English-language films with French subtitles are labelled 'VO' (*version originale*).

There are a few noteworthy movie theatres over and above mainstream cinemas showing Hollywood blockbusters:

CINÉMA DES CINÉASTES Map pp144–5

☎ 01 53 42 40 20; www.cinema-des-cineastes.fr, in French; 7 av de Clichy, 17e; adult €8.70, student & child €6.80, morning screenings €6; Ⓜ Place de Clichy

Founded by the three Claudes (Miller, Berri and Lelouch) and *Betty Blue* director Jean-Jacques Beneix, this is a three-screen theatre dedicated to quality cinema, be it French or foreign, but always avant-garde. Thematic showings, documentaries and meet-the-director sessions round out the repertoire. Don't miss the excellent Bar à Vins du Cinéma des Cinéastes (p294) on the 1st floor.

CINÉMATHÈQUE FRANÇAISE Map pp158–9

☎ 01 71 19 33 33; www.cinemathequefrancaise .com; 51 rue Bercy, 12e; adult/student/child under 12yr €6/5/3; ☺ box office noon-7pm Mon, Wed, Fri & Sat, to 10pm Thu, 10am-8pm Sun; Ⓜ Bercy

This national institution is a temple to the 'seventh art' and always leaves its foreign offerings – often rarely screened classics – in their original versions. The association is a nonprofit collective and also holds debates, cultural events, workshops and exhibitions. For information on its exhibitions see p157.

LA PAGODE Map pp128–9

☎ 01 45 55 48 48; 57bis rue de Babylone, 7e; adult/student €6/4; Ⓜ Vaneau

A classified historical monument, this Chinese-style pagoda was shipped to France, piece by piece, in 1895 by Monsieur Morin (the then proprietor of Le Bon Marché), who had it rebuilt in his garden on rue de Babylone as a love present for his wife. The wife clearly wasn't that impressed – she left him a year later. But Parisian *cinéphiles* who flock here to revel in its eclectic programme are. La Pagode has been a fantastic, atmospheric cinema since 1931 – don't miss a moment or two in its bamboo-enshrined garden.

LE CHAMPO Map pp110–11

☎ 01 43 54 51 60; www.lechampo.com, in French; 51 rue des Écoles, 5e; adult/student & under 20yr €7.50/6, 2pm matinée €5; Ⓜ St-Michel or Cluny la Sorbonne

This is one of the most popular of the many Latin Quarter cinemas, featuring classics and retrospectives looking at the films of actors and directors such as Alfred Hitchcock, Jacques Tati, Alain Resnais, Frank Capra and Woody Allen. One of the two *salles* (cinemas) has wheelchair access.

MK2 BIBLIOTHÈQUE Map pp162–3

☎ 08 92 69 84 84; www.mk2.com; 128-162 av de France, 13e; adult/student/under 18yr €9.90/6.80/5.90, everyone before noon €5.90; Ⓜ Bibliothèque

This branch of the ever-growing chain (nine outlets at last count) next to the Bibliothèque Nationale is the most ambitious yet, with 14 screens, a trendy café, brasserie, restaurant, late-night bar and a trio of shops specialising in DVDs, books and comics and graphic novels respectively. MK2 cinemas show blockbusters and studio films, so there's always something for everyone. Don't miss the new branches MK2 Quai de Seine (Map pp174–5; ☎ 08 92 69 84 84; 14 quai de Seine, 19e; Ⓜ Jaurès or Stalingrad) and MK2 Quai de Loire (Map pp174–5; ☎ 08 92 69 84 84; 7 quai de Loire, 19e; Ⓜ Jaurès or Stalingrad), which face one another opposite the canal and are linked by ferry boat.

UGC CINÉ CITÉ LA DÉFENSE Map p180

☎ 08 92 70 00 00; www.mk2.com; 15 Parvis de la Défense; adult/student/under 18yr €9.50/6.50/5.90, everyone before noon €5.50; Ⓜ La Défense Grande Arche

One of a dozen-odd UGC cinemas in Paris, this modern 16-screen venue inside the Centre Commercial des Quatre Temps shows all the latest box-office hits, many in VO, ie invariably English. IMAX fans, don't get excited – the screen inside the dome is a regular one. Descend one floor to refuel with food and drink in style.

OPERA

The Opéra National de Paris (ONP) splits its performance schedule between the Palais Garnier, its original home (completed in 1875), and the modern Opéra Bastille, which opened in 1989. Both opera houses also stage ballets and classical-music concerts performed by the ONP's affiliated orchestra and ballet companies. The season runs from September to July.

OPÉRA BASTILLE Map pp94–5

☎ 08 92 89 90 90, 01 72 29 35 35; www.opera -de-paris.fr, in French; 2-6 place de la Bastille, 12e; opera €5-150, ballet €5-80, concert tickets €10-65; Ⓜ Bastille

Despite some initial resistance to this 3400-seat venue, the main opera house in the capital, it's now performing superbly. While less alluring than the Palais Garnier (opposite), at least all seats have a view of the stage. Ticket sales begin at a precise date prior to each performance, with different opening dates for bookings by telephone, online or from the box office (Map pp94–5; 130 rue de Lyon, 11e; ☎ 10.30am-6.30pm Mon-Sat). Box office sales start 14 days before the performance date. The cheapest opera seats are €7 and are sold only from the box office. Note: on the first day they are released, box office tickets can be bought only from the opera house at which the performance is to be held. At Bastille, standing-only tickets for €5 are available 1½ hours before performances begin. Just 15 minutes before the curtain goes up, last-minute seats at reduced rates (usually €20 for opera and ballet performances) are released to people aged under 28 or over 60.

OPÉRA COMIQUE Map pp82–3

☎ 08 25 01 01 23; www.opera-comique.com; place Boïeldieu, 2e; tickets €6-95; Ⓜ Richelieu Drouot

This century-old hall has premiered many important French operas. It continues to host classic and less-known operas. Buy tickets online or from the box office (5 rue Favart, 2e; ☽ 11am-7pm Mon-Fri, to 2pm & 3-7pm Sat, 1hr before performances) on the southwest side of the theatre. Subject to availability, students and those under 28 can buy tickets for less than €15.

PALAIS GARNIER Map pp148–9
☎ 08 92 89 90 90; www.opera-de-paris.fr; place de l'Opéra, 9e; Ⓜ Opéra
The city's original opera house is smaller and more glamorous than its Bastille counterpart, and boasts perfect acoustics. Due to its odd shape, however, some seats have limited or no visibility. Ticket prices and conditions (including last-minute discounts) at the box office (☽ 11am-6.30pm Mon-Sat) are identical to those at the Opéra Bastille (opposite).

THEATRE
Most theatre productions, including those originally written in other languages, are performed in French in Paris. But there is the odd itinerant English-speaking troupe around, and some theatres, such as the celebrated Théâtre des Bouffes du Nord (right), stage the occasional English-language production.

COMÉDIE FRANÇAISE Map p86
☎ 08 25 10 16 80; www.comedie-francaise.fr, in French; place Colette, 1er; tickets €5-37; ☽ box office 11am-6pm; Ⓜ Palais Royal-Musée du Louvre
Founded in 1680 under Louis XIV, the 'French Comedy' theatre bases its reper

toire around the works of classic French playwrights such as Molière, Racine, Corneille, Beaumarchais, Marivaux and Musset, though in recent years contemporary and even – shock, horror! – non-French works have been staged.

There are three venues: the main Salle Richelieu on place Colette just west of the Palais Royal; the Studio Théâtre (Map p86; ☎ 01 44 58 98 58; Galerie du Carrousel du Louvre, 99 rue de Rivoli, 1er; ☽ box office 2-5pm Wed-Sun; Ⓜ Palais Royal-Musée du Louvre) and the Théâtre du Vieux Colombier (Map pp116–17; ☎ 01 44 39 87 00; 21 rue du Vieux Colombier, 6e; ☽ box office 11am-6pm; Ⓜ St-Sulpice).

Tickets for regular seats cost €11 to €37; tickets for the 65 places near the ceiling (€5) go on sale one hour before curtain time (usually 8.30pm) at the discount ticket window (Map p86) around the corner from the main entrance and facing place André Malraux. Those aged under 27 can purchase any of the better seats remaining one hour before curtain time for between €10 and €12 at the main box office.

THÉÂTRE DES BOUFFES DU NORD
Map pp152–3
☎ 01 46 07 34 50; www.bouffesdunord.com, in French; 37bis blvd de la Chapelle, 10e; adult €12-24, student & under 25yr €10-20; ☽ box office 11am-6pm Mon-Sat; Ⓜ La Chapelle
Perhaps best known as the Paris base of Peter Brooks' and Micheline Rozan's experimental troupes, this theatre in the northern reaches of the 10e and just north of the Gare du Nord also hosts works by other directors (eg Declan Donnellan, Stéphane Braunschweig, Krzysztof Warlikowski), as well as classical and jazz concerts.

top picks

- Espace St-Louis (p319)
- Hammam de la Mosquée de Paris (p318)
- Patinoire de l'Hôtel de Ville (p321)
- Piscine de la Butte aux Cailles (p322)
- Piscine Joséphine Baker (p323)
- Spa Nuxe (p318)
- Stade de France (p183)

SPORTS & ACTIVITIES

Hot, sticky sports and ice-cool Parisians seemingly don't go together. *Au contraire:* not only are Parisians mad about watching sport, they play it too. The only trifling difference between us and them is that they wouldn't be seen dead walking down the street in their tracksuit (or working out in their lunch hour).

As the French capital, Paris is privy to big games in world-class stadiums, and there are bags of opportunities to see great sporting moments unfold before your very eyes. Out of the arena, it's dead easy for all those closet *sportifs* (sportspeople) to stay fit (and sickeningly slim). Be it cycling, swimming, lounging on the beach, street blading with the masses or practising the silent art of t'ai chi in the Jardin du Luxembourg, this urban landscape is action-packed.

The best single source of information on sports – spectator and participatory – is the free, 500-page *Parisports: Le Guide du Sport à Paris* (www.sport.paris.fr, in French), published online and on paper by the Mairie de Paris (Paris Town Hall; Map pp98–9; ☎ 39 75; www.paris.fr; Hôtel de Ville, 29 rue de Rivoli, 4e; M Hôtel de Ville); *mairies* (town halls) in every arrondissement have information on sports in their own patch. For sports stadiums, venues, public spaces and associations surf www.parisinfo.com.

HEALTH & FITNESS

Whether you want to hobnob with the stars at a *spa de luxe* or dance the samba on the Seine, Paris has spaces to suit every whim. Spoil yourself.

HAMMAMS & SPAS

Nothing beats a lavender-and-ginger massage, perfumed foot soak or flop in a traditional Turkish bath (hammam) between sips of *thé à la menthe* (mint tea) after a hard day slogging the city sights.

ESPACE JOÏYA Map pp140–1
☎ 01 40 70 16 49; www.joiya.fr; 6 rue de la Renaissance, 8e; 30min/1hr/90min €45/80/115; ⏱ 10.30am-7pm Mon-Thu, 10.30am-9pm Fri & Sat; M Alma-Morceau
The creation of former Russian model mad about Asia, Julia Lemigova (she looks like Julia Roberts), this exclusive spa unwinds wound-up city slickers with detox and de-stress massages using natural and essential oils. The truly indulgent can go for a four-hand massage, followed by a bento box lunch (€25) in the stylish *salon de thé*. Or plump for both options: a 30-/60-minute massage and bento lunch costs €65/100.

HAMMAM DE LA MOSQUÉE DE PARIS Map pp110–11
☎ 01 43 31 38 20; www.la-mosquee.com; 39 rue Geoffroy St-Hilaire, 5e; admission €15; ⏱ men 2- 9pm Tue & 10am-9pm Sun, women 10am-9pm Mon, Wed, Thu & Sat, 2-9pm Fri; M Censier Daubenton or Place Monge
Massages at this atmospheric hammam cost €1 a minute and come in 10-, 20- or 30-minute packages. Should you fancy an exfoliating body scrub and mint tea, get the 10-/30-minute massage *formule* (€38/58). There are lunch deals for rumbling tummies. Bring a swimsuit but hire a towel/dressing gown (€4/5). No children under 12 years.

SPA HARNN & THANN Map pp82–3
☎ 01 40 15 02 20; www.harnn-spa.fr; 11 rue Molière, 1e; massage from €75; ⏱ 11am-9pm Mon-Wed, Fri & Sat, 11am-10pm Thu; M Pyramides
This relaxing 'natural home spa' is another heady one for the senses. Masseuses soothe muscles with traditional Thai massage techniques and an aromatic mix of plant and essential oils. Particularly inventive are its Wednesday Les Petit Duos – a 30-minute massage for one worn-out mum or dad plus kid (aged six to 12 years) – and its after-work *bien-être* (well-being) deal for couples, which includes a foot bath, massage *en duo* and dinner at a neighbouring Thai restaurant. A 20-minute lounge in the peacock-blue hammam costs €20.

SPA NUXE Map pp82–3
☎ 01 55 80 71 40; www.nuxe.com; 32 rue Montorgueil, 1e; massage from €75; ⏱ 9am-9pm Mon-Fri, 9am-7.30pm Sat; M Les Halles

PARKOUR & FREERUNNING

Should you be stopped dead in your tracks on the streets of Paris by a feline figure scaling two buildings with a death-defying leap, vaulting a statue or springing off a lamppost, no sweat: that's Parkour. Throw in a 360° backflip and triple somersault and you have its more flamboyant acrobatic brother, Freerunning.

Born in the Parisian suburbs, the craze of getting from A to B without letting *anything* get in your way has since gained a cult following in cities worldwide. And anything really means *anything*, be it a stairwell, metro station entrance, Vélib' bike stand or 25m gap between rooftops. One YouTube video tags it as 'dudes fiddling around with buildings' (a fair enough assumption), but this is a discipline fusing sport, art and philosophy with serious backbone. Plain dangerous, in fact, whether you do or don't know what you're doing.

Two godlike men with a cinematic screen presence and muscles to die for are behind the French-bred discipline, which some say was the natural progression of New York's 1970s breakdance: David Belle (b 1973; http://kyzr .free.fr/davidbelle) and Sébastien Foucan (b 1974; www.foucan.com). The two played together as kids growing up in the Parisian suburb of Lisses, 40km south of the centre, and in 1989 as fearless adolescents they put a name to their increasingly dare-devil street antics – Parkour, from the French military's *'parcours du combattant'* (obstacle courses).

But in the 1990s, then a fireman, Foucan found his outlook shifting subtly away from Belle's as the philosophical lure of martial arts and yearning for greater freedom of expression kicked in. Thus, in 2001, he came up with his own, more expressive brand of Parkour called Freerunning. While Belle and his followers (known as *les traceurs*) ruthlessly track the shortest, most efficient route from A to B, Foucan's team focuses on aesthetics and creativity of movement – hence the gravity-defying stunts and acrobatics choreographed in most Freerunning movements. As much a mental as physical challenge (indeed, 'obstacles' are not always what they seem), both brands advocate the extreme sport as a way of life in which inner balance plays as crucial a role as physical prowess.

Naturals when it comes to the silver screen, Belle and Foucan are both film stars. A black belt in Gong Fu, Belle struts his stunts as a do-gooder ghetto kid in Luc Besson's *Banlieue 13* (2004), aptly set in a drug- and gun-riddled Parisian suburb in 2010. Among Foucan's spellbinding credits are James Bond movie *Casino Royale* (2006) and Madonna's 2006 'Confessions' world tour.

A regular in *Elle* and other French glossies, this Zen spa lounging in a medieval wine cellar with old stone walls and wood-beamed ceilings is where stars and supermodels find peace. An orgy of 45-minute massages (Thai, Chinese, Californian, Yoga, Shiatsu), including rhythmic ones to music (€80); skin treatments; French pedicures and manicures; and so on.

GYMS

Many Paris gyms and fitness clubs allow one-off or short-term memberships.

CLUB MED GYM
☎ 08 20 20 20 20; www.clubmedgym.com, in French
In addition to 13 gyms, Club Med runs 'Club Med Waou' (basically, 'Club Med Wow') centres offering luxurious settings and spa facilities; check the website for locations. Club Med Gym branches include Palais Royal (Map p86; ☎ 01 40 20 03 03; 147bis rue St-Honoré, 1er; 7.30am-10pm Mon-Fri, 9am-7pm Sat, 9am-5pm Sun; Palais Royal-Musée du Louvre); and République (Map pp94–5; ☎ 01 47 00

69 98; 10 place de la République, 11e; 7.30am-10pm Mon-Fri, 8am-7pm Sat, 9am-5pm Sun; République), which is entered via rue du Faubourg du Temple.

ESPACE ST-LOUIS Map p105
☎ 01 43 26 93 99; www.espace-saint-louis.com, in French; 51-53 rue St-Louis en l'Île, 2e; 1/10/20 sessions €18/150/240; Pont Marie
Take your pick of keep-fit courses at this fun fitness space on an island: pilates, Hatha or Ashtanga yoga, Qi Gong, salsa, samba, flamenco, modern jazz. Pay €10 to try a one-hour *cour* or buy a carnet. Recommended are the classes aboard a *péniche* (barge) on the Seine; details online.

VIT'HALLES BEAUBOURG Map pp98–9
☎ 01 42 77 21 71; www.vithalles.com, in French; 48 rue de Rambuteau, 3e; admission €25, 10-entry carnet €199; 8am-10.30pm Mon-Fri, 9am-7pm Sat, 10am-7pm Sun; Rambuteau
This squeaky-clean health club gets fabulous reviews from local residents and blow-ins; it follows the Les Mills fitness programme.

ACTIVITIES

Entertainment weeklies *Pariscope* and *L'Officiel des Spectacles* (p302) list what's on.

CYCLING

Plenty more Parisians are pedal-powered thanks to Vélib' (see p389 for details); for imaginative and unusual cycling itineraries suggested by Parisians, subscribe to its monthly online newsletter and read the blog (http://blog.velib.paris.fr/blog, in French).

Including tracks in the Bois de Boulogne (16e) and Bois de Vincennes (12e), Paris has 370km of *pistes cyclables* (cycling lanes) running throughout the city, as well as a dedicated lane running parallel to about two-thirds of blvd Périphérique. On Sunday and holidays, large sections of road are reserved for pedestrians, cyclists and skaters under the scheme *Paris Respire* (below).

The Mairie de Paris (Map pp98–9; ☎ 39 75; www.paris.fr; Hôtel de Ville, 29 rue de Rivoli, 4e; Ⓜ Hôtel de Ville) is an invaluable source of information for cyclists: it allows free downloads online at www.velo.paris.fr of its *carte des itinéraires cyclables* (map of cycling itineraries) mapping every Parisian cycling path; pick up a paper version at local *mairies*. This is also the place to find itineraries, rules and regulations detailed in its free booklet *Paris à Vélo* (Paris by Bicycle). More detailed is *Paris de Poche: Cycliste et*

Piéton (Pocket Paris: Cyclist and Pedestrian; €3.50), sold in bookshops.

For information on guided bicycle tours, see p406.

Bicycle Hire

FAT TIRE BIKE TOURS Map pp166–7

☎ 01 56 58 10 54; www.fattirebiketoursparis.com; 24 rue Edgar Faure, 15e; 1hr/day/weekend/week €2.50/15/25/50; ☼ 9am-7pm; Ⓜ La Motte-Picquet Grenelle

Fat Tire is a friendly Anglophone outfit that rents three-speed cruisers, kids' bikes, trailers, tandems and so on. Show a driver's licence or passport and leave €250 deposit on your credit card.

GEPETTO & VÉLOS Map pp110–11

☎ 01 43 54 19 95; www.gepetto-et-velos.com, in French; 59 rue du Cardinal Lemoine, 5e; half-/full-day/weekend/week €7.50/14/23/50; ☼ 10am-7pm Tue-Sun; Ⓜ Cardinal Lemoine

New and secondhand bicycles plus repairs. To rent, show your passport and leave a €325 deposit.

MAISON ROUE LIBRE Map p86

☎ 01 44 76 86 43, 08 10 44 15 34; www.rouelibre.fr; 1 Passage Mondétour, 1er; 1hr/4hr/weekend €4/10/28, weekday/Sat or Sun/night from 5pm €10/15/7, electric bikes 1hr/4hr/weekday/Sat or Sun

---

PARIS BREATHES

Now a well-established operation, Paris Respire ('Paris Breathes') kicks motorised traffic off certain streets at certain times to let pedestrians, cyclists, in-line skaters and other non-motorised cruisers breathe. While it drives its usual traffic jams and pollution to other spots in the city instead, it makes Sundays very pedal-pleasurable.

The tracks listed here are off-limits to cars on Sunday and public holidays. For updates on exact routes and detailed maps see www.velo.paris.fr.

- **By the Seine:** from quai des Tuileries, 1e, to Pont Charles de Gaulle, 12e, on the Right Bank; and on the Left Bank from the eastern end of quai Branly near Pont d'Alma, 7e, to quai Anatole France, 7e (from 9am to 5pm).
- **Latin Quarter, 5e:** rue de Cluny and from place Marcelin Berthelot by the Sorbonne to the rue Mouffetard market via rue de Lanneau, rue de l'École Polytechnique and rue des Descartes (from 10am to 6pm).
- **Bastille, 11e:** Rue de la Roquette and surrounding streets (from 10am to 6pm July and August).
- **Montmartre and Pigalle:** all the streets in Montmartre, 18e, encircled by rue Caulaincourt, rue de Clignancourt, blvd de Rochechouart and blvd de Clichy (from 11am to 7pm April to August, 11am to 6pm September to March); and rue des Martyrs, 9e (from 10am to 1pm).
- **Canal St-Martin, 10e:** a particularly scenic area around quai de Valmy and quai de Jemmapes (from 10am to 6pm winter, 10am to 8pm summer); in July and August yet more streets running south from quai de Jemmapes become car-free.
- **Bois de Boulogne:** (from 9am to 6pm Saturday and Sunday) and Bois de Vincennes (from 9am to 6pm Sunday).
- **Jardin du Luxembourg, 6e:** immediate surrounding streets including parts of rue Auguste Compte, rue d'Assas, blvd St-Michel and rue des Chartreux (from 10am to 6pm March to November).

€6.50/16/16/26; 9am-7pm mid-Jan–mid-Dec; Les Halles
Sponsored by the city's public transport system, this is *the* place to rent a bike – pedal powered or electric (with which you can rent a €32 audioguide). Seniors, students and under-26s get a 10% discount. Insurance, helmet and baby seat are included. The deposit is €150, and you need some form of ID. Its outlet at Bastille (Map pp92–3; ☎ 01 44 71 54 54; 37 blvd Bourdon, 4e; Bastille) shares the same hours. From 10am to 6pm Sunday and public holidays April to October, bikes can also be rented from 'cyclobuses' (bikes stored on big buses) around the city, including Denfert-Rochereau (Map pp124–5; cnr rue Daguerre & av Général Leclerc, 14e; Denfert-Rochereau).

PARIS À VÉLO, C'EST SYMPA! Map pp94–5
☎ 01 48 87 60 01; www.parisvelosympa.com, in French; 22 rue Alphonse Baudin, 11e; half-day/10hr/weekend/week €10/13/25/60; 9.30am-1pm & 2-6.30pm Mon-Fri, 9am-7pm Sat & Sun Apr-Oct, 9.30am-1pm & 2-5.30pm Mon-Fri, 9.30am-6pm Sat & Sun Nov-Mar; St-Sébastien Froissart
Cringe-worthy name ('Paris by Bike, It's Nice!'), yes, but it rents tandems for the price of two bikes and organises great thematic bike tours around Paris. Deposit €250 (€600 for a tandem) with a credit card or your passport.

VÉLO CITO Map pp166–7
☎ 01 42 73 60 21; 97 rue Mademoiselle, 15e; www.velocito.fr, in French; day €25; 9.30am-1pm & 2-6.30pm Mon-Fri, 9am-7pm Sat & Sun Apr-Oct, 9.30am-1pm & 2-6pm Mon-Fri, 9am-6pm Sat & Sun Nov-Mar; Cambronne, Commerce & Vaugirard
The pedal-weary can opt for extra power with a smart electric bicycle to cruise around the city from this 15e outlet; rental is by the day only and you need to leave your passport as a deposit. Its Right-Bank branch (Map pp94–5; ☎ 01 43 38 47 19; 7 rue St-Ambroise, 11e; St-Ambroise) shares the same hours. Both distribute an excellent free map (1:53:000) detailing some lovely *pistes cyclables* starting at RER stations around Paris.

SKATING
Be it across Tarmac or ice, skating is big – see p303 for street spots to catch entertaining free demos. See opposite for details of traffic-free streets to cruise down on Sundays.

In-line Skating
Serious bladers use the bus lanes; others scoot along pavements and cycling lanes. Up to 15,000 take part in the weekly *randonnées en roller* (skating rambles).

The 30km Pari Roller Ramble (☎ 01 43 36 89 81; www.pari-roller.com, in French) kicks off on place Raoul Dautry, 14e (Map pp124–5; Montparnasse Bienvenüe) at 10pm Friday (arrive at 9.30pm), returning at 1am.

The Rollers & Coquillages Ramble (☎ 01 44 54 07 44; www.rollers-coquillages.org) afternoon skate departs from behind the Nomades bike shop (below) on Sunday at 2.30pm, returning around 5.30pm.

NOMADES Map pp92–3
☎ 01 44 54 07 44; www.nomadeshop.com, in French; 37 blvd Bourdon, 4e; half-/full- day weekdays €5/8, weekends €6/9, weekend €15, 5 days Mon-Fri €23, full week €30; 11.30am-7.30pm Tue-Fri, 10am-7pm Sat, noon-6pm Sun; Bastille
Paris' 'Harrods for roller-heads' rents and sells equipment and accessories, and gives courses at five different levels. Elbow and knee guards/helmets cost €1/2. Deposit of €150 or an identity card or passport.

Ice-Skating
From December to early March, the city maintains several pretty-as-a-picture outdoor *patinoires de Noël* (Christmas ice-skating rinks; www.paris.fr, in French). Access is free but *patins/casques* (skates/safety helmets) cost €5/3 to rent. Rinks include Patinoire de l'Hôtel de Ville (Map pp98–9; ☎ 39 75; place de l'Hôtel de Ville, 4e; noon-10pm Mon-Thu, noon-midnight Fri, 9am-midnight Sat, 9am-10pm Sun; Hôtel de Ville) and Patinoire de Montparnasse (Map pp124–5; ☎ 39 75; place Raoul Dautry, 14e; noon-8pm Mon-Fri, 9am-8pm Sat & Sun; Montparnasse Bienvenüe). The national library rink in the increasingly happening 13e, Patinoire de la Bibliothèque François Mitterand (cnr rue des Moulins & av de France; 9am-8pm late Dec–early Jan; Bibliothèque) opens for one month from late December to late January.

DJs turn Friday and Saturday evenings into something of an ice disco at the Patinoire Sonja Henie (Map pp158–9; ☎ 01 40 02 60 60; www.bercy.fr, in French; 8 blvd de Bercy, 12e; adult/under 26yr €4/3, Fri & Sat €6/4, skate hire €3; 3-6pm Wed, 9.30pm-12.30am Fri, 9.30pm-12.30am Sat, 10am-noon & 3-6pm Sun Sep-May; Bercy), an indoor ice-skating rink in the Palais Omnisports de Paris-Bercy.

Art Deco in style, 800 sq metres in size and worth the trip is Patinoire Pailleron (Map pp174–5;

☎ 01 47 20 27 70; 32 blvd Édouard Pailleron, 19e; adult before/after 8pm €4/6, carnet of 10 tickets before/after 8pm €34/26, skate hire €3; ☾ during school holidays except Jul & Aug noon-10pm Mon, Tue & Thu, 9am-10pm Wed, noon-midnight Fri, 9am-midnight Sat, 10am-6pm Sun; during term time noon-1.30pm & 4-10pm Mon, Tue & Thu, noon-10pm Wed, noon-1.30pm & 4pm-midnight Fri, noon-midnight Sat, 10am-6pm Sun), open year-round except July and August.

BOULES & BOWLING

Don't be surprised to see groups of earnest Parisians (usually men) playing *boules* (known as *pétanque* in southern France) – France's most popular traditional game, similar to lawn bowls – in the Jardin du Luxembourg (Map pp116–17) and other parks and squares with suitably flat, shady patches of gravel. The Arènes de Lutèce *boulodrome* (www.arenes delutece.com, in French) in a 2nd-century Roman amphitheatre in the Latin Quarter is a fabulous spot to absorb the scene. The player who tosses his *boules* (biased metal balls) nearest the small wooden *cochonnet* (jack) wins. Sports shops and supermarkets sell cheap sets of *boules*, should you have the urge to have a spin at it.

Come dark, tenpin bowling takes over. Prices for games depend on the time and day of the week. Among the best and/or most central alleys:

AMF BOWLING DE MONTPARNASSE Map pp124–5

☎ 01 43 21 61 32; www.bowling-amf.com, in French; 25 rue du Commandant René Mouchotte, 14e; games €4.50-6, shoes €2; ☾ 10am-2am Sun-Thu, 10-4am Fri, 10-5am Sat; Ⓜ Montparnasse Bienvenüe
This centre, just opposite Gare Montparnasse, has 16 lanes.

BOWLING MOUFFETARD Map pp110–11

☎ 01 43 31 09 35; www.bowling-mouffetard .abcsalles.com, in French; 13 rue Gracieuse & 73 rue Mouffetard, 5e; games €3.10-6.20, shoes €2; ☾ 3pm-2am Mon-Fri, 10am-2am Sat & Sun; Ⓜ Place Monge
Intimate, friendly place with eight lanes and two entrances; games are cheapest on weekday afternoons.

TENNIS

Again, the Mairie de Paris (☎ 39 75, reservations 01 71 71 70 70; www.tennis.paris.fr; open court per hr adult/under 26yr €6.50/4, covered court €12.50/7) is the contact.

The city runs some 170 covered and open tennis courts in dozens of locations (hours vary considerably); reserve by telephone or online. Courts include Luxembourg (Map pp110–11; ☎ 01 43 25 79 18; Jardin du Luxembourg, 6e; Ⓜ Luxembourg); Candie (Map pp94–5; ☎ 01 43 55 84 95; rue de Candie, 11e; Ⓜ Ledru Rollin); and Neuve St-Pierre (Map pp92–3; ☎ 01 42 78 21 04; 5 rue Neuve St Pierre, 4e; Ⓜ St-Paul).

SWIMMING

Paris has almost 40 public swimming pools. Most are short-length pools and finding a free lane to swim laps can be tricky. Opening times vary widely; Wednesday afternoon and weekends when kids are off school are the busiest. Unless noted otherwise, admission costs €2.60/21.50 for a single ticket/carnet of 10 and €1.50 a dip for Paris residents under 26 years.

Boys, no hiding what you don't have: Bermuda and boxer shorts are a no-go in public pools. With the exception of nudist Roger Le Gall, men and boys must don a pair of skin-tight trunks *(slips de bain)*. Most places also demand that everyone wears a *bonnet* (swimming hat), sold at most pools for a few euros.

FOREST HILL AQUABOULEVARD Map pp166–7

☎ 01 40 60 10 00; www.aquaboulevard.com, in French; 4-6 rue Louis Armand, 15e; adult/child 3-11yr €20/10; ☾ 9am-11pm Mon-Thu, 9am-midnight Fri, 8am-midnight Sat, 8am-11pm Sun; Ⓜ Balard
Aquaboulevard delights with water slides and shutes, waterfalls and wave pools in its fun-filled tropical 'beach' and aquatic park. The less frivolous can keep fit with tennis, squash, golf, gym and dance classes. No children under 3 years; last admission is 9pm.

PISCINE DE LA BUTTE AUX CAILLES Map pp162–3

☎ 01 45 89 60 05; 5 place Paul Verlaine, 13e; ☾ during school holidays 1-6pm Mon, 7am-7pm Tue & Wed, 7am-6pm Thu-Sat, 8am-6pm Sun; during term time 7am-8.30am, 11.30am-1.30pm & 4.30-7pm Tue, 7am-7pm Wed, 7am-8.30am & 11.30am-6.30pm Thu & Fri, 7am-8.30am & 10am-6.30pm Sat, 8am-6pm Sun; Ⓜ Place d'Italie
This positively stunning pool, built in 1924 and now a heritage listed building, takes advantage of the lovely warm water issuing from a nearby artesian well. Come summer, its two outdoor pools buzz with swimmers frolicking in the sun.

SPORTS & ACTIVITIES ACTIVITIES

PISCINE JOSÉPHINE BAKER Map pp162–3

☎ 01 56 61 96 50; quai François Mauriac, 13e;
admission Jul & Aug adult/concession first 2hr
€5/2.60, then per hr €5/2.60; ☼ 1-3pm & 5-9pm
Mon & Thu, noon-5pm & 7pm-midnight Tue & Fri,
1-9pm Wed, 10am-8pm Sat & Sun; Ⓜ Bibliothèque
or Quai de la Gare
Built over two years at a cost of €2 million,
this striking *piscine* afloat the Seine is style
indeed (named after the sensual 1920s
Afro-American singer, what else could it
be?). More of a spot to be seen than thrash
laps, the two 25m by 10m pools lure Parisians like bees to a honey pot in summer
when the roof slides back. Shut for work
since November 2007, the 90m-long metallic barge should reopen in 2008.

PISCINE KELLER Map pp166–7

☎ 01 45 71 81 00; 14 rue de l'Ingénieur Keller,
15e; adult/child €2.60/1.50; ☼ noon-10pm Mon &
Fri, 7-8.30am & noon-10pm Tue & Thu, 7am-8pm
Wed, 9am-9pm Sat, 9am-7pm Sun, slightly different
hours during school holidays; Ⓜ Charles Michels
This brand-new indoor pool with state-of-
the-art glass roof that slides back on warm
days opened in mid-April and is a particular
splash with Parisians keen to swim beneath
the stars.

PISCINE PONTOISE Map pp110–11

☎ 01 55 42 77 88; 19 rue de Pontoise, 5e;
adult/concession €3.70/2.20, 10-entry carnet
€30.20/19.40; ☼ during school holidays 7-8.30am
& 11am-11.45pm Mon, 7am-7.30pm & 8.15-
11.45pm Tue & Thu, 7-8.30am, 11.30am-7.30pm &
8.15pm-11.45pm Wed, 7-8.30am, 11am-8pm & 9
11.45pm Fri, 10am-7pm Sat, 8am-7pm Sun, shorter
hr during term time; Ⓜ Maubert Mutualité
A beautiful Art Deco–style indoor pool in
the heart of the Latin Quarter, Piscine Pontoise measures 33m by 15m and offers a €9
ticket for all in the evening, covering entry
to the pool, gym and sauna.

PISCINE ROGER LE GALL Map pp158–9

☎ 01 44 73 81 12; 34 blvd Carnot, 12e; ☼ during
school holidays 10am-8pm Mon, Tue, Thu & Fri,
8am-9pm Wed, 10am-7pm Sat, 8am-7pm Sun; during term time noon-2pm & 5-8pm Mon, Tue & Thu,
noon-2pm & 5-9pm Fri, noon-7pm Sat, 8am-7pm
Sun; Ⓜ Porte de Vincennes
With its grassy lawns to lounge about on
and twin-set of pools, indoor and out,
many readers reckon this is Paris' best (blvd
Périphérique is a tad close for our comfort).

It is notably the only public *naturiste* pool
in Paris where you can swim nude. In July
and August admission costs more.

SPECTATOR SPORT

Depending on what time of year you're here,
this is the city to see all types of matches and
events. Sports daily *L'Équipe* (www.lequipe.fr,
in French), and entertainment and activities
supplement *Figaroscope* (www.figaroscope.fr,
in French; published every Wednesday in *Le Figaro*), can tell you what's on; as can box offices –
which sell tickets for most sports events –
situated inside branches of Fnac and Virgin
Megastore (p302) for bigger events. Or follow the
'what's on' link at http://en.parisinfo.com.

FOOTBALL

Paris' magnificent Stade de France (p183; tickets €20 to
€100), north of the centre in St-Denis, is where
France's home matches kick off.
   The city's only top-division football team,
Paris-St-Germain (☎ 01 47 43 71 71; www.psg.fr), wears
red and blue and plays its home games at the
48,500-seat Parc des Princes (Map p178; ☎ 32 75, 01 47
43 72 56; www.leparcdesprinces.fr; 24 rue du Commandant Guil-
baud, 16e; tickets €20-80; ☼ box office 9am-7pm Mon-Fri & 3hr
before match; Ⓜ Porte de St-Cloud), built in 1970.

RUGBY

When at home Paris-based team Stade Français
CASG (☎ 01 40 71 71 00; www.stade.fr) plays north
at the small Stade Jean Bouin (Map pp132–3; ☎ 01
46 51 00 75; 26 av du Général Sarrail, 16e; tickets €5-35; box
office ☼ 11am-2pm & 3-7pm Tue-Fri, 2-7pm Mon & Sat;
Ⓜ Exelmans) and occasionally at the Stade de
France (p183). The finals of the Championnat
de France de Rugby take place in late May
and early June.

TENNIS

By far the glitziest annual sporting event in
Paris is the French Open, the second of four
Grand Slam tennis tournaments, held on clay
at the 16,500-seat Stade Roland Garros (Map p178;
☎ box office 08 25 16 75 16, from abroad +33 1 47 43 52
52; www.rolandgarros.com, in French; 2 av Gordon Bennett,
16e; Ⓜ Porte d'Auteuil) in the Bois de Boulogne
from late May to mid-June. Tickets are expensive and like gold dust; they go on sale
mid-November and bookings must be made
by March. One week prior to the competition

(on the first day of the qualifiers), remaining tickets are sold from the box office (9.30am-5.30pm Mon-Fri) at the entrance to the stadium.

The top indoor tournament is the Paris Tennis Open, usually held in late October or early November at the Palais Omnisports de Paris-Bercy (Map pp158–9; 01 40 02 60 60, box office 08 92 39 01 00; www .bercy.fr, in French; 8 blvd de Bercy, 12e; Bercy).

CYCLING

Joining the tens of thousands of spectators along the av des Champs-Élysées to watch the final leg of the world's most prestigious cycling race, the three-week Tour de France (www .letour.fr), is a must for those in Paris towards the end of July.

The 3000km-long route changes each year, but three things remain constant: the inclusion of the Alps, the Pyrenees and, since 1974, the race finish on av des Champs-Élysées. The final day varies from year to year but is usually

the 3rd or 4th Sunday in July, with the race finishing some time in the afternoon. If you want to see this exciting event, find a spot at the barricades before noon.

Track cycling, a sport at which France excels, is held in the velodrome of the Palais Omnisports de Paris-Bercy (Map pp158–9; 01 40 02 60 60; www .bercy.fr, in French; 8 blvd de Bercy, 12e; Bercy).

HORSE RACING

Spend a cheap afternoon relaxing at the races with Parisians of all ages, backgrounds and walks of life. The easiest racecourse to get to is Hippodrome d'Auteuil (Map pp132–3; 01 40 71 47 47; www .france-galop.com; Champ de Courses d'Auteuil, Bois de Boulogne, 16e; Porte d'Auteuil), host to steeplechases six times a month from February to late June or early July, and early September to early December. Standing on the lawn in the middle of the track is free, but a seat in the stands costs €3 or €4 (under 18s free).

GAY & LESBIAN PARIS

top picks

- Centre Gai et Lesbien de Paris Île de France (p328)
- Villa Papillon (p326)
- Le Dépôt (p327)
- Le Cox (p327)
- 3W Kafé (p327)

France is one of Europe's most liberal countries when it comes to homosexuality – in part because of the long French tradition of public tolerance towards groups of people who choose not to live by conventional social codes – and Paris is the epicentre.

While certainly not London, New York or even Berlin, the French capital is home to thriving gay and lesbian communities, and same-sex couples are a common sight on its streets, especially in the Marais district of the 4e. In 1999 the government enacted PACS (Pacte Civile de Solidarité) legislation, designed to give homosexual couples some of the legal protection (eg inheritance rights) it extends to married heterosexuals (though it falls well short of the laws since codified in Spain and the UK). In May 2001, Paris elected Bertrand Delanoë, a European capital's first openly gay mayor. He was returned to office for a second term in March 2008.

EATING

AUX TROIS ÉLÉPHANTS
Map pp82–3   Thai €€

☎ 01 42 33 53 64; 36 rue Tiquetonne, 2e; starters €7-12.50, mains €10-19.50; ☽ dinner to 11.30pm; Ⓜ Étienne Marcel

In a street where each restaurant is more original than the next, 'At the Three Elephants' takes the tart. Customers – a very mixed bag – are plunged into a highly exotic world where the extravagant 'hostesses' are equal to the dishes on offer. The subtle flavours of the *yum plameuk* (squid salad) and the *homok pla* (steamed fish served in a banana leaf; €10) are both excellent choices.

VILLA PAPILLON
Map pp82–3   Thai €€

☎ 01 42 21 44 83; 15 rue Tiquetonne, 2e; starters €7-9.50, mains €13-20; ☽ dinner to 11pm Mon-Fri, to 11.30pm Sat & Sun; Ⓜ Étienne Marcel

Offering Aux Trois Éléphants (see above) some very stiff competition is this new and relatively authentic Thai eatery just across rue Tiquetonne. Try the duck with Thai basil and the prawns cooked in Musulman-style curry. Lovely staff.

LE GAI MOULIN
Map pp98–9   French €€

☎ 01 48 87 06 00; www.le-gai-moulin.com, in French; 10 rue St-Merri, 4e; menus €12.90-20.90; ☽ dinner till midnight daily; Ⓜ Rambuteau

The much expanded 'Gay Mill' (we don't get it either – unless they mean 'rumours') serves 'classic but honest' French cuisine, including decently priced set menus, to a mainly (but not exclusively) gay clientele. With the tables this close, there's no chance of not making a friend or two between (or even during) courses. We love the piano bar downstairs on Tuesday evenings.

DRINKING & NIGHTLIFE

The Marais (4e), especially those areas around the intersection of rue Ste-Croix de la Bretonnerie and rue des Archives, and eastwards to rue Vieille du Temple, has been Paris' main centre of gay nightlife for over two decades. There are also a few bars and clubs within walking distance of blvd de Sébastopol. Other venues are scattered throughout the city.

The lesbian scene here is much less public than its gay counterpart, and centres around a few cafés and bars in the Marais.

In Paris, the need for exclusiveness appears to be relaxing – as is the general public's mentality towards homosexuality. Clubs are generally all gay friendly, while specifically gay venues are increasingly mixing things up – becoming some of the coolest spots in Paris. The bars and clubs listed here are almost exclusively gay or lesbian. For mixed clubs, see the Nightlife & the Arts chapter (p302).

LOUVRE & LES HALLES

LE TROISIÈME LIEU
Map p86   Bar

☎ 01 48 04 85 64; 62 rue Quincampoix, 4e; ☽ 6pm-2am Tue-Sun; Ⓜ Rambuteau

This friendly bar is a popular place for chic young lesbians and, at times, for everyone else. There's a large, colourful bar and big wooden tables at street level, with good-value canteen meals. The vaulted cellar below leaves space for dancing to DJs, rock/alternative music concerts and live singers. On the last Saturday of the month it opens at 2pm.

MARAIS & BASTILLE

3W KAFÉ Map pp98–9   Bar

☎ 01 48 87 39 26; www.3w-kafe.com, in French; 8 rue des Écouffes, 4e; ⏱ 5.30pm-2am; Ⓜ St-Paul

This glossy lesbian cocktail bar is the flagship venue on a street with several dyke bars. It's relaxed and elegant and there's no ban on men. If you're looking for something a bit more hardcore and 'exclusive', head for the 3W's sister-bar Les Jacasses (Map pp98–9; ☎ 01 42 71 15 51; 5 rue des Écouffes, 4e; ⏱ 5pm-2am Tue-Sun; Ⓜ St-Paul) just opposite.

INTERFACE BAR Map pp94–5   Bar

☎ 01 47 00 67 15; 34 rue Keller, 11e; ⏱ 3pm-2am; Ⓜ Ledru Rollin

No, not 'In yer face'… This is a laid-back gay bar that attracts locals and habitués of the nearby Gay & Lesbian Centre (p328). Unusualyl for a gay bar in Paris, it attracts customers in the afternoon and early evening, especially during happy hour (6pm to 9pm).

LE COX Map pp98–9   Bar

☎ 01 42 72 08 00; www.cox.fr, in French; 15 rue des Archives, 4e; ⏱ noon-2am Mon-Fri, 1pm-2am Sat & Sun; Ⓜ Hôtel de Ville

This small gay bar has become *the* meeting place for an interesting (and maybe interested) and cruisy crowd throughout the evening from 6pm. OK, we don't like the in-your-face name either, but what's a boy to do? Happy hour is 6pm to 9pm daily and the décor – be it a farm, be it a casino, be it a rodeo – changes every quarter.

LE QUETZAL Map pp98–9   Bar

☎ 01 48 87 99 07; 10 rue de la Verrerie, 4e; ⏱ 5pm-5am; Ⓜ Hôtel de Ville

This perennial favourite gay bar – one of the first in the Marais – is opposite rue des Mauvais Garçons (Bad Boys' Street), a road named after the brigands who congregated here in 1540. It's always busy, with house and dance music playing at night, and cruisy at all hours. During happy hour (5pm to 9pm) a pint costs €3.60.

LE SCARRON Map pp98–9   Bar

☎ 01 42 77 44 05; www.lescarron.com, in French; 3 rue Geoffroy l'Angevin, 4e; ⏱ 10pm-6am Wed-Sat; Ⓜ Rambuteau

This rather chic *bar de nuit* (night bar) hots up as the evening progresses, especially in the

vaulted basement. There's a rather subdued piano bar on the ground floor much more suited (key word) to quiet conversation.

AMNÉSIA Map pp98–9   Bar-Café

☎ 01 42 72 16 94; 42 rue Vieille du Temple, 4e; ⏱ 11am-2am; Ⓜ Hôtel de Ville

In the heart of the Marais, cosy, warmly lit Amnésia is an institution not easy to forget. Friendly and stylish, it remains resolutely popular with gay guys but is more mixed than many of its counterparts. There's an attractive lounge area upstairs and a tiny dance floor in the *cave* (wine cellar) downstairs with DJ music from the 1980s and 90s.

LITTLE CAFÉ Map pp98–9   Bar-Café

☎ 01 48 87 43 36; 62 rue du Roi de Sicile, 4e; ⏱ 10am-2am; Ⓜ St-Paul

Run by some of the eminent ladies from the much missed lesbian club Le Pulp on the Grands Boulevards, this modern wine bar-café is a new local favourite, with great coffee and meals. The clientele is relaxed, mixed and street smart, with a penchant for electronic music and good wine.

L'OPEN CAFÉ Map pp98–9   Bar-Café

☎ 01 42 72 26 18; www.opencafe.fr; 17 rue des Archives, 4e; ⏱ 11am-2am Sun-Thu, 11am-4am Fri & Sat; Ⓜ Hôtel de Ville

Until recently this Marais institution was the place for gay men of all ages to head after work, but the action seems to have shifted a few doors southwards to the Cox bar (left). Still, L'Open's large terrace and daytime schedule are drawing cards, as is the four-hour happy 'hour' starting at 6pm.

NYX Map pp98–9   Bar-Café

☎ 01 42 78 71 55; 30 rue du Roi de Sicile, 4e; ⏱ 5pm-2am Sun-Thu, 5pm-4am Fri & Sat; Ⓜ St-Paul

This lesbian café and lounge bar at the corner of rue des Écouffes (in what was once a *boulangerie*-patisserie) has a stylish vibe and an upbeat crowd. There's a DJ club downstairs that operates on Friday and Saturday nights.

LE DÉPÔT Map p86   Club

☎ 01 44 54 96 96; www.ledepot.com, in French; 10 rue aux Ours, 3e; admission €8.50-12.50; ⏱ 2pm-8am; Ⓜ Rambuteau or Étienne Marcel

With a cop shop just next door you'd think this strictly men-only bar and club over three floors would be a titch more subdued. Fat (actually, rather buffed) chance. It proudly waves its gay flag just metres from the red, white and blue ones of the *commissariat* (police station) and is perhaps just as much of an institution. It's a major men's pick-up joint, with theme nights, DJs and notorious backrooms.

RAIDD BAR Map pp98–9   Club
☎ 01 42 77 05 13; www.raiddbar.com; 23 rue du Temple, 4e; ☽ 5.30pm-5am; Ⓜ Hôtel de Ville
This is a club-bar that takes its cue from Splash in New York, with showering go-go boys behind glass and a terrace on which to cool off. It's a pretty attitude-y place and the drinks aren't cheap, but that's New York for you. Happy hour daily 5pm to 10pm.

TANGO Map pp92–3   Club
☎ 01 42 72 17 78; www.boite-a-frissons.fr; 13 rue au Maire, 3e; admission €7; ☽ 10.30pm-5am Fri & Sat, 6pm-midnight; Ⓜ Arts et Métiers
Billing itself as a *boîte à frissons* (quivering club), Au Tango brings in a mixed and cosmopolitan gay and lesbian crowd. Housed in a historic 1930s dancehall, its atmosphere and style is retro and festive. Dancing gets going when it opens at 10.30pm with waltzing, salsa and tango. From about 12.30am onwards DJs play. Sunday's gay tea dance is legendary.

SLEEPING

HÔTEL CENTRAL MARAIS
Map pp98–9 Hotel
☎ 01 48 87 56 08; www.hotelcentralmarais.com; 2 rue Ste-Croix de la Bretonnerie, 4e; s & d from €89, tr €109; Ⓜ Hôtel de Ville; ▯
This small hotel in the centre of gay Paris caters essentially for gay men, though lesbians are also welcome. It's in a lovely 17th-century building and its seven rooms are spread over several floors; there is no lift. Also, there is only one bathroom for every two rooms, though the room on the 5th floor has an en suite bathroom and toilet. Reception, which is on the 1st floor, is open from 8am to 5pm; after that check in around the corner at Le Central Bar (Map pp98–9; ☎ 01 48 87 99 33; 33 rue Vieille du Temple, 4e; ☽ 4pm-2am Mon-Fri, 2pm-2am Sat & Sun; Ⓜ Hôtel de Ville), which is the oldest (in every sense) gay bar still open in Paris.

FURTHER RESOURCES
Most of France's major gay organisations are based in Paris. If you require a more complete list than we are able to provide here, pick up a copy of *Genres*, an almost-annual listing of gay, lesbian, bisexual and transsexual organisations, at the Centre Gai et Lesbien de Paris Île de France (below) or consult *Le Petit Futé Paris Gay et Lesbien* guide (opposite).

Act Up Paris (☎ 01 48 06 13 89; www.actupparis.org, in French) Meetings open to the public are held every Tuesday at 7.30pm at the École des Beaux-Arts (Map pp128–9; Amphithéâtre des Loges, 14 rue Bonaparte, 6e; Ⓜ St-Germain des Prés).

Association des Médecins Gais (AMG; ☎ 01 48 05 81 71; www.medecins-gays.org, in French) The Association of Gay Doctors deals with gay-related health issues. Telephone advice on physical-health issues is available from 6pm to 8pm on Wednesday and 2pm to 4pm on Saturday. For counselling, call between 8.30pm and 10.30pm Thursday.

Centre Gai et Lesbien de Paris Île de France (CGL; Map pp92–3; ☎ 01 43 57 21 47; www.cglparis.org, in French; 63 rue Beaubourg, 3e; ☽ 6-8pm Mon, 3-8pm Tue & Thu, 12.30-8pm Wed, Fri & Sat, 4-8pm Sun; Ⓜ Rambuteau or Arts et Métiers) The Lesbian, Gay, Bisexual and Transsexual Centre, now in spanking-new premises just north of the Centre Pompidou, is your single best source of information in Paris. The large library of gay books and periodicals is open from 3pm to 8pm on Wednesday and 3pm to 6pm on Friday.

Écoute Gaie (☎ 0 810 811 057; www.france.qrd .org/assocs/ecoute-gaie, in French; ☽ 6-10pm Mon-Fri) Established in 1982, this is the oldest hotline for gays and lesbians in Paris.

SOS Homophobie (☎ 0 810 108 135, 01 48 06 42 41; www.sos-homophobie.org; ☽ 6-10pm Mon, Fri & Sun, 8-10pm Tue-Thu, 2-4pm Sat) This hotline takes anonymous calls concerning discriminatory acts against gays and lesbians.

Of gay and lesbian publications, *Têtu* (www .tetu.com, in French; €5) is a popular and widely circulating glossy monthly available at newsstands everywhere. Be on the lookout for bimonthly freebies like *2X* (www.2xparis .fr) and *Mâles-a-Bars* (www.males-a-bars. com, in French), which have interviews and articles (in French) and listings of gay clubs, bars, associations and personal classifieds. You'll find them stacked up at most gay venues. The monthly magazine *Lesbia* (€4.10), established almost 20 years ago, looks at lesbian women's issues and gives a rundown of what's happening around the country. Also for women, *La Dixième Muse* (The 10th Muse; www.ladixiememuse.com, in French; €4.20) is more culturally oriented.

The following guidebooks list pubs, restaurants, clubs, beaches, saunas, sex shops and cruising areas; they are available from Les Mots à la Bouche bookshop (p201).

Dyke Guide: Le Guide Lesbien (www.dykeguide.com, in French; €13;) The essential French-language guide for girls on the go in France and Paris.

Le Petit Futé Paris Gay et Lesbien (www.petitfute.com, in French; €14) A French-language guide that goes well beyond pursuits hedonistic, with political, cultural, religious and health listings along with bars and restaurants. Highly recommended.

Paris Gayment (www.parigramme.com, in French; €6) A French-language, 110-page sourcebook from the ones behind *Paris Est à Nous* pocket books about various aspects of life in the French capital and contains just about every address of interest to 'girls who love girls and boys who love boys and their friends'.

Spartacus International Gay Guide (www.spartacuswo rld.com; €28.95) A male-only guide to just about every country in the world, with more than 80 pages devoted to France, half of which cover Paris.

Among some of the better gay and lesbian websites include:

Dyke Planet (www.dykeplanet.com, in French) The best French-language website for gay women.

Gay France (www.gayfrance.fr, in French) Lots and lots of male-to-male chat and classifieds.

La France Gaie & Lesbienne (www.france.qrd.org, in French) 'Queer resources directory' for gays and lesbians.

Le Gay Paris (www.legayparis.fr) Not unlike Paris Gay (see below) but slightly more up to date.

Paris Gay (www.paris-gay.com) Decent overview of what's up and what's on in the French capital.

SLEEPING

top picks

- Hôtel St-Merry (p337)
- Hôtel Minerve (p344)
- Hôtel Alison (p352)
- Terrass Hôtel (p357)
- Hôtel Résidence des 3 Poussins (p353)
- Hôtel Jeanne d'Arc (p340)
- Hôtel Muguet (p351)
- Hôtel des 3 Collèges (p345)
- Hôtel d'Angleterre (p347)
- Hôtel La Demeure (p356)

SLEEPING

Paris has a very wide choice of accommodation options, counting some 76,500 beds in 1480 establishments that cater for all budgets throughout much of the city. There are four basic types: deluxe and top-end hotels, some of which count among the finest in the world; midrange hotels, many of which have personalities all of their own, and by and large offer very good value when compared with similarly priced places to stay in other European capitals; adequate but generally uninspiring budget hotels; and hostels, which run the gamut from cramped, airless cupboards to party places with bars worth a visit in their own right. In this chapter, accommodation options are listed according to the sections of the city as outlined in the Neighbourhoods chapter and appear in budget order, with the most expensive first. Prices are given for rooms with bathrooms unless otherwise noted.

The city of Paris levies a *taxe de séjour* (tourist tax) of between €0.20 (camp sites, 'NN' or unclassified hotels) and €1.50 (four-star hotels) per person per night on all forms of accommodation.

A note on the icons used in this chapter: Most hotels and hostels in Paris have some form of internet access available nowadays. We have included an internet icon (💻) only if the hotel has wi-fi (pronounced wee-fee in French) or allows guests to use a terminal in the lobby or reception area. Some establishments (usually hostels) charge their guests an access fee for this service, which we have usually noted in the review text.

Most hotels with two or more stars in Paris are equipped with a lift but not much more for those in wheelchairs. In this chapter most of the hotels marked with a wheelchair icon (♿) have one or two guestrooms fully equipped for disabled guests (bathrooms big enough for a wheelchair user to turn around in, access door on bath tubs, grip bars alongside toilets etc) though we've included a few with guestrooms on the *rez-de-chaussée* (ground floor) that can be accessed by anyone in a wheelchair and may serve at a pinch.

For information about the use of the non-smoking icon (🚭), see the boxed text, below.

ACCOMMODATION STYLES

Apartments & Flats

If you are interested in renting a furnished flat for anything from a night to a month, consult one of the many agencies listed under the heading 'Furnished Rentals' in the 'Hotels & Accommodation' section of the Paris Convention & Visitors Bureau (www.parisinfo.com) website. Accommodation for students and organisations that arrange it are listed under 'Young Paris'.

Websites of commercial agencies that let studios and apartments to visitors, and have been recommended by both readers and Lonely Planet staff members, include the following half-dozen:

A La Carte Paris Apartments (www.alacarte-paris -apartments.com)

Apartment in Paris (www.an-apartment-in-paris.com)

Lodgis.com (www.lodgis.com)

Paris Accommodation Service (www.paris-accommo dation-service.com)

Paris Apartments Services (www.paris-apts.com)

Paris Attitude (www.parisattitude.com)

Paris Stay (www.paristay.com)

For information about longer-term apartment and flat rentals in Paris, see p334.

SERVICED APARTMENTS

Serviced apartments – like staying in a hotel without a lot of the extras – are an excellent option for those staying longer than a week,

APARTMENTS AT YOUR SERVICE

The following are among the three most popular chains of serviced apartments in Paris.

Apart'hotels Citadines (☎ 0 825 333 332, from abroad 01 41 05 79 05; www.citadines.com; 🖂 🖳 ⬥) This fabulously successful (now international) chain has 17 properties in Paris, including those listed below. Prices vary depending on the season and the location but, in general, a small studio for two with fully equipped kitchen (fridge, microwave, dishwasher, crockery and cutlery) for just under a week costs from €103 to €289 per night and a one-bedroom flat sleeping four costs €175 to €462. For stays longer than six days there's a discount of 10% to 15%, and for 30 days or more about 20% to 25%. Central branches include: Bastille Nation (Map pp158–9; ☎ 01 40 04 43 50; bastillenation@citadines.com; 14-18 rue de Chaligny, 12e; Ⓜ Reuilly Diderot); Les Halles (Map p86; ☎ 01 40 39 26 50; leshalles@citadines.com; 4 rue des Innocents, 1er; Ⓜ Châtelet-Les Halles); Maine Montparnasse (Map pp124–5; ☎ 01 53 91 27 00; montparnasse@citadines.com; 67 av du Maine, 14e; Ⓜ Gaîté); Montmartre (Map p169; ☎ 01 44 70 45 50; montmartre@citadines.com; 16 av Rachel, 18e; Ⓜ Blanche); Opéra Grands Boulevards (Map pp82–3; ☎ 01 40 15 14 00; operaboulevard@citadines.com; 18 rue Favart, 2e; Ⓜ Richelieu Drouot); St-Germain des Prés (Map pp116–17; ☎ 01 44 07 70 00; stgermain@citadines.com; 53ter quai des Grands Augustins, 6e; Ⓜ St-Michel); and La Tour Eiffel (Map pp166–7; ☎ 01 53 95 60 00; eiffel@citadines.com; 132 blvd de Grenelle, 15e; Ⓜ La Motte Picquet Grenelle).

Residences FranceLoc (☎ 04 92 28 38 48; www.franceloc.fr; 🖳) Formally known as France Location (France Rental), this chain has serviced apartments throughout France, including two in Paris. Daily prices quoted here are for up to seven nights' stay; there is a discount of 10% from eight to 27 nights and 20% after that. Résidence Le St-Germain (Map pp110–11; ☎ 01 46 34 22 33; reservation@france-location.fr; 16 rue Boutebrie, 5e; 2-person studio €93-119, 4-person apt €143-158; Ⓜ St-Michel) has 11 fully equipped studios and apartments for between two and six people measuring from 17 to 55 sq metres. Résidence Passage Dubail (Map pp152–3; ☎ 01 44 89 66 70; residence-dubail@franceloc.fr; 5-7 Passage Dubail, 10e; 2-person studio €89, 4-person apt €139; Ⓜ Gare de l'Est) has studios and apartments measuring 16 to 30 sq metres, accommodating up to four people.

Adagio City Aparthotel (☎ 0 825 040 608; www.adagio-city.com; 🗶 🖂 🖳) Called Résidences Pierre & Vacances until recently, Adagio counts some 10 properties in greater Paris, including the Adagio Montmartre City Aparthotel (Map p169; 10 place Charles Dullin, 18e; pam@adagio-city.com; 2/3/4 person studios €131/144/169, 1/2 bed apt €205/259; Ⓜ Abbesses), an attractive *résidence* at the end of a leafy street in the heart of Montmartre with 76 studios and apartments for between two and six people. There's a 10% discount on stays of eight nights or more, and 20% on stays of 28 days or more.

particularly if you're part of a small group, and don't feel like emptying the trash yourself. There are quite a few of them around Paris; for a partial listing see the boxed text, above.

Hotels

Hotels in Paris are inspected by authorities at *département* (administrative division of France) level and classified into six categories – from no star to four-star 'L' (for *luxe*), the French equivalent of five stars. All hotels must display their rates, including TVA (VAT; valued-added tax) both outside the hotel and in guests' rooms.

Paris may not be able to boast the number of budget hotels it did a decade or so ago, but the choice is still more than ample, especially in the Marais, around the Bastille, near the major train stations and off the Grands Boulevards. Places with one star and those with the designations 'HT' (Hôtel de Tourisme) or 'NN' (Nouvelle Norme), which signifies that a hotel is awaiting its rating but remains of a certain standard of comfort, are much of

a muchness. Remember: the overall consideration at these places is cost, never quality. Be advised that some budget hotels in Paris do not accept credit cards.

Breakfast – usually a simple continental affair of bread, croissants, butter, jam and coffee or tea, though American-style breakfast buffets are becoming more popular – is served at most hotels with two or more stars and usually costs around €8.

Some hotels in Paris have different rates according to the season and are noted as such throughout the chapter. The high season is (roughly) from April to September while the low season is from October to March. There are usually bargains to be had during the late autumn (say, November) and winter months (January and February).

Hostels

Paris is awash with hostels, but such budget accommodation isn't as cheap as it used to be here. Beds under €25 are increasingly rare – especially in summer – so two people who don't mind sleeping in the same bed may find basic rooms in budget hotels a less-expensive proposition. Groups of three or four will save even more if they share two or three beds in a budget hotel.

Showers are always free at hostels in Paris, and rates include a simple breakfast. Internet access (from about €1 for 15 minutes) is available at almost all the hostels listed here. If you don't have your own sheet bag, sheets can be rented at most hostels for a one-off charge of around €3 (plus deposit).

Some of the more institutional hostels only allow guests to stay a maximum of three nights, particularly in summer. Places that have upper age limits (for example, 30 years old) tend not to enforce them except at the busiest of times. Only the official *auberges de jeunesse* (youth hostels), of which there are just two in all of Paris, require guests to present Hostelling International (HI) cards or their equivalent. Curfew – if enforced – is generally at 1am or 2am.

Homestays & B&Bs

Under an arrangement known as *hôtes payants* (literally 'paying guests') or *hébergement chez l'habitant* (lodging with the occupants of private homes), students, young people and tourists can stay with French families. In general you rent a room and, for an additional fee, have access to the family's kitchen in the evening. Half and full board is also usually available. For a list of homestay venues see opposite. Some private language schools (p398) can arrange homestays for their students.

Bed-and-breakfast (B&B) accommodation – known as *chambres d'hôte* in French – has never been anywhere near as popular in Paris as it has been in, say, London but that is changing. The city of Paris has inaugurated a scheme called Paris Quality Hosts (www.hqp.fr) to encourage Parisians to rent out their spare rooms. The idea is not just to offer visitors an alternative choice of accommodation but to ease the isolation of some Parisians, half of whom apparently live alone. Expect to pay anything from €65 a double. Most hosts will expect you to stay a minimum of three or four nights.

The following B&Bs are all members of the Paris Quality Hosts initiative. At least two have been recommended by readers.

Alcôve & Agapes (Alcoves & Feasts; ☎ 01 44 85 06 05; www.bed-and-breakfast-in-paris.com)

B&B Paris (☎ 01 47 34 01 50; www.2binparis.com)

Fleurs de Soleil (Sunflower; ☎ 06 62 37 97 85; www.fleursdesoleil.fr, in French)

Good Morning Paris (☎ 01 47 07 44 45; www.goodmorningparis.fr)

Longer-term Rentals

Small (15 to 30 sq metres) studios with attached toilet in central Paris start at about €20 per sq metre per month; expect to pay from about €800 for a one-bedroom flat and €600 for a studio. The per-metre cost theoretically decreases the larger the place, the further away it is from the city centre and if it is a walk-up (ie does not have access to a lift).

Under €500 a month will get you a tiny garret room with a washbasin but no landline telephone, proper cooking facilities or private toilet. There may not even be a communal shower. These rooms, often occupied by students, are usually converted *chambres de bonne* (maid's quarters) on the 6th or 7th floors of old apartment buildings without lifts, but in decent neighbourhoods.

The hardest time to find an apartment – especially a cheap one – in Paris is in September and October, when everyone is back from their summer holidays and students are searching for digs for the academic year. Moderately priced places are easiest to find towards the end of university semesters – ie between Christmas and early February and July to September.

If you've exhausted your word-of-mouth sources (expats, students, compatriots living temporarily in Paris), it's a good idea to check out the bulletin boards at the American Church (p408). People who advertise there are more likely to rent to foreigners, will usually speak at least some English and might be willing to offer a relatively short-term contract. *Fusac* (p405), a free periodical issued every two weeks, is another good source.

If you know some French (or someone who does), you'll be able to consult several periodicals available from newsagents: the weekly *De Particulier à Particulier* (www.pap.fr; €2.95) appears on Thursday, while the biweeklies *À Vendre, à Louer* (www.avendrealouer.fr, in French; €1.50) and *Se Loger* (www.seloger.com; €2.30) come out on Monday and Thursday respectively. You'll have to do your calling in French, though. If you have access to a phone, you could place a want ad in *De Particulier à Particulier* and have people call you.

FAMILY AFFAIR

Popular with students learning French are *pensions de famille,* which are similar to B&Bs but more intimate. In 1970 there were some 400 scattered around the city; today there are a mere nine family guesthouses. Four that come recommended by the Paris tourist office are the following:

Pension au Palais Gourmand (Map pp116–17; ☎ 01 45 48 24 15; www.au-palais-gourmand.fr; 3rd fl, 120 blvd Raspail, 6e; s & d €72.50-82.50, tr €107; Ⓜ Vavin or Notre Dame des Champs) The promisingly named 'At the Gourmet Palace' is on a busy street between the Jardin du Luxembourg and Montparnasse and is convenient to everything. Lunch or dinner is €13. Breakfast is included.

Pension les Marronniers (Map pp116–17; ☎ 01 43 26 37 71; www.pension-marronniers.com; 78 rue d'Assas, 6e; s €40-67, d €74-84; Ⓜ Vavin or Notre Dame des Champs; 🖳) In a pretty building facing the Jardin du Luxembourg, it has monthly rates at 20% less. Vegetarian meals and ones for those on special diets are also available. Rates included breakfast, as well as the use of microwave, fridge, washing machine and wi-fi.

Résidence des Palais (Map pp116–17; ☎ 01 43 26 79 32; www.hotelresidencedupalais.com; 2nd fl, 78 rue d'Assas, 6e; s/d/tr/q €56/63/78/110; Ⓜ Vavin or Notre Dame des Champs) This luxurious place is in the same building as the Pension Les Marroniers. Rates are cheaper after four days and still cheaper after a week. Breakfast is included.

Résidence Cardinal (Map pp148–9; ☎ 01 48 74 16 16; http://pensioncardinal.free.fr, in French; 2nd fl, 4 rue Cardinal Mercier, 9e; s/d/t €40/55/75; Ⓜ Liège or Place de Clichy) This place is on a quiet street with an old fountain at the end of it. Doubles with shower and toilet are €10 pricier. Rates include breakfast.

Allô Logement Temporaire (Map pp98–9; ☎ 01 42 72 00 06; www.allo-logement-temporaire.asso.fr; 1st fl, 64 rue du Temple, 3e; 🕐 noon-8pm Mon-Fri; Ⓜ Rambuteau) is a nonprofit organisation that links property-owners and foreigners looking for furnished apartments for periods of one week to one year. Small furnished studios of 15 to 18 sq metres cost around €600 per month while double that size is about €800, depending on the location. October, when university classes resume, is the hardest month to find a place, but over summer and into September it's usually possible to rent something within a matter of days. Before any deals are signed, the company will arrange for you to talk to the owner by phone, assisted by an interpreter if necessary. There is a €55 annual membership fee and, in addition to the rent and one month's deposit (paid directly to the owner), you'll pay a charge of €35 for each month you rent.

RESERVATIONS

During periods of heavy domestic or foreign tourism – Christmas and New Year, the winter school holidays (February to March), Easter, July and August – a hotel reservation can mean the difference between a bed in a room and a bench in the park. For really popular places – think location and/or price – book several months ahead.

Many hotels, especially budget ones, accept reservations only if they are accompanied by *des arrhes* (a deposit). Some places, especially

those with two or more stars, don't ask for a deposit if you give them your credit card number or if you send them confirmation of your plans by letter, fax or email in French or clear, simple English.

Most independent hotels will hold a room only until a set hour, rarely later than 6pm or 7pm without prior arrangement. If you're arriving later than expected and you haven't prepaid or given the hotel your credit-card details, let the staff know or they might rent your room to someone else.

The Paris Convention & Visitors Bureau (Office de Tourisme et de Congrès de Paris), particularly the Gare du Nord branch (p411) can find you a place to stay for the night of the day you stop by and will make the booking for free. The only catch is that you have to use a credit card to reserve a room Be warned: the queues can be very long in the high season.

ROOM RATES

When calculating accommodation costs, assume you'll spend from about a minimum of €40 for a washbasin-equipped double in a budget hotel (count on anything up to at least €70 if you want your own shower). Bear in mind that you may be charged extra (up to €3) to use communal showers in budget hotels. If you can't go without your daily ablutions, it can be a false economy staying at such places.

Midrange hotels in Paris offer some of the best value for money of any European capital city.

Hotels at this level always have bathroom facilities (showers or baths) unless noted otherwise. These hotels charge between €70 and €160 for a double and generally offer excellent value, especially at the higher end.

Top-end places run the gamut from tasteful and discreet boutique hotels to palaces with 100plus rooms and will cost two people €160 or more a night. And brace yourself at the very top end of the range; according to a comparison done by the *Wall Street Journal* of the price of a Saturday night in the most expensive suite of a five-star (in this case four-star 'L') hotel in eight cities around the world, Paris came out tops at €7600 (followed by New York at €6641, Tokyo at €5450 and London at €5334).

LOUVRE & LES HALLES

The area encompassing the Musée du Louvre and the Forum des Halles, effectively the 1er and a small slice of the 2e, is very central but don't expect to find tranquillity or many bargains here. But while it is more disposed to welcoming top-end travellers, there are some decent midrange places to choose from and the main branch of a popular hostel can also be found here.

Both airports are linked to nearby metro station Châtelet-Les Halles by the RER (Réseau Express Régional – regional train service).

HÔTEL MEURICE Map pp82–3 Hotel €€€
☎ 01 44 58 10 10; www.meuricehotel.com; 228 rue de Rivoli, 1er; s €620, d €730-910, ste from €990; Ⓜ Tuileries; ✕ ⊠ 🖳 ♿
With 160 rooms, many of them facing the Jardin des Tuileries, the Meurice's gold leaf and Art Nouveau glass positively glisten, and its ground-floor restaurant, Le Meurice, is a mainstay of good taste (in more ways than one). The domed Le Dali restaurant with its astonishing canvas and whimsical furnishings, is a light-hearted addition to this otherwise bastion of tasteful reserve.

BOOK ACCOMMODATION ONLINE
For more accommodation reviews and recommendations by Lonely Planet authors, check out the online booking service at www.lonelyplanet.com. You'll find the true, insider lowdown on the best places to stay. Reviews are thorough and independent. Best of all, you can book online.

HÔTEL RITZ PARIS Map pp82–3 Hotel €€€
☎ 01 43 16 30 30; www.ritzparis.com; 15 place Vendôme, 1er; s & d €730-880, ste from €970; Ⓜ Opéra; ✕ 🖳 🖭
So famous it's lent its name to the English lexicon, the incomparable, the unmistakable Ritz has 161 sparkling rooms and suites. Its L'Espadon restaurant has a Michelin star and the Hemingway Bar (p285) is where the American author imbibed once he'd made a name for himself. It's equally celebrated for its cooking school (p398).

HÔTEL COSTES Map pp82–3 Hotel €€€
☎ 01 42 44 50 00; www.hotelcostes.com; 239 rue St-Honoré, 1er; s & d €400-850, ste from €1250; Ⓜ Concorde; ✕ 🖳 🖭 ♿
Jean-Louis Costes' eponymous caravanserai remains an 'extravagant luxury hotel popular with the jet-set' (or so says Michelin). Outfitted in the signature Second Empire colours of purple and gold with a Byzantine twist, this 82-room hotel is still very much a darling of the rich and famous. A delightful restaurant takes pride of place in the stone-strewn central courtyard in the warmer months; the basement pool, with Art Deco-ish lounge chairs and lighting, is gorgeous; and the bar and its groovy music compilations are legendary.

GRAND HÔTEL DE CHAMPAIGNE Map p86 Hotel €€€
☎ 01 42 36 60 00; www.hotelchampaigneparis .com; 17 rue Jean Lantier, 1er; s €155-180, d & tw €189-235, tr €210-235; Ⓜ Châtelet; ✕ 🖳
This very comfortable, three-star hotel is housed in the former Hôtel des Tailleurs, a stonecutters' mansion built in 1562 on a quiet street between rue Rivoli and the Seine. Some of the 43 guestrooms (eg the Louis XIII–style room) are almost over the top but, well, this is Paris. Enjoy.

HÔTEL THÉRÈSE Map pp82–3 Hotel €€€
☎ 01 42 96 10 01; www.hoteltherese.com; 5-7 rue Thérèse, 1er; s €150, d & tw €180-250; Ⓜ Pyramides; ✕ 🖳
From the same people who brought you the Hôtel Verneuil (p350) the Thérèse also has chic individually decorated rooms – in this case 43 of them in eight basic colours. The décor is classic yet eclectic; larger rooms have tubs while smaller ones (and they are small) have showers. We love the linen panels on the windows that diffuse the light so nicely.

HÔTEL BRITANNIQUE Map p86 Hotel €€€
☎ 01 42 33 74 59; www.hotel-britannique.fr;
20 av Victoria, 1er; s €147, d €178-205; tr €233, ste
€263-306; Ⓜ Châtelet; ✕ 🖳
With all the plaid here and the panelled,
library-like lounge, you'd be excused for
thinking you'd hopped over what the French
called La Manche ('Sleeve', or English Channel). Still, the 39-room 'Britannic' remains a
Gallic oasis above the brouhaha of Châtelet,
and the rooms on the upper floors, some of
which have balconies, look straight down to
a row of plane trees. It's an excellent choice
if you want to be near everything.

LE RELAIS DU LOUVRE Map p86 Hotel €€€
☎ 01 40 41 96 42; www.relaisdulouvre.com;
19 rue des Prêtres St-Germain l'Auxerrois, 1er;
s €108, d & tw €165-198, tr €212, ste €237-430;
Ⓜ Pont Neuf; ✕ 🖳
If you are someone who likes style but
in a traditional sense, choose this lovely
21-room hotel just west of the Louvre and
south of the Église St-Germain l'Auxerrois.
The 10 rooms facing the street and the
church are on the petite side; if you are
looking for something more spacious, ask
for one of the five rooms ending in a '2'
and looking onto the garden/patio. Room 2
itself has access to the garden.

HÔTEL ST-MERRY Map p86 Hotel €€
☎ 01 42 78 14 15; www.hotelmarais.com;
78 rue de la Verrerie, 4e; d & tw €160-230, tr €205-
275, ste €335-407; Ⓜ Châtelet; 🖳
The interior of this 11-room hostelry,
with beamed ceilings, church pews and
wrought-iron candelabra, is a neogoth's
wet dream; you have to see the architec
tural elements of room 9 (flying buttress
over the bed) and the furnishings of 12
(choir-stall bed board) to believe them. On
the downside there is no lift connecting the
postage-stamp lobby with the four upper
floors, and it has no mod cons to speak of
except for recently introduced wi-fi.

HÔTEL VIVIENNE Map pp82–3 Hotel €€
☎ 01 42 33 13 26; www.hotel-vivienne.com;
40 rue Vivienne, 2e; s €60-114, d & tw €75-114;
Ⓜ Grands Boulevards; ✕ 🖳
This stylish hotel is amazingly good value
for Paris. While the 45 rooms are not huge,
they have all the modcons (some even
boast little balconies), and the public areas
are bright and cheery.

PRICE GUIDE
The symbols below indicate the cost per night of a
standard double room in high season.

€	under €70
€€	€71-160
€€€	over €160

HÔTEL DE LILLE Map p86 Hotel €
☎ 01 42 33 33 42; www.heoteldelille.net; 8 rue de
Pélican, 1er; s €35-38, d €43-50, tr €65-75;
Ⓜ Palais Royal-Musée du Louvre; ✕
This old-fashioned but spotlessly clean
13-room hotel is down a quiet side street
in a 17th-century building. A half-dozen of
the rooms have just a washbasin and bidet
(communal showers cost €3), while the rest
have en suite showers. The friendly and
helpful manager speaks good English.

CENTRE INTERNATIONAL DE SÉJOUR BVJ PARIS-LOUVRE Map p86 Hostel €
☎ 01 53 00 90 90; www.bvjhotel.com; 20 rue Jean-
Jacques Rousseau, 1er; per person dm €28, d €30;
Ⓜ Louvre-Rivoli; ✕ 🖳
This modern, 200 bed hostel run by the
Bureau des Voyages de la Jeunesse (Youth
Travel Bureau) has doubles and bunks in a
single-sex room for four to 10 people with
showers down the corridor. Guests should
be aged 18 to 35. Rooms are accessible
from 2.30pm on the day you arrive and all
day after that. There are no kitchen facilities. There is usually space in the morning,
even in summer, so stop by as early as you
can. All rooms are nonsmoking and internet access is available for €1 for 10 minutes.
The Centre International de Séjour BVJ Paris-Quartier
Latin (Map pp110–11; ☎ 01 43 29 34 80; 44 rue des Bernardins, 5e; per person dm €28, s/d €42/32; Ⓜ Maubert
Mutualité), its sister-hostel on the Left Bank,
has 100 beds in singles, doubles and single-
sex dorm rooms for four to 10 people. All
rooms have showers and telephones, and
rates include breakfast.

MARAIS & BASTILLE
The Marais is one of the liveliest parts of
the Right Bank and its top-end hostels are
among the city's finest. Despite massive
gentrification in recent years, there are also
some less expensive hotels left and the choice
of lower-priced one- and two-star hotels

top picks

BOUTIQUE HOTELS

- Hôtel La Manufacture (p356)
- Le Général Hôtel (right)
- Mayet Hôtel (p348)
- Hôtel du Petit Moulin (below)
- Kube Hôtel (p357)
- Select Hôtel (p343)

remains excellent. East of the Bastille, the relatively untouristy 11e is generally made up of unpretentious working-class areas and is a good way to see the 'real' Paris up close. Two-star comfort there is less expensive than in the Marais.

MURANO URBAN RESORT

Map pp92–3   Boutique Hotel €€€

☎ 01 42 71 20 00; www.muranoresort.com; 13 blvd du Temple, 3e; s €360, d €440-650, ste €750-1200; Ⓜ Filles du Calvaire; ⊠ ⊠ ▣ ☎
This 52-room 'urban resort' south of place de la République wears a classical 19th-century exterior but has the 21st century inside. And with public areas like a new spa with heated pool, a courtyard restaurant under glass, a cool jazz bar with DJ, and bedrooms that allow you to change their colour scheme, it might even be the 22nd.

HÔTEL DU BOURG TIBOURG

Map pp98–9   Boutique Hotel €€€

☎ 01 42 78 47 39; www.hoteldubourgtibourg.com; 19 du Bourg Tibourg, 4e; s €180, d €230-260, ste €360; Ⓜ Hôtel de Ville or St-Paul; ⊠ ▣
This stunning 30-room boutique hotel is in the Hôtel Costes stable and was also done up by über-designer Jacques Garcia. The result is romantic 'French' neogothic combined with Orientalia. Be aware that this place is built more for romance than business; rooms are not particularly large, except for the one suite.

HÔTEL DU PETIT MOULIN

Map pp98–9   Boutique Hotel €€€

☎ 01 42 74 10 10; www.hoteldupetitmoulin.com; 29-31 rue du Poitou, 3e; r €180-280, ste €350; Ⓜ Filles du Calvaire; ⊠ ▣ ♿
Oh, brave new world! This scrumptious boutique hotel (OK, we're impressed that

it was a bakery at the time of Henri IV) was designed from top to bottom by Christian Lacroix and features 17 completely different rooms. You can choose from medieval and rococo Marais sporting exposed beams and dressed in Toile de Jouy wallpaper, to a more modern *quartier* with contemporary murals and heart-shaped mirrors just this side of kitsch. 'The Little Mill' is a wonderful new addition to the northern end of the Marais and highly recommended.

LE GÉNÉRAL HÔTEL

Map pp94–5   Boutique Hotel €€€

☎ 01 47 00 41 57; www.legeneralhotel.com; 5-7 rue Rampon, 11e; s €143-163, d €173-203, tr €203-233, ste €243-273; Ⓜ République; ⊠ ⊠ ▣ ♿
This 48-room hotel is a symphony in white on the outside and bonbon box of cherry and chocolate tones within. The hotel's décor is fresh and fun, and the rooms are beautifully furnished. The light 'sculpture' in the bar off the lobby is memorable and amenities include a fitness centre and sauna.

CASTEX HÔTEL Map pp92–3   Hotel €€

☎ 01 42 72 31 52; www.castexhotel.com; 5 rue Castex, 4e; s/d €120/150, ste €220; Ⓜ Bastille; ⊠ ▣
Equidistant from the Bastille and the Marais, the 30-room Castex has modernised but managed to retain some of its 17th-century elements, including a vaulted stone cellar used as a breakfast room, terracotta tiles on the floor and Toile de Jouy wallpaper. Try to get one of the independent rooms (1 and 2) off the lovely patio; No 3 is a two-room suite or family room.

HÔTEL BASTILLE DE LAUNAY

Map pp94–5   Hotel €€

☎ 01 47 00 88 11; www.paris-hotel-launay.com; 42 rue Amelot, 11e; s €110, d €140-160; Ⓜ Chemin Vert; ▣
This 36-room hotel offers good value due to its central location just up from place de la Bastille. Rooms are smallish and much of a muchness, with classic two-star furnishings and carpets. Rooms ending in '1' face quiet rue Amelot and the steps up to busy blvd Beaumarchais.

HÔTEL DU VIEUX SAULE

Map pp92–3   Hotel €€

☎ 01 42 72 01 14; www.hotelvieuxsaule.com; 6 rue de Picardie, 3e; s €120, d €140-160, tr €180; Ⓜ Filles du Calvaire; ⊠ ⊠ ▣

This flower-bedecked 28-room hostelry in the northern Marais is something of a 'find' because of its slightly unusual location. The hotel has a small sauna, there is a tranquil little garden on full display behind glass off the lobby. Breakfast is served in the 16th-century vaulted cellar.

AUSTIN'S ARTS ET MÉTIERS HÔTEL Map pp92–3 Hotel €€
☎ 01 42 77 17 61; www.hotelaustins.com; 6 rue Montgolfier, 3e; s/d €108/148; M Arts et Métiers; ✉ 🖴

This three-star hotel southwest of place de la République and hard by the Musée des Arts et Métiers (p97) stands out primarily for its warm welcome and excellent service. The 29 rooms are minimally furnished but attractively done up in reds, yellows and blues. The brightest rooms face the street, while the largest ones overlook the courtyard. Choose 12 if, like us, you like a bathroom with a window. There is a sister hotel, Austin's St-Lazare Hôtel (p353) opposite Gare St-Lazare.

HÔTEL BASTILLE SPÉRIA
Map pp94–5 Hotel €€
☎ 01 42 72 04 01; www.hotel-bastille-speria.com; 1 rue de la Bastille, 4e; s €103-131, d €135-160, tw €152-170; M Bastille; ✂ 🖴

This 42-room hotel is within spitting distance of place de la Bastille offers good value for its location. The rooms are nothing to write home about but some of them (103, for example) sit on the corner and boast two windows. Bathrooms are modern and relatively large.

HÔTEL CARON DE BEAUMARCHAIS
Map pp98–9 Boutique Hotel €€
☎ 01 42 72 34 12; www.carondebeaumarchais .com; 12 rue Vieille du Temple, 4e; r €125-162; M St-Paul; ✉ ✂ 🖴

Decorated like an 18th-century private house contemporary with Beaumarchais, who wrote Le Mariage de Figaro (The Marriage of Figaro) at No 47 on this street, this award-winning themed hotel has to be seen to be believed. The small, museum-quality lobby, with its prized 18th-century pianoforte, gaming tables and original Beaumarchais manuscripts, sets the tone of the place. The 19 rooms aren't huge but are positively dripping in brocade, furniture decorated with tracery, and ormolu-framed mirrors. The welcome can verge on the scary.

HÔTEL DE LA BRETONNERIE
Map pp98–9 Hotel €€
☎ 01 48 87 77 63; www.bretonnerie.com; 22 rue Ste-Croix de la Bretonnerie, 4e; s & d €125-160, ste €185-210; M Hôtel de Ville; 🖴

This is a very charming three-star hotel in the heart of the Marais nightlife area dating from the 17th century. The décor of each of the 22 rooms and seven suites is unique, and some rooms have four-poster and canopy beds. Three 'duplex' suites on two levels are huge and can easily accommodate three or four people.

GRAND HÔTEL MALHER
Map pp98–9 Hotel €€
☎ 01 42 72 60 92; www.grandhotelmalher.com, in French; 5 rue Malher, 4e; s €95-120, d €115-140, ste €170-185; M St-Paul; 🖴 ♿

This welcoming establishment run by the same family for three generations has nicely appointed rooms and a small but pretty courtyard at the back. The hotel's 31 bedrooms are a decent size, and the bathrooms are modern and relatively large; most are equipped with a bath and a few with a shower. Rooms 1 and 2 give on to the courtyard.

HÔTEL SAINTONGE MARAIS
Map pp98–9 Hotel €€
☎ 01 42 77 91 13; www.hotelmarais.com; 16 rue Saintonge, 3e; s/d/tr €105/115/140, ste €170; M Filles du Calvaire; 🖴 ♿

This renovated 23-room hotel, with exposed beams, vaulted cellar and period furniture, is really more Oberkampf/République than the Marais. But with the Musée Picasso practically next door, let's not quibble. You'll get much better value for money here than in the more central parts of the Marais, including at the Saintonge's show-off sister property, the Hôtel St-Merry (p337).

HÔTEL ST-LOUIS MARAIS
Map pp92–3 Hotel €€
☎ 01 48 87 87 04; www.saintlouismarais.com; 1 rue Charles V, 4e; s €99, d & tw €115-140, tr €150, ste €160; M Sully Morland; 🖴

This especially charming hotel built within a converted 17th-century convent is more Bastille than Marais, but still within easy walking distance of the latter. Wooden beams, terracotta tiles and heavy brocade drapes tend to darken the 19 renovated rooms, but certainly add to the atmosphere. Be aware that this four-floor hotel has no lift.

HÔTEL BEAUMARCHAIS
Map pp94–5   Boutique Hotel €€

☎ 01 53 36 86 86; www.hotelbeaumarchais.com; 3 rue Oberkampf, 11e; s €75-90, d €110-130, tr €170-190; M Filles du Calvaire; ✗ 🖳
This brighter-than-bright 31-room boutique hotel, with its emphasis on sunbursts and bold primary colours, is just this side of kitsch. But it certainly makes for a different Paris experience, and there are monthly art exhibitions to which guests are invited to the *vernissage* (opening night). The rooms are of a decent size and the best are Nos 2 and 3 – a triple and a double in the courtyard.

HÔTEL DE NICE Map pp98–9   Hotel €€
☎ 01 42 78 55 29; www.hoteldenice.com; 42bis rue de Rivoli, 4e; s/d/tr €80/110/135; M Hôtel de Ville
This is an especially warm, family-run place with 23 comfortable rooms. Some have balconies high above busy rue de Rivoli. Reception is on the 1st floor. Every square inch of wall space is used to display old prints, and public areas and bedrooms are full of Second Empire–style furniture, Indian carpets and lamps with fringed shades.

HÔTEL DE LA PLACE DES VOSGES
Map pp98–9   Hotel €€
☎ 01 42 72 60 46; www.hotelplacedesvosges .com; 12 rue de Birague, 4e; s & d €90-95, ste €150; M Bastille; 🖳
This superbly situated 17-room hotel is an oasis of tranquillity due south of sublime place des Vosges. The public areas are impressive and the rooms warm and cosy. A tiny lift serves the 1st to 4th floors but it's stairs only from the ground floor and to the 5th floor. A boon to families is the suite on the top floor with choice views that can accommodate up to four people comfortably.

HÔTEL DU 7E ART Map pp92–3   Hotel €€
☎ 01 44 54 85 00; www.paris-hotel-7art.com; 20 rue St-Paul, 4e; s & d €85-145, tw €100-145; M St-Paul; 🖳
This themed hotel on the south side of rue St-Antoine is a fun place for film buffs – *le septième art* (the seventh art) is what the French call cinema – and boasts a B&W-movie theme throughout, right down to the tiled floors and the bathrooms. The 23 rooms

over five floors – there is no lift – are sizeable and quite different from one another. A single with just a washbasin is €65. Go for room 41 or 42 on the 4th floor; they both have windows facing in two directions.

HÔTEL PARIS FRANCE Map pp92–3   Hotel €€
☎ 01 42 78 00 04; www.paris-france-hotel.com; 72 rue de Turbigo, 3e; s €72-98, d €89-129, tw €89-159, tr €109-159; M Temple; ✗ 🖳
This hotel with the inspired name first opened in 1910 but you wouldn't win any prizes locating vestiges of the Belle Époque here. Rooms are nicely proportioned but try to get one facing the rear as rue Turbigo is a very busy street and even the double-glazing is challenged by the din.

HÔTEL CROIX DE MALTE
Map pp94–5   Hotel €€
☎ 01 48 05 09 36; www.hotelcroixdemalte-paris .com; 5 rue de Malte, 11e; s €75-85, d €85-95; M Oberkampf; ✗ 🖳
This cheery hotel will have you thinking you're in the tropics, not Paris. The breakfast room just off the lobby is bathed in light and looks out onto a tiny glassed-in courtyard with greenery and a giant jungle mural; Walasse Ting prints (of parrots mostly) complete the picture. The 40 rooms are in two little buildings, only one of which has a lift.

HÔTEL JEANNE D'ARC Map pp98–9   Hotel €€
☎ 01 48 87 62 11; www.hoteljeannedarc.com; 3 rue de Jarente, 4e; s €60-97, d €84-97, tr €116, q €146; M St-Paul; 🖳 🖳
This cosy 36-room hotel near lovely place du Marché Ste-Catherine is a great little base for your peregrinations among the museums, bars and restaurants of the Marais, and almost has a country feel to it (including heated towel rails). About the only thing wrong with this place is that everyone knows about it, so you'll have to book well in advance.

HÔTEL DAVAL Map pp94–5   Hotel €€
☎ 01 47 00 51 23; www.hoteldaval.com; 21 rue Daval, 11e; s/d/tr/q €76/82/105/118; M Bastille; ✗ 🖳
Always a favourite, this 23-room property is a very central option if you're looking for budget accommodation just off place de la Bastille. What's more, it's had a facelift that brings it up at least to the start of the 21st century. Rooms and bathrooms are on the

small side and if you're looking for some peace and quiet choose a back room (eg room 13).

HÔTEL PRATIC Map pp98–9 Hotel €€
☎ 01 48 87 80 47; www.hotelpratic.com; 9 rue d'Ormesson, 4e; s €75-105, d €81-121, tr €93-145; Ⓜ St-Paul; ✕
This 23-room hotel, which is opposite the delightful place du Marché Ste-Catherine, has been given another overhaul and the décor – exposed beams, gilt frames, half-timbered or stone walls – is almost too much. Rooms, dispersed over six floors, are rather pricey for what you get, though there are frequent promotions on their website. There's no lift here.

HÔTEL SÉVIGNÉ Map pp98–9 Hotel €€
☎ 01 42 72 76 17; www.le-sevigne.com; 2 rue Malher, 4e; s €67, d & tw €80-91, tr €107; Ⓜ St-Paul; ✕
This hotel in the heart of the Marais, and named after the celebrated 17th-century writer, the Marquise de Sévigné (whose letters give us such a wonderful insight into the Paris of her day) is excellent value for its location and price. The hotel's 29 rooms, spread over six floors and accessible by lift, are basic but comfortably furnished.

HÔTEL LYON MULHOUSE
Map pp94–5 Hotel €€
☎ 01 47 00 91 50; www.1-hotel-paris.com; 8 blvd Beaumarchais, 11e; s €65-90, d €78-110, tr €110-130; Ⓜ Bastille; ✕ ▯
This former post house, from where carriages would set out for Lyon and Mulhouse, has been a hotel since the 1920s. The 40 rooms, though not particularly special, are comfortable, quiet and of a good size; opt for room 12 with a door leading to a courtyard. Place de la Bastille is just around the corner.

HÔTEL BAUDELAIRE BASTILLE
Map pp94–5 Hotel €
☎ 01 47 00 40 98; www.paris-hotel-bastille.com; 12 rue de Charonne, 11e; s €55-66, d €62-76, tr €71-89, q €89-108; Ⓜ Bastille or Ledru Rollin; ▯
This independent one-star hotel is in an ancient building that is coy about showing its age except for the odd worm-chewed beam. The 46 rooms are of a decent size and spotless, though there is no lift. Rooms look out onto a quiet courtyard or the street but double-glazing more or less

keeps the noise where it belongs. Internet costs €2 for 15 minutes or €6 per hour.

GRAND HÔTEL DU LOIRET
Map pp98–9 Hotel €
☎ 01 48 87 77 00; hotelduloiret@hotmail.com; 8 rue des Mauvais Garçons, 4e; s €50-80, d €50-90, tr/q €100/110; Ⓜ Hôtel de Ville or St-Paul; ▯
This 27-room budget hotel in the heart of gay Marais is very popular with young male travellers, not just because it is within easy walking distance of just about everything after dark, but because it sits – or does it lie? – on the 'Street of the Bad Boys'. Seven of the rooms have neither private shower nor bath or toilet but share facilities off the corridors. Those rooms are a steal at €50. Internet access costs a whopping €3/5/9 for 15/30/60 minutes.

HÔTEL DE LA HERSE D'OR
Map pp92–3 Hotel €
☎ 01 48 87 84 09; www.hotel-herse-dor.com; 20 rue St-Antoine, 4e; basic s/d €45/60, with shower d/tr €76/96; Ⓜ Bastille; ▯
This friendly place east of place de la Bastille has 35 serviceable rooms off a long stone corridor lined with mirrors. It's very basic and cheap; the lower-priced rooms have washbasins only. Though there's wi-fi, those without laptops can check their emails at an internet terminal in the lobby for €2/6 for 15/60 minutes. And, in case you wondered, *herse* in French is not 'hearse' but 'portcullis'. So let's call it the 'Golden Gate Hotel'.

HÔTEL DE NEVERS Map pp94–5 Hotel €
☎ 01 47 00 56 18; www.hoteldenevers.com; 53 rue de Malte, 11e; s €39, d €45-55, tr €75-87; Ⓜ Oberkampf; ▯
This 32-room budget hotel around the corner from place de la République and within easy walking distance of the nightlife of Ménilmontant is under new management but remains excellent value. Hyper-allergenics may think twice about staying here, though: there are three cats on hand to greet you. Rooms at the low-end of the scale share bathing facilities.

HÔTEL RIVOLI Map pp98–9 Hotel €
☎ 01 42 72 08 41; 44 rue de Rivoli & 2 rue des Mauvais Garçons, 4e; s €35-55, d €44-55, tr €70; Ⓜ Hôtel de Ville
Long a Lonely Planet favourite (there's no pretending who we are – or are not – with

these guys), the Rivoli is forever cheery but not as dirt cheap as it once was, with 20 basic, somewhat noisy rooms. The cheaper singles and doubles have washbasins only, but use of the shower room in the hallway is free. Annoyingly – given that it is in the heart of the Marais nightlife area – the front door is locked from 2am to 7am. Reception is on the 1st floor.

MAISON INTERNATIONALE DE LA JEUNESSE ET DES ÉTUDIANTS
Map pp98–9   Hostel €

MIJE; ☎ 01 42 74 23 45; www.mije.com; per person dm €29, s/d/tr €47/34/30; ⊠ 🖳
The MIJE runs three hostels in attractively renovated 17th- and 18th-century *hôtels particuliers* (private mansions) in the heart of the Marais, and it's difficult to think of a better budget deal in Paris. Costs are the same for all three hostels, and include single-sex, shower-equipped dorms with four to eight beds per room as well as singles, twins and triples. Rooms are closed from noon to 3pm, and curfew is from 1am to 7am. The maximum stay is seven nights. Individuals can make reservations at any of the three MIJE hostels listed below by emailing (info@mije.com) or telephoning; reception will hold you a bed till noon. During summer and other busy periods, there may not be space after mid-morning. There's an annual membership fee of €2.50.

MIJE Le Fauconnier (Map pp92–3; 11 rue du Fauconnier, 4e; Ⓜ St-Paul or Pont Marie) has 125 beds and is two blocks south of MIJE Le Fourcy.

MIJE Le Fourcy (Map pp98–9; 6 rue de Fourcy, 4e; Ⓜ St-Paul), with 180 beds, is the largest of the three. There's a cheap eatery here called Le Restaurant, which offers a three-course fixed-price *menu* including a drink for €10.50.

MIJE Maubuisson (Map pp98–9; 12 rue des Barres, 4e; Ⓜ Hôtel de Ville or Pont Marie) – the pick of the three, in our opinion – is half a block south of the *mairie* (town hall) of the 4e and has 99 beds.

AUBERGE DE JEUNESSE JULES FERRY
Map pp94–5   Hostel €

☎ 01 43 57 55 60; www.fuaj.fr; 8 blvd Jules Ferry, 11e; per person dm & d €21; Ⓜ République or Goncourt; ⊠ 🔀 🖳
This official hostel three blocks east of place de la République is somewhat institutional and the rooms could use a refit,

but the atmosphere is fairly relaxed. The 99 beds are in two- to six-person rooms, which are locked between 10.30am and 2pm for housekeeping, but there is no curfew. You'll have to pay an extra €2.90 per night if you don't have an HI card or equivalent (€11/17 for those under/over 26).

AUBERGE INTERNATIONALE DES JEUNES
Map pp94–5   Hostel €

☎ 01 47 00 62 00; www.aijparis.com; 10 rue Trousseau, 11e; per person dm Jul & Aug €17, Mar-Jun & Sep-Oct €15, Nov-Feb €13; Ⓜ Ledru Rollin
This clean, friendly hostel just 700m east of place de la Bastille attracts a young, international crowd and gets full in the summer. Beds in dorms are for two to four people; the largest ones have shower and toilet en suite. Rooms are closed for cleaning between 11am and 4pm but there's no curfew. Internet access costs €2 for 15 minutes.

ALSO RECOMMENDED

Hôtel Verlain (Map pp94–5; ☎ 01 43 57 44 88; www.verlain.com; 97 rue St-Maur, 11e; s/d €115/125; Ⓜ Rue St-Maur; 🖳) Good-value and more-than-functional 38-room midrange hotel overlooking busy blvd de la République.

Hôtel des Arts (Map pp94–5; ☎ 01 43 79 72 57; www.paris-hotel-desarts.com; 2 rue Godefroy Cavaignac, 11e; s/d/tr €90/99/120; Ⓜ Charonne) Cosy hotel with 35 bright (and recently renovated) rooms convenient to the bars and restaurants of Bastille.

Garden Hôtel (Map pp94–5; ☎ 01 47 00 57 93; www.garden-hotel-paris.com; 1 rue du Général Blaise, 11e; s/d €60/78; Ⓜ St-Ambroise) If you're looking for peace and quiet but want to be within easy walking distance of Bastille and Ménilmontant, choose this hotel with 42 rooms overlooking a large leafy square. We're also suckers for a glass Art Deco entranceway.

Hôtel Américain (Map pp92–3; ☎ 01 48 87 58 92; www.paris-hotel-americain.com; 72 rue Charlot, 3e; s €62, d €72, tw €86; Ⓜ République) This cheapie facing a small square just off place de la République has 36 barebones rooms (singles with shower, doubles with bathtubs) and a lobby brightened up by a spot of modern art.

THE ISLANDS

The smaller of the two islands in the middle of the Seine, the Île St-Louis is by far the more romantic and has a string of excellent top-end hotels. It's an easy walk from central Paris. Oddly enough, the only hotel of any sort on the Île de la Cité is a budget one.

HÔTEL DE LUTÈCE Map p105 Hotel €€€

☎ 01 43 26 23 52; www.hotel-ile-saintlouis.com; 65 rue St-Louis en l'Île, 4e; s €150, d €170-189, tr €205-225; Ⓜ Pont Marie; ⊠ ⌨

An exquisite 23-room hotel, the Lutèce has an enviable spot on delightful Île St-Louis. It received a complete makeover in 2006 and has both friendly and helpful management. The comfortable rooms are tastefully decorated and the location is one of the most desirable in the city. The lobby/salon, with its ancient fireplace, wood panelling, antique furnishings and terracotta tiles, sets the inviting tone of the whole place.

HÔTEL ST-LOUIS Map p105 Hotel €€€

☎ 01 46 34 04 80; www.hotel-saint-louis.com; 75 rue St-Louis en l'Île, 4e; r €140-155, ste €220; Ⓜ Pont Marie; ⊠ ⊠ ⌨

One of several hotels lining posh rue St-Louis en l'Île, this hotel has 19 appealing but unspectacular rooms, though the public areas are lovely. The breakfast room in the basement dates from the early 17th century.

HÔTEL HENRI IV Map p105 Hotel €

☎ 01 43 54 44 53; 25 place Dauphine, 1er; s & d €52-76, tr €76; Ⓜ Pont Neuf or Cité; ♿

This decrepit place, with 15 worn rooms, is popular for its location, location and – above all else – location on the tip of the Île de la Cité. It would be impossible to find a hotel more romantically located at such a price in all of Paris – much less the Île de la Cité. While it's not the most salubrious of establishments, in its favour the rooms, all of which have showers, are large and the views over the square are wonderful. Book well in advance.

LATIN QUARTER & JARDIN DES PLANTES

There are dozens of attractive two- and three-star hotels in the Latin Quarter, including a cluster near the Sorbonne and another group along the lively rue des Écoles. Midrange hotels in the Latin Quarter are very popular with visiting academics, so rooms are hardest to find when conferences and seminars are scheduled (usually from March to June and in October). In general this area offers better value among top-end hotels than the better-heeled neighbouring 6e does. The Luxembourg and Port Royal RER stations are linked to both airports by RER and Orlyval.

The northern section of the 5e close to the Seine has been popular with students and young people since the Middle Ages. While truly budget places to stay are at a premium these days, there's at least a popular and well-maintained hostel to choose from.

HÔTEL HENRI IV RIVE GAUCHE
Map pp110–11 Hotel €€€

☎ 01 46 33 20 20; www.henri-paris-hotel.com; 9-11 rue St-Jacques, 5e; s/d/tr €157/175/198; Ⓜ St-Michel Notre Dame or Cluny La Sorbonne; ⊠ ⌨ ♿

This three-star hotel with 23 rooms awash with antiques, old prints and fresh flowers is an oasis in the Latin Quarter just steps from Notre Dame and the Seine. It's part of the same group as the Hôtel de Lutèce (left) on the Île de St-Louis and exudes 'country chic'; the lobby with its 18th-century fireplace, terracotta tiles and portraits could almost be in a manor house in Normandy. Front rooms have stunning views of the Église St-Séverin and its buttresses.

HÔTEL DE NOTRE DAME MAÎTRE ALBERT Map pp110–11 Hotel €€€

☎ 01 43 26 79 00; www.hotel-paris-notredame .com; 19 rue Maître Albert, 5e; s/d €155/165; Ⓜ Maubert Mutualité; ⌨

Hidden down a quiet side street of the Latin Quarter but just paces from the Seine, this hotel boasts some lovely public areas (we adore the tapestry in the lobby and the oriental carpets). However but the 34 rooms, most of which look out to rooftops and give off long narrow corridors, are less impressive. Still, room 27 is a decent size and very quiet.

SELECT HÔTEL Map pp110–11 Boutique Hotel €€€

☎ 01 46 34 14 80; www.selecthotel.fr; 1 place de la Sorbonne, 5e; d €139-175, tw €155-175, tr €179-189, ste €212; Ⓜ Cluny La Sorbonne; ⊠ ⊠ ⌨

Smack dab in the heart of the studenty Sorbonne area, the Select is a very Parisian Art Deco mini-palace, with an atrium and cactus-strewn winter garden, an 18th-century vaulted breakfast room and 67 stylish bedrooms. The rooms are not always

top picks

HOTELS WITH A GARDEN

as large as you'd hope for, but the design solutions are ingenious, making great use of a minimum of space. The 1920s-style cocktail bar with an attached 'library' just off the lobby is a delight.

HÔTEL ST-CHRISTOPHE
Map pp110–11   Hotel €€

☎ 01 43 31 81 54; www.charm-hotel-paris.com; 17 rue Lacépède, 5e; s €122-124, d €134-136; Ⓜ Place Monge; ✖ 🖥 ♿

This classy small hotel is located on a quiet street between rue Monge in the Latin Quarter and the Jardin des Plantes. The 32 rooms are hardly what you would call spectacular, but they are well-equipped and there are five sizes and shapes to choose from. The welcome is always particularly warm at this Logis de France 'charm hotel'.

HÔTEL DU LEVANT Map pp110–11   Hotel €€

☎ 01 46 34 11 00; www.hoteldulevant.com; 18 rue de la Harpe, 5e; s €100-120, d €118-145, tw €160, tr €175-215, q €235-255, ste €300-320; Ⓜ Cluny La Sorbonne or St-Michel; ✖ 🖥

It's hard to imagine anything more central than this 47-room hotel in the heart of the Latin Quarter; you'll never lack for a kebab day or night. The lobby, done up in yellows and reds, is warm and welcoming; the breakfast room is nicely decorated with a large *faux naïf* mural and lots of 19th-century fashion engravings. Rooms are of a decent size, with furnishings two steps beyond pure functional, and feature modern bathrooms.

HÔTEL DES GRANDES ÉCOLES
Map pp110–11   Hotel €€

☎ 01 43 26 79 23; www.hotel-grandes-ecoles.com; 75 rue du Cardinal Lemoine, 5e; s & d €110-135, tr €125-155; Ⓜ Cardinal Lemoine or Place Monge; ✖ ♿

This wonderful, very welcoming 51-room hotel just north of place de la Contrescarpe has one of the loveliest situations in the Latin Quarter, tucked away in a courtyard off a medieval street with its own private garden. Choose a room in one of three buildings but our favourites are those in the garden annexe, especially the five that are on the ground floor and have direct access to the garden (rooms 29 to 33).

HÔTEL MINERVE Map pp110–11   Hotel €€

☎ 01 43 26 26 04; www.parishotelminerve.com; 13 rue des Écoles, 5e; s €90-125, d €106-136, tr €156-158; Ⓜ Cardinal Lemoine; ✖ 🖥

We make no secret of our love affair with this 54-room hotel and the people (p348) who run it. Housed in two Haussman buildings and owned by the same family who run the Familia Hôtel (below) next door, the Minerva has a reception area kitted out in Oriental carpets and antique books, which the affable owner/manager collects, and some of the rooms have been enlarged. We like the frescoes of French monuments and reproduction 18th-century wallpaper. Some 10 rooms have small balconies, eight with views of Notre Dame and two have tiny courtyards that are swooningly romantic. Complimentary breakfast buffet is included.

HÔTEL ST-JACQUES Map pp110–11   Hotel €€

☎ 01 44 07 45 45; www.hotel-saintjacques.com; 35 rue des Écoles, 5e; s €92, d €105-137, tr €168; Ⓜ Maubert Mutualité; ✖ ✖ 🖥 ♿

This very stylish 38-room hotel has rooms with balconies overlooking the Panthéon. Audrey Hepburn and Cary Grant, who filmed some scenes of *Charade* here in the 1960s, would commend the mod cons that complement the original 19th-century details (trompe l'oeil ceilings that look like cloud-filled skies, an iron staircase and so on). The cabaret-themed breakfast room and comments book in the lobby is a welcome touch.

FAMILIA HÔTEL Map pp110–11   Hotel €€

☎ 01 43 54 55 27; www.familiahotel.com; 11 rue des Écoles, 5e; s €86, d & tw €103-124, tr €161-173, q €184; Ⓜ Cardinal Lemoine; ✖ 🖥

This very welcoming and well-situated family run hotel has sepia murals of Parisian landmarks in most rooms and is one of the most attractive 'almost budget' options on this side of the Seine. Eight rooms have little balconies, from which you can catch a glimpse of Notre Dame; the choicest rooms which carry a premium – are rooms 61, 62 and 65 (the last has a four-poster bed). We love the flower-bedecked window, the lovely parquet floors and the complimentary breakfast.

HÔTEL DU COLLÈGE DE FRANCE
Map pp110–11   Hotel €€

☎ 01 43 26 78 36; www.hotel-collegedefrance.com; 7 rue Thénard, 5e; s €89, d €99-135; M Maubert Mutualité; ▯
Close to its prestigious educational namesake, this hotel has 29 rooms that are basic and very similar; avoid the dark ones facing the courtyard and go for those overlooking the quiet street, especially the rooms with two windows. The lobby, with its fireplace, stained glass and statue of Joan of Arc (go figure – unless it's to remind visiting Brits of their dastardly deed) is welcoming.

HÔTEL DES 3 COLLÈGES
Map pp110–11   Hotel €€

☎ 01 43 54 67 30; www.3colleges.com; 16 rue Cujas, 5e; s €78-120, d €96-140, tr €130-160; M Luxembourg; ✕ ⌦ ▯
Under new (and enthusiastic) management, this 44-room hotel is a pleasant and reasonably priced place to located by the Sorbonne. Furnishings in the smallish rooms are simple – white with splashes of pastel – and some rooms share a WC. But we love the half-price (€4.50) express breakfast and room 63 with its beamed ceiling and – count 'em – three sun-splashed windows.

HÔTEL RÉSIDENCE HENRI IV
Map pp110–11   Hotel €€

☎ 01 44 41 31 81; www.residencehenri4.com; 50 rue des Bernardins, 5e; s & d €90-230, 1-/2-person apt €150-310, 3-/4-person apt €180-340; M Maubert Mutualité; ✕ ⌦ ▯ ♿
This exquisite late-19th-century hotel at the end of a quiet cul-de-sac near the Sorbonne has eight rooms and five two-room apartments – all with kitchenette (microwave, fridge, stove, crockery and cutlery). They are of a generous size – a minimum 17 sq metres for the rooms and 25 sq metres for the apartments – and all look out onto the street and leafy square, while the bathrooms all face a courtyard. Room 1 on the ground floor is wheelchair accessible. Rates vary widely; check the internet.

HÔTEL ESMERALDA Map pp110–11   Hotel €€
☎ 01 43 54 19 20; fax 01 40 51 00 68; 4 rue St-Julien le Pauvre, 5e; s €35-95, d €85-95, tr/q €110/120; M St-Michel
Tucked away in a quiet street with million-dollar views of Notre Dame (choose room 12!), this no-frills place – always just about to be renovated – is about as central to the Latin Quarter as you're ever likely to get. Its charm is no secret though, so book well ahead. At these prices and location, the 19 rooms – the three cheapest singles have washbasin only – are no great shakes, so expect little beyond the picture-postcard view through the window. There's no lift and some rooms share a toilet.

HÔTEL DE L'ESPÉRANCE
Map pp110–11   Hotel €€

☎ 01 47 07 10 99; www.hoteldelesperance.fr; 15 rue Pascal, 5e; s €71-80, d €80-90; M Censier Daubenton; ✕ ▯ ♿
Just a couple of minutes' walk south of lively rue Mouffetard is this quiet and immaculately kept 38-room hotel with faux antique furnishings and a warm welcome from a charming couple. Some of the larger rooms have two double beds.

HÔTEL CLUNY SORBONNE
Map pp110–11   Hotel €€

☎ 01 43 54 66 66; www.hotel-cluny.fr; 8 rue Victor Cousin, 5e; s & d €70-95, q €130-150; M Luxembourg; ▯
This hotel, surrounded by the prestigious buildings of the Sorbonne and where the poet Arthur Rimbaud dallied in 1872, has 23 rooms that could do with an upgrade, but the cheery yellow lobby and equally cheery staff make up for that. One of the choicest rooms is No 63 for four people, with memorable views of the college and the Panthéon.

HÔTEL GAY-LUSSAC Map pp110–11   Hotel €
☎ 01 43 54 23 96; hotel.gay-lussac@club-Internet.fr; 29 rue Gay Lussac, 5e; s/d with washbasin €50/60, s/d with shower €60/70, s/d/tr/q with shower & WC €65/78/98/110; M Luxembourg; ▯
Sacré bleu! The Gay-Lussac, a 35-room threadbare hotel with a certain amount of character in the southern part of the Latin Quarter, has entered into the modern age with a website, wi-fi throughout and a lick of paint. Though the single rooms are small, the others are very large indeed and have high ceilings. Furnishings are very basic and

the whole place could use a more ambitious refit, but the staff are friendly and helpful.

PORT ROYAL HÔTEL Map pp110–11   Hotel €

☎ 01 43 31 70 06; www.hotelportroyal.fr; 8 blvd de Port Royal, 5e; s €41-89, d €53-89; Ⓜ Les Gobelins; &

It's hard to imagine that this 46-room hotel, owned and managed by the same family since 1931, still only bears one star. The spotless and very quiet rooms overlook a small glassed-in courtyard (eg room 15) or the street (room 14) but we especially like room 11 with its colourful bed frame and pretty bathroom. Of course, this value-for-money place is no secret, so book ahead. Rooms at the lower end of the scale have washbasins only.

YOUNG & HAPPY HOSTEL

Map pp110–11   Hostel €

☎ 01 47 07 47 07; www.youngandhappy.fr; 80 rue Mouffetard, 5e; dm €23, d per person €26; Ⓜ Place Monge; ✂ ▢

This is a friendly though slightly frayed place in the centre of the Latin Quarter. It's popular with a slightly older crowd than when it opened as Paris' first independent hostel some two decades ago. The hostel rooms are shut tight between 11am and 4pm but reception stays open and there is no curfew. Beds are in cramped rooms with washbasins, and accommodate three to 10 people. In summer, the best way to get a bed is to stop by at about 8am. Internet access costs €2 for 30 minutes.

ST-GERMAIN, ODÉON & LUXEMBOURG

St-Germain des Prés is a delightful area to stay and offers some excellent midrange hotels. The three-star hotels in this area are around St-Germain des Prés. Not surprisingly in this well-heeled *quartier*, there is a serious shortage of budget accommodation, but what you will find is competitively priced.

RELAIS CHRISTINE Map pp116–17   Hotel €€€

☎ 01 40 51 60 80; www.relais-christine.com; 3 rue Christine, 6e; s & d €370-460, ste from €540; Ⓜ Odéon; ✂ ▢

Part of the Small Luxury Hotels (SLH) association, the Relais Christine is a beautiful property housed in what was once a

Catholic college. Special features include an unforgettable courtyard entrance off a quiet street with a garden behind it, as well as a spa and fitness centre built in and around an original 13th-century cellar. The 51 rooms are spacious and (unusual for a hotel of this category) the décor is more modern than classic.

LA VILLA Map pp116–17   Boutique Hotel €€€

☎ 01 43 26 60 00; www.villa-saintgermain.com; 29 rue Jacob, 6e; s & d €265-335, ste €445; Ⓜ St-Germain des Prés; ✂ ▢ &

This 31-room hotel helped set what has become almost a standard of the Parisian accommodation scene: small, minimalist, boutique. Fabrics, lighting and soft furnishings are all of the utmost quality and taste. Rooms are refreshingly modern (with a preference for chocolate browns, purples and burgundies) but subtly designed. Bathrooms are small but shimmering, and the lobby, with its popular bar, is large and bright.

RÉSIDENCE LE RÉGENT

Map pp116–17   Serviced Apartment €€€

☎ 01 56 24 19 21; www.residence-le-regent.com; 28 rue Monsieur le Prince, 5e; studio €265-295, 2-room apt €315-460, 3-room apt €525-610, 4-room apt 620-725; Ⓜ Odéon; ✂ ▢

This stunner of a *résidence*, on a quiet street of the Latin Quarter, has 16 superb apartments all looking onto a peaceful inner courtyard. They range in size from studios for two people to a four-room duplex apartment for a family of six. All have fully equipped kitchenettes (did we spot a potato peeler?) and dining areas.

L'HÔTEL Map pp116–17   Boutique Hotel €€€

☎ 01 44 41 99 00; www.l-hotel.com; 13 rue des Beaux Arts, 6e; s & d €255-640, ste €540-740; Ⓜ St-Germain des Prés; ✂ ✂ ▢ ⌨

With 20 rooms and a location tucked away in a quiet quayside street, this award-winning hostelry with the most minimal of names is the stuff of romance, Parisian myths and urban legends. Rock- and film-star patrons alike fight to sleep in room 16 where Oscar Wilde died in 1900 and now decorated with a peacock motif, or in the Art Deco room (No 36) of legendary dancer Mistinguett, with its huge mirrored bed. Rooms lead off a large circular atrium. Other features include a fantastic bar and restaurant under a glass canopy and, in the ancient cellar, a very modern swimming pool. Rates vary widely according to the seasons.

HÔTEL LE CLOS MÉDICIS

Map pp116–17   Hotel €€€

☎ 01 43 29 10 80; www.closmedicis.com; 56 rue Monsieur le Prince, 6e; s €165, d & tw €205-255, tr €290, ste €490; Ⓜ Luxembourg; ✕ ⧉ ▯ ♿

Someone has taken an 18th-century building and pushed it into the 21st century, with tasteful greys, blacks and burgundies in the 38 bedrooms. History stays for the most part in the lobby, with its antique furnishings, convivial bar and, in winter, open fireplace. The inner courtyard is a delight for drinks and/or breakfast in the warmer months.

HÔTEL D'ANGLETERRE

Map pp116–17   Hotel €€€

☎ 01 42 60 34 72; www.hotel-dangleterre.com; 44 rue Jacob, 6e; s €100-255, d €200-265, ste €285-320; Ⓜ St-Germain des Prés; ✕ ▯

The 'England Hotel' is a beautiful 27-room property in a quiet street close to busy blvd St-Germain and the Musée d'Orsay. The loyal guests take breakfast in the courtyard of this former British Embassy, where the Treaty of Paris ending the American Revolution was signed, and where Hemingway once lodged (see p193). Duplex suite 51 at the top has a beamed ceiling and room 12 a four-poster bed. Breakfast is included.

HÔTEL ST-GERMAIN DES PRÉS

Map pp116–17   Hotel €€€

☎ 01 43 26 00 19; www.hotel-paris-saint-germain .com; 36 rue Bonaparte, 6e; s & d €190-265, ste €325; Ⓜ St-Germain des Prés; ⧉ ▯

Situated just up from the cafés and hubbub of place St-Germain des Prés, this is a tastefully appointed 30-room hotel. Rooms can be somewhat small; if you need more space, splurge on a 'superior' room (numbers ending in 4 and 5) or a 'deluxe' room (ending in 6) or even go for the suite (room 26) with the baronial four-poster bed. Many guests come to lay their head where Henry Miller did (p193).

HÔTEL DES MARRONNIERS

Map pp116–17   Hotel €€

☎ 01 43 25 30 60; www.hotel-marronniers.com; 21 rue Jacob, 6e; s €115-181, d & tw €161-181, tr €216, q €256; Ⓜ St-Germain des Prés; ⧉ ▯

At the end of a small courtyard 30m from the main street, this 37-room hotel has a delightful conservatory leading on to a magical garden – a true oasis in the heart of St-Germain. From the 3rd floor up, rooms ending in 1, 2 or 3 look on to the garden; the rooms on the two uppermost floors – the 5th and the 6th – have pretty views over the courtyard and the roofs of central Paris.

HÔTEL AVIATIC Map pp116–17   Hotel €€

☎ 01 53 63 25 50; www.aviatic.fr; 105 rue de Vaugirard, 6e; r €149-270, ste €310-355; Ⓜ Montparnasse Bienvenüe; ✕ ⧉ ▯

This 42-room hotel with charming, almost Laura Ashley–style décor and a delightful canopied Art Deco entrance has been around since 1856, so it must be doing something right. The tiny 'winter garden' is a breath of fresh air (literally). Some rooms face the street and a quieter courtyard. For more space choose a 'superior' or 'deluxe' room.

HÔTEL DANEMARK

Map pp116–17   Boutique Hotel €€

☎ 01 43 26 93 78; www.hoteldanemark.com; 21 rue Vavin, 6e; s & d €148-168; Ⓜ Vavin; ✕ ⧉ ▯

This positively scrumptious boutique hotel southwest of the Jardin du Luxembourg has 15 very tastefully furnished rooms and eclectic contemporary décor contrasting with ancient stone walls. Public areas such as the reception and its corner rooms are full of vibrantly coloured furniture and objects that match and contrast. The bedrooms are well soundproofed and of a generous size (minimum 20 sq metres) for a boutique hotel in central Paris, and all have bathtubs.

HÔTEL LA SAINTE-BEUVE

Map pp116–17   Hotel €€

☎ 01 45 48 20 07; www.hotel-sainte-beuve.fr; 9 rue Ste-Beuve, 6e; s & d €145-295, ste €295-345; Ⓜ Rue Notre Dame des Champs; ⧉ ▯

The lift is as slow as cold treacle in this three-star hotel southwest of the Jardin du Luxembourg but the rooms are stylish and very well proportioned; both rooms 18 and 20 are good choices and the former has an especially large bathroom. The neoclassical style of the lobby is clean and soothing, and recalls the life and times of its eponymous former resident, the literary critic Charles Augustin Sainte-Beuve (1804–69).

SLEEPING ST-GERMAIN, ODÉON & LUXEMBOURG

ERICH GAUCHERON

The son of hotelier parents, Erich Gaucheron owns and operates what many consider to be among the most welcoming and well-run hotels in Paris, the two-star Familia and, just next door, the three-star Hôtel Minerve (p344).

What's the worst thing about being a hotelier? Dealing with people's expectations... Guests sometimes expect things we just can't provide. In America, hotels have big guestrooms, for example; there's a lot of land there. Those who have travelled to Europe know that this is not the case here.

OK, and for the saints among the sinners out there, what's the best thing about your job? Learning from guests. Whether they're from Norway, New Zealand or China, my guests and I share ideas. Because I can't travel everywhere, I move with my guests.

Just how difficult can people be? People are a lot more demanding these days because life is so much faster. In fact, it's as fast as the internet. But in the end nothing is difficult, you just need to take your time. My ambition is to anticipate any problem a guest may have beforehand.

Any, err, particularly odd requests? Well, yes, the usual things. But there's always a way to refuse a request nicely. The key is discretion. A hotelier must above all be discreet. But it's become more and more difficult finding such people.

OK, the question we've all been wanting to ask: what's the shelf life for sheets and bedspreads? For sheets, 1½ to two years. For bedspreads, four to five years.

If there were no room at the inns Familia or Minerve, where would you stay? Probably the (four-star) Hôtel de l'Abbaye Saint Germain (opposite). I find some of the great five-star hotels overly serviced; they actually try to give too much. I prefer the feel of a local hotel.

On my perfect day, find me... Poking through old books and antiques at the Marché aux Puces d'Aligre (p216) or attending one of the auctions at the Hôtel Drouot (p215). I don't go just to collect for the hotels but for my own pleasure as well.

Interviewed by Steve Fallon

HÔTEL DES 2 CONTINENTS
Map pp116–17   Hotel €€

☎ 01 43 26 72 46; www.hoteldes2continents.com; 25 rue Jacob, 6e; s €125-152, d €145-167, tw €145-185, tr €175-215; Ⓜ St-Germain des Prés;

The 'Two Continents Hotel' – the name pays homage to the Treaty of Paris having been signed at the nearby Hôtel d'Angleterre (p347) – is a very pleasant establishment with 41 spacious rooms in a quiet street. The mural in the beamed breakfast room, viewed through parted drapes, is an early morning eye-opener. About half of the rooms are air-conditioned.

HÔTEL LE CLÉMENT Map pp116–17   Hotel €€

☎ 01 43 26 53 60; www.clement-moliere-paris-hotel.com; 6 rue Clément, 6e; s & d €130-140, tr €155; Ⓜ St-Germain des Prés;

Excellent value for the style and tranquillity it offers, the Clément has 28 stylish rooms, some of which overlook the Marché St-Germain (eg room 100). Note though that the rooms at the very top floor have sloping ceilings. The people who run the hotel clearly know what they're doing; it's been in the same family for over a century.

MAYET HÔTEL Map pp116–17   Boutique Hotel €€

☎ 01 47 83 21 35; www.mayet.com; 3 rue Mayet, 6e; s €95-120, d €120-140, tr €160; Ⓜ Duroc;

Light-hearted and loads of fun, this 23-room boutique hotel with drippy murals and a penchant for oversized clocks and primary colours, has good sized rooms and bathrooms, most with tubs. It offers excellent value and free breakfast too.

HÔTEL DU LYS Map pp116–17   Hotel €€

☎ 01 43 26 97 57; www.hoteldulys.com; 23 rue Serpente, 6e; s/d/tr €100/120/140; Ⓜ Odéon

Located in a 17th-century *hôtel particulier*, this 22-room midrange hotel has been in the same family for six decades. We love the beamed ceiling and the *chinoiserie* wallpaper in the lobby; rooms to go for include the blue-toned room 13 with its striped ceiling and two windows, or the darker (but more atmospheric) room 14 in terracotta and with rustic old furniture.

WELCOME HÔTEL Map pp116–17   Hotel €€

☎ 01 46 34 24 80; www.welcomehotel-paris.com; 66 rue de Seine, 6e; s €76-97, d €105-115, tw €115-130; Ⓜ Mabillon;

The name says it all at this unpretentious 30-room hotel in the heart of St-Germain.

OK, rooms are not overly endowed in square metres and some of the ones at the uppermost levels have sloping roofs, but the price is right and the location couldn't be better.

HÔTEL DU GLOBE
Map pp116–17   Boutique Hotel €€
☎ 01 43 26 35 50; www.hotel-du-globe.fr; 15 rue des Quatre Vents, 6e; s €95-140, d €115-150, ste €180; Ⓜ Odéon; 🖳
This eclectic caravanserai has 14 small but nicely decorated rooms just south of the blvd St-Germain. Some of the rooms are verging on the miniscule, and there is no lift (but four floors to ascend via a very narrow staircase). Still, we're suckers for armour – there are at least two full sets here – and canopy beds (go for room 43).

HÔTEL DU DRAGON Map pp116–17   Hotel €€
☎ 01 45 48 51 05; www.hoteldudragon.com; 36 rue du Dragon, 6e; s/d €95/115; Ⓜ S-Germain des Pres or St-Sulpice; ☒ 🖳
There's no lift at this five-storey hotel, just a rickety-looking old wooden staircase that leads to the 28 brightly coloured rooms. The bedside lamps are on the low-budget side and we could live without the *faux*-fur bed coverings, but the bathrooms are large and well maintained. The piano lounge and tiny back patio are just made for relaxing.

HÔTEL DE SÈVRES Map pp116–17   Hotel €€
☎ 01 45 48 84 07; www.hoteldesevres.com; 22 rue de l'Abbé Grégoire, 6e; s €95-130, d €110-150, tr €140-160; Ⓜ St-Placide; 🖳 ♿
The deep kiss of a total makeover has turned a frog into a prince (or even princess). Well situated on a quiet street between Montparnasse and St-Germain, this 31-room hotel still offers some of the best value for money on the Left Bank. Rooms are of a decent size; deep browns, reds and yellows predominate, and the ones facing the courtyard are as bright as those on the street. We love the wrought iron bed frames as well as the friendly reception and its country/contemporary décor.

HÔTEL ST-ANDRÉ DES ARTS
Map pp116–17   Hotel €€
☎ 01 43 26 96 16; www.france-hotel-guide.com/ h75006saintandredesarts.htm; 66 rue St-André des Arts, 6e; s/d/tw/tr/q €69/89/93/113/124; Ⓜ Odéon
Located on a lively, restaurant-lined thoroughfare, this 31-room hotel is an excellent

choice if you're looking for reasonably priced, but, stylish accommodation in the centre of the action. The rooms are not particularly spectacular, but the public areas are very evocative of *vieux Paris* (old Paris), with their beamed ceilings, ancient stone walls and mock-Gothic chairs. Room rates include breakfast.

HÔTEL DE NESLE Map pp116–17   Hotel €€
☎ 01 43 54 62 41; www.hoteldenesleparis.com; 7 rue de Nesle, 6e; s €55-85, d €75-100; Ⓜ Odéon or Mabillon
The Nesle, a relaxed, colourfully decorated hotel in a quiet street west of place St-Michel, is such a fun place to stay. Most of its 20 rooms are painted with brightly coloured naive murals inspired by French literature. But its greatest asset is the huge (by Parisian standards) garden – a back yard really – accessible from the 1st floor, with pathways, trellis and even a small fountain. For a garden-facing room choose room 12.

ALSO RECOMMENDED
Hôtel de l'Abbaye Saint Germain (Map pp116 17; ☎ 01 45 44 38 11; www.hotelabbayeparis.com; 10 rue Cassette, 6e; r €215-340, ste €395 480; Ⓜ St-Sulpice) New to us, this four-star hotel southeast of Église St-Sulpice even impresses the experts (opposite).

Hôtel Le Petit Trianon (Map pp116–17; ☎ 01 43 54 94 64; 2 rue de l'Ancienne Comédie, 6e; s €39, s with shower €50, d €60-65, tr €75; Ⓜ Odéon) This old standby has 13 very basic rooms dispersed over six floors, with rooms 17 and 20 catching a fleeting glimpse of Notre Dame.

MONTPARNASSE
Located just to the east of Gare Montparnasse (the mammoth train station that also houses the Montparnasse Bienvenüe metro station), there are several two- and three-star places situated on rue Vandamme and rue de la Gaîté – though the latter is rife with sex shops and peep shows. Gare Montparnasse is served by Air France buses from both airports. Place Denfert Rochereau is also usefully linked to both airports by Orlybus, Orlyval and RER.

The budget places in the 14e don't usually see many foreign tourists because of the dearth of sights in the area, but that means the accommodation is usually better value for money.

HÔTEL DELAMBRE Map pp124–5   Hotel €€

☎ 01 43 20 66 31; www.hoteldelambre.com;
35 rue Delambre, 14e; s & d €80-115, ste €150-160;
Ⓜ Montparnasse Bienvenüe; ⌧ ▯ ⛔
This very attractive 30-room hotel just east
of Gare Montparnasse takes wrought iron
as a theme and uses it both in functional
pieces (bed frames, lamps, shelving) and
decorative items throughout. Room 7 has
its own little terrace while rooms 1 and 2
look onto a small private courtyard. The
writer André Breton (1896–1966) lived here
in the 1920s.

HÔTEL ODESSA Map pp124–5   Hotel €€

☎ 01 43 20 64 78; www.paris-hotel-odessa.com;
28 rue d'Odessa, 14e; s €75, d €90, tw €95, tr/q
€110/120; Ⓜ Montparnasse Bienvenüe
This hotel on the street of crêperies (p258)
has 42 unspectacular but bright and airy
rooms. Double-glazing keeps out the racket
of Montparnasse below, and the train station is a mere two minutes' away on foot.

HÔTEL DE L'ESPÉRANCE

Map pp124–5   Hotel €€
☎ 01 43 21 63 84; hotelesperance@yahoo.fr; 45 rue
de la Gaîté, 14e; s €55-70, d €85, tw €99; Ⓜ Gaîté
This 15-room place, along a street lined
with sex shops and other less-than-
salubrious establishments one usually finds
around train stations, has had a protracted
(and rather superficial) refit but remains
good value for what (and where) it is.

PETIT PALACE HÔTEL Map pp124–5   Hotel €€

☎ 01 43 22 05 25; www.paris-hotel-petit-palace
.com; 131 av du Maine, 14e; s €60-69, d/q €79/99;
Ⓜ Gaîté; ⌧ ▯
This friendly (and rather ambitiously
named) two-star hotel right on a main
boulevard south of Montparnasse has been
run by the same family for half a century.
It has 41 smallish but spotless rooms, all of
which have showers and toilets.

CELTIC HÔTEL Map pp124–5   Hotel €

☎ 01 43 20 93 53; hotelceltic@wanadoo.fr;
15 rue d'Odessa, 14e; s €45-56, d €63-70, tr €80;
Ⓜ Edgar Quinet
A cheapie of the old school and still resisting a website, this 29-room hotel is an
old-fashioned place with a small lift and an
up-to-date reception area with new furniture. The cheaper singles are pretty bare

and even the en suite doubles and triples
are not exactly *tout confort* (with all the
mod cons), but Gare Montparnasse is only
200m away.

HÔTEL DE BLOIS Map pp124–5   Hotel €

☎ 01 45 40 99 48; www.hoteldeblois.com; 5 rue
des Plantes, 14e; s €55-75, d €59-80, tw €58-66, tr
€70-85; Ⓜ Mouton Duvernet; ⌧ ▯
This 25-room establishment just off the av
du Maine has been completely overhauled
and is now a very pleasant and affordable
one-star just south of Gare Montparnasse.
Rooms, smallish but fully equipped, have a
shower or bath but some share use of the
toilet down the hall. Staff are very helpful
and friendly.

FAUBOURG ST-GERMAIN & INVALIDES

The 7e is a lovely arrondissement in which to
stay, but apart from the northeast section –
the area east of Invalides and opposite the
Louvre – it's fairly quiet here.

HÔTEL VERNEUIL Map pp128–9   Hotel €€€

☎ 01 42 60 82 14; www.hotelverneuil.com;
8 rue de Verneuil, 7e; s €140, d €170-220;
Ⓜ St-Germain des Prés; ⌧ ▯
Chic and cosy, this lovely hotel is in a
17th-century building in a quiet street
just off blvd St-Germain des Prés. It has 26
individually decorated rooms (half of which
have air conditioning) and the décor tries
hard to reflect this *quartier* full of galleries
and antique shops, with engravings and
original artwork on the walls throughout.
The beamed salon off the lobby feels like a
library in a private home and there is some
lovely stained glass in the hallways.

HÔTEL DE VARENNE Map pp128–9   Hotel €€€

☎ 01 45 51 45 55; www.hoteldevarenne.com;
44 rue de Bourgogne, 7e; s & d €137-177, tr €167-
187; Ⓜ Varenne; ⌧ ⌧ ▯
Very refined, very classic and very quiet,
this hotel tucked at the end of a courtyard
garden with fountain has something of a
country feel to it. Most of the two dozen
rooms spread over four floors look into the
courtyard and a very sizable choice is room
22. The Musée Rodin is within spitting
distance.

HÔTEL ST-DOMINIQUE

Map pp128–9   Hotel €€

☎ 01 47 05 51 44; www.hotelstdominique.com;
62 rue St-Dominique, 7e; s €115, d €135-155;
Ⓜ Invalides; ☒ ▢

This hotel, with its beamed ceilings, ancient stone walls, and large and leafy back patio, where breakfast is served in fine weather, is located between Invalides and the Eiffel Tower. Only some of the 37 rooms have had a refit, so insist on one of those (eg room 2). A very quiet choice is room 10, which looks out onto the patio.

HÔTEL MUGUET Map pp128–9   Hotel €€

☎ 01 47 05 05 93; www.hotelmuguet.com;
11 rue Chevert, 7e; s/d/tr €103/135/180; Ⓜ La Tour Maubourg; ☒ ☒ ▢

This hotel, strategically placed between Invalides and the Eiffel Tower, has 48 generous sized rooms that have been recently renovated. Room 63 is bathed in light and takes in the Église du Dôme (p127), while room 62 has a mansard ceiling but wins the lottery with views of the Eiffel Tower. The glassed in breakfast room has access to a delightful courtyard garden.

HÔTEL LENOX ST-GERMAIN

Map pp128–9   Hotel €€

☎ 01 42 96 10 95; www.lenoxsaintgermain.com;
9 rue de l'Université, 7e; s & d €130-220, ste €270-290; Ⓜ Rue du Bac; ☒ ▢

This hotel has 34 simple, comfortable rooms and a late-opening 1930s-style bar called the Lenox Club that attracts a chic clientele. The Art Deco décor (burlwood panelling and glass tabletops) is a treat, and the fine leather armchairs in the lobby are more than comfortable.

HÔTEL LINDBERGH Map pp128–9   Hotel €€

☎ 01 45 48 35 53; www.hotellindbergh.com;
5 rue Chomel, 7e; s & d €98-160, tr €156-180, q €166-190; Ⓜ Sèvres Babylone; ▢

We still haven't figured out why this *hotel de charme* is totally kitted out in Charles Lindbergh photos and memorabilia or named after him, but somehow it all works. The 26 guestrooms are done up in shades of chocolate and red, with silk fabric on the walls and rush matting on the floors. We like the room-number plates on the doors with little Paris landmarks, the ample-sized bathrooms and the very friendly staff.

GRAND HÔTEL LÉVÊQUE

Map pp128–9   Hotel €€

☎ 01 47 05 49 15; www.hotel-leveque.com;
29 rue Cler, 7e; s €60, d €90-115, tr €130; Ⓜ École Militaire; ☒

This partially renovated 50-room hotel is recommended less for its charms than its *bon rapport qualité prix* (good value for money) and an excellent location overlooking rue Cler and its market (p231). Choose any room ending in 1, 2 or 3, all of which have two windows overlooking the market. For those travellers seeking silence, your best bet is one of the rooms facing the courtyard but they're darker and smaller (eg room 10). Singles here are miniscule.

HÔTEL DU CHAMP-DE-MARS

Map pp128–9   Hotel €€

☎ 01 45 51 52 30; www.hotelduchampdemars .com; 7 rue de Champ de Mars, 7e; s/d/tw/tr €84/90/94/112; Ⓜ École Militaire; ☒ ▢

This charming 25-room hotel is on everyone's wish list so book a good month or two in advance if you want to wake up in the shadow of the Eiffel Tower. The attractive shop-front entrance leads into a colourful lobby done up in yellow and charcoal. Rooms on the lower floors can be downright cupboardlike, though; go up higher (in floors and price) and you might earn a glimpse of Mademoiselle Eiffel herself.

EIFFEL TOWER AREA & 16E ARRONDISSEMENT

Not surprisingly, these two very chic neighbourhoods are somewhat short on budget and midrange accommodation options.

HÔTEL SEZZ pp132–3   Boutique Hotel €€€

☎ 01 56 75 26 26; www.hotelsezz.com;
6 av Frémiet, 16e; s €280-335, d & tw €330-460, ste €440-660; Ⓜ Passy; ☒ ☒ ▢ ☒ ♿

Punning on the number of the posh arrondissement – 16 (*seize* in French) – in which it finds itself, this boutique bonanza is heavy on design (think Christophe Pillet), technology and *l'esprit zen* (zen spirit). The 27 rooms, more than half of which are suites, are spacious and done up in reds and blacks, and lots of glass. There's a hammam, Jacuzzi and massage room, and the bar specialises in champagne. Each guest has their own personal assistant during their stay.

ÉTOILE & CHAMPS-ÉLYSÉES

Like the 1er, the 8e is for the most part home to deluxe hotels, though there are a few top-end favourites in the vicinity of place Charles de Gaulle.

HÔTEL DE CRILLON

Map pp140–1   Hotel €€
☎ 01 44 71 15 00; www.crillon.com; 10 place de la Concorde, 8e; s €750, d €750-930, ste from €1200; M Concorde; ✕ 🔀 🖵 ⚒

This colonnaded 200-year-old 'jewel in the heart of Paris', whose sparkling public areas (including Jean-François Piège's Les Ambassadeurs restaurant, with two Michelin stars) are sumptuously decorated with chandeliers, original sculptures, gilt mouldings, tapestries and inlaid furniture, is the epitome of French luxury. The 147 rooms are spacious with king-sized beds and have floor-to-ceiling marble bathrooms with separate shower and bath. And Le Crillon is not just a pretty face; in 1778 the treaty in which France recognised the independence of the new USA was signed here by Louis XVI and Benjamin Franklin.

HÔTEL LE A

Map pp140–1   Boutique Hotel €€
☎ 01 42 56 99 99; www.paris-hotel-a.com; 4 rue d'Artois, 8e; r €355-431, ste €485-640; M St-Philippe du Roule; ✕ 🔀 🖵

The 26-room 'A' (think 'list') is an über-stylish minimalist hotel that doesn't have any of the attitude that generally goes with the concept. White, black and grey predominate and help 'frame' the fabulous contemporary art by painter Fabrice Hybert. The airy spaces (the breakfast area and bar are in a glassed-in courtyard), fireplace and real books (as opposed to decorative items) in the lobby for guests' use are as welcome as the nonsmoking floor, but rooms are on the petite side.

HÔTEL DES CHAMPS-ELYSÉES

Map pp140–1   Hotel €€
☎ 01 43 59 11 42; www.champselysees-paris-hotel.com; 2 rue d'Artois, 8e; s €105-115, d €117-130, tr €143-150; M St-Philippe du Roule; 🔀 🖵

A lovely hotel on a quiet street just up from the brash avenue of the same name, the Champs-Elysées offers 35 rooms with their own custom-made wooden furniture and renovated bathrooms done up in white tiles. We love the skylit lounge/study with the mural just off the lobby.

HÔTEL ALISON

Map pp140–1   Hotel €€
☎ 01 42 65 54 00; www.hotelalison.com; 21 rue de Surène, 8e; s €80-165, d €112-165, tw €135-145, tr €165, ste €204-290; M Madeleine; 🖵

This excellent-value 34-room midrange hotel, just west of place de la Madeleine, attracts with the bold colours of its carpets and furnishings and modern art in the lobby. Prices depend on whether rooms have bath or shower and the view. Double room 37 (€112), for example, looks on to rue Surène, while room 31 (€145) overlooks a leafy patio.

HÔTEL DE SÈZE

Map pp140–1   Hotel €€
☎ 01 47 42 69 12; www.hoteldeseze.com; 16 rue de Sèze, 9e; s €107-110, d & tw €120-150, tr €140; M Madeleine

On no account to be confused with its almost namesake, the posh Hôtel Sezz (pp132–3) in the 16e, this 25-room no frills establishment is excellent value for its location – it's so close to the place de la Madeleine you'll wake up smelling the coffee from Fauchon (p214). For a real treat, ask for the double with Jacuzzi.

CLICHY & GARE ST-LAZARE

These areas offer some excellent midrange and reasonably priced top-end hotels. The better deals are away from Gare St-Lazare but there are several places along rue d'Amsterdam beside the station worth checking out. Clichy offers a couple of very unusual places to stay in the budget category.

HÔTEL FAVART

Map pp82–3   Hotel €€
☎ 01 42 97 59 83; www.hotel-paris-favart.com; 5 rue Marivaux, 2e; s €100-130, d €130-160, tr €140-180, q €155-200; M Richelieu Drouot; ✕ 🔀 🖵

This stylish Art Nouveau hotel with 37 rooms facing the Opéra Comique feels like it never let go of the belle époque. It's an excellent choice if you're interested in shopping, being within easy walking distance of the grands magasins on blvd Haussmann. We like the prints on the walls in the lobby and the dramatic wrought-iron staircase leading up to the 1st floor, but not the fake books.

AUSTIN'S ST-LAZARE Map pp144–5   Hotel €€

☎ 01 48 74 48 71; www.hotelaustins.com; 26 rue d'Amsterdam, 9e; s/d €98/135; Ⓜ St-Lazare
This hotel, located conveniently opposite Gare St-Lazare, has 36 rooms. Just steps away are the department stores of the Grand Boulevards and the fine food shops of place de la Madeleine.

NEW ORIENT HÔTEL Map pp140–1   Hotel €€

☎ 01 45 22 21 64; www.hotelneworient.com; 16 rue de Constantinople, 8e; s €89-115, d €106-115, tw €115-140, tr & q €150; Ⓜ Europe; ☒ ☒ ▣
This delightful place is situated in a neighbourhood of the 8e north of Gare St-Lazare that seems to have only shops that sell musical instruments and/or sheet music. It has a lot of personality, especially in the public areas. The 30 guestrooms are not as nice, though several have Second Empire furnishings and decorative busts. Some, including twin room 7 and double room 8, even have little balconies.

HÔTEL BRITANNIA Map pp144–5   Hotel €€

☎ 01 42 85 36 36; www.hotelbritannia.com; 24 rue d'Amsterdam, 9e; s/d/tr €79/89/105; Ⓜ St-Lazare, ▣
This 46-room place with narrow hallways but pleasant, clean rooms is just opposite Gare St-Lazare and a quick walk to the *grands magasins* (department stores) on blvd Haussmann. The plaster reliefs of Roman citizens lining the entrance hall are from the Louvre and give the place something of a classical feel. Ask about the three-night packages.

HÔTEL AURORE MONTMARTRE

Map pp144–5   Hotel €€
☎ 01 48 74 85 56; www.montmartre-hotel-paris.com; 76 rue de Clichy, 9e; s €65-85, d €70-105, tr €99-140; Ⓜ Place de Clichy; ▣
The lobby and the lift may both be pint-sized and Montmartre ain't exactly one street over, but some of the 24 rooms of this hotel between place de Clichy and the Gare St-Lazare have balconies (eg room 54) overlooking the street and quite striking black-and-white bathrooms. And the price is certainly right for the location.

HÔTEL ELDORADO Map pp144–5   Hotel €

☎ 01 45 22 35 21; www.eldoradohotel.fr; 18 rue des Dames, 17e; s €35-57, d & tw €68-80, tr €80-90; Ⓜ Place de Clichy

This bohemian place is one of Paris' greatest finds: a welcoming, reasonably well-run place with 23 colourfully decorated and (often) ethnically themed rooms in a main building on a quiet street and in an annexe with a private garden at the back. We love rooms 1 and 2 in the garden annexe; the choicest rooms in the main building are Nos 16 and 17 with their own terraces leading out into the garden. Cheaper-category singles have washbasin only. The hotel's excellent Bistro des Dames (p263) is a bonus.

OPÉRA & GRANDS BOULEVARDS

The avenues around blvd Montmartre are popular for their nightlife area and it's a lively area in which to stay. It's very convenient for shopping as this is where you'll find Paris' premium department stores (p215).

HÔTEL RÉSIDENCE DES 3 POUSSINS

Map pp148–9   Hotel €€
☎ 01 53 32 81 81; www.les3poussins.com; 15 rue Clauzel, 9e; s/d & tw €137/152, 1- or 2-person studio €187, 3- or 4-person studio €222; Ⓜ St-Georges; ☒ ▣ &
A lovely hotel due south of place Pigalle, it has 40 rooms, half of which are small studios with their own cooking facilities. This place reeks of style – from the classical music in the lobby to the artistically designed lift up to the bedrooms – and the back patio is a delightful place in the warmer months for breakfast or a drink.

HÔTEL LANGLOIS Map pp148–9   Hotel €€

☎ 01 48 74 78 24; www.hotel-langlois.com; 63 rue St-Lazare, 9e; s €105-120, d & tw €120-140, ste €180; Ⓜ Trinité; ☒ ▣
Built in 1870, this 27-room hotel has kept its charming *belle époque* look. The rooms and suites (eg rooms 11 and 15) are large for a smallish hotel in Paris; most have sandstone fireplaces that, sadly, have been decommissioned, and many retain original bathroom fixtures and tiles. Room 64 has wonderful views of the rooftops of Montmartre.

HÔTEL DES ARTS Map pp148–9   Hotel €€

☎ 01 42 46 73 30; hdag@free.fr; 7 Cité Bergère, 9e; s/d/tr €84/92/102; Ⓜ Grands Boulevards; &
This quirky place with pink geraniums adorning each exterior window is in a quiet

little alley off rue du Faubourg Montmartre. It has 25 rooms recently redone in shades of plum and burgundy, and there seems to be a bird theme (vintage bird prints, caged parrot in the lobby) throughout.

HÔTEL PELETIER HAUSSMANN
OPÉRA Map pp148–9   Hotel €€
☎ 01 42 46 79 53; www.peletieropera.com; 15 rue Le Peletier, 9e; s €70-90, d €80-100, tr €86-110; Ⓜ Richelieu Drouot; ▢
This is a pleasant 26-room hotel just off blvd Haussmann and close to the big department stores. Attractive packages are available at the weekend, depending on the season. Internet access here costs €2 for 15 minutes.

HÔTEL CHOPIN Map pp148–9   Hotel €€
☎ 01 47 70 58 10; www.hotelchopin.fr; 46 passage Jouffroy & 10 blvd Montmartre, 9e; s €50-78, d €81-92, tr €109; Ⓜ Grands Boulevards
Dating back to 1846, the Chopin is down one of Paris' most delightful 19th-century *passages couverts* (covered shopping arcades) and a great deal for its location right off the Grands Boulevards (entrance at 10 blvd Montmartre). The sprawling 36-room hotel may be a little faded, but it's still enormously evocative of the *belle époque*. After 10pm, when the arcade closes, ring the *sonnette de nuit* (night doorbell).

HÔTEL VICTORIA Map pp148–9   Hotel €€
☎ 01 47 70 20 01; www.hotelvictoria.free.fr; 2bis Cité Bergère, 9e; s/d/tr €71/77/93; Ⓜ Grands Boulevards
This 107-room old-style hotel in a quiet alleyway just off the Grands Boulevards is a good choice if you're looking for central budget accommodation on the Right Bank. The rooms are generally unexceptional but of a good size, and the welcome is warm.

WOODSTOCK HOSTEL Map pp148–9   Hostel €
☎ 01 48 78 87 76; www.woodstock.fr; 48 rue Rodier, 9e; per person dm/d Oct-Mar €19/22, Apr-Sep €22/25; Ⓜ Anvers; ▢
This friendly hostel is just down the hill from raucous place Pigalle in a quiet residential quarter. Dorm beds are in rooms sleeping four to six people in bunk beds, and each room has washbasin only; showers and toilets are off the corridor. Rooms are shut from 11am to 3pm, and the (enforced) curfew is at 2am. The spanking eat-

in kitchen, situated down the steps from the patio has everything. Internet access is available for €2 for 30 minutes; wi-fi is free.

GARE DU NORD, GARE DE L'EST & RÉPUBLIQUE

The areas east and northeast of the Gare du Nord and Gare de l'Est have always had a more than ample selection of hotels; there are a few two- and three-star places around the train stations in the 10e that are convenient if you're catching an early train to London or want to crash immediately upon arrival. Place de la République is relatively convenient for the nightlife areas of Ménilmontant.

Gare du Nord is linked to Charles de Gaulle airport by RER and RATP (Régie Autonome des Transports Parisians) bus 350, and to Orly airport by Orlyval. Bus 350 to/from Charles de Gaulle airport also stops right in front of the Gare de l'Est.

HÔTEL FRANÇAIS Map pp152–3   Hotel €€
☎ 01 40 35 94 14; www.hotelfrancais.com; 13 rue du 8 Mai 1945, 10e; s €94-101, d €99-106, tr €134-141; Ⓜ Gare de l'Est; ✕ ✕ ▢
This two-star hotel facing the Gare de l'Est has 72 attractive, almost luxurious and very quiet rooms, some of which have balconies. The place has recently been freshened up; we love the new mock café breakfast area.

GRAND HÔTEL DE PARIS
Map pp152–3   Hotel €€
☎ 01 46 07 40 56; grand.hotel.de.paris@gofornet.com; 72 blvd de Strasbourg, 10e; s/d/tr/q €80/86/105/122; Ⓜ Gare de l'Est
The Grand Hôtel de Paris is a well-run establishment just south of Gare de l'Est on blvd de Strasbourg. It has 49 soundproofed rooms and a tiny lift, and is a pleasant place to stay if you're in the area. The quads are especially spacious and suitable for a small family; try room 53, or room 33 which has a small balcony.

HÔTEL LA VIEILLE FRANCE
Map pp152–3   Hotel €€
☎ 01 45 26 42 37; la.vieille.france@wanadoo.fr; 151 rue La Fayette, 10e; s €48, d €75-85, tr €120; Ⓜ Gare du Nord; ▢

This is an upbeat, 34-room place with relatively spacious and pleasant rooms, though with Gare du Nord so close it's bound to be somewhat noisy. Singles have washbasins only, but communal showers are free.

NORD-EST HÔTEL Map pp152–3 Hotel €
☎ 01 47 70 07 18; hotel.nord.est@wanadoo.fr; 12 rue des Petits Hôtels, 10e; s/d/tr/q €65/75/110/145; Ⓜ Poissonnière; 🖳
This unusual 30-room hotel is set away from the street and fronted by a small terrace. It is convenient to both Gare du Nord and Gare de l'Est. Internet access costs an extortionate €8/12 for 30/60 minutes.

SIBOUR HÔTEL Map pp152–3 Hotel €
☎ 01 46 07 20 74; www.hotel-sibour.com, in French; 4 rue Sibour, 10e; s €40-60, d €45-65, tr/q €80/110; Ⓜ Gare de l'Est
This friendly place has 45 well-kept rooms, including some which are a bit old-fashioned (the cheapest singles and doubles) and have washbasins only. Communal showers cost €3. Some of the rooms look down on pretty Église de St-Laurent. We love the trompe l'oeil mural in the breakfast room.

HÔTEL LIBERTY Map pp152–3 Hotel €
☎ 01 42 08 60 58; www.libertyhotel.net; 16 rue de Nancy, 10e; s €35-47, d €42-55, tw €42-58, tr €70; Ⓜ Château d'Eau
The Liberty is a 42-room hotel situated just south of Gare de l'Est with clean, partially renovated but very plain, functional rooms. The cheapest singles and doubles have washbasins only; communal showers cost €3.

PEACE AND LOVE HOSTEL
Map pp152–3 Hostel €
☎ 01 46 07 65 11; www.paris-hostels.com; 245 rue La Fayette, 10e; per person dm/d €25/30; Ⓜ Jaurès or Louis Blanc; 🖳
This modern-day hippy hangout is a groovy though chronically crowded hostel with beds in 21 smallish, shower-equipped rooms for two to four people. There's a great kitchen and eating area, but most of the action seems to revolve around the ground-floor bar (open till 2am), which boasts more than two dozen types of beer. Internet access costs from €1.

GARE DE LYON, NATION & BERCY

The development of Bercy Village, with its selection of restaurants and bars, has done much to resuscitate the 12e. The neighbourhood around Gare de Lyon has a few budget hotels and a popular independent hostel.

HÔTEL DU PRINTEMPS Map pp158–9 Hotel €
☎ 01 43 43 62 31; www.hotel-paris-printemps .com; 80 blvd de Picpus, 12e; s/d €50/60, tw €65-70, tr €75-80, q €88; Ⓜ Picpus; 🖳
It may not be in the centre of the action, but the 38-room 'Spring Hotel' offers excellent value for its standard and location, just steps from place de la Nation. What's more, there's an inhouse bar open day and night. Singles have showers but share a toilet; doubles have everything.

HÔTEL LE COSY Map pp158–9 Hotel €
☎ 01 43 43 10 02; www.hotel-cosy.com; 50 av de St-Mandé, 12e; s €40-65, d €50-99; Ⓜ Picpus; 🌣 🖳
This family-run budget hotel immediately southeast of place de la Nation positively oozes charm. The 28 rooms, though basic (the cheapest singles and doubles have washbasins only), are all different, decorated in warm pastels with original artwork by a young painter from Marseilles and have hardwood floors. If feeling flush, choose one of four 'VIP' rooms in the courtyard annexe, especially room 3 or 4 on the 1st floor.

HOSTEL BLUE PLANET Map pp158–9 Hostel €
☎ 01 43 42 06 18; www.hostelblueplanet.com; 5 rue Hector Malot, 12e; dm €21; Ⓜ Gare de Lyon; 🌣 🖳
This 43-room hostel is very close to Gare de Lyon – convenient if you're heading south or west at the crack of dawn or arriving in the wee hours. Dorm beds are in rooms for two to four people and the hostel closes between 11am and 3pm. There's no curfew. Internet access costs €3/6 for 30/60 minutes.

13E ARRONDISSEMENT & CHINATOWN

The 13e is where you'll find the Bibliothèque Nationale de France, as well as the *péniches* (barges) on the Seine fitted out with music clubs and restaurants. The southern 13e is a happy hunting ground for budget hotels.

HÔTEL LA DEMEURE Map pp162–3 Hotel €€€
☎ 01 43 37 81 25; www.hotellademeureparis.com; 51 blvd St-Marcel, 13e; s/d €165/202, ste €290; Ⓜ Les Gobelins; ✗ ⚇ ⌨

This self-proclaimed *hotel de caractère,* owned and operated by a charming father-son team who always seem to be at hand, is a bit away from the action at the bottom of the 5e. But the refined elegance of its 43 rooms, the almost 'clubby' public areas in warm red and orange tones and the wrap-around balconies of the corner rooms make it worth going the extra distance. Famed for those extra touches, the suite has an iPod, and the modern red fireplace in the lobby actually works.

HÔTEL LA MANUFACTURE
Map pp162–3 Boutique Hotel €€€
☎ 01 45 35 45 25; www.hotel-la-manufacture .com; 8 rue Philippe de Champagne, 13e; s €120-145, d €165-195, tr €195-230, q €266-278; Ⓜ Place d'Italie; ✗ ⚇ ⌨

The graceful, minimalist La Manufacture is located on the fringe of the Latin Quarter. The 57 individually decorated rooms adhere to clean lines and sport very bold plumage. Rooms on the top (7th) floor are the most spacious and coveted; room 71 boasts a view of the Panthéon while room 74 glimpses the Eiffel Tower. The lobby bar is a delight.

PARK & SUITES GRANDE BIBLI-
OTHÈQUE Map pp162–3 Serviced Apartment €€
☎ 01 53 61 62 00; www.mysuiteapparthotels .com; 15 rue de Tolbiac, 13e; ste with kitchenette for 1-/2-person €142, for 3-/4-person €151/158, €889/917/994 per week; Ⓜ Bibliothèque; ⌨

Close to the Bibliothèque Nationale de France (p161) these 70 fully equipped studios for up to four people are a good choice if you want to stay in the Bercy area. Rates drop to as low as €93/98/103 per night for longer stays.

GRAND HÔTEL DES GOBELINS
Map pp162–3 Hotel €€
☎ 01 43 31 79 89; www.hotel-des-gobelins.com; 57 blvd St-Marcel, 13e; s €90-100, d €105-150, tr €150-185; Ⓜ Gobelins; ✗ ⚇ ⌨

This three-star Logis de France hotel may be a bit out of the way but rue Mouffetard and its market (p231) is just minutes away.

Both the 45 rooms and the public areas are particularly stylish; framed fragments of 18th-century Gobelins tapestry and the painter Maladir's *Atelier à St-Petersbourg* add warmth to the already cosy lobby. You'll pay more for the air-conditioned 'superior' rooms facing the back than you will for the noisy ones on the boulevard.

15E ARRONDISSEMENT

The 15e, some people's least favourite arrondissement in Paris, offers some decent accommodation options, especially when it comes to chain hotels.

The 15e is home to two hostels under the same management and very well known among backpackers and budget travellers: the Aloha Hostel (see below) and the Three Ducks Hostel. Based on feedback from readers, Lonely Planet no longer recommends the Three Ducks, but the Aloha still gets the thumbs up.

HÔTEL AMIRAL FONDARY
Map pp166–7 Hotel €€
☎ 01 45 75 14 75; www.amiral-fondary.com, in French; 30 rue Fondary, 15e; s €74-90, d & tw €85-90; Ⓜ Av Émile Zola; ✗ ⚇ ⌨

This reasonably priced hotel in the far-flung (but well-served by metro) 15e is an excellent choice for the price. The 20 rooms are modest but well maintained; choose one looking onto the pretty (and very leafy) little courtyard that is such a delight in the warm weather.

HÔTEL CARLADEZ CAMBRONNE
Map pp166–7 Hotel €€
☎ 01 47 34 07 12; www.hotelcarladez.com; 3 pl du Généra Beuret, 15e; s €76-89, d €79-93, tw €83-95, ste €97-141; Ⓜ Vaugirard; ⌨

A small, very dynamic hotel overlooking an attractive square, the CC has 28 comfortable rooms that look onto a courtyard – the suite/apartment is in an annexe which has direct access to it from the street. While the former rooms are quieter, the latter are larger. The public areas have that 'just in from Indonesia' look; the complimentary coffee- and tea-making facilities are a nice touch.

ALOHA HOSTEL Map pp166–7 Hostel €
☎ 01 42 73 03 03; www.aloha.fr; 1 rue Borromée, 15e; per person dm/d Nov-Mar €19/23, Apr-Oct €23/26; Ⓜ Volontaires; ✗ ⌨

The Aloha is a laid-back hostel north of rue de Vaugirard. The rooms, which have two to six beds and sometimes a shower en suite, are locked from 11am to 5pm (though reception remains open) and curfew is at 2am. Kitchen facilities are available. Internet access costs €2 for 30 minutes, but wi-fi is free.

MONTMARTRE & PIGALLE

Montmartre, encompassing the 18e and the northern part of the 9e, is one of the most charming neighbourhoods in Paris. There is a bunch of top-end hotels in the area, and the attractive two-star places on rue Aristide Bruant are generally less full in July and August than in the spring and autumn.

The flat area around the base of the Butte de Montmartre has some surprisingly good deals. The lively, ethnically mixed area east of Sacré Cœur can be a bit rough; some people say it's prudent to avoid Château Rouge metro station at night. Both the 9e and the 18e have fine and recommended hostels.

KUBE HÔTEL Map p169 Boutique Hotel €€€
☎ 01 42 05 20 00; www.kubehotel.com; 1-5 passage Ruelle, 18e; s €250, d €300-400, ste €500-750; Ⓜ La Chapelle; ⊠ ⛛ 💻
The easternmost edge of the 18e, virtually the lap of Gare du Nord, is the last place in Paris you'd expect to find an über-trendy boutique hotel, but this 41-room hostelry manages to pull it off. The theme here is, of course, three dimensional square – from the glassed-in reception box in the entrance courtyard to the cube-shaped furnishings in the 41 guestrooms to the ice in the cocktails at the celebrated Ice Kube (p300) bar. The offspring of the stylish Murano Urban Resort (p338) the Kube might have been less openhanded with the florescent reds and *faux* fur, but if that's what it takes to get guests to trek all the way to La Chapelle, so be it.

TERRASS HÔTEL Map p169 Hotel €€€
☎ 01 46 06 72 85; www.terrass-hotel.com; 12 rue Joseph de Maistre, 18e; s & d €260-325, ste €355-375; Ⓜ Blanche; ⊠ ⛛ 💻
This very sedate, stylish hotel at the southeastern corner of Montparnasse Cemetery and due east of the Butte de Montmartre (Montmartre Hill) has 92 spacious and

well-designed rooms and suites, an excellent restaurant and bar, and quite simply the best views in town. For the ultimate Parisian experience, choose double room 608 for stunning views of the Eiffel Tower and Panthéon or room 802, which boasts its own private terrace. The rooms on floors 4, 5 and 6 were designed by Kenzo.

HÔTEL DES ARTS Map p169 Hotel €€
☎ 01 46 06 30 52; www.arts-hotel-paris.com; 5 rue Tholozé, 18e; s €75-95, d & tw €95-105, tr €160; Ⓜ Abbesses or Blanche; 💻
This friendly and attractive 50-room hotel, convenient to both place Pigalle and Montmartre, has gained another star and added a few euros to its rates. Towering over it is the old-style windmill Moulin de la Galette. The resident canine is very friendly indeed.

HÔTEL REGYN'S MONTMARTRE Map p169 Hotel €€
☎ 01 42 54 45 21; www.hotel-regyns-paris.com; 18 place des Abbesses, 18e; s €79-89, d & tw €91-111, tr €117-131; Ⓜ Abbesses; ⊠ 💻
This 22-room hotel is a good choice if you want to stay in old Montmartre and not break the bank. It's just opposite the Abbesses metro station, which happens to have one of the best preserved Art Nouveau entrance canopies designed by Hector Guimard (see p156), and outside the hotel is a lovely old plane tree. Some of the rooms have views out over Paris.

HÔTEL DU MOULIN Map p169 Hotel €€
☎ 01 42 64 33 33; www.hotelmoulin.com; 3 rue Aristide Bruant, 18e; s/d/tr €83/88/106; Ⓜ Abbesses or Blanche; 💻
This quiet little hotel has 27 good-sized rooms, with toilet and bath or a shower in both a main building and a garden annexe.

The Korean family who own the place are very kind. Check out their fun website.

HÔTEL UTRILLO Map p169   Hotel €€

☎ 01 42 58 42 58; www.hotel-paris-utrillo.com; 7 rue Aristide Bruant, 18e; s €73, d & tw €83-88, tr €105; Ⓜ Abbesses or Blanche; ▭ &

This friendly 30-room hotel, named after the 'painter of Montmartre' Maurice Utrillo (1883–1955) and decorated in primary colours, can boast a few extras such as a little courtyard and small sauna.

HÔTEL BONSÉJOUR MONTMARTRE

Map p169   Hotel €

☎ 01 42 54 22 53; www.hotel-bonsejour-montmartre.fr; 11 rue Burq, 18e; s €33-40, d €44-55, tr €58-65; Ⓜ Abbesses; ▭

At the top of a quiet street in Montmartre, this is a perennial budget favourite. It's a simple place to stay – no lift, linoleum or parquet floors – but welcoming, comfortable, very clean and getting a protracted (and much needed) facelift. Some rooms (eg Nos 14, 23, 33, 43 and 53) have little balconies attached and at least one room (No 55) offers a fleeting glimpse of Sacré Cœur. Communal showers cost €2.

STYLE HOTEL Map p169   Hotel €

☎ 01 45 22 37 59; fax 01 45 22 81 03; 8 rue Ganneron, 18e; s & d €35-50, tr/q €57/67; Ⓜ La Fourche

This 36-room hotel just north of place de Clichy and west of Cimetière de Montmartre is a titch rough around the edges (ie rough wooden floors, old runner carpets in the hallways) but is loaded with character and the welcome is always charming. There's a lovely double glassed-in courtyard, but no lift. The cheapest singles and doubles are equipped with washbasin only.

LE VILLAGE HOSTEL Map p169   Hostel €

☎ 01 42 64 22 02; www.villagehostel.fr; 20 rue d'Orsel, 18e; per person dm/d/tr €20/24/30/27; Ⓜ Anvers; ✗ ▭

A fine 25-room hostel with beamed ceilings, a lovely outside terrace and views of Sacré Cœur. Dormitory beds are in rooms for four to six people and all have shower and toilet. Kitchen facilities are available, and there's a popular bar too. Rooms are closed between 11am and 4pm for cleaning, but there is no curfew. Internet access is available for €1/3.50 for 15/60 minutes.

PRATIC HÔTEL Map p169   Hotel €

☎ 01 46 06 27 61; 31 rue Germain Pilon, 18e; s/d €18/24, d with shower €35; Ⓜ Abbesses

As cheap as chips with almost the same odeur, this 33-room ultra-budget place has price, location and a warm welcome in its favour.

EXCURSIONS

EXCURSIONS

Strike out into the Île de France (literally 'Island of France'), the romantically named 12,000-sq-km area around Paris. Framed by five rivers and rich in fairytale chateaux, breathtaking cathedrals and forest rife with game, it was here that the seed of the kingdom of France was sown in 1100.

Some day trips are obvious: Versailles (below), with its palace and equestrian academy, and Fontainebleau (p368), the other fabled chateau, are little more than half an hour away. Those who hate crowds should consider art-rich Chantilly (p373) with its heavenly stables, gardens and woodlands, or lesser-known Vaux-le-Vicomte (p372), created by the same architect who designed Versailles.

The other quick-flit heavyweight is Chartres (p377) and its cathedral, one of Western architecture's greatest achievements with its mesmerising medieval stained glass. Art lovers will find Giverny (p381), with the pink-and-green house and flower-filled garden lived in and painted by Monet from 1883 to 1926, equally inspiring. Strangely moving is Auvers-sur-Oise (p382), the place where van Gogh painted like mad for two months before dying in the bedroom of a cheap inn from a self-inflicted bullet wound: both painter shrines take little over an hour to get to. Then there's Champagne's gourmet tipple, Reims (p386).

Light relief (from serious art and architecture, not crowds) comes in the frenetic form of Disneyland Resort Paris (p384). The pricey theme park with painfully long queues might not be everyone's *tasse de thé* (cup of tea), but the fact that twice as many people visit Disneyland Paris – 14.5 million in 2007 – as visit the Eiffel Tower says something. Nearer Paris, Parc Astérix (p385) is a fractionally quieter, home-grown alternative to the American theme park.

INFORMATION

In Paris visit a tourist office (p411) or the Espace du Tourisme d'Île de France (Map pp82–3; ☎ 01 44 50 19 98; www.pidf.com; Galerie du Carrousel du Louvre; 99 rue de Rivoli, 1er; ☼ 10am-6pm; Ⓜ Palais Royal–Musée du Louvre).

Gem up on exactly where you're going with IGN's *Île de France* (1:25,000; €5.20) or its more compact *Paris et Ses Environs* (1:100,000; €3.90), sold at book and map shops (p198).

ORGANISED TOURS

Pressed for time or don't want to do it alone? Hop on an air-conditioned coach:

Cityrama (Map pp82–3; ☎ 01 44 55 61 00; www.pariscityrama.com; 2 rue des Pyramides, 1er; Ⓜ Tuileries) Half-day trips to Versailles (€45 to €62) or Chartres (€56); day trips combining Reims and Champagne vineyards (€147),

Versailles apartments with Chartres (€99) or Fontainebleau (€105), and Giverny with Auvers-sur-Oise (€109).

Paris Vision (Map pp82–3; ☎ 01 42 60 30 01; www.parisvision.com; 214 rue de Rivoli, 1er, Ⓜ Tuileries) Half-/day trips to Versailles or Giverny (€42/102 to €116), or Giverny and Versailles combined (€64/119). Many more including Champagne (€162), Disneyland (€79) and Astérix (€64). Coaches depart from its rue de Rivoli branch.

VERSAILLES

Seven hundred rooms, 67 staircases, 352 chimneys, 2153 windows, 6300 paintings, 2100 sculptures and statues, 15,000 engravings, 5000 decorative art objects and furnishings, 4.7 million chateau visitors annually: no wonder visiting France's most famous, grandest palace can be overwhelming. Six days a week (the chateau is shut Monday) tourist madness consumes the prosperous, leafy and bourgeois suburb of Versailles (population 85,300), political capital and seat of the royal court from 1682 until 1789, when Revolutionary mobs massacred the palace guard and dragged Louis XVI and Marie-Antoinette back to Paris to eventually lop off their heads.

It was during the reign of Sun King Louis XIV (1643–1715) that Château de Versailles (☎ 0 810 811 614; www.chateauversailles.fr; palace ticket adult/under 18yr €13.50/free, from 4pm/3pm in low/high season €10/

DAY TRIP PLANNER

In true French fashion, even the biggest of sights shut one day a week. Note the following when planning your week:

- Monday – Château de Versailles (right), Auvers-sur-Oise's van Gogh sights (p382) and Monet's house in Giverny (p381) all shut.
- Tuesday – Château de Fontainebleau (p368) and Château d'Auvers (p382) both shut.

AROUND PARIS

To Reims (60km) (see inset map)

Marne

La Ferté sous Jouarre

Coulommiers

N34

SEINE ET MARNE

N4

N19

A4

To Troyes (75km)

Meaux

N36

A5

TGV

Reims (p386)

Épernay

Marne

Troyes

Beauvais

PARIS

Versailles

Chartres

Meuln

Orléans

Évreux

Rouen

Seine

Auxerre

Seine

Disneyland Resort Paris (p384)

Vaux-le-Vicomte (p372)

V Nord

N2

Aéroport Roissy Charles de Gaulle

A104

Sud Est

TGV

Fontainebleau (p368)

To Lille (175km)

Forêt d'Ermenonville

Ermenonville

Paris Hélicoptère

N3

N19

N104

Melun

N7

Forêt de Fontainebleau

E

C

Parc Astérix (p385)

A1

SEINE ST-DENIS

43

VAL DE MARNE

N6

A6

Barbizon

To Dijon (250km)

Forêt de Chantilly

N6

Luzarches

N17

Écouen

Créteil

N104

N7

Seine

N

A

Chantilly (p377)

N1

St-Denis

A5

Évry

R

Persan

Beaumont

La Marne

PARIS

A6

Aéroport d'Orly

E

F20

Étampes

VAL D'OISE

A15

La Défense

HAUTS DE SEINE

A6

A10

TGV Atlantique

ESSONNES

Auvers-sur-Oise (p382)

Pontoise

Cergy

St-Germain en-Laye

Versailles (p360)

N10

D

E

To Orléans (75km)

A10

20 km

12 miles

N13

F

A13

Mantes la Jolie

N12

N10

Forêt de Rambouillet

Rambouillet

A11

EURE ET LOIR

Seine

L

Giverny (p381)

Vernon

YVELINES

Eure

To Le Mans (125km)

N10

Chartres (p377)

To Rouen (50km)

To Alençon (35km)

free, Passeport sold until 3pm adult/under 18yr €20/free Tue-Fri & €25/free Sat & Sun Apr-Oct, €16/free Nov-Mar; 9am-6.30pm Tue-Sun Apr-Oct, 9am-5.30pm Tue-Sun Nov-Mar) was built. The basic palace ticket and more elaborate Passeport both include an English-language audioguide and allow visitors to freely visit the palace's state apartments, chapel, the Dauphin's apartments and various galleries. The Passeport additionally gets you into the Grand Trianon and, in high season, the Grandes Eaux Musicales fountain displays. Enter the palace through Entrée A with a palace ticket; Entrée C with a Passeport.

top picks

TGV CITY ESCAPES

It costs, but if you're prepared to pay the pricey fare (the only downside of France's otherwise impeccable, super-speedy rail service; see p395), France is your oyster as far as flitting elsewhere for a day or weekend goes. Our top five urban flits:

- Lille (www.lille-tourism.com; €75-105 return; 1hr from Paris Gare du Nord) Lively Lille with its strong Flemish flavour, stylish shopping and student-driven nightlife, abuts Belgium. Hot date: first weekend in September during the mussel extravaganza, Braderie de Lille.
- Lyon (www.lyon-france.com; €122-126 return, 2hr from Paris Gare de Lyon) Don't tell Parisians, but France's second-largest city is its true gastronomic capital. Wonderful museums, Roman relics, a thriving cultural scene, magnificent markets and fabulous dining make Lyon a cultured must. Avoid August, when everything is shut.
- Marseille (www.marseille-tourisme.com; €191-266 return, 3hr from Paris Gare de Montparnasse) Raining in Paris, again? To cheer soggy spirits nothing beats watching the Mediterranean sun sink for another day over pastis (the local aniseed-flavoured aperitif) and bouillabaisse at Marseille's Vieux Port.
- Rennes (www.ville-rennes.fr; €104 return, 2hr from Paris Gare de Montparnasse) Crêperies, churches and half-timbered houses are the sweet lure of this picturesque old city, a university town and capital of Brittany.
- Tours (www.ligeris.com; €80 return, 1¼hr from Paris Gare de Montparnasse & Gare d'Austerlitz) It's not so much Tours — great cafés, buzzing bar life — as the mighty Loire Valley chateaux that can be reached from it. Essential viewing: Chenonceau and Chambord.

Intended to house his court of 6000 people, the sheer scale and décor of Versailles reflected not only the absolute power of the French monarchy but also Louis XIV's taste for profligate luxury and appetite for self-glorification. He hired four talented men to take on the gargantuan task: architect Louis Le Vau; Jules Hardouin-Mansart, who took over from Le Vau in the mid-1670s; painter and interior designer Charles Le Brun; and landscape designer André Le Nôtre, under whom entire hills were flattened, marshes drained and forests moved to create the seemingly endless gardens, ponds and fountains for which Versailles is so well known.

The vast chateau complex – get a map from the tourist office – divides into four main sections: the 580m-long palace building with its innumerable wings, halls and bedchambers and the King's and Queen's State Apartments; the vast gardens, canals and pools to the west of the palace; two smaller palaces known as the Grand Trianon and the Petit Trianon; and the Hameau de la Reine (Queen's Hamlet). Few alterations have been made to the chateau since its construction, bar most of the interior furnishings disappearing during the Revolution and many of the rooms being rebuilt by Louis-Philippe (r 1830–48), who opened part of the chateau to the public in 1837. The current €370 million restoration programme is the most ambitious yet and until it's completed in 2020 a part of the palace is likely to be clad in scaffolding when you visit. Families with babies and young children should note that pushchairs (prams), even folded, are not allowed inside the palace and tots under one must be contained in a sling.

Luxurious and ostentatious appointments – frescoes, marble, gilt and woodcarvings, with themes and symbols drawn from Greek and Roman mythology – ooze from every last moulding, cornice, ceiling and door in the palace's Grands Appartements du Roi et de la Reine (King's and Queen's State Apartments). But the opulence peaks in its shimmering, sparkling, amazing (insufficient superlatives for this one) recently restored Galerie des Glaces (Hall of Mirrors). This 75m-long ballroom with 17 giant mirrors one side and an equal number of windows the other has to be seen to be believed.

History and/or art buffs keen to delve deeper into life at court, music, Louis XV and XI's private apartments and so on can sign up for an informative lecture tour (0 810 811 614; adult with/without palace ticket, Passeport or ticket to the Domaine de Marie-Antoinette €7.50/14.50, under 18yr €5.50; ⊙ 9.45am-3.45pm Tue-Sun), some in English, at the main ticket office.

Château de Versailles gardens & park (Château de Versailles; admission free except Sat & Sun Apr-Oct during the Grandes Eaux Musicales; ⊙ 8.30am-8.30pm Apr-Oct, 8am-6pm Nov-Mar) are vast and the only way to see it all is to hire a four-person electric car (per hr €28; drivers must be over 23 and show their driver's licence); hop aboard the train shuttle (☎ 01 39 54 22 00; www.train-versailles.com; adult/11-18yr €6/4.50), which stops at the Petit Trianon, Grand Trianon and Grand Canal; or rent a bike (per hr €6, half-/full day €13.50/15) from the kiosk at the eastern end of the Grand Canal or next to the Grille de la Reine garden entrance.

The Hall of Mirrors peeps over part of the palace gardens, laid out in the formal French style between 1661 and 1700. Famed for their geometrically aligned terraces, flowerbeds, tree-lined paths, ponds and fountains, they are studded with 400 marble, bronze and lead statues sculpted by the most talented sculptors of the period – winter visitors won't get to see them, as these are covered at this time of year. Meandering, sheltered paths snake through the more pastoral English-style Jardins du Petit Trianon.

The gardens' largest fountains are the 17th-century Bassin de Neptune (Neptune's Fountain), a dazzling mirage of 99 spouting fountains 300m north of the palace, and the Bassin d'Apollon (Apollo's Fountain), built in 1668 at the eastern end of the Grand Canal. The straight side of the Bassin de Neptune abuts a small, round pond graced by a winged dragon. Emerging from the water in the centre of the Bassin d'Apollon is Apollo's chariot, pulled by rearing horses. A truly magical, must-experience are the Grandes Eaux Musicales (Château de Versailles; adult/11-18yr/under 10yr €7/5.50/free; ⊙ 11am-noon & 3.30-5.30pm Sat & Sun Apr-Sep) and Grandes Eaux Nocturnes (Château de Versailles; adult/11-18yr/under 10yr €7/5.50/free; ⊙ 9.30-11.30pm Sat & Sun Jul & Aug) fountain displays set to the sweet tones of baroque and classical composers throughout the grounds in summer. The grand finale of these fabulous fountain dances to soul-stirring classical music sees the Bassin de Neptune flow for 10 minutes from 5.20pm. Set the soul stirring still further with the fountains' fabulous summertime performances at night! Brilliantly lit, it is a performance to remember. Reserve tickets in advance at the Billetterie Spectacle (☎ 01 30 83 78 89; www.chateauversaillesspectacles.fr; place d'Armes; ⊙ 10am-6pm Tue-Sun Apr–mid-Sep) in front of the

TRANSPORT: VERSAILLES

Distance from Paris 21km

Direction Southwest

Travel time 35 minutes by RER/train

Car A13 from Porte de St-Cloud, exit 'Versailles Château'

Bus 171 (€1.40 or one metro/bus ticket) from the Pont de Sèvres (15e) metro station to place d'Armes every six to nine minutes 5am to midnight

RER train Fastest way: the RER line C5 (€2.80) from Paris' Left Bank RER stations to Versailles-Rive Gauche station is 700m southeast of the chateau; trains run every 15 minutes until shortly before midnight. Less convenient: RER line C8 (€2.80) stops at Versailles-Chantiers station, a 1.3km walk from the chateau.

SNCF train From Paris' Gare St-Lazare (€2.80) SNCF operates 70-odd trains a day to Versailles-Rive Droite, 1.2km from the chateau. Versailles-Chantiers is likewise served by half-hourly SNCF trains daily from Gare Montparnasse (€2.80); trains on this line continue to Chartres (€10.90, 45 to 60 minutes). An SNCF package *(forfait loisir)* covering Paris metro, return train journey to/from Versailles and chateau admission costs €19.20.

chateau or on the same day directly at garden entrances.

The Grand Canal, 1.6km long and 62m wide, is oriented to reflect the setting sun and is traversed by the 1km-long Petit Canal, thus forming a cross-shaped body of water with a perimeter of over 5.5km. Louis XIV used to hold boating parties here. In summer you can paddle around the Grand Canal in four-person rowing boats; the dock is at the canal's eastern end. The Orangerie, built below the Parterre du Midi (a flowerbed) on the southwestern side of the palace, houses exotic plants in winter.

In the middle of the vast 90-hectare park, about 1.5km northwest of the main palace, is the Domaine de Marie-Antoinette (Marie-Antoinette's Estate; Château de Versailles; adult/adult after 5pm/under 18yr €9/5/free Apr-Oct, adult/under 18yr €5/free Nov-Mar; ⊙ noon-6.30pm Apr-Oct, noon-5.30pm Nov-Mar). High-season tickets cover admission to the Grand Trianon, the Hameau de la Reine, Marie-Antoinette's dairy, theatre, English garden and so on; low-season tickets only cover the Grand Trianon and Petit Trianon gardens, which, notably, are both free on the first Sunday of the month from November to March. The

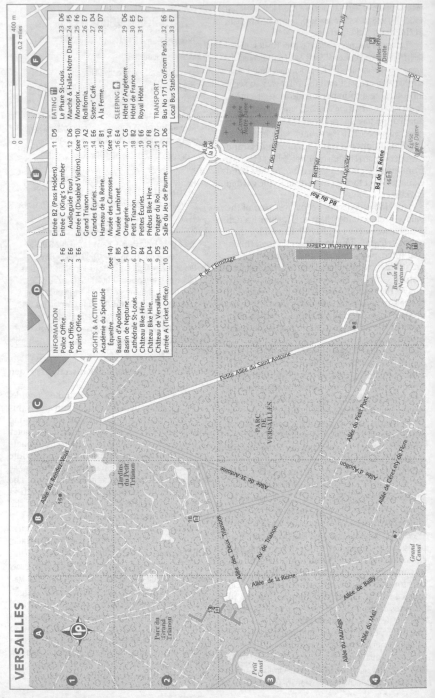

VERSAILLES

INFORMATION		EATING 🍴	
Police Office	1 F6	Le Phare St-Louis	23 D6
Post Office	2 E6	Marché & Halles Notre Dame	24 F5
Tourist Office	3 E6	Monoprix	25 F6
		Rollifornia	26 E7
SIGHTS & ACTIVITIES		Sisters' Café	27 D4
Académie du Spectacle		À la Ferme	28 D7
Équestre	(see 14)		
Bassin d'Apollon	4 B5	SLEEPING 🛏	
Bassin de Neptune	5 D4	Hôtel d'Angleterre	29 D6
Cathédrale St-Louis	6 D7	Hôtel de France	30 E5
Château Bike Hire	7 B4	Royal Hôtel	31 E7
Château Bike Hire	8 D4		
Château de Versailles	9 D5	TRANSPORT	
Entrée A (Ticket Office)	10 D5	Bus No 171 (To/From Paris)	32 E6
Entrée B2 (Pass Holders)	11 D5	Local Bus Station	33 E7
Entrée C (King's Chamber			
Audioguide Tour)	12 D6		
Entrée H (Disabled Visitors)	(see 10)		
Grand Trianon	13 A2		
Grandes Écuries	14 E6		
Hameau de la Reine	15 B1		
Musée des Carrosses	(see 14)		
Musée Lambinet	16 E4		
Orangerie	17 C6		
Petit Trianon	18 B2		
Petites Écuries	19 E6		
Phébus Bike Hire	20 F8		
Potager du Roi	21 D7		
Salle du Jeu de Paume	22 D6		

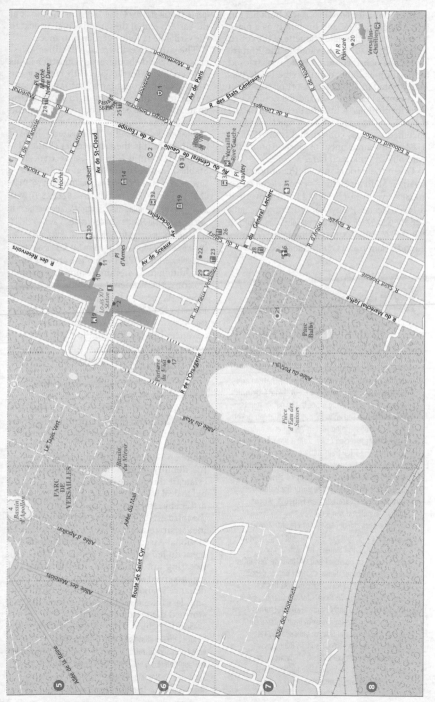

365

pink-colonnaded Grand Trianon was built here in 1687 for Louis XIV and his family as a place of escape from the rigid etiquette of the court. Napoleon I had it renovated in the Empire style. The ochre-coloured Petit Trianon (closed until summer 2008), dating to the 1760s, was redecorated in 1867 by consort of Napoleon III, Empress Eugénie, who added Louis XVI–style furnishings. A little further north on the estate is the Hameau de la Reine, a mock village of thatched cottages constructed from 1775 to 1784 for the amusement of Marie-Antoinette, who played milkmaid here.

Given the park is so vast, the only way of seeing it all to hire a four-person electric car (per hr €28); drivers must be over 23 and show their driver's licence); hop aboard the train shuttle (☎ 01 39 54 22 00; www.train-versailles.com; adult/11-18yr €6/4.50), which stops at the Petit Trianon, Grand Trianon and Grand Canal; or rent a bike

(per hr €6, half-/full day €13.50/15) from the kiosk at the eastern end of the Grand Canal or next to the Grille de la Reine garden entrance.

The attractive town of Versailles criss-crossed by wide boulevards is another Louis XIV creation. In the late 17th century the three wide thoroughfares that fan out east-wards from place d'Armes in front of the chateau – av de St-Cloud, av de Paris and av de Sceaux – were separated by two vast stable blocks. Versailles' celebrated school of architecture fills the Petites Écuries (Little Stables) today; but it is to the Grandes Écuries (Big Stables) – stage to the prestigious Académie du Spectacle Équestre (Academy of Equestrian Arts; ☎ 01 39 02 07 14, advance ticket reservations 08 92 68 18 91; www .acadequestre.fr, online tickets http://acadequestre.fnac spectacles.com, in French; Grandes Écuries, 1 av Rockefeller; Les Matinales (morning training sessions) adult/under 18yr €9.50/6.50; ⏲ 10.30am & 11.15am Sat & Sun, additional days during school holidays) – that the crowds dash. In addition to its 45-minute morning training sessions, the academy presents spectacular Reprises Musicales (musical equestrian shows; adult/12-18yr/under 12yr €25/21/16; ⏲ 6pm Sat, 3pm Sun & 3pm some Thu), for which tickets sell out weeks in advance; call for information and reservations. Training sessions and shows include a stable visit. For more information, see the boxed text, opposite.

Nearby, the Salle du Jeu de Paume (Royal Tennis Court Room; ☎ 01 30 83 77 88; 1 rue du Jeu de Paume; admission free; ⏲ 12.30-6.30pm Sat & Sun Apr-Oct) was built in 1686 and played a pivotal role in the Revolution a century later. It was in Versailles that Louis XVI convened the États-Généraux made up of over 1000 deputies representing the nobility, clergy and the so-called third estate (ie the middle classes) in May 1789 in a bid to deal with national debt and to moderate dissent by reforming the tax system. But when the third estate's reps were denied entry, they met separately on the tennis court, formed a National Assembly and took the famous Serment du Jeu de Paume (Tennis Court Oath), swearing not to dissolve it until Louis XVI had accepted a new constitution. This act of defiance sparked demonstrations of support and, less than a month later, a mob in Paris stormed the prison at Bastille.

South, behind a stone wall, slumbers the Potager du Roi (King's Kitchen Garden; ☎ 01 39 24 62 62; www.potager-du-roi.fr, in French; 10 rue du Maréchal Jof-fre; adult weekday/weekend €4.50/6.50, 6-18yr €3 Apr-Oct, admission all Nov-Mar €3; ⏲ 10am-6pm Tue-Sun Apr-Oct, 10am-6pm Tue & Thu, 10am-1pm Sat Nov-Mar), laid out

top picks

TO MAKE VERSAILLES VISITS LESS HELLISH

- To avoid disappointment, resign yourself to queu-ing for everything, be it tickets for the chateau and getting into it (two vastly different things), renting an electric car or taking a pee in the public toilets.
- It can't be stressed enough: buy your chateau ticket in advance of stepping foot in Versailles – online (www.chateauversailles.fr), from a branch of FNAC (p302) or any SNCF train station/office (see p395).
- Should you arrive in Versailles ticket-less, bulldoze straight to the tourist office to buy a Passeport (p360), which allows you to enter the palace through Entrée C (rather than Entrée A, where queues are always longer).
- By noon both queues spiral out of control: visit the palace first thing in the morning or after 4pm; avoid Tuesday and Sunday, its busiest days.
- Save money by downloading Château de Versailles podcasts and other digital content before depar-ture from www.podcast.chateauversailles.fr.
- Don't miss the show! Tickets for the Grandes Eaux Musicales (p363) and Grandes Eaux Nocturnes (p363) can be like gold dust in high season. Gem up on what's on and reserve your seat by tel-ephone or online (☎ 01 30 83 78 89; www .chateauversaillesspectacles.fr). Advance reserva-tions are even more imperative for Bartabas' masterful equestrian displays (right).

MASTER OF CEREMONY

The press might well portray him as an impulsive bad boy when it comes to rampaging local government offices, demanding increased subsidies for his equestrian school (as was the case in December 2007). But in the ring Bartabas – passionate, highly respected horse trainer, choreographer and film director of world renown – is the master of his own exquisitely orchestrated ceremony.

'Bartabas is the founder, artistic director and teacher of the Academy. His philosophy is to develop a great artistic direction in all its forms in each rider, to give that rider sufficient autonomy to train, care and respect the horses,' explains academy equerry and teaching assistant Laure Guillaume. 'He is the heart of the academy – nothing is undertaken without his support.'

Each day in the red-brick vaulted stables at Versailles (built in 1693 to house King Louis XIV's 600 horses), some 15 equerries of Bartabas' Academy of Equestrian Art (Académie du Spectacle Équestre) are put through their paces. Students train for three years in song, dance, artistic fencing, plastic arts and *kyudo* (Japanese archery) before becoming an *écuyer titulaire* (qualified rider) – of which there are currently just five. Indeed, in the chandelier-lit ring during Les Matinales, Laure (b 1970), with the academy since 1991, looks like she's stepped right out of an equestrian painting. Wearing a pale-green riding jacket with ornately trimmed cuff beneath a dark-green wool cape with fur collar, this poised horsewoman with perfect chignon and enviably high cheekbones cuts a dashing figure.

'The hardest thing at the academy is to go from a course in riding to singing, then *kyudo* – it requires an enormous amount of concentration, but you quickly adapt,' Laure says, adding that riders work six days a week, with weekends being devoted to Bartabas' signature spellbinding *spectacles* (shows).

Most of the 40 mounts – Pas de Deux, Treize et Trois, Kimono, Nord and Dali to name a few – are of the same chalk-coloured, blue-eyed Lusitanian breed kept by Louis XIV. The stubbier zebra-styled horses who gallop dramatically towards audiences during the morning training sessions to the sound of baroque music are Argentine Criollos – the hardy traditional mount of the South American cowboy and polo player. Champagne is a short stocky Quarter Horse, Edwin a thoroughbred Arab, and the six in the well-bred cavalry named after solar system planets are Sorayas.

'Horses are selected according to their race, colour and aptitudes: Lusitanians are excellent in dressage, and Criollos, very handy and fast, are used for artistic fencing,' explains Laure. 'Certain horses are also selected *sur un coup de cœur* (on love at first sight),' she adds. For riders, the academy must be more than just a school or a job. 'Riders are recruited on equestrian ability, which must be very high, and also for their desire to make the Academy their life's philosophy.'

Bartabas was first noticed during in his teens in the late 1970s at Avignon's fringe theatre festival, Off. He went on to form his own equestrian theatre, aptly called Zingaro ('gitan' or 'gypsy' in Italian), and established the academy at Versailles in 2003 to both safeguard and dispel his art.

---

on 9 hectares of land in the late 17th century to meet the enormous catering requirements of the court. It retains its original patch divisions and many old apple and pear orchards, producing 70 tonnes of vegetables and fruit a year.

In the same *quartier*, one of Versailles' prettiest, is the neoclassical Cathédrale St-Louis (☎ 01 39 50 40 65; 4 place St-Louis; ☷ 8.30am-noon & 2-7.45pm), a harmonious if austere work built between 1743 and 1754, and made a cathedral in 1802. It is known for its 3636-pipe Cliquot organ and is decorated with some interesting paintings and stained-glass panels. To the northeast of the chateau just around the corner from the Versailles–Rive Droite train station, and housed in a lovely 18th-century residence, the Musée Lambinet (Lambinet Museum; ☎ 01 39 50 30 32; www.musee-lambinet.fr; 54 blvd de la Reine; adult/child €5.30/2.50, 1st Sun of the month free; ☷ 2-6pm Tue, Thu, Sat & Sun, 1-6pm Wed, 2-5pm Fri) displays 18th-century furnishings (ceramics, sculpture, paintings

and furniture) and objects connected with the history of Versailles, including the all-important Revolutionary period.

INFORMATION

Post Office (av de Paris)

Tourist Office (☎ 01 39 24 88 88; www.versailles -tourisme.com; 2bis av de Paris, Versailles; ☷ 9am-7pm Tue-Sun, 10am-6pm Mon Apr-Sep, 9am-6pm Tue-Sat, 11am-5pm Sun & Mon Oct-Mar) Sells the Passeport (p360) to Château de Versailles, a detailed visitor's guide (€8.50) and also an IGN walking map of the area (€9.50).

EATING

Rue Satory is lined with restaurants serving cuisine from everywhere, Indian, Chinese, Lebanese, Tunisian and Japanese included.

Rollifornia (☎ 01 39 50 67 61; rollifornia@hotmail.fr; 9 rue du Satory; lunch menus €10; ☷ lunch & dinner to 10.30pm) The dynamic choice of Versailles' sometimes stuffy dining scene: this young funky Korean quick-eat joint with designer pea-green and white interior cooks up California rolls stuffed with imaginative combos.

Sisters' Café (☎ 01 30 21 21 22; 15 rue des Réservoirs; menus €10-15; ⏰ lunch & dinner to 11pm Mon-Sat, noon-11pm Sun) Another break with French tradition, this relaxed 1950s-styled space cooks up club sandwiches, chicken fajitas, spinach salads and great weekend brunches. Mustard and ketchup (tomato sauce) are table standards.

Le Phare St-louis (☎ 01 39 53 40 12; 33 rue du Vieux Versailles; menus €11-16; ⏰ lunch & dinner to 11pm) This cosy Breton place heaves. Pick from 15 savoury *galettes* (buckwheat pancakes; €6.70 to €8) and 40-odd different sweet *crêpes*, including the Vieux Versailles (€5.60) topped with redcurrant jelly, pear and ice cream then set ablaze with Grand Marnier.

À La Ferme (☎ 01 39 53 10 81; 3 rue du Maréchal Joffre; starters/mains €6/14, menus €17.50 & €21.80; ⏰ lunch & dinner to 11pm Wed-Sun) Cow-hind seats and rustic garlands strung from old wood beams add a country air to 'At the Farm', temple to grilled meats and cuisine from southwest France.

For picnic supplies:

Marché & Halles Notre Dame (place du Marché Notre Dame; inside ⏰ 7am-1pm & 3.30-7pm Tue-Sat, outside ⏰ 7.30am-2pm Tue, Fri & Sun) Indoor and outdoor food market.

Monoprix (9 rue Georges Clemenceau)

SLEEPING

Hôtel De France (☎ 01 30 83 92 23; www.hotelfrance-ver sailles.com; 5 rue Colbert; s/d/tr €137/141/174) If you're going to stay in this regal town, you may as well go the whole hog and plump for a canopied bed and floral bedspread in a three-star 18th-century townhouse. It's old, old-fashioned and across from the chateau.

Royal Hôtel (☎ 01 39 50 67 31; www.royalhotelversailles .com; 23 rue Royale; d €58-69, tr/q €92/110) In the delightful St-Louis neighbourhood, this 35-room hotel displays character and a fondness for patterned wallpaper. The smallish rooms mix bulk furnishings with old-fashioned touches and there are self-catering studios for keen cooks.

Hôtel d'Angleterre (☎ 01 39 51 43 50; www.hotel-an gleterre-versailles.com; 2bis rue de Fontenay; d €50-88, ste €120) On a quiet street away from the chateau mayhem sits this good-value 18-room hotel – look for the burnt-copper canopy above the entrance. The cheapest rooms only have a shower; rooms 15 and 23 are family friendly.

FONTAINEBLEAU

The smart town of Fontainebleau (population 17,811) grew up around its elegant Renaissance chateau, one of France's largest royal residences, around which the beautiful Forêt de Fontainebleau (p371) fans out. The chateau is less crowded and pressured than Versailles and its forest – rich in walking, cycling, rock climbing, horse-riding opportunities and game – is as big a playground as it was in the 16th century.

The town's lifeblood is international graduate business school Insead (www.insead.edu), which brings in some 2000 students a year and seals Fontainebleau's reputation as a nice respectable middle-class place to be – for the French and expats alike. The town has an Anglican church, its own Wednesday-morning English school and a dynamic pick of swish cafés, bars and cultural happenings. No wonder so many work in Paris but choose to live in this safe, healthy living space oozing, as many a local will tell you, 'a certain Swiss ambience'.

Château de Fontainebleau (☎ 01 60 71 50 70; www .musee-chateau-fontainebleau.fr, in French; place Général de Gaulle; adult/18-25yr/under 18yr €8/6/free, 1st Sun of the month free for all; ⏰ 9.30am-6pm Wed-Mon Jun-Sep, 9.30am-5pm Wed-Mon Oct-May), with its 1900 rooms, is one of France's most beautifully decorated and furnished chateaux. Walls and ceilings are richly coated with wood panelling, gilded carvings, frescoes, tapestries and paintings. The parquet floors are of the finest woods, the fireplaces are decorated with exceptional carvings, and many of the pieces of furniture are originals dating back to the Renaissance. An informative 1½-hour audioguide leads visitors around the main areas of the palace (whose list of former tenants or visitors is like a who's who of French royalty) and two guided tours (adult/18-25 years €12.50/11; 1¼ hours) take visitors to the Petits Appartements and Musée Napoléon 1er (10.30am and 3.30pm daily) and the Second-Empire salon and Musée Chinois de l'Imperatice Eugénie (11.30am and 2.30pm daily). Sign up for both tours (€19/16) and you get into the main part of the chateau for free. You can access the chateau gardens & courtyards (⏰ 9am-7pm May-Sep, 9am-6pm Mar, Apr & Oct, 9am-5pm Nov-Feb) for free.

The first chateau on this site was built in the early 12th century and enlarged by Louis IX a century later. Only a single medieval tower survived the energetic Renaissance-style reconstruction undertaken by François I

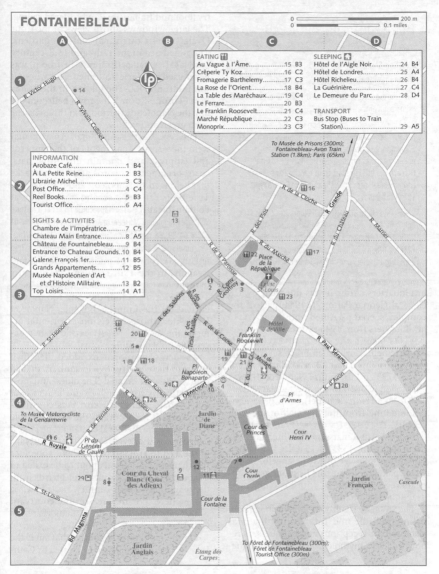

FONTAINEBLEAU

0 ____ 200 m
0 ____ 0.1 miles

EATING 🍴
Au Vague à l'Âme...................15 B3
Crêperie Ty Koz.....................16 C2
Fromagerie Barthelemy..........17 C3
La Rose de l'Orient.................18 B4
La Table des Maréchaux..........19 C4
Le Ferrare.............................20 B3
Le Franklin Roosevelt.............21 C4
Marché République.................22 C3
Monoprix..............................23 C3

SLEEPING 🛏
Hôtel de l'Aigle Noir...............24 B4
Hôtel de Londres....................25 A4
Hôtel Richelieu......................26 B4
La Guérinière........................27 C4
Le Demeure du Parc...............28 D4

TRANSPORT
Bus Stop (Buses to Train
   Station)..............................29 A5

INFORMATION
Arobaze Café..........................1 B4
À La Petite Reine.....................2 B3
Librairie Michel.......................3 C3
Post Office..............................4 C4
Reel Books..............................5 B3
Tourist Office..........................6 A4

SIGHTS & ACTIVITIES
Chambre de l'Impératrice.........7 C5
Chateau Main Entrance.............8 A5
Château de Fountainebleau.......9 B4
Entrance to Chateau Grounds..10 B4
Galerie François 1er................11 B5
Grands Appartements.............12 B5
Musée Napoléonien d'Art
   et d'Histoire Militaire............13 B2
Top Loisirs............................14 A1

(r 1515–47), whose superb artisans, many of them brought over from Italy, blended Italian and French styles to create what is known as the First School of Fontainebleau. The *Mona Lisa* once hung here amid other fine artworks of the royal collection.

During the latter half of the 16th century, the chateau was further enlarged by Henri II (r 1547–59), Catherine de Médicis and Henri IV (r 1589–1610), whose Flemish and

French artists created the Second School of Fontainebleau. Even Louis XIV got in on the act: it was he who hired Le Nôtre to redesign the gardens.

Fontainebleau, which was not damaged during the Revolution (though its furniture was stolen or destroyed), was beloved and much restored by Napoleon Bonaparte. Napoleon III was another frequent visitor. During WWII the chateau was turned into a German headquarters. After it was liberated by US General George Patton in 1944, part of the complex served as Allied and then NATO headquarters from 1945 to 1965.

Visits take in the state apartments (Grands Appartements), which embrace several outstanding rooms. Louis XV wed Marie Leczinska in 1725 and the future Napoleon III was christened in 1810 in the spectacular Chapelle de la Trinité (Trinity Chapel), with ornamentation dating from the first half of the 17th century. The Galerie François 1er (François I Gallery), a jewel of Renaissance architecture, was decorated from 1533 to 1540 by Il Rosso, a Florentine follower of Michelangelo. In the wood panelling, François I's monogram appears repeatedly, along with his emblem, a dragonlike salamander.

The Salle de Bal (Ballroom), a 30m-long room dating from the mid-16th century that was also used for receptions and banquets, is renowned for its mythological frescoes, marquetry floor and Italian-inspired coffered ceiling. The large windows afford views of the Cour Ovale (Oval Courtyard) and the gardens. The gilded bed in the 17th- and 18th-century Chambre de l'Impératrice (Empress' Bedroom) was never used by Marie-Antoinette, for whom it was built in 1787. The gilding in the Salle du Trône (Throne Room), the royal bedroom before the Napoleonic period, is in three shades: gold, green and yellow.

The Petits Appartements (Small Apartments) were the private apartments of the emperor and empress and contain uniforms, hats, coats, ornamental swords and knick-knacks that belonged to Napoleon and his relatives. True buffs can get a second dose of him at Fontainebleau's Musée Napoléonien d'art et d'histoire Militaire (Napoleonic Museum of Art & Military History; ☎ 01 60 74 64 89; 88 rue St-Honoré; adult/under 12yr €4/free; ☯ museum 2-5.30pm Tue-Sat, garden 10am-6pm or 7pm Tue-Sat), six rooms of military uniforms and weapons in the 19th-century Villa Lavaurs in town.

In 1863 a set of four drawing rooms were created for the Empress Eugénie, Napoleon III's wife, whose collection of oriental art forms the Musée Chinois de l'Imperatice Eugénie, accessible only by guided tours.

As successive monarchs added their own wings to the chateau, five irregularly shaped courtyards were created. The oldest and most interesting is the Cour Ovale, no longer oval but U-shaped due to Henri IV's construction work. It incorporates the keep, the sole remnant of the medieval chateau. The largest courtyard is the Cour du Cheval Blanc (Courtyard of the White Horse), from where you enter the chateau. Napoleon, about to be exiled to Elba in 1814, bid farewell to his guards from the magnificent 17th-century double-horseshoe staircase here. For that reason the courtyard is also called the Cour des Adieux (Farewell Courtyard).

On the northern side of the chateau is the Jardin de Diane, a formal garden created by Cath-

THE FOREST OF FONTAINEBLEAU

The Forêt de Fontainebleau, a 20,000-hectare wood surrounding the town, is among the region's loveliest. National walking trails GR1 and GR11 are excellent for jogging, walking, cycling and horse riding, and for climbers the forest is a veritable paradise. Rock climbing enthusiasts have long come to its sandstone ridges, rich in cliffs and overhangs, to hone their skills before setting off for the Alps. There are different grades marked by colours, with white representing easy climbs (suitable for children) and black representing climbs up and over death-defying boulders. The website http://bleau.info has stacks of information on climbing in Fontainebleau.

To give it a go, contact Top Loisirs (☎ 01 60 74 08 50; www.toploisirs.fr in French; 16 rue du Sylvain Collinet) about equipment hire and instruction. Two gorges worth visiting are the Gorges d'Apremont, 7km northwest near Barbizon, and the Gorges de Franchard, a few kilometres south of Gorges d'Apremont. The tourist office sells Fontainebleau Climbs (€25), translated into English.

The area is covered by IGN's 1:25,000 scale Forêt de Fontainebleau map (No 2417OT; €9.70). The tourist office sells the Guide des Sentiers de Promenades dans le Massif Forestier de Fontainebleau (€12), whose maps and French text cover 19 forest walks, and Librairie Michel (below) sells À Pied en Famille – Autour de Fontainebleau (FFRP), which maps 18 family walks, 2.5km to 5km long.

erine de Médicis. Le Nôtre's formal, 17th-century Jardin Français (French Garden), also known as the Grand Parterre, is east of the Cour de la Fontaine (Fountain Courtyard) and the Étang des Carpes (Carp Pond). The informal Jardin Anglais (English Garden), laid out in 1812, is west of the pond. The Grand Canal was excavated in 1609 and predates the canals at Versailles by over half a century.

Should you be around longer than a day, you might catch one of the monthly guided visits the tourist office organises of an eclectic trio of lesser-known sights: Fontainbleau's Musée National des Prisons (National Museum of Prisons; ☎ 01 60 74 99 99; adult/child €8.60/6.50; ☯ guided tour 3pm last Fri of month), a gruesome portrait of French prisons from the 17th century to the present in a magnificent 19th-century prison with 30 cells; its Musée Motocycliste de la Gendarmerie (Police Motorcycle Museum; ☎ 01 60 74 99 99; Camp Guymener; adult/child €8.60/6.50; ☯ guided tour quarterly); and the Centre Sportif d'Equitation Militaire (Sporting & Military Horseriding Centre; (☎ 01 60 74 99 99; allée Maintenon; adult/child €8.60/6.50; ☯ guided tour 10.30am last Wed of month), where mounted French army officers and 50 military horses are trained each year.

INFORMATION

À La Petite Reine (☎ 01 60 74 57 57; 32 rue des Sablons; hire per half-/full day €13/16; ☯ 9am-7.30pm Tue-Sat) Bike hire for adults and kids; a helmet or a child's seat each costs €3.

Arobaze Café (☎ 01 60 72 24 52; www.arobazecafe.com, in French; 5 rue de Ferrare; per hr €3; ☯ 10am-10pm Mon-Sat, 2-8pm Sun) Internet café with 30 machines.

Forêt de Fontainebleau Tourist Office (Antenne Forestière; ☎ 01 60 74 99 99; Carrefour du Coq, La Faisanderie; ☯ 9am-12.30pm & 1.30-6.30pm Fri, Sat & Sun May-Oct) Seasonal tourist office in the forest to assist walkers, cyclists and other forest ramblers.

Librairie Michel (☎ 01 64 22 27 21; 15 rue de la Paroisse; ☯ 9.30am-1pm & 2.30-7pm Mon-Sat, 10.30am-1pm Sun) Maps, travel and walking guides, including ones for the forest (above).

Post Office (2 rue de la Chancellerie)

Reel Books (☎ 1 64 22 85 85; 9 rue de Ferrare; ☯ 11am-7pm Tue-Sat) English bookshop with new and secondhand titles, and a great noticeboard crammed with ads aimed at the large local Anglophone community.

Tourist Office (☎ 01 60 74 99 99; www.fontainebleau-tourisme.com; 4 rue Royale; ☯ 10am-6pm Mon-Sat, 10am-1pm & 2-5.30pm Sun May-Oct, 10am-1pm Sun Nov-Apr) A converted petrol station west of the chateau. It sells loads of walking guides and maps; offers 30-minute self-paced audioguide tours (€4.60, 30 minutes) of the chateau interior, its parks and gardens or of the Forêt de Fontainebleau (2km); and takes prepaid bookings for monthly visits of the National Prison Museum, Police Motocycle Museum and Sporting and Military Horseriding Centre. It also has a limited number of bikes for hire (€5/15/19 per hour/half-day/day); reserve in advance.

EATING

There are lovely café terraces on which to soak up the sun across from the chateau on place Napoléon Bonaparte, behind the old-fashioned merry-go-round, and there are a couple of drinking options on rue de la Corne. Rue de Montebello tours the world with Indian, Lebanese and other international cuisine.

La Rose de l'Orient (☎ 06 08 88 36 49; 20 rue de Ferrare; mezzes per piece €1, sandwiches €4, grills €7.50; ☒ 10.30am-8pm Tue-Sat) This Lebanese eatery is the spot for a fast cheap lunch courtesy of two sisters, one of whom cooked for diplomats in Paris before launching into business alone. Five plastic tables inside or take away a mezzes-and-pita-bread picnic.

Au Vague à l'Âme (☎ 01 60 72 10 32; 39 rue de France; lunch menus €11.50 & €16, dinner menus €25; ☒ lunch Tue-Sun, dinner to 1am Tue-Sat) This cheerful café-restaurant with a vague nautical theme is the place for Breton specialities, including mussels, fresh oysters and an oyster terrine to die for.

Le Ferrare (☎ 01 60 72 37 04; 23 rue de France; starters €5-7.50, mains €13-17; ☒ 10am-1am Mon-Sat) If you want to know where locals lunch, pile into this quintessential brasserie with typical fare and a blackboard full of Auvergne specialities. Tripe anyone?

Le Franklin Roosevelt (☎ 01 64 22 28 73; 20 rue Grande; starters €5-8, mains €13-19; ☒ 10am-1am Mon-Sat) If the Fontainebleau regular is not in Le Ferrare, it's a dead cert you'll find him here. Another great brasserie, with wooden panelling, red banquet seating and oodles of atmosphere, the Franklin keeps weekday punters happy with a good-value €10 *plat du jour* (daily special).

La Table des Maréchaux (☎ 01 60 39 55 50; 9 rue Grande; starters €15-20, mains €23-30, menu lunch Mon-Fri €32, dinner €40; ☒ lunch & dinner to 11pm) Tucked in fancy Hôtel Napoléon, this romantic restaurant with its flowery interior-courtyard garden is a must in summer. Cuisine is inventive: traditional French inspired by foreign flavours and exotic spices.

Crêperie Ty Koz (☎ 01 64 22 00 55; 18 rue de la Cloche; small/large crêpes & galettes €3-7/5.80-10.20, 1L pichet cider €9.40; ☒ lunch & dinner to 10pm or 10.30pm Tue-Sun) Tucked in an attractive courtyard, this Breton hidey-hole cooks up sweet *crêpes* and savoury *galettes* whipped up with traditional black wheat. Order a regular *simple* or double-thickness *pourleth* and wash it down with some traditional Val de Rance cider.

SLEEPING

La Guérinière (☎ 01 60 71 97 57; balestier.gerard@wanadoo .fr; 10-12 rue de Montebello; d incl breakfast €60, extra bed €20; ☒) This charming B&B provides some of the best-value accommodation in town. Owner Monsieur Ballestier speaks English

and has five rooms, each named after a different flower and dressed in white linens and period wooden furniture. Coquelicot (meaning 'poppy'), with its white walls and exposed beams, is particularly charming.

Hôtel de l'Aigle Noir (☎ 01 60 74 60 00; www.hotel aiglenoir.fr; 27 place Napoléon Bonaparte; s/d €160/170; ☒ ☐ ☒ ☒) Rich elegance and smart service with a gorgeous pool, grand Empire-style furnishings, and plush suites are the trademarks of this sparkling-white 17th-century mansion, across from the chateau.

Hôtel de Londres (☎ 01 64 22 20 21; www.hotel delondres.com; 1 place du Général de Gaulle; d €90-120) Classy, cosy and beautifully kept, the London is charmingly furnished in warm reds and royal blues and has been in the same family for 70-odd years. The priciest rooms have balconies with dreamy chateau view.

Le Demeure du Parc (☎ 01 64 22 24 24; www.hotel fontainebleau.fr; 6 rue Avon; d €90-120; ☒) Adjacent to the chateau park, this hotel languishes in a 17th-century residence where Jean Racine once laid his head. The swimming pool overlooked by its excellent restaurant, Le Village Café, is magical.

Hôtel Richelieu (☎ 01 64 22 26 46; richelieu.bacchus@ wanadoo.fr; 4 rue Richelieu; d €48-65) The rooms without windows are best avoided at this clean and welcoming but bland, 18-room hotel. Bacchus swigs wine next door and has a sterling reputation.

VAUX-LE-VICOMTE

Privately owned Château de Vaux-le-Vicomte (☎ 01 64 14 41 90; www.vaux-le-vicomte.com; adult/child 6-16yr €12.50/9.90, family ticket €39, candlelight visit €15.50/13.70; ☒ 10am-1pm & 2-6pm Mon-Fri & 10am-6pm Sat & Sun mid-Mar–early Nov, candlelight visits 8pm-midnight Fri Jul & Aug, 8pm-midnight Sat May–mid-Oct) and its magnificent French-styled gardens, 20km north of Fontainebleau, were designed and built as a precursor to Versailles by Le Brun, Le Vau and Le Nôtre between 1656 and 1661.

Unfortunately, Vaux-le-Vicomte's beauty turned out to be the undoing of its owner, Louis XIV's minister of finance Nicolas Fouquet: Louis, seething with jealousy that he had been upstaged at the chateau's official opening, had Fouquet thrown into prison, where he died in 1680.

Today visitors swoon over the beautifully furnished chateau interior, including its fabulous dome. In the vaulted cellars an exhibition looks at Le Nôtre's landscaping of the formal

TRANSPORT: VAUX-LE-VICOMTE

Distance from Paris 60km

Direction Southeast

Travel time An hour by car or by RER and taxi.

Car N6 from Paris and then A5a (direction Melun and exit 'Voisenon'); from Fontainebleau N6 and N36.

RER train Line D2 from Paris (€7) to Melun, 6km southwest, then taxi (€15 to €20) or chateaubus shuttle three to five times daily Saturday and Sunday April to October (single/return €3.50/7).

gardens, complete with elaborate fountain displays (⟡ 3-6pm 2nd & last Sat of month Apr-Oct) and lit by thousands of candles after dark. The collection of 18th- and 19th-century carriages in the chateau stables, included in the chateau visit, forms the Musée des Équipages (Carriage Museum). While the chateau interior shuts for lunch weekdays, the French-styled gardens remain open and can be strolled. Weekends and school holidays, rent prince, princess or musketeer costumes for the kids to prance around in. Fun seasonal events include Easter-egg hunts.

CHANTILLY

Don't come Tuesday, when Chantilly's beautiful chateau bathed in parkland and its grandiose stables fit for a king are closed.

Enviably situated 48km north of Paris, this elegant old town (population 11,200) is small, select and spoilt. Its chateau sits in a sea of parkland, gardens, lakes and forest packed with walking opportunities; its race track is one of those prestigious hat-and-frock addresses in Europe; and that deliciously sweetened thick *crème* called Chantilly was created here. Given its large and lively English community (the town has its own Anglican church, vicar, tearoom, cricket club etc), it's thoroughly apt that Chantilly is twinned with the horse-racing town of Epsom in Surrey.

Château de Chantilly (☎ 03 44 27 31 80; www.chateaudechantilly.com; adult/under 18yr €9/free; ⟡ chateau 10am-6pm Wed-Mon Mar-Oct, 10.30am-5pm Wed-Mon Nov-Mar, park 10am-6pm Wed-Mon), left in a shambles after the Revolution, is of interest mainly because of its beautiful gardens and collection of superb paintings. It consists of two attached buildings, entered through the same vestibule. Admission includes unlimited strolling around the chateau's vast gardens and a visit of the chateau interior, richly adorned with paintings (look out for the Raphaël and Delacroix), 16th-century stained glass, porcelain, lace and tapestries. Pricier combination tickets, available April to November, include a boat or mini-train ride adult/under 18 years (€14/3) or both (€19/6); a ticket covering just park and ride costs adult/under 18 years €10/3.

The Petit Château was built around 1560 for Anne de Montmorency (1493–1567), who served six French kings as *connétable* (high constable), diplomat and soldier and died while fighting Protestants during the Counter-Reformation. The highlight of a visit is the Cabinet des Livres in the Appartements des Princes (Princes' Suites), a repository of 700 manuscripts and over 30,000 volumes, including a Gutenberg Bible and a facsimile of the *Très Riches Heures du Duc de Berry*, an illuminated manuscript dating from the 15th century that illustrates the calendar year for both the peasantry and the nobility. The chapel, to the left as you walk into the vestibule, has woodwork and stained-glass windows dating from the mid-16th century and was assembled by the duke of Aumale in 1882.

The attached Renaissance-style Grand Château, completely demolished during the Revolution, was rebuilt by the duke of Aumale, son of King Louis-Philippe, from 1875 to 1885. It forms the Musée Condé, a series of unremarkable 19th-century rooms adorned with paintings and sculptures haphazardly arranged according to the whims of the duke – he donated the chateau to the Institut de France on the condition the exhibits were not reorganised and would be open to the public. The most remarkable works, hidden in the Sanctuaire, include paintings by Raphael, Filippino Lippi and Jean Fouquet.

The chateau's stunning but long-neglected gardens were once among France's most spectacular. The formal Jardin Français (French Garden), whose flowerbeds, lakes and Grand Canal were laid out by Le Nôtre in the mid-17th century, is northeast of the main building. To the west, the 'wilder' Jardin Anglais (English Garden) was begun in 1817. East of the Jardin Français is the rustic Jardin Anglo-Chinois (Anglo-Chinese Garden), created in the 1770s. Its foliage and silted-up waterways surround the Hameau, a mock village dating from 1774 whose mill and half-timbered buildings inspired the Hameau de la Reine at Versailles.

CHANTILLY

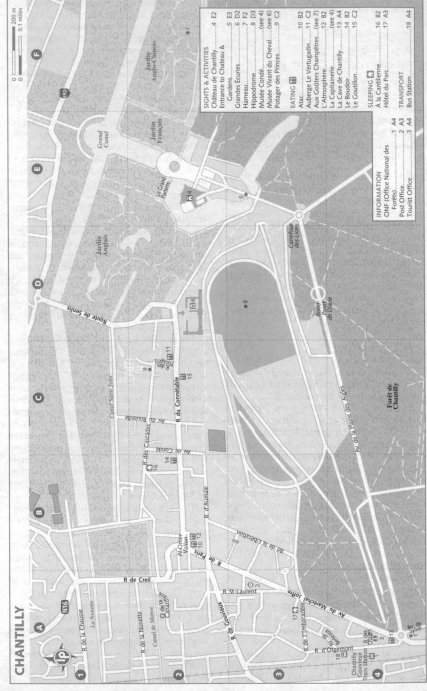

SIGHTS & ACTIVITIES	
Château de Chantilly	4 E2
Entrance to Chateau &	
Gardens	5 E3
Grandes Écuries	6 D2
Hameau	7 F2
Hippodrome	8 D3
Musée Condé	(see 4)
Musée Vivant du Cheval	(see 6)
Potager des Princes	9 C2

EATING 🍴	
Atac	10 B2
Auberge Le Vertugadin	11 C2
Aux Goûters Champêtres	(see 7)
L'Atmosphère	12 B2
La Capitainerie	(see 4)
La Cave de Chantilly	13 A4
Le Boudoir	14 B2
Le Goutillon	15 C2

SLEEPING 🛏	
À la Cantilienne	16 B2
Hôtel du Parc	17 A3

TRANSPORT	
Bus Station	18 A4

INFORMATION	
ONF (Office National des	
Forêts)	1 A4
Post Office	2 A3
Tourist Office	3 A4

0   200 m
0   0.1 miles

The chateau's Grandes Écuries (Grand Stables), built between 1719 and 1740 to house 240 horses and over 400 hounds, are next to Chantilly's famous Hippodrome (racecourse), inaugurated in 1834. Today the stables house the Musée Vivant du Cheval (☎ 03 44 27 31 80; www.museevivantducheval.fr; Grandes Écuries, rue du Connétable; adult/4-17yr €9/7; ⏲ 10.30am-6.30pm Mon & Wed-Fri, 10.30am-7pm Sat & Sun Apr-Oct, 2-6pm Mon & Wed-Fri, 10.30am-6.30pm Sat & Sun Nov-Mar), whose 30 pampered and spoiled equines live in luxurious wooden stalls built by Louis-Henri de Bourbon, the seventh Prince de Condé, who was convinced he would be reincarnated as a horse (hence the extraordinary grandeur!). Displays cover everything from riding equipment to horse toys to portraits, drawings and sculptures of famous nags. The last tickets for the museum are sold one hour before it closes. Every visitor, big and small, will be mesmerised by the 30-minute Présentation Équestre Pédagogique (Introduction to Dressage) – a Chantilly must-do included in the admission price. Presentation times are: 11.30am, 3.30pm and 5.15pm Wednesday to Monday from April to October; 11.30am Monday and Wednesday to Friday, and 11.30am, 3.30pm and 5.15pm Saturday and Sunday from November to March. Even more magical and highly sought-after are the handful of equestrian shows performed in the stables each year; tickets are like gold dust and can be reserved online.

Less in demand but equally entertaining are the plays and theatrical pieces staged during July and August in the open-air Theatre de la Faisanderie (www.theatredelafaisanderie.com) of the Potager des Princes (☎ 03 44 57 39 66; www.potagerdesprinces.com; 17 rue de la Faisanderie; adult/under 18yr €7.50/4, ⏲ 2-7pm Wed-Mon Mar Nov). Arrive before 5.30pm, when the last tickets of the day are sold. Hidden behind an old stone wall, these lovely little-known gardens embrace a watery and romantic Jardin Fantastique crossed with bridges and grottoes; an exotic Jardin Japonais, a flower-filled

TRANSPORT: CHANTILLY

Distance from Paris 48km

Direction North

Travel time 25 minutes by train

Car By motorway, Autoroute du Nord (A1/E19), exit No 7 'Survilliers-Chantilly'; by national road, N1 then N16 from Porte de la Chapelle/St-Dénis.

SNCF train Paris' Gare du Nord is linked to Chantilly (€7) by SNCF trains, departing almost hourly between 6.30am and 10.30pm.

Verger (vegetable garden), several Italianate waterfalls, a 19th-century rose garden and puppet theatre (shows Wednesday, Saturday and Sunday). The rabbit obstacle-course races held in the Lapinodrome – a rabbit village with church, town hall etc – will raise a smile, be it one of amusement or sheer disbelief.

South of the chateau is the 6300-hectare Forêt de Chantilly (Chantilly Forest), once a royal hunting estate and now crisscrossed by a variety of walking and riding trails. In some areas, straight paths laid out centuries ago meet at multi-angled carrefours (crossroads). Long distance trails that pass through the Forêt de Chantilly include the GR11, which links the chateau with Senlis 10km northeast, an attractive medieval town of winding cobblestone streets, Gallo-Roman ramparts and towers and a lovely cathedral; the GR1, which goes from Luzarches (famed for its cathedral, parts of which date from the 12th century) to Ermenonville; and the GR12, which goes northeastward from four lakes known as the Étangs de Commelles, to the Forêt d'Halatte.

The tourist office sells IGN's indispensable walking map Forêts de Chantilly, d'Halatte and d'Ermenonville (No 2412OT; 1:25,000; €9.50) and the ONF (Office National des Forêts; National Forests Office) has information on walks and mountain-bike trails in the forest.

CHÂTEAU DE WHIPPED CREAM

Like every other self-respecting French chateau three centuries ago, the palace at Chantilly had its own hameau (hamlet), complete with laitier (dairy) where the lady of the household and her guests could play milkmaids. But the cows at Chantilly's dairy took their job rather more seriously than their fellow bovine actors at other faux dairies, and news of the crème Chantilly (sweetened whipped cream) served at the hamlet's teas became the talk of aristocratic 18th-century Europe. The future Habsburg Emperor Joseph II clandestinely visited this 'temple de marbre' (marble temple), as he called it, to taste the stuff in 1777, and when the Baroness of Oberkirch tasted the goods she cried: 'Never have I eaten such good cream, so appetising, so well prepared.' Sample it in any café or restaurant in town.

INFORMATION & ORIENTATION

The chateau is just over 2km northeast of the train station; cut along av de la Plaine des Aigles through a section of the Forêt de Chantilly or take the longer route through town along Chantilly's principal thoroughfare, av du Maréchal Joffre.

ONF (Office National des Forêts; ☎ 03 44 57 03 88; www .onf.fr, in French; 1 av de Sylvie) The National Forests Office is almost always shut, given its guardian practically lives in the forest; call ahead to find out about its organised forest walks.

Post Office (26 av du Maréchal Joffre)

Tourist Office (☎ 03 44 67 37 37; www.chantilly-tour isme.com; 60 av du Maréchal Joffre; ☽ 9.30am-12.30pm & 1.30-5.30pm Mon-Sat, 10am-1.30pm Sun May-Sep, 9.30am-12.30pm & 1.30-5.30pm Mon-Sat Oct-Apr) Ample information on Chantilly, including accommodation lists and a trio of *promenades* leaflets outlining walks through town, along Chantilly's two canals and around the racecourse.

EATING

Aux Goûters Champêtres (☎ 03 44 57 46 21; Château de Chantilly; lunch menus €19.50, €32 & €41.50; ☽ 11am-7pm Wed-Mon Apr-Nov) A wonderful spot for a summery lunch in the sun, this fine restaurant sits in the windmill of the park's *hameau* (hamlet). Its chief claim to fame: its *crème Chantilly* whipped up for the past 20 years by prized local chef Jean-Michel Duda.

Le Goutillon (☎ 03 44 58 01 00; 61 rue du Connétable; starters €8-10, mains €15-25; ☽ lunch & dinner to 11pm Mon-Sat) With its red-and-white checked tablecloths, simple wooden tables and classic bistro fare, Le Goutillon is a cosy French affair much loved by local expats. It's as much wine bar as munch hole.

Auberge Le Vertugadin (☎ 03 44 57 03 19; www.res taurantlevertugadin.fr; 44 rue du Connétable; starters €14-38, mains €20-32, menus €28; ☽ lunch & dinner to 11pm Mon-Sat, lunch Sun) Old-style and elegant, this ode to regional cuisine – think meat, game and terrines accompanied by sweet onion chutney – fills a white-shuttered townhouse. A warming fire roars in the hearth in winter, and summer welcomes diners to its walled garden.

Le Boudoir (☎ 03 44 55 44 49; 100 rue du Connétable; lunch menus €7.50-16; ☽ 11am-6pm Mon, 10am-7pm Tue-Sat, 11am-7pm Sun) This relaxed *salon de thé* (tearoom) with sofas to lounge on and magazines to read is the place to sample *crème Chantilly* in all its decadence: go for one of several hot chocolate types topped with the lashings of the stuff, a *chococcino* (a cream-topped mix of coffee and chocolate) or chocolate fondue served just for two. Le Boudoir also serves perfect light lunches – salads, savoury tarts, gourmet savoury platters and wok-cooked dishes.

L'Atmosphère (☎ 03 44 60 58 75; 5 rue de Paris; starters €5-8, mains €10-14, menus €12.20, €16 & €24; ☽ lunch & dinner to 11.30pm Mon-Sat) A refreshingly youthful spirit pervades this contemporary eating space, the restaurant of Café Noir around the corner on place Omer Vallon. Interior décor is funky and Mediterranean dining is beneath a glass roof or in a cobbled courtyard.

La Capitainerie (☎ 03 44 57 15 89; www.restaurantfp -chantilly.com; Château de Chantilly; lunch menus €15.50-29.50; ☽ lunch Wed-Mon) Enviably nestled beneath the vaulted stone ceiling of the chateau kitchens, La Capitainerie captures history's grandeur and romance. Fare is traditional and includes *crème Chantilly* at every opportunity. Its weekend *formule buffet à volonté* (help-yourself-to-as much-as-you want buffet deal; €19.50) is good value. Afternoon tea from 3pm.

For picnic supplies:

Atac (5 place Omer Vallon; ☽ 9am-6pm)

La Cave de Chantilly (69 av du Maréchal Joffre)

Weekly food market (place Omer Vallon; ☽ 8.30am-12.30pm Wed & Sat)

SLEEPING

The tourist office has a list of uninspired chain hotels in town.

À la Cantilienne (☎ 03 44 58 05 76; www.chantilly-cham bres-dhotes.fr, in French; 15 rue des Cascades; d €95-125, extra bed €25; P) A five-minute stroll from the high wall of the princes' kitchen garden sits this delightful B&B, the family home of Monsieur and Madame Vergne-Hyttenhove aplomb a grassy hillock. Its two spacious rooms both peep out on the pretty garden that languishes out back.

La Ferme de la Canardière (☎ 03 44 62 00 96, 06 20 96 43 89; www.fermecanardiere.com, in French; 20 rue du Viaduc; s/d €130/150; P ☻) Delicately embroidered cushions, country-style furnishings and a colour scheme of soft creams and beiges cast a romantic air over the country home of Sabine and Thierry – everything one would hope for in a French B&B. In summer allow plenty of time for breakfast on the terrace before plunging in for a quick dip.

CHARTRES

Step off the train in Chartres (population 42,000) and the two very different spires – one Gothic, the other Romanesque – of its magnificent 13th-century cathedral instantly beckon. Rising from rich farmland to dominate this charming medieval town, Chartres' Cathédrale Notre Dame (☎ 02 37 21 22 07; www.diocese -chartres.com; place de la Cathédrale; ☺ 8.30am-7.30pm, Sunday mass 9.15am, 11am & 6pm) is a must-see. Its brilliant-blue stained glass and collection of relics, including the Sainte Voile (holy veil) said to have been worn by the Virgin Mary when she gave birth to Jesus, have lured pilgrims since the Middle Ages. Up until 4pm daily, the shop below the North Tower inside the cathedral rents informative, 25-/45-/70-minute English-language audioguide headsets costing €3.20/4.20/6.20 – you'll need to leave your passport or other ID as a deposit. Guided tours in French (adult/10 to 18 years €6.20/4.20) and English also depart from the shop.

One of the crowning architectural achievements of Western civilisation, this 130m-long cathedral was built in the Gothic style during the early 13th century to replace a Romanesque cathedral devastated by fire in 1194. Construction took only 30 years, resulting in a high degree of architectural unity. It is France's best-preserved medieval cathedral, having been spared postmedieval modifications, the ravages of war and the Reign of Terror.

Its three entrances all have superbly ornamented triple portals, but the western Portail Royal is the only one that predates the fire. Carved between 1145 and 1155, its superb statuary, whose features are elongated in the Romanesque style, represents the glory of Christ in the centre, and the Nativity and Ascension to the right and left, respectively. The structure's other main Romanesque feature is the 105m-high Clocher Vieux (Old Bell Tower; South Tower), begun in the 1140s. It is the tallest Romanesque steeple still standing.

A visit to the 112m-high Clocher Neuf (New Bell Tower; Cathédrale Notre Dame, North Tower; adult/18-25yr/under 18yr €6.50/4.50/free, admission free on 1st Sun of some months; ☺ 9.30am-noon & 2-5.30pm Sun May-Aug, 9.30am-noon & 2-4.30pm Sun Sep-Apr) is worth the ticket price and steep climb up the spiral stairway. Access is just behind the cathedral bookshop. A 70m-high platform on the flamboyant Gothic spire, built from 1507 to 1513 by Jehan de Beauce

after an earlier wooden spire burned down, affords superb views of the three-tiered flying buttresses and the 19th-century copper roof, turned green by verdigris.

Extraordinary are the cathedral's 172 stained-glass windows, mostly 13th-century originals, covering 2.6 sq km and forming one of Europe's most important medieval stained-glass collections. The three most important, dating to 1150, cast a magical light over the west entrance, below the rose window. Survivors of the 1194 fire, they are renowned for the depth and intensity of their blue tones, famously called 'Chartres blue'. To see stained glass close up, nip into the Centre International du Vitrail (International Stained-Glass Centre; ☎ 02 37 21 65 72; www .centre-vitrail.org; 5 rue du Cardinal Pie; adult/16-18yr/under 15yr €4/3/free; ☺ 9.30am-12.30pm & 1.30-6pm Mon-Fri, 10am-12.30pm & 2.30-6pm Sat & Sun), in a half-timbered former granary.

The cathedral's 110m-long crypt (Cathédrale Notre Dame; guided tour adult/7-18yr €2.70/2.10; ☺ tours 11am Mon-Sat & 2.15pm, 3.30pm, 4.30pm & 5.15pm daily late Jun–late Sep, 11am Mon-Sat & 2.15pm, 3.30pm & 4.30pm daily Apr–late Jun & late Sep–Oct, 11am Mon-Sat & 4.15pm Nov-Mar), a tombless Romanesque structure built in 1024 around a 9th-century predecessor, is the largest crypt in France. Guided tours in French (with written English translation) lasting 30 minutes are available year-round. Summertime guided tours of the crypt (in French with written English translation) depart from La Crypte (☎ 02 37 21 56 33; 18 Cloître Notre Dame, Chartres; ☺ Apr-Oct), the cathedral-run souvenir shop. From November to March, tours depart from the shop inside the cathedral.

TRANSPORT: CHARTRES

Distance from Paris 88km

Direction Southwest

Travel time 55 to 70 minutes by train

Car A6 from Paris' Porte d'Orléans (direction Bordeaux-Nantes), then A10 and A11 (direction Nantes), exit 'Chartres'.

SNCF train More than 30 SNCF trains a day (20 on Sunday) link Paris' Gare Montparnasse (€12.90) with Chartres, all of which pass through Versailles-Chantiers (€10.90, 45 to 60 minutes). The last train back to Paris leaves Chartres a bit after 9pm weekdays, just before 9pm on Saturday and sometime after 10pm on Sunday.

CHARTRES

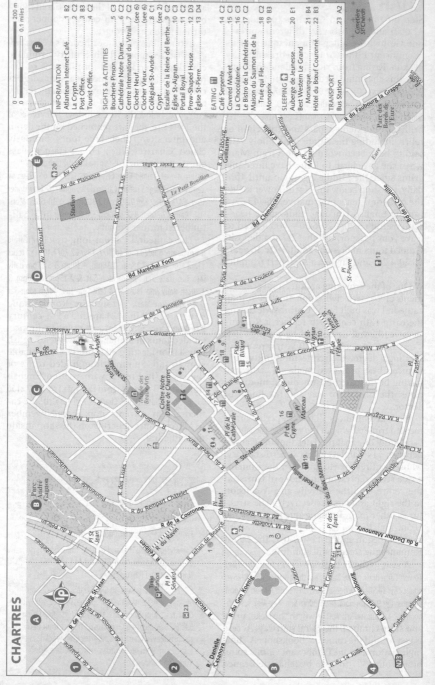

INFORMATION	
Atlanteam Internet Café	.1 B2
La Crypte	.2 C2
Post Office	.3 B3
Tourist Office	.4 C2

SIGHTS & ACTIVITIES	
Boucherie Pinson	.5 C3
Cathédrale Notre Dame	.6 C2
Centre International du Vitrail	.7 C2
Clocher Neuf	(see 6)
Clocher Vieux	(see 6)
Collégiale St-André	.8 C1
Crypt	(see 2)
Escalier de la Reine del Berthe	.9 C2
Église St-Aignan	.10 C3
Portail Royal	.11 C2
Prow-Shaped House	.12 D3
Église St-Pierre	.13 D4

EATING 🍴	
Café Serpente	.14 C2
Covered Market	.15 C3
La Chocolaterie	.16 C2
Le Bistro de la Cathédrale	.17 C2
Maison du Saumon et de la	
Truie qui File	.18 C2
Monoprix	.19 B3

SLEEPING 🛏	
Auberge de Jeunesse	.20 E1
Best Western Le Grand	
Monarque	.21 B4
Hôtel du Bœuf Couronné	.22 B3

TRANSPORT	
Bus Station	.23 A2

The most venerated object in the cathedral is the Sainte Voile (Holy Veil) relic, originally part of the imperial treasury of Constantinople but offered to Charlemagne by the Empress Irene when the Holy Roman Emperor proposed marriage to her in 802. It has been in Chartres since 876, when Charles the Bald presented it to the town. Indeed, the cathedral was built because the veil survived the 1194 fire. It is contained in a cathedral-shaped reliquary and is currently displayed in a small side chapel off the eastern aisle.

Chartres' Musée des Beaux-Arts (Fine Arts Museum; ☎ 02 37 90 45 80; 29 Cloître Notre Dame, Chartres; adult/12-18yr/under 12yr €4.20/2.80/free; ☽ 10am-noon & 2-6pm Mon & Wed-Sat, 2-6pm Sun May-Oct, 10am-noon & 2-5pm Mon & Wed-Sat, 2-5pm Sun Nov-Apr), accessed via the gate next to the cathedral's north portal, is in the former Palais Épiscopal (Bishop's Palace), built in the 17th and 18th centuries. Its collections include 16th-century enamels of the Apostles made for François I, paintings from the 16th to 19th centuries and polychromatic wooden sculptures from the Middle Ages.

Chartres' carefully preserved old town is northeast and east of the cathedral along the narrow western channel of the River Eure, spanned by a number of footbridges. From rue Cardinal Pie, the stairways called Tertre St-Nicolas and rue Chantault, the latter lined with medieval houses, lead down to the empty shell of the 12th-century Collégiale St-André, a Romanesque collegiate church that closed in 1791 and was damaged in the early 19th century and again during WWII.

Along the river's eastern bank, rue de la Tannerie and its extension rue de la Foulerie are lined with flower gardens, millraces and the restored remnants of riverside trades: wash houses, tanneries and the like. Rue aux Juifs (Street of the Jews) on the western bank has been extensively renovated. Half a block down the hill there's a riverside promenade. Up the hill, rue des Écuyers has many structures dating from around the 16th century, including a half-timbered, prow-shaped house at No 26 with its upper section supported by beams. At No 35 is the Escalier de la Reine Berthe (Queen Bertha's Staircase), a towerlike covered stairwell clinging to a half-timbered house that dates back to the early 16th century.

There are some lovely half-timbered houses north of here on rue du Bourg and to the west on rue de la Poissonnerie; look for the magnificent Maison du Saumon (Salmon House) at Nos 10 to 14, with its carved consoles of the eponymous

salmon, the Archangel Gabriel and Mary and Archangel Michael slaying the dragon.

From place St-Pierre you get a good view of the flying buttresses holding up the 12th- and 13th-century Église St-Pierre. Once part of a Benedictine monastery founded in the 7th century, it was outside the city walls and thus vulnerable to attack; the fortresslike, pre-Romanesque bell tower attached to it was used as a refuge by monks, and dates from around 1000. The fine, brightly coloured clerestory windows in the nave, choir and apse date from the early 14th century.

To the northwest on place St-Aignan, Église St-Aignan is interesting for its wooden barrel-vault roof (1625), arcaded nave and painted interior of faded blue and gold floral motifs (c 1870). The stained glass and the Renaissance Chapelle de St-Michel date from the 16th century.

Le Petit Chart' Train (☎ 02 37 25 88 50; lepetitchartrain@wanadoo.fr; adult/3-10yr €5.50/3; ☽ 10.30am-6pm Apr-Oct), Chartres' electric tourist train, covers the main sights in 35 minutes; it departs from in front of the tourist office.

INFORMATION

Atlanteam (☎ 02 37 36 62 15; 13bis rue Jehan de Beauce; €1/2/3.60 per 15/30/60min; ☽ 10.30am-midnight Mon-Sat, 2pm-midnight Sun) Internet café.

Post Office (3 blvd Maurice Violette)

Tourist Office (☎ 02 37 18 26 26; www.chartres-tourisme.com; place de la Cathédrale; ☽ 9am-7pm Mon-Sat, 9.30am-5.30pm Sun Apr-Sep, 10am-6pm Mon-Sat,

THE BUTCHER OF CHARTRES

There's nothing sinister about the butcher of Chartres. Boucherie Pinson, the medieval town's oldest *boucherie,* tucked behind cherry-red and chocolate ironwork at 4 rue du Soleil d'Or, is all about good, honest, old-fashioned charm.

The shop has been in business since 1892, and Roland Pinson has wielded the proprietor's knife with precision since 1958. He might well be in his late 70s, but it's clear from the ferocious passion with which he discusses his cuts that he is here to stay.

'It's my life,' he says with a wry smile, as if it could possibly be anything but. A historic relic, this butcher's shop is a blast to the past. There is no cash register (just a paper ledger), no digital scales, no meat behind glass or hiding the nasty bits in a back room (fat trimmed from Pinson's legendary *entrecôte* and other joints are popped in a wooden drawer). Hunks of meat hang on hooks above a long wooden chopping block, chopped so much it's U-shaped. White marble clads all four walls bar one in which a 1930s refrigerated larder – the nearest thing to modernity – is embedded. The patterned mosaic floor is original.

Customers, fiercely loyal, have grown up with this shop. Each is greeted first by Madame Pinson, well wrapped in winter coat, hat and scarf (there doesn't appear to be any heating in the shop) – kiss, kiss, one on each cheek – followed by Monsieur Pinson between chops. He wears a shirt and tie underneath his bloodied apron and service is endearingly slow.

'Do you have any calf kidneys today Roland?' 'No, only lamb.' It's not all about an attentive personal service. As EU regulations (to which this butcher's shop, being a protected historical monument, appears immune) are fast seeing certain meat cuts disappear, this butcher of Chartres is one of France's last bastions of *une bouffe d'autrefois* (cuisine of yesteryears).

10am-1pm & 2.30-4.30pm Sun Oct-Mar) Rents 1½-hour English-language audioguide tours (€5.50/8.50 for one/two) of the medieval city and has info on binocular rental, cathedral lectures in English etc.

EATING

Maison du Saumon et de la Truie qui File (☎ 02 37 36 28 00; 10-14 rue de la Poissonnerie; menus €29.80, €31.60 & €32.90; ☟ lunch Tue-Sun, dinner to 11.30pm Tue-Sat) Inhabiting Chartres' most photographed half-timbered building, this medieval landmark cooks up a bit of everything, ranging from Polish stuffed cabbage rolls and Hungarian ghoulash to Alsatian sauerkraut and Moroccan *tajines* (€18.50). Kids get roast chicken and veg in their *menu* (€9).

Le Bistro de la Cathédrale (☎ 02 37 36 59 60; 1 Cloître Notre Dame; starters €10-15, mains €15-20; ☟ lunch & dinner to 10.30pm, closed Sun Sep-Easter) Our favourite in the shadow of the cathedral, this stylish wine bar is the place for a long lazy lunch over a glass or three of wine. Tasty morsels to soak it up are chalked on the boards inside and out.

Café Serpente (☎ 02 37 21 68 81; 2 Cloître Notre Dame; starters €6-14.80, mains €15-20; ☟ 10am-11pm) Its location slap-bang opposite the cathedral ensures this brasserie and *salon de thé* is always full. Cuisine is traditional and its chef also constructs well-filled sandwiches (€3.80 to €5.80).

La Chocolaterie (☎ 02 37 21 86 92; 14 place du Cygne; ☟ 8am-7.30pm Tue-Sat, 10am-7.30pm Mon & Sun) Leave the tourists behind. Revel instead in local life at this bar-cum-chocolate-shop overlooking the open-air flower market in place du Cygne. Its coloured macaroons – orange, apricot, pistachio, pineapple and so on in flavour – are to die for, as are its sweet homemade *crêpes,* brownies and Madeleine sponge cakes.

Self-Catering

Covered Market (place Billard; ☟ 7am-1pm Wed & Sat)

Monoprix (21 rue Noël Ballay & 10 rue du Bois Merrain; ☟ 9am-7.30pm Mon-Sat) Department store with ground-floor supermarket.

SLEEPING

The tourist office has a list of guesthouses and B&Bs in town.

Best Western Le Grand Monarque (☎ 02 37 18 15 15; www.bw-grand-monarque.com; 22 place des Épars; s €101-175, d €121-175, tr €175, ste €206-249; P) With its sage-green shutters piercing a façade dating to 1779, lovely stained-glass ceiling and treasure-trove of period furnishings, old B&W photos and knick-knacks, the Grand Monarch is a historical gem – well worn but charming nonetheless. Dining is fine in its gourmet restaurant, George (starters €12 to €23, mains €30 to €35, menus €47 and €65).

Hôtel du Bœuf Couronné (☎ 02 37 18 06 06; 15 place Châtelet; s/d with washbasin €30/35, s/d with bathroom €46/57; ☟ mid-Jan–mid-Dec) The red-curtained entrance lends a vaguely theatrical air to this two-star Logis de France guesthouse in the centre of everything. Its summertime terrace restaurant cooks up cathedral-view dining (half-board €64 per person) and the Dicken's Blues bar is right next door.

Auberge de Jeunesse (☎ 02 37 34 27 64; www.auberge -jeunesse-chartres.com; 23 av Neigre; dm incl breakfast €13; reception ⓨ 2-10pm) An easy 1.5km stroll north-east from the train station via blvd Charles Péguy and blvd Jean Jaurès or a trip aboard bus 5 (direction Mare aux Moines) to the Rouliers stop brings you to Chartres' well-run hostel. Rates include breakfast with cathedral view, but sheets are €2.

GIVERNY

The prized drawcard of this tiny village (pop-ulation 544), northwest of Paris en route to Rouen, is the Maison de Claude Monet (House of Claude Monet; ☎ 02 32 51 28 21; www.fondation-monet.com; 84 rue Claude Monet, Giverny; adult/7-12yr/under 7yr €5.50/4/ free, ⓨ 9.30am-6pm Tue-Sun Apr-Oct), the home and flower-filled garden of one of the leading im-pressionist painters and his family from 1883 to 1926. Here Monet painted some of his most famous series of works, including *Décorations des Nymphéas* (Water Lilies). Unfortunately, the hectare of land that Monet owned here has become two distinct areas, cut by the Chemin du Roy, a small railway line that has been converted into the D5 road.

The northern area of the property is Clos Normand, where Monet's famous pastel pink-and-green house and the Atelier des Nymphéas (Water Lilies Studio) stand. These days the studio is the entrance hall, adorned with pre-cise reproductions of his works and ringing with cash-register bells from busy souvenir stands. Outside are the symmetrically laid-out gardens. Visiting the house and gardens is a treat in any season. From early to late spring, daffodils, tulips, rhododendrons, wisteria and irises appear, followed by poppies and lilies. By June, nasturtiums, roses and sweet peas are in blossom. Around September, there are dahlias, sunflowers and hollyhocks.

From the Clos Normand's far corner a tun-nel leads under the D5 to the Jardin d'Eau (Water Garden). Having bought this piece of land in 1895 after his reputation had been estab-lished (and his bank account had swelled), Monet dug a pool, planted water lilies and constructed the famous Japanese bridge, since re-built. Draped with purple wisteria, the bridge blends into the asymmetrical foreground and background, creating the intimate atmosphere for which the 'Painter of Light' was famous.

About 100m northwest of the Maison de Claude Monet is the Musée d'Art Américain (Ameri-can Art Museum; ☎ 02 32 51 94 65; www.maag.org; 99 rue Claude Monet, Giverny; adult/12-18yr/under 12yr €5.50/4/free; ⓨ 10am-6pm Tue-Sun Apr-Oct), a modern building displaying a fine collection of the works of many of the American impressionist painters who flocked to France in the late 19th and early 20th centuries.

INFORMATION

For online information, see www.giverny-art .com and www.ville-vernon27.fr for informa-tion on Vernon, 7km northwest of Giverny.

Vernon Tourist Office (☎ 02 32 51 39 60; tourisme .vernon@wanadoo.fr; 36 rue Carnot; ⓨ 9am-12.30pm & 2-6pm Mon-Sat, 10am-noon Sun May-Oct, 9am-12.30pm & 2-5.30pm Tue-Sat Nov-Apr) The closest tourist office is in Vernon; travelling by train, stop here before continuing to Giverny.

EATING & SLEEPING

Many Giverny restaurants and hotels are only open in season.

Auberge du Vieux Moulin (☎ 02 32 51 46 15; www .vieuxmoulingiverny.com, 21 rue de la Falaise, Giverny; salads €12, lunch Mon-Fri €15; ⓨ lunch Tue-Sun Sat Apr-Oct) The lovely little 'Old Mill Inn', a couple of hundred metres east of the Maison de Claude Monet, is an excellent place for lunch and has a lovely terrace.

TRANSPORT: GIVERNY

Distance from Paris 76km

Direction Northwest

Travel time 45 minutes by train to Vernon, then 20 by bus or bicycle

Car Route A13 from Paris' Port de St-Cloud (direc-tion Rouen), exit No 14 to route N15 (direction Vernon & Giverny)

SNCF train From Paris' Gare St-Lazare there are two early-morning SNCF trains to Vernon (€11.90), from where seasonal shuttle buses (☎ 02 32 71 06 39; €4 return; ⓨ Apr-Oct) continue from the station to Giverny, 7km northwest. Miles more fun is to hire a bike for €12 a day from the café facing the station on place de la Gare, Bar-Restaurant du Chemin de Fer (☎ 02 32 21 16 01; ⓨ 6.30am-11pm); take your passport as a deposit. Between 5pm and 9pm there's roughly one train an hour back to Paris.

Hôtel La Musardière (☎ 02 32 21 03 18; 123 rue Claude Monet; s/d/tr/q €67/79/100/110) This two-star 10-room hotel evocatively called the 'Idler' is set amid a lovely garden less than 100m northeast of the Maison de Claude Monet. Dining in its summer restaurant (*menus* €26 and €36) is a pleasure.

AUVERS-SUR-OISE

On 20 May 1890 the painter Vincent Van Gogh left a mental asylum in Provence and moved to this small village (population 6940) north of Paris. He came here to reacquaint himself with the light with which he was so familiar in his native Holland, and to be closer to his friend and benefactor Dr Paul Ferdinand Gachet (1828–1909), whose house, the Maison du Docteur Gachet (☎ 01 30 36 81 27; rue du Docteur Gachet; adult/18-25yr/under 18yr €4/3.50/free; ⏱ 10.30am-6.30pm Wed-Sun Apr-Oct), can be visited. He set to work immediately, producing at least one painting or sketch every day until his death on 29 July, two months after his arrival.

Today Auvers-sur-Oise is predominantly a shrine to the great impressionist painter. Foremost is the Maison de Van Gogh (☎ 01 30 36 60 60; info@vangoghfrance.com; adult/12-18yr/under 12yr €5/3/free; ⏱ 10am-6pm Tue-Sun Mar-Oct), actually the Auberge Ravoux, where the artist stayed during his 70 days here. Bar the seasonal restaurant on the ground floor, for the most part it's empty. However, there's an excellent video on Van Gogh's life and work, and the bedroom in which he fatally wounded himself is strangely moving.

Northwest is the Maison-Atelier de Daubigny (☎ 01 34 48 03 03; 61 rue Daubigny; adult/under 12yr €5/free; ⏱ 2-6.30pm Thu-Sun Easter–early Nov), the house studio of artist Charles-François Daubigny (1818–78), who began the practice of painting *en plein air* (outside), pre-empting the impressionists. He decorated the walls of his studio from top to bottom with help from painters Camille Corot (1796–1875) and Honoré Daumier (1808–79), and the result is stunning. To learn more about the forays and frolics of Daubigny, his friends and pupils, visit the small Musée Daubigny (☎ 01 30 36 80 20; rue de la Sansonne; adult/under 18yr €4/free; ⏱ 2-6pm Wed-Fri, 10.30am-1pm & 2-6pm Sat & Sun Apr-Oct, 2-5pm Wed-Fri, 10.30am-1pm & 2-6pm Sat & Sun Nov & mid-Jan–Mar), above the tourist office in the delightful Manoir des Colombières.

Heading west is the sprawling 17th-century Château d'Auvers (☎ 01 34 48 48 45; www.chateau-auvers .fr; rue de Léry; adult/6-18yr €11.50/7.50; ⏱ 10.30am-6pm Tue-Fri & 10.30am-6.30pm Sat & Sun Apr-Sep, 10.30am-4.30pm Tue-Fri & 10.30am-5.30pm Sat & Sun Oct-Dec & mid-Jan–Mar), whose inspired, enormously informative audiovisual presentation on Van Gogh and other impressionists who found their way to Auvers is essential for anyone wanting to truly immerse themselves in the Van Gogh era. En route nip into the Musée de l'Absinthe (☎ 01 30 36 83 26; 44 rue Callé; adult/15-18yr/under 15yr €4.50/3.80/free; ⏱ 1.30-6pm Wed-Fri, 11am-6pm Sat & Sun mid-Jun–mid-Sep, 11am-6pm Sat & Sun mid-Sep–Nov & Mar–mid-Jun) to discover the history of the liqueur that possibly contributed to Van Gogh's downfall (below).

Finally, there's the Église Notre Dame (rue Daubigny; ⏱ 9.30am-6pm), subject of Van Gogh's *L'Église d'Auvers* (1890), and the cemetery (Chemin des Vallées) where he and his brother Théo are buried.

Chateau aside, practically everywhere is shut in winter.

ABSINTHE: SPIRIT OF THE AGE

In its heyday absinthe was akin to the marijuana of the 1960s or the cocaine of the '80s. But until it became the drink of choice among artists, artistes and the underclasses (and thus gained in notoriety), absinthe had been a bourgeois favourite, sipped quietly and innocuously in cafés around the land. It was only when the creative world discovered the wormwood-based liqueur and its hallucinogenic qualities that it took off, and everyone from Paul Verlaine, Arthur Rimbaud, Oscar Wilde, Édouard Manet, Edgar Degas, Henri de Toulouse-Lautrec and, of course, Vincent Van Gogh wrote about it, painted it and/or drank it. Whether or not it was the *fée verte* (green fairy), as absinthe was known during the *belle époque,* that pushed Van Gogh off the edge is not known; some say he was so poor he couldn't even afford this relatively cheap libation and instead sometimes ate paint containing lead, which may have driven him mad.

More than anything else, the easy availability and low cost of the spirit led to widespread alcoholism and in 1915, having just entered into war against Germany and its allies, France found it prudent to ban the drink altogether. Incredibly, it wasn't until 1998 that absinthe became legal again in France (and the EU).

Try it for €3.70 a 2cL shot at Auvers' Café de la Paix (opposite).

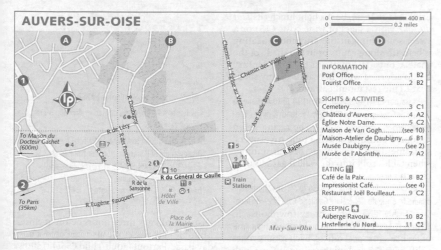

AUVERS-SUR-OISE

INFORMATION
Post Office.................................1 B2
Tourist Office.............................2 B2

SIGHTS & ACTIVITIES
Cemetery..................................3 C1
Château d'Auvers....................4 A2
Église Notre Dame...................5 C2
Maison de Van Gogh.........(see 10)
Maison-Atelier de Daubigny....6 B1
Musée Daubigny................(see 2)
Musée de l'Absinthe...............7 A2

EATING
Café de la Paix........................8 B2
Impressionist Café..............(see 4)
Restaurant Joël Bouilleaut.......9 C2

SLEEPING
Auberge Ravoux....................10 B2
Hostellerie du Nord...............11 C2

INFORMATION

Post Office (place de la Mairie)

Tourist Office (☎ 01 30 36 10 06; www-auvers-sur-oise
.com, in French; rue de la Sansonne; ☺ 9.30am-12.30pm
& 2-6pm Tue-Sun Apr-Oct, to 5pm or 5.30pm Nov-Mar) Ask
for its excellent free brochure, *Parcours des Peintres de la
Vallée de l'Oise*, which maps out the spots where Van Gogh,
Daubigny and others painted. Mid-March to October it runs
guided Van Gogh tours around the village, departing at
3pm on Sunday (€5.50).

EATING & SLEEPING

There's a Moroccan place opposite the station, Thai at the chateau end of the village
and a *crêperie* neighbouring Café de la Paix,
all open year-round.

Auberge Ravoux (☎ 01 30 36 60 60; 52 rue du Général de
Gaulle; 2-/3-course menu €29/37; ☺ lunch Wed-Sun & dinner
to 9.30pm Fri & Sat Mar–early-Nov) What could be a
more appropriate way to celebrate the life of
Vincent Van Gogh than by having lunch or
dinner in the house in which he died? Auberge
Ravoux has been a *café d'artistes* (artists' café;
or so it claims) since 1876, so it predates Van
Gogh's fateful sojourn by more than a dozen
years. Reservations essential.

Café de la Paix (☎ 01 30 36 73 23; 11 rue du Général de
Gaulle; starters €8-10, mains €8.50-15, lunch menus €12.80 &
€18.90; ☺ 7am-8.30pm Wed-Sun, 7am-3pm Mon) Across
the road from Auberge Ravoux, locals pile
into the 1950s village cinema, now a café-
restaurant with stage and wooden floor where
jazz concerts take centre stage at weekends.
Food covers the whole gamut, from brasserie-

style grills to more-refined restaurant dishes,
and it has a few hotel rooms up top.

Impressionist Café (☎ 01 30 36 71 31; Château d'Auvers;
starters €10-12, mains €14.50-20, lunch menus €16 & €20;
☺ lunch Tue-Sun) A delightful spot to eat and

TRANSPORT: AUVERS-SUR-OISE

Distance from Paris 35km

Direction North

Travel time 60 to 70 minutes by train, bus or RER/bus

Car Route A15 from Paris' Porte de Clichy, exit 7 to
route N184 (direction Beauvais), exit 'Méry-sur-Oise'

Bus From mid-April to mid-October Les Cars Air
France (☎ 01 74 25 08 12) operates a direct bus
several times a week from place de la Porte Maillot
(Map pp144–5) to Auvers-sur-Oise.

RER train Line A3 from Gare de Lyon or Châtelet-
Les Halles (€5.40) to Cergy Préfecture station, then
Val d'Oise bus 95-07 (destination Butry) to rue du
Général de Gaulle. The last bus (☎ 01 34 25 30 81)
back to Paris leaves Auvers around 8pm weekdays
(7pm weekends).

SNCF train Suburban train from Gare du Nord or
Gare St-Lazare to Pontoise or Persan Beaumont
then a connecting train to Auvers-sur-Oise; the
last train to Paris leaves just after 9pm weekdays
(10.30pm weekends). April to October, the SNCF
runs a direct train (30 minutes) on Sunday departing
from Gare du Nord at 9.56am and leaving Auvers
at 6.15pm; the SNCF package (adult/10-17yr/6-9yr
€16.10/14.20/10.20) including return transport from
Paris and chateau admission is available year-round.

drink *à la château*, be it a light lunch (its *plat du jour* with a glass of wine costs €15) or a sweet something in the afternoon. Seating is beneath stone vaults or in the shade of the chateau outside; don't miss the 17th-century grotto adorned with thousands of tiny shells next to the restaurant entrance.

Restaurant Joël Bouilleaut (☎ 01 30 36 70 74; 6 rue du Général de Gaulle; menus €49 & €79; ☾ lunch & dinner Tue-Fri, dinner Sat, lunch Sun; ✖ ♿) The racing-green canopied entrance sets the tone for Auvers' stiff, fine-dining restaurant, best in summer when tables spill into the walled garden with church view.

Hostellerie du Nord (☎ 01 30 36 70 74; www.hostellerie dunord.fr; 6 rue du Général de Gaulle; d €95-125; ☾ Mon-Sat; ✖ ♿) The 17th-century townhouse in which this eight-room inn slumbers was one of France's first post offices. Each room evokes a different artist: sloping-ceilinged Van Gogh faces the church the artist so famously painted; Ferrière showcases flowery watercolours for sale by the local artist; and Ferré – the only room to have a terrace – is for sculpture lovers. No rooms available on Sunday evening, when the entire place closes. Free wi-fi.

DISNEYLAND RESORT PARIS

It took almost €4.6 billion and five years of hard graft to turn the beet fields east of the capital into Europe's first Disney theme park, which opened amid much fanfare and controversy in 1992. Rocky start now a million moons away, what started out as Euro-Disney sees visitors (mostly families) pour into the park to scare themselves silly in the blood-curdling Tower of Terror, dance in a High School Musical, dive with Nemo, hit 70km/h in a Space Mountain rocket, shake Winnie the Pooh's paw and share a fiesta of other magical moments with Mickey and his Disney mates. The park celebrated its 15th anniversary in 2007, but as its marketing bumph boasts, 'the party never stops…'

One-day admission fees at Disneyland Resort Paris (☎ 01 60 30 60 60 53; www.disneylandparis.com; adult/3-11yr €46/38; ☾ Disneyland Park 10am-8pm Mon-Fri early May–mid-Jun & Sep-Mar, 9am-11pm early Jul-Aug; Walt Disney Studios Park 9am-6pm late Jun–early Sep, 10am-6pm Mon-Fri & 9am-6pm Sat & Sun early Sep–late Jun) include unlimited access to all rides and activities in *either* Disneyland Park or Walt Disney Studios Park. Those who opt for the latter can enter

TRANSPORT: DISNEYLAND RESORT PARIS

Distance from Paris 32km

Direction East

Travel time 35 to 40 minutes by RER train

Car Route A4 from Porte de Bercy, direction Metz-Nancy, exit No 14

RER train Line A4 to Marne-la-Vallée/Chessy, Disneyland's RER station, from central Paris (€7.50, adult/3 to 11 years €47/39 incl park admission). Trains run every 15 minutes or so, with the last train back to Paris just after midnight.

Disneyland Park three hours before it closes. Multiple-day passes are also available: a one-day Passe-Partout (adult/child €56/48) allows entry to both parks for a day and its multi-day equivalents (two days €103/84, three days €128/105) allow you to enter and leave both parks as often as you like over nonconsecutive days used within one year. Some shows and activities such as breakfast, lunch or dinner with the Disney characters (from €22/15 per adult/child) cost extra. Admission fees change season to season and a multitude of special offers and accommodation/transport packages are always available.

Anyone who abhors long queues, go elsewhere: queues here are hideous and can make it hard going for those with younger children in tow. Buy your tickets at tourist offices or train stations in Paris beforehand to avoid at least one queue (for tickets); once in, reserve your slot on the busiest rides using FastPass, the park's ride reservation system (limited to one reservation at a time).

Disneyland comprises three areas plus a golf course: Disney Village, with its hotels, shops, restaurants and clubs; Disneyland Park, with its five theme parks; and Walt Disney Studios Park, which brings film, animation and TV production to life, most recently in the walking, talking, life-sized shape of alien puppy Stitch and the dimly lit rollercoaster ride, Crush's Coaster. Fans of the film *Cars* will love the Cars Race Rally. RER and TGV train stations separate the first two, and the studios neighbour Disneyland Park. Moving walkways whisk visitors to the sights from the far-flung car park.

Disneyland Park's *pays* (lands) include Main Street USA, a spotless avenue just inside the main entrance reminiscent of Norman Rockwell's idealised small-town America c 1900; Frontierland, a re-creation of the 'rugged, untamed American West' with the legendary Big Thunder Mountain ride (minimum height 1.02m); and Adventureland, which evokes the Arabian Nights, the wilds of Africa and other exotic lands portrayed in Disney films, including that of the Pirates of the Caribbean; the spiralling 360-degrees rollercoaster, Indiana Jones and the Temple of Peril, is the biggie here (minimum height 1.40m). Pinocchio, Snow White and other fairy-tale characters come to life in Fantasyland, while Discoveryland is the spot for high-tech attractions and massive-queue rides like Space Mountain: Mission 2 (minimum height 1.32m), Star Tours and the *Toy Story 2*–inspired Buzz Lightyear Laser Blast, apparently still the hottest thing since sliced bread.

Before hot-footing it to Disney, devote a good hour on its website planning your day – which rides, shows, characters etc you really want to see.

EATING & SLEEPING

No picnics allowed at Disneyland Paris! But there are ample themed restaurants to pick from, be it Buzz Lightyear's Pizza Planet (Discoveryland), Planet Hollywood or the *Happy Days*–inspired Annette's Diner (Disney Village), the meaty Silver Spur Steakhouse or Mexican Fuente del Oro (Frontierland) and the sea-faring Blue Lagoon restaurant (Adventureland) for future pirates. Most have *menus* for children (around €10) and adults (€20 to €30); opening hours vary. To avoid another queue, pick your place online and reserve a table in advance (☎ 01 60 30 40 50).

The resort's seven own American-themed hotels (central booking ☎ 01 60 30 60 30) and a handful of others are linked by free shuttle bus to the parks. Rates vary hugely, peaking in July and August and around Christmas; on Friday and Saturday nights and during holiday periods April to October; and on Saturday night mid-February to March. The cheapest rates are Sunday to Thursday January to mid-February, mid-May to June, September, and November to mid-December.

Advertised rates are for a minimum of two, three or four nights and supplementary nights can be added – rates include park admission. Lucky hotel guests are often entitled on designated days to two 'Magic hours' in Disneyland Park when the park is closed to regular punters. Consider Disney's Hotel New York for Big Apple 1930s Art Deco, its Newport Bay Club for a nautical theme, Hotel Cheyenne

for Hollywood, and Santa Fe for some deep southwest. Otherwise, try the prince or the pauper of the sleeping scene:

Disneyland Hôtel (d 2-night/3-day package per adult €483-720; 🖳) The flagship of Disneyland Resort Paris accommodation, this 496-room Victorian palace stares in all its majesty at Sleeping Beauty's 43m-tall castle.

Disney's Davy Crockett Ranch (d 2-night/3-day package per adult €242-361) As 'relaxing' as you're gonna' get at Disney, this trapper's village is not bad. Imagine 535 log cabins planted in a 57 hectare-large wood with limited self-catering facilities (fridge, microwave). Cabins sleep up to six.

PARC ASTÉRIX

Just beyond Roissy Charles de Gaulle airport, this seasonal theme park splits into seven 'zany zones', the Gaulish Village, the Roman Empire, Ancient Greece and so on. Rides are numerous, invariably hair-raising and as much a hit with kids as the various shows, spectacles and devilishly Gaullist pranks throughout the day.

INFORMATION

Parc Astérix (☎ 08 26 30 10 40; www.parcasterix.com, in French; adult/3-11yr/under 3yr €37/27/free, parking €7; 🕙 10am-8pm early Apr, 10am-7pm Jun-Aug, 10am-7pm Wed, Sat & Sun Sep–early Oct) Tickets including admission and all transport to/from the park (adult/3-11yr €41.60/27) are available at most RER and SNCF stations in central Paris.

TRANSPORT: PARC ASTÉRIX

Distance from Paris 36km

Direction Northeast

Travel time 50 to 60 minutes by shuttle, RER train and bus

Car Route A1, Parc Astérix, exit between exit Nos 7 and 8

Shuttle The park operates a daily navette (shuttle; ☎ 01 48 62 38 33; adult/3-11yr return €19/13) departing from outside the Louvre (metro Palais Royal) at 8.45am and from Parc Astérix at 6.30pm.

RER train & bus Line B3 from Châtelet or Gare du Nord to Aéroport Roissy Charles de Gaulle 1 train station, then take the Courriers Île-de-France shuttle bus (☎ 01 48 62 38 33; adult/3-11yr return €6.90/5), departing from the bus station, platform 3, every half-hour between 9.30am and 6.30pm (7pm from the park).

REIMS

This city of 202,600 people some 144km northeast of Paris has two claims to fame. It is by far the largest and most attractive of the major champagne-producing centres, affording travellers a smorgasbord of things to see and do as well dining and accommodation options. At the same time, as the so-called Coronation City, Reims – pronounced something like 'rance' – is the place where, over the course of a millennium (816 to 1825), some 34 sovereigns – among them 25 kings – began their reigns as Christian rulers.

The focal point of these pompous occasions was Cathédrale Notre Dame (www.cathedrale-reims.com, in French; place du Cardinal Luçon; 7.30am-7.30pm, closed to visitors Sun morning), a Gothic edifice begun in 1211 – on a site occupied by churches since the 5th century – and mostly completed 100 years later. The most famous event to take place here was the coronation of Charles VII, with Joan of Arc at his side, on 17 July 1429. The tourist office rents audioguides (1/2 people €5/9) with self-paced tours of the cathedral. Tours of the cathedral tower (adult/12-25yr €6.50/4.50; Tue-Sat & afternoon Sun early May–early Sep, Sat & afternoon Sun mid-Mar–early May & early Sep-Oct) can be booked at the Palais du Tau.

Very badly damaged by artillery and fire during WWI, the 138m-long cathedral, a Unesco World Heritage Site, is more interesting for its dramatic history than its heavily restored architectural features. The finest stained-glass windows are the western façade's 12-petalled great rose window, its almost cobalt-blue neighbour below it, and the rose window in the north transept arm (to the left), above the flamboyant Gothic organ case (15th and 18th centuries) topped with a figure. Nearby is

a 15th-century wooden astronomical clock. There's a window by Chagall (1974) in the central axial chapel (behind the high altar) portraying Christ and Abraham and, two chapels to the left, a statue of Joan of Arc. Persons strong-of-thigh might want to climb the 250 steps of the cathedral tower on a one-hour tour.

Next door, the Palais du Tau (03 26 47 81 79; www.palais-du-tau.fr, in French; 2 place du Cardinal Luçon; admission free until end Jun 2008, then adult/under 18yr €6.50/ free; 9.30am-6.30pm Tue-Sun early May–early Sep, 9.30am-12.30pm & 2-5.30pm Tue-Sun early Sep–early May), a former archbishop's residence constructed in 1690, was where French princes stayed before their coronations and where they hosted sumptuous banquets afterwards. Now a museum, it displays truly exceptional statues, ritual objects and tapestries from the cathedral, some in the impressive Salle du Tau.

The rich collections of the Musée des Beaux-Arts (03 26 47 28 44; 8 rue Chanzy; 10am-noon & 2-6pm Wed-Sun), housed in an 18th-century building, include one of only four versions of Jacques-Louis David's world-famous *Death of Marat* (yes, the bloody one in the bathtub), 27 works by Camille Corot (only the Louvre has more), lots of Barbizon School landscapes, Art Nouveau creations by Émile Gallé and two works each by Monet, Gauguin and Pissarro.

No visit to Reims would be complete without a tour of a champagne *cave* (cellar) and eight *maisons* (houses or producers) offer guided tours of their premises that end, *naturellement*, with a tasting session. Of the Reims trinity, Mumm (03 26 49 59 70; www.mumm.com; 34 rue du Champ de Mars; tours adult/under 12yr €8/free; tours 9am-10.50am & 2pm-4.40pm daily Mar-Oct, Sat only Nov-Feb) is most easily accessible from the centre, while Taittinger (03 26 85 84 33; www.taittinger.com; 9 place St-Niçaise; tours adult/under 12yr €10/free; tours 9.30am-noon & 2pm-4.30pm, closed Sat & Sun mid-Nov–mid-Mar) and Pommery (03 26 61 62 55; www.pommery.fr; 5 place du Général Gouraud; tours adult/student & 12-17yr/under 12yr €10/7/free; tours 9.30am-7pm Apr–mid-Nov, 10am-6pm Sat & Sun mid-Nov–Mar) are under 2km to the southeast.

INFORMATION

Tourist Office (03 26 77 45 00; www.reims-tourisme .com; 2 rue Guillaume de Machault; 9am-7pm Mon-Sat, 10am-6pm Sun mid-Apr–mid-Oct, 10am-6pm Mon-Sat, 11am-4pm Sun mid-Oct–mid-Apr) The Reims City Card (€14) gets you a champagne house tour, an all-day bus ticket, entry to four municipal museums, including Musée des Beaux-Arts, and a guided tour of the cathedral.

TRANSPORT: REIMS

Distance from Paris 144km

Direction Northeast

Travel time 45 minutes by TGV, 1½ to 1¾ hours by normal train or car

Car Route A4 from Paris' Porte de Bercy (direction Metz)), exit No 23 (Reims-Centre)

Train Up to 15 daily trains link Reims with Paris' Gare de l'Est (€22.70, 1¾ hours); seven of them are TGVs (45 minutes, €28). Information and tickets in the city centre are available at the Boutique SNCF (1 cours Jean-Baptiste Langlet; 9am-7pm Mon-Fri, 10am-6pm Sat).

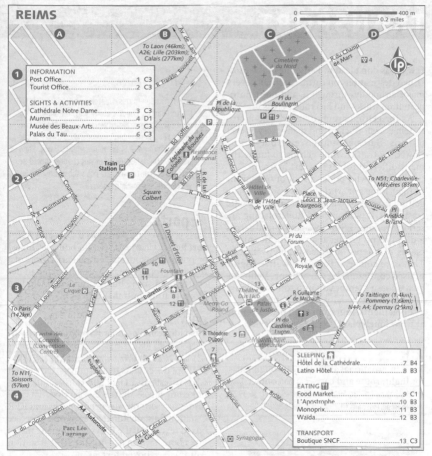

REIMS

INFORMATION
Post Office.................................1 C3
Tourist Office.............................2 C3

SIGHTS & ACTIVITIES
Cathédrale Notre Dame..............3 C3
Mumm......................................4 D1
Musée des Beaux-Arts................5 C3
Palais du Tau............................6 C3

SLEEPING
Hôtel de la Cathédrale...............7 B4
Latino Hôtel..............................8 B3

EATING
Food Market..............................9 C1
L 'Apostrophe...........................10 B3
Monoprix.................................11 B3
Waïda.....................................12 B3

TRANSPORT
Boutique SNCF.........................13 C3

EATING & SLEEPING

L'Apostrophe (☎ 03 26 79 19 89; 59 place Drouet d'Erlon; starters €6.50-15.10, mains €14.50-25, lunch menus €14; ⏱ lunch & dinner to 11.30pm) This stylish café-brasserie in the centre of Reims dispenses French and international cuisine as well as some mean *piscines* (enormous cocktails for several people). A perennial favourite thanks to its chic atmosphere, summertime terrace and good value. Open as a café straight through from 9am to 1am.

Waïda (☎ 03 26 47 44 49; 5 place Drouet d'Erlon; ⏱ 7.30am-7.30pm Wed-Sun) An old-fashioned *salon de thé* and confectionery with mirrors, mosaics and marble. This is the place to buy a box of a box of *biscuits roses* (pink biscuits; €3.30), traditionally nibbled with champagne.

Hôtel de la Cathédrale (☎ 03 26 47 28 46; www.hotel-cathedrale-reims.fr; 20 rue Libergier; s/d/q €54/62/78; ✕ 🖳) Charm, graciousness and a resident Yorkshire terrier greet guests at this hostelry run by two musicians. The 17 tasteful rooms are smallish but pleasingly chintzy and some have been recently renovated. There are four floors but no lift. Go for room No 14 with two windows or No 43 with views of Basilique St-Rémi and the hills to the south.

Latino Hôtel (☎ 03 26 47 48 89; www.latinocafe.fr; 33 place Drouet d'Erlon; s & d €54-74, apt €130; ✕ 🅿 🖳) This budget boutique hotel above a buzzy musical café has a dozen gaily painted guestrooms (think cherry and pumpkin) over five floors but no lift. The furnishings are fun, the welcome exceptionally warm and we love the quotes from the great and the good (Gandhi, Boris Vian) painted on the hall walls. The apartment on the top floor looking straight onto the cathedral can accommodate up to five people.

Few roads don't lead to Paris, one of the most visited destinations on earth. Practically every major airline flys through it, and most European train tracks and bus routes cross it.

As for getting around – easy! The metro system is vast, efficient and spans every pocket of Paris. Buses are more scenic but can be slowed by traffic, while getting to know the many different routes is an art in itself.

For those who prefer a spot of fresher air in their lungs, or who simply want to make getting from A to B a historical and aesthetic feast in itself, walking and Rollerblading are serious options. With city sights spread across a distance no greater than 10km, the major places of interest are pleasurably walkable. That is, of course, if Paris' innovative, highly praised communal bicycle scheme, Vélib' (opposite), doesn't tempt you into some footloose and fancy-free pedal-powered action.

Book flights, tours and train tickets online at www.lonelyplanet.com/travel_services.

AIR

Most international airlines fly through Paris; for flight, route and carrier info contact Aéroports de Paris (☎ 39 50, from abroad +33 1 70 36 39 50; www.aeroportsdeparis.fr).

top picks

ONLINE TICKET RESOURCES

No great deal to be struck going straight to the airline website? See what these online airline ticketing resources throw up.

- Anyway (www.anyway.fr, in French)
- Bargain Holidays (www.bargainholidays.com)
- Cheap Flights (www.cheapflights.co.uk)
- easyvols (www.easyvols.com, in French)
- ebookers (www.ebookers.com)
- e-mondial (www.e-mondial.com, in French)
- Go Voyages (www.govoyages.com, in French)
- Last Minute (www.lastminute.com)
- Opodo (www.opodo.com)
- Travelocity (www.travelocity.com)
- Voyages SNCF (www.voyages-sncf.com, in French)

THINGS CHANGE...

The information in this chapter is particularly vulnerable to change. Check directly with the airline or a travel agent to make sure you understand how a fare (and ticket you may buy) works and be aware of the security requirements for international travel. Shop carefully. The details given in this chapter should be regarded as pointers and are not a substitute for your own careful, up-to-date research.

Airports

Paris is served by Aéroport d'Orly and Aéroport Roissy Charles de Gaulle, both well linked by public transport to central Paris. More of a trek is Aéroport de Beauvais, which handles charter and some budget carriers, including Ryanair and Central Wings.

ORLY

The older, smaller of Paris' two major airports, Aéroport d'Orly (ORY; Map pp78–9; ☎ 39 50, from abroad +33 1 70 36 39 50; www.aeroportsdeparis.fr), is 18km south of the city. Its two terminals, Orly Ouest (Orly West) and Orly Sud (Orly South), are linked by a free shuttle bus service that continues to/from the airport car parks and RER C station Pont de Rungis-Aéroport d'Orly (see boxed text, p390); the Orlyval automatic metro links both terminals with the RER B station Antony (see boxed text, p390).

Need to get from Orly to Roissy Charles de Gaulle (or vice versa)? See below.

ROISSY CHARLES DE GAULLE

Aéroport Roissy Charles de Gaulle (CDG; ☎ 39 50, from abroad +33 1 70 36 39 50; www.aeroportsdeparis.fr), 30km northeast of central Paris in the suburb of Roissy, has three *aérogares* (terminals) – aptly numbered 1, 2 and 3 – and two train stations served by commuter trains on RER line B3: Aéroport Charles de Gaulle 1 (CDG1), which serves terminals 1 and 3, and the sleek Aéroport Charles de Gaulle 2 (CDG2) for terminal 2. A free shuttle bus links the terminals with the train stations.

To get to/from Charles de Gaulle and Orly, take the RER line B3 to the Antony stop then pick up the Orlyval automatic metro (adult/child four to ten years €9.30/4.65) or hop aboard the Air France shuttle bus 3 (adult/child 2-11yr €16/8; ☺ 6am or 7am–10.30pm) linking the two airports. Both journeys take an hour, as does a taxi (€50 to €60). See p390).

BEAUVAIS

Charter companies and Ryanair, Central Wings and various other budget airlines land/take off at Aéroport Paris-Beauvais (BVA; ☎ 0 892 682 066; www.aeroportbeauvais.com), 75km north of central Paris.

BICYCLE

Two-wheeling has never been so good in the city of romance thanks to Vélib' (a crunching of *vélo*, meaning bike, and *liberté*, meaning freedom), a self-service bike scheme whereby you pick up a pearly-grey bike for peanuts from one roadside Vélib' station, pedal wherever you're going, and park it right outside at another.

A runaway success since its launch in 2007, Vélib' (☎ 01 30 79 79 30; www.velib.paris.fr; day/week/year subscription €1/5/29, bike hire 1st/2nd/3rd & each additional half-hr free/€2/4) has revolutionised how Parisians get around. Its 1451 *stations Vélib'* across the city – one every 300m – sport 20-odd bike stands a head (at the last count there were 20,600 bicycles in all flitting around Paris) and are accessible around the clock.

To get a bike, you need a Vélib' account: One- and seven-day subscriptions can be done on the spot at any station with any major credit card providing it has a microchip and pin number (be warned North Americans!).

BIKES ON PUBLIC TRANSPORT

Bicycles are not allowed on the metro except on line 1 on Sunday and public holidays. You can, however, take your bicycle to the suburbs on some RER lines on weekdays before 6.30am, between 9am and 4.30pm, after 7pm, and all day on the weekend and on public holidays. More lenient rules apply to SNCF commuter services. Contact SNCF (p395) for details.

As deposit you'll need to pre-authorise a direct debit of €150, all except €35 of which is debited if your bike is not returned or is reported as stolen). If the station you want to return your bike to is full, swipe your card across the multilingual terminal to get 15 minutes for free to find another station. Bikes are geared to cyclists aged 14 and over, and are fitted with gears, antitheft lock with key, reflective strips and front/rear lights. Bring your own helmet though!

For more information on cycling in Paris, and a list of rental outlets where you can rent wheels for longer periods of time, see p320. Guided bicycle tours are listed on p406.

BOAT

For pleasure cruises on the Seine, Canal St-Martin and Canal de l'Ourcq, see p406.

For a more flexible, hop-on-and-off approach, sail with the Compagnie de Batobus (☎ 08 25 05 01 01; www.batobus.com; adult 1-/2-/3-day pass €12/14/17, student €8/9/11, child 2-16yr €6/7/8;

TRANSPORT BICYCLE

CLIMATE CHANGE & TRAVEL

Climate change is a serious threat to the ecosystems that humans rely upon, and air travel is the fastest-growing contributor to the problem. Lonely Planet regards travel, overall, as a global benefit, but believes we all have a responsibility to limit our personal impact on global warming.

Flying & Climate Change

Pretty much every form of motor transport generates CO_2 (the main cause of human-induced climate change) but planes are far and away the worst offenders, not just because of the sheer distances they allow us to travel, but because they release greenhouse gases high into the atmosphere. The statistics are frightening: two people taking a return flight between Europe and the US will contribute as much to climate change as an average household's gas and electricity consumption over a whole year.

Carbon Offset Schemes

Climatecare.org and other websites use 'carbon calculators' that allow travellers to offset the greenhouse gases they are responsible for with contributions to energy-saving projects and other climate-friendly initiatives in the developing world – including projects in India, Honduras, Kazakhstan and Uganda.

Lonely Planet, together with Rough Guides and other concerned partners in the travel industry, supports the carbon offset scheme run by climatecare.org. Lonely Planet offsets all of its staff and author travel.

For more information check out our website: www.lonelyplanet.com.

GETTING INTO TOWN

Getting into town is straightforward and inexpensive thanks to a fleet of public-transport options, listed under airport headings. Bus drivers sell tickets.

Pricier, door-to-door alternatives include taxi (€40 to €50 between central Paris and Orly, €40 to €60 to/from Charles de Gaulle, €110 to €150 to/from Beauvais; see p395 for taxi telephone numbers); or a private minibus shuttle such as Allô Shuttle (☎ 01 34 29 00 80; www.alloshuttle.com), Paris Airports Service (☎ 01 55 98 10 80; www.parisairportservice.com) or PariShuttle (☎ 01 53 39 18 18; www.parishuttle.com). Count on around €25 per person (€40 between 8pm and 6am) for Orly or Charles de Gaulle and €150 for one to four people to/from Beauvais. Book in advance and allow ample time for other pick-ups and drop-offs.

Aéroport d'Orly

Unless noted otherwise, these options to/from Orly call at both terminals.

Air France bus 1 (☎ 08 92 35 08 20; www.cars-airfrance.com; adult single/return €9/14; ☼ 6am-11.30pm from Orly, 5.45am-11pm from Invalides) This *navette* (shuttle bus) runs every 15 minutes to/from the eastern side of Gare Montparnasse (Map pp124–5; 30 to 45 minutes) and Aérogare des Invalides (Map pp128–9; 30 to 45 minutes) in the 7e. On the way into the city, passengers without baggage stowed in the coach hold can ask to get off at metro Porte d'Orléans (Map pp78–9) or metro Duroc (Map pp128–9).

Jetbus (☎ 01 69 01 00 09; adult/under 5yr €5.70/free; ☼ 6.20am-11.10pm from Orly, 6.15am-10.30am from Paris) Jetbus runs every 15 to 25 minutes to/from metro Villejuif Louis Aragon (Map pp78–9; 55 minutes), a bit south of the 13e on the city's southern fringe, from where a metro/bus ticket gets you into town.

Noctilien bus 31 (☎ 08 92 68 77 14, 08 92 68 41 14 in English; adult/4-9yr €6/3; ☼ 12.30am-5.30pm) Part of the RATP's night service, Noctilien bus 31 links Gare de Lyon (Map pp158–9), place d'Italie (Map pp162–3) and Gare d'Austerlitz (Map pp158–9) with Orly-Sud. It runs every hour and journey time is 45 minutes to an hour.

Orlybus (☎ 08 92 68 77 14; adult/4-11yr €6.10/3.05; ☼ 6am-11.50pm from Orly, 5.35am-11.25pm from Paris) This RATP bus runs every 15 to 20 minutes between both terminals and metro Denfert- Rochereau (Map pp78–9; 30 minutes) in the 14e, making several stops in the eastern 14e en route.

Orlyval & RER B (☎ 08 92 68 77 14; adult/4-10yr €9.30/4.65; ☼ 6am-11pm) From either terminal take the Orlyval automatic rail to the RER B station Antony, then RER B4 north (35 to 40 minutes to Châtelet, every four to 12 minutes). Orlyval tickets are valid for the subsequent RER and metro journey.

RATP bus 183 (☎ 08 92 68 77 14; adult/4-9yr €1.50/0.75 or 1 metro/bus ticket; ☼ 6am-9.40pm from Orly, 5.35am-8.35pm from Porte de Choisy) The cheapest means of getting to/from Orly Sud, this slow public bus links the South Terminal with metro Porte de Choisy (Map pp78–9; one hour), on the southern edge of the 13e, every 35 minutes.

RER C & shuttle (☎ 08 90 36 10 10; adult/4-10yr €6/4.25; ☼ 5.30am-11.50pm) From the airport, hop aboard an airport shuttle bus (every 15 to 30 minutes) to the RER station Pont de Rungis-Aéroport d'Orly, then RER C2 train to

☼ 10am-9.30pm May-Aug, 10am-7pm Sep–mid-Nov & mid-Mar-Apr, 10.30am-4.30pm mid-Nov–mid-Dec & Feb–mid-Mar, 10.30am-5pm mid-Dec–Jan). Its fleet of glassed-in trimarans dock at small piers along the Seine and tickets are sold at each stop or tourist offices. For those keen to combine boat with bus, its Paris à la Carte deal allows two/three consecutive days of unlimited travel on Batobus boats and Open Tour buses (p407) for €37/40. Boats depart every 15 to 30 minutes from various stops:

Champs-Élysées (Map pp140–1; Port des Champs-Élysées, 8e; Ⓜ Champs-Élysées Clemenceau)

Eiffel Tower (Map pp132–3; Port de la Bourdonnais, 7e; Ⓜ Champ de Mars-Tour Eiffel)

Hôtel de Ville (Map pp98–9; quai de l'Hôtel de Ville, 4e; Ⓜ Hôtel de Ville)

Jardin des Plantes (Map pp110–11; quai St-Bernard, 5e; Ⓜ Jussieu)

Musée d'Orsay (Map pp128–9; quai de Solférino, 7e; Ⓜ Musée d'Orsay)

Musée du Louvre (Map p86; quai du Louvre, 1er; Ⓜ Palais Royal-Musée du Louvre)

Notre Dame (Map pp110–11; quai de Montebello, 5e; Ⓜ St-Michel)

St-Germain des Prés (Map pp116–17; quai Malaquais, 6e; Ⓜ St-Germain des Prés)

Paris' Gare d'Austerlitz (50 minutes). Coming from Paris, be sure to get the shuttle at Pont de Rungis that goes to the correct terminal.

Aéroport Roissy Charles de Gaulle

Air France bus 2 (☎ 08 92 35 08 20; www.cars-airfrance.com; single/return €13/18; ☺ 5.45am-11pm) Links the airport every 15 minutes with the Arc de Triomphe outside 1 av Carnot, 17e (Map pp140–1; 35 to 50 minutes) and the Palais des Congrès de Paris, 17e (Map pp144–5; 35 to 50 minutes).

Air France bus 4 (☎ 08 92 35 08 20; www.cars-airfrance.com; single/return €14/22; ☺ 7am-9pm from CDG, 6.30am-9.30pm from Paris) Links the airport every 30 minutes with Gare de Lyon (Map pp158–9; 45 to 55 minutes) and Gare Montparnasse (Map pp124–5; 45 to 55 minutes).

Noctilien night bus (☎ 08 92 68 77 14; adult/4-9yr €7.50/3.75; ☺ 12.30am-5.30pm) Part of the RATP night service, Noctilien buses 120, 121 (linking Montparnasse, Châtelet, Gare du Nord) and 140 (linking Gare du Nord and Gare de l'Est) go to Roissy-Charles de Gaulle hourly.

RATP bus 350 (☎ 08 92 68 77 14; adult/4-9yr €4.50/2.25 or 3 metro/bus tickets; ☺ 5.45am-7pm each direction) Links Aérogares 1 and 2 with Gare de l'Est (Map pp152–3; one hour, every 30 minutes) and Gare du Nord (Map pp152–3; one hour, every 30 minutes).

RATP bus 351 (☎ 08 92 68 77 14; adult/4-9yr €4.50/2.25 or 3 metro/bus tickets; ☺ 7am-9.30pm from the airport, 8.30am-8.20pm from Paris) Links the eastern side of place de la Nation (Map pp78–9) with Roissy-Charles de Gaulle (55 minutes, every 30 minutes).

RER B (☎ 08 90 36 10 10; adult/4-11yr €8.20/5.80; ☺ 5am-midnight) RER line B3 links CDG1 and CDG2 with the city (30 minutes; every 10 to 15 minutes). To get to the airport take any RER line B train whose four-letter destination code begins with E (eg EIRE) and a shuttle bus (every five to eight minutes) takes you to the correct terminal. Regular metro ticket windows can't always sell RER tickets to the airport so you may have to buy one at the RER station where you board.

Roissybus (☎ 08 92 68 77 14; adult €8.60; ☺ 5.45am-11pm) Direct public bus linking several points at both terminals with rue Scribe, next to Palais Garnier, in the 9e (Map pp148–9; 45 to 60 minutes, every 15 minutes).

Aéroport Paris-Beauvais

Express Bus (☎ car park 08 92 68 20 64, airport 08 92 68 20 66; one way €13) Leaves Parking Pershing (Map pp144–5), west of the Palais des Congrès de Paris, three hours before flight departures (board 15 minutes before) and leaves the airport 20 to 30 minutes after arrivals, dropping passengers south of the Palais des Congrès on place de la Porte Maillot (Map pp144–5). Journey time is one to 1¼ hours and tickets can be purchased up to 24 hours in advance online (http://ticket.aeroportbeauvais.com), at the airport from Ryanair (☎ 03 44 11 41 41) and at a kiosk in the carpark. Only plane ticket holders can board the bus, so leave the farewell troops at home.

BUS

Local Buses

Paris' bus system, operated by RATP (see p393), runs from 5.45am to 8.30pm Monday to Saturday; after that another 20 lines continue until 12.30am. Services are drastically reduced on Sunday and public holidays, when buses run from 7am to 8.30pm. Among many *service en soirée* (evening service) routes – distinct from the Noctilien overnight services described on right – are route 26 between the Gare St-Lazare and Cours de Vincennes via Gare du Nord and Gare de l'Est; route 38 linking Gare du Nord, Châtelet and Porte d'Orléans via blvd St-Michel; route 92 from Gare Montparnasse to place Charles de Gaulle and back via Alma Marceau; and route 95 between Porte de Montmartre and Porte de Vanves via Opéra and St-Germain. The same fares and conditions apply on evening routes as for regular daytime services. Most evening routes finish at around midnight.

Night Buses

Night buses pick up the traffic after the last metro (around 1am Sunday to Thursday, 2.15am Friday and Saturday). Buses depart hourly from 12.30am to 5.30pm. The RATP runs 42 night bus lines on its improved

VOGUÉO

That's the name of Paris' brand-spanking-new river metro *(métro fluvial)*, set to sail along the Seine from the end of June 2008 for an initial two-year trial period.

Navettes (shuttle boats) will yo-yo between Gare d'Austerlitz (Map pp162–3) and the École Vétérinaire de Maisons Alfort, southeast of central Paris in the Val de Marne – a 40-minute journey door to door – and will initially stop at Bibliothèque Nationale de François Mitterrand, 13e (Map pp162–3), Bercy, 12e (Map pp158–9) and Port d'Ivry (Map pp78–9). Boats will run every 20 minutes (every 30 minutes between 10am and 5pm) from 7am to 8.30pm Monday to Friday, and every 30 minutes from 10am to 8pm Saturday and Sunday. One-week Navigo Découverte travel passes will be valid aboard; otherwise pay €3 for a single fare.

Noctilien network (www.noctilien.fr has information, maps and itineraries in English), including direct or semidirect services out to the suburbs. The services pass through the main *gares* (train stations) and cross the major axes of the city before leading out to the suburbs. Many go through Châtelet (rue de Rivoli and blvd Sébastopol). Look for blue N or Noctilien signs at bus stops. There are two circular lines within Paris (the N01 and N02) that link four main train stations, St-Lazare, Gare de l'Est, Gare de Lyon, Montparnasse (but not Châtelet), as well as popular nightspots Bastille, the Champs-Elysées, Pigalle and St-Germain.

The buses are equipped with security surveillance systems linked to local police, and RATP staff members are posted at major points to help passengers. Do remain alert, however, and watch your bags and pockets – especially on weekends when the post-drinking crowd circulates.

Noctilien services are free if you have a Mobilis or Paris Visite (p394) pass for the zones in which you are travelling. Otherwise you pay a certain number of standard €1.50 metro tickets, depending on the length of your journey: the driver can sell you tickets and will explain how many you need to get to your destination.

Tickets & Fares

Short bus rides embracing one or two bus zones cost one metro/bus ticket (€1.50); longer rides require two tickets. Transfers to other buses or the metro are not allowed on the same ticket. Travel to the suburbs costs up to three tickets, depending on the zone. Special tickets valid only on the bus can be purchased from the driver.

Whatever kind of single-journey ticket you have, you must *oblitérer* (cancel) it in the *composteur* (cancelling machine) next to the driver. If you have a Mobilis or Paris Visite (p394) pass, flash it at the driver when you board. Do *not* cancel the magnetic coupon that accompanies your pass.

Long-Distance Buses

Eurolines (Map pp110–11; ☎ 01 43 54 11 99; www.eurolines .fr, in French; 55 rue St-Jacques, 5e; ☉ 9.30am-6.30pm Mon-Fri, 10am-1pm & 2-5pm Sat; Ⓜ Cluny-La Sorbonne), an association of more than 30 national and private bus companies that links Paris with points all over Western and Central Europe, Scandinavia and Morocco, can organise ticket reservations and sales. The Gare Routière Internationale de Paris-Galliéni (Map pp78–9; ☎ 08 92 89 90 91; 28 av du Général de Gaulle; Ⓜ Gallieni), the city's international bus terminal, is in the inner suburb of Bagnolet.

CAR & MOTORCYCLE

The quickest way of turning your stay in Paris into an uninterrupted series of hassles is to drive. If driving the car doesn't destroy your holiday sense of spontaneity, parking the thing certainly will.

Driving

While driving in Paris is nerve-wracking, it's not impossible – except for the faint-hearted or indecisive. The fastest way to get across the city is usually via the blvd Périphérique (Map pp78–9), the ring road that encircles the city.

Hire

You can get a small car (eg a Renault Twingo or Opel Corsa) for one day for no more than €100, including unlimited mileage and insurance. Most of the larger companies have offices throughout Paris and at airports and main train stations, including Gare de Nord (Map pp152–3; Ⓜ Gare de Nord). Several are represented at Aérogare des Invalides (Map pp128–9; Ⓜ Invalides) in the 7e.

Avis (☎ 08 02 05 05 05; www.avis.fr, in French)

Budget (☎ 08 25 00 35 64; www.budget.fr, in French)

Europcar (☎ 08 25 35 83 58; www.europcar.fr, in French)

Hertz (☎ 08 25 88 92 65; www.hertz.fr)

National Citer (☎ 08 25 16 12 12; www.citer.fr)

Sixt (☎ 08 20 00 74 98; www.sixt.fr, in French)

Smaller agencies often offer more-reasonable rates and have several branches throughout Paris. Find a complete list in the *Yellow Pages* (www.pagesjaunes.fr, in French) under 'Location d'Automobiles: Tourisme et Utilitaires'.

ADA (☎ 08 25 16 91 69; www.ada.fr, in French) ADA has a dozen branches in Paris including 8e arrondissement (Map pp140–1; ☎ 01 42 93 65 13; 72 rue de Rome, 8e; M Rome) and 11e arrondissement (Map pp94–5; ☎ 01 48 06 58 13; 34 av de la République, 11e; M Parmentier).

easyCar (www.easycar.com) This budget agency has cars at competitive prices from branches at main train stations including Montparnasse (Map pp124–5; Parking Gaîté, 33 rue du Commandant René Mouchotte, 15e; M Gaîté). Branches are in underground car parks and are fully automated systems; book in advance and fill in the forms online.

Rent A Car Système (☎ 08 91 70 02 00; www.rentacar .fr, in French) Rent A Car has 16 outlets in Paris, including Bercy (Map pp158–9; ☎ 01 43 45 98 99; 79 rue de Bercy, 12e; M Bercy) and 16e arrondissement (Map pp132–3; ☎ 01 42 88 40 04; 84 av de Versailles, 16e; M Mirabeau).

If you've got the urge to look like you've just stepped into (or out of) a black-and-white French film from the 1950s, a motor scooter will fit the bill perfectly.

Free Scoot (Map pp94–5; ☎ 01 44 93 04 03; www.free -scoot.com, in French; 144 blvd Voltaire, 11e; ⏰ 9am-1pm & 2-7pm Mon-Fri; M Voltaire) Rents 50cc scooters per day/24 hours/weekend/week from €30/35/75/145, and 125cc scooters for €45/55/110/245. Prices include third-party insurance as well as two helmets, locks, raingear and gloves. To rent a 50/125cc scooter you must be at least 21/23 and leave a credit card deposit of €1300/1600. Freescoot runs a seasonal branch in the 5e arrondissement (Map pp110–11; ☎ 01 44 07 06 72; 63 quai de la Tournelle, 5e; ⏰ 9am-1pm & 2-7pm Mon-Sat mid-Apr–mid-Sep; M Maubert Mutualité).

Parking

In most parts of Paris, street parking costs €1 to €3 an hour and is limited to a maximum of two hours. Municipal public car parks, of which there are 140 in Paris, charge between €1.70 and €2.80 an hour or €20 to €25 per 24 hours. Most open 24 hours.

Parking attendants dispense fines ranging from €11 to €35, depending on the offence

and its gravity, with great abandon. To pay a fine, buy a *timbre amende* (fine stamp) for the amount written on the ticket from any *tabac* (tobacconist), stick a stamp on the preaddressed coupon and post it in a postbox.

METRO & RER NETWORKS

Paris' underground network, run by RATP (Régie Autonome des Transports Parisians), consists of two separate but linked systems: the Métropolitain, aka the *métro*, with 14 lines and 373 stations (one more will open in 2008 and another in 2010); and the RER (Réseau Express Régional), a network of suburban lines (designated A to E and then numbered) that pass through the city centre. When giving the names of stations in this book, the term 'metro' is used to cover both the Métropolitain and the RER system within Paris proper.

Information

Metro maps of various sizes and degrees of detail are available for free at metro ticket windows; several can also be downloaded for free from the highly informative, comprehensive and useful RATP website (www.ratp.fr).

For information on the metro, RER and bus systems, contact RATP (☎ 3246, 0 892 693 246; www.ratp.fr, in French; ⏰ 7am-9pm Mon-Fri, 9am-5pm Sat & Sun).

Metro

Each metro train is known by the name of its terminus. On maps and plans each line has a different colour and number (from 1 to 14); Parisians usually refer to the line number.

Signs in metro and RER stations indicate the way to the correct platform for your line. The *direction* signs on each platform indicate the terminus. On lines that split into several branches (like lines 3, 7 and 13), the terminus of each train is indicated on the cars with backlit panels, and often on the increasingly common electronic signs on each platform giving the number of minutes until the next train.

Signs marked *correspondance* (transfer) show how to reach connecting trains. At stations with many intersecting lines, like Châtelet and Montparnasse Bienvenüe, walking from one train to the next can take a long time.

Different station exits are indicated by white-on-blue *sortie* (exit) signs. You can get your bearings by checking the *plan du quartier* (neighbourhood maps) posted at exits.

Each line has its own schedule, but trains usually start at around 5.30am, with the last train beginning its run between 12.35am and 1am (2.15am on Friday and Saturday).

RER

The RER is faster than the metro but the stops are much further apart. Some attractions, particularly those on the Left Bank (eg the Musée d'Orsay, Eiffel Tower and Panthéon), can be reached far more conveniently by the RER than by the metro.

RER lines are known by an alphanumeric combination – the letter (A to E) refers to the line, the number to the spur it will follow somewhere out in the suburbs. As a rule of thumb, even-numbered RER lines head for Paris' southern or eastern suburbs, while odd-numbered ones go north or west. All trains whose four-letter codes (indicated both on the train and on the lightboard) begin with the same letter share the same terminus. Stations served are usually indicated on electronic destination boards above the platform.

Tickets & Fares

The same RATP tickets are valid on the metro, the RER (for travel within the city limits), buses, trams and the Montmartre funicular. A ticket – white in colour and called *un ticket* – costs €1.50 if bought individually and €11.10 for adults (half-price for children aged four to nine years for a *carnet* (book) of 10. Tickets are sold at all metro stations; ticket windows and vending machines accept most credit cards.

One metro/bus ticket lets you travel between any two metro stations (no return journeys) for a period of 1½ hours, no matter how many transfers are required. You can also use it on the RER for travel within zone 1. A single ticket can be used to transfer between buses, but not to transfer from the metro to bus or vice-versa.

Always keep your ticket until you exit from your station; you may be stopped by a *contrôleur* (ticket inspector) and will have to pay a fine (€25 to €50 on the spot or €47 to €72 within two months) if you don't have a valid ticket.

TRAVEL PASSES

If you're staying a week or more, the cheapest and easiest way to use public transport in Paris is to get a combined travel pass that allows unlimited travel on the metro, RER and buses for a week, a month or a year. You can get passes for travel in two to eight urban and suburban

zones but, unless you'll be using the suburban commuter lines extensively, the basic ticket valid for zones 1 and 2 should be sufficient.

The Navigo system (www.navigo.fr, in French), like London's Oyster or Hong Kong's Octopus cards, provides you with a refillable weekly, monthly or yearly unlimited pass that you can recharge at Navigo machines in most metro stations; swipe the card across the electronic panel as you go through the turnstiles. Standard Navigo passes, available to anyone with an address in Paris, are free but take up to three weeks to be issued; ask at the ticket counter for a form. Otherwise pay €5 for a Nagivo Découverte, issued on the spot but – unlike the Navigo pass – not replaceable if lost or stolen. Both passes require a passport photo and can be recharged for periods of one week or more.

A weekly ticket *(coupon hebdomadaire)* pass costs €16.30 for zones 1 and 2 and is valid from Monday to Sunday. It can be purchased from the previous Thursday until Wednesday; from Thursday weekly tickets are available for the following week only. Even if you're in Paris for three or four days, it may work out cheaper than buying carnets and will certainly cost less than buying a daily Mobilis or Paris Visite pass (see below). The monthly ticket *(coupon mensuel*; €53.50 for zones 1 and 2) begins on the first day of each calendar month; you can buy one from the 20th of the preceding month. Both are sold in metro and RER stations from 6.30am to 10pm and at some bus terminals.

TOURIST PASSES

The Mobilis and Paris Visite passes are valid on the metro, RER, SNCF's suburban lines (opposite), buses, night buses, trams and Montmartre funicular railway. No photo is needed, but write your card number on the ticket. Passes are sold at larger metro and RER stations, SNCF offices in Paris, and the airports.

The Mobilis card coupon allows unlimited travel for one day in two/three/four/five/six zones and costs €5.60/7.50/9.30/12.50/15.90. Buy it at any metro, RER or SNCF station in the Paris region. Depending on how many times you plan to hop on/off the metro in a day, a *carnet* might work out cheaper.

Paris Visite allows unlimited travel (including to/from airports) as well as discounted entry to certain museums and other discounts and bonuses. Passes are valid for either three, five or eight zones. The zone 1 to 3 pass costs €8.50/14/19/27.50 for one/two/three/five days. Children aged four to 11 years pay €4.25/7/9.50/13.75.

TAXI

The *prise en charge* (flagfall) is €2.10. Within the city limits, it costs €0.82 per kilometre for travel between 10am and 5pm Monday to Saturday (*Tarif A*; white light on meter). At night (5pm to 10am), on Sunday from 7am to midnight, and in the inner suburbs the rate is €1.10 per km (*Tarif B*; orange light on meter). Travel in the outer suburbs is at *Tarif C*, €1.33 per kilometre. There's a €2.75 surcharge for taking a fourth passenger, but drivers often refuse for insurance reasons. The first piece of baggage is free; additional pieces over 5kg cost €1 extra. When tipping, round up to the nearest €1.

Flagging down one of Paris' 15,500-odd licensed taxis can be hard, particularly after 1am. Some 'freelance' (illegal) taxis nip around town but are not organised (like minicabs are in London) and offer no guarantee on price or safety.

To order a taxi, call Paris' central taxi switchboard (☎ 01 45 30 30 30, passengers with reduced mobility 01 47 39 00 91; ☺ 24hrs) or reserve online with Alpha Taxis (☎ 01 45 85 85 85; www.alphataxis.com), Taxis Bleus (☎ 01 49 36 29 48, 08 91 70 10 10; www.taxis-bleus.com) or Taxis G7 (☎ 01 47 39 47 39; www.taxisq7.fr, in French).

TRAIN
Suburban

The RER and the commuter lines of the SNCF (Société Nationale des Chemins de Fer; ☎ 08 91 36 20 20, 08 91 67 68 69 for timetables; www.sncf.fr) serve suburban destinations outside the city limits (ie zones 2 to 8). Purchase your ticket *before* you board the train or you won't be able to get out of the station when you arrive. You are not allowed to pay the additional fare when you get there.

If you are issued with a full-sized SNCF ticket for travel to the suburbs, validate it in one of the time-stamp pillars *before* you board the train. You may also be given a *contremarque magnétique* (magnetic ticket) to get through any metro-/RER-type turnstiles on the way to/from the platform. If you are travelling on a Mobilis or Paris Visite (opposite) pass, do *not* punch the magnetic coupon in one of the time-stamp machines. Most but not all RER/SNCF tickets purchased in the suburbs for travel to the city allow you to continue your journey by metro. For some destinations, tickets can be purchased at any metro ticket window; for others you have to go to an RER station on the line you need to buy a ticket.

Mainline & International

Thanks to very fast TGV (*train à grande vitesse*) trains, of which the French are inordinately proud, many of the most exciting and scenic cities in provincial France are all within a few hours of the capital from one of six major train stations, each with its own metro station: Gare d'Austerlitz (13e), Gare de l'Est (10e), Gare de Lyon (12e), Gare du Nord (10e), Gare Montparnasse (15e) and Gare St-Lazare (8e). Each station handles passenger traffic to different parts of France and Europe. Information for SNCF mainline services (☎ 36 35, 08 92 35 35 35; www.voyages-sncf.com) is available by phone or internet.

The super-speedy Eurostar (☎ 08 36 35 35 39; in UK 0875 186 186; www.eurostar.com) links Gare du Nord with London's sizzling new St-Pancras International train station in a lightening two hours and not much longer with dozens of other regional stations in the UK; through-ticketing to/from Paris and 68 regional stations in the UK is now possible. Gare du Nord is likewise the point of departure/terminus for Thalys (☎ 36 35, 08 92 35 35 36; www.thalys.com) trains to Brussels, Amsterdam and Cologne.

Mainline stations in Paris have left-luggage offices or lockers (*consignes*). They cost €4/7.50/9.50 per 48 hours for a small/medium/large bag, then €5 per day per item. Most left-luggage offices and lockers open from around 6am to 11pm.

TRAM & FUNICULAR

Paris has three tram lines (www.tramway.paris.fr, in French), although the majority of visitors are unlikely to use them: T1 links the northern suburb of St-Denis with Noisy le Sec on RER line E2 via metro Bobigny Pablo Picasso on metro line 5; T2 runs south along the Seine from La Défense to the Issy Val de Seine RER station on line C; and T3 traces a 7.9km-long curve around the southern edge of Paris from Point to Garigliano (15e), through Porte de Versailles (where it links with the T2), Porte d'Orléans, Porte d'Italie and up to Porte d'Ivry. Normal metro tickets and passes remain valid here and function in the same way as on the buses. Buy tickets at automatic machines at each tram stop.

One form of transport that most travellers will use is the Montmartre funicular, which whisks visitors up the southern slope of Butte de Montmartre from square Willette (metro Anvers) to Sacré Cœur.

BUSINESS HOURS

Small businesses are open daily, except Sunday and sometimes Monday. Hours are usually 9am or 10am to 6.30pm or 7pm, often with a midday break from 1pm to 2pm or 2.30pm. Shops that open Monday usually get started late (eg at 11.30am).

Banks usually open from 8am or 9am to between 11.30am and 1pm, and then 1.30pm or 2pm to 4.30pm or 5pm, Monday to Friday or Tuesday to Saturday. Exchange services may end 30 minutes before closing time.

Most post offices open 8am to 7pm weekdays and 8am or 9am till noon on Saturday.

Supermarkets open Monday to Saturday from 8.30/9am to 8pm, though a few now open on Sunday morning as well. Small food shops are mostly closed on Sunday and often Monday too, so Saturday afternoon may be your last chance to stock up on certain types of food (eg cheese) until Tuesday.

Restaurants keep the most convoluted hours of any business in Paris; for details see p228.

Most museums are closed one day a week: usually Monday or Tuesday. Some museums have a weekly *nocturne* in which they remain open until as late as 10pm one night a week, including the Louvre (Wednesday and Friday) and the Musée d'Orsay (Thursday).

CHILDREN

Paris is extraordinarily kid-friendly. Be it playing tag around Daniel Buren's black and white columns at Palais Royal (p88), laughing with puppets in Jardin de Luxembourg (p119), sailing down the Seine (p407) or resting little legs with a city sightseeing tour via one of its two above-ground metro lines (2 and 6), there really does seem to be a cheap childish pleasure around every corner here.

Some restaurants serve a *menu enfant* (set children's menu), usually for children under 12, though often starters or the savoury crêpes served in neighbourhood brasseries are more imaginative *(steak haché* and fries gets tiresome after two days). *Cafétérias* (p226) are a good place to bring kids if you just want to feed and water them fast and cheaply, as are French chain restaurants (p229).

Kids aged between six and 12 and keen to cook and consume their own creations can do so at Alef-Bet (p249).

Information

Pariscope and *L'Officiel des Spectacles* (p302) both have decent 'Enfants' sections covering the week's shows, theatre performances and circuses for kids. Online see the exhaustive site, www.cityjunior.com (in French).

The newspaper *Libération* (p54) produces an English translation of its bimonthly supplement *Paris Mômes* (www.parismomes.fr, in French) called *Paris with Kids*. It has listings and other useful information aimed at kids up to age 12; focusing on the 'unusual' is its philosophy.

Lonely Planet's *Travel with Children* by Cathy Lanigan includes useful advice for travelling parents.

Sights & Activities

Many museums organise educational, fun-packed *ateliers enfants* (kids' workshops) for children from aged four or six and upwards. Sessions cost €3 to €10, last a couple of hours, and must be booked in advance; some are in English. Favourites include hands-on art workshops at Les Arts Décoratifs (p84), Musée de la Halle St-Pierre (p171), Musée d'Orsay (p130), Palais de Tokyo (p135) and Centre Pompidou (p88); money- and medal-making at the Musée de la Monnaie de Paris (p120); meeting marine life at the Centre de la Mer (p109); learning about animals with activities and film at the Musée National d'Histoire Naturelle (p113); and calligraphy, Arab music and mosaics at the Institut du Arabe Monde (p112).

Building an Eiffel Tower, Parisian church or entire village from thousands of miniature wooden planks is what kids do at the innovative Centre Kapla (Map pp152–3; ☎ 01 43 56 13 38; www .kapla.com/centre_kapla.html; 27 rue de Montreuil, 11e; sessions €10; ☉ 10.30am-6pm Wed, Sat & school holidays; Ⓜ Faidherbe-Chaligny). It runs three 1½ hour building sessions daily; book in advance.

Around Paris, the mesmerising equestrian displays and stable visits at Versailles (p360) and Chantilly (p373) make magical half-day trips; the Disney (p384) and Astérix theme parks (p385) need at least a full day.

See the Neighbourhoods chapter for details on the following suggestions:

Children's Playgrounds Port de Plaisance de Paris-Arsenal (Map pp158–9; 4e; Ⓜ Bastille); Jardin du Luxembourg (Map pp116–17; 6e; Ⓜ Luxembourg); Square Willette (Map p169; Montmartre, 18e; Ⓜ Anvers)

CineAqua (Map pp132–3; 2 av des Nations Unies, 16e; Ⓜ Trocadéro)

Cité de la Musique (Map pp174–5; 221 av Jean Jaurès, 19e; Ⓜ Porte de Pantin) Saturday-morning educational concerts, music discovery workshops, concerts and shows for children.

Cité des Sciences et de l'Industrie (Map pp174–5; Parc de la Villette, 19e; Ⓜ Porte de la Villette) Including the Géode, Cinaxe and planetarium.

Eiffel Tower (Map pp132–3; Parc du Champ de Mars, 7e; Ⓜ Champ de Mars-Tour Eiffel)

Exploradôme & Jardin d'Acclimatation (Map p178; Bois de Boulogne; Ⓜ Les Sablons) Interactive science, art and multimedia; plus a funfair to fill a day.

Ménagerie du Jardin des Plantes (Map pp110–11; Jardin des Plantes, 5e; Ⓜ Jussieu or Gare d'Austerlitz) Near the Musée National d'Histoire Naturelle.

Musée de la Curiosité et de la Magie (Map pp92–3; 11 rue St-Paul, 4e; Ⓜ St-Paul) Magic shows.

Palais de la Découverte (Map pp140–1; Champs-Élysées, 8e; Ⓜ Champs-Élysées Clemenceau)

Parc Zoologique de Paris (Map p177; Bois de Vincennes; Ⓜ Porte Dorée)

Babysitting

L'Officiel des Spectacles (p302) lists *gardes d'enfants* (baby-sitters) available in Paris.

Au Paradis des Petits (☎ 01 43 65 58 58) From €7 per hour (€10 subscription fee).

Baby Sitting Services (☎ 01 46 21 33 16) From €6.80 per hour (€11.90 subscription), €60 for 10 hours or one day.

Étudiants de l'Institut Catholique (Map pp116–17; ☎ 01 44 39 60 24; 21 rue d'Assas, 6e; Ⓜ Rennes) From €7.50 per hour (plus €2 for each session).

Fondation Claude Pompidou (☎ 01 40 13 75 00) Specialises in looking after children with disabilities.

CLIMATE

The Paris basin lies midway between coastal Brittany and mountainous Alsace and is affected by both climates. The Île de France region, of which Paris is the centre, records among the lowest annual precipitation (about

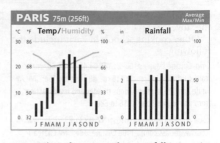

640mm) in the nation, but rainfall is erratic; you're just as likely to be caught in a heavy spring shower or an autumn downpour as in a sudden summer cloudburst. Paris' average yearly temperature is just under 12°C (2°C in January, 19°C in July), but the mercury sometimes drops below zero in winter and can climb into the 30s in the middle of summer.

You can find out the weather forecast in French for the Paris area by calling ☎ 0 892 680 275. The national forecast can be heard on ☎ 0 899 701 234 in French or ☎ 0 899 701 111 in one of 11 different languages. Call charges for either number are €1.35 then €0.35 per minute. Another number (French only) is ☎ 3250 charged at €0.34 per minute. The summary can also be read for free on the website of Météo France (www.meteofrance.com, in French).

COURSES
Cooking

What better place to discover the secrets of *la cuisine française* than in Paris, the capital of gastronomy? Courses are available at different levels and lengths of time and the cost of tuition varies widely. One of the most popular – and affordable – for beginners is the Les Coulisses du Chef Cours de Cuisine Olivier Berté (Map pp82–3; ☎ 01 40 26 14 00; www.coursdecuisineparis .com; 2nd fl, 7 rue Paul Lelong, 2e; Ⓜ Bourse), which offers three-hour courses (adult/12 to 14 years €100/30) at 10.30am from Wednesday to Saturday with an additional class from 6pm to 9pm on Friday. 'Carnets' of five/20 courses cost €440/1500.

Much more expensive are the Paris Cooking Classes with Patricia Wells (www.patriciawells.com; US$5000) led by the incomparable American food critic and author at her cooking studio in rue Jacob, 6e. The class runs from Monday to Friday, is limited to seven participants and includes market visits, tastings, local transport and daily lunch. See the boxed text on p213. For information about getting the kids in front of the stove, see p249.

Other cooking schools in Paris include the following:

Coin-Cuisine (Map pp166–7; ☎ 01 45 79 01 40; www .coin-cuisine.fr, in French; 110 rue du Théatre, 15e; M Av Émile Zola) Courses of various themes and levels lasting from one to four hours (€16 to €80).

Cook'n with Class (Map p169; ☎ 06 31 73 62 77; www .cooknwithclass.com; 21 rue Custine, 18e; M Château Rouge) Morning/evening/full-day classes available for €135/135/200.

École Le Cordon Bleu (Map pp166–7; ☎ 01 53 68 22 50; www.cordonbleu.edu; 8 rue Léon Delhomme, 15e; M Vaugirard or Convention) Dating back to 1895, the Cordon Bleu school has professional courses as well as one-day themed workshops (€160) on topics like terrines and *viennoiserie* (baked goods), and two- (€299) and four-day courses (€869) on classic and modern sauces and the secrets of bread and pastry making.

École Ritz Escoffier (Map pp82–3; ☎ 01 43 16 30 50; www.ritzescoffier.com; 15 place Vendôme, 1er M Concorde) This prestigious cooking school is based in what is arguably Paris' finest hotel (though you also enter from 38 rue Cambon, 1er). A four-hour Saturday themed workshop (petits fours, truffles, carving fruit and vegetables, pairing food and wine etc) costs €135; a two-day introductory course is €920.

Language

All manner of French-language courses, lasting from two weeks to a full academic year, are available in Paris, and many places begin new courses every month or so.

Alliance Française (Map pp116–17; ☎ 01 42 84 90 00; www.alliancefr.org; 101 blvd Raspail, 6e; 🕑 8.30am-7pm Mon & Tue, 8.30am-6pm Wed-Fri; M St-Placide) French courses (minimum two weeks) at all levels begin every two weeks; registration (€55) takes place five days before. *Intensif* courses meet for four hours a day, start at 9am and 1.30pm and cost from €400/700 for two weeks/one month; *extensif* courses involve three hours of class for three days a week, start at the same two times and cost from €176/332.

Cours de Langue et Civilisation Françaises de la Sorbonne (Map pp110–11; ☎ 01 44 10 77 00, 01 40 46 22 11; www.ccfs-sorbonne.fr; Galerie Richelieu, office C391, 17 rue de la Sorbonne, 5e; 🕑 10am-noon & 2-4pm Mon-Fri; M Cluny La Sorbonne or Maubert Mutualité) The Sorbonne's prestigious French Language and Civilisation Course has courses for all levels. A four-week summer course starts at €530, while 20 hours a week of lectures and tutorials costs €1300 per semester. Instructors take a very academic (though solid) approach to language teaching.

Eurocentres (Map pp116–17; ☎ 01 40 46 72 00; www .eurocentres.com; 13 passage Dauphine, 6e; 🕑 8.15am-6pm Mon-Fri; M Odéon) Intensive courses lasting two/four weeks with 10 to 14 participants cost from €660/1272. New courses begin every two, three or four weeks.

Inlingua (Map pp128–9; ☎ 01 45 51 46 60; www .inlingua-paris.com; 109 rue de l'Université, 7e; 🕑 7.30am-8.15pm Mon-Fri, 9am-1.30pm Sat; M Invalides) Individual and group lessons for all levels, from 'first contacts' through to that linguistic state we all aspire to, 'full control'. It has seven centres, including in La Défense and Versailles. French lessons for kids too.

Institut Parisien de Langue et de Civilisation Françaises (Map pp140–1; ☎ 01 40 56 09 53; www .institut-parisien.com; 2nd fl, 29 rue de Lisbonne, 8e; 🕑 8.30am-5pm Mon-Fri; M Monceau) Four-week courses with a maximum of 10 students per class cost €148/222/296/370 for 10/15/20/25 hours a week plus an enrolment fee of €40.

Langue Onze (Map pp94–5; ☎ 01 43 38 22 87; www .langueonzeparis.com; 15 rue Gambey, 11e; 🕑 11am-5pm Mon-Fri; M Parmentier) Well-received independent language school with two-/four-week intensive courses of four hours' instruction a day for €390/630; evening classes (four hours a week) start at €175 for four weeks. Classes have a maximum of nine students.

CUSTOMS REGULATIONS

Duty-free shopping within the EU was abolished in 1999; you cannot, for example, buy tax-free goods in, say, France and take them to the UK. However, you can still enter an EU country with duty-free items from countries *outside* the EU (eg Australia, the USA) where the usual allowances apply: 200 cigarettes, 50 cigars or 250g of loose tobacco; 2L of still wine and 1L of spirits; 50g of perfume and 250cc of eau de toilette.

Do not confuse these with *duty-paid* items (including alcohol and tobacco) bought at normal shops in another EU country (eg Spain or Germany) and brought into France, where certain goods might be more expensive. Here allowances are generous: 800 cigarettes, 200 cigars, 400 small cigars or 1kg of loose tobacco; and 10L of spirits (more than 22% alcohol by volume), 20L of fortified wine or *aperitif*, 90L of wine or 110L of beer.

DISCOUNT CARDS

Museums, the national rail service SNCF (Société Nationale des Chemins de Fer), ferry companies and other institutions give discounts to those aged under 26 (ie holders of the International Youth Travel Card, IYTC), students with an International Student Identity Card (ISIC; age limits may apply) and *le troisième age* (usually those aged over 60). Look for the words *tarif réduit* (reduced rate) or *demi-tarif* (half-price tariff) and then ask if you qualify. Those under 18 years of age get an even wider range of discounts, including free admission to the *musées nationaux* (national museums). Some 22 museums are free on the first Sunday of every month, though not necessarily year-round. For specifics, see p102.

The Paris Museum Pass (www.parismuseumpass.fr; 2/4/6 days €30/45/60) is valid for entry to some 38 venues in Paris – including the Louvre, Centre Pompidou, Musée d'Orsay as well as the Musée du Quai Branly and Cité de l'Architecture et du Patrimoine. Outside the city limits but still within the Île de France region, it will get you into another 22 places, including the basilica at St-Denis (p182) and parts of the chateaux at Versailles (p360) and Fontainebleau (p368). The pass is conveniently available online as well as from the participating venues, branches of the Paris Convention & Visitors Bureau (p411), Fnac outlets (p302), RATP (Régie Autonome des Transports Parisiens) information desks and major metro stations.

ELECTRICITY

France runs on 220V at 50Hz AC. Plugs are the standard European type with two round pins. French outlets often have an earth (ground) pin in which case you may have to have a French adapter to use a two-pin European plug. The best place for adapters and other electrical goods is the Bazar de l'Hôtel de Ville (p203) department store near Hôtel de Ville or any branch of the electronics chain Darty (☎ 0 821 082 082; www.darty.fr, in French; ☒ 10am-7.30pm Mon-Sat), which has a République branch (Map pp92–3) 1 av de la République, 11e; Ⓜ République) and a Ternes branch (Map pp144–5; 8 av des Ternes, 17e; Ⓜ Ternes).

EMBASSIES
French Embassies & Consulates

Almost all of the French embassies and consulates listed following have information posted on the internet at www.france.diplomatie.fr.

Australia embassy (☎ 02-6216 0100; www.ambafrance-au.org; 6 Perth Ave, Yarralumla, ACT 26000); consulate (☎ 02-9268 2400; www.ambafrance-au.org; 26th fl, St Martin's Tower, 31 Market St, Sydney, NSW 2000)

Belgium embassy (☎ 02-548 8700; www.ambafrance-be.org; 65 rue Ducale, 1000 Brussels); consulate (☎ 02-548 8811; www.ambafrance-be.org; 42 blvd du Régent, 1000 Brussels)

Canada embassy (☎ 613-789 1795; www.ambafrance-ca.org; 42 Sussex Dr, Ottawa, Ont K1M 2C9); consulate (☎ 416-847 1900; www.consulfrance-toronto.org; Suite 2200, 2 Bloor St East, Toronto, Ont M4W 1A8)

Germany embassy (☎ 030-590 03 90 00; www.ambafrance-de.org; Parizer Platz 5, 10117 Berlin); consulate (☎ 069-795 09 60; www.consulatfrance.de/francfort; Zeppelinallee 35 60325 Frankfurt am Main)

Ireland embassy (☎ 01-277 5000; www.ambafrance-ie.org; 36 Ailesbury Rd, Ballsbridge, Dublin 4)

Italy embassy (☎ 06-686 011; www.ambafrance-it.org; Piazza Farnese 67, 00186 Rome); consulate (☎ 06-686 011; www.ambafrance-it.org; Via Giulia 251, 00186 Rome)

Netherlands embassy (☎ 070-312 58 00; www.ambafrance-nl.org; Smidsplein 1, 2514 BT The Hague); consulate (☎ 020-530 69 69; www.consulfrance-amsterdam.org; Vijzelgracht 2, 1000 HR Amsterdam)

New Zealand embassy (☎ 04-384 2555; www.ambafrance-nz.org; 13th fl, Rural Bank Bldg, 34-42 Manners St, Wellington)

South Africa embassy Apr-Jan (☎ 012-425 1600; www.ambafrance-rsa.org; 250 Melk St, New Muckleneuk, 0181 Pretoria); embassy Feb-Mar (☎ 021-422 1338; www.ambafrance-za.org; 78 Queen Victoria St, 8001 Cape Town)

Spain embassy (☎ 91-423 8900; www.ambafrance-es.org; Calle de Salustiano Olozaga 9, 28001 Madrid); consulate (☎ 93-270 3000; www.consulfrance-barcelone.org; Ronda Universitat 22b, 08007 Barcelona)

Switzerland embassy (☎ 031-359 2111; www.consulfrance-geneve.org; Schlosshaldenstrasse 46, 3006 Berne); consulate (☎ 01-268 8585; www.consulatfrance-zurich.org; Signaustrasse 1, 8008 Zürich)

UK embassy (☎ 020-7073 1000; www.ambafrance-uk.org; 58 Knightsbridge, London SW1X 7JT); consulate (☎ 020-7073 1200; www.consulfrance-londres.org; 21 Cromwell Rd, London SW7 2EN)

USA embassy (☎ 202-944 6000; www.ambafrance-us.org; 4101 Reservoir Rd NW, Washington, DC 20007); consulate (☎ 212-606 3600; www.consulfrance-newyork.org; 934 Fifth Ave, New York, NY 10021)

Embassies & Consulates in Paris

It's important to realise what your own embassy – the embassy of the country of which you are a citizen – can and cannot do to help you if you're in trouble. In general, it won't be much help if the trouble you're in is even remotely your own fault. Remember that you are bound by French law while visiting Paris. Your embassy will not be sympathetic if you commit a crime locally, even if such actions are legal in your own country.

In genuine emergencies you might get some assistance, but only if other channels have been exhausted. For example, if you need to get home urgently, a free ticket home is exceedingly unlikely – the embassy would expect you to have insurance. If you have all your money and documents stolen, it might assist with getting a new passport, but a loan for onward travel is usually out of the question.

The following is a list of selected embassies and consulates in Paris. For a more complete list, consult the *Pages Jaunes* (Yellow Pages; www.pagesjaunes.fr, in French) under 'Ambassades et Consulats' or the website of the tourist office (www.parisinfo.com).

Australia embassy (Map pp166–7; ☎ 01 40 59 33 00; 4 rue Jean Rey, 15e; Ⓜ Bir Hakeim)

Belgium embassy (Map pp140–1; ☎ 01 44 09 39 39; 9 rue de Tilsitt, 17e; Ⓜ Charles de Gaulle-Étoile)

Canada embassy (Map pp140–1; ☎ 01 44 43 29 00; 35 av Montaigne, 8e; Ⓜ Franklin D Roosevelt)

Germany embassy (Map pp140–1; ☎ 01 53 83 45 00; 13-15 av Franklin D Roosevelt, 8e; Ⓜ Franklin D Roosevelt); consulate (Map pp132–3; ☎ 01 53 83 46 70; 28 rue Marbeau, 16e; Ⓜ Porte Maillot)

Ireland embassy (Map pp132–3; ☎ 01 44 17 67 00; 4 rue Rude, 16e; Ⓜ Argentine)

Italy embassy (Map pp128–9; ☎ 01 49 54 03 00; 47-51 rue de Varenne, 7e; Ⓜ Rue du Bac); consulate (Map pp132–3; ☎ 01 44 30 47 00; 5 blvd Émile Augier, 16e; Ⓜ La Muette)

Japan embassy (Map pp140–1; ☎ 01 48 88 62 00; 7 av Hoche, 8e; Ⓜ Courcelles)

Netherlands embassy (Map pp128–9; ☎ 01 40 62 33 00; 7 rue Eblé, 7e; Ⓜ St-François Xavier)

New Zealand embassy (Map pp132–3; ☎ 01 45 00 24 11; 7ter rue Léonard de Vinci, 16e; Ⓜ Victor Hugo)

South Africa embassy (Map pp128–9; ☎ 01 53 59 23 23; 59 quai d'Orsay, 7e; Ⓜ Invalides)

Spain embassy (Map pp140-1; ☎ 01 44 43 18 00; 22 av Marceau, 8e; Ⓜ Alma-Marceau)

Switzerland embassy (Map pp128–9; ☎ 01 49 55 67 00; 142 rue de Grenelle, 7e; Ⓜ Varenne); consulate (Map pp166–7; ☎ 01 45 66 00 80; 13 rue du Laos, 15e)

UK embassy (Map pp140-1; ☎ 01 44 51 31 00; 35 rue du Faubourg St-Honoré, 8e; Ⓜ Concorde); consulate (Map pp140-1; ☎ 01 44 51 31 02; 18bis rue d'Anjou, 8e; Ⓜ Concorde)

USA embassy (pp140-1; ☎ 01 43 12 22 22; 2 av Gabriel, 8e; Ⓜ Concorde); consulate (Map pp82-3; ☎ 0 810 264 626; 2 rue St-Florentin, 1er; Ⓜ Concorde)

EMERGENCY

The following numbers are to be dialled in an emergency. See p403 for hospitals with 24-hour accident and emergency departments.

Ambulance (SAMU; ☎ 15)

EU-wide emergency hotline (☎ 112)

Fire brigade (☎ 18)

Police (☎ 17)

Rape crisis hotline (Viols Femmes Informations; ☎ 0 800 05 95 95; ⏱ 10am-7pm Mon-Fri)

SOS Helpline (☎ 01 47 23 80 80; ⏱ in English 3-11pm daily)

SOS Médecins (☎ 01 47 07 77 77, 24hr house calls 0 820 33 24 24; www.sosmedecins-france.fr)

Urgences Médicales de Paris (Paris Medical Emergencies; ☎ 01 53 94 94 94; www.ump.fr, in French)

Lost Property

All objects found anywhere in Paris – except those picked up on trains or in train stations – are brought to the city's Bureau des Objets Trouvés (Lost Property Office; Map pp166–7; ☎ 0 821 00 25 25; www .prefecture-police-paris.interieur.gouv.fr/demarches/article/service_objets_trouves.htm, in French; 36 rue des Morillons, 15e; ⏱ 8.30am-5pm Mon-Thu, 8.30am-4.30pm Fri; Ⓜ Convention), which is run by the Préfecture de Police. Since telephone enquiries are impossible, the only way to find out if a lost item has been located is to go there and fill in the forms in person.

Items lost on the metro are held by station agents (☎ 3246; ⏱ 7am-9pm Mon-Fri, 9am-5pm Sat & Sun) before being sent to the Bureau des Objets Trouvés. Anything found on trains or stations is taken to the lost-property office (usually attached to the left-luggage office) of the relevant station. Phone enquiries (in French) are possible:

Gare d'Austerlitz (☎ 01 53 60 71 98)

Gare de l'Est (☎ 01 40 18 88 73)

Gare de Lyon (☎ 01 53 33 67 22)

Gare du Nord (☎ 01 55 31 58 40)

Gare Montparnasse (☎ 01 40 48 14 24)

Gare St-Lazare (☎ 01 53 42 05 57)

HOLIDAYS

There is at least one public holiday a month in France and, in some years, up to four in the month of May alone. Be aware, though, that unlike in the USA or UK, where public holidays usually fall on (or are shifted to) a Monday, in France a *jour férié* (public holiday) is celebrated strictly on the day on which it falls. Thus if May Day falls on a Saturday or Sunday, no provision is made for an extra day off.

The following holidays are observed in Paris:

New Year's Day (Jour de l'An) 1 January

Easter Sunday & Monday (Pâques & Lundi de Pâques) Late March/April

May Day (Fête du Travail) 1 May

Victory in Europe Day (Victoire 1945) 8 May

Ascension Thursday (L'Ascension) May (celebrated on the 40th day after Easter)

Pentecost/Whit Sunday & Whit Monday (Pentecôte & Lundi de Pentecôte) Mid-May to mid-June (Seventh Sunday and Monday after Easter)

Bastille Day/National Day (Fête Nationale) 14 July

Assumption Day (L'Assomption) 15 August

All Saints' Day (La Toussaint) 1 November

Armistice Day/Remembrance Day (Le Onze Novembre) 11 November

Christmas (Noël) 25 December

INSURANCE

A travel insurance policy to cover theft, loss and medical problems is a good idea. There is a wide variety of policies available, so check the small print. EU citizens on public-health insurance schemes should note that they're generally covered by reciprocal arrangements in France.

You may prefer a policy which pays doctors or hospitals directly rather than you having to pay on the spot and then claim it back later. If you have to claim later make sure you keep all documentation. Ensure that your policy covers ambulances or an emergency flight home.

Paying for your airline ticket with a credit card often provides limited travel accident insurance, and you may be able to reclaim the payment if the operator doesn't deliver. Ask your credit card company what it's prepared to cover.

INTERNET ACCESS

Paris has a surfeit of internet cafés. Among the biggest, best and/or most central:

Baby Connect (Map pp116–17; ☎ 01 40 62 98 00; 56 rue de Babylone, 7e; per 15/30/60min €1/2/4; ⏰ 10am-8pm Mon-Sat; Ⓜ St-François Xavier) Very near La Pagode cinema.

Cyber Cube (Map pp124–5; ☎ 01 56 80 08 08; www .cybercube.fr; 9 rue d'Odessa, 14e; per 15/30min €1/2, per 5/10hr €30/40; ⏰ 10am-10pm; Ⓜ Montparnasse Bienvenüe) One of three branches; expensive but convenient to Gare Montparnasse.

Cyber Latin (Map pp116–17; ☎ 01 42 22 89 35; 35bis rue de Fleurus, 6e; per 15/30/60min €1.25/2.25/4, per 5/10/20hr €17/34/56; ⏰ 9.30am-7.30pm Mon-Fri, 11.30am-7.30pm Sat; Ⓜ St-Placide) Just west of the Jardin du Luxembourg.

Cyber Squ@re (Map pp92–3; ☎ 01 48 87 82 36; info@ cybersquare-paris.com; 1 place de la République; per 5/15/30/60min €0.75/2.30/3.80/6, per 10/20hr €45/76; ⏰ 10am-8pm Mon-Sat; Ⓜ République) This small but convivial place on two levels is entered from passage Vendôme.

Manga Square (Map p86; 28 blvd de Sébastopol, 4e; per 1hr €3, per 5/10 hr €15/27.50; ⏰ 1-10pm; Ⓜ Les Halles) Groovy cyber café in a shop selling Japanese comic books.

Milk (Map pp110–11; ☎ 0 820 00 10 00; www.milklub .com; 17 rue Soufflot, 5e; daytime per 1/2/3/5hr €4/7/9/12, night time per 3/10hr €6/13; ⏰ 24hr; Ⓜ Luxembourg) This branch of a minichain of seven internet cafés, including a big Les Halles branch (Map p86; 31 blvd de Sébastopol, 1er; ⏰ 24hr; Ⓜ Les Halles), is bright, buzzy and open round the clock.

Netvision (Map pp116–17; ☎ 01 43 25 13 90; 10 Gît le Cœur, 6e; per 1min €0.07, 20min €1.40; ⏰ 10am-8pm; Ⓜ St-Michel) On a quiet street west of the blvd St-Michel.

Phon'net (Map pp94–5; ☎ 01 42 05 10 73; 74 rue de Charonne, 11e; per 1/5/15/30hr €5/16/30/45; ⏰ 10am-midnight; Ⓜ Charonne or Ledru Rollin)

Taxiphone Internet (Map p169; ☎ 01 42 59 64 14; 2 rue de La Vieuville, 18e; per 5/10/20/30/60min €0.50/1/2/3/4, per 5hr €10; ⏰ 9am-10pm Mon-Sat; Ⓜ Abbesses) One of the few internet cafés in high-rent Montmartre.

Web 46 (Map pp98–9; ☎ 01 40 27 02 89, fax 01 40 27 03 89; 46 rue du Roi de Sicile, 4e; per 15/30/60min €2.50/4/7, per 5hr €29; ☯ 10am-11pm Mon-Fri, 10am-9pm Sat, noon-11pm Sun; Ⓜ St-Paul) Pleasant, very well-run café in the heart of the Marais.

Zeidnet (Map pp110–11; ☎ 01 44 07 20 15; www .zeidnet.com; 18 rue de la Bûcherie, 5e; per 10/30/60min €1/2.50/4; ☯ 10.30am-11pm; Ⓜ Maubert-Mutualité) Small and personal, handy to Notre Dame.

LAUNDRY

There's a *laverie libre-service* (self-service laundrette) around every corner in Paris; your hotel or hostel can point you to one in the neighbourhood. Machines usually cost €3.50 to €4.50 for a small load (around 6kg) and €5.50 to €8 for a larger one (about 10kg). Drying costs €1 for 10 to 12 minutes. Some laundrettes have self-service *nettoyage à sec* (dry-cleaning) machines.

You usually pay at a *monnayeur central* (central control box) – not the machine itself – and push a button that corresponds to the number of the washer or dryer you wish to operate. Some machines don't take notes; come prepared with change for the *séchoirs* (dryers) as well as the *lessive* (laundry powder) and *javel* (bleach) dispensers.

The control boxes are sometimes programmed to deactivate the machines 30 minutes to an hour before closing time.

Among centrally located self-service laundrettes are the following:

C'Clean Laverie (Map pp94–5; 18 rue Jean-Pierre Timbaud, 11e; ☯ 7am-9pm; Ⓜ Oberkampf)

Julice Laverie 56 rue de Seine, 6e; ☯ 7am-11pm (Map pp116–17; Ⓜ Mabillon); 22 rue des Grands Augustins, 6e; ☯ 7am-9pm (Map pp116–17; Ⓜ St-André des Arts)

Lav' Net (Map pp110–11; 88 bis blvd du Port-Royal, 5e; Ⓜ Port-Royal)

Laverie Libre Service 7 rue Jean-Jacques Rousseau, 1er, near the BVJ Paris-Louvre hostel (Map p86; ☯ 7.30am-10pm; Ⓜ Louvre-Rivoli); 14 rue de la Corderie, 3e (Map pp92–3; ☯ 8am-9pm, Ⓜ République or Temple); 35 rue Ste-Croix la Bretonnerie, 4e (Map pp98–9; ☯ 7am-9pm, Ⓜ Hôtel de Ville); 25 rue des Rosiers, 4e (Map pp98–9; ☯ 7.30am-10pm; Ⓜ St-Paul); 216 rue St-Jacques, 5e, three blocks southeast of the Panthéon (Map pp110–11; ☯ 7am-10pm; Ⓜ Luxembourg) 63 rue Monge, 5e, south of the Arènes de Lutèce (Map pp110–11; ☯ 6.30am-10pm; Ⓜ Place Monge) 3 rue de la Montagne Ste-Geneviève & 2 rue Jean de Beauvais, 5e (Map pp110–11; ☯ 7am-11pm; Ⓜ Maubert-Mutualite); 116 rue d'Assas, 6e (Map pp116–

17; ☯ 7am-10pm; Ⓜ Mabillon); 94 rue du Dessous des Berges, 12e (Map pp162–3; ☯ 7.30am-10pm; Ⓜ Bibliothèque); 92 rue des Martyrs, 18e (Map p169; ☯ 7.30am-10pm; Ⓜ Abbesses); 4 rue Burq, 18e, west of the Butte de Montmartre (Map p169; ☯ 7.30am-10pm; Ⓜ Blanche)

Laverie Libre Service Primus 40 rue du Roi de Sicile, 4e(Map pp98–9; ☯ 7.30am-10pm Ⓜ St-Paul); 83 rue Jean-Pierre Timbaud, 11e; ☯ 7.30am-10pm (Map p155; Ⓜ Couronnes)

Laverie Miele Libre Service (Map pp94–5; 4 rue de Lappe, 11e; ☯ 7am-10pm; Ⓜ Bastille)

Laverie SBS (Map pp152–3; 6 rue des Petites Écuries, 10e; ☯ 7am-10pm; Ⓜ Château d'Eau)

Salon Lavoir Sidec (Map p169; 28 rue des Trois Frères, 18e; ☯ 7am-8.50pm; Ⓜ Abbesses)

LEGAL MATTERS
Drink Driving

As elsewhere in the EU, the laws in France are very tough when it comes to drinking and driving, and for many years the slogan has been: '*Boire ou conduire, il faut choisir*' (roughly – to make it rhyme in English too – 'To drive or to booze, you have to choose'). The acceptable blood-alcohol limit is 0.05%, and drivers exceeding that amount but still under 0.08% (the limit in the UK and Ireland) face a fine of €135; over 0.08% and it could cost you €4500 (or a maximum of two years in jail). Licences can also be immediately suspended. If you cause an accident while driving under the influence, the fine could be increased to €30,000. And if you cause serious bodily harm or commit involuntary manslaughter, you face 10 years in jail and a fine of up to €150,000.

The Police

Thanks to the Napoleonic Code on which the French legal system is based, the police can search anyone they want to at any time – whether or not there is probable cause.

France has two separate police forces. The Police Nationale, under the command of departmental prefects (and, in Paris, the Préfet de Police), includes the Police de l'Air et des Frontières (PAF; the border police). The Gendarmerie Nationale, a paramilitary force under the control of the Ministry of Defence, handles airports, borders and so on. During times of crisis (eg a wave of terrorist attacks), the army may be called in to patrol public places.

The dreaded Compagnies Républicaines de Sécurité (CRS) – riot-police heavies to be avoided at all costs – are part of the Police Nationale. You often see hundreds of them, each bigger and butcher than the next and armed with the latest riot gear, at marches or demonstrations. Police with shoulder patches reading 'Police Municipale' are under the control of the local mayor.

The American concept of neighbourhood cops walking their beat or the British bobby giving directions does not exist whatsoever in France; police here are to maintain order, not mingle and smile. If asked a direct question, a French policeman or policewoman will be correct and helpful but not much more; assisting tourists is not part of their job description. If the police stop you for any reason, be polite and remain calm. They have wide powers of search and seizure and, if they take a dislike to you, they may choose to use them all. Be aware that the police can, without any particular reason, decide to examine your passport, visa, *carte de séjour* (residence permit) and so on. Do *not* challenge them.

French police are very strict about security. Do not leave baggage unattended; they are quite serious when they say that suspicious objects will be summarily blown up. Your bags will be inspected and you will have to pass through security gates not only at airports but also at many public buildings (including certain museums and galleries) throughout the city. If asked to open your bag or backpack for inspection, please do so willingly – it's for your (and our) safety ultimately.

MAPS

The most ubiquitous (and user-friendly) pocket-sized street atlas available is L'Indispensable's *Paris Practique par Arrondissement* (€4.90), though the similar *Paris Utile* (€4.50) from Blay Foldex has its supporters. More detailed is Michelin's *Paris Poche Plan* (No 50; €2.20). All of these are usually available from newsstands and the Espace IGN (p213).

MEDICAL SERVICES

If you are not an EU citizen, it is imperative that you take out travel insurance before your departure. EU passport holders have access to the French social security system, which reimburses up to 70% of medical costs.

Hospitals

There are some 50 *assistance publique* (public health service) hospitals in Paris. If you need an ambulance, call ☎ 15; the EU-wide emergency number (with English speakers) is ☎ 112. For emergency treatment, call Urgences Médicales de Paris (☎ 01 53 94 94 94) or SOS Médecins (☎ 01 47 07 77 77 or 0 820 332 424). Both offer 24-hour house calls costing between €35 and €90 depending on the time of day and whether you have French social security.

Hospitals in Paris include the following:

American Hospital in Paris (off Map pp144–5; ☎ 01 46 41 25 25; www.american-hospital.org; 63 blvd Victor Hugo, 92200 Neuilly-sur-Seine; Ⓜ Pont de Levallois Bécon) Private hospital offering emergency 24-hour medical and dental care.

Hertford British Hospital (off Map pp144–5; ☎ 01 46 39 22 22; www.british-hospital.org; 3 rue Barbès, 92300 Levallois-Perret; Ⓜ Anatole France) A less-expensive private English-speaking option than the American Hospital.

Hôpital Hôtel Dieu (Map p105; ☎ 01 42 34 82 34; www.aphp.fr, in French; 1 place du Parvis Notre Dame, 4e; Ⓜ Cité) One of the city's main government-run public hospitals (Assistance Publique Hôpitaux de Paris); after 8pm use the emergency entrance on rue de la Cité.

Dental Clinics

For emergency dental care contact either of the following:

Hôpital de la Pitié-Salpêtrière (Map pp162–3; ☎ 01 42 16 00 00; rue Bruant, 13e; Ⓜ Chevaleret) The only dental hospital with extended hours – from 6am to 10.30pm. After 5.30pm use the emergency entrance at 83 blvd de l'Hôpital, 13e (metro St-Marcel).

SOS Dentaire (Map pp162–3; ☎ 01 43 37 51 00; 87 blvd de Port Royal, 13e; Ⓜ Port Royal) A private dental office that offers services when most dentists are off-duty (8pm to 11pm weekdays, 9.45am to 11pm weekends).

Pharmacies

Pharmacies with extended hours:

Pharmacie Bader (Map pp116–17; ☎ 01 43 26 92 66; 12 blvd St-Michel, 5e; ☾ 9am-9pm; Ⓜ St-Michel)

Pharmacie de La Mairie (Map pp98–9; ☎ 01 42 78 53 58; 9 rue des Archives, 4e; ☾ 9am-8pm; Ⓜ Hôtel de Ville)

Pharmacie des Champs (Map pp140–1; ☎ 01 45 62 02 41; Galerie des Champs, 84 av des Champs-Élysées, 8e; ☾ 24hr; Ⓜ George V)

Pharmacie des Halles (Map p86; ☎ 01 42 72 03 23; 10 blvd de Sébastopol, 4e; ☼ 9am-midnight Mon-Sat, 9am-10pm Sun; Ⓜ Châtelet)

Pharmacie Européenne (Map pp144–5; ☎ 01 48 74 65 18; 6 place de Clichy, 17e; ☼ 24hr; Ⓜ Place de Clichy)

MONEY

France is among the 15 member-states of the EU (Austria, Belgium, Cyprus, Finland, Germany, Greece, Ireland, Italy, Luxembourg, Malta, the Netherlands, Portugal, Slovenia and Spain) that have adopted the euro (abbreviated € and pronounced *eu*-roh in French) as its national currency. One euro is divided into 100 cents (*centimes* in French). There are seven euro notes in different colours and sizes; they come in denominations of €5, €10, €20, €50, €100, €200 and €500. The designs on the recto (generic windows or portals) and verso (imaginary bridges, map of the EU) are exactly the same in all 15 countries and symbolise openness and cooperation.

The eight coins in circulation are in denominations of €1 and €2, then one, two, five, 10, 20 and 50 cents. The 'head' side of the coin, on which the denomination is shown, is identical throughout the euro zone; the 'tail' side is specific to each member-state, though euro coins can be used anywhere that accepts euros, of course. In France the €1 (silver centre with brassy ring) and €2 (brassy centre with silver ring) coins portray the tree of liberty; the 10, 20 and 50 cent coins (all brass) have *la Semeuse* (the Sower), a recurring theme in the history of the French franc; and the one, two and five cent coins (all copper) portray Marianne, the symbol of the French Republic.

Exchange rates are given in the Quick Reference section on the inside front cover of this book. The latest rates are available on websites such as www.oanda.com and www.xe.com. For a broader view of the local economy and costs in Paris, see p15.

ATMs

You'll find an ATM, which here is known as as a DAB (*distributeur automatique de billets*) or *point d'argent*, linked to the Cirrus, Maestro, Visa or MasterCard networks, virtually on every corner. Those without a local bank account should know that there is usually a transaction surcharge of around €3 for cash withdrawals. You should contact your bank to find out how much this is before using ATMs too freely.

Changing Money

In general, cash is not a very good way to carry money. Not only can it be stolen, but in France it doesn't usually offer the best exchange rates. What's more, in recent years ATMs and the euro have virtually wiped out *bureaux de change* and even centrally located banks rarely offer exchange services these days.

That said, some banks, post offices and *bureaux de change* pay up to 2.5% or more for travellers cheques, more than making up for the 1% commission usually charged when buying the cheques in the first place.

Post offices that have a Banque Postale can offer the best exchange rates, and they accept banknotes (commission €4.50) in various currencies as well as travellers cheques issued by Amex (no commission) or Visa (1.5%, minimum €4.50).

Commercial banks usually charge a similar amount per foreign-currency transaction. For example BNP Paribas charges €5.95 for cash while Société Générale takes €5.40 (or €11.40 if you don't bank with them). The rates charged on travellers cheques vary but neither BNP Paribas or Société Générale charge a fee to change travellers cheques in euros.

In Paris, *bureaux de change* are usually faster and easier, open longer hours and give better rates than most banks. It's best to familiarise yourself with the rates offered by the post office and compare them with those on offer at *bureaux de change*, which are not generally allowed to charge commissions. *Bureaux de change* charge anything between 6% and 13% plus €3 or €4 on cash transactions and 6% to just under 10% (plus €3) to change travellers cheques.

Among some of the better *bureaux de change*:

American Express Bureau de Change (Map pp148–9; ☎ 01 47 77 79 50; 11 rue Scribe, 9e; ☼ 9am-6.30pm Mon-Sat; Ⓜ Auber or Opéra)

Best Change (Map p86; ☎ 01 42 21 46 05; 21 rue du Roule, 1er; ☼ 9.30am-7pm Mon-Sat; Ⓜ Louvre Rivoli) Three blocks southwest of Forum des Halles.

CCO (Map pp82–3; ☎ 01 42 66 24 44; 12 blvd de Capucines, 9e; ☼ 9am-5.30pm Mon-Fri, 9.30am-4pm Sat; Ⓜ Opéra); Opéra branch (Map pp148–9; ☎ 01 47 42 20 96; 9 rue Scribe, 9e; ☼ 9am-5.30pm Mon-Fri, 9.30am-4pm Sat; Ⓜ Opéra)

European Exchange Office (Map p169; ☎ 01 42 52 67 19; 6 rue Yvonne Le Tac, 18e; ☼ 10am-noon & 2-6pm Mon-Sat; Ⓜ Abbesses) A few steps from the Abbesses metro station.

Le Change du Louvre (Map p86; ☎ 01 42 97 27 28; 151 rue St-Honoré, 1er; ⊙ 10am-6pm Mon-Fri; Ⓜ Palais Royal-Musée du Louvre) This moneychanger is on the northern side of Le Louvre des Antiquaires (p80).

Multi Change (Map pp116–17; ☎ 01 42 22 45 00; 180 blvd St-Germain, 6e; ⊙ 9am-6.30pm Mon-Sat; Ⓜ St-Germain des Prés) Just west of Église St-Germain des Prés.

Société Touristique de Services (Map pp110–11; ☎ 01 43 54 76 55; 2 place St-Michel, 6e; ⊙ 9am-8pm Mon-Fri, 10am-8pm Sat; Ⓜ St-Michel) A bureau de change in the heart of the Latin Quarter.

Credit Cards

In Paris, Visa/Carte Bleue is the most widely accepted credit card, followed by MasterCard (Eurocard). Amex cards can be useful at more upmarket establishments. In general, all three cards can be used for train travel, restaurant meals and cash advances.

When you get a cash advance on your Visa or MasterCard account, your issuer charges a transaction fee, which can be high; check with your card issuer before leaving home. Some banks charge a commission of 4% (minimum around €6) for a cash advance though BNP Parisbas does it for free (though the card-holder's issuing bank will probably do so) to a maximum of €1000. American Express takes a 5% commission on cash advances on Visa cards.

Call the following numbers if your card is lost or stolen. It may be impossible to get a lost Visa or MasterCard reissued until you get home so two different credit cards are generally safer than just one.

Amex (☎ 01 47 77 72 00, 01 71 23 08 38)

Diners Club (☎ 0 820 82 05 36, 0 800 22 20 73)

MasterCard/Eurocard (☎ 0 800 90 13 87, 01 45 67 84 84)

Visa/Carte Bleue (☎ 0 892 70 57 05, 0 800 90 20 33)

Travellers Cheques

The most flexible travellers cheques are issued by American Express (in US dollars or euros) and Visa, as they can be changed at many post offices.

Amex offices charges a commission on all travellers cheques of about 4% (minimum €2). If your Amex travellers cheques are lost or stolen while you are in Paris, call ☎ 0 800 83 28 20 (24-hour, toll-free). Reimbursements can be made at the main American Express office (Map pp148–9; ☎ 01 47 77 79 50; www.americanexpress.fr, in French; 11 rue Scribe, 9e; ⊙ 9am-5.30pm Mon-Sat; Ⓜ Auber or Opéra).

NEWSPAPERS & MAGAZINES

Among English-language newspapers widely available in Paris are the *International Herald Tribune* (€2.50), which is edited in Paris and has very good coverage of both French and international news; the *Guardian* and the more compact *Guardian Weekly*; the *Financial Times*; the *Times of London*; and the colourful (if lightweight) *USA Today*. English-language news weeklies that are widely available include *Newsweek, Time* and the *Economist*. For information about the French-language press, see p54.

The Paris-based *Fusac* (*France USA Contacts*), a freebie issued every two weeks, consists of hundreds of ads placed by companies and individuals. To place one yourself, contact Fusac (Map p124–5; ☎ 01 56 53 54 54, www.fusac .fr; 26 rue Bénard, 14e; ⊙ 10am-7pm Mon-Fri; Ⓜ Alésia or Pernety),still going strong after two decades. It is distributed free at Paris' English-language bookshops, Anglophone embassies and the American Church (Map pp128–9; ☎ 01 40 62 05 00; www .acparis.org; 65 quai d'Orsay, 7e; reception ⊙ 9am-noon & 1-10pm Mon-Sat, 2-7.30pm Sun; Ⓜ Pont de l'Alma or Invalides), which functions as a kind of community centre for English speakers and is an excellent source of information on au pair work, short-term accommodation etc. The free *Paris Times* (www.theparistimes.com), published monthly, is also worth a look. See the website for a full list of distribution points.

ORGANISED TOURS

If you can't be bothered making your own way around Paris or don't have the time, consider a tour by air, bus, boat, bicycle or on foot. There's no reason to feel sheepish or embarrassed about taking a guided tour. They are an excellent way to learn the contours of a new city, and even experienced guidebook writers have been known to join them from time to time. Most useful are the buses and other conveyances that allow you to disembark when and where you want and board the next one that suits you. They usually offer little or no commentary aside from calling out the stop names but offer the most freedom to do what you want.

True couch potatoes will head for Paris Story (Map pp148–9; ☎ 01 42 66 62 06; www.paris-story.com; 11bis rue Scribe, 9e; adult/student & 6-17yr/family €10/6/26, under 6 yr free; ⊙ 10am-6pm; Ⓜ Auber or Opéra), which includes a 50-minute audiovisual romp through Paris' 2000-year history on the hour, with headset commentary in 14 languages; an interactive model of Paris called Paris Miniature; and Paris Experience, a gallery of five themed video clips.

Air

Hot-air balloon Ballon Eutelsat (Map pp166–7; ☎ 01 44 26 20 00; www.aeroparis.com, in French; Parc André Citroën, 2 rue de la Montagne de la Fage, 15e; Mon-Fri adult/3-11 yr/12-17yr €10/5/9, Sat & Sun €12/6/10, under 3yr free; ☯ 9am-5.30pm to 9.30pm (seasonal); Ⓜ Balard), in the Parc André Citroën in southwestern Paris, lifts you 150m off the ground and offers fabulous views of Paris and the Seine. But don't expect to get very far; the helium-filled balloon remains firmly tethered to the ground. Be sure to call in advance as the balloon does not ascend in windy conditions.

A company called iXAir (Map pp166–7; ☎ 01 30 08 80 80; www.ixair.com, in French; 4 av de la Porte de Sèvres, 15e; Ⓜ Porte de Sèvres) at the Héliport de Paris next to the Aquaboulevard in the 15e offers circuits by helicopter over the city lasting between 25 and 45 minutes for €128 to €195. You should book 10 to 15 days ahead.

Bicycle

Fat Tire Bike Tours (Map pp166–7; ☎ 01 56 58 10 54; www.fattirebiketoursparis.com; 24 rue Edgar Faure, 15e; ☯ office 9am-6pm; Ⓜ La Motte-Picquet Grenelle) offers daytime bike tours of the city (adult/student €24/22; four hours), starting at 11am daily from mid-February to early January, with an additional departure at 3pm from April to October. Night bicycle tours (adult/student €28/26) depart at 7pm on Sunday, Tuesday, Thursday and Saturday from mid-February to mid-March and in November and at the same time daily from mid-March to October. A day and night combination tour costs €48 for adults and €44 for students.

Participants can meet at the Fat Tire Bike Tours office, where you can store bags, log on to the internet and get tourist information, but tours actually depart from opposite the Eiffel Tower's South Pillar at the start of the Champ de Mars; just look for the yellow signs. Costs include the bicycle and, if necessary, rain gear.

The same company runs City Segway Tours (www.citysegwaytours.com) which, though not on bicycles, involve two-wheeled, electric-powered conveyances. Segway tours (€70), which follow an abbreviated route of the bike tours and last four hours, depart at 9.30am from mid-February to early January, with an extra tour at 6.30pm from April to October. You must book these tours in advance.

Bike tours lasting three hours from cycle shop Gepetto & Vélos (Map pp110–11; ☎ 01 43 54 19 95; www.gepetto-et-velos.com, in French; 59 rue du Cardinal Lemoine, 5e; tours €25; ☯ 9am-1pm & 2-7.30pm Tue-Sat, 10am-1pm & 2-7pm Sun; Ⓜ Cardinal Lemoine) include guide, bicycle and insurance. There is also a branch in the Latin Quarter (Map pp110–11; ☯ 01 43 37 16 17; 46 rue Daubenton, 5e; ☯ 9am-1pm & 2-7.30pm Tue-Sat; Ⓜ Censier Daubenton).

RATP-sponsored Maison Roue Libre (Map p86; ☎ 0 810 44 15 34; www.rouelibre.fr; Forum des Halles, 1 passage Mondétour, 1er; adult/under 26 yr €27/20, with own bike €17; ☯ 9am-7pm Feb-Oct, 10am-6pm Wed-Sun Nov & Jan; Ⓜ Les Halles) has as many as 15 different themed bike tours from 12km to 26km lasting from three to eight hours. Tours operate on certain weekend days throughout the year starting at 10am, 2pm or 8pm. Consult the website for exact details. The Bastille branch (Map pp92–3; ☎ 0 810 44 15 34; 37 blvd Bourdon, 4e; Ⓜ Bastille) keeps the same hours but shuts Wednesday and Thursday in winter.

Paris à Vélo, C'est Sympa! (Map pp94–5; ☎ 01 48 87 60 01; www.parisvelosympa.com, in French; 22 rue Alphonse Baudin, 11e; ☯ 9.30am-1pm & 2-6pm Mon-Fri, 9am-1pm & 2-7pm Sat & Sun Apr-Oct, 9.30am-1pm & 2-5.30pm Mon-Fri, 9am-1pm & 2-6pm Sat & Sun Nov-Mar; Ⓜ St-Sébastien Froissart) This association with the cringey name (Paris by Bike is Nice!) has five different three-hour bike tours available for €34/28/18 for adult/12 to 25 years/under-12 years. Prices include bicycle and insurance.

Boat

Be it on what Parisians call *la ligne de vie de Paris* (the lifeline of Paris or the Seine) or the rejuvenated canals to the northeast, a boat cruise is the most relaxing way to watch the city glide by.

CANAL CRUISES

Canauxrama (Map pp158–9 & Map pp174–5; ☎ 01 42 39 15 00; www.canauxrama.com, in French; Bassin de la Villette, 13 quai de la Loire, 19e; Mon-Fri adult/6-12yr/student & senior €15/8/11, under 6yr free, admission afternoon Sat & Sun €15; ☯ Mar-Nov; Ⓜ Jaurès) has barges that run from Port de Plaisance de Paris-Arsenal, 12e, opposite 50 blvd de la Bastille, to Parc de la Villette, 19e, along charming Canal St-Martin and Canal de l'Ourcq. Departures are at 9.45am and 2.30pm from Port de Plaisance de Paris-Arsenal during the season and, in summer only, at 9.45am and 2.45pm from Bassin de la Villette. The cruise last 2½ hours.

Paris Canal Croisières (Map pp174–5; ☎ 01 42 40 96 97; www.pariscanal.com; Bassin de la Villette, 19-21 quai de la Loire, 19e; adult/4–11yr/senior & 12-25yr €17/10/14, under 4yr free; ☾ late Mar–mid-Nov; Ⓜ Jaurès or Musée d'Orsay) has 2½-hour cruises from quai Anatole France (7e), northwest of Musée d'Orsay, at 9.30am and departing from Parc de la Villette for the return trip at 2.30pm.

RIVER CRUISES

On the Right Bank just east of Pont de l'Alma, **Bateaux-Mouches** (Map pp140–1; ☎ 0142259610; www.bateaux mouches.com, in French; Port de la Conférence, 8e; adult/senior & 4-12yr €9/4, under 4yr free; ☾ mid-Mar–mid-Nov; Ⓜ Alma Marceau), the most famous river-boat company in Paris, runs nine 1000-seat glassed-in tour boats, still the largest on the Seine. Cruises (70 minutes) depart eight times a day between 10.15am and 3.15pm and then every 20 minutes till 11pm April to September and 10 times a day between 10.15am and 9pm the rest of the year. Commentary in French and English.

From its base northwest of the Eiffel Tower, **Bateaux Parisiens** (Map pp132–3; ☎ 0 825 01 01 01; www .bateauxparisiens.com; Port de la Bourdonnais, 7e; adult/3-11yr €10.50/5, under 3yr free; ☾ every half hr 10am-10.30pm Apr-Sep, hourly 10am-10pm Oct-Mar; Ⓜ Pont de l'Alma) runs one-hour river cruises with recorded commentary in 13 different languages.

La Marina de Paris (Map pp128–9; ☎ 01 43 43 40 30; www .marinadeparis.com; port de Solferino, quai Anatole France, 7e; Ⓜ Musée d'Orsay) offers lunch cruises at 12.15pm (€51) and dinner cruises at 6.30pm (€45 and €59) and 9pm (€79). They last about 2¼ hours and a menu for those under 12 (€39) is available at all meals.

Vedettes du Pont Neuf (Map p105; ☎ 01 46 33 98 38; www.pontneuf.net; square du Vert Galant, 1er; adult/4-12yr €11/6; ☾ every half hr 10.30am-noon, 1.30-8pm & 9-10.30pm mid-Mar-Oct; Ⓜ Pont Neuf), whose home dock is at the far western tip of the Île de la Cité (1er), has one-hour boat excursions year-round. From November to mid-March there are 13 departures from 10.30am to 10pm Monday to Thursday and 15 departures until 10.30pm Friday to Sunday.

Bus

In season, RATP **Balabus** (☎ 3246; www.ratp.fr; €1.40 or 1 metro/bus ticket; ☾ departures 12.30-8pm from La Défense, 1.30pm from Gare de Lyon Sun Apr-Sep), designed for tourists, follows a 50-minute route to/from Gare de Lyon (Map pp158–9) and La Défense

(Map p180), passing many of central Paris' most famous sights.

Located just opposite the western end of the Louvre, **Cityrama** (Map pp82–3; ☎ 01 44 55 60 00; www.pariscityrama.com; 2 rue des Pyramides, 1er; adult/4-11yr €18/9; ☾ tours 10am, 11.30am & 2.30pm; Ⓜ Tuileries) runs 1½-hour tours of the city, accompanied by taped commentaries in 16 languages, three times a day year-round.

L'Open Tour (Map pp148–9; ☎ 01 42 66 56 56; www.paris cityrama.com; 13 rue Auber, 9e; 1 day adult/4-11yr €26/13, 2 consecutive days €29/13; Ⓜ Havre Caumartin or Opéra), now part of the same group, runs open-deck buses along four circuits (central Paris, 2¼ hours; Montmartre-Grands Boulevards, 1¼ hours; Bastille-Bercy, one hour; and Montparnasse-St-Germain, one hour) daily year-round. You can jump on and off at more than 50 stops On the 'Grand Tour' of central Paris, with some 20 stops on both sides of the river between Notre Dame and the Eiffel Tower, buses depart every 10 to 15 minutes from 9.30am to 7pm April to October and every 25 to 30 minutes from 9.45am to 6pm November to March. Holders of the Paris Visite card (p394) pay €22 for a one-day pass.

Walking

If your French is up to it, the sky's the limit on specialised and themed walking tours available in Paris. Both *Pariscope* and *Officiel des Spectacles* (p302) list a number of themed walks (usually €10) each week under the heading 'Conférences' or 'Visites Conférences'. They are almost always informative and entertaining, particularly those run by Paris Passé, Présent (☎ 01 42 58 95 99; http://parispassepresent.free.fr) and Écoute du Passé (☎ 01 42 82 11 81, 06 83 89 18 25).

Long-established and highly rated by readers, **Paris Walks** (☎ 01 48 09 21 40; www.paris-walks.com; adult/under 15yr/student under 21 from €10/5/8) has tours in English of several different districts, including Montmartre at 10.30am on Sunday and Wednesday (leaving from metro Abbesses, Map p169) and the Marais at 10.30am on Tuesday and 2.30pm on Sunday (departing from metro St-Paul, Map pp98–9). There are other tours focusing on people and themes, eg Hemingway, medieval Latin Quarter, fashion, the French Revolution and – yum-yum – chocolate.

PHOTOGRAPHY

Kodak and Fuji colour-print film is available in supermarkets, photo shops and certain Fnac stores, but it is relatively expensive compared with a lot of other countries so it might pay to stock up before you leave home. Developing a 24-exposure film costs around €13 but can be almost twice that if you want your photos in a hurry. Printing 50 digitals (10cm x 13cm) costs between €9.50 and €12 plus €2 for developing.

It's getting increasingly difficult to find express photo labs in Paris. One place with labs for both traditional and digital work and highly recommended by professionals is Négatif+ (Map pp148–9; ☎ 01 45 23 41 60; www.negatifplus .com, in French; 104-106 rue La Fayette, 10e; �}8am-7.30pm Mon-Fri, 10am-1pm & 2-7.30pm Sat; Ⓜ Poissonière).

PLACES OF WORSHIP

The following places offer services in English. For a more comprehensive list of churches and other places of worship, check the *Pages Jaunes* (Yellow Pages; www.pagesjaunes.fr). or the website of the tourist office (http:// en.parisinfo.com/guide-paris/worship).

Adath Shalom Synagogue (Map pp166–7; ☎ 01 45 67 97 96; www.adathshalom.org, in French; 8 rue George Bernard Shaw, 15e; Ⓜ Dupleix) Conservative Jewish.

American Cathedral in Paris (Map pp140–1; ☎ 01 53 23 84 00; www.americancathedral.org; 23 av George V, 8e; Ⓜ Alma Marceau) Protestant.

American Church in Paris (Map pp128–9; ☎ 01 40 62 05 00; www.acparis.org; 65 quai d'Orsay, 7e; Ⓜ Invalides) Nondenominational Protestant.

Church of Jesus Christ of the Latter Day Saints (Map pp174–5; ☎ 01 42 45 29 29; 64-66 rue de Romainville, 19e; Ⓜ Porte des Lilas) Mormon.

First Church of Christ Scientist (Map pp124–5; ☎ 01 47 07 26 60; 36 blvd St-Jacques, 14e; Ⓜ St-Jacques) Christian Scientist.

Mosquée de Paris (Map pp110–11; ☎ 01 45 35 97 33; www.mosquee-de-paris.org, in French; 2bis place du Puits de l'Ermite, 5e; Ⓜ Censier Daubenton or Place Monge) Muslim.

St Joseph's Catholic Church (Map pp140–1; ☎ 01 42 27 28 56; www.stjoeparis.org; 50 av Hoche, 8e; Ⓜ Charles de Gaulle-Étoile) Roman Catholic.

Sri Manikar Vinayakar Temple (Map p169; ☎ 01 40 34 21 89; 72 rue Philippe de Girard, 18e; Ⓜ Marx Dormoy) Hindu.

POST

Most post offices (*bureaux de poste*) in Paris are open from 8am to 7pm weekdays and 8am or 9am till noon on Saturday. *Tabacs* (tobacconists) usually sell postage stamps.

The main post office (Map pp82–3; www.laposte.fr, in French; 52 rue du Louvre, 1er; �}24hr; Ⓜ Sentier or Les Halles), five blocks north of the eastern end of the Musée du Louvre, is open round the clock, but only for basic services such as sending letters and picking up poste restante mail (window 11; €0.54 per letter). Other services, including currency exchange, are available only during regular opening hours. Be prepared for long queues after 7pm and at the weekend. Poste restante mail not specifically addressed to a particular branch post office will be delivered here. There is a one-hour closure from 6.20am to 7.20am Monday to Saturday and from 6am to 7am on Sunday.

Each arrondissement has its own five-digit postcode, formed by prefixing the number of the arrondissement with '750' or '7500' (eg 75001 for the 1er arrondissement, 75019 for the 19e). The only exception is the 16e, which has two postcodes: 75016 and 75116. All mail to addresses in France *must* include the postcode. Cedex (*Courrier d'Entreprise à Distribution Exceptionelle*) simply means that mail sent to that address is collected at the post office rather than delivered to the door.

Domestic letters weighing up to 20/50g cost €0.55/0.88. Postcards and letters up to 20/50g sent within the EU cost €0.65/1.25 and €0.85/1.70 to the rest of the world.

RADIO

You can pick up a mixture of the BBC World Service and BBC for Europe in Paris on 648 kHz AM. The Voice of America (VOA) is on 1197 kHz AM and 96.9 MHz FM. You can pick up an hour of Radio France Internationale (RFI) news in English three times a day (7am, 2.30pm and 4.30pm) on 738 kHz AM.

Pocket-sized short-wave radios and the internet make it easy to keep abreast of world news in English wherever you are. The BBC World Service can be heard on 6195 kHz, 9410 kHz and 12095 kHz (a good daytime frequency), depending on the time of day. BBC Radio 4 broadcasts on 198 kHz LW, and carries BBC World Service programming in the wee hours of the morning. The VOA broadcasts in English at various times of the day on 7170 kHz, 9535 kHz, 9760 kHz, 9770 kHz, 11805 kHz, 15205 kHz and 15255 kHz.

The following are some of the more popular French-language radio stations:

FIP (105.1MHz FM) Eclectic mix of musical genres, with some news and cultural info; a favourite with Parisians and part of France Inter.

France Info (105.5 MHz FM; www.france-info.com) Operates 24-hour, all-news radio.

France Inter (87.8 MHz FM; www.radiofrance.fr/france inter/accueil) Talk-back station specialising in music, news and entertainment.

Paris Jazz (88.2 MHz FM; www.comfm.com/live/radio /parisjazz) Jazz and blues.

Radio FG (98.2 MHz FM; www.radiofg.com) The station for house, techno, garage, trance, club news and gigs.

Radio Nova (101.5 MHz FM; www.novaplanet.com) Latino, clubs, modern beats.

TSF (89.9 MHz FM; www.tsfjazz.com) Popular jazz station.

RELOCATING

If you're considering moving to Paris and you are not a citizen of the EU you must have both a *carte de séjour* (residence permit; p412) and an *autorisation de travail* (work permit; p414). Neither is easy to come by.

For practical information on living and working in employment in Paris and France, pick up a copy of *Live and Work in France* by Victoria Pybus, now in its 5th edition, or *Living and Working in France: A Survival Handbook* by David Hampshire.

The fortnightly *Fusac* (p405) is an excellent source for job-seekers.

SAFETY

In general, Paris is a safe city and random street assaults are rare. The so-called Ville Lumière (City of Light) is generally well lit, and there's no reason not to use the metro until it stops running at some time between 12.30am and just past 1am. As you'll notice, women *do* travel alone on the metro late at night in most areas, though not all who do so report feeling 100% comfortable.

Metro stations that are best avoided late at night include Châtelet-Les Halles and its seemingly endless corridors, Château Rouge in Montmartre, Gare du Nord, Strasbourg St-Denis, Réaumur Sébastopol, and Montparnasse Bienvenüe. *Bornes d'alarme* (alarm boxes) are located in the centre of each metro/RER platform and in some station corridors.

Nonviolent crime such as pickpocketing and thefts from handbags and packs is a problem wherever there are crowds, especially packs of tourists. Places to be particularly careful include Montmartre (especially around Sacré Cœur); Pigalle; the areas around

Forum des Halles and the Centre Pompidou; the Latin Quarter (especially the rectangle bounded by rue St-Jacques, blvd St-Germain, blvd St-Michel and quai St-Michel); below the Eiffel Tower; and anywhere on the metro during rush hour. Take the usual precautions: don't carry more money than you need, and keep your credit cards, passport and other documents in a concealed pouch, a hotel safe or a safe-deposit box.

Vigipirate is a security plan devised by the Paris city council to combat terrorism. Both citizens and visitors are asked to report any abandoned luggage or package at all times. When the full Vigipirate scheme is put into action, public litter bins are sealed, left-luggage services in train stations and at airports are unavailable, checks at the entrances to public buildings and tourist sites are increased, and cloakrooms and lockers in museums and at monuments are closed.

TAXES & REFUNDS

France's value-added tax (VAT) is known as TVA *(taxe sur la valeur ajoutée)* and is 19.6% on most goods except medicine and books, for which it's 5.5%. Prices that include TVA are often marked TTC *(toutes taxes comprises; literally 'all taxes included')*.

If you're not an EU resident, you can get a TVA refund provided that: you're aged over 15; you'll be spending less than six months in France; you purchase goods worth at least €175 at a single shop on the same day (not more than 10 of the same item); the goods fit into your luggage; you are taking the goods out of France within three months after purchase; and the shop offers *vente en détaxe* (duty-free sales).

Present a passport at the time of purchase and ask for a *bordereau de vente à l'exportation* (export sales invoice) to be signed by the retailer and yourself. Most shops will refund less than the full amount (about 14%) to which you are entitled, in order to cover the time and expense involved in the refund procedure.

As you leave France or another EU country, have all three pages of the *bordereau* validated by the country's customs officials at the airport or at the border. Customs officials will take one sheet and hand you two. You must post one copy (the pink one) back to the shop and retain the other (green) sheet for your records in case there is any dispute. Once the shop where you made your purchase receives its stamped copy, it will send you a *virement* (fund transfer) in the form you have requested. Be prepared for a wait of up to three months.

If you're flying out of Orly or Roissy Charles de Gaulle, certain shops can arrange for you to receive your refund as you're leaving the country though you must complete the steps outlined preceding. You must make such arrangements at the time of purchase.

For more information contact the customs information centre (☎ 0 820 02 44 44; www.douane.minefi .gouv.fr; 🕑 8.30am-6pm Mon-Fri).

TELEPHONE

There are no area codes in France – you always dial the 10-digit number. Telephone numbers in Paris always start with ☎ 01. Mobile phones through France commence with ☎ 06.

Once the domain of France Télécom, the domestic *service des renseignements* (directory enquiries or assistance) is now offered by over a dozen operators on six-digit numbers starting with 118 (France Télécom, for example, uses ☎ 118 710, 118 711, 118 712 and 118 810). For a complete listing in French consult www.allo118.com.

Note that while numbers beginning with ☎ 0 800, 0 804, 0 805 and 0 809 are toll-free in France, other numbers beginning with '8' are not. A number starting with ☎ 0 810 or 0 811 is charged at local rates (€0.078 then €0.028) while one beginning with ☎ 0 820 and 0 821 cost €0.12 per minute, or even €0.15 if the prefix numbers are ☎ 0 890. The ubiquitous ☎ 0 892 numbers are billed at an expensive €0.34 per minute whenever you call. ☎ 0 899 numbers cost €1.35 per connection then €0.34 per minute, Numbers beginning with ☎ 0 897 cost a flat €0.562 per call.

Most four-digit numbers starting with 10, 30 or 31 are also free of charge.

France's country code is ☎ 33. To call a number in Paris from outside France, dial your country's international access code (usually ☎ 00 but exceptions include ☎ 011 from the USA and ☎ 001 from Hong Kong), then ☎ 33 and then the local number, omitting the first '0'.

To call abroad from Paris, dial France's international access code (☎ 00), the country code (see right), the area code (usually without the initial '0', if there is one) and the local number. International Direct Dial (IDD) calls to almost anywhere in the world can be placed from public telephones. The international reduced rate applies from 7pm to 8am weekdays and all day at the weekend.

For international directory enquiries, dial ☎ 3212. Note that the cost for this service is €3 per call. Instead consult the phone book on the internet (www.pagejaunes.fr).

Selected country codes

Australia	☎ 61
Belgium	☎ 32
Canada	☎ 1
Germany	☎ 49
Ireland	☎ 353
Italy	☎ 39
Netherlands	☎ 31
New Zealand	☎ 64
South Africa	☎ 27
Spain	☎ 34
Switzerland	☎ 41
UK	☎ 44
USA	☎ 1

Mobile Phones

France uses the GSM 900 network, which is compatible with the rest of Europe, Australia and New Zealand but not with the North American GSM 1900 (though many North Americans now have GSM 1900/900 phones that do work in France) or the totally different system in Japan. If you have a GSM phone, check with your service provider about using it in France, and beware of calls being routed internationally, which can make a 'local' call very expensive indeed.

It's usually most convenient to buy a local SIM card from one of the major providers such as Orange/France Telecom (☎ 0 800 83 08 00 or ☎ +33 1 41 43 79 40 outside France; www.orange.fr, in French) has a €59 package that includes a Sony Ericsson MP3 mobile phone, a local phone number and €5 of call time.

For more time, you can buy a prepaid Mobicarte recharge card (€5 to €100) from *tabacs* (tobacconist) and other places you'd buy a *télécarte* (phonecard); Mobicartes from €25 upward offer extra talk time (€5 bonus for €25, €10 bonus for €35, up to €50 extra for €100). If you don't mind changing your telephone number to a French one during your stay, you can also buy a local SIM card for your mobile (provided it's not blocked) for €20 (plus 10 minutes' talk time) and recharge with Mobicartes as you go along. The biggest outlet is La Boutique Orange (Map pp140–1; 16 place de la Madeleine, 8e; 🕑 10am-7pm Mon-Sat; Ⓜ Madeleine).

Phonecards

All public phones can receive both domestic and international calls. If you want someone to call you back, just give them France's country code and the 10-digit number, usually written after the words 'Ici le...' or 'No d'appel' on the tariff sheet or on a little sign inside the phone box. Remind them to drop the '0' of the initial '01' of the number. When there's an incoming call, the words 'décrochez – appel arrive' (pick up receiver – incoming call) will appear in the LCD window.

Public telephones in Paris usually require a télécarte (phonecard; €7.50/15 for 50/120 calling units), which can be purchased at post offices, tabacs, supermarkets, SNCF ticket windows, metro stations and anywhere you see a blue sticker reading 'télécarte en vente ici' (phonecard for sale here).

You can buy prepaid phonecards in France such as Allomundo (www.allomundo.com, in French) that are up to 60% cheaper for calling abroad than the standard télécarte. They're usually available in denominations of up to €15 from tabacs, newsagents, phone shops and other sales points, especially in ethnic areas such as rue du Faubourg St-Denis (10e), Chinatown (13e) and Belleville (19e and 20e). In general they're valid for two months but the ones offering the most minutes for the least euros can expire in just a week.

TIME

France uses the 24-hour clock in most case, with the hours usually separated from the minutes by a lower-case 'h'. Thus, 15h30 is 3.30pm, 00h30 is 12.30am and so on.

France is on Central European Time, which is one hour ahead of (ie later than) GMT. During daylight-saving time, which runs from the last Sunday in March to the last Sunday in October, France is two hours ahead of GMT.

Without taking daylight-saving time into account, when it's noon in Paris it's 11pm in Auckland, 11am in London, 6am in New York, 3am in San Francisco and 9pm in Sydney.

TIPPING

French law requires that restaurant, café and hotel bills include a service charge (usually between 12% and 15%); for more information on tipping at restaurants and cafés, see p228. Taxi drivers expect small tips of between 5% and 10% of the fare though the usual proce-

dure is to round up to the nearest €1 regardless of the fare.

TOILETS

Public toilets in Paris are signposted toilettes or WC. The tan-coloured, self-cleaning cylindrical toilets you see on Parisian pavements are open 24 hours and are free of charge. Look for the words libre ('free'; green-coloured) or occupé ('occupied'; red-coloured).

Café-owners do not appreciate you using their facilities if you are not a paying customer. When desperate, try a fast-food place, major department store or even a big hotel. There are free public toilets in front of Notre Dame cathedral, near the Arc de Triomphe, east down the steps at Sacré Cœur, at the northwestern entrance to the Jardins des Tuileries and in some metro stations. Check out the wonderful Art Nouveau public toilets, built in 1905, below place de la Madeleine, 8e (Map pp140–1). In older cafés and bars, you may find a toilette à la turque (Turkish-style toilet), which is what the French call a squat toilet.

TOURIST INFORMATION

The main branch of the Paris Convention & Visitors Bureau (Office de Tourisme et de Congrès de Paris; Map pp82–3; ☎ 0 892 68 30 00; www.parisinfo.com; 25-27 rue des Pyramides, 1er; ⊙ 9am-7pm Jun-Oct, 10am-7pm Mon-Sat & 11am-7pm Sun Nov-May, closed May Day; Ⓜ Pyramides) is about 500m northwest of the Louvre.

The bureau also maintains a handful of centres elsewhere in Paris, listed following (telephone numbers and websites are the same as for the main office). For details of the area around Paris, contact Espace du Tourisme d'Île de France, p360.

Anvers (Map p169; opp 72 blvd Rochechouart, 18e; ⊙ 10am-6pm, closed Christmas Day, New Year's Day & May Day; Ⓜ Anvers)

Gare de Lyon (Map pp158–9; Hall d'Arrivée, 20 blvd Diderot, 12e; ⊙ 8am-6pm Mon-Sat, closed May Day) In the arrivals hall for mainline trains.

Gare du Nord (Map pp152–3) 18 rue de Dunkerque, 10e; ⊙ 8am-6pm, closed Christmas Day, New Year's Day & May Day; Ⓜ Gare du Nord) Under the glass roof of the Île de France departure and arrival area at the eastern end of the station.

Syndicate d'Initiative de Montmartre (Map p169; ☎ 01 42 62 21 21; 21 place du Tertre, 18e; ⊙ 10am-7pm; Ⓜ Abbesses) This locally run tourist office and shop is in Montmartre's most picturesque square and open year-round.

Information offices beyond central Paris include those at La Défense and St-Denis:

Espace Info-Défense (Map p180; ☎ 01 47 74 84 24; www.ladefense.fr; 15 place de la Défense; ✆ 9am-5.15pm Mon-Fri; Ⓜ La Défense Grande Arche) La Défense's tourist office has reams of free information, including the useful *Discover La Défense* brochure and details on cultural activities.

Office de Tourisme de St-Denis Plaine Commune (Map p182; ☎ 01 55 87 08 70; www.saint-denis-tourisme .com, in French; 1 rue de la République; ✆ 9.30am-1pm & 2-6pm Mon-Sat, 10am-2pm Sun Oct-Mar, 10am-1pm & 2-4pm Sun Apr-Sep; Ⓜ Basilique de St-Denis) This helpful tourist office is 100m west of the basilica.

TRAVELLERS WITH DISABILITIES

Paris is an ancient city and is thus not particularly well equipped for *les handicapés* (disabled people): kerb ramps are few and far between, older public facilities and bottom-end hotels usually lack lifts, and the metro, dating back more than a century, is inaccessible for those in a wheelchair (*fauteuil roulant*). But efforts are being made and early in the new millennium the tourist office launched its 'Tourisme & Handicap' initiative in which museums, cultural attractions, hotels and restaurants that provided access or special assistance or facilities for those with physical, mental, visual and/or hearing disabilities would display a special logo at their entrances. For a list of the places qualifying, visit the tourist office's website (www .parisinfo.com) and click on 'Practical Paris'.

Information & Organisations

The SNCF has made many of its train carriages more accessible to people with physical disabilities. A traveller in a wheelchair can travel in both the TGV (*train à grande vitesse*; high-speed train) and in the 1st-class carriage with a 2nd-class ticket on mainline trains provided they make a reservation by phone or at a train station at least a few hours before departure. Details are available in the SNCF booklet *Le Mémento du Voyageur Handicapé* (Handicapped Traveller Summary) available at all train stations. For advice on planning your journey from station to station contact the SNCF service Acces Plus (☎ 0 890 64 06 50; www .accessibilite.sncf.com, in French).

For information on accessibility to all forms of public transport in the Paris region,

get a copy of the *Guide Practique à l'Usage des Personnes à Mobilité Réduite* (Practical Usage Guide for those with Reduced Mobility) from the Syndicat des Transports d'Île de France (☎ 0 810 64 64 64; www.stif-idf.fr). Its Info Mobi (www.infomobi.com, in French) is especially useful. Also helpful is the RATP's Assistance Voyageurs à Mobilité Réduite (Assistance for Travellers with Reduced Mobility; ☎ 01 53 11 11 12).

For information about what cultural venues in Paris are accessible visit the website of Access Culture (www.accessculture.org).

Access in Paris, a 245-page guide to the French capital for the disabled, was being updated at the time of research and should be available from Access Project (www.accessinparis .org; 39 Bradley Gardens, West Ealing, London W13 8HE, UK) by the time you read this.

The following organisations can provide information to disabled travellers:

Association des Paralysées de France (APF; ☎ 01 40 78 69 00; www.apf.asso.fr, in French; 17 blvd Blanqui, 75013 Paris) Brochures on wheelchair access and accommodation throughout France, including Paris.

Groupement pour l'Insertion des Personnes Handicapées Physiques (GIHP; ☎ 01 43 95 66 36; www .gihpnational.org, in French; 10 rue Georges de Porto Riche, 75014 Paris) Provides special vehicles outfitted for people in wheelchairs for use within the city.

Mobile en Ville (☎ 06 82 91 72 16; 1 rue de l'Internationale; www.mobile-en-ville.asso.fr, in French; B.P. 59, 91002 Evry) Association set up in 1998 by students and researchers with the aim of making independent travel within the city easier for people in wheelchairs.

VISAS

There are no entry requirements for nationals of EU countries. Citizens of Australia, the USA, Canada and New Zealand do not need visas to visit France for up to three months. Except for people from a handful of other European countries (including Switzerland), everyone, including citizens of South Africa, needs a so-called Schengen Visa, named after the Schengen Agreement that has abolished passport controls among 22 EU countries and has also been ratified by the non-EU governments of Iceland, Norway and Switzerland. A visa for any of these countries should be valid throughout the Schengen area, but it pays to double check with the embassy or consulate of each country you intend to visit.

Visa fees depend on the current exchange rate but transit and the various types of short-stay (up to 90 days) visas all cost €60, while a long-stay visa allowing stays of more than 90 days costs €99. You will need: your passport (valid for a period of three months beyond the date of your departure from France); a return ticket; proof of sufficient funds to support yourself; proof of prearranged accommodation; a recent passport-sized photo; and the visa fee in cash payable in local currency.

If all the forms are in order, your visa will usually be issued on the spot. You can also apply for a French visa after arriving in Europe – the fee is the same, but you may not have to produce a return ticket. If you enter France overland, your visa may not be checked at the border, but major problems can arise if the authorities discover that you don't have one later on (for example, at the airport as you leave the country).

Carte de Séjour

If you are issued a long-stay visa valid for six months or longer, you should apply for a *carte de séjour* (residence permit) within eight days of your arrival in France. Students must apply in person for a *carte de séjour* at the Centre des Étudiants Étrangers (Foreign Student Centre; Map pp166–7; ☎ 01 53 71 51 68; 13 rue Miollis, 15e; ⏰ 8.30am 4.30pm Mon-Thu, 8.30am-4pm Fri; Ⓜ Cambronne or Ségur). Arrive early – the queues can be mammoth.

Those holding a passport from one of the original EU member-states and seeking to take up residence in France no longer need to acquire a *carte de séjour*; their passport or national ID card is sufficient. Citizens of any one of the 10 so-called accession countries that joined the EU in 2004 who wish to stay permanently must for the time being apply to the Service Étranger (Foreigner Service) office on the ground floor next to *escalier F* (stairway F) in the Préfecture de Police (Map p105; ☎ 01 53 71 51 68; www.prefecture-police-paris.interieur.gouv.fr, in French; 1 place Louis Lépine, 15e 4e; ⏰ 8.30am-4.50pm Mon-Thu, 8.30am-4.15pm Fri; Ⓜ Cité) for guidance.

Foreigners with non-EU passports must go to one of two offices, depending on the arrondissement in which they're living or staying. The offices are open from 9am to 4.30pm Monday to Thursday and from 9am to 4pm on Friday. The office that deals with 1er to 10e and 15e to 18e Arrondissements is Hôtel de Police (Map pp144–5; ☎ 01 44 90 37 17; 19-21 rue Truffaut, 17e; Ⓜ Place de Clichy or La Fourche); for 11e to 14e and 19e to 20e Arrondissements go to Hôtel de Police (Map pp124–5; ☎ 01 53 74 14 06; 114-116 av du Maine, 15e 14e; Ⓜ Gaîté).

Long-Stay & Student

If you would like to work, study or stay in France for longer than three months, apply to the French embassy or consulate nearest to you for the appropriate *long séjour* (long-stay) visa. For details of au pair visas, which must be arranged *before* you leave home (unless you're an EU resident), see p414.

Unless you hold an EU passport, it's extremely difficult to get a visa that will allow you to work in France. For any sort of long-stay visa, begin the paperwork in your home country several months before you plan to leave. Applications cannot usually be made in a third country nor can tourist visas be turned into student visas after you arrive in France. People with student visas can apply for permission to work part-time; enquire at your place of study.

Visa Extensions

Tourist visas *cannot* be extended except in emergencies (such as medical problems). If you have an urgent problem, you should call the Service Étranger (Foreigner Service) at the Préfecture de Police (see left) for guidance.

If you don't need a visa to visit France, you'll almost certainly qualify for another automatic three-month stay if you take the train to, say, Geneva or Brussels and then re-enter France. The fewer recent French entry stamps you have in your passport the easier this is likely to be.

If you needed a visa the first time around, one way to extend your stay is to go to a French consulate in a neighbouring country and apply for another one there.

WOMEN TRAVELLERS

In 1923 French women obtained the right to – wait for it – open their own mail. The right to vote didn't come until 1945 during De Gaulle's short-lived postwar government, and a woman still needed her husband's permission to open a bank account or get a passport until 1964. It was in such an environment that Simone de Beauvoir wrote *Le Deuxième Sexe* (The Second Sex) in 1949.

Younger French women especially are quite outspoken and emancipated but self-confidence has yet to translate into equality in the workplace, where women are not infrequently passed over for senior and management positions in favour of their male colleagues. Women attract more unwanted attention than men, but female travellers need not walk around Paris in fear: people are rarely assaulted on the street. However, the French seem to have given relatively little thought to sexual harassment (harcèlement sexuel), and many men still think that to stare suavely at a passing woman is to pay her a compliment.

Information & Organisations

France's women's movement flourished as in other countries in the late 1960s and early 1970s, but by the mid-80s had become moribund. For reasons that have more to do with French society than anything else, few women's groups function as the kind of supportive social institutions that exist in English-speaking countries.

La Maison des Femmes de Paris (Map pp158–9; ☎ 01 43 43 41 13; http://maisondesfemmes.free.fr in French; 163 rue de Charenton, 12e; ☺ office 9am-7pm Mon-Fri; Ⓜ Reuilly Diderot) is a meeting place for women of all ages and nationalities, with events, workshops and exhibitions scheduled throughout the week.

France's national rape-crisis hotline (☎ 0 800 05 95 95; ☺ 10am-7pm Mon-Fri) can be reached toll-free from any telephone, without using a phonecard. It's run by a group called Collectif Féministe contre le Viol (Feminist Collective Against Rape; CFCV; www.sosviol.com).

In an emergency, you can always call the police (☎ 17). Medical, psychological and legal services are available to people referred by the police at the Service Médico-Judiciaire (☎ 01 42 34 86 78; ☺ 24hr) of the Hôtel Dieu (p403).

WORK

Although there are strict laws preventing non-EU nationals from being employed in France, it's possible to work 'in the black' (ie without the legally required documents). Au pair work is popular and can be done legally even by non-EU nationals.

To work legally in France you need a carte de séjour (p412). Getting one is almost impossible if you aren't a citizen of the EU, unless you are a full-time student. At the same time non-EU nationals cannot work legally unless they obtain an autorisation de travail (work permit) before arriving in France. This is no easy matter, as a prospective employer has to convince the authorities that there is no French person – or other EU national, for that matter – who can do the job being offered to you.

In addition to the fortnightly Fusac (p405), an excellent source for job-seekers, the following agencies might be of some assistance.

Agence Nationale pour l'Emploi (National Employment Agency; ANPE; www.anpe.fr, in French), France's national employment service, has lists of job openings and branches throughout the city. The ANPE Hôtel de Ville branch (Map pp98–9; ☎ 01 42 71 24 68; 20bis rue Ste-Croix de la Bretonnerie, 4e; ☺ 9am-5pm Mon-Wed & Fri, 9am-noon Thu; Ⓜ Hôtel de Ville) assists those residing in the 1er, 4e and 12e arrondissements.

Centres d'Information et de Documentation Jeunesse (CIDJ; Youth Information & Documentation Centres; www.cidj.com, in French) offices have information on housing, professional training and educational options, and notice boards with work possibilities. Its Paris headquarters (Map pp166–7; ☎ 01 44 49 12 00, 0 825 090 630; 101 quai Branly, 15e; ☺ 10am-6pm Mon-Wed & Fri, 1-6pm Thu, 9.30am-1pm Sat; Ⓜ Champ de Mars-Tour Eiffel) is a short distance southwest of the Eiffel Tower.

Doing Business

If you are going to Paris on business, it's a good idea to contact one of the main commercial offices or your embassy's trade office in Paris before you leave home, to establish contacts and make appointments. These include the following:

American Chamber of Commerce (Map pp140–1; ☎ 01 56 43 45 67; www.amchamfrance.org; 1st fl, 156 blvd Haussmann, 75008 Paris)

Australian Trade Commission (Map pp166–7; ☎ 01 40 59 33 85; www.austrade.gov.au; 4 rue Jean Rey, 75015 Paris)

Canadian Government Department of Commercial & Economic Affairs (Map pp140–1; ☎ 01 44 43 29 00; www.amb-canada.fr; 35-37 av Montaigne, 75008 Paris)

Chambre de Commerce et d'Industrie de Paris (Map p86; CCIP; ☎ 01 55 65 40 03, 0 820 012 112; www.ccip.fr, in French; Bourse de Commerce, 2 rue de Viarmes, 75001 Paris)

France-Canada Chamber of Commerce (Map pp128–9; ☎ 01 43 59 32 38; www.ccfc-france-canada.com, in French; 5 rue Constantine, 75007 Paris)

Franco-British Chamber of Commerce & Industry (Map pp140–1; ☎ 01 53 30 81 30; www.francobritishchamber.com; 3rd fl, 31 rue Boissy d'Anglas, 75008 Paris)

Irish Embassy Trade Office (Map pp132–3; ☎ 01 44 17 67 04; www.embassyofirelandparis.com; 4 rue Rude, 75016 Paris)

New Zealand Embassy Trade Office (Map pp132–3; ☎ 01 45 01 43 10; www.nzembassy.com/france; 7ter rue Léonard de Vinci, 75116 Paris)

and word counts. What more could a boy want? As always, I like to dedicate my share of Paris to my partner Michael Rothschild, a veritable walking *Larousse Gastronomique*.

NICOLA WILLIAMS

The overwhelmingly graciousness, good humour and willingness to help of the many (very busy) Parisians and others I interviewed during my forays in the capital cannot be emphasised enough: *Un grand grand merci* to NetVibes.com founder and CEO Tariq Krim and his assistant Laure Chouillou; Patricia Wells (www.patriciawells.com); Romee de Goriainoff (The Experimental Cocktail Club); Virginie Violet (La Scène Bastille); vintage fashion experts Françoise Auguet (Ragtime) and Lawrence Carlier (Le Dépôt-Vente de Buci); Christophe at Le Pré Verre. Outside Paris, many thanks to Roland Pinson at the Boucherie Pinson in Chartres; Laëtitia Rousseaux at Château d'Anvers; Bartabas, Laure Guillaume and Marie-Hélène Arbour at the Académie du Spectacle Équestre in Versailles; and Sue Dumand (Reel Books) for an invaluable lowdown on the Fontainebleau scene. Kudos to my coordinating author Steve Fallon, font of Paris knowledge and super-heroic to work with. And on the home front a flurry of heartfelt *bisous* to Sally Elliott for revealing her Paris haunt favourites; my parents Ann and Paul Williams; and Matthias for holding the fort while I was gone, valiantly testing out Paris for kids with Niko, aged six, and Mischa, aged four, and last but far from least, sparking off the love affair to start with.

OUR READERS

Many thanks to the travellers who used the last edition and wrote to us with helpful hints, useful advice and interesting anecdotes:

Steven Andreoff, Ian & Miranda Andrews, Ben Andrews & Emma Haycraft, Zoe Ash, Magdalena Balcerek, Isaiah Bier, Robin Bomet, Romke Bontekoe, Stephen Boswell, William Botkin, Paula Bradway, Bleddyn Butcher, Jenny & Wei Ch'Ng, Helen Chou, Barbara Clayton, Laura Cochrane, Matthew Corks, Jenny Cornet, Florent Dargnies, Howard Davies, Lydia

SEND US YOUR FEEDBACK

We love to hear from travellers – your comments keep us on our toes and help make our books better. Our well-travelled team reads every word on what you loved or loathed about this book. Although we cannot reply individually to postal submissions, we always guarantee that your feedback goes straight to the appropriate authors, in time for the next edition. Each person who sends us information is thanked in the next edition – and the most useful submissions are rewarded with a free book.

To send us your updates – and find out about Lonely Planet events, newsletters and travel news – visit our award-winning website: www.lonelyplanet.com/contact.

Note: We may edit, reproduce and incorporate your comments in Lonely Planet products such as guidebooks, websites and digital products, so let us know if you don't want your comments reproduced or your name acknowledged. For a copy of our privacy policy visit www.lonelyplanet.com/privacy.

Du Rieu, Beth Eli, Roberto Finazzi, Wendy Foster, Elin FröGeli, Frances Gendlin, Melissa Graovac, Susanne Harms, Karina Hellmann, Sue Henderson, Robert Holder, Roger Holstein, Carol Hoyle, Anders Jeppsson, Alice Kacperska, Christoph Kaupat, Birte Klitte, Florian Krisch, Jason Lam, Blank Leonard, Bethe Lewis, Ulrike Liebrenz, Christine Lovasz-Kaiser, Jonathan Man, Dan Miller, Joyce Roberta Miller-Alper, Cheryl Northey, David O'Connell, Prudence Peiffer, Danielle Perry, Nancy Rios, Shannon Roy, Rebecca Schweder, Mary Seifert, Sidharth Shah, Rebecca Sonntag, Bob Stenning, Janice Swab, Linda Tomasone, Marlo & Valerie Toups, Una Ui Dhuinn, Georges Valat, Mayda Velez, Luka Vidovi, John Wade, Long Wang, Thomas Weinmann

ACKNOWLEDGMENTS

Many thanks to the following for the use of their content: Paris Metro Map © 2008 RATP

Notes

INDEX

INDEX

13e arrondissement & Chinatown 161, 164, **162-3**
  accommodation 355
  drinking 297-8
  food 274-6
15e arrondissement 165, **166-7**
  accommodation 356-7
  drinking 298
  food 276-7
  shopping 217
16e arrondissement, *see* Eiffel Tower Area & 16e Arrondissement

A

Abélard, Pierre 33
absinthe 382
Académie Française 119
accommodation 328, 332-58, *see also* Sleeping *subindex*
  Clichy & Gare St-Lazare 352-3
  Étoile & Champs-Élysées 352
  Faubourg St-Germain & Invalides 350-1
  Gare de Lyon, Nation & Bercy 355-6
  Gare du Nord, Gare de l'Est & République 354-5
  internet resources 332

000 map pages
000 photographs

Latin Quarter & Jardins des Plantes 343-6
longer-term rentals 334
Louvre & Les Halles 336-7
Marais & Bastille 337-42
Montmartre & Pigalle 357-8
Montparnasse 349-50
Opéra & Grands Boulevards 353-4
St-Germain, Odéon & Luxembourg 346-9
activities 318-24, *see also* Sports & Activities *subindex*
addresses 85
agricultural fair 13
air travel 388-9
airports 388-9
ambulance 400
Amélie 44
amusement parks 384-5
Ancien Régime 22
annoyances 123
antiques, *see* Shopping *subindex*
apartments 332-3, *see also* Sleeping *subindex*
aquariums, *see* Sights *subindex*
Arc de Triomphe 138, **69**
Arc de Triomphe du Carrousel 85
architecture 45-51
  Art Nouveau 48
  Baroque 47
  Carolingian 46
  contemporary 49-50
  Gallo-Roman 45-6
  Gothic 46-7
  Merovingian 46
  modern 48-9
  Neoclassicism 48
  Renaissance 47
  Romanesque 46
area codes, *see inside front cover*
Arènes de Lutèce 109
arrondissements 51, 74
arts 33-45, *see also* Arts *subindex*
  architecture 45-51
  dance 45, 312-13
  film 43-4, 313-14

literature 33-8
metro, art inside 226
music 42-3, 307-12
philosophy 38-9
sculpture 41, 181
theatre 44-5, 315-16
visual arts 39-41
Assemblée Nationale 127
Astérix 385
ATMs 404
auberges 225
Auvers-sur-Oise 382-4, 383
av des Champs-Élysées 138, **69**

B

B&Bs 334, *see also* Sleeping *subindex*
babysitting 397
Balabus 407
ballet 312
ballooning, *see* Sports & Activities *subindex*
Balzac, Honoré 136, 193
bargaining 198
bars 225, 284-300, *see also* Drinking *subindex*
Basilique de St-Denis 182-3
Basilique du Sacré Cœur 168, **62**
Bastille, *see* Marais & Bastille
Bastille Day 14
Bateaux Parisiens 407, **8**
Bateaux-Mouches 407
bathrooms 411
Baudelaire, Charles 35
Belle, David 319
Belleville, *see* Ménilmontant & Belleville
Bercy, *see* Gare de Lyon, Nation & Bercy
bicycle travel, *see* cycling
bistros 226, *see also* Eating *subindex*
Black, Cara 35
blogs 17
blues 309-10
boat travel 389-90
  tours 406-7
Voguéo 392
Bois de Boulogne 177, 178
Bois de Vincennes 176, 177
books 31, 33, 34, 36, 37, 48

bookshops, *see* Shopping *subindex*
boucheries 380, **5**
boules 322, *see also* Sports & Activities *subindex*
Bourse de Commerce 90
boutique hotels, *see* Sleeping *subindex*
bowling 322, *see also* Sports & Activities *subindex*
brasseries 226, *see also* Eating *subindex*
bread 233
Breton, André 36
Brown, Dan 88, 195
buffets 226
bureaux de change 404-5
bus travel 391-2
  tours 407
business hours 198, 228, 396, *see also inside front cover*

C

cabaret 303, *see also* Nightlife *subindex*
cafés 226, *see also* Drinking, Eating *subindexes*
Camus, Albert 36
canal cruises 406-7
Canal St-Martin 151, **70**
Canauxrama 406-7
car travel 392-3
carnet de voyage 394
Catacombes 122
Cathédrale de Notre Dame de Paris 104, **8, 71**
cathedrals, *see* Sights *subindex*
celebrations 222
cell phones 410-11
cemeteries, *see* Sights *subindex*
Centre Pompidou 88-9, **58**
Cézanne, Paul 40
chain restaurants 229, *see also* Eating *subindex*
champagne 386
Champs-Élysées, *see* Étoile & Champs-Élysées
chansons françaises 42, 310-12
Chantilly 373-6, 374

000 map pages
000 photographs

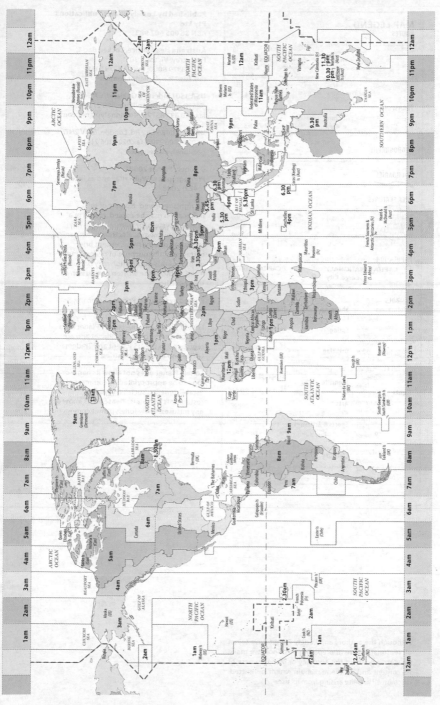

439

MAP LEGEND
ROUTES

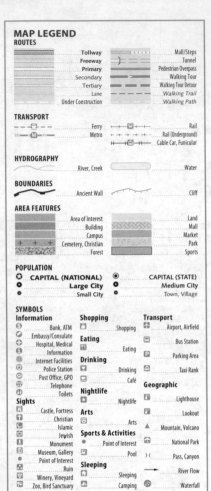

Tollway	Mall/Steps
Freeway	Tunnel
Primary	Pedestrian Overpass
Secondary	Walking Tour
Tertiary	Walking Tour Detour
Lane	Walking Trail
Under Construction	Walking Path

TRANSPORT

Ferry	Rail
Metro	Rail (Underground)
	Cable Car, Funicular

HYDROGRAPHY

River, Creek	Water

BOUNDARIES

Ancient Wall	Cliff

AREA FEATURES

Area of Interest	Land
Building	Mall
Campus	Market
Cemetery, Christian	Park
Forest	Sports

POPULATION

CAPITAL (NATIONAL)	CAPITAL (STATE)
Large City	Medium City
Small City	Town, Village

SYMBOLS

Information
- Bank, ATM
- Embassy/Consulate
- Hospital, Medical
- Information
- Internet Facilities
- Police Station
- Post Office, GPO
- Telephone
- Toilets

Sights
- Castle, Fortress
- Christian
- Islamic
- Jewish
- Monument
- Museum, Gallery
- Point of Interest
- Ruin
- Winery, Vineyard
- Zoo, Bird Sanctuary

Shopping
- Shopping

Eating
- Eating

Drinking
- Drinking
- Café

Nightlife
- Nightlife

Arts
- Arts

Sports & Activities
- Point of Interest
- Pool

Sleeping
- Sleeping
- Camping

Transport
- Airport, Airfield
- Bus Station
- Parking Area
- Taxi Rank

Geographic
- Lighthouse
- Lookout
- Mountain, Volcano
- National Park
- Pass, Canyon
- River Flow
- Waterfall

Published by Lonely Planet Publications Pty Ltd
ABN 36 005 607 983

Australia Head Office, Locked Bag 1, Footscray, Victoria 3011,
☎ 03 8379 8000, fax 03 8379 8111,
talk2us@lonelyplanet.com.au

USA 150 Linden St, Oakland, CA 94607,
☎ 510 250 6400, toll free 800 275 8555,
fax 510 893 8572, info@lonelyplanet.com

UK 2nd fl, 186 City Rd, London, EC1V 2NT,
☎ 020 7106 2100, fax 020 7106 2101,
go@lonelyplanet.co.uk

© Lonely Planet 2008
Photographs © Will Salter and as listed (p422) 2008

Printed by Hang Tai Printing Company. Printed in China.